THE RISE OF
Magic
IN EARLY MEDIEVAL EUROPE

THE RISE OF

Magic

IN EARLY MEDIEVAL EUROPE

VALERIE I. J. FLINT

PRINCETON UNIVERSITY PRESS • PRINCETON, NEW JERSEY

Copyright © 1991 by Princeton University Press
Published by Princeton University Press, 41 William Street,
Princeton, New Jersey 08540

Library of Congress Cataloging-in-Publication Data

Flint, Valerie I. J. (Valerie Irene Jane), 1936–
The rise of magic in early medieval Europe / Valerie I. J. Flint.
p.   cm.
Includes bibliographical references.
ISBN 0-691-03165-7 (alk. paper)
1. Magic—Europe—History. 2. Europe—Religious life and customs.
3. Church history—Middle Ages, 600–1500. 4. Civilization,
Medieval. I. Title.
BF1593F45   1990
133.4′3′0940902—dc20   90-34843   CIP

This book has been composed in Linotron Goudy Old Style

Princeton University Press books are printed on acid-free paper,
and meet the guidelines for permanence and durability of the
Committee on Production Guidelines for Book Longevity
of the Council on Library Resources

Printed in the United States of America by
Princeton University Press, Princeton, New Jersey

10 9 8 7 6 5 4 3 2 1

To the Memory of My Mother **IRENE A. B. FLINT**

Contents

Acknowledgments

MY DEBTS, institutional and personal, are very great. Outstanding among them are the ones I owe to Princeton. A Membership at the Institute for Advanced Study first gave me the idea for the book. Two subsequent semesters at the History Department of Princeton University (the first assisted by the Fulbright Foundation, the second by a Davis Fellowship), and much hospitality there during the Auckland long vacations, enabled me to plunge into the work for it. The staff of the Institute Library, the Firestone Library, and the Speer Library of the Princeton Theological Seminary provided help and resources that would be very hard to equal. Among the many individual persons who gave ideas and encouragement during these Princeton expeditions, I should like especially to thank Professors Peter Brown, Giles Constable, Mary Douglas, John Gager, Tony Grafton, Richard Kieckhefer, Kenneth Lockridge, Theda Perdue, Richard Rouse, Lawrence Stone, Robert Webb, Drs. Mary Rouse, Managing Editor of *Viator*, Lois Drewer and Robert Melzack of the Princeton Index of Christian Art, Mss. Joanna Hitchcock, Executive Editor of the Press, Lauren Lepow, Copy Editor of the Press, Jean Preston, Curator of manuscripts of the Firestone Library (who shouldered the additional burden of housing me), Joan Daviduk, Alice Lustig, Jean Silver, Yoma Ullmann, and my co-Fellows at the Davis Center, class of '88. Some of the views expressed here upon the medieval rescue of astrology were in fact first aired at the Davis Center Seminar and have appeared in preparatory form in "The Transmission of Astrology in the Early Middle Ages," *Viator* 21 (1990).

I owe much as well to the University of Auckland, which, far as it is in space from the more obvious sources of energy for medieval studies, can make heroic efforts to compensate for this in spirit. The Leave Committee and the Head of the History Department, Professor Nicholas Tarling, accorded the permissions necessary to enable me to accept the Fellowships. The University Research Committee provided borrowing funds and a long vacation air fare. Sympathetic colleagues turned Nelsonian eyes to my many late returns and contributed invaluable insights from their own work. So too did students, undergraduate as well as graduate. The University Librarian, Mr. Peter Durey, con-jured funds from nowhere for the purchase of special collections. The University Library, the accessions and interloans sections especially, responded with unflagging efficiency to demands that must have seemed endless. In the History Department office Mss. Barbara Batt typed and retyped, Josie Underhill copied and recopied, Sisilia Tonga did everything else and saved us from losing our tempers. My friend and colleague Professor Philip Rousseau read the whole manuscript through in final draft, made helpful suggestions, and saved me from many infelicities of expression and from downright error. I owe him particular thanks.

Finally, for arousing my interest in medieval history in the first place, for attempting to train it, and for sustaining it ever since, my gratitude to Sir Richard Southern is enduring and very deep. These debts are all far greater than I can repay. They make it abundantly clear, furthermore, that the inadequacies which remain are those of the author.

Abbreviations

AS   J. Bollandus, *Acta Sanctorum Quotquot Toto Orbe Coluntur* (Antwerp, 1643–; repr., Brussels, 1965–)

CC   *Corpus Christianorum Series Latina* (Turnholt, 1953–)

EETS   Early English Text Society

Mansi   J. D. Mansi, *Sacrorum Conciliorum Nova et Amplissima Collectio*, 31 vols. (Florence and Venice, 1757–1798; repr., Paris, 1899–1927)

MGH   *Monumenta Germania Historica*

MT   My translation

PG   *edit.* J. P. Migne, *Patrologia Graeca* (Paris, 1857–1866)

PL   *edit.* J. P. Migne, *Patrologia Latina* (Paris, 1878–1890)

RS   Rolls Series

SRM   *Scriptores Rerum Merovingicarum*

SS   *Scriptores*

The terms *edit.* and *transl.* are used throughout to show that the given work contains both a full edition (as opposed to a transcription) and a translation from the Latin.

Introduction

CHAPTER 1

The Scope of the Study

MAGIC may be said to be the exercise of a preternatural control over nature by human beings, with the assistance of forces more powerful than they. This combination of human and superhuman power will sometimes employ strange instruments and is always liable to produce remarkable and unaccustomed results. Thus we may expect an element of the irrational, and of the mysterious too, in a process that deserves to be called magical.

Magic, in certain of its forms, came into fifth-century Europe, when this study begins, under a very black cloud indeed; for *magia* had long been current in the Roman Empire as a term of condemnation, and fierce efforts had been made to bury all its trappings and practitioners deep in a dark sea of oblivion. I speak advisedly of *magia* as "magic in certain of its forms." *Magia* is a foreign word, used in a period remote from the modern one; it may not, then, in content or in intent, always be exactly translated by *magic*. Sometimes there is a closeness. Sometimes, of course, *magic* is employed now simply as a term of abuse: but at least as often, I would contend, it is used to describe a type of excitement, or wonder, or sudden delight, that is not only wholly proper but without which life might be seriously the poorer. As such it can become a term of high praise, and one that might denote a certain spiritual elevation.

This distinction of values, and different weighting of terms, existed in early Europe as it does now, and to a greatly intensified degree. The word *magia* weighed heavily, and so few of the activities ranged under this rubric could readily be rescued from the burden of imperial proscription. But some could. And not only could they be, but many people became increasingly convinced that they had to be, and that in pursuit precisely of the enrichment of human life with which some today incline to link the word *magic*; in pursuit, that is, of those gifts persons might receive "merely by remaining unwittingly in an undem-

ocratic state of grace."[1] This is, in the main, what this book is about.
It is about a double process. One, firstly, of a rejection of *magia*, a
rejection shared both by imperial Rome and by many of its most powerful medieval heirs; and then, and centrally, a complex second one of
the second thoughts of some of Rome's early medieval successors.
These second thoughts led, I shall attempt here to prove, not merely
to the halting of the process of rejection and to the tolerance of certain
"magical" survivals, but to the active rescue, preservation, and encouragement of very many of these last; and all for the furtherance of
a relationship between people and the supernatural that, it was fervently believed, would improve human life.

As we try to follow this process of rescue, moreover, a further line
of argument will be added. The reader deserves advance warning of
this. It is that in their attempt to find a place for unreason deeper than,
rather than this side of, reason, the early Middle Ages in Europe dis-
play a good deal more enlightenment about the emotional need for
that magic which sustains devotion and delight than does the post-
Reformation Western world in general, or, come to that, the "Enlightenment" itself. This shocking proposition requires more proof for its
sustenance than can be given to it here, but its enunciation is perhaps
a start. The title I have chosen does, within this context, help to express my very strong conviction that some, at least, of the wiser spirits
within the early medieval Christian Church were alerted to the benefits of the emotional charge certain sorts of magic offered and tried hard
to nourish and encourage this form of energy; and they were alerted
too (again perhaps to a greater degree than some of their successors) to
the advantages the accommodation of non-Christian magical practices
afforded in the matter of the peaceful penetration of societies very different from their own.

At root, then, this cannot help but be in large part a book about
cultural compromise in matters of religious emotion, although the historian will very properly tremble at the terms. Emotional history is not
easily extracted from the written records as we have them, and to step
aside from these is very hazardous. The process was, moreover, a symbiotic one, involving much mutual enlargement of soul, and much
adjustment on both sides of the cultural barrier set up by the condemnation of magia. A symbiotic process of this kind is not, again, that

[1] Elizabeth Bishop, "Gregorio Valdes," in *edit*. R. Giroux, *Elizabeth Bishop: The Collected Prose* (New York, 1984), p. 59.

most amenable to historical inquiry, and especially not when the written record is as one-sided as it is here. But where there are risks, perhaps there are rewards too.

I have touched upon the foreignness of late Roman–medieval terms, and upon the difficulties we can ourselves face when we try to speak of magic. This problem must now be pressed a little further and certain additional hazards addressed, hazards inseparable from the use of words that range widely and carry a freight of religious feeling. *Magia* does not, in the written sources for the period, describe the magic of this period in all of its forms. Many other words, very variously weighted both in time and social context, will be needed; *auguria* and *auspicia*, for example, and *incantatio* or—one of the most testing and informative perhaps of all—*astrologia*. Some portions of the magic that came to be rescued were once specifically condemned or misconstrued as *magia*; some were not. Again, *magia*, weighted as it was, could not in the early Middle Ages conceivably be changed from a term of condemnation to one of commendation; and no single substitute Latin term for the magic to be encouraged could be found. Instead a number of other formulations had to be employed, for reasons which, though confusing on one level, are illuminating on another. For magic to be rehabilitated in its exalted sense, and for such complex purposes, it became necessary that it be distinguished clearly and decisively from *magia*, and all the more so if the activities associated with this rehabilitated form of magic bore a resemblance to practices denounced by the latter word and had to cross frontiers fortified in part by borrowed imperial defenses. It might pleasingly, then, be distinguished, and disguised for the crossing, by not one but a series of names. It might be called, for instance, *miracula* or *mirabilia*, *mysterium* or even *gratia*. The Latin written sources, in short, upon which the medievalist must for the most part rely, use many different terms, none of which is exactly represented by the English word *magic*. All of the Latin terms I have chosen to use in this study, however, both the pejorative and the restorative (and some, of course, changed from one to the other), may be subsumed beneath this English word in its extended sense; and they might even deepen our own use and understanding of it.

Nonetheless, in choosing a single modern English word as a starting point, and one so loosely employed as this often is, one inevitably does some damage; damage not merely to the variety of the ways in which magic was defined and perceived within the period under present scrutiny, but to a whole host of other concerns, especially pressing to historians and anthropologists, about how magic *is* meaningfully to be defined and discussed.[2] Sometimes, for example, *paganism* or *primitive religion* will seem to many to be better descriptions than *magic* for the phenomena I shall seek to explore, and sometimes they may be—but not, I think, very often, for these terms too, though familiar, carry with them that very burden of implicit condemnation from which I am trying here to free the single word. At an opposite extreme, the equation in English of *miracle*, or *grace*, or *mystery* with *magic* may give offense to some. I can only plead that *magic* is helpful as a sounding word for the exploration of the many ways in which a hopeful belief in preternatural control reached the early Middle Ages. It has been chosen as one way into a time, and as one approach to sensibilities that were preoccupied to an extraordinary degree with the preternatural, and which had some surprisingly subtle and socially sensitive uses for it. That it is a terminologically difficult way I readily agree.

Any decision about whether a given event is preternatural or not, and elements of it irrational, will depend, of course, upon the views of nature and of reason current when it takes place. Further chasms of language and of discipline open before one's feet. In general, however, this much may perhaps be said. Where nature is thought to encompass all that is not purely *human* nature, where its forces appear to be hostile and where reasoned knowledge of its working is small, the possibilities for preternatural intervention will be feared. Conversely, as nature lessens, as it were, in stature, where its influence appears to be benign, and where human scientific knowledge of its workings has grown, the scope for the preternatural may diminish—but so too may the awe and terror it inspires. Under the first dispensation we may expect competition for the power that magic as a form of control seems to hold out, but anxiety about its practice and alarm at its practitioners. Under the second, the need for such magic may seem to be less urgent, but, paradoxically, that which it has to offer may be a little easier peacefully and generally to accept. I shall try to suggest that, in the period with which we shall be concerned, we begin with the first state of affairs, but we end with the second. By the year 1100 certain practices, objects, and aims which had at one point in their spans of existence most certainly fallen into the dreaded dimension of the magical had become

[2] A helpful introductory discussion of these concerns may be found in H. Geertz and K. Thomas, "An Anthropology of Religion and Magic. Two Views." *The Journal of Interdisciplinary History* 6 (1975–1976), 71–109. See also the illuminating remarks in G.E.R. Lloyd, *Magic, Reason and Experience* (Cambridge, 1979), pp. 1–4.

the object of reverent attention. The means by which this transformation came about are not simple ones, nor are they easy to discover. Many factors contributed to that enlargement of confidence which led to the calming of fear, but the threads of pre-Christian and non-Christian magic and its defenders may be seen to run through the process; and some of them may be followed.

I have used the word *scientific*. Magic and science are, of course, very old enemies, and it will always be the aim of science, in the sense in which we generally understand the term, to eliminate the irrationality and the mysteries of magic. There is a time, however, when the two can and do walk together. Experimental science, in pursuit of its own most respectable purposes, will do much to preserve many of the objects and practices formerly confined to magia, or otherwise distrusted, and so to rescue them. This is one of the activities a less fearful atmosphere will encourage, and this treading of the borderline between magic and science is one of the means by which the old magic will be allowed to emerge. Magic in some of its forms (though never, of course, under the name *magia*) may, on the other hand, be seen as a corrective to the excessive rationalism of science, and to the social and intellectual distances its guardians might create around themselves. It might come, therefore, to be rescued for this end too. Yet again, science may help in that process of discrimination which detaches and condemns the grosser forms of magical practice, while preserving those thought capable after all of making contributions to Christianity.[3] Science can serve its old enemy in many ways and sometimes in spite of itself.

The mention of magic and science brings us to another borderline, perhaps the most formidable of all: that which divides both magic and science from religion. Sometimes such a borderline may amount to an impassable frontier, ringed about with every sort of weaponry; but at

---

[3] Pliny, for instance, is appealed to by Bede for "scientific" directions about the cutting of wood. *De Temporum Ratione* xxviii, xxix; *edit.* C. W. Jones, *Bedae Opera De Temporibus* (Cambridge, Mass., 1943), pp. 231–235. In areas where trees were thought to be sacred, of course, such actions were often accompanied by pagan magical ritual, and Bede's method may have been one way of countering this. An opposite process, one in which science is used to render respectable certain practices formerly ranged among those to be condemned, will be observed when we come to speak of astrology. For comments of exceptional interest upon the permeability of the boundaries between magic and science in Greek society, and the impossibility of declaring that the second invariably combated the first, see Lloyd, *Magic*, pp. 15–58. Many of these comments may be applied with equal force to the early Middle Ages.

others it becomes a little less forbidding, and then magic, albeit, as I have said, a little disguised, may be allowed to slip across it and reappear on the other side in all the panoply of respectability. As at the definitions of *magic, preternatural,* and *nature,* so still more at the definition of *religion* the historian pales; but here, once more, one must attempt, for the purposes of the discussion, a preliminary definition and distinction. Religion, then, at its best perhaps demands of its practitioners a disposition rather different from that required by magic at its mightiest. Religion in this sense requires reverence, an inclination to trust, to be open and to please, and be pleased by, powers superior in every way to humankind; magic may wish to subordinate and to command these powers. On this reckoning, religion and magic are again at opposite ends of a spectrum, as are magic and science. Yet both magic and religion can be seen to be deeply and most intimately involved with human beings' efforts to come to terms with that in their surroundings which they can never reduce to proportions rationally manageable, and, at their joint best, to rejoice in it. Thus some of the possibly strange means and instruments which are of use to the one may also, under a different dispensation, be of help to the other. This discussion, in that it sets itself to deal with the ways in which magic was brought into the early Middle Ages in the service of religion, will concern itself primarily with only one part of the traffic: that from condemned magic (perhaps by way of experimental science) to magic recognized as friendly to humans and capable of making positive contributions to the ways in which they must live together. There were certainly disputes about this traffic. Some noticed with dismay a reverse process, one in which true religion seemed to be likely to be subjected to magic at its worst. At the end of the period with which we shall be occupied, we are confronted with the spectacle of an archbishop of York, no less, who met an untimely end in a garden near his home. Under Archbishop Gerard's cushion was found a work of astrology deeply suspect to many of his compatriots—the *Mathesis* of Julius Firmicus Maternus—which he had been in the habit of reading there, secretly, of an afternoon. Only a few lines were needed for the conjuring up of this pagan pastoral idyll and the mysterious death at its end, and they are lines heavy with an old fear.[4] The powers of the old magic by this account had been neither tamed, nor Christianized; still

---

[4] *Edit.* N.E.S.A. Hamilton, *Willelmi Malmesbiriensis Monachi De Gestis Pontificum Anglorum,* RS (London, 1870), p. 259.

less should they be invited in. They are regarded as capable, certainly, of ensnaring archbishops, and perhaps even of killing them. Some sorts of magic, then, although they had friends in high places at the end of the early Middle Ages, had also enemies, as they had at the beginning. Clear inroads had, nonetheless, been made.

Archbishop Gerard, in the view of the narrator, William of Malmesbury, went a little far; but most of the inroads discernible to us, and many in reality, were made by the most prominent of the members of the infant European Christian Church. At first sight this may seem surprising. Christian proselytizers and legislators were often even more fervent than their Roman predecessors in their condemnation of *magia*—or *magi* or *malefici*—and were enthusiastic users of the machinery these predecessors had constructed for this purpose. At second it is less so, and this for two reasons. Firstly, in that the term *magia* did not apply to all existing forms of magic (as we have defined it), the Christian Church, as the most active and organized of the religions of early medieval Europe, inherited a position of enormous ambiguity, an ambiguity it was called upon at least in some part to resolve. It had to attend, then, most carefully to this magia, once it took up the term for its own use. Secondly, and more important, the church often needed, and believed in, certain sorts of magic, and even, on occasion, magic of the type condemned as *magia*. I have tried already to suggest that, given certain conditions, the borderlines between magic and religion can become blurred. When, furthermore, a religion is weak or in its infancy, and in want of additional emotional force, and when its opposition, battered as it may be, firmly declines simply to wither away, much of the preexisting magical world may be seen to be essential to this religion's growth and confidence. Then the borders will be both blurred and deliberately broken. This situation confronts us often in this period. The nascent European Christian Church came profoundly to care, at different times and in different places, for competing ways with the supernatural. It was, therefore, vigorous in its selection and rescue of that in non-Christian magic it thought would serve it, as well as in its rejection of that which it thought would not.

For these reasons, and particularly, of course, because so much of the written evidence is derived from Christian scriptoria, the attitudes of the Christian Church will be pivotal to this pursuit of the rise of magic. So fierce and filled with energy, moreover, was this church's sense of approbation, and of disapprobation, that I shall allow it to determine much of the structure of the book. In each of the central parts I shall first discuss that in the magic yet to rise which gave most cause for disapproval (not least because it refused to go away); and then, in second place, that which, by all sorts of mechanisms, came to be encouraged. There are dangers attached to these decisions which go beyond even those which attend the terms to be used. The early medieval Christian Church will be treated on occasion as a far more monolithic structure than it was in fact; and any inquiry that depends as deeply as this one must upon surviving written sources can resemble an attempt to understand, for example, the magical inheritance of a remote island people primarily through the observations and known intentions of the missionaries who went to them. All of this needs to be recognized. Further, I have divided the chapters themselves by subject. I shall plunder the source material primarily, then, for the light it might cast upon particular *categories* of magic condemned yet rescued; and, in pursuit of these categories, I shall range freely across the period and across Western Europe, from the fifth century to the eleventh. This decision risks the diversion of attention from, and certainly involves the inadequate treatment of, complex and subtle variations of time and place and scale, and the tensions between and within them. Compensation must, and I hope will, be made in future by more detailed studies more carefully placed in time, and by an enhanced understanding of the practices of similar peoples living now, where this is possible.

Setting aside, for the moment, the unconscious, I shall permit one conscious idiosyncrasy some scope. The footnotes to the text will mainly refer to the primary sources, and to an English translation of these sources where one is available. Secondary work will creep into them only when I find it to be of the utmost critical importance. This policy might make the task of consulting sources a little less onerous than it can sometimes be and should preserve that sense of direct contact which is as vital to readers as it is to magicians. It will do so, however, at the cost of much acknowledgment of debt. I have decided upon it with reluctance for my debts are very great.

The primary sources, I must add, are for both magicians and readers equally diverse. The reader must depend, of course, mainly upon the written, but so much of this is still in need of careful editors that our knowledge of its impact upon contemporaries can be very slight. The lack of well-edited texts is a desperate one, especially in the case of studies such as this. There was at times a demonstrably inverse relationship between urgency of expression and immediacy of result. The great tirade against magic, for example, of the distinguished Carolingian churchman Rabanus Maurus (d. 856), his *On the Magic Arts*,[5] seems to have had little impact upon his contemporaries. We have no modern edition of this text, but I have looked carefully for other early manuscripts and found none. Thus, a treatise that appears at first sight temptingly to represent an authoritative expression of the attitude to magic of the ninth-century continental Saxon church will, by a manuscript editor, be shown to have been taken far less seriously than its fervor might seem to deserve or lead us to expect. It will be shown also to be highly derivative. Hazards such as these make one very wary. Perhaps Rabanus was surrounded by persons skeptical of the threat which so alarmed him, and whose attitudes differed from his. Perhaps, on the other hand, the sources upon which he drew were thought to serve the purpose better in the original than in the form in which Rabanus offered them. Perhaps the fervor came, in reality, from his fierce sources and from Rabanus rather than from the situation the archbishop in fact confronted.[6] It is hard to be sure. There are more caveats still to be borne in mind when we confront the written evidence in its present state. It is tempting, for instance, to separate written sources firmly into categories, literary, perhaps, and legal ones, and to give rather more credence to the latter than to the former. In a highly articulated and sophisticated society such as that of the later Roman Empire this separation may have a certain limited virtue; but in less developed ones it breaks down entirely. There are, and were in the early Middle Ages, societies in which the written law is far less compelling than, for example, the often poetic utterance of respected elders. Again, even when we have the written record, and are as certain as we can be of its form and contents and that it is widely copied, the matter is not ended. Wide copying does not mean wide reading, and many impressive codices may have lain for long years gathering dust upon the shelves of monastic book cupboards because only the abbot, or the librarian, or indeed the donor, had an interest in them.

Thus, though time and circumstances make one dependent so largely upon the written record (and I shall discuss the written record

---

[5] *PL* 110,1095–1110. The *De Magicis Artibus* is at present known only in a single manuscript, MS Vat. Ottobon. Lat. 3295ff., 59ʳ–68ᵛ, bound with Rabanus's *Penitential*. The copy dates from the third quarter of the ninth century and is perhaps from Mainz. I owe this information to Professor Raymond Kottje.

[6] I shall discuss Rabanus's *De Magicis Artibus* more fully in chap. 3.

for this period much more fully below), we are still miserably ill-equipped to understand it, and the kind of crude separation and weighting of which I have just spoken is one against which the modern reader (and writer) must guard especially carefully. And there is one last preliminary point to be made about these sources—perhaps the most important of all. Even were the written materials more widely available and easier to use than they are, to gain a true sense of the power of magic for good or ill by this means would still be very hard. Touching or looking at a Carolingian crystal, walking through an ancient maze, entering the cloister of a great monastic church is, even now, far more effective. So is even a short stay among peoples touched little or not at all by the power of post-Reformation Europe or by that of the printing press. The societies with which I shall be concerned were, overwhelmingly, oral ones, by which I mean that the most important of the transactions within and about them were conducted through the medium of spoken words and gestures, and had an immediacy now almost lost to us. One way to its recovery may well be by means of the studies anthropologists have made of societies seemingly similar. With very great trepidation, I shall try to walk a little along this way.

It will, finally, have become clear from all I have set out here, that the whole of so enormous, indeed limitless, a subject cannot be covered in a single book. If the last word upon it ever comes to be said, it will not be said by me. This introduction prefaces an exercise that is itself an introductory one. I mean to try to cut some new openings into the forest, to tap a few extra sources of energy, to look afresh at some of the written sources, and to suggest a few paths which a historical interest in unreason's social role might profitably follow. My own concern, and the concern I hope the present inquiry to excite, is immediately, of course, with unreason and the supernatural in early medieval Europe; but I hope we might deduce, too, that there were and are places for them elsewhere, even now and even in so apparently "rational" a society as our own. There are forces better recognized as belonging to human society than repressed or left to waste away or growl about upon its fringes. There are resources it can be impoverishing to exclude. To refuse to give space to unreason can be insanity in its purest form. Too large a space, of course, is disastrous. But so is too small a one. Many of our forebears knew this.

The Legacy of Attitudes

ALARM

AT THE BEGINNING of the period, that is, in the first four centuries of the Christian era, we hear almost nothing from the magicians themselves. We do hear, on the other hand, enormous amounts from those they terrified, disgusted, or simply annoyed. Thus magia, so-called, had a very poor start indeed. Denunciations of the magical arts and their practitioners echo and reecho. They are richly to be found in Roman "science," Roman literature, and Roman law.

One of the most thorough and discursive of the denouncers of magic is Pliny the Elder. Pliny, by A.D. 77, had completed his monumental *Natural History* and had thus dealt, as he proclaimed in the preface, with no fewer than twenty thousand matters of note. Among these twenty thousand, the magical arts and their practitioners figured prominently (especially in the opening chapters of Book XXX, but in many other sections of the thirty-seven book compilation as well). He speaks at length of "magicas vanitates" and of the "magi" (a word often synonymous with "imposters") who practice them, and he praises the great service the Romans had already done and were still doing in sweeping them away. The British, he notes in passing, were especially attached to magic before the Romans attended to them. One item on the rather slender list of Nero's contributions to the sum of human happiness is, according to Pliny, his proof of the worthlessness of magic by his abandonment of it.[1] Suetonius reinforces Pliny's account of imperial proscription and general disapproval, manifested in the burning by Augustus of the books of the diviners ("fatidicorum"), with a very few select exceptions.[2]

[1] *Natural History* XXX,iv–v; *edit.* and *transl.* W.H.S. Jones, *Pliny Natural History* viii (Loeb Classical Library, 1963), 286–289.

[2] *Augustus* 31; *edit.* and *transl.* J. C. Rolfe, *Suetonius* (Loeb Classical Library, 1951), p. 170.

If Pliny was horrified, however, he was also fascinated, and ready to pour out his scandalized observations. A position so evidently emotional makes for good reading, and all the panoply of Shakespearean enchantment is spread out for our delight. Here is a passage from his section upon magic medicinal cures. For lumbago,

> an overseas spotted lizard, with head and intestines removed, is boiled down in wine with half an ounce by weight of black poppy, and this broth is drunk. Green lizards with feet and head cut off, are taken in food, or three snails, beaten up with their shells and boiled down in wine with fifteen peppercorns. They [the "magi"] break off, in the opposite way to the joint, the feet of an eagle, so that the right foot is attached as an amulet for pains in the right side, the left foot for those in the left side. The multipede too, that I have called oniscos, is another remedy, the dose being a denarius by weight taken in two cyathi of wine. The Magi prescribe that an earth worm should be placed upon a wooden plate that has been split beforehand and mended with a piece of iron, soaked in water that has been taken up in the dish, and buried in the place from which it was dug out. Then the water in the plate is to be drunk, which they say is a wonderful remedy for sciatica.[3]

None of this is encouraging. The equipment of Pliny's medical magicians, often singled out for mockery, is, indeed, always very remarkable and sometimes very repellent. It consists largely of parts of animals, as we have seen—ground bones, hair, skin, blood, eyes, ashes, and the like—often chosen, as are here the eagle's feet, for the supposedly sympathetic resemblance the object selected is held to have to the effect to be produced.

Accused in the second century A.D. of having secured a rich wife by sorcery, Apuleius, in his *Apologia*, expressed a distaste for the art equal to that of Pliny and, as he did so, recorded both some of the ancient condemnations of it and his own sense of what, in its essence, he felt magic truly to be.

> Now this magic of which you accuse me is, I am told, a crime in the eyes of the law, and was forbidden in remote antiquity by the Twelve Tables because in some incredible manner crops had been charmed away from one field to another. It is then as mysterious an art as it is loathly and horrible;

---

[3] *Natural History* XXX,xviii; *edit.* Jones, *Pliny*, viii,310–313.

it needs as a rule night watches and concealing darkness, solitude absolute and murmured incantations.[4]

Clearly here magic is maliciously manipulative. It connotes the dark and the alone, and it connives at the unjust. As with Pliny so with Apuleius, the art takes on its apparatus of fearfulness and its atmosphere of dread. Both Pliny and Apuleius attest to the use in it of "sympathetic" objects, wands and ligatures, magical plants, potions and substances, mystic words, letters and incantations.[5] The results of the successful practice of the art in its extended form include, it is claimed, vanishings, changes of shape, stature, and sex, transformations into other creatures (usually horrible), night visions and flyings (often on curious vehicles), the raising of storms, the scattering of thunderbolts, the transporting of crops and cattle, the exciting and extinguishing of love, abortions, the inflicting of injury and death. That branch of the magical art which occupies itself in divination—the most prized response to magical incantation, according to Apuleius—calls also upon the flights of birds, the whinnyings of horses, sneezes, the direction of smoke, thunder, entrails, lot casting, dreams, stars, planets, extraordinary or monstrous births. Diviners choose, like magi in general, special equipment and instruments to help them, objects again related in some sympathetic way to the ends for which information is sought. Here we come upon crystal balls, carved images, gems, minerals, and actions adjusted to the phases of the moon or the courses of the planets through the zodiac.

The Roman poets do much to sustain this atmosphere of manipulation, isolation, mystery, and fear. Virgil makes the magical arts responsible for Dido's death of love for Aeneas, fatally overriding her own true life-preserving will.[6] To this most moving evocation of the cruel arts of the enchantress Lucan adds a picture of a witch fit to freeze the blood. Like the *Aeneid*, Lucan's *Civil War* enjoyed enormous popularity as a school text in the last centuries of the empire and in the early

---

[4] *Apologia* 47; transl. H. E. Butler, *The Apologia and Florida of Apuleius of Madaura* (Oxford, 1909), p. 84.

[5] Pliny's views are comprehensively expressed in his *Natural History*, Book XXX. Among the objects and substances of which Apuleius speaks are (taken from Virgil *Aeneid* IV) soft garlands, rich herbs, male scent, threads, laurel, clay and wax. *Apologia* 26, 30; transl. Butler, *The Apologia*, pp. 56, 62.

[6] *Aeneid* iv, ll. 483ff.; edit. and transl. H. R. Fairclough, *The Aeneid of Virgil* i (Loeb Classical Library, 1960), 428–429.

Middle Ages, and it is worth, therefore, dwelling a little upon this picture, the very stuff of which the wicked witch still is made.

Dear to the deities of Erebus, she inhabited deserted tombs, and haunted graves from which the ghosts had been driven. Neither the gods of heaven, nor the fact that she was still living, prevented her from hearing the speechless converse of the dead, or from knowing the abodes of hell and the mysteries of subterranean Pluto. Haggard and loathly with age is the face of the witch; her awful countenance, overcast with a hellish pallor and weighed down by uncombed locks, is never seen by the clear sky; but if storm and black clouds take away the stars, then she issues forth from rifled tombs and tries to catch the nocturnal lightings. Her tread blights the seeds of the fertile cornfield, and her breath poisons air that before was harmless. . . . She buries in the grave the living whose souls still direct their bodies; while the years are still due to them from destiny, death comes upon them unwillingly, or she brings back the funeral from the tomb with procession reversed, and the dead escape from death. . . . But, when the dead are coffined in stone, which drains off the moisture, absorbs the corruption of the marrow and makes the corpse rigid, then the witch eagerly vents her rage on all the limbs, thrusting her fingers into the eyes, scooping out glee-fully the stiffened eyeballs, and gnawing the yellow nails on the withered hand. [7]

We must allow a good deal here, of course, for the needs and purposes of epic poetry, and for Lucan's hatred of that war between Caesar and Pompey which drove its proponents to consult such creatures. Allowance made, however, we do gain a certain clear insight into the reactions expected of an imaginative and educated Roman, and an impression of how an especially vivid image might be released into the air, to take on a being of its own, and to be taken up and used later both by Lucan's immediate sympathizers and admirers, and by others.

Fed on such horrors, accusations of magic and sorcery quickly showed themselves amenable to use as tools, tools for the delineation and suppression of those the governing classes of the later Roman Empire took to be their own chief enemies (real or imagined). Such expedients were particularly welcome in times of social and political uncertainty, and of governmental instability. [8] In the fourth and fifth

[7] *Civil War* (Pharsalia) vi, ll. 511–568; *edit.* and *transl.* J. D. Duff, *Lucan* (Loeb, Classical Library, 1928), pp. 341–345.

[8] Essential to an understanding of this use of magic is P. Brown, "Sorcery, demons and the rise of Christianity: From Late Antiquity into the Middle Ages," in *edit.*

centuries A.D. we hear a good deal from writers such as Ammianus Marcellinus and from such compilations as the *Theodosian Code* about the prohibition by law of practices described as magical, and the expulsion or death of those associated with them. Magic was linked with mystery and secrecy in these texts, as it was by Pliny and Apuleius, and secrecy with almost certain treason. Magic, accordingly, came increasingly to be represented by the word *maleficium*, which gradually replaced the initially more neutral *magia*. The *Theodosian Code* proscribes both *maleficium* and the *malefici* who indulge in it.

> No person shall consult a soothsayer [haruspex], or an astrologer [mathematicus] or a diviner [hariolus]. The wicked doctrines of augurs and seers [vates] shall become silent. The Chaldeans and wizards [magi] and all the rest whom the common people call magicians [malefici], because of the magnitude of their crimes, shall not attempt anything in this direction. The inquisitiveness of all men for divination shall cease forever. For if any person should deny obedience to these orders, he shall suffer capital punishment, felled by the avenging sword.[9]

In the *Code maleficium* becomes a markedly comprehensive term, including all forms of prognostication, simple and complex, regardless of method, and all practitioners who could by any manner of means be called magicians. As a class, magi were given less than no status under this dispensation. Catullus had long seen the magus as the product of an illicit union of a mother with her son.[10] Bred in an unacceptable manner and likely to behave in dangerous ways, such magi could be given no quarter. Scientific, apologetic, literary, and legal sources are, of course, wholly disparate in nature, and it would be a great mistake to believe that the Roman poets were always listened to or that the laws were always enforced. Coming at us as it does, however, from so many different angles, the information its discreditors give about magic in this early period does have a singular unity. Magic is real and threatening. It is always potentially evil and it may become uncontainable. Its adepts must be destroyed.

M. Douglas, *Witchcraft Confessions and Accusations* (London, 1970), pp. 17–45, reprinted in P. Brown, *Religion and Society in the Age of St. Augustine* (London, 1972), pp. 119–146.

⁹ *Theodosian Code* 9,16,4; transl. C. Pharr, *The Theodosian Code* (Princeton, 1952), p. 237. The additional gloss equates the diviner with "the invoker of demons."

¹⁰ XC,3–6; edit. and transl. F. W. Cornish, *The Poems of Gaius Valerius Catullus* (Loeb Classical Library, 1914), p. 164.

A parallel and reinforcing process of condemnation (and one of especial importance, of course, to the early Middle Ages) is to be found in the Bible, in Judaic and apocryphal literature, and in many of the writings of the early Christian Fathers. The God of the Old Testament had repeatedly expressed his aversion to divination (Num. 22:7, 23:23), to augury and to necromancy (Deut. 18:10), to mediums and to wizards (Lev. 19:31, 20:6, 27), and to all forms of enchantment and shape shifting (Exod. 7:10–12). He is active in the defense of his own servants against the threats posed by evil magicians, in the well-known story of the battle between Moses and the magicians of Pharaoh in Exod. 7:10–13, for example, in which the rods of the magicians are swallowed up by Aaron's superior serpent. Certain uncanonical books maintained similar views about the inherent wickedness of magical practice. The pseudepigraphical Book of Enoch, for instance, insisted that the human race was taught the magical arts by *fallen* angels (they taught them, in fact, to their wives, chosen from the daughters of men, and thus the damage was done).

> And they began to go in unto them and to defile themselves with them, and they taught them charms and enchantments, and the cutting of roots, and made them acquainted with plants. . . . Semjaza taught enchantments, and root-cuttings, Armaros the resolving of enchantments, Baragijal [taught] astrology, Kokabel the constellations, Ezeqeel the knowledge of the clouds, Aragiel the signs of the earth, Shamsiel the signs of the sun, and Sasiel the course of the moon. And as men perished they cried, and their cry went up to heaven.[11]

One of the most famous and most chilling of the biblical stories of magical manipulation is that of Saul and the witch of Endor (1 Sam. 28:8–25). King Saul, the story goes, having banished soothsayers and diviners from Israel, felt a need for their guidance after all and turned to an enchantress to conjure up the spirit of the dead Samuel to help him. The text tells us that the enchantress did indeed conjure up the ghost of Samuel. The early Fathers will not allow it. Augustine has two explanations: either it was the devil, by divine permission, who brought back Samuel, or the ghost was not Samuel at all, but a diabolical delusion.[12] He favors the second solution. At all events, the

[11] The Book of Enoch VI,1, VIII,3–4; *transl.* R. H. Charles, *The Apocrypha and Pseudepigrapha of the Old Testament* ii (Oxford, 1913), 191–192.

[12] *Ad Simplicianum* II,iii,1–2; *edit.* A. Mutzenbecher, *Sancti Aurelii Augustini De Diversis Quaestionibus ad Simplicianum*, CC (Turnholt, 1970), pp. 81–84.

"pythonissa" did not call up the dead Samuel on her own. No human being, on this argument, could have of him or herself such power (though we might note that this conclusion is supported rather by the commentators than by the text itself). Another especially vivid and popular story about magical practice is that of the duel between Peter and Simon Magus, adumbrated in Acts 8:9, but most enthusiastically elaborated upon in the various apocryphal Acts of Peter. According to one such account Simon challenges Peter to a trial of magic before Nero, in which the challenger fails disastrously. Frustrated by Peter's successful attacks upon his fraudulent cures, Simon proposes to fly before Peter and an admiring crowd. He does indeed fly "above all Rome and the temples thereof and the mountains," but Peter's prayers have him fall to his death.[13] In another famous contest, that between Paul and Elymas in Acts 13:6–12 for the conversion of the governor of Cyprus, Elymas, described again as a "magus," is blinded by Paul. Persons described as "magi" are always on the losing side in this tradition. In the Vulgate Bible such magicians are also frequently described as "malefici," as they are, for instance, in the Exodus story of Aaron and the magicians of Pharaoh. Even the Magi of Matthew make a poor showing against all this and seem, to many early commentators at least, to become truly respectable only when they can be seen to have abandoned their arts at the discovery of the Christ Child,[14] or when there is a doubt about their ever having been magi at all, in the full sense, that is, of pracitioner of the magical arts.[15]

The anxiety felt by commentators about the evident favor found by Matthew's Magi in the eyes of the Christian God, an anxiety to which we shall return, might serve to remind us that, of all the forbidden magical arts, astrology excited perhaps the liveliest alarm in this early period. There is much evidence of this. Tacitus records senate resolutions from the first century A.D. that ordered the expulsion, and in some cases the execution, of astrologers explicitly so named (they were usually called "mathematici"), and of "magi" along with them,[16] and

---

[13] Acts of Peter (Vercelli Acts) XXXII; transl. M. R. James, The Apocryphal New Testament (Oxford, 1924), pp. 331–332.

[14] For example, Origen, Contra Celsum I,58; transl. H. Chadwick, Contra Celsum (Cambridge, 1953), p. 53.

[15] Opus Imperfectum in Matthaeum II; PG 56,637.

[16] Annales II,xxxii; edit. and transl. J. Jackson, Tacitus ii (Loeb Classical Library, 1931), 431. See also the fine collection of passages on astrology in J.E.B. Mayor, Thirteen Satires of Juvenal with a Commentary ii (London, 1900), 329–331, and the

the passage from the *Theodosian Code* I have already cited shows how ready were late imperial legislators to add astrology to the list of condemned magical practices. It is to the Jewish and Christian sections of premedieval society, however, that we owe the most explicit denunciations of it to reach the Middle Ages. The fatalism astrology encouraged was perhaps the main reason for the dislike it aroused, especially among Christians concerned to emphasize the reality of active divine grace and free will. Astrology's claim to some degree of intellectual rigor and subtlety may have been felt as an additional threat to Christians not exactly noted for their support of the intellectual life, while the generally held notion that it originated in Babylonia did nothing to help its cause. In his *City of God* Augustine devoted nine magisterial chapters to arguments against astrology alone.[17]

I have mentioned the interpretation Augustine advanced so firmly upon the matter of Saul and the witch of Endor. Saul was the victim of demonic manipulation and delusion (though, like Job, under God's providence, of course). With this we may turn finally to one aspect of the religious dispositions current in the late empire which was of particular importance to the fate of magic in the early Middle Ages. That enormous variety of religious cults which had survived into this empire—Zoroastrian, Neoplatonic, Jewish, Gnostic, Christian—had one strong link between them. This link lay in the belief in demons as spirits of evil. Demons, whether they lived in the upper or the lower air, in the known world, in people, or in hell, were held to be real and powerful agents of human misfortune, and the possessors of supernatural powers. They flew or floated about, awaiting their many opportunities. There were armies of them. They caused plagues and famines, tempests, stormy seas, sicknesses, and deaths.[18] The apocryphal Book of Enoch and the Pseudo-Clementine *Homilies* (believed, of course, to be by the real Clement, Saint Peter's successor) were largely responsible for the spread of a story about demons that gained especially wide credence in the period. This story is an extension of the account of the illicit intercourse between lustful fallen angels and the daughters of men. The daughters bore giants, whose souls, surviving the flood, be-

---

perceptive pages on Roman and early Christian astrology in S. J. Tester, *A History of Western Astrology* (Boydell, Suffolk, 1987), pp. 49–56.

[17] *City of God* V,i–ix; *edit. and transl.* W. H. Green, *Saint Augustine City of God* ii (Loeb Classical Library, 1963), 132–181.

[18] See, for example, Origen, *Contra Celsum* I,31, VIII,27,32; *transl.* Chadwick, *Contra Celsum*, pp. 30–31, 471, 474–475.

came demons, eternally tormented and tormenting. John Cassian, though he moves away somewhat from this tradition, does much to keep alive an awareness of it, and to give it firm biblical and patristic support. He deals with demons in Book VIII of his *Conferences*, written by 420 at the instance of Honoratus, bishop of Lérins. Beginning with a reference to 6:11–12 (a passage often employed in matters demonic)—

> Put on the whole armor of God, that you may be able to stand against the wiles of the devil. For we are not contending against flesh and blood, but against the principalities, against the powers, against the world rulers of this present darkness, against the spiritual hosts of wickedness in the heavenly places—

and with a question from the obliging pupil Germanus about how it was that such malevolent influences could have been a part of God's creation, Cassian binds together wicked demons and the magic arts in something of the manner of the Book of Enoch. Rank upon rank of demons fell, he says, with Isaiah's Lucifer and Ezekiel's prince of Tyre (Isa. 14:12–14, Ezek. 28:12–19). Human beings can control demonic malice in only two ways. They can subjugate it by their own sanctity, or they can invoke it, by sacrifices and incantations. Invocation involves, of course, cooperation. Practices of the latter kind, "strange and malefic arts and tricks and magical superstitions," were, Cassian insists, actually instigated by demons, who took advantage of the spiritual debasement of the sons of Seth when these married the daughters of Cain.[19] We shall return again to this passage, and particularly to the stark opposition it sets out between sanctity and magic, for it stands behind much of that belief in the special attachment demons had to magic which preoccupied so many in the early Middle Ages. Indeed, the magical arts were expected in some sources to play a major part in the protection and service of Antichrist himself.[20]

By the time they reached the early Middle Ages, then, *magia* and *magus* and still more *maleficium* and *maleficus* and all the other words for magician carry a very heavy freight of condemnation. Were the practices or the persons ever to cross the barriers to respectability, a way would have to be found of relieving them of this load.

---

[19] *Edit.* E. Pichéry, *Jean Cassien Conferences* ii (Paris, 1958), 9–37.
[20] *Edit.* E. Sackur, *Sibyllinische Texte und Forschungen* (Halle, 1898), p. 185.

HOPE

Antiquity did, however, preserve old strains of defense. The word *magos* was, after all, first borrowed for Greek from the Persian, where it described a Median priest and, as such, one held in great respect and ultimately associated with the divine protection of Persian society.[21] If the *magoi* as a caste fell from favor because of their association with the invasion of Greece,[22] the memory of their early function and greatness was never wholly effaced. The gods needed special servants, and if the gods needed them, so, still more, did the people, although a discredited name for such supernatural services may need eventually to be replaced by a different one. Apuleius, again, and in another section of his argument, points to the two uses of the same word *magus* and expects his readers to remember the creditable side of the function, as they denounce the discreditable.

> If what I read in a large number of authors be true, namely, that magician is the Persian word for priest, what is there criminal in being a priest and having due knowledge, science and skill in all ceremonial law, sacrificial duties, and the binding rules of religion?[23]

The magician may, then, as priest, be legitimately involved in the invocation of certain preternatural forces, and for certain ends.

Also, for all the condemnations of seers we can find in them, Roman literature and Roman law kept a special place for some of the forms of divination. The art seems to gain greatly in respectability, for instance, if it is associated with particular persons, or devoted to purposes deemed socially appropriate. August imperial personages were seen to indulge in a singularly primitive form of divination, and to indulge in it without fear of opprobrium. Suetonius, their biographer of the early second century A.D., is kind to them about it. The deified Augustus, he tells us, was especially attentive to certain aspects of the diviners' lore.

> Certain auspices and omens he regarded as infallible. If his shoes were put on in the wrong way in the morning, the left instead of the right, he considered it a bad sign. If there chanced to be a drizzle of rain when he was

---

[21] Herodotus, *Histories* I,132; *edit.* and *transl.* A. G. Godley, *Herodotus* i (Loeb Classical Library, 1926), 172–173.

[22] Ibid., VII,19; iii,332–333.

[23] *Apologia* 25; *transl.* Butler, *The Apologia*, p. 55.

starting on a long journey by land or sea, he thought it a good omen, be-
tokening a speedy and prosperous return. But he was especially affected by
prodigies. When a palm tree sprang up between the crevices of the pave-
ment before his house, he transplanted it to the inner court beside his
household gods and took great pains to make it grow. . . . He also had
regard to certain days, refusing ever to begin a journey on the day after a
market day, or to take up any important business on the Nones; though in
the latter case, as he writes to Tiberius, he merely dreaded the unlucky
sound of the name.[24]

Julius Caesar could mock certain types of magic, and some portents, it
is true. He laughed at the so-called sacred trees whose timber he
needed for the siege of Marseilles,[25] and at the idea that the escape of
a victim proposed for sacrifice portended evil;[26] but, at the same time,
he clearly believed in some of the signs prophesying his own death,
particularly those associated with the movements of horses, and the
flights of birds, and with dreams.[27]

Before his account of the Thessalian witch, Lucan, too, has a revealing passage about the ways of looking into the future he himself
thought appropriate. He speaks of Sextus, one of Caesar's opponents
in Thessaly, and of the means of inquiry Sextus had ignored before he
resorted to the witch.

> Fear urged him on to learn beforehand the course of destiny; he was impa-
> tient of delay and distracted by all that was to come. But he sought not the
> tripods of Delos nor the caverns of Delphi . . . he asked not who could read
> the future by means of entrails, or interpret birds, or watch the lightnings
> of heaven and investigate the stars with Assyrian lore—he sought no
> knowledge which, although secret, is permissible. To him were known the
> mysteries of cruel witchcraft which the Gods above abominate, and grim
> altars with funereal rites.[28]

For Lucan, clearly, properly constituted oracles and certain means of
divination, including, it seems, astrology, were allowable. Here, activities quite properly described in one sense as magical, and which, as
we saw from the Theodosian Code, were at times roundly condemned,

---

[24] Augustus II,xcii; transl. Rolfe, Suetonius, i,261–263.
[25] Lucan Civil War III, ll.399–453; transl. Duff, Lucan, pp. 143–147.
[26] Julius I,lix; transl. Rolfe, Suetonius, i,81–83.
[27] Ibid., I,lxxxi; p. 107.
[28] Civil War VI,ll.423–432; transl. Duff, Lucan, pp. 335–337.

are seen as respectable alternatives to something worse: "cruel witch-craft." Cruelty, however that was to be defined, invalidated the magic. The human wish to see into the future deserved and obtained, on the other hand, the correct forms of assistance. The "haruspices" remained at their posts in Rome. Some of the divinatory aspects of the magical arts could thus be seen and accepted as the fulfillment of a fundamental human need, and those expert in them as benefactors of humanity.

Certain types of intercessor, then, and certain forms of human aspiration which could easily be associated with the magical, were defended in this early period and on ground of legitimate need. We may add to the number of these defensible items. If aspirations to political success in the future could justify some rather extraordinary procedures and beliefs, human hopes for the cure of present physical ills could allow of still more. Skill in interpreting signs could quite properly invade other areas of insufficiency—those, for instance, of providing food and medicine. From the behavior of animals, or clouds, changes in the weather might perhaps be predicted, and measures accordingly taken. Some concerned observers were very careful to distinguish this procedure from any of the practices in which astrologers engaged. Columella made this point particularly clearly.

> Warning about the duties of each month, dependent on a consideration of the stars and sky, is necessary. . . . Against this observation I do not deny that I have disputed with many arguments in the books which I wrote *Against the Astrologers*. But in those discussions the point which was being examined was the impudent assertion of the Chaldaeans that changes in the air coincide with fixed dates, as if they were confined within certain bounds; but in our science of agriculture scrupulous exactitude of that kind is not required, but the prognostication of future weather by homely mother-wit, as they say, will prove as useful as you can desire to a bailiff, if he has persuaded himself that the influence of a star makes itself felt sometimes before, sometimes after, and sometimes on the actual day fixed for its rising or setting. For he will exercise sufficient foresight if he shall be in a position to take measures against suspected weather many days beforehand.[29]

The art of astrology is eliminated here, but the stars and sky do manage, nonetheless, to enter legitimately upon the scene of what we

---

[29] *De Re Rustica* XI,i,31–32; *edit.* and *transl.* E. S. Forster and E. H. Heffner, *Lucius Junius Moderatus Columella on Agriculture and Trees* iii (Loeb Classical Library, 1955), 68–69.

might call forward planning. In another part of his full (and avidly read) agricultural directions, Columella advises planting when the moon is waning "for this frees the crop from weeds" and so becomes an avatar of a powerful body of opinion which would associate the moon in particular with influence upon growth and decay.[30] Even the *Theodosian Code* can make a distinction between arts aimed at the injury of humans (which arts are called magic ones), and predictive measures aimed to protect crops from the elements or to assist in cures. The latter, directed solely and laudably at the saving of divine and human labor from waste, are carefully defended.

> The science of those men who are equipped with magic arts and who are revealed to have worked against the safety of men or to have turned virtuous minds to lust shall be punished and deservedly avenged by the most severe laws. But remedies sought for human bodies shall not be involved in criminal accusation, nor the assistance that is innocently employed in rural districts in order that rains may not be feared for the ripe grape harvest or that the harvests may not be shattered by the stones of ruinous hail, since by such devices no person's safety or reputation is injured, but by their action they bring it about that divine gifts and the labors of men are not destroyed.[31]

The defense here of medical remedies dignifies another form of divination, one more familiarly known as diagnosis. No one would deny that, for instance, the onset of spots was a portent which could be interpreted and acted upon to the profit of all. Thus, again, certain apparently specialized and relatively secret arts, and materials that were magical in the sense that they sought to control illness and the elements in apparently supernatural ways, could be preserved in the service of a highly reputable end. Apuleius here becomes a positive advocate of such distinctions and of the materials, especially, they rescue.

> If it please you, we will assume with Aemilianus that fish are useful for making magical charms as well as for their usual purposes. But does that prove that whoever acquires fish is *ipso facto* a magician? On those lines it might be urged that whoever acquires a sloop is a pirate, whoever acquires a crowbar a burglar, whoever acquires a sword an assassin. You will say that there is nothing in the world, however harmless, that may not be put to

[30] Ibid., II,v,i; p. 137.
[31] *Theodosian Code* 9,16,3; transl. Pharr, *The Theodosian Code*, p. 237.

some bad use, nothing so cheerful that it may not be given a gloomy meaning. And yet we do not on that account put a bad interpretation on everything, as though for instance you should hold that incense, cassia, myrrh, and similar other scents are purchased solely for the purpose of funerals; whereas they are also used for sacrifice and medicine.[32]

There is a doubleness of attitude in all this which, while it dismisses much magical practice and material, allots to some of it a privileged place.

The poets, too, recognize the validity, indeed the desirability, of procedures seemingly magical when they are used to encourage and to cure. Ovid tells in the Fasti a cheering little story of the use of magical means by the goddess Carna to protect and heal a child from the vicious attacks of enchanted birds. The protection involved mystic gestures with arbutus leaves and whitethorn, sprinklings with water, the disemboweling of a sow, all with the most beneficent of results.[33] Evil enchantment asks here for good enchantment. Curative magic, perhaps because it was hopeful (and, so far as was known, harmless), because it did not require of its practitioners the excesses that some other magical efforts required, and because it was presumed to help, rather than invade, the proper operation of human good intentions, seems to have enjoyed a relative immunity from attack. Cato preserves some very remarkable remedies for sick oxen, including the demand that both the ox and he who administers the remedies be standing and fasting. Varro advances respectable incantations: one for sore feet, for instance ("The pain go into the ground and may my feet be sound"), which also demands fasting of the chanter.[34] Even Pliny has moments in which he reports the prescriptions of the magi without the annoyance which usually accompanies his accounts of their practices.

For snake bites efficacious remedies are considered to be fresh dung of sheep boiled down in wine and applied, and mice cut in two and placed on the wound. The nature of mice is not to be despised, especially in their agreement, as I have said, with the heavenly bodies, for the number of their liver filaments becomes greater or less with the light of the moon. The Magi

[32] Apologia 32; transl. Butler, The Apologia, p. 65.

[33] Fasti VI, ll. 101–168; edit. and transl. J. G. Frazer, Ovid's Fasti (Loeb Classical Library, 1951), pp. 325–331.

[34] Cato, On Agriculture LXX, Varro, On Agriculture I, ii, 28; edit. and transl. W. D. Hooper and H. B. Ash, Marcus Porcius Cato On Agriculture, Marcus Terentius Varro On Agriculture (Loeb Classical Library, 1934), pp. 78–81, 182–183.

declare that if a mouse's liver in a fig is offered to pigs, that animal will follow the offerer, adding that it has a similar effect on a human being also, but that the spell is broken by adding a cyathus of oil.[35]

Pliny's words here cannot be taken as signs of his adherence to the views of the magi, but they are neutral and so seem to suggest that, in this particular area, there lies a borderland in which magicians and healers may come close to one another.

Simultaneously with the strong current of the denunciation of magic in Roman literature and Roman law, then, we see flowing a counter-current that is beginning to rescue certain of the denounced practices and materials. This countercurrent follows a different course and end from some of those condemned as magical and has started to call into its service two special sources of strength which might, properly guided, become tributaries to the actual rise of a changed form of magic. In its trust in oracles and in some of the forms of divinatory prediction, this movement has begun to draw upon religious aspiration, and, in its efforts for the proper care of crops, in its recognition of the power of certain objects, and in its zealous pursuit of cures, it has begun also to edge (though tentatively and, through sympathetic magic, dangerously) toward experimental science. It has penetrated, in short, that no-man's-land between magic, science, and religion in which all three can come together and in which much magic might be salvaged and valued.

Of all the Roman sources to whose ambivalent attitudes to magic I have tried to draw attention here, Pliny is the most instructive. This is partly because his account of magic is so extensive, partly because of the eagerness with which his work (or, to put the matter more properly, largely unacknowledged portions of it) was seized upon in medieval Europe, and partly because, denouncer of magic as he can be, he cannot, in the last resort, wholly make up his mind about it. This last state of affairs may account, indeed, and more fully than we have realized, for that eagerness with which he was, in fact, seized upon in the period of our concern. For all his fervor of condemnation, Pliny's *Natural History* is full of fine examples of that which could be rescued from the no-man's-land, influences and specifics in which he as a rational and religious man clearly believed, and which were therefore available when other rational and religious persons came also to believe that magic, of a kind, had a Christian place. Pliny was sure of the

---

[35] *Natural History* XXIX,xv; transl. Jones, *Pliny*, viii,220–223.

force, for instance, of the evil eye,[36] and he is also responsible for the persistence well into the Middle Ages of the conviction that menstrual blood had a special power.

> Contact with it turns new wine sour, crops touched by it become barren, grafts die, seeds in gardens are dried up, the fruit of trees falls off, the bright surface of mirrors in which it is merely reflected is dimmed, the edge of steel and the gleam of ivory are dulled, hives of bees die, even bronze and iron are at once seized with rust.[37]

Pliny obviously considered this to be scientific knowledge, as he did certain medicinal cures that are, on the face of it, quite as remarkable as the ones of the magi he condemned.

> The bite of a human being is considered to be a most serious one. It is treated with ear wax, and (let noone be surprised) this, if applied locally and at once, is also good for the stings of scorpions and for the bites of serpents, being more efficacious if taken from the ears of the sufferer. Hangnails too are said to be cured in this way; the bite of serpents by a human tooth ground to powder.[38]

There are many more such examples. Magnificent opportunities are provided here for the Christianization, under the guise of science or simply of "authority," of practices extremely close to magical ones, both as they existed in Pliny's day, and as they were employed by competing early medieval non-Christian magicians. This is a theme to which we shall frequently return. Pliny on the dragon is, in his distinction between the "lies" of the Magi and true knowledge (a distinction that could arguably be lost), and in the opportunities he offers for the preservation and justification of very peculiar activities and beliefs, particularly fine.[39]

[36] Ibid., VII,ii,16–17; transl. Rackham, Pliny, ii,516–517.

[37] Ibid., VII,xv,64; ii,548–549.

[38] Ibid., XXVIII,viii; transl. Jones, Pliny., viii,30–31.

[39] "Its head, buried under the threshold of doors after the gods have been propitiated by worship, brings, we are assured, good luck to a home; those rubbed with an ointment of his eyes, dried and beaten up with honey, are not panic-stricken, however nervous, by phantoms of the night; the fat of the heart, tied in the skin of a gazelle on the upper arm with deer sinew, makes for victory in law suits; the first vertebra smooths the approach to potentates; and its teeth, wrapped in the skin of a roe and tied on with deer sinew, make masters kind and potentates gracious. But all these are nothing compared with a mixture that the lying Magi assert makes men invincible, composed of: the tail and head of a dragon, hair from the forehead of a lion and lion's marrow,

When we turn, lastly, to that Jewish and Christian tradition in which we found the condemnations, we can find there too some chinks of light for magic redeployed. For example, the Christian Fathers can also express an interest (based largely on Genesis) in the effect of the planets on growth and decay. Origen was sure that the heavenly bodies exercised a powerful influence upon the earth, and so, for that matter, was Saint Ambrose.[40] And, loud as he was in his denunciation of astrology, Saint Augustine himself was prepared to admit that the stars and the planets had some influence.[41] Here one can see in the Fathers some small deference to the tributary of science, though in the service of sustaining hopes, of course, essentially religious. This is one of the ways in which magic—turned science—would come to be accepted, even treasured, in the Christian Middle Ages.

And the elect of God can, when we look closely, be allowed to indulge in practices absolutely and unambiguously magical. In the battle with the magicians of Pharaoh, for instance (Exod. 7:8–13), which the magicians predictably lost, Aaron did precisely as they did. He performed a shape shift. He changed his own rod into a serpent; but in his case the practice was legitimate. Similar occurrences and transformations are to be found in the apocryphal Acts. Saints Simon and Jude engage in a contest with two Persian magicians, again involving serpents and magic.

> They [the magicians] were enraged and called in a host of snakes. The apostles were hastily summoned, and made the snakes all turn on the magicians and bite them: they howled like wolves. "Kill them outright" said the king; but the apostles refused, and instead made the serpents suck out all their venom, which hurt still more. And for three days in the hospital the wizards continued screaming.[42]

---

foam of a victorious racehorse, and the claw of a dog, all attached in deer hide with deer sinew and gazelle sinew plaited alternately. To expose these lies will be no less worth while than to describe their remedies for snake bite." Ibid., XXIX,xx; viii,226–227.

[40] *Contra Celsum* V,10–12; *transl.* Chadwick, *Contra Celsum*, pp. 271–274. Ambrose, *Ep.* XXXIV; *PL* 16,1121.

[41] *City of God* V,vi; *transl.* Green, *Saint Augustine*, ii,156–157.

[42] *Apostolic History of Abdias* xvi–xvii; *transl.* James, *The Apocryphal*, p. 465. For full references to Old Testament magic in the canon, and notice too of the ambiguities inherent in these references, see H. C. Kee, *Medicine, Miracle and Magic in New Testament Times* (Cambridge, 1986), pp. 17–19.

Stories of the latter sort were not, of course, supposed to enjoy that credit reserved for the biblical canon, but it was hard to enforce the distinction and on occasion the distinction was, indeed, hard to find. Christ had, after all, made beasts act in remarkable ways and changed water into wine,[43] in addition to his cures of the sick and his provision of inexplicable quantities of food.

Furthermore, although divination, Roman style, is repeatedly denounced in this tradition, the very reverse is true of that which is called prophecy. Origen shows himself sympathetic, if a little patronizingly so, to the need the Jewish people felt for their prophets.

> While, therefore, the heathen were using divination, whether by omens or auguries or by birds or by ventriloquists, or even by those who profess to divine by means of sacrifices or Chaldaean astrologers, all of these things were forbidden to the Jews. But if the Jews had had no knowledge of the future to console them, they would have been led by the insatiable desire of man to know the future, would have despised their own prophets for having nothing divine about them, and would not have accepted any prophet after Moses nor recorded their words. But of their own accord they would have turned to heathen divination and oracles, or even attempted to establish something of the kind among themselves. Consequently, there is nothing inappropriate about the fact that the prophets among them uttered predictions even about everyday matters for the consolation of those who wanted that kind of thing.[44]

Here there is a distinct, and indeed touching, softening of the heart toward a people humbly seeking simply to avoid despair, a softening easily extendable to later persons seeking to avoid it in a similar way. Thus prophecies and prophetic dreams (especially those of Daniel and of Joseph, and of persons who dreamed under like conditions) will be allowed to play a major part in the unfolding of the message of salvation to Jews and early medieval European Christians alike. Though dignified by Holy Writ, and disciplined by an organization larger than that which disciplined the emperor, the attitude of Origen here is not wholly unlike that of Caesar.

Divination under the name of science or prophecy, and shape shifts and amazing transformations in pursuit of the triumph of good over

---

[43] Matt. 8:32, John 2:1–10. See Kee, *Medicine*, pp. 75–79 and 115–125, and idem, *Miracle in the Early Christian World* (New Haven, 1983), pp. 183–241 for the New Testament opportunities given for the practice of magic.

[44] *Contra Celsum* I, 36; transl. Chadwick, *Contra Celsum*, p. 35.

evil can, then, in Jewish and early Christian literature, be seen to allow for the making of distinctions between magic that is bad and magic
that, under another name and in different hands, might be good. Once
such a distinction is made, then the positive adoption and encouragement of certain magical remains and practices comes to be possible.
We have the beginning of a salvaging process parallel to those beginnings we have already begun to see in Roman literature and Roman
law, and one which, in certain respects and emphases, even goes beyond the latter. The operations of a little science and much religion
might now allow a good deal of magic to slip across the borders.

Augustine is triumphant in the process, and we might, finally, look
at Augustine's attitude for itself a little more closely, for it was of enormous importance to the rise of magic in medieval Europe. Augustine
had, after all, performed great feats of rescue himself in matters supernatural, before it ever came to be realized how aptly his works were
suited to serve medieval needs. His attitude is expressed most fully in
his *City of God.* Nowhere, of course, does Augustine call that which
he rescues and encourages magic; he hates anything called "magia" or
"maleficium." Nonetheless, he has in this work two major, and very
evident, concerns in which something very like the ancient magia
must play a part. These two are, firstly, the preservation of human
beings from despair, and, secondly, the preservation of hope and reverent wonder. As we saw, Augustine vigorously eliminated astrology
from consideration as a possibly respectable means of divining; but he
did support prophecy, taking on Cicero, no less.

> Cicero, in undertaking to refute the Stoics, considers himself helpless
> against them unless he can do away with divination. This he attempts to
> do by denying that there is any knowledge of the future. He argues with
> might and main that there is no such foreknowledge, either in man or in
> God, and that there is no way of predicting events. By this course, he both
> denies the foreknowledge of God and essays to overthrow all prophecy,
> using futile arguments even when the truth of prophecy is clearer than day-
> light. . . . We can much better put up with those who maintain even that
> destiny lies in the stars than with the man who strikes out all foreknowledge
> of the future.[45]

This is an interesting concession, and one which shows how passionately concerned Augustine was for the preservation of a form of predic-

[45] *City of God* V, ix; transl. Green, *Saint Augustine,* ii, 166–169.

tion which would sustain Christian faith in the future. He insists, above all, upon the vital importance to man of that mysterious control of the preternatural which inspires wonder. Commenting upon the famous passage in Exodus, and the battle of Moses and Aaron against the magicians of Pharaoh, he says this:

> On this occasion the wizards of Pharaoh, that is, the king of Egypt who was oppressing the people with his tyranny, were allowed to perform some miracles, simply that they might be outdone by even greater marvels. For they worked their deeds by the sorceries and magic incantations to which the bad angels, that is the demons, have devoted themselves. But Moses, as much more powerful as more righteous, in the name of God who made heaven and earth, with angels as his ministers overcame them with ease. Then the magicians failed with the third plague, and the full number of ten plagues was completed by Moses in a great array of miraculous works, whereupon the bad hearts of Pharaoh and the Egyptians gave way and they let God's people go.[46]

There is enormous wealth in this passage and in the one that immediately follows it in the text. The adjective *magicus* accompanies the work of the bad angels; yet the control of preternatural events given to Moses and Aaron in this case is essentially similar—except that it is called "miracula." It is magic made respectable, because it is performed in the service of human salvation, which must partake, for Augustine, of that joy which comes from amazement.

Augustine, of course, revels in that which mazes the mind. One section of his *City of God* was especially frequently copied in the Middle Ages, in separation, sometimes, from the whole, and as a part of that marvels literature which can be used to stigmatize early medieval persons as essentially superstitious, "unscientific," and naive (if charmingly so). It is worth quoting in full here, both because it sums up so well Augustine's own attitude to the marvelous, and because it forms an excellent transition to my own contention that the medieval attitude to the marvelous and the magical had about it more than mere naïveté;

> They say that the salt of Agrigentum in Sicily melts when it is brought to a fire, as if dissolved in water, but when brought to water it crackles, as if in fire. They say that there is a spring among the Garamantes whose water

---

[46] Ibid., X,viii; transl. D. S. Wiesen, *Saint Augustine*, iii,282–283.

is so cold in the daytime that it cannot be drunk, and so hot at night that it cannot be touched. In Epirus there is another spring in which lighted torches are extinguished, as in other springs, but extinguished torches are lit in the spring, a thing not found elsewhere. They say that a stone of Arcadia is called asbestos (unquenchable) because when once set on fire it cannot be extinguished. The wood of a certain fig tree in Egypt does not float in water like other wood, but sinks. And, what is more marvellous, when it has been at the bottom for some time it rises again to the surface of the water, although when water-soaked it ought to be heavier than the weight of liquid. Apples in the land of Sodom grow and come to the appearance of maturity, but when they are bitten or squeezed the skin bursts in pieces and they vanish in smoke and ashes. Pyrites, a Persian stone, burns the hand which holds it if it is pressed too hard and hence derives its name from the Greek word for fire. In the same land of Persia is found the stone selenite, whose inner lustre waxes and wanes with the moon. In Cappadocia the mares are also impregnated by the wind, and their offspring do not live more than three years. Tylos, an island of India, is preferred to all other lands because no tree which grows there is ever stripped of its covering of leaves.[47]

This passage forms a central part of Augustine's argument against the paramountcy of reason and for the need for wonder. It was not always used to fight reason and skepticism in the early Middle Ages, for then the main enemy was a different one; but it *was* important in the sustaining of a Christian form of wonder, and to this end it was fervently employed. It might be remarked that these are all "magic" springs, and stones, and minerals, and fruits, and trees, and beasts; that they will have an echo, that is, in medieval non-Christian forms of magic and provide a ready opportunity for a Christian counterpart to them. And in these chapters of the *City of God* we have a summary of where lay, for Augustine, the dividing line between condemnable and essential magic. "Veneficia," "maleficia," "malefici" diminish, defraud, give pain. In league with demons, they conceal the true good from humankind. "Mira" and "miracula," on the other hand, overcome fear and pain, and encourage hope and open happiness. Yet, undeniably, they contain magic of a kind. Augustine recognizes that magicians and good Christians may do similar things. The difference lies in their means and ends.

[47] Ibid., XXI,v; *transl.* Green, *Saint Augustine*, vii,24–29.

It is one thing for magicians to perform miracles, another for good Christians, and another for evil Christians. Magicians do so through private contracts, good Christians through a public righteousness and evil Christians through the "ensigns" or symbols of this public righteousness.[48]

Certain ends, according to this argument, do not merely justify the use of magic; they actually require it.

Thus, although the words *magia* and *magus* had so long been used as terms of abuse that no part of them could now be rehabilitated, the case was entirely otherwise with a quite remarkable number of the materials and practices these words described, even before the early Middle Ages in Europe begin. These materials and practices might, in much compelling theory, be revivified and reincorporated into a search for a better life. Even at the height of the most hysterical of early condemnations, therefore, there remained movements of resistance, and not always underground. A people, if it was to dare to hope in the future, needed encouragement to look into it. It needed its religious leaders and its prophets and some, at least, of their methods of prediction. Human physical frailty and the vulnerability of human beings to the devices of malevolent demons might still cry out for the help and for the friendship of sympathetic substances, for good enchantments and for the skills of those practiced in their use. The generous consideration of the demands of human helplessness in literature such as this, provided that the helplessness was agreed both to be real and to be best satisfied in this way (and provided that the demands were made in a spirit of humility before the gods or God), brought powerful impulses to bear upon the rescue of magic, no matter, sometimes, how extraordinary its form. Thus, signs and portents and predictions, lot casting, planetary influences, shape shifts, dreams, the strangest of animal and herbal remedies, and the most wondrous of substances, all of these were given passage through to the Middle Ages on viable craft, and sometimes on the most substantial and impressive and undoubtedly Christian of vehicles.

Societies and individuals will frequently differ in their understanding of real need. They will differ, too, in their views of that which constitutes an appropriate request of the gods and of those who are qualified to make it. It would be foolish to suggest that early medieval Christian Europe was presented with, or could adopt, an united front

[48] *Eighty-Three Different Questions* 79,4; transl. D. L. Mosher, *Saint Augustine. Eighty-Three Different Questions* (Washington, 1982), p. 203.

upon so complex a combination of issues. But though there were certainly (and repeatedly expressed) alarms about magic, the legacy from antiquity did, in the end, assist hope in it to prevail. As the conversion of Europe progressed, moreover, that hope became, though slowly and not unmixed with fear, better informed and stronger. And, crucially, the early medieval church had one extra, and especially pressing, ingredient in the social complex to consider, an ingredient which made it turn to these earlier supports for magic with a positive enthusiasm. The supports we have just discussed are important ones to medieval Europe, but it is this extra social ingredient that is the vital one. We will turn to it in chapter 4.

CHAPTER 3

The Sources for the Early Middle Ages

THE SOURCES IN GENERAL

THE SOURCES which have something to tell us about medieval attitudes to magic are legion, and I shall not exhaust them.[1] I propose here to indicate, however, and where possible to date, those upon which I shall chiefly rely and to draw attention to those categories which might be most informative. One firm general criterion has guided this selection of sources: their influence within the period must be attested, and preferably widely so. The firm use of this criterion will sometimes lead me to place great weight upon materials which were in fact written before the early Middle Ages began. Many of the works of the Fathers, for instance, and certain nonpatristic sources (notably the *Natural History* of Pliny), are, though distinct from the period in strict chronology, of immense importance to it. Thus, many of the names mentioned in the preceding section will follow us through the book. From among the many materials for magic produced and widely disseminated within the period itself, I have made a second selection. I have drawn mainly upon the writings of those placed upon the frontiers between non-Christian and Christian magic: people who worked, as it were, at the coal face, where non-Christian belief was especially resistant, and in many ways impressive, and where the drive, and indeed the need, for conversion was accordingly intense. The views of persons such as these might be expected to have been formed and conveyed with an increased force. I have therefore singled out for particular attention materials from Visigothic Spain in the late sixth and early seventh centuries, from Merovingian France and Lombard Italy, from the Carolingian kingdoms in the eighth and the ninth centuries, from Anglo-Saxon and Anglo-Scandinavian England in the eighth,

---

[1] Although my own selection and emphases will be rather different, a useful introductory collection of sources for the period may be found in W. Boudriot, *Die altgermanische Religion in der amtlichen kirchlichen Literatur des Abenlandes vom 5. bis 11. Jahrhundert* (Bonn, 1928), pp. 7–24.

and again in the tenth and early eleventh centuries, and from northern Germany at the same period. This rushing from coal face to coal face means that I shall necessarily place more emphasis upon particular en-counters than is strictly just to the area and the period as a whole. It will also involve the passing over of many important narrower and deeper questions: questions, for example, about the exact transmission and reception of texts, (legal, conciliar, and sermon texts in particu-lar), and about the local information to be gleaned both from these and from treatises less obviously concerned with magic.[2] A lot of work needs to be done on the composition, the manuscript traditions, and the detailed diffusion of miracle collections; commentaries on certain books of the Bible; certain sermons on the Magi, the Greater Litany, the Ascension, and Saint John's Eve; certain types of history (those which contain miracles and portents especially). I have not done this; but this preliminary work on the borderlands, and upon the more ob-vious of the encounters between Christian and non-Christian magic, will, I hope, help to show us how much we might eventually learn from closer studies.

Nor have I distinguished between so-called popular and so-called learned sources, though this time not for reasons of time and personal limitation, but of conviction. Such distinctions can be, in matters concerning belief in the supernatural, unhelpful. When applied to a particular text or "superstitious" practice, for instance, the word pop-ular can imply that this text, or that action, belonged exclusively to the uneducated or to those lacking in social status; yet, as was the case with Caesar, even the most cultivated and exalted might find them-selves prey at moments to unsophisticated fears and simple hopes, and to remedies for these fears, and supports for these hopes, which partake of the irrational or magical. Nobiles will often share curious beliefs with rustici, although it may, on occasion, be politic for preachers to pre-tend that only the latter are at fault. When Archbishop Martin of Braga, for instance, wrote his sermon De Correctione Rusticorum in the late sixth century, the kings of Galicia were as nearly "rustic" in the matter of believing in pre-Christian practices as were their subjects; but the archbishop was far too adroit to say so. Lords often gave as much weight as did their retainers to so-called popular superstitions.[3]

[2] An exemplary discussion of the type of narrower and deeper question to which I refer is that by A. L. Meaney, "Aethelweard, Aelfric, the Norse Gods and Northum-bria," Journal of Religious History 6 (1970), 105–132.
[3] Canon XXII of the Council of Orléans of 549, for example, envisages the opposi-

Likewise, in the hands of a good speaker, or an enthusiastic child or relative or friend, "learned" material may easily be communicated to the uneducated, and we would do well to assume that there was a good deal of energetic talk about a subject so close to the lives of so many as magic.

Thanks to the work of social anthropologists it is now possible for the historian to acquire an ear for the echoes of an oral society, and for the impact upon it of certain sorts of written text. We might thus learn to suspect, for instance, that so-called school poetry, those passages and stories from Virgil and Lucan, perhaps, which we have already singled out, and which were provably taught at certain periods in many monastic schools, might very easily have been used to record and transmit a knowledge of magic, and that well down the social and the learned scale as well. So might other works heavy with supernatural reference, such as Virgil's eighth *Eclogue*, or the *De Divinatione* of Cicero. The frequency with which the reading of pagan authors and their "perniciosa dogmata"[4] were condemned in the early Middle Ages tends to dull us to the fact that real dangers still lay in them; but they ought to alert us to it instead. Some few lines in Lucan (close to the ones I cited earlier about the witch), had, we know, an impact.

> By these witches . . . the clear moon, beset by dread incantations, grew dim and burned with a dark and earthy light, just as if the earth cut her off from her brother's reflection, and thrust its shadow athwart the fires of heaven. Lowered by magic, she suffers all that pain, until from close quarters she drops foam upon the plants below.[5]

Lucan's magical substitute here for the scientific explanation of a lunar eclipse (an explanation he clearly knew about) found an echo in a "popular" magical belief well attested in the early Middle Ages. According to this, the darkening of the moon in this way was always the work of an enchantress, who drew it down into a dark cavern, and so caused it pain. To Lucan, the contrast between the magical and the scientific explanation had been an obvious one, but later the scientific explanation became quite lost to the magical one and had to be delib-

---

tion of local lords to the suppression of these, and the *Life* of Lupus of Sens (d. ca. 625) has Lupus converting a "dux" from such practices; Mansi, IX,135; AS Sept. i,259.

4 Isidore, *Sententiae*; PL 83,877.

5 *Civil War* (Pharsalia) vi,499–506; *edit. and transl.* J. D. Duff, *Lucan* (Loeb Classical Library, 1928), pp. 340–341.

erately revived in order to counter the latter.[6] It is not possible, of course, to argue with any degree of conviction that the passage from Lucan gave rise to the belief, but it could certainly have helped to keep alive folk memories of it, and to sustain the semi-educated in a twilight between condemned "magical" beliefs and "authoritative" evidence of their credibility.[7] This dimension to the teaching and reception of the so-called school poets is an important one and needs to be kept carefully in mind. An intricately constructed frontier between acceptable and unacceptable magical belief, but within the world of general education, is at issue here. The social consequences of "learning" such as this, received at second hand, are hard in any case to assess and even harder in a period so remote; but that there were some there is no doubt. The medieval church would have to worry about this frontier too. We shall, I hope, occasionally be able to make out its contours; but it is one which is again rather obscured than distinguished by the categories "learned" and "popular."

Within the general criterion of wide influence, then, keeping the borderland settings in mind, and putting this last particular form of distinction firmly aside, the sources I shall in general use may be divided into four: legal, doctrinal, literary, and scientific. The legal sources will be plundered greatly for the first chapters of each of the three latter parts of the book: for those chapters, that is, which deal primarily with persistence and condemnation. Four preliminary points may be made about these legal sources. We do not always know, of course, whether the ordering of the legislation as it reaches us reflects in fact the priorities of the legislators; but magic is not, in them, in general an overriding preoccupation. It appears to occupy a lesser place in the process of prohibition and punishment than, for example, murder or arson or counterfeiting, or, in ecclesiastical codes, simony and clerical marriage. This state of affairs is important, for it brings me to my second point. That magic occupied this lesser place suggests that it might have been allowed a greater freedom, and its practitioners a larger latitude, than the taking of certain condemnatory canons out of context can imply. Such comparative leniency was of great service to the situation in general of magic in the early Middle Ages, and, of course, to its rise. My third point has to do with the fact that these

---

[6] This belief will be more fully discussed in chap. 5.

[7] Virgil's *Eclogue* VIII,ll.69–71 reinforces the belief once again; *edit.* and *transl.* E. V. Rieu, *Virgil, the Pastoral Poems* (Harmondsworth, Middlesex, 1967), pp. 96–97.

legal sources are often laconic. Laconic utterance should not be mistaken for lack of information or concern; quite the reverse. It may mean, on the contrary, that nothing more needs to be said in elucidation, so familiar is the subject and so well known the practices. I think it often does mean this in the case of magic. Fourthly, secular and ecclesiastical sources should, where possible, be looked at in tandem and seen, on occasion, as complementary. Silence in ecclesiastical law codes, for example, may indicate not a lack of concern on the part of the church but a satisfactory concern on the part of the state,[8] and many "secular" codes were, of course, supervised or written by ecclesiastics. Special outbursts on the part of the one or the other may indicate, on the other hand, a division of views. The legal sources are difficult, in their present state, to interpret in their every detail, but they do yield important guiding information about attitudes to, and conflicts about, magic and its practitioners, and sometimes, when carefully dated and placed, they may yield information which is specific.

For secular "barbarian" legal sources, I shall draw greatly upon the laws of the Visigoths, especially upon the *Breviarium Alaricianum* (put together early in the sixth century), which formed the foundation of so many other collections, including the laws of the Bavarians and Lombards.[9] Much of this compilation and the lost earlier one of Euric (ca. 483) found its way into the *Forum Judicum* or *Visigothic Code* of the mid-seventh century,[10] and the two contribute in valuable ways to our understanding of the state of affairs faced by persons such as Archbishops Martin of Braga and Isidore of Seville. I shall draw, too, directly upon the Lombard collections put together between 643 (the date usually assigned to Rothair's *Edict*) and 755,[11] upon the laws of

[8] And, of course, the reverse. Sometimes we find that magic is given especial attention in church councils because the secular penalties seem too harsh. A decree of the Council of Merida, 666, condemns resoundingly, for instance, resort to secular penalties for magic on the part of priests; Mansi, XI,83–84.

[9] M. Conrat (Cohn), *Breviarium Alaricianum* (Aalen, 1963). This magnificent volume sets out the sources of the *Breviarium* as well as a German translation of the text.

[10] This is accessible in an English translation by S. P. Scott, *The Visigothic Code* (Boston, 1910), but the translation is extremely unreliable. The edition by Conrat, n. 9 above, complete with its source work, and all those to be found in the *MGH Leges* point clearly to the shortcomings of simple translations, even when they are good ones. My references to the Visigothic Laws, therefore, will usually be to the Latin texts.

[11] Transl. K. Fischer Drew, *The Lombard Laws* (Philadelphia, 1976).

the Salian and Ripuarian Franks,[12] and upon those of the Anglo-Saxons.[13] Very many of the laws of the Anglo-Saxon kings of England contain references to and condemnations of magical practices. This is especially true of those put together under the formidable eye of Archbishop Wulfstan of York (d. 1023), such as Ethelred v and its Latin paraphrase, Ethelred vi and some of Ethelred's later codes, the so-called *Laws of Edward and Guthrum*, and the secular code of Canute (1020–1023). Here the line between secular and ecclesiastical laws becomes a very slender one indeed.[14]

In the matter of strictly ecclesiastical legislation, and in addition to the canons of specific councils, four individual compilations are particularly important: the eighty-four "capitula" of Archbishop Martin of Braga (appended to the text of the Second Council of Braga of 572, and perhaps drawn up shortly after it, and later incorporated into the *Hispana*);[15] the tantalizing *Indiculus Superstitionum*, a list of thirty condemnable magical practices appended to a copy of the canons of the Council of Leptinnes (ca. 743);[16] the *De Ecclesiasticis Disciplinis* of Regino of Prüm (written ca. 906 in response to a request by the archbishop of Trier for a book of reference to guide him upon his visitations);[17] and the *Decretum*, especially Books X and XIX, of Bishop Burchard of Worms (put together between the years 1008 and 1012 as a more general guide for bishops).[18] Ecclesiastical penitentials (and Book XIX of the *Decretum* is in fact a penitential) are of course of great value too. Among these the so-called Roman penitential of Halitgar of Cambrai, together with the penitential of Rabanus Maurus, were

---

[12] Transl. T. J. Rivers, *Laws of the Salian and Ripuarian Franks* (New York, 1986).

[13] Transl. F. L. Attenborough, *The Laws of the Earliest English Kings* (Cambridge, 1922) and A. J. Robertson, *The Laws of the Kings of England from Edmund to Henry I* (Cambridge, 1925).

[14] Excellent texts and translations of these and related legislation may now be found in *edit.* and *transl.* D. Whitelock, M. Brett, C.N.L. Brooke, *Councils and Synods* i (Oxford, 1981), especially pp. 312, 341–342, 366, 371, 439–440, 488–489.

[15] Edit. C. W. Barlow, *Martini Episcopi Bracarensis Opera Omnia* (New Haven, 1950), pp. 123–144.

[16] This may be read in translation in J. T. McNeill and H. M. Gamer, *Medieval Handbooks of Penance* (New York, 1938), pp. 419–421.

[17] PL 132,185–370.

[18] PL 140,831–854, 943–1014. Parts of Regino's *De Ecclesiasticis Disciplinis* and of Burchard's *Decretum* XIX (the *Corrector*) may be read in translation in McNeill and Gamer, *Medieval Handbooks*, pp. 314–345. The excerpts are, however, exceedingly selective and the translation, on occasion, questionable. I shall generally refer, then, to the Latin texts.

exceptionally widely used and so have been called upon frequently.[19] Archbishop Wulfstan drew heavily upon penitentials[20] and seems to have been the author of a little handbook for confessors in which concern about magic was prominent.[21]

By "doctrinal" sources I mean sermons, treatises, and commentaries upon books of the Bible, and the canonical and apocryphal Scriptures themselves. Outstanding contributors of views upon magic through sermons and moral exhortation are Archbishop Caesarius of Arles (d. 543), Archbishop Martin of Braga once again (d. 579), Pirmin, monk of Reichenau (d. ca. 754), and the fiery Anglo-Saxon educators and homilists Aelfric of Eynsham (d. 1020) and, once more, Archbishop Wulfstan of York (d. 1023). Caesarius had excellent ways of speeding the circulation of his own sermons and of the sermon collections he made. He would press them upon visitors to Arles (especially upon those who came asking for letters of reference from him), and he would thoughtfully substitute the name of a great doctor of the church (that of Augustine most often) for his own as author.[22] Both methods seem to have worked wonderfully well. Caesarius's influence on later preachers can be very clearly marked, and the imprint of his views upon magic may be found in works that are not openly homiletic at all. The *Life of Eligius* (d. 660), written largely by Saint Eligius's disciple Saint Ouen (d. 684), is one such. When Saint Ouen has Saint Eligius preach upon magic, he has him do so largely in Caesarius's words.[23] It is likely that Caesarius's sermons, too, stand behind some of the thirty chapter headings of the *Indiculus Superstitionum*.[24] Not

[19] McNeill and Gamer, *Medieval Handbooks*, translate the penitentials attributed to Halitgar and Rabanus, as well as other important disciplinary collections and penitentials. Again, however, the Latin editions are in fact indispensable. There is an excellent collection in F.W.H. Wasserschleben, *Die Bussordnungen der abendländischen Kirche* (Halle, 1851). The penitentials (and the popularity) of Halitgar and Rabanus are discussed, and an important further expansion of them edited, in R. Kottje, *Die Bussbücher Halitgars von Cambrai und des Hrabanus Maurus* (Berlin, 1980).

[20] Whitelock, Brett, and Brooke, *Councils and Synods* i, 319–320.

[21] R. Fowler, "A Late Old English Handbook for the Use of a Confessor," *Anglia* 83 (1965), 1–34.

[22] G. Morin, "The Homilies of Caesarius of Arles," *Orate Fratres* 14 (1938–1940), 484–486.

[23] *Vita Eligii Noviomagensis* II, 16a, 17; *edit.* B. Krusch, and W. Levison MGH SRM iv (Hanover and Leipzig, 1902), 705–708.

[24] At least nine may have been drawn from Caesarius's categories. R. Boese, *Superstitiones Arelatenses e Caesario Collectae* (Marburg, 1909), p. 35.

surprisingly, many others (and notably Pirmin) also bear his mark.[25] Caesarius was the main source for an anonymous Latin sermon against pagan magic, which may have stemmed from the eighth century or shortly before, that quickly entered into *Florilegia*.[26] He was the main source, too, for a similar one, long attributed to Saint Augustine, which was remarkably explicit about forbidden magic, and which will be referred to frequently.[27] Springing perhaps from the same milieu which produced the *Indiculus Superstitionum*,[28] this *Homilia de Sacrilegiis* is striking testimony not only to the strength and obduracy of outlawed magical practices, but also, and more interestingly, to the evident ineffectiveness of condemnation *tout simple*. Caesarius's sermons are copied too into the eighth-century *Homiliary* attributed to Bishop Burchard of Wurzburg (d. 753/54), co-worker against pagan practice with Saint Boniface in Germany.[29] Aelfric, for his utterances on magic, was greatly indebted to Caesarius,[30] and Wulfstan of course to Aelfric. Sermon material such as this is instructive if used carefully, but dangerous if one tries to pin it too forcefully, and without detailed source and context work, to a particular place or person. Caesarius's long shadow reached into many corners, and perhaps on occasion convenience, rather than true contemporary feeling, prompted the repetition of his vehement words. It is hard always to be sure. Ten of his sermons seem to have been excerpted especially widely.[31]

[25] Boese draws attention to echoes in sermons attributed to Burchard of Würzburg (d. 754) and sermons by Rabanus; ibid., pp. 36–40.

[26] W. Levison, *England and the Continent in the Eighth Century* (Oxford, 1946), pp. 78–79. The discussion of this sermon forms part of an appendix intriguingly called "Venus, a Man."

[27] Edit. C. P. Caspari, *Homilia de Sacrilegiis. Aus einer Einsiedeler Handschrift des achten Jahrhunderts herausgegeben und mit kritischen und sachlichen Anmerkungen, sowie mit einer Abhandlung begleitet* (Christiania, 1886).

[28] Ibid., pp. 70, 73.

[29] A sermon from this *Homiliary* against magical practice, and attributed to Burchard of Würzburg (Sermon XXIV) is edited by J. G. Ekhart, *Commentarii in Rebus Franciae Orientalis* i (Würzburg, 1729), 844. It is in fact Sermon 52 of Caesarius.

[30] Thus J. C. Pope, *Homilies of Aelfric. A Supplementary Collection* ii, EETS (Oxford, 1968), 671n.

[31] Sermon 54 seems to have been the most popular. The others are 6, 12, 13, 33, 52, 184, 189, 192, 193. The numbering follows that given by G. Morin, *Sancti Caesarii Arelatensis Sermones*, CC (Turnholt, 1953). These sermons may be read in translation in M. M. Mueller, *Saint Caesarius of Arles. Sermons*, (Washington, 1956–1973). Boese, *Superstitiones* provides a most useful general introduction to the influence of Caesarius, but the sermon numbering he uses is the older *PL* one, and some of the

Shortly after the Second Council of Braga in 572, over which he presided, and in addition to compiling his "capitula," Archbishop Martin of Braga wrote a sermon for the guidance of Bishop Polemius of Astorga. This sermon, the De Correctione Rusticorum, tackled the problem of pagan magical survivals directly and offered a countering cosmology (modeled in large part upon the De Catechizandis Rudibus of Saint Augustine). Such a countering cosmology, we might note, was an excellent method of meeting opposition of this kind, and when, in the Middle Ages, we come across spurts of interest in Christian cosmology, we might with good reason take these as indicators of the presence of a strongly non-Christian threat. The De Correctione Rusticorum clearly met a demand many felt to be pressing, and it spread like wildfire, often losing the name of the original author in the process.[32] Like the sermons of Caesarius, it was certainly known to the biographer of Eligius, Saint Ouen of Rouen, in the seventh century, and, in the eighth, it influenced the anonymous sermons I have mentioned and had reached southern Germany in time for Pirmin to use it in his Scarapsus. This Scarapsus is, in its turn, also a collection of moral directives, this time based primarily upon material taken from the canonical books of the Bible.[33] Strictures against the practice of magic are prominent among these, and it is likely that Pirmin was writing for that same world against which the Indiculus Superstitionum, the anonymous sermons, and some of the earlier penitentials were directed.

Whether he did or did not know the Scarapsus directly,[34] Aelfric certainly had access to those sermons of Martin of Braga and Caesarius which Pirmin had himself consulted, and Aelfric too set himself to put these to immediate practical use. Aelfric's debt to Martin of Braga is evident in part of his sermon De Falsis Diis,[35] and his debt to Caesarius

echoes he attributes to Caesarius's influence are very slight and could come from legal or penitential sources.

[32] The Latin text of this sermon is printed, and the proliferation of the manuscripts of it are discussed, by Barlow, Martini Episcopi Bracarensis, pp. 159–203. It may be read in translation in C. W. Barlow, Iberian Fathers i (Washington, 1969), 71–85.

[33] De Singulis Libris Canonicis Scarapsus; PL 89, 1029–1050.

[34] Pope, Homilies of Aelfric, disagrees with Barlow, Martini Episcopi Bracarensis, and thinks he did not.

[35] Pope, Homilies of Aelfric, pp. 669–670. It was through Aelfric that this material got into the Old Icelandic Hauksbok; A. R. Taylor, "Hauksbok and Aelfric's De Falsis Diis," Leeds Studies in English 3 (1969), 101–109. A part of the De Falsis Diis may be read in translation in edit. A. S. Cook and C. B. Tinker, Select Translations from Old English Prose (Cambridge, Mass., 1908), pp. 186–191.

in that on the Passion of Saint Bartholomew. These and many others of his sermons,[36] and also sections of his other works (the *De Auguriis* from his *Lives of the Saints*, for example, which is also based in part upon Caesarius),[37] give us vivid insights into the ways in which some anxious (and infuriated) preachers approached the problem of magic in Anglo-Scandinavian England. The vehemence of Caesarius here did, I think, match Aelfric's own. Archbishop Wulfstan attended to magic in the law codes we know he drew up and supervised and in his directions to confessors, as we have seen; and he did so again in some of his sermons. His famous *Sermon of the Wolf to the English*, his *De Falsis Diis* (an adaptation of that of Aelfric), and his *De Baptismate*[38] are the most notable purveyors in sermon form of his views on magical practices.

For biblical commentaries I have looked to the same periods and frontiers, and I have, in the matter of the canonical books, given priority to those which tell of the more spectacular of the encounters between magicians and the servants of the Christian God. Foremost among such encounters is the story in Exod. 7 about Moses and the magicians of Pharaoh, closely followed by that in 1 Sam. 28 about the raising of the dead Samuel by the witch of Endor. The interventions of the angel Raphael as healer in the Book of Tobit and the magical methods recommended there are worth particular attention, more of it, in fact, than they have been given here. Isidore, Gregory the Great, Bede, and Rabanus have much to offer in their various commentaries on such books and passages, as they have in some of their other biblical commentaries. Information may be garnered both directly from the sources each uses and the positions each takes up, and, indirectly, through their tendencies (and this tendency is especially striking in Bede's commentary on Tobit) to disappear into allegory once the subject of magic becomes pressing. The reasons why an allegorical expla-

[36] The fullest Anglo-Saxon and English version of the Catholic Homilies is still that by B. Thorpe, *The Homilies of the Anglo-Saxon Church* (London, 1844–1846). We lack a complete translation into English of the Catholic and the Supplementary Homilies.

[37] This debt was first discovered by M. Förster, "Altenglische Predigtquellen, I," *Archiv für das studium der neueren Sprachen und Literaturen* 116 (1906), 307–308. The *De Auguriis* may be read in translation in W. W. Skeat, *Aelfric's Lives of the Saints*, EETS (London, 1881), pp. 364–383.

[38] For this see especially the notes to her edition in D. Bethurum, *The Homilies of Wulfstan* (Oxford, 1957), pp. 319–320. Wulfstan's sermons are here printed in the original. A translation of the *Sermon of the Wolf* may be found in Cook and Tinker, *Select Translations*, pp. 194–203.

nation of certain passages of the Bible becomes at times the predominant one deserve a great deal more discussion; but embarrassment at the sheer strength of that magical practice which prevailed when the commentaries were written may well be one of these reasons. In the matter of the apocryphal Scriptures I have laid most emphasis upon those which tell of the achievements of spectacular magicians, Simon Magus above all, and upon those which were assuredly widely known, either for themselves or through popularly read transmitters such as Cassian. Because they were so preoccupied with the supernatural and enjoyed such an enormous vogue, I have chosen, finally, to draw heavily upon the doctrinal material contained in the so-called Pseudo-Clementine literature. Consisting of the *Homilies* and *Recognitions*, this literature purported (and was believed, even though it was in fact put together in the fourth century) to be by the apostle Clement himself, successor to Peter, and so to carry an exceptional authority. It was translated into Latin in the fifth century by Rufinus, and the number of manuscripts surviving now attests to its immense importance to the period.[39]

My "literary" category is a catch-all for sources which decline to be ranged under any of the other headings, and it is beginning to resemble Pandora's box. Foremost among these unrangeable sources are saints' lives and miracle collections. These are resistant to firm categorization and dating once again, partly because they are, of course, full of exempla, and partly because they borrow from one another in ways that cause even the analogous complications of sermon literature to pale into insignificance. In that they deal so openly and so convincedly in every sort of wonder and preternatural event, however, they are of the very first importance to an understanding of the rise of magic; indeed, I have come to believe that they may be the most important of the sources we have, a belief that renders the state in which we find them at present (sometimes poorly edited, hard of access, and very rarely translated into English) doubly frustrating. Much magnificent work has been done upon the passing of certain stories from life to life, but from the point of view of magic, non-Christian versus Christian, I suspect that the true interest of such stories may lie less in their ancestry than in the grouping of particular types together (about healing

[39] The surviving manuscript evidence is set out in B. Rehm, *Die Pseudoklementinen* (Berlin, 1965), pp. xvii–xcic. The Clementine literature may be read in English in transl. T. Smith, *The Clementine Homilies* (Edinburgh, 1870), and idem, *The Writings of Tatian and Theophilus and the Clementine Recognitions* (Edinburgh, 1867).

through special means, as it might be, or the interventions of certain animals and birds, or the control of the weather) at particular times and in particular places. I shall draw here only upon pockets of these saints' lives and collections of miracles, and these, again, the "frontier" ones: those drawn from periods, that is, in which the opposition between non-Christian and Christian magical practice was felt particularly strongly. I shall depend very heavily, therefore, upon Merovingian saints' lives, especially the one to which I have already drawn attention, the *Life* of Saint Eligius of Noyon, and the many accounts of the miraculous activities of saints and confessors written by Gregory of Tours (d. 594).[40]

Some of the later *Acta* of the martyrs seem also to be instructive, and so do similar hagiographical writings by such as Bede, Alcuin, and Aelfric. I shall pay considerable attention in addition to the more notable and widely popular accounts of spectacular wonder-workers. Among these I would single out the *Life of Saint Martin of Tours* by Sulpicius Severus (begun in about 393 or 394 but a best-seller throughout the period) and the *Dialogues* of Pope Gregory the Great, especially the section (Book II that is) which treats of the life and miracles of Saint Benedict of Nursia.[41] The *Dialogues*, and also the sermons of Pope Gregory, are extraordinarily important as a source for Christian magic, for not merely are they written by a pope preoccupied to an exceptionally high degree with the problems of conversion and reconciliation, and with barbarian conversion and reconciliation especially, but they reflect these preoccupations fully in the complexity of their make-up and references, deceptively simple at first glance as some of these seem to be.

[40] *Edit.* B. Krusch and W. Levison, *Vita Eligii Episcopi Noviomagensis*, MGH SRM iv (Hanover and Leipzig, 1902), 634–749. Gregory's major works are also edited by Krusch in ibid., i (parts 1 and 2) (Hanover 1885). The *Decem Libri Historiarum* is translated by O. M. Dalton, *The History of the Franks by Gregory of Tours* (Oxford, 1927), and the *Liber Vitae Patrum* by E. James, *Gregory of Tours: Life of the Fathers* (Liverpool, 1985).

[41] The best edition and translation (into French) of the *Life of Saint Martin* is J. Fontaine, *Sulpice Sévère, Vie de Saint Martin* (Paris, 1967–1969). The *Life* and other works of Sulpicius may be read in English translation in A. Roberts, *The Works of Sulpitius Severus* (Washington, 1955). The best edition and translation of Gregory's *Dialogues* is, again, a French one, A. de Vogüé and P. Antin, *Grégoire le Grand, Dialogues* (Paris, 1978–1980). A recent effort to deny to Pope Gregory the authorship of the *Dialogues* has not commanded assent. The *Dialogues* will be discussed more fully in chap. 11.

I have mentioned the possibly deep effect well down the social and learned scale of works more obviously literary: of pre-Christian works such as the *Aeneid* of Virgil, with Servius's commentary, for instance, of certain of his *Eclogues,* and of the works of others such as Ovid or Cicero, Apuleius or Statius or Lucan. The immensely popular writings of the Christian poet Prudentius (d. ca. 410) might be expected to have had an even more profound effect, for Prudentius could offer all (or almost all) the linguistic and rhythmic attractions of the others without their pagan disabilities. I shall often turn to these school-books, then, and to their commentaries and glosses, for information both about condemned magical practices and about the possible allure that still lay in them for those open to their influence. Sometimes one can catch sight, in a gloss, of a view that may well be contemporary. A tenth-century glossator on Lucan can say, for example (when commenting upon the powers witches could wield in the matter of causing earthquakes and celestial convulsions), "effectum magicis *posse* fieri"—"such happenings *can* be brought about by magic."[42] Lucan and Virgil certainly did much to reinforce the belief, unquestioned throughout the period and forcefully driven home by many chroniclers, that comets portend direful changes, especially in kingdoms. This particular belief, I shall argue, had a direct effect upon one of the most spectacular of the magical rescues we shall discuss: the rescue of astrology.[43] Thus, some investigation into that which we can learn from school material such as this does seem to be appropriate.

One should, however, be a little more guarded about that which saga material can tell us for this period, full though the sagas are of tempting stories about witches and the supernatural. We know that the Norse and Icelandic sagas were composed primarily for entertainment, and that they were written down, at the earliest, in the thirteenth century, and so (on the face of it at least) after the conversion to Christianity of their authors and audiences. Many of these authors had as their object the discrediting of earlier ways with the supernatural, and, in the service of this discredit, perhaps the exaggeration of some of these ways. For this reason, as well as for many others, they are appallingly difficult to use as sources for this particular inquiry. I have used them, therefore, very sparingly. This being said, in their

---

[42] *Civil War* (Pharsalia) VI,ll.481–482; *transl.* Duff, *Lucan,* pp. 338–339. *Edit.* J. Endt, *Adnotationes super Lucanum* (Leipzig, 1909), p. 228nn.

[43] *Civil War* I,ll.525–529; *transl.* Duff, *Lucan,* pp. 40–41. And see below, chap. 6.

sheer preoccupation with magic, and in the clarity with which they draw attention to the everyday character, as it were, of the operations of witches and wizards upon the local scene, they do throw welcome extra light upon that situation which, I hope to prove, called forth such a complex response from the Christian Church.

It is, as I have tried to suggest, and as I hope has already become clear in the case of Pliny, extremely difficult wholly to set aside certain works as purely scientific ones, and so to discuss them separately. Very many stand on the borders between magic and that which Thorndike (in that magisterial work which stands at the basis of so much else) called "experimental science," and he has named and numbered them with a deftness which even now has no peer.[44] It is useless to repeat, and impossible to outdo, his work here; but I would draw attention to another way of looking at the scientific texts he cites and so of making some limited, and different, use of them again. Thorndike was interested primarily in the resemblances he could find between "primitive magic" and "experimental science," and in the ways in which the two might work together to promote the rise of science proper. He did not, then, look too closely at how the two might divide, or to the ways in which this science proper might be used in fact as a counter to magical excess; and he was certainly not at all interested in the purposeful rise of magic. Approached from another angle, however, Christian "scientific" texts in general might be used in a manner similar to that I have already suggested for certain types of Christian cosmology: as indicators, that is, of the presence of that powerful and pressing magical opposition to Christianity which will provoke new thought about the place of magic within the church itself.

One of the aims of science is, as I have said, the elimination of the magical, in the sense of the irrational. I have attempted recently to argue that the composition of such scientific works as the early treatises *De Natura Rerum* may have been in part inspired by the need for a more sober, indeed dampening, approach to the supernatural than some of those which were current when these treatises were written, current both within and without the Christian Church.[45] When used in this way—upside down, as it were—scientific texts can be extremely helpful as a means of showing us just how strong these opposing pressures

[44] L. Thorndike, *A History of Magic and Experimental Science* i (New York, 1923).

[45] V.I.J. Flint, "Thoughts about the Context of Some Early Medieval Treatises *De Natura Rerum*," in *Ideas in the Medieval West: Texts and their Contexts* (London, 1988), no. III.

were, how urgent was the need to overcome them, and how committed some persons were to a Christian-scientific rather than to a Christian-magical means of doing this. Such treatises could, furthermore, actually excite by reaction that response within the church we seek primarily to follow here: a response that turned certain churchmen away from scientific counters to non-Christian magical practice and actively toward a Christianized form of magic in their stead. Christianity, especially when under Pauline influence, was, after all, deeply anti-intellectual and passionately concerned to establish the rights of irrationality in a controllable form. Scientific works are complex objects for the social historian to use, but, through their contents, their immediate contexts, and the subjects to which they pay particular attention, they can give us vital information both about the practices they were, in fact, attacking, and about the various nonscientific Christian reactions they provoked. Some took their rise *from* magic, it is true; but others countered magic, and still others impelled the rise of magic of a different sort. I shall come to suggest that astronomical, astrological, and medical treatises are especially important in this respect.

We come finally to those treatises which deal with magic directly. Written material of this kind is in short supply, but the efforts of four particular authors of it do reward attention. The first of these authors is Isidore of Seville (d. 638). Isidore provided in his *Etymologies*, written shortly before his death, a section headed *De Magis*, in which he purported to summarize succinctly all the knowledge currently available to be gathered about forbidden magical practices.[46] Because of the immense success in the early Middle Ages of the *Etymologies* as a whole, and because of Isidore's ability here as a summarizer, his section *De Magis* became the standard description of magical practices for later authorities. Thus, it constituted a central part of three later works directly concerned with magic: the *De Magicis Artibus* of Rabanus Maurus (d. 856),[47] the *De Divortio Lotharii et Tetbergae* of Archbishop Hincmar of Rheims (d. 881),[48] and that section of the *Decretum* of Bishop Burchard of Worms (d. 1025) in which magic is described in general terms.[49]

[46] *Etymologiarum* VIII,ix; *edit*. W. M. Lindsay, *Isidori Hispalensis Episcopi Etymologiarum sive Originum Libri XX* (Oxford, 1911).

[47] *PL* 110,1097–1099.

[48] Chapter XV; *PL* 125,718–719.

[49] Book X,41–42; *PL* 140,839–840.

These excursions into direct description (and condemnation) are, not surprisingly, all undertaken by persons who confronted the problems of pagan magical survivals especially immediately, and this gives them an extra claim to consideration here; but this is not all. Much more important (and illuminating) is the fact that each work subsequent to Isidore borrows from his section *De Magis*, but each does so in a slightly different way. The difference between the versions given by Isidore and by Rabanus is especially striking and revealing. I shall end this chapter, then, with Isidore, and devote to him and to his immediate heirs a separate section; this firstly because Isidore sets out clearly and simply that view of non-Christian magicians and their arts which was to become the orthodox early medieval Christian one, and secondly because the process of adaptation which can be discerned even in the treatment of this relatively short passage might serve to alert one to the wealth to be gleaned in general from such adaptations and to inspire more work upon them.

ISIDORE, *DE MAGIS*

The *Etymologies* were devised as a sort of warehouse of precious knowledge, stored against leaner days and to be taken from the shelves at need. Isidore's description there of magical practices seems partly to be borrowed from the *Theodosian Code*, from the *Breviarium* of the Visigoth Alaric, from Virgil and Lucan, Prudentius and the Bible, but many may well also have been directly encountered, for we can find rulings against them in the canons of Martin of Braga. The compilation is, in short, though somewhat bookish, not wholly so; it may reasonably be (and was) received as the informed and practical observations of a conscientious pastor of souls. I give a full summary of it here for two reasons. Firstly, it has not yet been translated into English. Secondly, though pruned to its essentials, it does give quite a full description of that magic medieval Christians both feared and yet felt called upon to deal with.

Magic, in all its vanity, originally reached the human race through the intermediacy of the evil angels, says Isidore. The first exponent of the magical arts for whom we have a name was Zoroaster, King of Persia. Democritus much expanded the magical expertise received from Zoroaster, just when Hippocrates was perfecting the "disciplina" of medicine (this opposition between magic and "disciplina" is an interesting one, for it seems to indicate an attitude toward discipline which helped Isidore, I shall later argue, to rescue certain forms of magic). The Assyrians, he goes on (citing Lucan), whose king Ninus defeated and killed Zoroaster, paid magic even more attention. Thus it spread throughout the world. Such magic purported to offer knowledge that is hidden, either in the future or in the infernal regions, and to this end "aruspicia" and "augurationes" were invented, and so were the taking of oracles and the raising of the dead. Magicians became, as a result, powers in the land, magicians such as those whom Moses opposed,[50] or such as Circe, who changed the companions of Ulysses into beasts,[51] or the ones who through sacrifices to Zeus Lycaeus were enabled to turn other people into animals,[52] or Virgil's Massylian witch who could enchant the waters and the stars, and conjure earthquakes and human emotions. Isidore gives some indication that he believed that such things were indeed possible. He returns to the Bible with the instance of Saul and the witch of Endor, and the raising by the witch of the dead Samuel (1 Sam. 28) and then brings out a little more Christian evidence in the form of Prudentius's account of the raising of the dead by Mercury.[53] This particular section later, and interestingly, gave rise to a certain alarm.

Isidore then describes with gusto the practices of his "magi," a term he equates with "malefici." In general, they upset the elements, disturb the minds of men, even kill by enchantment alone, boasting, with the support of demons, of this manner of dealing with enemies. Such malefici make use, he says, of blood and sacrifices and dead bodies especially (surely Isidore is calling upon direct observation here).[54] Necromancers in particular call up the dead with charms and ask them questions with the help of blood from wounds, which demons love. Such blood, mixed with water, is, in fact, the sign of the necromancer. Hydromancers call up the shades of demons in water to consult them, also with the help of blood; blood, indeed, looms especially large in

[50] A reference to Exod. 7:10–12.

[51] Virgil, *Eclogues* VIII,69–70 (the same section that gave support to the magical account of the darkening of the moon); *transl.* Rieu, *Virgil*, pp. 96–97. Isidore does not give these references himself but clearly expects them to be well-known ones.

[52] Possibly a reference to Pausanias, viii,38; *edit.* and *transl.* W.H.S. Jones, *Pausanias Description of Greece* iv (Loeb Classical Library, 1933), 90–96.

[53] *Contra Orationem Symmachi* I,ll.90–93; *edit.* and *transl.* H. J. Thomson, *Prudentius* i (Loeb Classical Library, 1949), 356–357.

[54] See, for example, *Recc. Erv. Chind.* VI,2,5, in which encompassing death by magic is strictly forbidden; *edit.* K. Zeumer, MGH *Legum* 1, *Leges Visigothorum* (Hanover and Leipzig, 1902), 260.

Isidore's enumeration of the tools magicians use. He then takes from Varro a fourfold division of the divinatory arts (geomancy, hydromancy, aeromancy, pyromancy, each calling upon one of the four elements: earth, water, air, and fire) and proceeds to describe magicians of other types. Enchanters use words, and "arioli" call up demons through sacrifices. "Haruspices" are so called because they deal in the days and hours suitable for the undertaking of great enterprises and predict the future from the entrails of animals. "Augures" look to the flights and cries of birds for such predictions, and so do "auspices." Such signs are thought to be particularly pertinent to journeys. "Astrologi" make predictions from the stars and "genethliaci" pay special attention to days of birth and how the zodiac and planets stand in relation to these. They seek in this way, he adds, to predict personal behavior and events, and are vulgarly also called "mathematici." The Magi of the Gospels were, says Isidore, prominent astrologers, and indeed this science was legitimate until the coming of Christ. After Christ's coming, however, it was no longer held permissible to make such predictions. "Horoscopi" try to speculate about the fates of individuals from the exact hours of their births. Isidore devotes quite some space to his description of astrology, which he terms a "superstitio." I shall come to suggest that the problem of astrology was certainly a contemporary one and occupied him forcefully. He goes on to speak of lot casters ("sortilegi") who make predictions through certain sorts of writings, including writings of a sacred kind (Isidore calls this "false religion"), and "salisatores" who predict good or ill from the involuntary movements of limbs. Efforts to penetrate the hidden secrets of the future, to Isidore, make up the bulk of magical lore, but he reserves a special final burst of outrage for medical magic, in which all magicians dabble, he implies, and which he contrasts with the "ars medicorum" ("the learning of real doctors"), rather as he contrasts the "disciplina" of Hippocrates with the activities of the earliest magicians. Caesarius had made similar distinctions. Medical magic, as opposed to medicine proper, Isidore tells us, consists in the binding or hanging onto people of "execrable remedies," perhaps including written characters, perhaps involving incantations. Such activities are wholly demonic and are derived purely from an evil cooperation between human beings and the wicked angels. Christians must have nothing whatever to do with them.

This is a thorough enough description and denunciation, and as such it passes into the works of the three successors I have mentioned—but with interesting changes. Rabanus uses the passage twice, once in his *De Universo*,[55] the second time in a work even more important and revealing to us, his *De Magicis Artibus*. In each he makes amendments to Isidore's account of biblical magic and reinforces his own position, which is different, with considerable strength. When discussing the raising of the dead Samuel by the witch of Endor, for example, Isidore had in fact left the matter open. It might have been diabolical delusion, he says—and yet, on the other hand, it just might have happened; Mercury, according to Prudentius's poem, could, after all, raise the dead. The position Isidore takes up here is contrary to that of Saint Augustine, who, as we saw, had declared his view that the raising of Samuel was the work not of humans but of demons, purely and simply, and it is contrary to that he had himself adopted in his earlier *Quaestiones in Vetus Testamentum*, in which he follows Augustine verbatim.[56] It looks as though Isidore might have changed his mind; but if so it is a change that does not impress Rabanus. Rabanus, in his *De Magicis Artibus*, misses out this particular passage and also Isidore's quotation from Prudentius, and he substitutes instead a firm statement to the effect that all magical tricks rely on illusion and are not to be confused with fact. The same fierceness characterizes his discussion of the biblical account of Moses and the magicians of Pharaoh. Isidore had treated this quite cursorily, and as a small part of his discussion of pagan magical tricks in general. Rabanus includes this passage, as he had not that on Samuel, but later comes specially back to it, as he does to Samuel too; and when he does so he treats us to a veritable feast of authorities, all designed to prove, once again, that magicians can have no such powers of themselves.[57] In his reliance on

[55] XV,iv; *PL* 111,422–424.

[56] Augustine, *Ad Simplicianum* II,iii; *edit.* A. Mutzenbecher, *Sancti Aurelii Augustini De Diversis Quaestionibus ad Simplicianum*, CC (Turnholt, 1970), pp. 80–81. Isidore, *Quaestiones in Vetus Testamentum, In Regum* I,xv; *PL* 83,407–410.

[57] I have been unable fully to recover all of the sources Rabanus used for his *De Magicis Artibus*, but those I have been able to identify are, in order: *Pl* 110,1097B–1099A; Isidore, *Etymologiae* VIII,ix (excerpted as I have indicated), *edit.* Lindsay, *Isidori Hispalensis*, 1099B–C; perhaps Maximus of Turin, *Sermo* XXXI, *edit.* A. Mutzenbecher, *Maximi Episcopi Taurinensis Collectionem Sermonum Antiquam*, CC (Turnholt, 1962), pp. 122–123, 1099D; Augustine, *Quaestiones in Heptateuchum* II,xxi, *edit.* I. Fraipont, *Sancti Aurelii Augustini Quaestionum in Heptateuchum Libri VII*, CC (Turnholt, 1958), pp. 77–78, 1100A–1101A; Ambrosiaster, *Quaestiones Veteris et Novi Testamenti* CXXVII, *edit.* A. Souter, *Pseudo-Augustini Quaestiones Veteris et Novi Testamenti CXXVII* (Vienna and Leipzig, 1908), pp. 54–56, 1101B–C; Augustine,

Ambrosiaster, rather than Augustine, for his treatment of the problem of the raising of Samuel, and in his repeated insistence that the raising was delusory, Rabanus seems deliberately to turn to the fiercest expression available to him of the position adopted by Augustine, and in so doing doubly to reproach Isidore for the latter's seeming open-mindedness. Rabanus had become, in the De Magicis Artibus, even more fanatical upon this subject than he had been in the De Universo. We may see here the long shadow of contemporary magicians who really did claim to be able to raise the dead, and whose claims Rabanus felt it to be his special responsibility to rebut.[58] Supernatural power to revive dead men, and to lay or bring back ghosts, features strongly in the saga literature, and Rabanus was physically closer to the peoples from which this literature sprang than was Isidore.

The views expressed in the De Magicis Artibus may not be truly representative ones. Certainly it was not, as I have already noted, a widely copied treatise, and Rabanus's position may have seemed to some a little excessive. One explanation of the initially surprising lack of enthusiasm for Rabanus's little work on magic may be found in the closeness with which he drew upon sources already sufficiently known; but another may lie in the accident of his own geographical position (in the thick of the battle against non-Christian practice), and still another in the extreme conservatism of his opinions in the face of certain contemporary Christian attitudes that were, perhaps, less directly confrontational. Rabanus expressed a particular vehemence and conservatism in his choice of sources. Ambrosiaster, for example, allowed far less discussion of the problem of Samuel and the witch of Endor than Augustine did, and less too than Bede did in his own commentary on the selfsame passage, which Rabanus must surely have known.[59] The strong positions of such as Ambrosiaster could generate opposition as well as support, though it might be well for such opposition to take a practical form rather than too explicit a written one. Still one more

---

Quaestiones in Heptateuchum V,xviii, edit. Fraipont, Sancti, p. 287, 1101C–1107B; Augustine, De Divinatione Daemonum iii,7–10,14, edit. J. Zycha, Sancti Aurelii Augustini de Fide et Symbolo . . . (Vienna, 1900), pp. 603–618.

[58] The anonymous Homilia de Sacrilegiis, for example, contains a ruling against the consulting of "pitonissas"; III,5, Caspari, Homilia, p. 6. The very first practice the Indiculus Superstitionum condemns is that of "sacrilege at the graves of the dead"; McNeill and Gamer, Medieval Handbooks, p. 419.

[59] Edit. D. Hurst, Bedae Venerabilis Opera. Opera Exegetica ii (2), CC (Turnholt, 1970), pp. 256–257.

reason for the unenthusiastic reception of Rabanus on magic may lie in the fact that he annexed his conservatism to a penitential which sought to punish witchcraft far more leniently than did the secular authorities. Rabanus's insistence that witches had no true power was perhaps connected with this desire for leniency. It would be unacceptable to those who saw witchcraft as a threat demanding stronger measures, and unacceptable too to those who felt that a belief in the power of witchcraft was a belief that could be turned to good. We shall return to such questions again and again, and to this last one very shortly. For the moment, Rabanus's use of Isidore may serve to remind us that even the most apparently simple acts of textual transmission may in fact reflect sensibilities which are very deep indeed, and not easy immediately to recover.

The *De Divortio Lotharii et Tetbergae* of Archbishop Hincmar of Rheims was the product of a political crisis. King Lothar II, of the area later known as Lotharingia, was married to a barren wife and, wishing to divorce her, connived at accusations against her. The accusations, one of incest in particular, would, if upheld, render the marriage null and allow Lothar to marry his mistress of long standing, Waldrada. Archbishop Hincmar sprang to the defense of the unhappy Theutberga, Lothar's wife, after the first arraignments in 860, and he sprang in part with the help of Isidore. He needed, as a portion of this defense, to deal with the vexed question of the supposed magical abilities of witches, especially with those of female witches, for Lothar's mistress was suspected of using witchcraft in the affair. It served Hincmar's case to insist that she had actually done so, and he does seem, indeed, to have believed that witches had real powers. Thus, in his borrowings from Isidore he exchanges, this time, Isidore's references to Circe and to the witch of Endor for matters far more up-to-date and insists that, far from their being delusory in any sense (a matter Isidore had, after all, left open), the powers of the many contemporary witches of whom he speaks were all too evident. He makes telling little additions to Isidore's text, intruding a condemnation of weaving and measuring magic, and of juggling and trompe l'oeil, and expanding upon Isidore's dislike of diviners by mentioning how they indulge in divinations from animals' shoulder blades and from inspecting the livers of their animal victims.[60] These additions must surely come from contemporary obser-

[60] "Aruspices, qui horas in agendis negotiis et operibus custodiunt, qui exta pecudum et fibras atque spatulas, vel caetera quaeque inspiciunt, et ex eis futura praedicunt. . . . Sunt et praestigiatores, qui alio nomine obstrigilli vocantur, quod praestrin-

vation. Once more, Isidore's message is subtly changed, but this time the direction of the change is a different one, and we may even dare to suspect that Hincmar and Rabanus, close as they were to one another in time and even place, held conflicting views about the nature of claimed magical abilities, and so also, perhaps, about the remedies for these.

The *Decretum* of Burchard of Worms, put together, as I have said, between the years 1008 and 1012, uses Isidore slightly differently again. Burchard in fact takes Isidore's section *De Magis* from Rabanus, complete with Rabanus's own adaptations, and with Rabanus's additions from Augustine's *De Divinatione Daemonum* and from Ambrosiaster too, and attributes the whole to Augustine.[61] Thus here patristic authority is annexed, once more and clearly, to a conservative position on the powers of witches—but the penalties for witchcraft are, in Burchard, very gentle ones indeed. They are certainly a great deal more lenient than, for example, those recommended under Pope Innocent VIII or in the fifteenth-century *Malleus Maleficarum*.[62] This combination of skepticism about the powers of "malefici" and leniency toward their punishment, though, of course, a logical one, is of great interest in this context. Rabanus's *De Magicis Artibus*, and so his use of Isidore, was joined, as I have said, to his penitential, and that of Burchard had a penitential with it and was written with ecclesiastical sanctions, as opposed to secular ones, to the fore. Hincmar's, on the other hand, was annexed to a tirade and fashioned for circumstances which did not exactly encourage the archbishop to mildness. The different purposes for which Isidore's help was sought and the different ways in which his original passage *De Magis* was employed are once again reflected in the nature of the selections made.

The sources for magic, in short, are complex to use even when they reach us in their seemingly most straightforward forms, and the most

---

gant vel obstringant humanorum aciem oculorum, sicut isti qui de denariis quasi jocari dicuntur, quod omnino diabolicum est. . . . Ad haec omnia pertinent et ligaturae exsecrabilium remediorum . . . vel quibuscunque mensuris mensurandis: et quas superventas feminae in suis lanificiis vel textilibus operibus nominant"; PL 125,718–719.

[61] *Decretum* X,41–47; PL 140,839–851.

[62] This point is made by C. Vogel, in an article essential to all understanding of the *Decretum*. C. Vogel, "Pratiques superstitieuses au début du XIe siècle d'après le Corrector sive Medicus de Burchard évêque de Worms (965–1025)," in *Études de civilisation médiévale (IXe–XIIe siècles). Mélanges offerts à Edmond-René Labande* (Poitiers, 1974), 751–761.

apparently simple of borrowings from them may have many levels of understanding to offer, once one looks for them. In the last resort, also, they defy categorization, even categorization of the loose kind I have used. Burchard, for instance, a "legal" source par excellence, borrows from materials that are in one sense "literary," and Augustine's *De Divinatione Daemonum* can command, under certain circumstances, the force of law. In any event, our early written sources tell at most part of the story. We must attempt to recover the rest by other means.

CHAPTER

4

The Situation

BEHIND THE ATTITUDES to magic we saw developing under the late empire, and beneath the great names whose writings we have briefly discussed, we can trace the faint, but ever more insistent, influence of a third powerful presence. This presence, though hard fully to recover and harder still exactly to describe, is of an outstanding importance to our appreciation of the rise of magic. It consists of a host of faceless, and often nameless, diviners, soothsayers, sorcerers, and seers—potent sources of a type of influence that deserves the description "magical" by the fact that so very much of their local eminence sprang from their perceived ability to manipulate the supernatural. Persons such as these certainly deserve to be called religious leaders in a sense; and yet at first (and, in the eyes of many, at last as well), they could not be incorporated within the structure of the Christian religion as it came to early medieval Europe.

These leaders—we might dare to call them for the moment "witch doctors," for this both conveys to the mind that combination of awe-inspiring supernatural ability and local influence which was their chief attribute and gives us a hint, at least, of possible modern parallels—seem, when we look for them, to have been very widely to be found. Much anthropological work upon recent and contemporary village societies and their "witches" has wisely (and repeatedly) warned us that this may have been the case.[1] To discover just how prevalent such competing leaders were, and of how intricate a web of expectations their authority may have been compounded, can, nonetheless, come as something of a revelation to medievalists not always conditioned to look for such sources of social control. Faceless and nameless presences

[1] I have found two collections of essays here most helpful: *edit.* M. Douglas, *Witchcraft Confessions and Accusations* (London, 1970), and *edit.* M. Stephen, *Sorcerer and Witch in Melanesia* (Melbourne, 1987). I am deeply in debt to Professor Douglas for much generous discussion.

are not those which leap first to the historian's eye; and yet, when they are found, and especially when they are found in large numbers and filled with energy, they are of the first importance and extraordinarily instructive. In matters concerning medieval magic this revelation is, I would contend, a literally vital one. It brings a greater life to our largely Christian written sources and encourages us now to reach out a little further beyond them than we are always accustomed to do; and it gives us crucial insights into the type of society these sources confronted. It might thus allow us to see some of these written sources, especially those with overtly magical concerns (I think of hagiographical ones especially) as, in part at least, reactions to this presence, and to understand these too, then, a little better.

It seems, in truth, that early medieval Europe was remarkably well supplied with influential and respected harioli, auspices, sortilegi, and incantatores. Gregory of Tours is (sometimes despite himself, and always to the end of pouring scorn upon their practices by contrasting them with edifying Christian ones) very helpful indeed in introducing us to this state of affairs. Incantatores and harioli afford Gregory especial distress (and many compensating moments of triumph). The wife of one Serenatus, for instance, becomes ill on her way home from the fields and cannot speak. Her friends summon "harioli" in their anxiety, and these in their turn apply "ligamina" of herbs and say over her "words of enchantment" (to no effect at all). Gregory's niece Eustemia knows better. She removes the ligamina and replaces them with oil and wax from the tomb of Saint Martin, with instant success.[2] There are many dimensions to this little report, of course, and to others like it, and we shall return to some of them; but here the elements which claim our notice are the immediacy and confidence with which harioli are sought (and found), and their instant (and in intention helpful) response to trouble. Gregory, although he deplores recourse to persons such as these, seems to take it as a customary course of action, requiring not explanation, but defeat. He tells many more stories of this kind. A boy falls sick with the fever; again a "hariolus" is called, and he "murmurs incantations, throws lots, ties ligatures round the sufferer's neck." The boy dies; and when another sickens Gregory himself takes charge. He administers dust (mixed in water) from the tomb of

[2] *De Virtutibus S. Martini* IV, 36; *edit.* B. Krusch, MGH SRM i(2) (Hanover, 1885), 208–209.

the martyr Julian, again successfully.[3] A young man becomes ill when hunting, and his kinsmen, fearing that he has been bewitched, call "harioli" and "sortilegi" to his aid ("as countryfolk do"). These go about their tasks in their accustomed way, tying on ligatures and administering potions. Only a visit to the church of Saint Martin, however, produces the desired effect.[4]

Each of these stories conveys a single message: the Christian saints are faced with a strong and numerous opposition, and one in which many people (and people, we might remark, of noble as well as humbler status) have faith. The *Vita Iuniani Confessoris* tells us of one Ruricius, a powerful local magnate. His "fideles" take him to "medici" when he becomes ill and also, "which was worse," consult "maleficos ac praecantatores" (who cost a lot of money).[5] He too, of course, is cured only by the prayers of the saint. One Ursio breaks his arm when hunting and is rushed to "medici" and "incantatores" (a frequent method of double insurance, or so it seems), who prove unable to help him. Oil from the lamps burning at the tomb of Saint Praeiectus, however, heals the break.[6] There are many more such examples of the prevalence, and sometimes the fear, of witch doctors in Merovingian France.[7] Caesarius becomes very annoyed when persons elect to seek out "soothsayers" and "seers" and "diviners" and "enchanters" (and especially so when Christian priests and religious respond in such roles to their requests) instead of receiving the Sacrament and being anointed with oil at church; and he reveals, as he gives vent to his annoyance, that such recourse was very frequent and that such diviners were remarkably easily to be found.[8] The *Life of Eligius* tells the same tale (often, of course, in Caesarius's words). The rushing after

[3] *Liber de Passione et Virtutibus Sancti Juliani Martyris* 46a; ibid., 132.

[4] *De Virtutibus S. Martini* I,26; ibid., 151.

[5] *Vita Iuniani Confessoris Commodoliacensis* 6; *edit.* B. Krusch, MGH SRM iii (Hanover, 1896), 378.

[6] This healing encourages the making of generous donations in return. Financial as well as devotional considerations are here very clearly at stake. *Passio Praeiecti Episcopi et Martyris Arverni* 38; *edit.* B. Krusch and W. Levison, MGH SRM v (Hanover and Leipzig, 1910), 247.

[7] When Queen Fredegonde, for example, loses two sons in an epidemic, her immediate explanation is "maleficium"; Gregory of Tours, *History of the Franks* V,29; *transl.* O. M. Dalton, *The History of the Franks by Gregory of Tours* ii (Oxford, 1927), 211–212.

[8] Sermon 50; *transl.* M. Mueller, *Saint Caesarius of Arles, Sermons* i (Washington, 1956), 253–254.

conjurors of magic characters, diviners, lot casters, and enchanters "in matters of illness or in any other matter" is the first, and seemingly the worst, iniquity for which Eligius castigates his audience.[9]

Pirmin of Reichenau in the eighth century repeats and reaffirms Eligius's message: do not consult "praecantatores et sortilegos, et karagios, aruspices, divinos, ariolos, magos, maleficos," or look to auguries from sneezes or from the cries of birds.[10] In ca. 775 Cathulf wrote to Charlemagne to enlist his support against the prevailing numbers of "maleficos, veneficos, tempestarios, strigas, phitonissas."[11] The anonymous *Homilia de Sacrilegiis*, as we saw, denounced "divinos vel divinas, id est pitonissas."[12] In the tenth century Ratherius of Verona is only one of many still angrily objecting to "auguriis" and "praecantationibus," to the deceptions of "malefici" in general and to the willingness of people to believe in them,[13] and in the early eleventh Wulfstan, archbishop of York, intensifies the attacks found in earlier Anglo-Saxon law codes upon "incantatores . . . magos, phitonicos et veneficos necne idolorum cultores."[14] Wulfstan has a variety of different words, both Latin and Anglo-Saxon, for a scourge he clearly thought both numerous and powerful. Although he considered Norwegians to be the very worst of offenders, Adam of Bremen, writing in the later eleventh century, found witches everywhere.[15]

[9] *Vita Eligii Episcopi Noviomagensis* II,16a; *edit.* B. Krusch and W. Levison, MGH SRM iv (Hanover and Leipzig, 1902), 705.

[10] *Scarapsus; PL* 89,1041.

[11] *Edit.* E. Dümmler, MGH *Epistolae Karolini Aevi* ii (Berlin, 1895), 504.

[12] C. P. Caspari, *Homilia de Sacrilegiis. Aus einer Einsiedeler Handschrift des achten Jahrhunderts herausgegeben und mit kritischen und sachlichen Anmerkungen, sowie mit einer Abhandlung begleitet* (Christiania, 1886), p. 6.

[13] *Praeloquium*, I,iv; *PL* 136,152.

[14] *Edit.* D. Whitelock, M. Brett, C.N.L. Brooke, *Councils and Synods* i (Oxford, 1981), 366. In his *Sermon of the Wolf* Wulfstan lays stress on the great number of followers the servants of "false gods" had; *transl.* A. S. Cook and C. B. Tinker, *Select Translations from Old English Prose* (Boston, 1908), p. 195.

[15] "Although all barbarism overflows with their numbers, the Norwegian land in particular was full of these monsters. For soothsayers and augurs and sorcerers and enchanters and other satellites of Antichrist live where by their deceptions and wonders they may hold unhappy souls up for mockery by the demons"; *transl.* F. S. Tschan, *History of the Archbishops of Hamburg-Bremen* (New York, 1959), p. 94. The original Latin conveys Adam's horror even more vividly and is especially interesting in that it employs the term "miraculum" to describe some of the magical effects these "malefici" brought about: "Quorum numero cum tota barbaries exundet, precipuo vero Norvegia regio monstris talibus plena est. Nam et divini et augures et magi et incantatores cete-

Occasionally, too, we are afforded glimpses into life at a barbarian court of a sort that put us in mind of contemporary village chieftains and their sorcerers (and those of their opponents). Saint Vaast of Arras (d. ca. 539) discomfited enchanters and augurers at a dinner party given for King Lothar by making the sign of the cross over some enchanted ale and having it spill itself onto the floor, to the embarrassment of the assembly.[16] Paschasius Radbert, in the ninth century, tells us of a state of affairs which prevailed for a time at the court of the emperor, Louis the Pious.

> There was witchcraft everywhere. Policy was based not on sound judgment, but on auspices, and forward planning on auguries. . . . Lot casters, seers, interpreters of omens, mimers, dream mediums, consulters of entrails, and a whole crowd of other initiates in the malefic arts were driven out of the palace.[17]

Paschasius is expansive about the presence of such persons at court because there was a crisis, and because the "malefici" were singled out for persecution. Louis had married a second wife, Judith, and her stepsons had become jealous of her, even accusing the queen herself of witchcraft. Her supposed supporters, then, were similarly accused and punished (a classic case, we might remark, of witchcraft accusations).[18] The most striking aspect for us here of this little scrap of evidence, or so it seems to me, is that it is the driving away of these supposed "malefici," and not the fact that they could be discovered or were many, which attracts Paschasius's attention. He is not at all surprised that, once they came to be looked for, such persons were to be found. An unfortunate situation gave them a prominence which was painful, but the presence of them and their crafts in circumstances less extraordinary was only to be expected. They would be on hand as a matter of course, and they would scatter only when their activities

---

rique satellites Antichristi habitant ibi, quorum prestigiis et miraculis infelices animae ludibrio demonibus habentur." *Gesta Hammaburgensis Ecclesiae Pontificum*; edit. B. Schmeidler, *Adam von Bremen. Hamburgische Kirchengeschichte* (Hanover and Leipzig, 1917), p. 117.

[16] *Vita Vedasti Episcopi Atrebatensis Duplex* 8; edit. Krusch, MGH SRM, iii, 422–423.

[17] *Vita Walae*; edit. G. H. Pertz, MGH SS ii (Hanover, 1829), 553–554 (MT).

[18] A case, that is, of "accusations clustered in areas of ambiguous social relations"; edit. Douglas, *Witchcraft Confessions*, p. xvii. Such accusations do not always render witches vulnerable, of course. Sometimes they reinforce them in their positions of power. I am indebted to Professor Steven Sargent for reminding me of these distinctions.

came especially to be resented. Perhaps, after a short time (and when their accusers had failed in their own objectives), they would reassemble, strengthened by the persecution or, more significantly, by the failure of the Christian authorities to provide an adequate substitute for them.

By the time Archbishop Hincmar came to write his *De Divortio Lotharii et Tetbergae*, more gathering at court than scattering seems to have been apparent. Again, we owe this evidence to a crisis. Hincmar's concern to save the marriage of Lothar II (Louis the Pious's grandson) led him to dilate both upon the powers and the numbers of those manipulators of the supernatural who would injure this marriage. That such would be available, again, he takes entirely for granted, and he presents us with an enormous array of them and of their practices. They would conjure with bones, and with ashes and dead coals, and with hair from human heads or genitals. They would apply colored threads, or herbs, or bits of snail shell or snakes, chanting the while.[19] They would dress themselves up in many-colored garments, and drive themselves demented by consuming special foods and drinks. They would allow themselves to be hypnotized by "strigae," or sucked dry by vampires, or changed into members of the opposite sex. We must allow something here of course for the passion of the polemicist; but a truly wild inaccuracy would hardly have served his cause. "Viri malefici vel incantatrices feminae" were, according to Hincmar, absolutely everywhere, and they offered to those who wished to consult them a tremendous variety of services.

The parallels to be drawn at this point with the varied practices of modern village "sorcerers" are inescapable. I think especially of Aisaga, "man of knowledge," and of a portrait worth quoting at some length, partly because it is so beautifully written, partly because it is of a figure which has some echoes in the ones we have in Hincmar, and, indeed, in Gregory of Tours; but one seen this time through sympathetic eyes.

> His solitary hours—which seem so empty—are in fact filled with a subtle but continuous interaction with the realm of unseen powers. The plants that he tends in his house garden are not "just for decoration"; they provide the necessary ingredients for magical potions, like the insect tied up by one leg hanging over his fire and the dried bird's wing, and the lizard skin, thrust into the thatch over his veranda. The songs he sings to himself for

---

[19] *De Divortio* XV; PL 125,717.

hours on end are spells of various kinds; the soft muttering which can be overheard from my veranda when he retires for the night is not the old man talking to himself, as one might surmise, but a ritual invocation of the spirits of his fathers and grandfathers. The cries of birds, the chirps of insects, the sudden appearance of a firefly or a bat in the evening gloom, are all communications from the other world for a "man of knowledge," imbuing his working consciousness with constant awareness of other realities. This morning he has heard, for the third time in a row, the bird *ifi* calling in a bush towards the near end of the village; this is a sign of imminent death for someone in his clan. In the early evening a cicada shrills from the roof of his veranda, or a bat swoops low overhead; they are A'aisa's messengers. A sneeze, ringing in the ears, a throbbing of the veins in one's upper arm, all are meaningful to the "man of knowledge."[20]

We shall never find so full, still less so sensitive, a description in our surviving medieval Christian sources, but beneath the hostility with which these last are permeated we can discover many persons like Aisaga. He is a dream medium too, as well as an enchanter, an augurer, a mixer of magical potions, a guardian of powerful relics, a caster of spells. Much here is reminiscent of Isidore's *De Magis*.

It is at this point in his tirade aginst these multifarious magicians, indeed, that for good measure Hincmar launches into his repetition of Isidore, adding to the latter's "magi" the weaving and measuring witches, and those who made predictions from the livers and shoulder blades of animal victims. This copying does not, however, diminish the force of Hincmar's remarks. On the contrary, he seems to have found Isidore's list, appropriately varied, still to be applicable; and his use here of Isidore enhances the impression he has already given of a presence which was real, and pressing, and numerous. Seen from the other side, moreover, this presence might have had a great deal to offer to those who were ill, or in any way anxious or distressed. Aisaga, furthermore, could add to his other abilities the capacity to inspire an admiration and devotion in his followers by an impressive and real asceticism.[21] It is, at the very least, possible that some of our medieval "magi" also lived lives which commanded respect of this sort.[22] Hinc-

[20] M. Stephen, "Master of Souls: A Mekeo Sorcerer," *in edit.* Stephen, *Sorcerer and Witch*, p. 55.

[21] Ibid., p. 57.

[22] Maximus of Turin, for example, gives us a vivid description of a fifth-century "Dianaticus" or "aruspex": "All shaggy with extra hair, his breast bare and his cloak

mar would not tell us if they did, for he is hostile;[23] but his treatise
cannot but show, yet once again, that very many non-Christian manipulators of the supernatural were thought by him to be abroad in the
world in which he lived, and that he expected, despite his own horror
at them, many people to respect, and follow, and consult them. The
description of Aisaga may at least begin, I hope, to help us to understand why, and to suggest that in a sensitive process of conversion
these leaders might need to be invited to play a continued part. They
might, indeed, be very well fitted to do so.

Reports of the existence, and the appeal, of large numbers of such
leaders are by no means confined to hagiography, fierce individual pastors, or moments of crisis. Isolated prayers and blessings sometimes
confirm such presences for us by showing us the fear they might inspire
(or which might be aroused by their Christian critics).[24] Much more
spectacularly, both ecclesiastical and secular legal collections are
found condemning soothsayers, seers, diviners, enchanters, lot casters, and the like with a sonority and a consistency which almost deafen
us to their true significance by the very weight of repetition. Hincmar
includes a fair selection of such condemnation in *Interrogatio* XVII of
his treatise.[25] Canon XXIX of the Fourth Council of Toledo, over
which Isidore presided, is a good straightforward example of such rul-

---

reaching only to his thighs, he looks like a gladiator ready for a fight, sword in hand.
But he is in fact far worse than a gladiator, for the latter is under orders to do battle
with another, whereas this man is driven to do battle with himself. A gladiator attacks
the other man's body; this man tortures his own. His cruel god urges him on to tear
his own limbs to pieces, and when you see him dressed like this and covered with
blood you wonder is he in truth gladiator or priest?" Maximus wishes to dismiss this
figure as a mere drunken peasant, but, looked at in another way, this was a man clearly
prepared to undergo great pain in the interests of his priestly office. *Sermon* CVII,2;
edit. A. Mutzenbecher, *Maximi Episcopi Taurinensis Collectionem Sermonum Antiquam*,
CC (Turnholt, 1962), pp. 420–421 (MT). We can make out similar features in the
"imposters" Gregory of Tours and Saint Boniface present to their audience for their
outrage; see below, chaps. 6 and 8.

[23] He does speak, however, of that phenomenon whereby "malefici" in fact possessed by demons may nonetheless simulate great virtue: *De Divortio*, XV; PL 125,721.

[24] Such a prayer is to be found in a tenth-century manuscript from Schäftlarn: "I
ask in Christ's name that you will not let this place and parish be harmed by heavy
rains or ice or storm or the murmurings of enchanters," A. Franz, *Die Kirchlichen Benediktionen im Mittelalter* ii (Graz, 1909), 75. After all, such enchanters did threaten
these critics severely by offering a kind of alternative liturgy.

[25] PL 125,726–729.

ings and gives us a little further insight into the difficulties with which the ecclesiastical authorities were faced. It legislates against the type of compromise which had caused Caesarius to protest.

> If a bishop, or priest, or deacon, or anyone whomsover in clerical orders is caught consulting "magi" or "aruspices" or "arioli" or (most certainly) "augures" or "sortilegi" or those who profit by such arts or practice other such, he shall be immediately deprived of his dignity and placed under the yoke of monastic discipline, and shall redeem himself of his crime of sacrilege through perpetual penance.[26]

Some Christian leaders were, quite clearly, inclined to make common cause with those they should have shunned—an interesting and seemingly frequent combination of circumstances, and one with which this book will centrally be occupied. It is the reverse of that which can, on occasion, be found occurring now.[27] Not surprisingly, names describing these malefici are to be found, and frequently, in ecclesiastical pen-

---

[26] Mansi, X,611 (MT). A useful set of references to rulings against priests who made common cause with magicians may be found in D. Harmening, Superstitio. Überlieferungs—und theoriegeschichtliche Untersuchungen zur kirchlich-theologischen Aberglaubensliteratur des Mittelalters (Berlin, 1979), pp. 222–225.

[27] In "The Problem of Evil among the Lele. Sorcery, Manicheeism and Christian Teaching in Africa," Mary Douglas gives a spine-chilling account of how Christian teaching on the devil was recently, among the Lele, so manipulated by certain missionaries as to bring about a reign of terror there, to the end of hunting down supposed diabolically controlled sorcerers by means of a species of confession. She writes: "Now, in 1987, instead of deriding the ancient religion as a bunch of absurd superstitions, I found catholics profoundly believing in its efficacy as the work of the devil. Ordained priests of the Catholic Church were leading the hunt against malefactors whom they termed sorcerers. Sorcerer had come to mean anyone who practises the old religion. They identified sorcerers by occult means and forced them to confess. The new teaching is not that fear of sorcery is a delusion, but that sorcery is Satan's weapon. As Satan's servants, sorcerers are a grimly real menace. They have to be exorcised, but for some reason which has nothing to do with Christian teaching, the exorcism will not take effect unless the sorcerer confesses." This paper was first given in Oxford, at the Centre for African Studies Conference on Religion and Symbolism, in 1987. I am grateful to Professor Douglas for allowing me to read and quote from it before publication. It is a masterly exposition and discussion of present-day conflict between Catholicism and African magic, and of the dangers inherent in too forced a confrontation of the two, and one deeply relevant to the developments to be discussed below. Abuses of this kind there certainly were in this period, but I have not found that they prevailed.

itentials.[28] Persons called "arioli," "auspices," "vaticinatores," "divini," "aruspices," "sortilegi," "tempestarii," "and persons similar to these" appear too, and again often, as problems in secular law codes.[29] In one of these a careful distinction is made between the sorts of questions judges might be allowed to put to such "diviners" and that type of consultation which has augury in mind.[30] Such a distinction implies the existence of especially large numbers of such practitioners, numbers too great for them all to be excluded from the ordinary judicial processes.

The words I have left in the original Latin are not all capable of precise and consistent translation, though some, especially some of those used by Hincmar, will reward a closer scrutiny later. Distinctions between *witch* and *sorcerer*, and between those supernatural powers which are inherited and those which are acquired, distinctions helpful in certain sorts of anthropological investigation, are, sadly, of no help here as yet, for we cannot be certain about them; nor do all of the persons described, moreover, find a reflection in such as Aisaga.[31] I have kept reciting the names, however, and in this amorphous heap, to try to keep before our eyes three characteristics they seemingly all had in common. They were, for all the subdistinctions it may be possible to make between them, all in some sense "magicians," and thus non-Christian magical practitioners of a convincing kind, distinguished in our Christian sources by many derogatory names (or sometimes called simply "maleficus"),[32] are to be seen often going about their business. Secondly, they were a source of great concern to Christians and hard to accommodate within the church; and, thirdly, there

---

[28] In, for example, the so-called Roman penitential, attributed to Halitgar, V, VI; F. W. H. Wasserschleben, *Die Bussordnungen der abendländischen Kirche* (Halle, 1851), pp. 367–368.

[29] They are fiercely penalized, for instance, in the Visigothic Laws, and these again give the impression that they were very widely available for consultation and employment. *Recc. Erv. Chind.* VI.2.1–5; *edit.* K. Zeumer, *MGH Legum 1, Leges Visigothorum* (Hanover and Leipzig, 1902), 257–260.

[30] *Recc. Erv. Chind* VI.2.2; ibid., p. 258.

[31] It is, nonetheless, necessary to quibble with some of the English renderings of the Latin. Thus "jugglers" will not quite do, I think, for "caragios," nor simply "soothsayer" always for "ariolus," still less "wizard" for "mathematicus"; J. T. McNeill and H. M. Gamer, *Medieval Handbooks of Penance* (New York, 1938), pp. 229, 305–306. We might look to Isidore's definitions as a general guide.

[32] For instance, *Vita Iuniani Confessoris Commodoliacensis* 6; *edit.* Krusch, *MGH SRM,* iii, 378.

were very many of them. We should be quite wrong to draw such a conclusion from anthropological parallels, from persecution and outbursts, or from repetitive and hostile legislation alone, and we certainly cannot extrapolate across the whole of Europe a picture drawn from the rulings of individual councils, kings, or peoples, and uttered at separate times. When these different types of information are put together, however, and especially when we give living anthropological parallels a greater weight than we are sometimes accustomed to do, then all do combine to produce an engrossing picture of energetic, and sought after, non-Christian supernatural activity. To suggest that we are concerned here mainly, or even partly, with "pagan survivals" is to put the matter altogether too feebly. This is not a case of faint and lingering traces and last gasps, but of a whole alternative world of intercession. It is true that the manipulators of the supernatural we find in this world called upon many traditional sympathies and methods; but they operated very firmly in the present. They were enthusiastic, vigorous, and competitive, and their sphere of action was the lively and intimate circle of the contemporary village community. Many persons were accustomed to call upon these "sorcerers," and to do so in the very first instance. Rooted and vigorously alive custom and habit are the most difficult of all to change. This state of affairs needs to command a far greater degree of our attention than it has done hitherto.

The first few anecdotes, all taken from Merovingian sources, showed how avidly magi were sought out in matters of sickness. Sickness seems, indeed, to have provided a major sphere of influence for such practitioners, and across a wide expanse of time. Aelfric, for example, following Caesarius, condemns with an especial clarity the habit of going to diviners to ask advice on health.[33] According to Gregory of Tours sorcerers such as these could be seen both as potential curers of sickness, and as potential causes of it; and their services might, on occasion, be expensive.[34] Other types of magical skill were asked for in the pursuit of matters of the heart,[35] or, to put the matter less romantically, the commerce of marriage (and the misuse of love-related

[33] Edit. W. W. Skeat, Aelfric's Lives of the Saints i, EETS (London, 1881), 370, 375.

[34] Much evidence of a prevailing belief that illness was brought about by witchcraft may be found in Gregory's writings, in the De Virtutibus S. Martini III, 27, for instance, and Liber de Virtutibus S. Iuliani 45; edit. Krusch, MGH SRM, i, 189, 131. Such beliefs accord to harioli and incantatores an enormous amount of power and, of course, make persons exceedingly wary of causing them any offense.

[35] Aelfric; edit. Skeat, Aelfric's Lives, i, 370, 375.

skills was sometimes thought to be the cause of death as it can be too in modern societies).[36] Still others were expected to attend to the weather (fending off storms, producing rains), and others again to the planning of great enterprises. All such magicians (and of course a single one might attend to many different needs) were, in short, preoccupied with, and consulted in cases of, the very deepest of human concerns. They might channel substantial resources to the pursuit of their ends, and they might call upon considerable reservoirs of hope and fear.

The idea that a belief in witchcraft can spring from a need to account for (and if possible solace) misfortune and anxiety, and from a desire for the support of hopeful expectations, is, thanks to the labors primarily of anthropologists, an idea now familiar to us. And it is one that explains admirably the popularity of many of those magi at whom we have looked already. It solves many pressing questions about the persistence and the prevalence of the early non-Christian practitioners of magic we have briefly surveyed; and it throws into the sharpest relief at the same time both the strength and the nature of that competition with which the early medieval church must now contend. We cannot with certainty categorize those who consulted such persons as purely rustic and naive; and we cannot with confidence dismiss such practitioners as mere "gangsters of the supernatural,"[37] no matter what the Christian polemicists might ask us to believe. This aspect of the matter is of the very greatest importance. The Christian authorities were, in early medieval Europe, in competition with quite other persons of recourse; and that for a deep emotional (and also a financial) hold over the profoundest of personal anxieties and aspirations. They were ambitious, moreover, for a hold of their own which was to a large degree identical with that these other persons already commanded, and this at a time when the church's own problems of leadership were by no means entirely resolved. Christians, of course, also sought to solace fear and misfortune, to offer hope, to inspire, above all, devotion. They sought to bid for a trust, for a right to uplift the spirit and to assist

[36] See the so-called Roman penitential of Halitgar, 31; McNeill and Gamer, Medieval Handbooks, p. 305. "In the hands of the unskilled practitioner love magic, it is thought, can be made much more potent than it need be, such that it accidentally kills, rather than attracts, the woman at whom it is directed"; R. Bowden, "Sorcery, Illness and Social Control in Kwoma Society," in edit. Stephen, Sorcerer and Witch, p. 190.

[37] I take this felicitous phrase once again from Stephen, Sorcerer and Witch, p. 7.

in times of need, which had in fact been given to others, and to many others; but they sought to displace these others, and to focus their adherents upon the Christian "organization" alone. Looked at in this light, then, the problem posed to the early medieval Christian Church by magic was one of truly gargantuan dimensions. It was a matter of setting aside these multifarious and vigorous competing persons and objects without dispelling the emotions and expectations which had sustained them. It thus required that an attempt be made to retain in full that distinction and loyalty the competing magi were so successful in attracting, and yet to appropriate it for different or converted leaders (leaders who might come, we might add, to compete among themselves). It could become a matter too, then, of providing an adequate substitute for the resources lost, and one that would convincingly compel so large a return. And the task was not gargantuan alone—but urgent.

In the heroic ages of Christian conversion the dramatic, and, it must be said, the most superficial, methods of dealing with such competition seem, to ardent spirits, to have been preferred above all others. Eliminate it, destroy all remnants of its shrines and practices, discredit and outlaw all of its leaders, and begin afresh. I use the present tense when speaking of these attitudes, for they are rarely totally absent, and they are with us still today. In the Middle Ages they are richly to be found, especially in hagiographical sources. They seem to belong in general to an early stage of enthusiasm (though not, of course, only to an early time, for possible encounters of this sort will often recur),[38] not least because increasing experience, and the wisdom it brings, cannot but modify them. The elimination of devotion and its transference at the same time are not, after all, readily combinable activities. Such methods are, however, powerful in their impact while they last.

We find much evidence of the heroic approach among the Merovingians. The *Life of Eligius* is very revealing here. Eligius discovered an active group of non-Christian religious enthusiasts, complete with established and aggressive local leaders, quite close to Noyon. He ordered them to desist from their habitual practices and to accept baptism. They were furious and threatened him, and he called upon God to frighten them instead. God won the battle of terror by driving Eli-

---

[38] In the Philippines, for example, in the early stages of the Spanish missions there, this heroic approach seems to have been the most popular; J. L. Phelan, *The Hispanization of the Philippines. Spanish Aims and Philippine Responses 1565–1700* (Madison, 1959), pp. 53–54. I owe this reference to my colleague, Dr. Barbara Andaya.

gius's opponents (and especially their leaders—more than fifty of them in all, the writer tells us) raving mad. Eligius explained that this was a sign of God's glory,[39] but presumably the new congregation was without at least fifty of the old. There are many more such accounts. Saint Valery (d. 620) in one of his wanderings came upon a temple, complete with congregation. At his command the great structure collapsed at a single push, to the (understandable) resentment of its devotees. All attempts on their part to retaliate, however, were, through divine intervention, rendered ineffective. The opposition (again clearly considerable) retired in disarray.[40] Saint Radegunde (d. 587), on her way to a dinner party, was told that she was passing close to a pagan temple. She accordingly made a slight detour, ordered her servants to burn it down, and sat unmoved upon her horse before a huge multitude of hostile Franks who were waving swords and clubs at them all (the immobility of her horse at this sight is taken to be a similar sign of divine intervention).[41] Saint Bavo of Ghent (d. ca. 655) pulled down a temple, broke up its statues, and, as a result (we are asked to believe), brought back all the surrounding inhabitants to the Christian faith.[42] Saint Gall of Clermont (d. ca. 551) burned down a temple almost single-handedly, and the admiration this act evoked in Gregory of Tours led him incidentally to describe the misfortunes that this temple, and the statues or images in it, solaced, and the manner in which they did so.

> There was a temple there filled with various adornments, where the barbarians of the area used to make offerings and gorge themselves until they vomited; they adored idols there as if they were gods, and placed there wooden models of parts of the human body wherever some part of the body was touched by pain.

The many who valued the shrine pursued Saint Gall with drawn swords, and to such purpose that he had to hide in the nearby royal palace. The king calmed everyone down, but Saint Gall was later ashamed that he had not faced the martyrdom he was sure would oth-

[39] Vita Eligii II,20; edit. Krusch and Levison, MGH SRM, iv,711–712.
[40] Vita Walarici Abbatis Leucaenensis 22; ibid., pp. 168–169. This is an eleventh-century life, but the sentiments seem unchanged.
[41] Vita Sanctae Radegundis II,2; edit. B. Krusch, MGH SRM ii (Hanover, 1888) 380.
[42] Vita Bavonis Confessoris Gandavensis 4; edit. Krusch and Levison, MGH SRM, iv,537.

erwise have followed.[43] The Irish Saint Gall burned down a temple too and, to add insult to injury, threw all the offerings he found there into Lake Tuggen. Again its adherents sought to kill the saint, and he in his turn called down a dreadful curse upon their heads.[44] Saint Gall's biographer here, Walafrid Strabo, appears in the ninth century still to approve of such behavior; indeed, it was not far removed from that exhibited at the destruction of the Saxon Irminsul in 772 (although Charlemagne thoughtfully removed the offerings of gold and silver he found there) and which God was seen to approve by sending a miraculous supply of water for the army.[45]

Each of these stories praises power and its subsequent triumph, many have God send signs to confirm the message, and some of these signs are such as to render large numbers of the opposition wholly unable (being mad or driven away entirely) to subscribe to the new faith. Confrontation is forced, the opposition is defeated, and we are left to infer that the new power, under God, holds undivided sway. Occasionally this power is allowed to inflict actual death. When Bishop Wilfred of Ripon, in the seventh century, confronted a "magus" (one who sought to curse him and his followers from a high place "and to bind their hands by means of his magical arts") one of the bishop's companions hurled a stone from a catapult at the magus and killed him.[46] The parallels with David and Goliath are obvious and were recognized by Wilfred's biographer, but the message is obvious too. This was an excellent and well-attested way in which to deal with magi. They were to be humiliated, terrified, robbed of their following, and, if necessary, killed.

To my mind, and, far more important, to the minds of many contemporaries, such melodramas and such "miracles" served primarily to demonstrate how very effective in fact were the forces they purported to overcome, and to throw into sharp relief the real dangers such violent methods must inevitably have brought in their train.[47] To few

[43] Gregory of Tours, *Vitae Patrum* VI,2; *transl.* E. James, *Gregory of Tours: Life of the Fathers* (Liverpool, 1985), pp. 53–54.

[44] *Vita Galli Auctore Walahfrido* I,4; *edit.* Krusch and Levison, MGH SRM, iv,287–288.

[45] *Annals of the Kingdom of the Franks* 772; *transl.* P. D. King, *Charlemagne: Translated Sources* (Lancaster, 1987), p. 75.

[46] *Edit. and transl.* B. Colgrave, *The Life of Bishop Wilfred by Eddius Stephanus* (Cambridge, 1927), pp. 28–29.

[47] Dangers frighteningly illustrated by Douglas, "The Problem of Evil among the

people could, or can, such solutions recommend themselves as long-term ones, and certainly not for problems which deal in "magic" and are of the order confronted by the early medieval Christian Church. The wholesale destruction of places and discomfiture of persons once revered, does not, of itself and inevitably, induce respect for their replacements; nor does it always light the heart with joyful expectation. The humiliation of a loved leader, the requiring that he suffer loss of face, certainly does not automatically result in affection for his humiliator. By the very fact of its destroying so very many of the sanctions that hold a society together, and among these some they need still, such forcefulness might very easily recoil upon its perpetrator's head, upon that of the institution he or she represents, and, above all, upon that of the very society they seek to transform for the better.[48] Given the numbers and the scope of that non-Christian opposition which was abroad in early medieval Europe, and about which our written sources furnish so much evidence (albeit for the most part to different ends), far subtler, more varied, and often more gentle methods of approach were needed.

I shall argue that this need was recognized in the early Middle Ages. It was recognized by persons perhaps even more purposeful (though more quietly so) than the dramatic destroyers, and perhaps to a greater extent than it would be at a later date. It came to be accepted (quickly, indeed, by some) that where there was loss and a need for replacement in the matter of the older practices and practitioners, the replacement proposed would have to be one both sympathetically constructed and acceptable to the losers. It must be one upon which the losers might rely at least as securely as they had upon the former source of help. It must be of a sort that would neither give them reason to relapse nor reduce them to an acceptance which was cynical; and it must not, above all, cause loss of face.

Lele." Again, the shortcomings of such an approach are commented upon by Phelan, *The Hispanization*, pp. 70–71.

[48] Much illumination upon this point may be found, once more, in Douglas, "The Problem of Evil among the Lele," and also in the work of Stephen, this time in her essay "Contrasting Images of Power": "Accepting Christian teaching that sorcery was evil, Hanuabadans foreswore the use of it. As a result, they began to feel exposed to the sorcerers of less sophisticated neighbouring groups who continued to ply their black arts. . . . Fears increased as people accused relatives and neighbours of using hired sorcerers to harm them. Making no headway against the belief in sorcery, Christianity has succeeded only in damaging its legitimacy and the cultural controls that formerly guided its use." In Stephen, *Sorcerer and Witch*, p. 279.

The problems of disappointment and loss of face, of relapsing, and of a positively modern cynicism were, in fact, serious ones in the age of "heroic" conversion.[49] Our early sources, it is true, do not give us this impression at first reading; but then this was hardly exactly their aim. When we look at them more closely, however, even those who seem most enthusiastic about the ravage-and-burn method of approach do let slip suggestive little scraps of information. Both Saint Omer (d. ca. 699) and Saint Amand (d. ca. 675), for example, faced obdurate relapsers. The latter confronted persons who had returned to their former ways so enthusiastically as to throw the saint into the Scheldt several times as he urged them back to Christianity.[50] After the death of King Ethelbert of Kent, the people of London returned to the service of persons Bede calls "idolatrous high priests."[51] Gregory of Tours describes a cynic lying on a boat deck in a storm and refusing to pray to Saint Martin, a vignette that has a certain charm.[52] The *Codex Carolinus* contains a rather fierce letter from Pope Hadrian I to Charlemagne, written in response to the latter's anxiety about relapsers in his kingdom. The pope's first instinct is clearly to refer his correspondent to canon law (here to the penances prescribed in Dionysius Exiguus), but then he relents a little and admits that much depends upon the circumstances which surround and cause the apostasy.[53] Ultimately he allows the responsibility for deciding upon the measures to be adopted to rest with the local bishop.

In this last example the problem was clearly recognized to be one of a great complexity; but the road to an enduring solution to problems

[49] Once more, there are certain very striking parallels with the Christianization of the Philippines. There too the early aggressions of the "heroic" period had to be tempered in the face of possible apostasy, and accommodations made with preexisting non-Christian religious practices where this was possible. J. L. Phelan, "Prebaptismal Instruction and the Administration of Baptism in the Philippines during the Sixteenth Century," In *edit.* G. H. Anderson, *Studies in Philippine Church History* (Ithaca, N.Y., 1969), pp. 26, 37–39.

[50] *Vita Audomari* 5, *Vita Amandi Episcopi* I, 13; *edit.* Krusch and Levison, *MGH SRM*, v, 756, 436–438. Both reacted by tearing down temples nonetheless. Early councils speak often, and with distress, of converts reverting to their old ways; for example, canon XXII of the Council of Lyons, 567, Mansi, IX, 803.

[51] *Ecclesiastical History* II, vi; *edit.* and *transl.* B. Colgrave and R. A. B. Mynors, *Bede's Ecclesiastical History of the English People* (Oxford, 1969), pp. 154–155.

[52] *De Virtutibus S. Martini* I, 9; *edit.* Krusch, *MGH SRM*, i, 144.

[53] *Edit.* E. Dümmler, et al., *Epistolae Merowingici et Karolini Aevi* i (Berlin, 1892), 609. The letter is dated by its editor to the years 781–786.

such as these—one which neither gave excuse for, nor provoked, apostasy of this kind—was hard to find, and this partly because it was lit by far fewer immediate excitements (and royal friends, perhaps) than the high road of dramatics. Beneath the heroics and the harsher examples of God's "glory," however, we can begin, it is heartening to discover, to make out successful travelers along a second, more difficult, way; and it was this way that, in the end, led to the rise of magic.

This second way provided for magic's rise by not merely tolerating the older and competing magical practices—but calling them actively to its aid (though never, of course, under that name). This is the way I hope we might chiefly here retrace. It had long been recognized, by the talented and by the thoughtful, to be one which deserved support. Saint Augustine of Hippo had written movingly in favor of it,[54] and we have a particularly forthright advocate of it, significantly, in Pope Gregory the Great. In a famous letter, written to Abbot Mellitus (then on his way to barbarian England), Gregory spells out a course of action which is almost the complete reverse of that espoused by Saint Eligius and his like, and is one which gives us clear indications of the complexities this different path might involve. It was a widely copied letter and is worth setting out almost in full.

> When Almighty God has brought you to our most reverent brother Bishop Augustine, tell him what I have decided after long deliberation about the English people, namely that the idol temples of that race should by no means be destroyed, but only the idols in them. Take holy water and sprinkle it in these shrines, build altars and place relics in them. For if the shrines are well built, it is essential that they should be changed from the worship of devils to the service of the true God. When this people see that their shrines are not destroyed they will be able to banish error from their hearts and be more ready to come to the places they are familiar with, but now recognizing and worshipping the true God. And because they are in the habit of slaughtering much cattle as sacrifices to devils, some solemnity ought to be given to them in exchange for this. So on the day of the dedication of the holy martyrs, whose relics are deposited there, let them make themselves huts from the branches of trees around the churches which have

---

[54] "Keeping up the good habits idolaters practiced, cherishing the things and buildings they cherish too; this is not following in their footsteps. . . . Quite the contrary. In doing this we make something our own which never belonged to them, and give it back to the one true God, consecrating it in all manner of ways to his honor and that of his saints, and all for his greater glory." *Ep.* 47; *PL* 33,185 (MT).

been converted out of shrines, and let them celebrate the solemnity with religious feasts. Do not let them sacrifice animals to the devil, but let them slaughter animals for their own food to the praise of God, and let them give thanks to the Giver of all things for His bountiful provision. Thus while some outward rejoicings are preserved, they will be able more easily to share in inward rejoicings. It is doubtless impossible to cut out everything at once from their stubborn minds: just as the man who is attempting to climb to the highest place, rises by steps and degrees and not by leaps.[55]

This passage is a very rich one, and the further exploration of its wealth will form the substance of much of this book. I quote it here, however, as an introduction to those ways of conversion which fell short of total suppression. There might be substitutions under the direction of the church[56]—almost, indeed, imitations. Much might be left to look, at least, the same. Stubborn loyalty has its place; it might even be a virtue. Local pride and honor, habit, hope, and enthusiasm must, above all, be cherished. Gregory and, it must be said, Bede who so carefully includes this letter, are both extremely skillful spokesmen for this more complex, adaptive, approach; and they had, I hope to argue, many fellow travelers.

It was an approach that was full of pitfalls. Indeed, some of the priest consulters of harioli whom Caesarius and Isidore condemn seem to have been victims of just such enthusiasms, well meant, but in their cases taken to excess. Too much and too close an imitation of the people and practices to be replaced could be confusing, and it might so blur the distinction between the old and the new religious magic that the frontier between them would dissolve completely, and the new, rather than convert the old, revert to it instead. This was a danger to which even the most optimistic and diplomatic of churchmen must remain alive. It would involve them in difficult balancing choices, and in pastoral decisions of the utmost delicacy. Devils of the kind that were used so to trouble the Lele were, for example, available for abuse here too, through a misreading (perhaps willful) of Pope Gregory's directions. A belief in demons could always be manipulated in

---

[55] Bede, *Ecclesiastical History* I,xxx; *transl.* Colgrave, *Bede's Ecclesiastical History*, pp. 106–109.

[56] Interestingly, princes may still terrify non-Christians and tear down their shrines; ibid. I,xxxii, pp. 112–113. Gregory seems here to be drawing a distinction between ecclesiastical and secular policies, and so to emphasize the larger opportunities for compromise that were open to churchmen.

such a manner as to instill a numbing terror rather than a salutory circumspection. The success of the gentler and more complex way would depend to a frightening degree upon the abilities and the sympathies of churchmen in the field; but it was a way which held out much promise, and it had many able persons who wished to follow it.

Saint Vaast, who revealed and then replaced some magicians he found at an entertainment for King Lothar, seems to have been just such a one. He was apparently a widely popular guest and enjoyed convivial company (an attribute of the great Remigius too, and one more characteristic of saints in general, perhaps, than we are always led to suppose).[57] Saint Vaast's biographers tell us clearly that he believed in loving cooperation and example, not power. Only *after* he had made the sign of the cross over the enchanted ale at King Lothar's dinner party, and had it reveal the enchanter's charm by pouring itself onto the floor, did he make points about the supernatural power of the cross as opposed to that of enchanters and diviners. The particular enchanter involved was not, as far as we can tell, either deliberately, or deeply, humiliated. After Saint Vaast's explanation of the untoward event, the dinner party went on as planned. We can recover neither the exact social status of the "incantator" nor the ritual words and gestures he had used to accompany the charm, but it is unlikely that either was very far removed from those proposed by Saint Vaast for their replacement. Social ease, friendly association, and effective adaptation are the chief characteristics of this little encounter—not dislocation. Certainly that deliberate and aggressive confrontation which is so much a part of other "conversion" tales is here ruled out entirely. On this level the little story is an extraordinarily instructive one. Alcuin is one of Saint Vaast's admirers and biographers. It is to persons such as this, and to those who chose to write their *Lives*, that we should look most closely when we try to understand the rise of Christian magic.

Three stimuli above all, I would suggest, as a final introductory

[57] Saint Vaast was generous and amusing, it seems; *Vita Vedasti* 8; *edit.* Krusch, MGH SRM, iii,422–423. Hincmar, justifying him on the basis of Job 29:24, "And the light of my countenance they cast not down," noted that Saint Remigius, too, liked to laugh, and that this "grace" made people wish to follow and to serve him: *Vita Remigii.* 5; ibid., 266. Archbishop Hincmar, of course, had had much experience of dealing with the followers the supernatural opposition could command and might be expected, therefore, to be alerted to compensating sympathetic qualities in Christian churchmen.

foray, encouraged the taking of this far more difficult road. The first sprang from the scale of the problem and has been to some little degree discussed. I cannot sufficiently emphasize the importance, in sheer prevalence and numbers and in the range of their activities, of the opposing magicians. I revert to it once more because this is the aspect of the situation that I wish, in this section, most vehemently to stress. For all the hopes of those most inclined to the heroic approach, these magicians could not in fact be removed at one blow, nor even by very many; and they showed little sign of obligingly going away. Nor could they, as I have said (and as I hope in some cases to be able further to show quite clearly), always be dismissed as rustic or unlearned. They had skills that were evidently valued, and that were, in some part at least, both recondite and impressive. Those who came to replace them could by no means always equal them in such skills; and they might not, furthermore, even be available (or not in sufficient numbers) reliably to give solace to misfortune.[58] Wherever conditions such as these prevailed, then, and they may have prevailed very widely, it became wise at least to consider a different approach. Perhaps the opposing magi might be won over into allegiance? Methods a little like those of Saint Vaast or Saint Remigius must then have been at a premium. And where winning them over was not possible, they might instead be either equaled or outshone. On Gregory's model, the outshining must be accomplished by means which would attract, and would not alienate, that following these magi had so clearly commanded; means which would reorder, and not disappoint, its cherished expectations. This daunting task had its supporters from the first, and their conviction could only gain in strength as the shortcomings of other approaches became ever more apparent.

The second stimulus sprang from the uses to which miracle stories might be put in a society that was so largely oral and so deeply concerned with magic. This we shall come to discuss with, I hope, an ever increasing enthusiasm. In miracle literature, the medieval church found itself possessed of a remarkable resource. "Miracles," together with a belief of a certain sort in demons, held out a means for the

[58] We know little about the numbers of Christian priests available at any one time, but it is unlikely that they could often match those of the opposition. Boniface, for example, at the very height of his success in Germany in the mid-eighth century, is greatly troubled by the lack of suitable priests and pours out his worries to Archbishop Egbert of York; transl. E. Emerton, *The Letters of Saint Boniface* (New York, 1940), pp. 168–169.

making of a common cause with these non-Christian magi that many came deeply to need. Thus both were seized upon with vigor for this end. At the simplest level, a little further thought about the nature of God's "glory" and about the "miracula" by which it might best be made manifest led to a change of choice of miracle illustration by that very pope we have seen supporting the change in tactics toward competing expressions of religious sensibility. Gregory the Great, a tremendous supporter and purveyor of miracle stories, especially in his *Dialogues*, issued warnings to Augustine of Canterbury against too ready a reliance on, and a pride in, vainglorious sorts of miracle, and again these views, and other related ones on miracles, were given special treatment by Bede.[59] Bede, in his turn, gave the mission of Augustine rather shorter shrift than might have been expected and reported the different miracles of Aidan (miracles of a type which, I shall come to suggest, were more nearly related to contemporary magical concerns than were those of Augustine of Canterbury) far more sympathetically. Both spokesmen are defenders of a form of Christian magic that would find many other supporters. Miracles of particular kinds, fashioned and placed with care, became (and in part in conscious contrast to their different employment in the times of heroic enthusiasms) an ideal means of reordering, instead of eliminating, the revered and sought after magical powers of malefici, and of improving upon, rather than denying, the rewards these last had to offer.[60] The paradox whereby miracles recording triumphs over the non-Christian opposition may have inspired the support, by means of miracle again, of a quite different form of approach to this opposition is worth extended and serious attention.

The third stimulus springs from the observed fates of condemned malefici, and concerns a quite other, indeed almost opposite, aspect of the problem of magical competition. Witches could suffer severely, as we have seen, both from judicial process, and as a result of mere suspicion, and there would come to be a limit to the lengths to which the persecution of these opposing practitioners could be allowed to go and still allow itself the name of Christian. Wilfred's followers could kill a magus with impunity, as we have seen, at least in the eyes of his biog-

[59] Bede, *Ecclesiastical History* I,xxxi; *transl.* Colgrave, *Bede's Ecclesiastical History*, pp. 108–111.

[60] It is toward a solution of this order that Professor Douglas points in the case of present day Lele "magic"; "The Problem of Evil among the Lele."

rapher Eddius Stephanus.[61] Sulpicius Severus shows us, in his *Chronicle*, that many bishops favored the death penalty for Priscillian, charged with magic. Sulpicius too, however, points to the fact that Saint Martin himself did not favor so harsh a punishment.[62] A revealing little passage from the Lombard *Edict* of Rothair (ca. 643) points out that he and his advisors thought it un-Christian to exact the death penalty for supposed magical practices (in this case cannibalistic witchcraft). Many others make observations to this effect.[63] Aelfric tells how Saint Peter refused to allow the crowd to take vengeance upon the magician Simon Magus, for Christians "should requite evil with good,"[64] and Alcuin—in a letter written in 804 to an unknown bishop, in which he is concerned especially with the evils of contemporary divinatory practices—draws a specific distinction between the punishment for such practices licensed under the old law (here again that of death, licensed by Deut. 18:10–12) and those appropriate to the age of grace.[65]

The problem of the appropriate treatment of non-Christian leaders of this kind, both those who were merely suspected of magical expertise and those who actually practiced it, excited, quite clearly, substantial discussion and disagreement, and encouraged among some (among whom Saint Peter was seen by many to be numbered) the exhibition of skills that were superior, yet similar. To such persons the imitation yet outclassing of the competition seems to have been preferable to

[61] Bede, interestingly, says nothing of this, confining himself to a benevolent weather miracle instead. *Ecclesiastical History* IV,xiii; transl. Colgrave, *Bede's Ecclesiastical History*, pp. 372–375.

[62] *Chronicle* l; transl. A. Roberts, *The Works of Sulpitius Severus* (Grand Rapids, Mich., 1955), p. 121. Ambrose was also of Martin's mind.

[63] Rothair, *Edict*, title 376; transl. K. Fischer Drew, *The Lombard Laws* (Philadelphia, 1973), pp. 126–127. In the canons attributed to Saint Patrick—possibly drawn up in the seventh century, and widely circulated through their inclusion in the *Collectio Hibernensis*—there is to be found strong provision against too ready a belief in witchcraft, possibly with an eye to the persecution such a belief might unleash: "A Christian who believes that there is a vampire in the world, that is to say, a witch, is to be anathematised; whoever lays that reputation upon a living being, shall not be received into the church until he revokes with his own voice the crime that he has committed and accordingly does penance with all diligence." McNeill and Gamer, *Medieval Handbooks*, p. 78. The cannibalistic witch, or *striga*, will be further discussed in chap. 9.

[64] *Of the Passion of the Apostles Peter and Paul*; edit. and transl. B. Thorpe, *The Homilies of the Anglo-Saxon Church* i (London, 1844), 373.

[65] *Ep.* 267; edit. Dümmler, *MGH Epistolae Karolini Aevi*, ii,426.

measures of a more drastic kind. The danger of secular, rather than religious, scapegoating (often under cover of the general term *malefi-cus*), added further to the church's concerns. Gerberga, for instance, friend of the suspected wife of Louis the Pious, Judith, was actually drowned on the orders of Judith's jealous stepson King Lothar "more maleficorum."[66] In such cases forceful intervention on behalf of the threatened maleficus might be the answer chosen by the church. In the early ninth century, for example, Archbishop Agobard of Lyons actively stepped in to save the lives of suspected allies of supposed weather magicians, "tempestarii," whose victims sought to lynch them.[67] Sometimes the penalties specified by the ecclesiastical laws for the control of competing magi were a good deal less severe than those to which the secular authorities might resort, and it may well be that this was deliberate and reflects a felt need on the ecclesiastical side to temper the ferocity of the secular power.[68] To agree that non-Christian magicians must be silenced was one thing; to allow a capricious secular chieftain or, still worse, a village mob to do the silencing was quite another. Once again a further solution lay in a little controlled and judicious compromise with the practices condemned, rather than in the wholesale and brutal extermination of those who practiced them. The need to protect opposing magicians from a type of persecution neither side could (though, of course, for different reasons) wholly countenance, impelled, then, Christians to rethink their positions and to allow some parts of the old magic to survive in a christened form, along with its practitioners. This particular protective pressure is perhaps the most paradoxical of them all.

Finally, the problem of a different kind of scapegoat, that of the scapegoat for disappointed hopes, especially in matters of illness, seems also to have led to concessions and to efforts toward compromise. Both Gregory of Tours and Fredegar tell us, for example, how very easy it was for "medici" or erring "herbarii" to be killed by disappointed cli-

[66] Nithard, *Historiarum Libri IIII* I,v, and *Vita Hludovici Imperatoris; edit.* Pertz, MGH SS, ii,639, 653.

[67] *De Grandine et Tonitruis* ii; *edit.* L. Van Acker, *Agobardi Lugdunensis Opera Omnia,* (Turnholt, 1981), p. 4.

[68] As well as capital punishment, we have the public beatings, shaving of the head, and forced parading in this state about the locality prescribed for condemned "malefici" by the Visigoths: *Recc. Erv. Chind.* VI,2,4; *edit.* Zeumer, MGH *Legum,* i,259. Not even the most severe of the penances for malefici to be found in the penitentials seems quite to equal these.

ents should their prescriptions prove unavailing, or should the clients suspect the prescribers of malpractice.[69] A decree of the Council of Merida, 666,[70] rules specifically against the taking by priests of such chances of retribution. It seems that certain members of the clergy had, when they became ill, been inclined to blame their illness upon the magical practices of certain dissidents within their households, and to order that the suspects be tortured (this in accordance with the prevailing secular rules for the finding of witches). The council orders that suspected "malefici" be brought instead before the bishop. In circumstances such as these, the incentives for many to sympathize, even to try to make common cause with, the condemned, rather than with condemners liable to overstep the mark, were likely to be increased, and the hope of success in their conversion was possibly increased then too. We might reasonably suppose that humane considerations of this order also often acted upon Christian attitudes to magic and might, once again, have encouraged a greater indulgence in some cases toward its non-Christian forms than that permitted by a simpler view and a simpler situation.

The rise we seek to discuss, then, and, I trust, to describe, was very greatly conditioned by the unrelenting pressure of competing non-Christian magi upon the early church in Europe, and by the many different responses the reality of this competition, and the variety (and sometimes the savagery) of the counters it brought forth, both required and received. We shall, I hope, come to see with especial clarity that those "superstitious" practices the early medieval church eventually made its own, "superstitions" which were so vilified at the time of the Reformation and beyond,[71] had their origins in circumstances far from

[69] Lots of "medici" were killed when they failed to cure Austrechilde, wife of Guntram, of dysentry: *Chronicle of Fredegar* III,82; *edit.* Krusch, *MGH SRM*, ii,115. Mummolus, who failed to cure the son of Queen Fredegond, was tortured to death. Gregory of Tours, *History of the Franks* VI,25; *transl.* Dalton, *The History*, ii,265–266.

[70] Mansi, XI,83–84.

[71] The reciting of Creeds and Paternosters as a cure for sickness, a practice actually prescribed by Caesarius to anxious women as an acceptable Christian substitute for unacceptable magical practice, was, in 1597, taken as a sign that a woman was a witch; P. Hair, *Before the Bawdy Court* (London, 1972), p. 133 (and see also pp. 153 and 176). A cure for a sick horse which involved cutting the sign of the cross upon the beast, and which enjoyed the Christian authority of Bald's *Leechbook* in the early tenth century, required, in 1528, confession and atonement. G. L. Kittredge, *Witchcraft in Old and New England* (Cambridge, Mass., 1927), p.37. For a discussion of the place of the *Leechbook* and allied treatises, see below, chap. 9.

the Reformation in time and were formed in an atmosphere utterly remote from it in spirit. Many of these so-called superstitions were, in the early Middle Ages, formulated with discipline, skill, and great religious and social sensibility; they were supported by persons concerned to sustain devotion, and to combat ill-informed and brutal persecution, through a disciplined and sympathetic response to valued, though not yet Christian, contemporary practices. There is an irony of a very particular kind to be observed in the fact that these very same "superstitions" later became themselves the object of persecution of a peculiarly undisciplined and primitive kind. The force of this irony needs now to be appreciated in all its strength. The great majority of those very practices which were (in the period of the European witch hunts especially) to be so ferociously outlawed, and at such a cost to human life, at their beginnings were often forged for the protection and even enhancement of this life, and for purposes further-reaching, more intricate, and far more humane than their later critics were ever prepared, or perhaps able, to realize.

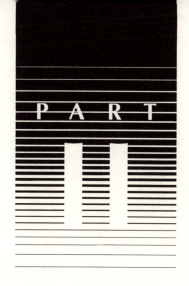

PART

II

The Magic of the Heavens

The Magic That Persisted:
Condemned Magical
Agencies

I SHOULD make it clear at the outset that this definition of the heavens is a negative one. I mean by the heavens everything except the earth we tread. Such a distinction between heaven
and earth is, in magical matters, artificial, for the powers intimate to
the heavens were thought to be capable of influencing every aspect of
life on earth, and to be the superior ones. It is made in part, then, for
convenience, but I hope that it will, in fact, make it all the clearer
that the attitudes to the magic of the heavens we shall see taking shape
before us here were of a quite outstanding importance in the formation
of views upon other kinds of medieval magic too.

The magic of the heavens poured into Christian Europe, and it
could be activated in many different ways. It might spring from the
stars or from the planets. Airy *daimones* might bring it to bear upon
humans. It could be borne by projectiles from the heavens such as
comets and falling stars, by lightning flashes or thunderclaps, in pestilence or harvest-bearing rains, vapors, storms, on the arrows of elves.
It might be traced in the movements and calls of creatures of the lower
air, such as birds, or in the smoke of sacrifices. It could be made manifest in dreams. Some of it was readily reconcilable with the Christian
dispensation, indeed helpful to it. Some was anathema and yet refused
to die. To kill the second species of magic without dissipating the
strength Christianity might derive from the first was a task of appalling
difficulty, no matter with what precise type we have to deal; but in the
case of the magic of the heavens the problem was especially severe.
Pagan ways with fear and hope, and sometimes very similar Christian
ones, confront us immediately once we look up into the awe-inspiring
regions above the earth; and all the incipient conflicts about, and compromises that can be made with, magic are to be found in essence here

and with an especial intensity. Because this was so, much more heavenly magic of an older kind came to be made welcome in the early Middle Ages than we should, perhaps, initially have expected.

DIVINATION

Common to the antimagic legislation of the whole of our period, and to most of it a pressing concern, was divination. Divination was central to Greco-Roman religion and to much pre-Christian Germanic religion too, and energetic response to the invocations of the many types of diviner seems to have been a major activity of the pre- and non-Christian gods. To most of their adherents it was the most beneficial of all their activities. Divination from the heavens took many forms. There was astrology, predictions from thunder and eclipses, from the flights and cries of birds, and from the directions the smoke from sacrifices took in the air. None of this could the early medieval church abide, for the mere mention of divinatory inquiry could call up a memory, or a present threat, of divinities and priestly invokers of a character most alarming to the new religion. It therefore attacked it wholesale.

One of the most thoroughgoing and vehement condemnations of divinatory practices is to be found in the *Life* of Eligius of Noyon, in a passage which leans heavily upon an earlier outburst by Caesarius of Arles. Passages such as these are worth a little prefatory attention here, even though they are not strictly confined to the magic of the heavens, and this for two particular reasons. Firstly, they put into a nutshell, if a somewhat commodious one, those means of prediction distinguished spokesmen for the Western church felt to be especially obnoxious; and, secondly, the outbursts are both so early and such very angry ones. To Eligius, as we have seen, the remedy lay in the suppression and destruction of the objectionable practices and in the substitution of simple nondivinatory Christian alternatives. The energy with which both Caesarius and Eligius described the practices condemned deserves special notice, for it shows with trenchant clarity how very delicate and complex a path the more moderate would have to tread, especially were they to have thoughts about sanctioning Christianized forms of inquiring into, and reassuring oneself about, the future. The adequate containment of outrage is never easy; it is all the less so when the outrage seems to be so clearly justified and has at the very outset occupied the center of the stage.

Eligius was not troubled by delicacies suggesting compromise, or tenderness toward the faint of heart.

I detest above all things and I absolutely insist that no one give credence to sacrilegious pagan customs. No pretext, no illness, nothing whatsoever can permit of the presumption of your approaching or questioning lot casters or seers or soothsayers or enchanters. Such wickedness will instantly deprive you of baptismal grace. Likewise, you may not look to signals such as sneezes to tell you what to do, nor ask answers of the cries of birds when going on a journey. Instead, for whatever you undertake, be it a journey or be it some other enterprise, sign yourself in the name of Christ, and say the Creed or the Lord's Prayer with reverence and in trust, and then nothing will be able to harm you. No right-minded Christian can possibly pay attention to the day on which he leaves, or returns to, his home, because all days were made by God. Nor may he heed the day or the state of the moon when he begins on something.

There follow some fierce views upon pagan rituals (especially the New Year ones) and upon pagan gods, and then he inveighs against divinatory and talismanic exercises once more.

No one should pronounce on his own fate or fortune, or suggest that this is determined at birth. The common people call this last practice "nascentia" and believe that a person's birth affects his character. No one should do such things for God "will have all men to be saved, and to come unto the knowledge of the truth" (1 Tim. 2:4), and He governs all things in His wisdom and did so before the world was made. And when someone becomes ill, do not seek out enchanters, or diviners, or soothsayers or lot casters, or place devilish charms at springs or trees or crossroads. The one who is ill should trust in God's mercy alone and receive the sacrament of the body and blood of Christ in faith and reverence. He should ask some holy oil of his church and have his body anointed in the name of Christ, and thus, as the apostle says, "The prayer of faith shall save the sick, and the Lord shall raise him up." (James. 5:15). In this way, he will be healed not only in body but in spirit, and that which the Lord promised in his Gospel shall be fulfilled in him: "And all things, whatsoever ye shall ask in prayer, believing, ye shall receive."[1]

[1] *Vita Eligii Episcopi Noviomagensis* II,16a; *edit.* B. Krusch and W. Levison, MGH SRM iv (Hanover and Leipzig, 1902), 705 and 707. (MT). The references to Caesarius's sermons are (in this order) to Sermons 54, 192, 33, and 13.

Though both Eligius and Caesarius speak of the pagan gods, there is no need to call always, or even primarily, upon the classical pantheon of divinities for an explanation of such beliefs. Practices of this sort can form a part of folk religion in areas very distant in time and place from medieval Europe.[2] It is their essence, and not their derivation, which deserves attention.

I have quoted from the sermon of Eligius at some length because it sums up so very aptly that which some members of the Christian Church felt to be so objectionable about divination, and that which they felt to be its best remedy. The emphasis on faith and trust is especially to be noted, for it helps to bring us to the crux of the problem. The practice of divination contained within it two especial insults to Christianity: one to the doctrine of human free will, the other to the doctrine of divine providence. In that the diviner based much of his art upon the supposition that the future was determined, and so could be known, he reduced human free will to a mere act of adjustment to this supplied foreknowledge of the inevitable. And when he sought to discover God's provision for humankind in advance—as though God could not be trusted to govern human fate for the creature's good, and as though people could not be required to have faith in this good government and to hope for its results—the diviner undermined belief in providence. Martin of Braga puts the Christian position on these questions succinctly. "God did not order man to know the future, but that he should always live in fear of Him and ask Him for guidance and help in his life. God alone possesses foreknowledge of events."[3] According to such views, divination was at best superfluous, and at worst blasphemous and degrading. It was both a powerful way of intervening in the supernatural, and one profoundly unacceptable to Christians.

[2] Again, parallels of great interest can be found in the religious practices of the pre-Spanish Philippines: "If, on leaving the house, they met someone sneezing, they returned to their houses, even if they had travelled a whole day, or even if they had just reached their destination, as if the sneezing was on the road. If this happened when they were about to start their work, they left off working immediately. If they heard a bird singing on any such occasions which seemed an ill omen to them they would return even if they had walked for many days. This was true even if it was an entire army that had marched off to war. They would fight under no circumstances, disregarding whatever advantages they had." A quotatation from Aduarte, translated in P. Fernandez, *The History of the Church in the Philippines (1521–1898)* (Manila, 1979), p. 4. Again, I am indebted to my colleague Dr. Barbara Andaya.

[3] *Reforming the Rustics* 12; transl. C. W. Barlow, *Iberian Fathers* i (Washington, 1969), 78.

The sermon writers were hardly alone in their vitriolic denunciations of divination. The sources in general are full of such views. Isidore, of course, gave looking into the future as the foremost occupa-
tion of the magi he described, and so did Isidore's imitators.
Occasionally Isidore's words are quoted verbatim in church councils.
The canons attributed to Pope Gregory III, for instance, and tentatively dated to 731, use Isidore's definitions of augurers ("those who
look to the flights and cries of birds for their messages"), harioli ("those
who offer sacrifice on the altars of idols"), and auspicia ("the signs
people look for when they are about to embark upon a journey") for
the types of divination they condemn first and by name. Those who
take to augurers or "harioli," or look superstitiously for "auspicia," rules
Gregory, are to do penance for three years (which penance might,
however, be reduced for humane reasons—an interesting addition).
He adds to these condemned categories "divinationes" in general, incantations, and the "making of vows outside the church." Gregory
seems here to be bringing clarity and comparative leniency to a shorter
pronouncement made by his predecessor and copied later into Burchard.[4]

Despite Isidore's help, these categories are hard for us to clarify or to
use consistently, for they seem on occasion to be interchangeable, or
to be subsumed under the more general *auguria* or *divinationes*.[5] They
always seem to mean looking to the future, however, and we may take
sermons, treatises, and canons such as these as a starting point for our
efforts to reconstruct some of the beliefs and activities they condemn,
confident that anxiety about divination within the Western church
was widely shared. Divination was the sticking point; that irrational
combination of arrogant scrutiny and persisting fear which inhibited
trusting faith in the Christian God.

Diviners did not of course restrict themselves to divination by means
of heavenly events; but by reason of the superior powers thought to be
vested in the heavens, divination that called upon these realms had a
peculiarly important effect on Christian responses, both emotional and

---

[4] Canon XVI; Mansi, XII,292. "Anyone paying attention to hariolos, aruspices, or
enchanters, or using phylacteries is to be excommunicated." Council of Rome, 721,
canon XII; Mansi, XII,264. (MT). Burchard, *Decretum* X,xxiiii; *PL* 140,836.

[5] The tenth-century Berne glosses on Lucan, for example, give the "aruspex" and
the "augur" the same function, that of interpreting the signs given by birds. An "aruspex" also reads entrails. H. Usener, M. *Annaei Lucani Commenta Bernensia* (Leipzig,
1869), pp. 73, 206.

institutional. Divination as a whole was an excellent candidate for frontline condemnation, and for, at first, relatively simple and repressive countering methods. But on some fronts this simplicity gave way to a type of complexity that wished to accommodate, rather than eliminate, the impulse to look into the future. Some Christians felt themselves impelled to legitimate certain heavenly divinatory practices. They did so to tap, rather than repress, those earlier and deeply rooted hopes and enthusiasms, and to soothe pervasive fears by methods perhaps more generally convincing than those offered by Eligius. We may look a little more closely now at the different forms in which non-Christian divination pressed upon Christianity, in order to appreciate a little better the selections made.

ASTROLOGY

I propose to begin the discussion of divination from the heavens with that taking of auspicia which concerned signs derivable from the bodies in the upper heavens, the sun and moon and stars and other planets, known by the general term *astrology*. Astrology deserves pride of place for two reasons. Firstly, pre-Christian cosmography saw these heavenly bodies as physically higher than all others, and perhaps morally so, for they inhabited a superior region. This region was both nearer to their creator or mover (who was highest of all) and one which might become the abode of superior beings, and of men made into gods or heroes. Plato's cosmology, transmitted through the *Timaeus* and the commentary on it by Chalcidius (or through such derivative works as the *De Deo Socratis* of Apuleius), Cicero's *Dream of Scipio*, with the commentary by Macrobius, or the beginning of Lucan's *Civil War* Book IX and its glosses, brought to the early Middle Ages a picture of the heavens that resembled nothing so much as a layer cake, of upper air, or ether, reaching down to the moon; and then of darkened middle air, reaching from the moon to the earth and man. The upper air was peopled by godlike beings, and the middle by "daimones" good and bad.[6] The middle air, the earth, and humankind were dependent for their light upon the luminaries of the upper air. The four elements might accommodatingly be arranged among the layers, with fire predominant in the upper air (or ether), then air predominant, then water, then earth. Augustine, in his discussion of the res-

[6] Ibid., pp. 47–48.

urrection of the body in the *City of God* reports as much disparagingly. "Hence they say that since the earth, going up from our level, is first, and water above the earth second, and air above the water third, and heaven above the air fourth there can be no earthly body in heaven."[7] For this last reason especially, this pre-Christian hierarchical arrangement of the heavens could be troublesome to Christians. Certain aspects of it, however, notably the high and powerful positions of the heavenly bodies, were acceptable, and we find even today an echo of it in the persistent and tiresome image of God the Father peering down from the clouds.

My second reason for beginning with this aspect of divination is that the problem of quite how widely divination from the heavenly bodies was practiced in the early Middle Ages is still a remarkably contentious one, and I propose to add to this contention. It has been argued, for example, that there was little interest in, or fear of, astrology in the Latin West before the ninth and tenth centuries, a lack of interest caused partly by the lack of textbooks for its service. This failure of interest in astrology is echoed, it has been held, in conciliar legislation, which contains few outright condemnations of its practice.[8] I would modify this argument, firstly, then add another of my own. In pursuit of the modification, it may be said that the lack of surviving textbooks on astrology is not an insuperable problem. Much can be transmitted verbally or by means of charts and tables, easily used to impress and as easily lost, and it is all the more likely to be so transmitted when there is condemnation in the air. "Scripta" such as these, and wielded by non-Christian astrologers, are mentioned by Cassiodorus and by Isidore.[9] And there was, I would contend, in fact consistent condemnation of astrology, both conciliar and literary, although

---

[7] *City of God.* XXII,xi; *edit.* and *transl.* W. M. Green, *Saint Augustine City of God Against the Pagans* vii (Loeb Classical Library, 1972), 258–259.

[8] M.L.W. Laistner, "The Western Church and Astrology during the Early Middle Ages," *Harvard Theological Review* 34 (1941), 251–275.

[9] For references to objectionable and non-Christian astrological "scripta," see R.A.B. Mynors, *Cassiodori Senatoris Institutiones* (Oxford, 1937), pp. 156–159, and Isidore, *Etymologiae* III,lxxi,38–39; *edit.* W. M. Lindsay, *Isidori Hispalensis Episcopi Etymologiarum sive Originum Libri XX* (Oxford, 1911). Keith Thomas speaks of the "small collection of tattered magical recipes and astrological figures bequeathed by some earlier practitioner" with which a sixteenth-century astrologer might operate: K. Thomas, *Religion and the Decline of Magic* (Harmondsworth, Middlesex: Penguin, 1973), p. 358. His early medieval counterpart was quite capable of operating in a similar manner, as are Indian astrologers, for instance, now.

sometimes this condemnation is disguised beneath those general terms describing divinatory practices to which I have drawn attention. The terminology varied, but there is sufficient mention of astrology to be found in the records of councils, in sermons, and even in some treatises to indicate that it provoked an anxiety far more constant than has been previously allowed.

Early councils only occasionally, it is true, allow astrology clearly defined a canon or two to itself. Such a one is the council held at Braga between the years 560 and 565. Canons 9 and 10 of this council condemn generally those who believe that the fate of humans is controlled by the stars, and specifically those "mathematici" who associate the twelve signs of the zodiac with parts of the bodies and souls of humans, and with the "names of the patriarchs."[10] The Council of Braga aimed this part of its strictures primarily at a specific heresy, that of Priscillian (d. ca. 385/86) and his followers, who had excited an admiration of ancient astrology too strong for, and a belief in the powers of the demons in the heavens outrageous to, those who believed in the Christian God. Horror at the Priscillianists stood behind many an early condemnation of astrology.[11] That is not to say, however, that this horror was confined to them. Quite the contrary. It is likely, indeed, that the name was used as a convenient cover for astrology in general. Gregory the Great, for instance, when speaking of the Magi, seems to regard the term *Priscillianist* simply as a synonym for astrologer.[12] By the same process, the phrasing of this canon of the Council of Braga, initially derived from those directed at Priscillianists, passed into the contemporary definition of "superstitious" astrology formulated by Isidore (to which we shall shortly come) and also into many of the more popular canon law collections. The Priscillianists, in sum, helped to release into the early Middle Ages a term and a set of definitions which could be applied to astrologers in general when Priscillianists as a sect had long disappeared, and it is likely that they were so applied. By the mid-sixth century the term *Priscillianist* may have been something of an anachronism; but the astrological commitment it described was not.

The sermon of Saint Eligius takes us well on into the seventh century when he singles out "nascentia" (most likely the casting of horoscopes) for condemnation, and Aldhelm (d. 709) and perhaps even

[10] Mansi, IX, 775.
[11] Thus, for example, Pope Leo the Great; PL 54, 679.
[12] XL Homiliarum in Evangelia x; PL 76, 1111–1112.

Bede, into the eighth.[13] Fredegar takes it as quite natural that the Emperor Heraclius should have an interest in astrology, and that King Dagobert should listen to his predictions.[14] And then there are, in addition, the terms *haruspex* and *auspicia*, and even *augurium* and *divinatio*. *Haruspex* is a word peculiarly susceptible of being applied to an astrologer, for the haruspex was defined by Isidore in his section *De Magis* as an observer of the days and hours on which to do things, and Augustine associated the choice of favorable or unfavorable times with the practice of astrology.[15] Haruspices appear very often as subjects of conciliar condemnation in our period.[16] The Laws of the Visigoths contain rulings specifically against those who consult "haruspices" about the fates of kings,[17] and although the "auspicia" to which they looked may often have been sought through other forms of divining, it would be quite incorrect to restrict the word to these.[18] It may well be, in short, that we can deduce that non-Christian astrologers were sought after and active in very many areas of Europe and throughout the period which concerns us, and if we allow ourselves to associate the haruspex, especially, with astrological portents as well as with the scrutiny of omens of other kinds, then one problematic distinction, that between the paucity of conciliar condemnation of astrology and the contrasting abundance of such condemnation in the case of other kinds of divination, disappears.

Such a conclusion seems to be reinforced when we notice the widespread copying of some of those earlier works most condemnatory of astrology. Among those copied, the works of two authors stand out:

[13] *Etymologiae* III,xxvii; *edit.* Lindsay, *Isidori Hispalensis. Vita Eligii Episcopi Noviomagensis* II,16; *edit.* Krusch and Levison, *MGH SRM* iv,707. Aldhelm condemns "mathematici" in his *De Metris et Enigmatibus ac Pedum Regulis* and comments upon the "ridiculosa stoliditas" of belief in their powers; *edit.* R. Ehwald, *MGH Auctorum Antiquissimorum* xv (Berlin, 1919), 72–73. Bede made a comparison between the divisions of time as he described them, and those employed by astrologers, which may well have had contemporary reference: *De Temporum Ratione* iii; *edit.* C. W. Jones, *Bedae Opera De Temporibus* (Cambridge, Mass., 1943), p. 183.

[14] *Chronicle* IV,65; *edit.* B. Krusch, *MGH SRM* ii (Hanover, 1888), 153.

[15] *City of God* V,vii; *transl.* Green, ii,158–161.

[16] In addition to the councils I have already mentioned, augurers and "aruspices" were condemned in canon XXIX of the Fourth Council of Toledo in 633, for example, and the canons of this council were frequently copied; Mansi, X,627.

[17] *Recc. Erv. Chind.* VI,2,1; *edit.* K. Zeumer, *MGH Legum* 1, *Leges Visigothorum* (Hanover and Leipzig, 1902), 257.

[18] This point is made by J. Fontaine, "Isidore de Séville et l'astrologie," *Revue des Études Latines* 31 (1953), 281–282.

Saint Augustine and the author of the Pseudo-Clementine *Recognitions*. Augustine uttered many words expressing a horror of astrology, some of which I have already mentioned.[19] Besides the famous chapters in Book V of the *City of God*, one repository of these words is especially important. This is Augustine's letter to Januarius (written ca. 400), a letter which was exceptionally popular in the early Middle Ages. In this letter Augustine answers certain queries put to him about the correspondence with the solar and lunar calendars of certain Christian observances. It sets out with great clarity Augustine's views upon those directions from the heavens which may be accepted in good faith by Christians and those which may not. The idea that the stars have power over human free will may not. "We do not forecast the outcome of our acts, then, by the sun or the moon, or by yearly or monthly periods, lest we be shipwrecked in the most dangerous storms of human life, cast by our free will onto the rocks of a wretched slavery." The activities indulged in by astrologers are, to him, wholly to be distinguished from that observation of the heavenly bodies which is of practical service to farmers and sea pilots. "Everyone understands that there is a great difference between observing the stars as natural phenomena in the way that farmers and sailors do . . . and the superstitions of men who study the stars, not to forecast the weather, or to find their way . . . but to steer into the predestined outcome of events."[20] Of course, had everyone indeed so understood, then Augustine would not have found it necessary to write these words; nor would they have been so avidly transmitted.

The Pseudo-Clementine *Recognitions*, a treatise to whose exceptional popularity within our period I have already drawn attention, puts the position without even Augustine's secondary allowances. Astrologers, declares the author, operate "not knowing that it is not the course of the stars but the operation of demons, that regulate these things; and those demons, being anxious to confirm the error of astrology, deceive men to sin by mathematical calculations, so that when they suffer the punishment of sin, either by the permission of God or by legal sentence, the astrologer may seem to have spoken truth." The whole science is to be discredited. "The issue of human doings is uncertain, because it depends upon freedom of will. For a mathematician

[19] They are conveniently collected together in L. de Vreese, *Augustine en de Astrologie* (Maastricht, 1933).

[20] Letter 55 to Januarius; *transl.* W. Parsons, *Saint Augustine, Letters* i (Washington, 1951), 271–273.

[astrologer] can indeed indicate the desire which a malignant power produces; but whether the acting or the issue of this desire shall be fulfilled or not, noone can know before the accomplishment of the thing, because it depends upon freedom of will."[21] We notice that demons are involved again here, as they are with the Priscillianists, but they are put in their place as subject, in the last resort, to properly ordered human free will.

Whether in legislation or in well-known sermons and literary treatises, then, sufficient material condemnatory of astrology was current in the early Middle Ages in Europe for it to be reasonable to suppose that astrology, viewed as magic, persisted, as did those other forms of divination which were always admitted to be strong. We may now turn to the argument I wish to add. It is this. Astrological magic did not merely persist; it was actually given strength. And it was given this strength, paradoxically, by the very persistence of those other forms of divination of which mention has already been made. Astrology's extra strength came from the possibility that, in some of its manifestations, it might be used in Christian hands as a counter to these other, far more alarming, forms of divination; it might be called upon, that is, as a reinforcement to, not a contradiction of, that freedom of the will many thought to be threatened by such practices. Certainly in some hands astrology focused and intensified the offense that divination in general caused to Christian beliefs and sensibilities; but in others it could be used to mitigate this offense and to counteract the non-Christian diviners' worst excesses.[22] This question, and this claim, are very large ones, and, as with so many of these large questions, still await a closer scrutiny of the surviving manuscript evidence and extensive exploration of early medieval views on providence and freedom; but they bear too heavily upon the shape and balance of surviving, and actively rescued, magic, and so upon its rise, to permit the omission of that which we can say about them now.

When speaking more narrowly of the biblical Magi, I shall come to suggest that early and patristic condemnation of them and their supposed astrological practices was not sustained everywhere at white

---

[21] IX,xii and X,xii; transl. T. Smith, The Writings of Tatian and Theophilus and the Clementine Recognitions (Edinburgh, 1867), pp. 409, 434.

[22] In his Confessions, for example, even Augustine drew a distinction between astrologers and soothsayers in favor of the former because, as he himself said, astrologers did not invoke spirits. Nor did they offer sacrifices. Transl. R. C. Pine-Coffin, Saint Augustine Confessions IV,2–3 (London, 1961), pp. 72–73.

heat. This is true too of many of the condemnations of astrology. Extremely important in this respect (indeed, he perhaps prepared the way for the rehabilitation of the science of the Magi) is Isidore of Seville. Isidore, the same who saw so much to object to in the practices of other types of diviner (including aruspices in one of their guises), and who presided over the Fourth Council of Toledo in which they were so roundly condemned, played a major part in rendering astrology respectable. It seems highly likely that the two activities were connected. Isidore is responsible for a famous distinction between astronomy and astrology, and a division within astrology itself which allowed one part of it to be adopted with enthusiasm by Christians. This distinction passed into the *De Universo* of Rabanus, and so, again, to a wide readership.[23]

Astronomy, says Isidore, is concerned with the revolutions of the heavens; the rising, setting, and movements of the constellations, and their names; and the laws which govern all these activities.[24] Astrology is concerned with the powers such movements involve.[25] Astrology may be subdivided into the natural and the superstitious. Natural astrology concerns itself with the courses of the sun and moon and stars, and their places in time; with, that is, the type of observation Augustine himself had thought acceptable on behalf of farmers, travelers, and pilots, and which were necessary to the ecclesiastical *computus*. Natural astrology comes here, of course, very close to astronomy. Superstitious astrology concerns itself with augury, however, and this is improper. This is the forbidden domain of the "mathematici," who try to tell the future from the stars and who associate the signs of the zodiac with parts of the human body and soul (here we return to the Priscillianists). They think too that they can predict the birth and behavior of humans from the movement of the stars.[26] Predictions of this kind were forbidden; and yet, it seems, they were currently most popular.[27] In this context, to subdivide was a wise way in which to proceed, even if such a procedure was capable of infecting some of those

[23] *PL* 111,423. Rabanus expressed with great firmness the view that the magi were not "malefici"; see below, chap. 11.

[24] *Etymologiae* III,xxiv,xxviii; *edit.* Lindsay, *Isidori Hispalensis.*

[25] *Differentiae* II,xxix,152; *PL* 83,94. Essential to this observation and to all understanding of Isidore's position is J. Fontaine, "Isidore de Séville," pp. 271–300.

[26] *Etymologiae* III,xvii; *edit.* Lindsay, *Isidori Hispalensis.*

[27] J. Fontaine, "Isidore de Séville," pp. 281–282.

who followed it (Isidore included) with something which might seem to many a dangerous taint.

In that, according to my own thesis, some part of the old magic of the heavens becomes now respectable and a part of the salvage from the world of the old magicians, it becomes too the property of the next chapter, and integral to that magic which was to rise. We may follow its fortunes further, then, there. The general argument about astrology deserves additional stress here, however, because the divisions and subsequent career of astrologia are a fine example of how, on occasion, certain species of condemned and outlawed magic could so react the one upon the other that the determined persistence of some kinds could lead to changes of mind about the essential wickedness of others—and sometimes even to the positive encouragement of these last. Some kinds of magic might come to seem evils of a lesser sort than others. They might even be seen as a welcome weapon in the war against activities especially and undeniably discreditable.

In natural astrology, then, we shall see some of the old astrological magic coming through into the Middle Ages on the coattails of astronomy, and, more especially and importantly, in a new and wholly proper guise as a Christian "scientific" counter to non-Christian magical divination in its least acceptable forms. Scientific astrology will be materially assisted on its way by Isidore, but he only begins the process. If a form of the old magic can be renamed science and Christianized under such pressures, then its different respectable clothing allows it to cross a very formidable frontier indeed. Many other types of magic, formerly condemned, might come to make such a crossing, in a like disguise and sometimes for similar reasons.

Before leaving Isidore, we might note that another form of the old magic of the heavens acted upon him too and encouraged him in the process of selection; and that this also was capable of acting upon others. This time the pressure came not from astrological divination but from folk magic. We learn about it in a poem King Sisebut wrote to Isidore to thank him, significantly, for his earlier scientific treatise, the *De Natura Rerum*.[28] Sisebut proposed to explain another heavenly phenomenon scientifically: the phenomenon of the lunar eclipse. He wished to do so, he tells Isidore, in order to counter a popularly held belief in the power of sorcery. This popular belief held that, when the moon was in eclipse, it was in fact in trouble, being drawn down into

[28] This was written in 612/613, and so well before the *Etymologiae*.

a cave of the underworld by a sinister woman wielding a magic mirror to attract it. The moon had need of sympathetic magic if it was to be rescued; it required shouts and cries to comfort it and to distract the sorcerer.[29] The belief was ancient and evidently widely known. Maximus of Turin gives us an account of it. Even good Christians seem to think, says Maximus, that if they do not shout, God will somehow lose the moon.[30] It is referred to in the tantalizing *Indiculus Superstitionum* of the mid-eighth century,[31] and Burchard still finds it necessary in the eleventh century to condemn those who indulge in shouts and magical rites when the moon is obscured, and to inflict relatively severe penances for breaches of this prohibition.[32]

Sisebut reached for astronomy, that science so close to Isidore's natural astrology, to offer another explanation; but sometimes, and interestingly, a practical compromise was allowed. Instead of banging boards together or blowing through conch shells, one might sing psalms or, specifically, the *Miserere*.[33] Not everyone turned, then, to science in response to such a situation. Eligius of Noyon, in the sermon already cited, and still in the part borrowed from Caesarius, also condemns the shouting that the moon's disappearance calls forth. He reaches, however, not for astronomy but to a belief in the all-encompassing will of God as a counter. God created the moon to temper the darkness of the night, and God decides when the moon shall be obscured and, indeed, rules all its relations with persons.[34]

This explanation might have been more satisfying to some than Sisebut's scientific one, and the singing of psalms sufficient; but both of these simpler, more credulous, responses can have the appearance of a sort of sleight of hand whereby a new, rather facile form of Christian

[29] The relevant part of Sisebut's poem, with a translation into French, is in J. Fontaine, *Isidore de Séville, Traité de la Nature* (Bordeaux, 1960), pp. 330–331.

[30] Maximus of Turin, *Sermo XXX, De Defectione Lunae*; edit. A. Mutzenbecher, *Maximi Episcopi Taurinensis Collectionem Sermonum Antiquam*, CC (Turnholt, 1962), pp. 117–119.

[31] Chapter 21, "De lunae defectione quod dicunt *Vince luna*." Edit. G. H. Pertz, MGH *Leges* i (Hanover, 1835), 20; transl. J. T. McNeill and H. M. Gamer, *Medieval Handbooks of Penance* (New York, 1938), p. 420, and nn.

[32] *Decretum* X,xxxiii; *PL* 140,837.

[33] "Si quis *vince luna* clamaverit aut pro tonitrua tabula aut coclea batederit aut qualibet sonum fecerit preter psalmodia aut 'miserere mei deus' dixerit." Quoted from an early penitential by A. Franz, *Die Kirchlichen Benediktionen im Mittelalter* ii (Graz, 1909), 39.

[34] *Vita Eligii*, edit. Krusch and Levison, MGH SRM iv,707.

supernatural intercession apes, rather than displaces, the non-Christian. There is room for tension here. The simple "will of God," on the one side, and "science," on the other, can on occasion be at war with one another as counters to unacceptable yet pervasive forms of magic. Often they were, as indeed often they are, the products of different mentalities. When simple faith in the Christian God is insufficient, however, or an older faith in supernatural practices too strong, or substitutes such as psalmody inadequate as recompenses for the old excitements, the new religion will have need of magic rehabilitated as "science," such as astrology. Though this may once have been condemned by Christians, its new purpose will give it a new dignity. In such ways and for such purposes the old magic does not merely persist in science; it invades it, and for reasons which have far deeper social roots, and were liable to be more divisive, than is generally realized.

That non-Christian magic of the heavens which rested itself on divination from the heavenly bodies, then, was both heavily condemned and peculiarly persistent in the earlier part of the period. Gradually, by friction and contrast with other condemned and persistent, but far less acceptable, magical practices, sections of it ("natural" astrology, for instance) became not merely credible but positively helpful to Christians. I have spent some little time upon the problem of astrology both because it is such a problem, and because it is also such a good preliminary example of the forging and sifting processes that "purified" parts of the old magic and so gave it passage and increasing acceptability in medieval Europe. It is a good example too of the motives that made for such rescues. In the case of the magic of the heavens the problems were especially severe, and the solutions proposed were especially difficult and contested. One solution required, however, that much more of the old heavenly magic be brought through and placed firmly into Christian hands than could ever have been expected at the outset.

DEMONS

A mention of demons has crept in to the discussion of divination from the heavenly bodies; necessarily so, for recourse to the idea of demonic temptation was one way of coping with the problem of astrological fatalism. This aspect of the condemned magical powers inherent in the heavens is hardly less contentious, and is perhaps even more revealing, than the problem of astrology; and again, its social dimensions are peculiarly important to an adequate understanding of the assisted rise, under Christian auspices, of certain aspects of non-Christian magical beliefs. It is not hard to show that demons, related to the old pagan daimones, persisted into early medieval Europe, and still less difficult to show that they were condemned. There is, however, another, deeper and more complex, level on which demons need to be confronted: one which requires both that we give them a preliminary mention here, and that we discuss them a good deal more fully in the next chapter, when they come to play an exceedingly active, if largely perverse, role in further decision making about magic.

It was necessary in matters of magic to retain the old daimones, for reasons intimately related to that forging and sifting process we have just begun to investigate. Also, in that these daimones came to be rescued very largely for the purposes they could serve within the context of magical selection, their role is in some ways similar to that which, I have suggested, was played by astrology. The distinctions between the two, however, and the manner in which these distinctions acted upon each other in complementary ways, are greatly more illuminating. I have just suggested that astrology, in one of its guises, was rescued in order to combat "scientifically" some of the least acceptable forms of magic. Demons, on the other hand, in one of theirs, were retained for their help in isolating those wicked forms of magic for which a scientific answer seemed neither desirable to Christians nor available to them; and, of course, the moment one introduces the daimones, one introduces the psychological. It is in this sense that the two rescues were complementary. Like astrology, demons were intimately involved in that magic which was to rise, and they formed, indeed, a part of it—but a very different part.

Christian fear of non-Christian magic, the availability, as it were, of demons, and also (as I suggested in the introductory section) Christian compassion for the fate of humans accused of magical manipulation, acted upon one another in a peculiarly powerful way. The demons of the middle air rushed into the early Middle Ages when Christians found themselves pressed, and especially when they found themselves pressed by magic. Mercilessly to misappropriate Voltaire, it may be said that if demons had not existed it would have been necessary to invent them. I shall treat here of the simple survival into the early Middle Ages of beliefs in the supernatural powers of demons and the resources they contributed to the cause of condemnation, resources which were tenaciously retained. In the next chapter, I shall attempt to explore some of the deeper motives which stood behind the active rescue of these demons. This rescue allowed them to emerge, somewhat refined in their own fire, into the Christian magical world and to have a considerable impact upon it.

The daimones, good and bad, of the pre-Christian world were, by the beginning of the period, generally held to dwell in that murky layer of the middle air which reached from the moon to the earth (not that they were restricted to that layer, by any means, but it was thought to be their usual habitat). Ancient beliefs in demons survived as long as there was record of them, again oral or written, and a willing eye or ear. Plato's *Timaeus* (40–42) once more, with Chalcidius's commentary, supplied a picture of the making and placing of these daimones, as beings intermediate between gods and men, that was available certainly to scholars, and to many others. Macrobius, in his *Saturnalia*, drew special attention to their divinatory powers.

> Plato refers to spirits [daemones] and gods, jointly by name, either because the gods are "daemones," that is to say "gifted with knowledge of the future" or, as Posidonius writes in his work *On Heroes and Spirits*, because their nature springs from and shares in the heavenly substance—this word for spirits being then derived from "daiomenos," which may mean either "burning" or "sharing."

To Macrobius, here, divinatory powers are wholly good and Plato's demons admirable. This, to look ahead, would call for comment. The little work *De Deo Socratis* by Apuleius also brought Plato's demons in simple form to those too faint-hearted to tackle Chalcidius. Apuleius stresses the superiority of demons to other creatures of the air, such as birds, both by reason of the heights to which they can fly (birds are, after all, unable to climb higher than all mountains) and by reason of their mental capacities.[35] The educated world was fully able, then, to be conversant with these views. Nor was it difficult to bring daimones to the uneducated. Many a grove, or spring, or tree, had, as we shall see in later chapters, its lower daimon temporarily assigned to that particular place on the earth. Such beliefs responded to movements of the human spirit not easily quelled and with danger repressed. It was not surprising, then, that Christians felt it necessary to address themselves to the ancient demons with care.

[35] *Transl.* P. V. Davies, *Macrobius, The Saturnalia* I,23 (New York and London, 1969), p. 150; *edit.* P. Thomas, *Apulei Platonici Madaurensis Opera Quae Supersunt* iii (Stuttgart, 1970), 16, 21–23.

Though demons of the air as such cannot be found in the Old Testament, nor in pre-Christian Jewish apocrypha, Rabbinic Judaism allows of them, and biblical support for demonic wickedness or *daemonium* seemed, to those who wished to find it, sufficient to bring the two together. I mentioned earlier the strength of expansions of the Genesis story, of Isaiah, and of Ezekiel, and I shall do so later when speaking of the magus Ham. In the New Testament, evil demons were frequent opponents of Christ, and such phrases as Paul's "prince of the power of the air" and "wickedness in high places" (Eph. 2:2 and 6:12) could be, and were, used to give them even greater reality. Paul's beliefs early made an impact upon Christian hagiography. *The Life of Antony*, written in the mid-fourth century and often attributed to Athanasius, had, in its Latin translation by Evagrius, a profound effect on Augustine; it also enjoyed an enormous and enduring independent imaginative success in our period. In it, turbulent and wicked demons of the lower air occupy the center of the stage. In the *Life*, Antony himself describes them fully in his address to his fellow monks (after quoting Eph. 6:12).

> Great is the number of them in the air around us, and they are not far from us. . . . They also din loudly, emit silly laughs and hiss. If noone pays any attention to them, they wail and lament as though defeated. . . . the attack and appearance of the evil ones is full of confusion, accompanied by crashing, roaring and shouting, it could well be the tumult produced by rude boys and robbers.[36]

The idea that demons made loud noises may have given added force to an ecclesiastical tendency to condemn noisy activities in general, and especially those attached to suspect magical beliefs. The dominion these demons exercised over the lower air might also on occasion, says the *Life*, allow them to block the passing of souls upward to the heavens.[37] The *Life of Antony* here assists powerfully in the transmission of that pre-Christian cosmography of which I spoke earlier. The *Life of Antony* is, in addition, anxious to explain away the apparent divinatory powers demons possess. There is nothing supernatural or magical about these, it points out. They are attributes merely of the aery bodies and superior speed of demons. Thus, for example, demons can give advance warning of visitors because demons can see them set off upon their journeys, and arrive at their chosen destinations, before others

[36] *Transl.* R. T. Meyer, *St. Athanasius, the Life of St. Antony* (Westminster, Md., and London, 1950), pp. 38, 43, 50.
[37] *Transl.* Meyer, *St. Athanasius*, pp. 75–76.

do.[38] This special demonic interest in "predicting" the action of trav-elers may explain why divinations associated with journeys were so often singled out in church councils for proscription. It was always helpful, too, to be able to turn to these real demons as a means of explaining away any successes human diviners might seem to have had, especially in a period when diviners were especially prevalent. Augustine will play a crucial role in the rescue of demons for this very purpose.

I have called attention already to another group of works which had a particular influence on demonology and on the early Middle Ages— those apocryphal and Pseudo-Clementine treatises which, although put together well before the early medieval period begins, must have answered many needs within it, so avidly were they copied and trans-mitted. These are full of sustenance for a belief in demons, and the need for "demonization" was clearly one of the needs to which they responded. The Book of Enoch, for instance, declared that an earth-born branch of demons survived the flood, and that these were able to add their souls to the spirits of the lower air (this even though the lustful angels who generated them were chained by God in the dark places of the earth). The Book of Jubilees gives reinforcement to the view that there remains in the lower air an unbound and evil demonic legion ready to tempt human beings to the deadliest of sins.[39] The specific proposition, that these demons were the progeny of fallen an-gels and the "daughters of men" before the flood, did not gain ortho-dox acceptance, but it possibly left its mark upon that belief in incubi and succubi which was to cause anxiety to later commentators on Gen-esis. Rabanus, for instance, is inclined to make room for the possibility of demonic intercourse with women.[40]

Moral failings might always be illustrated by demonic assaults (and, at a pinch, explained away). This fact helped the survival of demons greatly. Cassian is especially interesting here, in both his *Conferences* and his *Institutes*. Certainly his sense of the high moral purposes of monasticism and the enormity of failures to live up to these, together with the avidity with which his works were read, did a very great deal to perpetuate beliefs in wicked demons. Cassian's descriptions are

[38] Ibid., pp. 46–48.

[39] 1 Enoch 10:1–11, 15:11, The Book of Jubilees 11:5; *transl.* R. H. Charles, *The Apocrypha and Pseudepigrapha of the Old Testament* ii (Oxford, 1913), 29, 193–194, 198.

[40] *Commentaria in Genesim* II,v; *PL* 107,512.

vivid, and they actively propagated the view that the monastic life was in large part a war against the demons, a view enthusiastically taken up by Pope Gregory the Great, with consequent effect.[41] Once the idea had taken root, the institution fed the theory, and Benedictine monasteries, especially, became both spiritual and physical strongholds against demons and so against the worst of their magic also—sometimes to the extent of their tolerating the less bad in the manner of a sop to Cerberus. This last feature of the medieval monastic impact on magical survivals will become increasingly evident as we go on. Initially, however, demons do much to project monks into this embattled role, and Cassian and Gregory are preeminent in giving these demons life for them.

Again, in Cassian, we have the now familiar picture of the extreme malice and the supreme capacity of demons, their aery speed, their subtle intelligence, and their ready ability to impregnate a thick and heavy mass, like the flesh. Their superior perceptions enable them accurately to assess, furthermore, each individual's particular susceptibilities. For instance, observes Cassian with an appropriateness horribly universal, if someone constantly looks out the window to see where the sun is in the sky, and so how near the next meal is, a mere mortal can deduce that this person is greedy. How much more, then, can the infinitely more subtle demons see? One of Cassian's illustrations of demonic expertise gives us an insight into the expertise of ancient burglars too. Burglars, he tells us, who want both to keep the house in darkness and yet to steal the best treasures, throw fine sand about the rooms and deduce, from the sound it makes upon each object it strikes, the value of the object. Of this standard is the skill of demons, who throw a fine sand of evil suggestion among the treasures of the human heart and divine what they may steal.[42] Unlike the usual balance of burglars and house owners, however, demons are overwhelming in their numbers, and they are not, as we, subject to physical exhaustion or the need to care for their families and earn their daily bread. Cassian

---

[41] *Collations* VII,xxi; *transl.* E. Pichéry, *Jean Cassien Conférences* i (Paris, 1955), 262–265. Gregory describes Satan as constantly on the lookout for battles, and especially so with monks; e.g., *Dialogues* II,viii,13, *edit.* A. de Vogüé, *Grégoire le Grand, Dialogues* ii (Paris, 1979), 171. The temptations of Job, too, provide Gregory with rich material, for the exploration of some of which he is clearly dependent on Cassian, e.g., II,38; *transl.* A. de Gaudemaris, *Grégoire le Grand Morales sur Job* i (Paris, 1975), pp. 314–317.

[42] *Collations* VII,xii–xiii,xv–xvi; *transl.* Pichéry, *Jean Cassien*, i,256–257, 259–260.

has some interesting and comforting observations to make upon the need to beware, in this context, of demonic incitement to overwork.[43] He is also eloquent about the activities of the midday demon of Ps. 90:6 (Vulgate), and in a way which takes him beyond even the exegesis of that psalm which was to be adopted by Augustine and his followers. Though based upon a Septuagint mistranslation from the Hebrew, the Vulgate midday demon was real to Cassian as a tempter of monks. Here the temptation is to dereliction: too little effort rather than too much. Every day at noon, this demon might infect his hapless victim with every sort of discomfort, from a simple disinclination to do his housework and reading, to a positive wish to leave. Cassian ensured, then, in this way too, that demons were believed in as an ever active presence. Hincmar of Rheims, in the ninth century, sees Cassian's midday demon as capable of tempting not merely monks but all manner of persons to fruitless self-indulgence.[44]

Isidore, as so often, produced an apt summary of that early medieval view of demons which drew widest acceptance. It is to be found in his *Etymologies*, in the section on the gods of the pagans. He asserts, like Macrobius and perhaps depending on him, that "daemonas" were so named by the Greeks for their foreknowledge and explains, like the *Life of Antony*, that this is achieved by their superhuman capacities and longevity. Isidore stresses his beliefs in the aery bodies of demons, and that before the Fall they were celestial creatures only to plunge into the prison of the lower air with the devil and his wicked followers, there to remain until the day of judgment. He had found them in an earlier section, of course, peculiarly adept in the magical arts.[45]

The old demons persisted into the Middle Ages, then, and occupied a prominent place in the early medieval magical world, partly because there was a cosmological structure and a scriptural basis ready to support them, but largely because they were a useful means of isolating persons and practices the Christian world in particular wished to proscribe—or protect. Medieval Christians have the dubious distinction of confining the term *demon* with absolute firmness to wicked spirits alone, and of insisting upon their particular malevolence to human-

---

[43] *Collations* VIII,xii, IX,v–vi; ibid., ii,19–20, 45–46. House improvement, especially, seems to attract the attention of demons, who delight in driving their victims to anxious exhaustion over their efforts at this.

[44] Cassian, *Institutes* X,1–3; edit. J. C. Guy, *Jean Cassien Institutions Cénobitiques* (Paris, 1965), pp. 384–391. Hincmar, *De Divortio Lotharii et Tetbergae; PL* 125,720.

[45] *Etymologiae* VIII,xi,15–17, ix,10; edit. Lindsay, *Isidori Hispalensis*.

kind. These demons do us a signal service here, however, for they are very useful in illuminating that in the old magic which was decisively to be cast out, those of its practitioners who needed special treatment, and that within the Christian dispensation which called out for a compensatory form of magic (one additionally commendable in that it might help to defeat the demons). Such magic might lie within the domain of angels. Old daemones, subdivided into evil demons and good angels are centrally involved in the process of both rejecting and selecting from non-Christian magic. We shall pursue their activities in this sphere.

DISTURBANCES OF THE LOWER AIR

We have looked so far primarily at the persistence into medieval Europe of that non-Christian magic of the heavens which is associated with the arts of divination, and at aery demons, apparently expert in these arts (though certainly not in these alone). We may turn now to other areas in which demons, together with people's aspirations to manipulate the preternatural, and their understandable reluctance to relinquish ancient and well-tried means of doing this, cause them to look up above the earth. The arts of divination from the heavens could be exercised upon many other aspects of these heavens. That hierarchical arrangement according to which demons had found their places was reflected in the values put upon these other celestial actors too. In that these occupied a lower place, they were often understood to be lesser in importance, and to be subordinated, in their different ways, to the efforts of the stars and planets and, especially, to the demons. They had their own parts to play in magic nonetheless. Again, the main offenses lay in divination: divination, that is, from thunder and lightning, from the flights and cries of birds, and from the ways of, and smoke from, sacrifices burned in the superior element of fire. In an interesting tenth-century gloss on the *Consolation of Philosophy* by Boethius (V, iv, 2) these three are linked together: "Divination and augury may be divided into three parts; into 'aruspicinam' which is performed with entrails, into 'fulguritiam' which is concerned with thunder, and into 'oscinis' which concerns the cries of birds."[46] Each of these condemned activities had a long past, and some of them enjoyed a lively medieval present.

[46] H. Naumann, *Notker's Boethius* (Strassburg, 1913), p. 58.

Divination by storms and thunder was a part of the special lore of the Etruscans, whereby they drew directions from the sound and appearance of storms and the direction of thunder and lightning, as they did also from the flights of birds. The view that the powers which operate thunderstorms and hailstorms are supernatural ones is very ancient and very pervasive.[47] So is the belief that human beings may manipulate and propitiate such storms. Seneca pours scorn upon such belief but gives us at the same time a full account of it at Cleonae on the Peloponnese.

It is incredible that at Cleonae there were "hail officers" appointed at public expense who watched for hail to come. When they gave a signal that hail was approaching, what do you think happened? Did people run for woolly overcoats or leather raincoats? No. Everybody offered sacrifices according to his means, a lamb or a chicken. When those clouds had tasted some blood they immediately moved off in another direction. . . . Are you laughing at this? Here is something to make you laugh even more. If someone did not have a lamb or a chicken he laid hands on himself, which could be done without great expense. But do not think the clouds were greedy or cruel. He merely pricked his finger with a well-sharpened stylus and made a favourable offering with this blood, and the hail turned away from his little field no less than it did from the property of a man who had appeased it with sacrifices of larger victims. . . . But how can the power in a little drop of blood be so great that it penetrates to the heights and influences of clouds? It is much easier to say: it is an untrue fable. But the people of Cleonae passed judgement on those who had been delegated the task of forecasting storms, because through their negligence vines were beaten down or crops flattened. And among ourselves, in the Twelve Tables there is the warning: "None may make incantations against another's crop."[48]

There is an interesting subcommentary here upon the services such "hail officers" rendered to society as scapegoats, and upon the vulnerability of such magicians in general to perhaps excessively harsh punishment. Pliny brings much information of this kind into our period. He tells of the prophetic power of thunderbolts and presents a full description of the various processes their interpretation involved. He

---

[47] Pliny, *Natural History* II,liii–liv; *edit.* and *transl.* H. Rackham, *Pliny Natural History* i (Loeb Classical Library, 1949), 274–279. And see E. E. Evans-Pritchard, *Witchcraft, Oracles and Magic among the Azande* (Oxford, 1937), pp. 390–391.

[48] Seneca, *Natural Questions* IVB,6–7; *transl.* T. H. Corcoran, *Seneca, Natural Questions* ii (Loeb Classical Library, 1972), 54–57.

writes as though he believed in both the power and the means of interpretation.[49]

The art of divining from and propitiating disturbers of the lower air retained in certain areas sufficient strength to bring down the wrath of eminent ecclesiastics—largely, one suspects, ineffectively. Paul the Deacon (d. ca. 799), for example, refers to Lombard faith in such auguries, adding his own, that they belonged to the devil. At the marriage of the Lombard king Authari to Theudelinda in the late sixth century, he tells us, "a certain tree in this place which was situated in the royal inclosures, was hit during a violent gale by a stroke of lightning with a great crash of thunder, and Agilulf had then as a soothsayer a certain servant of his who by diabolical art understood what future happenings strokes of lightning portended."[50] The soothsayer predicted that Theudelinda would become the wife of Agilulf. Agilulf was suitably horrified at the suggestion, but, says Paul, sure enough the marriage took place after Authari's death in all respectability and apparent happiness (and Theudelinda, of course, became the recipient of the *Dialogues* of Gregory the Great). This thunder and lightning, then, was the precursor of great prosperity to the church, an aspect upon which Paul, understandably, does not dwell. The fact that he mentions the portent at all, however, suggests a certain ambiguity in his approach to the question. Many echoes of beliefs such as these may be found in the rulings about them we find being made in our period. Rulings against them are evident, for example, in barbarian law codes, in ecclesiastical councils, and in sermons and treatises. A treatise produced in about the years 815–817 by Archbishop Agobard of Lyons is an especially important example of these last.[51]

Among barbarian law codes, those issued by the Visigoths show a good deal of anxiety about the practices of supposed invokers of tempests, and so do those of the Bavarians.[52] The Visigothic *Forum Iudicum*, promulgated in the mid-seventh century, includes a condemna-

---

[49] *Natural History* II,xviii: "Heavenly fire is spit forth by the planet [i.e., the sun] as crackling charcoal flies from a burning log, bringing prophecies with it"; *transl.* Rackham, *Pliny*, i,226–227. Pliny describes the practice of augury from thunder and lightning in II,lv; ibid., 278–281.

[50] Paul the Deacon, *History of the Lombards* III,xxx; *transl.* W. D. Foulke, *Paulus Diaconus, History of the Lombards* (Philadelphia, 1907), p. 141.

[51] *De Grandine et Tonitruis*; *edit.* L. Van Acker, *Agobardi Lugdunensis Opera Omnia*, CC (Turnholt, 1981), pp. 3–15.

[52] *Recc. Erv. Chind.* VI,2,4; *edit.* Zeumer, *MGH Legum*, i,259.

tion of persons who maliciously bring tempests down upon another's property. This ruling goes back in part to the *Lex Romana Visigothorum* of the early sixth century and spells out clear and savage penalties. The malefactor is to undergo a flogging, a shaving of the head, and a parade in this state about the neighboring farms. The laws of the Bavarians fine him as well. These laws do not speak merely of pretending to raise tempests, but of actually doing so, a testimony to profound conviction. The First Council of Braga, in 561, drew attention to, and condemned, an even deeper level of anxiety about supernatural influences and storms. Anathema is declared against anyone who believes that the devil causes lightning or thunder or tempests or droughts.[53] This belief is traceable to a Priscillianist doctrine, reported by Orosius, and of Gnostic origin. "For it says that there is a certain Light-Virgin whom God, when he wants to grant rain to men, shows to the Prince of Darkness who, as he desired to grasp her, sweats with excitement and makes rain and, when he is deprived of her, causes thunder by his groaning."[54] We are some way here from the flesh-and-blood malefactors the secular law codes deal with, but we are certainly concerned with a faith in heavenly magic undesirable to Christians, and with a seemingly persistent faith.[55] Other councils and penitentials return to the simpler "emissores tempestatum" and levy penances of up to seven years. As with the moon, so in the case of storms, a good deal of noise was sometimes thought to be helpful, and shouts and the blowing of conch shells and trumpets to drive them away attracted the disapproval of pastors.[56] Storm raisers and those who encourage them are still being condemned by Ratherius of Verona and by Burchard, although the penance the latter require is a relatively light one.[57]

The clearest account we have, however, comes from Archbishop

[53] Canon viii; Mansi, IX,775.

[54] I reproduce here the translation of the relevant section of Orosius's *Commonitorium* given in H. Chadwick, *Priscillian of Avila* (Oxford, 1976) p. 194.

[55] This doctrine is condemned in later penitentials, for example, the *Silense* and the *Vigilanum*, both possibly of the ninth century. McNeill and Gamer, *Medieval Handbooks*, p. 289.

[56] See the penitential ascribed to Bede and the eighth-century Burgundian penitential in ibid., pp. 227, 275. The *Indiculus Superstitionum* has a heading "On storms and horns and conch shells' (xxii); ibid. p. 420 (I have emended the translation). A ninth-century penitential reproves those who shout or blow trumpets against tempests; Franz, *Die Kirchlichen*, ii,39.

[57] Ratherius, *Praeloquium* I,10, and *Sermo* VIII, *De Ascensione Domini*; PL 136,158,739. Burchard, *Decretum* XIX; PL 140,961.

Agobard. He is clearly infuriated by a storm-raising superstition which claimed a large number of his supposed faithful. In this region, says Agobard (that is, in the region around Lyons), almost everyone believes that when they hear thunder "tempestarii" are going about their business. He makes a point of including in his "almost everyone" the grand as well as the poor: one of the many indications that faith in so-called rustic magic was not confined to peasants. These tempestarii, he continues, are thought to be able to control tempests and hail-storms. Through incantations they are supposed to raise a special wind, one which can draw down storms and hail to cut down harvests. They then sell the harvests to persons (presumably alerted to the pickings) who sail from a land called Magonia in ships that fly among the clouds. The crops are loaded upon the ships, payment is made by the airborne sailors, and they sail back whence they have come. Agobard adds that he has even had produced before him four persons, three men and a woman, whom their captors declared to have fallen from the ships and whom they wanted to stone.[58] Middlemen are involved in the whole practice, men who pretend to be able to buy off the tempestarii and are accordingly paid to do so, and as a result (and here perhaps we come upon the main reason for Agobard's lengthy explanation and his anger) tithes and alms remain unrendered.[59] His response is scathing. He presents (with the help of Augustine's *De Trinitate*) a list of biblical quotations to show that God alone can send down storms, and that it is heresy to attribute such powers to men, unless to prophets and to men so holy that God will listen to their prayers. We may deduce that characters such as the tempestarii and their henchmen do not fall within these categories.[60]

This short treatise is full of interest, not only because of the details Agobard gives but because of the range of responses to pre- and non-Christian magic with which it presents us. At the one extreme we have simple credulity and its merciless financial exploitation by a protection racket worthy of the Mafia; at the other, attempts to confound this credulity by Christian written authority, together with interpretations of supernatural incidents not themselves wholly unconnected with financial gain. Agobard tells us nothing here about the type of penalty he would recommend for such delinquency, but if his attitude to other

[58] *De Grandine et Tonitruis; edit.* Van Acker, *Agobardi Lugdunensis*, p. 4.
[59] Ibid., p. 14.
[60] Ibid., p. 13.

deviations from the Christian faith is anything to go by, it is unlikely to have been a light one. It would have inclined perhaps a good deal more to Visigothic rulings than to Burchard.[61] Yet, at the same time, the archbishop was clearly not about to let lynch law run its normal course. We are able to see here, and rather clearly, a few more of the difficulties involved in attempts to overcome non-Christian magical beliefs. It might seem to many that exploitation by the racketeers was punishment enough. Considerations such as these may lie behind much of the leniency of Burchard, for example. There remained, on the other hand, the need to rob the exploiters of both their credibility and their ardor for profit. It is hard to believe that Agobard's biblical quotations and his assertions about the nature of God and of truth were quite equal to this task. Interestingly, he reaches neither for the examples of modern saints and holy men (all his examples are Old Testament ones), nor for "scientific" explanations such as those King Sisebut, for instance, opposed to popular superstitions about the moon. Yet both possible sources of help lay ready to hand. There were many *Lives* telling of the triumphs of saints and martyrs over storms and racketeers, and accessible to Agobard (and to which we shall turn in the succeeding chapters), and there were scientific answers in treatises such as the *De Natura Rerum* of Isidore or of Bede.[62] Agobard seems in truth to have made a deliberate choice, and to have preferred the giving of all power to God and to his Old Testament saints; but this is only one choice among many, and we would do well to suspect immediately that not all would have agreed with it.

Nor did they. The author of the curious little *Book of Thunder*[63] (which used to be ascribed to Bede but is now thought perhaps to be a ninth-century abbreviated translation of a Greek work by John Ly-

[61] Agobard is noted, for instance, for his severity toward Jews, although his strictures in this case seem to have been largely ignored. See B. Blumenkranz, *Les Auteurs Chrétiens Latins du Moyen Age* (Paris, 1963), pp. 152–168, for full references to Agobard's views here. Agobard may well have been more severe in general than was commonly acceptable. His is a singular position and would reward far fuller treatment.

[62] The chapters on storms and hail in these treatises *De Natura Rerum* reduce the problem wholly (except for Isidore's allegorical excursions), and I am sure deliberately, to its natural dimensions. For Isidore see chapters xxix, xxx, xxxv especially; Fontaine, *Isidore de Séville, Traité*, pp. 278–283, 290–291. For Bede, chapters xxviii, xxviiii, xxxiv; edit. C. W. Jones, *Bedae Venerabilis Opera, Opera Didascalica* i, CC (Turnholt, 1975), pp. 219–220, 222.

[63] *De Tonitruis*; PL 90,609–614.

dus)[64] is aware that his task is a topical and dangerous one; he expresses the fear that he will be accused of a wicked interest in magic for treating of such a subject. He treats of it nonetheless, for all his declared alarms, and with apparent relish. His work consists entirely of predictions based on the times and directions of thunder, albeit simple ones and with a certain Christian bias. Indeed, the little treatise is an important example of the type of justification of such activities with which we shall deal in the chapters to come. That the translator, or compiler, felt the need to say something defensive, but that he produced the treatise anyway, shows that there was both unease and fascination about divination by thunder in the circles in which he lived, and that Christian answers were advanced which differed radically from those offered by Archbishop Agobard, and even by Bede himself.

All of this is much to our purpose. The task of dealing with such magical beliefs was far from simple, and the possible approaches to this task were bewildering in their variety, and complicated further by the status and personal views both of condemner and condemned. Faith is a delicate commodity, and if too much gentleness could allow harmful beliefs to persist when they should not, and open the way to unscrupulous exploitation, too much ferocity could do harm of another kind to a trusting disposition much treasured by the church. The removal of the persons of the tempestarii, for example, would not, as many saw, of itself remove belief in them. Anxieties so deep-seated required a focus. And yet, at another extreme, a revealing little scrap of evidence from a far later period shows what might happen should clerical involvement go too far. In 1080 Pope Gregory VII writes in a letter of reproach to King Haakon of Denmark: "You ascribe to your priests the inclemency of the weather, foulness of the air and certain ills of the body."[65] Officers were able to control storms and pestilence—good officers, then, or so it seems King Haakon thought, should control them for good. Fear of misunderstandings such as this may in part explain why Archbishop Agobard's own answers reposed so securely in Old Testament times. If Christian persons, and especially priests, were to be defended from such transferences (transferences of which Seneca made fun, but which could have serious consequences), and if good

---

[64] For a discussion of this text and a possible late ninth-century date for it (and attribution to the court of Charles the Bald), see C. W. Jones, *Bedae Pseudepigrapha* (New York, 1938), pp. 45–47.

[65] Transl. E. Emerton, *The Correspondence of Pope Gregory VII* (New York, 1932), p. 153.

faith and hope were to be preserved, extremely subtle and judicious measures were needed. That there are many different Christian responses to thunder divination and to conjuring with the weather to be found in the early Middle Ages, and that, despite the attitudes of such as Archbishop Agobard, compromise magic of a kind will come to play a part in them, should not cause too much surprise.

The mention of "certain ills of the body" and, especially, of the sensitivity and graded tolerance needed in that combat against magic which sought to preserve a sense of hope, brings us briefly to the questions of pestilence brought by the air (and often associated with thunder), and of "elfshot"; for the treatment of this aspect of the magic of the heavens is, in this context, most rewarding. The idea that illness could fall from the air, or be inflicted by missiles shot through the air by malevolent supernatural agencies, was (and is) as pervasive as belief in the supernatural origins of storms. It may be traced backward at least as far as the *Iliad*, wherein the arrows of Apollo brought pestilence upon the Greeks camped before Troy; and Evans-Pritchard, of course, found among the Azande a belief in "witches [who] shoot objects, called *ahu mangu*, things of witchcraft, into the bodies of those whom they wish to injure. This leads to pain in the place where the missile is lodged, and a witch doctor, in his role of leech, will be summoned to extract the offending objects, which may be material objects or worms and grubs."[66] In the early Middle Ages the same notion was contained in the idea of elfshot, a term applied to little arrows thought to be sent through the air by elves to cause harm. We find mention of elfshot in Anglo-Saxon sources above all, many of which prescribe cures for the illness inflicted, and some of which involve priests in a role not dissimilar to that ascribed to the Zande witch doctors. *Lacnunga*, for example, contains this direction: "If a horse or other beast be 'shot': take dock seed and Scottish wax. Let a mass-priest sing twelve masses over them, and put holy water on them. And put it then on the horse or whatever beast it be."[67] It is easy to see here how vulnerable priests were made, by such recommendations, to charges of failure and reproaches of the sort Gregory VII condemns; yet the risk was clearly thought by many to be an acceptable one. We are here again in the no-man's-land between rejected and accepted magic, and

---

[66] Evans-Pritchard, *Witchcraft*, p. 38.

[67] *Lacnunga* CXVIIIa; transl. J.H.G. Grattan and C. Singer, *Anglo-Saxon Magic and Medicine* (Oxford, 1952), p. 169.

once more in danger of trespassing upon the preserve proper to the next chapter; but the danger is instructive, for it is from this very no-man's-land that we learn best the quality of the dilemma with which the ecclesiastical authorities, especially, were constantly faced. If a belief is deeply rooted, then failure either to eradicate it wholly or to respond to it may expose the believer to quacks or racketeers. What then is to be done? The Anglo-Saxon sources are especially full of an attitude toward elfshot, and many related anxieties about non-Christian magic, which was very different from that adopted by Agobard toward the tempestarii. They manifest a readiness both to assess the strength and harmfulness of the belief, and to risk a response well short of its total eradication and, the punishing of its adherents—or, alternatively, of "science." Non-Christian magic contained commodities both delicate and deeply valuable, commodities which would prompt some, at least, to urge that they could be brought through into Christianity with both safety and advantage.

MAGICAL FLIGHT

Divination from the flights and cries of birds must have been a direct legacy from antiquity. The theory of this, along with the cosmology which supported it, was well within the reach of early Europe. Cicero tells of it, for example:

> I need not remind you of that most famous and worthy man, our guest-friend, King Deiotarus, who never undertook any enterprise without first taking the auspices. On one occasion, after he had set out on a journey for which he had made careful plans beforehand, he returned home because of the warning given him by the flight of an eagle. The room in which he would have been staying, had he continued on his road, collapsed the very next night. This is why, as he told me himself, he had time and again abandoned a journey, even though he might have been travelling for many days.[68]

Origen commented, albeit critically, upon Celsus's belief that birds were dearer to God than people and closer to communion with him,[69] and the lightness of birds and their nearness to the superior elements

---

[68] Cicero, *De Divinatione* I,XV; *edit. and transl.* W. A. Falconer, *Cicero. De Senectute, De Amicitia, De Divinatione* (Loeb Classical Library, 1923), pp. 252–255.

[69] *Contra Celsum* IV,88; *transl.* H. Chadwick, *Contra Celsum* (Cambridge, 1953), pp. 253–254.

of the upper air (though they were not, of course, so near as demons) rendered them excellent as messengers of those divinities supposed to live there. Readers of Pliny, Servius, and Cicero might discover many of the particulars of this type of augury. Cicero passes on the division of birds into "alites," birds such as the eagle, hawk, or osprey, thought to convey messages by their flight, and "oscines," such birds as ravens, crows, and owls, who gave omens by their cries and by the positions in which they uttered these cries: whether they cried on the right-hand side of the augurer or on the left. To Roman augurers at the time of Cicero the left was in general the favorable side, for the augurer faced south and so had his left toward the sunrise (some species, such as the raven, however, were favorable when on the right). Such complexities added refinement to the augurer's skills—and status to the augurer.[70] Pliny regarded the croak of the crow as unlucky when uttered during its breeding season, that is, after midsummer. He tells us too that woodpeckers and, especially, cocks are birds of very great importance in the art of augury.[71] Servius stresses the eagle: "If an owl or a woodpecker gives one auspice and then an eagle gives another, the auspice given by the eagle will be the stronger. There are many grades of auspice."[72]

Auspicia seems frequently to be the plural noun associated with haruspices, or aruspices, people who, according to Isidore, seek for signs to tell them the hours and days on which things are to be done. Some of these were perhaps astrologers; others seem to have exercised themselves in the simpler arts of divining. The habit of looking to the flights and cries of birds for auguries, and not just when setting out on journeys, is condemned in two separate places by Martin of Braga.[73] Eligius objects to it, as we saw, and again we can find in Paul the Deacon information about Lombard beliefs upon the matter, and from a time and place close to the rulings of Gregory III against the looking for signs for journeys. In the year 735, Paul tells us, King Liutprand of the Lombards was thought to be dying, and so the Lombards chose his

[70] Cicero, De Divinatione I,xxxix,liii; transl. Falconer, Cicero, pp. 316–317, 354–355.

[71] Natural History X,xiii,xx,xxiv; transl. Rackham, Pliny, iii,310–311, 318–319, 322–323.

[72] Commenting on the Aeneid III,374; Servianorum in Vergilii Carmina Commentariorum, Editionis Harvardianae iii (Oxford, 1965), 147 (MT).

[73] Reforming the Rustics, chapters 12 and 16; transl. Barlow, Iberian Fathers, pp. 78, 82.

nephew, Hildeprand, to succeed him. "When they handed to him the staff, as is the custom, a cuckoo bird came flying and sat down on the top of the staff. Then to certain wise persons it appeared to be signified by this portent that his government would be useless."[74] Liutprand too was worried; but fortunately he recovered. He exercised prudence, however, and kept Hildeprand with him in the government. Burchard reveals that such portents were still observed in the early eleventh century.

> Have you believed that which some believe? Namely, that if, when they are on a journey, a crow sings while it is flying from their left to their right, the outcome of the journey will be prosperous? And if, when they are looking for somewhere to stay, an owl flies in front of them, the omens are good, and to be trusted in place of trust in God? If you have yourself done or believed in such things, then you must do five days' penance on bread and water.[75]

As usual with Burchard, the penance for delicts of this sort is not severe. He is slightly harsher upon those who believe in the power of the cock, but not seriously so.

> Are you frightened to go out before dawn when you should, declaring that you should wait and not venture forth before cockcrow, because it is dangerous, for unclean spirits have more power to harm before cockcrow than after? And do you believe that the crowing of the cock can do more to repel and quiet these spirits than that divine power which is in man in his faith, and in the sign of the cross? If you do, then ten days' penance on bread and water.[76]

Auguries from signs such as these are clearly unimportant to Burchard; but they have, as clearly, persisted.

Auguries from birds, then, formed a significant part of the paraphernalia of the diviner from the heavens in our period. They were treated with varying degrees of seriousness, depending upon circumstances, the office and importance of the practitioner or inquirer, and the priorities of the legislator. The full lore of the Tuscan augurers, as passed on to us for example by Pliny,[77] and their division of the field of vision by their temples into happy and unhappy houses through which birds

---

[74] *History of the Lombards.* VI,lvi; transl. Foulke, *Paulus Diaconus*, pp. 300–301.

[75] *Decretum* XIX; PL 140,970–971 (MT).

[76] Ibid., 971 (MT).

[77] *Natural History* II,lv; transl. Rackham, *Pliny* i,280–281.

and thunderbolts might fly, is perhaps unlikely to have been conveyed intact. It had never, of course, been unquestioned as a practice,[78] nor had it been exactly organized. Sufficient belief of the kind Celsus expressed, however, and sufficient practice of the sort Pliny described seem to have been prevalent to render them worthy of consistent conciliar notice.[79]

The efforts of the harioli have similarly ancient precedents. Isidore describes their altar sacrifices as "funesta," meaning most probably the blood sacrifices of certain animals in pursuit of directions from the gods (described here by the orthodox Isidore as demons). It seems likely that Isidore had in mind the taking of auspices from the entrails, an activity with which he also associated haruspices. Gregory III seems to make the same connection, and to return to it in a later canon (xxvi). Councils speak of two sorts of forbidden animal sacrifices, both associated with diviners, enchanters, and auspicia, as, indeed, they are here. The first are the general divinatory sacrifices traceable to antiquity. The second are blood sacrifices for the dead, which took place upon specified anniversaries and to which we shall return in a later chapter.

We are reasonably well-informed, and from many of the sources already mentioned, about what the general divinatory sacrifices entailed. The sacrificial animal was treated as a temple in little, and certain portions of its entrails were thought peculiarly capable of conveying divine messages. The liver was the most important part. We have this on no less an authority than the *Timaeus* (71C). Pliny singles it out too, and (though here as part of a belief worthy only of mockery), so does Cicero.[80] Pliny provides us with insights into the complexities this art could involve.

[78] "In the kinds of birds and signs employed, need I assert that divination is compounded of a little error, a little superstition, and a good deal of fraud?" *De Divinatione* II,xxxix; *transl.* Falconer, *Cicero*, pp. 464–465.

[79] And, perhaps, architectural. It seems to me doubtful that the resolute exclusion of large windows from Romanesque churches derived solely from structural limitations. It may have sprung partly at least from a desire to eliminate the augural aspect of the temple building.

[80] *Natural History* XI,lxxx; *transl.* Rackham, *Pliny*, iii,560–561. *De Divinatione* II,xii,xiii; *transl.* Falconer, *Cicero*, pp. 400–405. A vivid account of a blood sacrifice and of the alarms which attended an unfavorably shaped liver is to be found in Lucan, *Civil War* I,618–638; *edit.* and *transl.* J. D. Duff (Loeb Classical Library, 1928), pp. 48–49.

When the late lamented Augustus was sacrificing at Spoleto on the first day he was in power the livers of six victims were found with the bottom of their tissue folded back inward, and this was interpreted to mean that he would double his power within a year. It is also of gloomy omen when the head of the liver is accidentally cut—except at a period of trouble and alarm, when it removes anxieties.[81]

Pliny also speaks of the importance to augurers of bulls' gall in the matter of whether or not to embark on sea voyages.[82] Oxen seem to have taken pride of place as sacrificial animals, but birds, chickens especially, were by no means exempt, and pigs (mentioned by Varro) appear as sacrifices condemned in Salic Law.[83]

Auspices might also be asked by the harioli of the state of the entrails after burning, and in particular of the direction of the smoke that rose into the air during this process, after the initial dismemberment of the victim had been made. The ways of the smoke in the air were thought to be very important. Isidore's pyromancy (taken from Varro) distinguishes this form of divination, but it may generally have been understood as a part of the art of the hariolus. If the liver became distorted in the fire or, still worse, consumed by the heat, this too was a bad omen.[84] If the tail of the creature became crooked, this indicated hardship to come; if it stood upright, this meant victory. Pyromancy did not confine its inquiries to animal sacrifices. Food, too, could be cast into the fire to see what the smoke or flames might portend. We seem to have a distant memory, and indeed a domestication, of this kind of activity again in Burchard. "Have you done as many people do? They sweep the place where they light the fire in their houses and throw grains of corn onto the warm place. If the grains jump up into the air, then there is danger on the way. If they stay still, all is well."[85] Again, Burchard treats it lightly. Ten days on bread and water is the

---

[81] *Natural History* XI,lxxiii; *transl.* Rackham, *Pliny*, iii,550–553.

[82] *Natural History* XI,lxxv; ibid., pp. 554–555.

[83] Titulus II,6; *edit.* K. A. Eckhardt, *Lex Salica* (Weimar, 1953), p. 106. The tenth-century Berne glosses on Lucan draw attention to the sacredness of the groves in which pigs were castrated; *edit.* Usener, *M. Annaei Lucani*, p. 191.

[84] Livy, *Ab Urbe Condita* XLI,xv; *edit.* and *transl.* E. T. Sage and A. C. Schlesinger, *Livy* xii (Loeb Classical Library, 1938), 229. Suetonius, *On Augustus*; *edit.* and *transl.* J. C. Rolfe, *Suetonius* i (Loeb Classical Library, 1914), 122–123.

[85] *Decretum* XIX; PL 140,965. (MT). According to Lucan, the augurer Arruns sprinkled meal before he sacrificed the bull; *transl.* Duff, *Lucan*, pp. 46–47.

penance for divination by popcorn. But inviting professional diviners home to practice their arts, or encouraging them to practice these arts in a larger arena, is of more serious concern. In the *Decretum* proper, Book X (as opposed to the private and confessional *Corrector*, in Book XIX), he repeats fierce earlier rulings against the takers of auspices in general and prescribes penances of up to seven years.[86]

One last form of contending with the supernatural forces thought to inhabit the heavens seems to have earned for a long time universal condemnation; this is the attempt to put things or persons up into the air. The idea that the heavens were the habitation of demons, together with the persistent (and encouraged) memory of the antics of Simon Magus, doubtless did much to prolong this attitude. Conjuring things up into the sky became a distinguishing attribute of a black magician, and Gregory the Great, for example, gave, in his *Dialogues*, currency to this belief by his story of the acts and fate of Basilius the monastic magician. Basilius manifested his demonic powers, and his dislike of his abbot, who had seen through him from the first, by suspending the abbot's house in the air (although he confessed himself unable to harm any of its inhabitants by doing so).[87] He was later burned at the stake by an outraged citizenry. Such stories did nothing to encourage scientific investigation into the possibilities of flight. It is worth noticing, however, that the first serious exponent of the science of aviation in the West in our period, Eilmer of Malmesbury, was also an astrologer of distinction as well as a Benedictine monk.[88] Eilmer fell from the tower of Malmesbury during his test flight and broke his leg in the manner of the end of Simon Magus (according to one account, that is, of the latter's end); but Eilmer was held in great esteem for all he did. Eilmer seems to have profited by that reversion to science as one means of combating the worst of the old magic which recommended itself to many of the subtler thinkers of the early Middle Ages, and perhaps it was his status as a Benedictine that allowed him to take this path. William of Malmesbury did not treat him as he did Archbishop Ge-

[86] Ibid., X; *PL* 140,833–834.

[87] *Dialogues* I,4,6; transl. de Vogüé, *Grégoire le Grand*, ii,42–43. Basilius, in company with another magician, Praetextatus, is mentioned independently by Cassiodorus in his letters: ep. xxii, xxiii; *PL* 69,624–625.

[88] The full story of Eilmer, who made his experiments in the early eleventh century, is told by L. White, "Eilmer of Malmesbury, an Eleventh Century Aviator," *Technology and Culture* 2 (1961), 97–111.

rard. We shall come back again and again to this slender strand of science, to the privileged position of Benedictines in matters supernatural, and to the effect these both had upon the establishing of a hierarchy, both of the magical beliefs to be rescued and of their potential rescuers.

One last type of rising into the heavens did cause sustained alarm, an alarm which varied in intensity but was, in the last event, unable to be subdued by science. This took the form of a belief in flying dreams. The most often reported, and seemingly the most widespread of these, were associated with Diana, Roman goddess of the moon. Diana dreams were, apparently, confined to women. They are spoken of very fully by Regino and by Burchard. Sporadic reference to a cult of Diana, especially in France, and not restricted to women, may be found throughout the early Middle Ages,[89] and it may be that anxiety for Diana's welfare prompted the shoutings at eclipses of the moon to which attention was earlier drawn. As has frequently been pointed out, Diana could easily be associated, and indeed equated, with other female goddesses, such as the Greek Hecate accompanied by her hounds or the German Holde, as beings and beasts who moved freely in the air between the earth and the moon. The flying dreams associated with Diana, and other similar dreams, expressed the belief that human beings, assisted by supernatural agencies, could themselves inhabit the heavens and could perform there feats both enjoyable and dreadful. Regino sets out the contents of the Diana flying dream as it appeared to confessors.

> Wicked women who have given themselves back to Satan and been seduced by the phantasm and illusions of demons believe and declare that they can ride with Diana the pagan goddess and a huge throng of women on chosen beasts in the hours of night. They say that in the silence of the night they can traverse great stretches of territory, that they obey Diana as though she were their mistress and that on certain nights she calls them to her special service.[90]

[89] Saint Kilian, for example, met his death when attempting to convert the East Franks from her cult; AS, Julii ii,616. *The Life of Caesarius* associates Diana with a sort of madness which attacks women at night. *Vita Caesarii* II,18; *edit.*, B. Krusch, MGH SRM iii (Hanover, 1896), 491. A "Dianaticus" might also be a "haruspex," and Gregory of Tours can equate Diana with the midday demon: *Vita Patrum Iurensium Romani, Lupicini, Eugendi* III,11; *edit.* Krusch, ibid., 159 and n.

[90] *De Ecclesiasticis Disciplinis* II,ccclxiv; *PL* 132,352 (MT).

Burchard repeats Regino's anxieties in his own *Corrector*.[91] Both of them pour scorn on such dreams and condemn them. "Who is there who has not been taken out of himself in dreams and nightmares and seen in his sleep things he would never see when awake? Who is imbecile enough to imagine that such things, seen only in the mind, have a bodily reality?" Both draw attention to the capacity, exhibited by Ezekiel and Saint Paul, to distinguish between dreams of this kind and reality. Both are equally sure, however, that such dreams persist. In separate places Burchard speaks of distinct flying and riding dreams, one connected with Holde, and another, again seemingly confined to women, in which the dreamers believe they can fly up into the clouds with demons and indulge in battles, giving and receiving phantom wounds.[92]

The penalties Burchard prescribes for these beliefs are relatively light: one year's penance for flying with Holde, and for flying with Diana or indulging in demonic combats, two years. It is worse if there is active blasphemy involved.

> Do you believe this, in common with many women who are followers of Satan? Namely that, in the silence of the night, when you are stretched out upon your bed with your husband's head upon your breast you have the power, flesh as you are, to go out of the closed door and traverse great stretches of space with other women in a similar state of self-deception? And do you believe that you can kill, though without visible arms, people baptized and redeemed by the blood of Christ, and can cook and eat their flesh, after putting some straw or a piece of wood or something in the place of the heart? And then that you can resuscitate them after you have eaten them and make them live again? If yes, then you must do forty days of penance, that is, a Lent, on bread and water for seven consecutive years.[93]

Besides the more obvious horrors, the idea of resuscitating the dead would have caused a frisson in the breasts of readers, for example, of Augustine and of Isidore on Saul and the witch of Endor.[94] We shall return to this. The mention of the putting of straw or a piece of wood

---

[91] *PL* 140,963–964.

[92] Ibid., 973–974. Wounds and illnesses are often to be found in Shamanic dreams: see L. and B. D. Paul, "The Maya Midwife as Sacred Professional: a Guatemalan Case," *American Ethnologist* 2 (1975), 707–726.

[93] *PL* 140,973 (MT).

[94] For example, Isidore, *Quaestiones in Libros Regum* II,xx, *PL* 83, 407, in which he quotes Augustine to Simplicianus verbatim.

in place of the heart recalls Petronius on the "strix," the horrible flying creature which devoured babies, leaving a straw doll in their place, or Ovid on the same part bird, part sorceress in the *Fasti* or *Amores*. Hincmar of Rheims clearly believed in the strix, which he too thought was female, and of supernatural power and malevolence.[95] A "stria" or "striga" in barbarian law codes frequently incurs a charge of cannibalism.[96] The deeds of a strix are demonic and are almost all associated with the power to fly through the dark and airy realms of demons. We shall return to this also, but for the moment I advance these separate alarms together to show how filled with supernatural powers (and supernatural powers of a frightening sort) was the non-Christian lower air, and how seriously, then, the early medieval Christian Church must take these powers.

The fact that in these particular flying dreams the leaders of such flights are, in the early Middle Ages, seemingly always female,[97] and so too are those who follow them in their journeys through the night skies, might tempt one to connect them with the psychology of female repression, and especially with the repression of feminine aspirations by this church. Two features of this evidence should be borne, however, most carefully in mind when one is assaulted by such a temptation. Firstly, the dreams are discussed strictly within the context of an ecclesiastical discipline anxious to safeguard its wards from aery demonic influences in which it genuinely believed. Secondly, the penalties recommended here are gentler than those to be found in secular laws for deviations verging upon witchcraft and thus are rather protective than truly punitive. The relative lightness of the penalties Burchard recommends is, in fact, deserving of far more notice than is the fact that he singles out women for condemnation. Both Burchard and Regino are, moreover, insistent that these are merely *dreams*. Flying dreams are not the worst form of intrusion into the heavens. The

---

[95] Petronius, *Satyricon* 134; transl. W. Arrowsmith (Ann Arbor, Mich. 1959), p. 166. Ovid, *Fasti* VI,131–168; transl. J. G. Frazer, *Ovid's Fasti* (Loeb Classical Library, 1951), pp. 326–331. *Amores* I,viii, for the witch Dipsas who flies by night; transl. G. Showerman, *Ovid, Heroides and Amores* (Loeb Classical Library, 1977), p. 347. Hincmar, *De Divortio Lotharii et Tetbergae*, xv; PL 125,717.

[96] *Lex Salica* titulus lxlvi; edit. Eckhardt, *Lex Salica*, p. 236. *Leges Alamannorum*, *Pactus* XIII; edit. K. A. Eckhardt, MGH *Leges* v (Editio Altera, Hanover, 1966), 24. See also Charlemagne's Saxon Capitulary, chapter 6. This may be read in translation in H. R. Loyn and J. Percival, *The Reign of Charlemagne* (London, 1975), p. 52.

[97] As distinct, for example, from the flying witches of the Azande; Evans-Pritchard, *Witchcraft*, pp. 34–35.

dreams of sorceresses about their magical heavenly journeys are of far less concern to both Regino and Burchard than, for example, the real efforts of diviners (male or female) or of tempestarii to compel the heavens to answer their commands. Of course, there were better dreams to have than dreams of flying with Diana—we shall look at some of these—but, that being said, dreams such as the Diana ones were not of the first importance, and the attitude of the authorities to them is indulgent, more indulgent than it is to rituals and statues to Diana. The magic of the heavens is dangerous because the heavens are full of demons, but less dangerous in certain dreams than in reality, and, to Burchard at least, of less danger still when confined to dreaming women. Dreams fell into a category of heavenly magic toward which the authorities felt able to be relatively relaxed. There were far worse forces abroad, and far more frightening demons. It was well then to concede where concession was possible, and here women, as a category, enabled such concession to be made. There was, furthermore, not merely no repression in such an attitude, but, on the contrary a good deal of positive courage. Women, as Hincmar had shown, were vulnerable to witchcraft persecution. Here their vulnerability was very greatly lessened. They *dreamed* they were flying with witches; that is all. Some of the rescued magic of the earth too, I shall later suggest, had as one of its effects the much needed protection of women's rights at secular law.[98] Such small hints of patronage as there are in the church's attitude may surely be offset by such considerations as these. This dimension of the rise of magic in early medieval Europe, the beneficial effect it had, that is, upon aspects of the social position of women, is an exceptionally important one. Again, the early medieval attitude to non-Christian magic, and the circumstances which caused some of it then to be encouraged, distinguish this period sharply and with a poignant irony, from the circumstances of, and sufferers from, its sixteenth- and seventeenth-century "decline."

The old magic of the heavens persisted into early Europe in many forms, and the vigor with which it did so, and the need to preserve that which was good in the faith it commanded, led to much subtlety in the Christian approach, and to many divisions within it. Tolerably innocent forms of non-Christian magical beliefs came to be distinguished from those less innocent, and the degrees of acceptance or penalty required by each came, accordingly, to be differentiated and

[98] See below, chap. 9.

refined. Some of the magic distinguished as innocent by these processes might be allowed to survive; indeed it might even be a help in defeating the more destructive forms. Science might assist in the divisions to be made and the defeats to be inflicted. Complicated processes were afoot, some of which may now be followed to their resolutions.

The Magic That Was Needed: Rescued Means of Magical Intervention

IT WAS IMPOSSIBLE to reject all aspects of the pre- or non-Christian magic of the heavens out of hand. For one thing, Christianity had no full-fledged scheme with which to replace them. Genesis, to be sure, with its story of the creation of the world in six ordered days, provided a promising outline, but sections even of Genesis were markedly unclear in their precise meanings, and parts of it (such as 6:1–4, as we have seen) were contested by scriptural traditions still of great authority. And for another, of course, beliefs in an order that transcended the material order, and habits that encouraged the looking to the heavens for help, even divinatory help, needed rather to be cherished than set aside. Both were at least concomitant with reverence, and this fact, taken together with the further manifest truth that so many of the non-Christian magical practices which involved the heavens quite simply refused to die, required a more muted approach than the stridency of the first stage of conversion enthusiasm. Many medieval Christians, moreover, still fell short of that trusting belief in divine providence espoused by Eligius, and of that acceptance of the full responsibilities human free will imposed with which the Fathers opposed the divinatory arts. Perhaps this would always be so. For this last reason too, then, some of the old beliefs and habits might have to be indulged to help such persons on their way.

The process whereby certain aspects of the magic of the heavens came to be indulged, and indeed encouraged by Christian leaders, cannot be truly understood without some insight into the contemporary strength of earthly magic too; for horrified resistance to far grosser earthly beliefs (at some of which we shall look in the next chapter) was an issue of major importance when it came to decision making about magic in general by the Christian Church. For some medieval Christians the repression of every aspect of magical practice was still the only answer; but for others negotiation was possible, and for this the non-Christian heavens might actually provide resources, for those wise enough to notice them. Thus, "gross," condemned, and earth-bound magic was, through the reactions it provoked, centrally engaged in the rescue of much of the magic of the heavens. Tempered belief in the powers of the sun, moon, and stars, and in the influence of demons and angels, and Christian invocation of, and control over, storms and rains and pestilences, came to seem to these others an excellent way of combating the prevalence and popularity of the non-Christian earthly magic purveyed by conjurers and witch doctors and necroman-cers, love charms and potions, spells and the powers of the dead. And there was, in addition, a great deal in the content of the magic of the heavens that was of itself attractive and could be rendered at least in-offensive and perhaps again helpful to Christians. This was plundered with more eagerness than we have always understood.

ASTROLOGY

One of the most spectacular rescues in the history of magic's rise in the early Middle Ages is the rescue of astrology. From being bowed almost to extinction by the heavy weight of patristic condemnation, astrology became a perfectly acceptable, indeed encouraged, object of learned inquiry. I tried to argue in the preceding chapter that the rescue of astrology was in fact thought to be desirable in a remarkably short time, and that the early lack of manuals on the subject, a lack which Laistner sees as evidence of a failure of astrological practice, is evi-dence of no such thing. The reappearance of such manuals in the tenth, and especially the eleventh, centuries is marked, certainly. It may mean, however, not that an interest in astrology had reappeared after many centuries' eclipse, but that its scrutiny and even practice had fallen into different hands. I think it does mean this; and I would reaffirm that divination by means of the stars and the planets and the signs of the zodiac was enthusiastically practiced throughout our pe-riod, and that the ways in which, and the reasons why, it was quickly made respectable are among the most instructive we have before us.

The rescue of astrology was, of course, in part accomplished by wordplay. Isidore's distinction between "natural" and "superstitious" astrology paved the way, as we saw, for the rehabilitation of "natural" astrology and made it possible for the terms *astronomia* and *astrologia* to become, under certain conditions, interchangeable. We do not owe the rescue solely, or even primarily, however, to semantics. Astrology was made respectable in the early Middle Ages for three particular reasons. Firstly, there were in existence forms of non-Christian magic thought more destructive both mentally and socially than astrology, and against which astrology might prove to be an active compromise and counter. Secondly, once it became desirable to make an honest science of astrology, supporting materials could be found for the decision to do so; and they could be found, moreover, in sacred as well as in scientific writings. Thirdly, astrology properly understood exercised the mind to a high degree. Such exercise might be seen as a quite acceptable ingredient of asceticism, and an appropriate way of freeing the spirit from the miring of the earth and of associating it with the angels, provided that it be undertaken with due purpose, and in the context of a style of life in other respects undeniably virtuous. This last state of affairs may be one (though not, of course, the only) reason why, when we do have certain sorts of astrological direction committed to writing in our period, they are committed to writing so often by monks. It was perhaps Archbishop Gerard of York's misfortune in this respect that his style of life was not beyond reproach. Observers could, quite independently, find excellent occasions for moral disapproval, and it was therefore easy for them to range his astrological interests among these. The reputation of Gerbert of Aurillac suffered in the same way and at some of the same hands.[1] The position of astrology was necessarily precarious, and those who continued to find in it a wicked form of magic could always lay their hands upon good reasons to condemn it. There were persons, however, who, almost from the earliest, could see not only that it might not be magic in its destructive sense at all, but that it could be both a widely acceptable answer to that magic which must indubitably be outlawed, and a positive inducement to intellectual achievement and religious devotion. The translating of such insights into action was not easy; but it was possible and it did, in the end, yield results.

Three views believed to be scientifically based assisted in the rehabilitation of astrology on many different levels, and in the scrutiny of

[1] Archbishop Gerard of York had a reputation for lasciviousness, and William of Malmesbury had reasons to dislike him too for his refusal to submit his province to the primacy claimed by Canterbury. The same William regarded Gerbert as a renegade monk. *Edit.* N.E.S.A. Hamilton, *Willelmi Malmesbiriensis Monachi De Gestis Pontificum Anglorum* RS (London, 1870), pp. 259–260; *edit.* W. Stubbs, *Willelmi Malmesbiriensis Monachi de Gestis Regum Anglorum*, i, RS (London, 1887), 193–195.

its surviving texts. Firstly, in that the heavenly bodies, the stars and the planets, influenced growth and decay and the changes of the seasons, it could be, and was, argued (and with an increasing fervor) that a knowledge of their movements might be both of medical and agricultural benefit. It might be especially so in contrast to deeply dubious prevailing non-Christian magical practices, such as the use of ligatures and the charming of crops. Secondly, the moon, in its nearness to earth and in its capacity to penetrate the murky demon-filled air, was firmly believed to have, in its waxing and waning, an especially powerful effect. Thirdly, comets and falling stars had long been acknowledged to be important to events on earth, and this supposedly proven fact slipped easily into the mental ground prepared by the other two beliefs. All these heavenly bodies, then, deserved respect and attention.

Isidore was, once again, crucial to the restoration to propriety of one manifestation of this respect and attention: the scrutiny of the stars and planets for medical purposes. It might be remembered that, in the section of his *Etymologies* devoted to magical practices, he had found the use of ligatures in medicine especially execrable.[2] In another section of these same *Etymologies* Isidore positively advocated medical astronomy, with its contemplation of the laws, the stars, the changes of the seasons, as a means of understanding the workings of the human body.[3] The medical aspects of the Christianization of astrology are important ones and will be better seen in their true context when we come to treat of non-Christian earthly magic and the remedies it advocated; but we might note meanwhile that Isidore was a most enthusiastic early medieval propagator of the notion, derived from Greek science, that the body of a man is a microcosm of the universe and reflects in little all the constituent parts of it. Isidore seemingly gave the word *microcosmus* its first Latin form. If, then, the forces of the universe permeate human beings, then those first created and immensely powerful bodies of the heavens might be expected to influence humanity especially intensely. It can, indeed, be shown that Isidore believed in this permeation, this power, and this intense influence, even to the extent of admitting of the possibility that the heavenly bodies could be signs to and about humankind in virtue of the sympa-

[2] See above, chap. 3.

[3] *Etymologiae* IV, 13–14; *edit.* W. M. Lindsay, *Isidori Hispalensis Episcopi Etymologiarum sive Originum Libri XX* (Oxford, 1911).

thy that binds the universe, and that they might themselves have souls.[4]

Priscillianist enthusiasms for astrology went, as we saw in the first section of this chapter, too far, and they brought down upon their heads the anathemas of the mid-sixth-century Council of Braga. This council objected specifically to the notions that the twelve patriarchs might have the signs of the zodiac assigned to them, and that these signs ruled the health and sickness of certain set parts of the body. The Priscillianists were condemned chiefly for their views about the overweening power of Satan, and this tainted their other beliefs; but once the Priscillianists themselves had retreated, attitudes to astrology might, and in fact did, change. Medical astrology, of a sort, early found its advocates. Some of the forms this advocacy took might, to judge from our manuscript records of it, seem little removed from the sort of superstitious faith in ligatures Isidore condemned. But they were different in kind. They used mental rather than physical conjurations. And they rested upon things thought to be known for certain about the power of the moon.

"Scientific" knowledge about the moon, in contrast with those magical beliefs we have briefly surveyed, played a vital part in the rescue of astrology. Lunar influence over growth and decay was a firm ingredient of scientific orthodoxy, for the moon was, after all, the planet nearest to earth and was considered to be much bigger than the earth. Its influence might then be expected to be strong. Such views were ancient, reaching back at least as far as Hesiod, but Pliny and Augustine were perhaps their most forceful conveyors to this period. Pliny gave the moon prominence in his advice, for example, to agriculturalists.

All cutting, gathering and trimming is done with less injury to the trees and plants when the moon is waning than when it is waxing. Manure must not be touched except when the moon is waning, but manuring should chiefly be done at new moon or at half moon. Geld hogs, steers, rams, and kids when the moon is waning. Put eggs under the hen at the new moon. Make ditches at full moon, in the night time. Bank up the roots of trees at

[4] J. Fontaine, "Isidore de Séville et l'astrologie," *Revue des Études Latines* 31 (1953), 283–285. In his *De Natura Rerum* xxiii Isidore can say that the planets are called "errantia" not because they err themselves but because they cause men to err; *edit.* J. Fontaine, *Isidore de Séville, Traité de la Nature* (Bordeaux, 1960), pp. 258–259.

full moon. In damp land sow seed at the new moon and in the four days round that time. . . ."[5]

Pliny's influence was greatly assisted by Augustine's acceptance of the fact that farmers needed to consult the movements and behavior of the heavenly bodies.

> We see that the seasons of the year change with the approach and the receding of the sun. And with the waxing and waning of the moon we see certain kinds of things grow and shrink, such as sea urchins and oysters, and the marvellous tides of the ocean.[6]

Augustine's words here were uttered, it is true, within the context of a general condemnation of the science of the mathematici, and he goes on to point out that "choices of the will are not subject to the positions of the stars"; but the door had been opened a chink.

Such naturalistic explanations of the moon's effects were useful in counteracting the excesses of Diana worshipers, and this may be one reason for their perpetuation. Again Isidore and Bede did not fail. In the De Temporum Ratione Bede quoted Ambrose and Basil with great approval on the power of the moon, especially over winds and waters and growing things. He advocated the taking of great care that wood, for example, be cut at the correct phase of the moon, if it was to be used in shipbuilding or preserved from termites; and he drew attention to the marvelous capacity of moonlight to penetrate Persian selenite, or moonstone, and to make its luster wax and wane with that of the moon (here Bede probably draws upon the City of God XXI,v, which is itself dependent upon Pliny). It was at this point that he adduced his famous observations on the tides and the ways of the moon with these.[7] It is a very long step indeed, of course, from such observations to the science of astrology fully armed, and Isidore was particularly careful to point out that the moon exercised its powers strictly within the control of Divine Providence. Perhaps he feared that others might object to how close to the edge of Christian orthodoxy he had drawn. Bede issued a clear condemnation of astrology too, as we have seen,

---

[5] Natural History XVIII,lxxv; edit. and transl. H. Rackham Pliny Natural History v (Loeb Classical Library, 1950), 390–391.

[6] City of God V,vi; edit. and transl. W. M. Green, Saint Augustine City of God Against the Pagans ii (Loeb Classical Library, 1963), 156–157.

[7] Isidore, De Natura Rerum xix; edit. Fontaine, Isidore de Séville, Traité, pp. 246–247. Bede, De Temporum Ratione xxviii,xxix; edit. C. W. Jones, Bedae Opera De Temporibus (Cambridge, Mass., 1943), pp. 231–235.

and that in the same *De Temporum Ratione*;[8] but he issued only one, and there may be in that also an instinct for self-defense which was stronger than his conviction that astrology in all its manifestations should be outlawed. If star lore taught that the stars governed human fate entirely, then its doctrine would indeed be foreign to the Christian faith, as Bede declared. But if it merely brought to light sure influences and enabled people to take these influences into account when making their choices, and if, in addition, it enabled the more expert of Christians to face, and indeed outplay, the ever present haruspices or augures, on their own ground, then the matter might be different. At least such beliefs about the power of the moon could enable the door to be opened perhaps one inch more.[9]

Anglo-Saxon sources are especially rich in evidence of both fear of, and trust in, the moon. Pliny's view that the moon was important to the growth of plants finds many echoes, for example in the *Anglo-Saxon Herbal*: "[Periwinkle] must be plucked when the moon is nine nights old, or eleven nights, thirteen nights or thirty nights, and when it is one night old."[10] Isidore's recommendations that the movements of the heavenly bodies be taken seriously when it comes to medical diagnosis and cure find a clear response in these and other sources. Bloodletting may only take place during certain lunar phases. Bede has the saintly John of Beverley very cross about a bleeding on the fourth day of the moon's waxing. A nun from Watton had become seriously ill. John was outraged. "You have acted foolishly and dangerously to bleed her on the fourth day of the moon; I remember how Archbishop Theodore of blessed memory used to say that it was very dangerous to bleed a patient when the moon is waxing and the Ocean tide flowing." The nun recovered only as a result of his prayers.[11] *Lacnunga*, among many early treatises, dilates upon the danger of bloodletting on Mondays.[12] Cures for lunacy involve, as one might expect, similar careful

[8] iii; *edit*. Jones, *Bedae Opera*, pp. 183–184.

[9] I have tried elsewhere to argue that, in his *De Natura Rerum*, Bede did indeed show a good deal more interest in astrological motifs than one might expect: V.I.J. Flint, "Thoughts about the Context of Some Early Medieval Treatises *De Natura Rerum*," in idem, *Ideas in the Medieval West* (London, 1988) III, pp. 22–24.

[10] clxxix (MT); *edit*. and *transl*. O. Cockayne, *Leechdoms, Wortcunning and Starcraft of Early England* i, RS (London, 1864), 314.

[11] *Ecclesiastical History* V,3; *edit*. B. Colgrave and R.A.B. Mynors, *Bede's Ecclesiastical History of the English People* (Oxford, 1969), pp. 460–461.

[12] clxxxix; *transl*. J.H.G. Grattan and C. Singer, *Anglo-Saxon Magic and Medicine* (Oxford, 1952), p. 199. Professor James John has drawn my attention to a *calendarium*, found in a manuscript datable to the early years of the eleventh century (and coming

reference. "For a lunatic take this wort [clovewort], and wreathe it with a red thread about the man's neck, when the moon is on the wane."[13]

Collections of medical prognostics from the moon are very commonly to be found in surviving manuscripts, such as this one from an eleventh-century Canterbury manuscript, BL Cotton Tiberius A III, fol. 38a (a famous codex to which we shall have cause to return): "When the moon is one night old, he who is attacked by disease will be dangerously attacked. If disease attacks him on a two night old moon, he will soon be up. If sickness attacks him when the moon is three nights old he will be confined to bed and he will die."[14] And so on until the thirtieth night. Belief in the value of such reckonings inspired the composition of whole books which followed the moon through the thirty days of its life, assigning recommendations and characteristics to each day. Sometimes they were accompanied by spheres, such as the curious (and widely copied) little *Sphere of Pythagoras* (or *Sphere of Apuleius*). This sphere, in manuscripts, took the form of a circle divided by a line across the middle. Above and below the line were three compartments each, among which the numbers one to thirty were divided. Described as a "sphere of life and death or of all sick people and their questions," it was worked by adding the sum of the letters of the sick person's name (each letter had a number assigned to it) to the day of the moon on which he or she became sick, and then dividing the sum by thirty. Should the resulting number fall below the line, it signified death, and if above it, life. Further calculations involving the compartments, and lunar tables matching the numbers found, might throw light upon the length and extent of the illness.[15] It is hard to see what, if any, comfort the sufferer derived from such activities, but they certainly gave the calculator power of a sort through which the pretensions of the local medicine man or woman might temporarily have been thwarted. This may have been one im-

---

perhaps, and interestingly, from the environs of Liège), in which days unsuitable for bloodletting are clearly marked. G. I. Lieftinck, *Manuscrits Datés Conservés dans les Pays-Bas* i (Amsterdam, 1964), 46–47, and pls. 34–35.

[13] *Anglo-Saxon Herbal* x,2 (MT); *edit.* Cockayne, *Leechdoms*, i,100–101.

[14] (MT) *Edit.* Cockayne, *Leechdoms*, iii,182.

[15] An excellent illustration of such a sphere, together with directions for its use and lunar prognostic tables, is to be found in MS London B.L. Cotton Caligula A xv, fols. 121v–122. The lunar prognostics are printed and discussed by M. Förster, "Beiträge zur mittelalterlichen Volkskunde VIII," *Archiv für das Studium der neueren Sprachen* 129 (1912), 30–49.

portant reason for their appearance in monastic manuscripts. It was, I think, to look ahead for a moment, a major reason for the rehabilitation of astrology from condemned non-Christian mumbo jumbo to respectable Christian science.

Often prognostics based upon the moon went well beyond mere medical ones. Thus:

> The fourth day of the moon. Let blood in the morning. This is a good day on which to begin undertakings and to send boys to school. Whoever tries to run away will be speedily recaptured and whoever falls ill will quickly die, with almost no hope of recovery. Boys born on this day will be fornicators and so will girls. If you have a dream on it, good or bad, it will come true.[16]

Lunaria of this kind, sometimes with a token Christian reference to the birthday of a biblical figure, were exceedingly popular. We have surviving texts of them from the ninth century onward and some indication that they may have been in fashion from as early as the third.[17] Sometimes they took cognizance of the relation of the moon to the signs of the zodiac—"Do not shave when the moon is in the sign of Aries"—sometimes of the position of the moon in relation to the planets. Happily they did not always agree among themselves. Parents of incipient fornicators, for example, might have the relief of turning to another prognostication.[18] We cannot know quite how seriously they were taken, but they were carefully copied in monastic scriptoria. Yet, at the same time, behavior which depended upon the moon attracted hostile attention in ecclesiastical councils and in sermons. We may surely see here a division in the Christian ranks, and evidence of a greater willingness at a local level than at a central one to make compromises with older beliefs. We shall explore this divisive aspect of the matter far more thoroughly when we turn to the magic of the earth. One thing is certain, however, and that is that beliefs in the moon, and lunaria, were important ingredients in the mounting pressure for serious attention to be paid to astrology.

The third "scientific" view assisting in the rehabilitation of astrol-

---

[16] From a late eleventh-century Vatican manuscript, Vat. Lat. 3101 from Bavaria, printed in E. Svenburg, *De Latinska Lunaria* (Gothenburg, 1936), p. 31 (MT).

[17] E. Svenburg, *Lunaria et Zodiologia Latina* (Gothenburg, 1963), p. 6.

[18] "A child [born on the fourth day of the moon] will be an important servant of the realm"; Svenburg, *De Latinska*, p. 31 (from the eleventh-century MS B. L. Cotton Titus D XXVII).

ogy, the idea, that is, that comets and falling stars might be portents, particularly of disaster, was, again, perhaps most effectively transmitted to the Middle Ages by Pliny. Pliny gives evidence of such portended disasters in human history (though he is careful to say that such influences did not wholly govern them).[19] This view was also taken up by Isidore, by Bede, and by their copious following with enthusiasm. Isidore, while obviously approving of the idea, quite cheerfully ascribes it to the supposedly forbidden "Genethliaci."[20] Comets, thus dignified, became popular with historians too as a satisfying preface to, and often implied reason for, disasters of a possibly more complex origin. Medieval chroniclers employed them gladly, and so comets shine through histories as portents of war, pestilence, famines, and the fall of kingdoms. We have very many examples of this way of using them.[21] On this convenient (if intellectually sometimes slightly dubious) pretext as well, then, comets were able to insinuate themselves, probably even more effectively than through the scientific texts alone, into the learned and the popular imagination. Gregory of Tours insisted that one could differentiate between types of comet. "When it seems to have a flaming diadem, it portends the death of a king. When it has a long ray like a sword, glowing red, and spreads its hair abroad darkly, it announces ruin to the country."[22] Whether helped primarily by the political and intellectual exigencies of historians (as I think), or because it was set out in scientific treatises De Natura Rerum, insistence

[19] Natural History II,xxiii; edit. Rackham, Pliny, i,234–239.

[20] Isidore, Etymologiae III,lxxi, 16; edit. Lindsay, Isidori Hispalensis. De Natura Rerum xxvi,13; edit. Fontaine, Isidore de Séville, Traité, pp. 272–275. Bede, De Natura Rerum xxiiii; edit. C. W. Jones, Bedae Venerabilis Opera, Opera Didascalica i, CC (Turnholt, 1975), 216.

[21] Comets heralded the inroads of Saracens into Gaul, according to Bede, and portended "dire disaster to east and west alike." Ecclesiastical History V,23; edit. Colgrave and Mynors, Bede's Ecclesiastical History, pp. 556–557. Paul the Deacon ascribed a particularly severe pestilence in Rome to the appearance of a brilliant comet. History of the Lombards V,xxxi; transl. W. J. Foulke, Paulus Diaconus, History of the Lombards (Philadelphia, 1907), p. 235. The early eleventh-century historian Adhémar of Chabannes is a particularly good example of one who takes readily to explanation by means of signs in the heavens. See, for instance, his entry for the year 1010: "His temporibus signa in astris, siccitates noxiae, nimiae pluviae, nimiae pestes, et gravissimae fames, defectiones multae solis et lunae apparuerunt." These foretold, according to Adhémar, the destruction of the Holy Sepulcher. Adhemari Historiarum Libri III iii,46–47; edit. D. G. Waitz, MGH SS iv (Hanover, 1841), 136–137.

[22] De Cursu Stellarum xxxiv; edit. B. Krusch, MGH SRM i(2) (Hanover, 1885), 419 (MT).

on the influence of comets certainly did a great deal further to fortify belief in the power the heavenly bodies in general had over human-kind, and thus, when the time was right, to reinforce the mounting enthusiasm for the rescue of astrology.

One additional factor in the building up and justification of an interest in the heavenly bodies lay in the practical needs of the ecclesiastical computus and monastic horarium. Cassian, when speaking of demons, gave us a vivid example of the timing of the next meal by the sun; Gregory of Tours, in turn, tells us how important was the observation of the stars' position in the night sky in determining the times at which to rise for the night offices. His *De Cursu Stellarum* (in which he described the two kinds of comet) was in fact written primarily for the help of the monk whose responsibility it was to wake everyone up for those offices which normally occurred in darkness. The appropriate hour was determined by noting the place in the sky—a place that varied from month to month—of specific stars and constellations. Gregory describes these stars and constellations, includes illustrations, and then gives directions for their proper interpretation and use. For example: "If [in the month of December] you ring the bell for matins when you see Arcturus rise, then thirty psalms may be sung without difficulty."[23] Thus, splendidly illustrated copies of such treatises on the stars and heavenly bodies as the *Aratea* of Cicero, the *Astronomica* of Hyginus, and the *Arati Phaenomena* of Germanicus Caesar, became standard works in monastic libraries, and we have many startlingly beautiful surviving copies of them.[24] Often they are accompanied by maps, some of which had an agreeable tendency to place the observer up in the firmament and have him look down on the constellations, like Scipio in his dream.[25] At the very least, these needs and these

[23] *De Cursu Stellarum* xxxv; ibid., p. 421.

[24] References to and descriptions (with plates) of such manuscripts are contained in F. Saxl and H. Meier, *Verzeichnis astrologischer und mythologischer illustrierter Handschriften des lateinischen Mittelalters* (Heidelberg, 1915–). An English translation of the volumes bearing upon manuscripts held in England was made in 1953 by H. Bober. Among these MSS B. L. Harley 647 of the ninth century and 2506 of ca. 1000 (originally from Fleury) are striking examples of the type of text to which I refer. A magnificent representation of the ninth-century Leiden Aratus manuscript (MS Voss. lat. Q 79) is available in R. Katzenstein, *The Leiden Aratea: Ancient Constellations in a Medieval Manuscript*, J. Paul Getty Museum (Malibu, 1988).

[25] Certain maps accompanying Isidore's *De Natura Rerum* in tenth- and eleventh-century manuscripts for example, are drawn from this perspective, most probably from antique exemplars. W. M. Stevens, "Isidore's Figure of the Earth," *Isis* 71 (1980),

treatises helped to focus watchful and admiring attention upon the skies, and they again helped to make the notion of the heavenly bodies' power over human lives more palatable, and so astrology more acceptable as a legitimate exercise than even Isidore had hoped. The calculation, too, of the days of the movable feasts, especially Easter, required reckonings from the sun and the moon, and manuscripts assembled for the purposes of these calculations, usually called "computi," are rich sources of medical astronomy, of lunaria, and of astronomical and sometimes of astrological knowledge.

Such manuscripts, which as a whole contain a great mine of material still to be worked on, and which vary greatly among themselves in computistical and astrological complexity, become an excellent gauge of the state of affairs and attitudes prevailing in separate areas, and even in separate communities. It may be no accident, for instance, that the great Benedictine abbeys of Bavaria—which, to look ahead for a moment, most probably produced one of the earliest surviving manuscripts we have of the *Mathesis* of Julius Firmicus Maternus (that astrological treatise which was the downfall of Archbishop Gerard)[26]—are also among the richest we have in star guides and computistical texts. There are many examples of these. A striking one is an early ninth-century codex from the abbey of Saint Peter's, Salzburg, a well-thumbed book contained a medley of astronomical material from Bede, Hyginus, scolia on Germanicus, Pliny: little bits, indeed, of the works of many of those contributors we have distinguished in isolation as pressures building toward the rehabilitation of astrology.[27] Much of Pliny's *Natural History* reached the Middle Ages only as a result of its inclusion in computistical collections. Thus, much as the enthusiasm of historians for the use of comets as aids to historical explanation helped to perpetuate a belief in their influence, so did the practical requirements of the computus help to provide space and incentive for the recording of much about the heavenly bodies that was not exclusively computistical, and much that many used to find frankly magical.

The mention of the ecclesiastical computus and the requirements of the liturgy bring us to one last aid to the process (another intensely

---

268–277. Two ninth-century celestial hemispheres, attached to a star book and most probably used for teaching, are reproduced in F.V.M. Cumont, "Astrologica," *Revue Archéologique* 5 (1916), 11–16.

[26] MS Bayerische Staatsbibliothek clm. 506, of the eleventh century.

[27] MS Bayerische Staatsbibliothek clm. 210.

practical one, although dressed up in theory) of justifying serious thought about the stars and the planets: liturgical music. This is illustrated well in a letter for which a ninth-century date seems appropriate, and which shows a clear sympathy for astrology. The author explains his conviction that the planets, especially, affect human action.

> We can understand how it is that this or that planet brings prosperity or adversity. Thus, Jupiter, which is most in concord with the sun, and Venus, in its numerical ratio and nature, with the moon, are thought to conduce to human health. This is not because they think about whether to confer good or ill, but because certain things about the future are shown by the transits of the planets. Their pauses and their retrograde motions make clear certain aspects of the future, rather as birds give signs through their flights and their stillnesses, and their types and their cries and their feathers, although they do not know that they do so.[28]

The careful denial of reason to the planets and the reference to the signs of birds are both of interest, but the most important point to notice here is that the author writes this paragraph immediately after a disquisition upon the harmony of the spheres. He introduces his astrological beliefs, that is, after expressing a view common to medieval musical theorists especially, that the distances between the planets produce intervals, and their motions, sound; and, in the numerical ratios of these intervals, all produce concords similar to those produced by the musical scale.[29] Humans were thought to be drawn to this music and to try to create some semblance of it upon earth. Such a view was sometimes recognized as akin to condemned astrology, and not everyone agreed with it,[30] but the impact was sufficient for us to be able to find that codices concerned with musical theory and with the music of the liturgy not infrequently contain items of an astrological interest also.[31]

Music, therefore, and especially the music the liturgy required, gave

---

[28] *Edit.* E. Dümmler, MGH *Epistolae Karolini Aevi* ii (Berlin, 1902), 198–199 (MT).

[29] Macrobius was a familiar source for such a view, especially his *Commentary on the Dream of Scipio* II,iii–iv; *transl.* W. Stahl, *Macrobius, Commentary on the Dream of Scipio* (New York, 1952), pp. 193–199.

[30] Cassiodorus, for example, was wary of it: *Expositio in Psalterium*, Psalm cxlviii; *PL* 70,1047.

[31] Such a codex is London, B.L. Add. 17808, of the eleventh century, which binds treatises on music together with directions upon how to use the astrolabe, and with the frankly astrological *Liber Alchandrei*.

its participants and audiences one further excuse for pondering upon the influences of the planets. We cannot suppose that medieval ecclesiastical music invariably put one in mind of the superior music of the spheres; only that the connection could be made, and that sometimes, when it was made, it brought with it thought about the power of the heavenly bodies too. It is worth remarking, also, that psalmody would come to be thought an acceptable noise (if, that is, one must indulge in forms of noise) in Christian approaches to sympathetic magic for the moon, and in Christian efforts to provide a supernatural counter to storms.[32] Here music again assists (though differently) in the adjustment of attitudes to magic, and in the acceptance of aspects of it formerly condemned.

And materials supporting a scrutiny of the heavenly bodies for directions about human behavior could, in the final resort, be found, once one looked, even in the Bible, especially in Genesis. Light itself was, after all, created on the first day, and the great luminaries in the firmament on the fourth. God himself set the sun and the moon, moreover, "to rule over the day and over the night, and to sign the seasons and the days and nights" (Gen. 1:3–5, 14–18). He created these well before he created man, and, according to those Christian cosmologies we have already noticed, they were higher up in the heavens than were the demons. Much of the stuff of which astrology was made could, then, rightly hold a most important place in the mind of those who placed the Bible in the forefront of Christian learning and reverence, and who felt that demons had to be contained by superior powers. In other places in the Old Testament, moreover, God himself could be seen to use the heavenly bodies as signs and even as determinants. Thus he moved the sun as a sign to Hezekiah of his healing (2 Kings 20:10–11) and made the sun and the moon stand still for Joshua (Josh. 10:12–13). Of course humankind may not worship the heavenly bodies in place of God (thus Deut. 4:19), but people might be expected to be in awe of them and to be alerted to God's possible use of them. The zodiac, to be sure, is not to be found as such in the Scriptures, but, once again, ingenious exegesis might make it a fellow traveler, and the twelve signs do appear, as for example in 2 Kings 23:5. Parallels could be drawn between these signs of the zodiac and the twelve precious stones in Exod. 28:15–21 and 39:9-14. It was a short step then to their additional association with Joseph's dream of the eleven stars in Gen.

[32] See below, chap. 7.

37:9, with the patriarchs—that is, the twelve sons of Jacob—and with, then, the twelve tribes of Israel and even the apostles.[33] Certain individual signs could readily be assigned, too, to single biblical figures: the Ram, for example, to Abraham, the Lion to Daniel, Taurus and Sagittarius to Joseph (Gen. 19:24 and Deut. 13:7). The evangelist signs from Ezek. 1:10 and Rev. 4:7 found their echo in the zodiac, in the man (Aquarius), Taurus, and Leo. Two of the evangelists, Matthew and John, were, of course, apostles. In that many of the authors of the Scriptures may themselves have been sensitive to astrological lore,[34] earnest seekers after astrological precedent could be expected to find at least some justification there, then, once they turned to the Scriptures for such help. The Bible provided no direct incentives for the study of astrology, it is true; but neither did it plant insuperable obstacles in its way.

The lack of classical written works containing material on astrology, works such as the *Astronomicon* of Manilius or the *Mathesis* of Julius Firmicus Maternus, began to be remedied only gradually and, judging from the manuscripts that survive, perhaps only in the late tenth and the eleventh centuries. But, to say nothing of the incentives we have already discussed, seventeen manuscripts of the whole or parts of Isidore's *De Natura Rerum* have come down from the period before the ninth century; and from the ninth century onward we hear rumblings which grow into a roar as opposition to astrological interests within the Latin church crumbles under the weight of the reasons for its rehabilitation, and of efforts to provide for this. From the ninth century we have copies of the *Sphere of Pythagoras*, speedily followed by other versions of lunar calculations of this type. It is from the ninth century also that we can trace an increasing desire to find Christian equivalents for the signs of the zodiac, as though the zodiac was now attracting the kind of attention which should be turned to a Christian account. Thus the Ram represents Abraham's offering (Gen. 22:1–14), the Bull Jacob's struggle with the angel (Gen. 32:25ff), the Twins Adam and

---

[33] Philo Judaeus was of great importance to exegesis of this kind, although he was himself a ferocious opponent of astrology. Such associations are sometimes a guide to the seriousness with which astrology was viewed in general. Vital information on the texts bearing upon the Christianization of the zodiac is to be gained from W. Hübner, *Zodiacus Christianus*, Beiträge zur klassischen Philologie 144 (Konigstein, 1983).

[34] See, for example, S. Weinstock, "The Geographical Catalogue in Acts II, 9–11," *Journal of Roman Studies* 38 (1948), 43–46.

Eve, the Crab Job's sores (Job 2:7), and so on.[35] Christianizing of this sort had been tried before,[36] but not, it seems, quite on this scale. The crucial turning point for the rehabilitation of astrology may have come, indeed, in the ninth century. This seems to have marked, as I shall also suggest, the turning point for the rehabilitation of the Magi of Saint Matthew as respectable astrologers, and it is perhaps understandable that the Christian Carolingians, confronted as they were by the peculiarly turbulent and impenitent paganism of the Saxons and Slavs, should have been active in arranging controlled compromises of such a kind. Simply by being there, and particularly by being there in great numbers, competing magicians hold up the process of conversion, cause, as it were, a catch of breath, and make space for choices. These moments (some of them very extended ones) and these choices allow parts of the old magic to slip through and take up, paradoxically, a position far more stable and permanent than the circumstances which set it on its way. Astrology, for all the reasons we have discussed, and finally for this last one, was a prime candidate for such a crossing.

In the tenth century, certainly, we have a rush toward respectability for astrology. We begin to have circulated written directions for the use of the astrolabe, manuscripts of the treatises I have mentioned, and compilations containing astrological material from Arab sources, such as the perplexing MS Paris B.N. Lat. 17686.[37] The distinguished Benedictine scholar Abbo of Fleury (d. 1004) may take a place beside the more famous Gerbert of Aurillac (d. 1003) in the history of the active sponsoring of "natural astrology." In the tenth century too the lost astronomical handbook of Boethius—who had expressed a certain sympathy for astrological assumptions in his De Consolatione Philosophiae and whose execution may have been prompted in part by such sympathies—became sought after again following a long period of obscurity.[38] From the tenth century come tangible examples, one espe-

---

[35] These and other equivalents are set out in Hübner, Zodiacus Christianus, pp. 69–85 and 194–208.

[36] By, for example, Bishop Zeno of Verona in ca. 400 and by his ninth-century imitator Pacificus. Ibid., pp. 11–12 and also idem, "Das Horoskop der Christen," Vigiliae Christianae 29 (1975), 120–127.

[37] This manuscript and other, related, ones are discussed in A. Van de Vyver, "Les plus anciennes traductions latines médiévales (x–xi siècles) de traités d'astronomie et d'astrologie," Osiris 1 (1936), 658–691.

[38] De Consolatione Philosophiae IV, 51–55, for example; edit. and transl. H. F. Stewart et al., Boethius (Loeb Classical Library, 1973), pp. 360–361. Gerbert was pleased to

cially spectacular, of the coming together in apparent harmony of Christian associations which were, in an earlier period, specifically condemned. An ivory reliquary from Quedlinburg in northern Germany, possibly a gift of the emperor Otto I, has a Christianized zodiac of a special type carved upon its sides. These sides depict the twelve apostles, bordered by precious stones, and, placed above each apostle, a zodiac sign. In the center of the front panel is a medallion of Christ.[39] The latter may be meant to represent Christ the "sun of justice" (Mal. 4:2) replacing the sun as the center of the zodiac. Christ and apostles together were meant most probably to be seen to surpass the planets and the zodiac as guides, but to be involved with them nonetheless, rather as the Astrologer-Magi of Matthew were perhaps meant to be seen as outdoing older magicians on the Franks Casket of the seventh/eighth centuries.[40] The position of astrology was still precarious and responses to it divided,[41] but the Quedlinburg reliquary and its companion pieces are speaking examples of the importance now assumed by astrological motifs, and of how far opinion has moved from the uncompromising outrage earlier expressed at such associations.

An interesting little text, datable, it seems, to the late eleventh century, On the Make-up of the Celestial and Terrestrial Universe, gives us an excellent idea of the state of affairs which prevailed before the

have found a copy of the Astrologia at Bobbio. H. Lattin, The Letters of Gerbert (New York, 1961), p. 54.

[39] The Quedlinburg reliquary is illustrated and described in A. Goldschmidt, Die Elfenbeinskulpturen aus der Zeit der karolingischen und sächsischen Kaiser i (Berlin, 1914), pp. 32–33 and pl. XXIV. Goldschmidt draws attention to four more reliquary fragments showing apostles and zodiac signs, and all from the tenth century. The Quedlinburg reliquary was possibly made in Fulda, and the metalwork and cameo were perhaps added in the early eleventh century and, interestingly, to render the whole a little more Christian in appearance: P. E. Schramm and F. Mütherich, Denkmale der deutsche Könige und Kaiser i (Munich, 1962), 153, and H. Keller, "Zum sogennanten Reliquienschrein Ottos des Grossen in Quedlinburg," Dumbarton Oaks Papers 41 (1987), 261–264. I owe these references to Drs. Lawrence Nees and Robert Melzack. A reverse process may be detected in a manuscript of the late tenth century, probably from the Fleury of Abbot Abbo. Here, zodiac illustrations are actually intruded into the decoration of Eusebius's canon tables: C. Nordenfalk, "A Tenth Century Gospel Book in the Walters Art Gallery," in edit. U. E. McCracken et al., Gatherings in Honor of Dorothy E. Miner (Baltimore, 1974), pp. 139–170.

[40] See below, chap. 11.

[41] The Berne glosses on Lucan, for example, are still, though not hostile, wary: "All mathesis is a matter for conjecture." H. Usener, M. Annaei Lucani Commenta Bernensia (Leipzig, 1869), p. 42.

twelfth century turned to the Arabs with such excitement. This text seems very probably to have been put together as a result of school-room lectures and so may be taken to represent actual teaching.[42] It is striking in its concern with, and sympathy for, astrology. The four elements of earth, water, air, and fire still predominate as the basis of the discussion (on the plan of ancient cosmographies), and that section of the text which deals with the heavens is initially arranged as a steady ascent through the elements up to the ether, the abode of the planets and the stars. The whole is suitably prefaced by a reference to the compound of these elements in man, to man as microcosm in fact, and we spend much of our time agreeably suspended above the earth as we do in some of the maps I mentioned earlier. The lecturer, or compiler of the text, loses little time before he mentions geographical astrology (but without the denunciation of astrological measurements of time Bede had thought it proper to make),[43] and he brings us far more information about the planets and the zodiac than Bede or Isidore had ever offered. Nor is he above a straight-faced use of material drawn from sources well known to be opposed to astrology. He chooses, for example, four horoscopes from the Pseudo-Clementine *Recognitions* but neatly omits the arguments against astrology with which the author of the *Recognitions* had surrounded these. Thus:

> When Venus and the Moon are with Saturn in Saturn's houses, that is, in Capricorn and Aquarius, whatever females are born by day with that horoscope will be masculine women, quick to take up farming, waging war and building houses, and, neglecting the scents, sandals and clothing belonging to women, they seek that which is common to men. Nor are they effectively opposed in this by their husbands.[44]

To those who knew their *Recognitions*, and it seems, as we have seen, that there were many such, this use of the text would have conveyed a clear message.

[42] This has recently been edited and translated by C. Burnett, *Pseudo-Bede: De Mundi Celestis Terrestrisque Constitutione. A Treatise on the Universe and the Soul*, Warburg Institute Surveys and Texts x (London, 1985). My remarks are dependent upon his discussion and apparatus. It remains just conceivable that this treatise was written in the ninth century, and in South Germany (perhaps even at Reichenau): H. W. Hine, "Seneca and Anaxagoras in Pseudo-Bede's De Mundi Celestis Terrestrisque Constitutione," *Viator* 19 (1988), 111–127.

[43] Ibid., p. 23.

[44] Ibid., p. 55. I have emended the translation very slightly. The *De Mundi Celestis Terrestrisque Constitutione* interestingly omits that part of the Clementine horoscope which tells that such women commit adultery with whom they please as well.

The influence of the Arabs and the accessibility of their libraries and translators to such as Gerbert and his fellow enthusiasts have for long been blamed for, or credited with, the eventual incursion of astrology into the West. The importance of the Arabs cannot be doubted; and yet the greatest of the incentives may lie in truth elsewhere. It is more than conceivable that astrology owed its rehabilitation in the early medieval West primarily to the problems posed to and by Benedictine monks—and non-Christian magic; that, in short, the monks made their rather simpler efforts in the direction of astrological divination, in the form of divining spheres and lunaria and the like, primarily to make friends, and indeed Christians, of the people of the countryside in which they settled, and among whom the old magic persisted in so many of its forms. Such friendships, and such inducements to follow the Christian faith, required the making of accommodations with dearly held magical beliefs, and astrology, in its less refined forms, could help them to make these accommodations. It may also be that that increasing sophistication of astrological theory which took place in Northern Europe, especially Lorraine, was in one part prompted by the interest certain bishops came to take in the education of their clergy (and by the intellectual and political choices attendant on this interest), and in another part by alarm at the too simple practices of certain Benedictines. In the surviving codices, indeed, there is some evidence of such a distinction of origin and purpose.[45]

None of these hypotheses can be turned into certainties, but it can be proposed with some firmness that the revival of astrology both "popular" and "scientific" owed a great deal to the active interest ninth- and tenth-century Christians still had in persisting divinatory practices, and that, to the Christian Church, astrological lore was an appropriate way of distracting attention from the more menacing of the forms of supernatural intercession with which it was surrounded. Some of its leaders reacted toward simpler forms of astrological divination, some toward astrological science. Astrology of a simple kind could cohabit with, and perhaps dignify, the less harmful and certainly popular elements of rustic superstition, such as beliefs in the power of the moon; it could be practically and, when it came to it, even scripturally supported, and it could allow a certain authority over such beliefs to communities attempting to live a life of Christian excellence. Astrol-

---

[45] Compare, for instance, the contents of MS B. L. Cotton Titus D. xxvi with those of MS B. L. Harley 2506. I have set out the evidence which supports this suggestion in V.I.J. Flint, "The Transmission of Astrology in the Early Middle Ages," *Viator* 21 (1990), 1ff.

ogy of a more scientific kind, though it might inspire reactions and even resentment, might also help to avoid confusion with forbidden rustic practices and might allow Christians to capture a divinatory authority they badly needed.

The power and persistence of other forms of the old magic, and the pastoral anxieties and ambitions both of the Benedictine Order and of bishops, were at least as important as the Arabs to the rescue of astrology. Isidore was a herald of an enterprise taken up with enthusiasm by those who needed to outplay the non-Christian sorcerers and diviners who pressed upon them.

DEMONS

I have suggested that the demons of the lower air came into the early Middle Ages in part because there were scriptural and philosophical foundations for a belief in them, and in part (I suspect, indeed, in the main) because they were useful as a means of isolating evil from good, and of inspiring an appropriate fear of it. For all these reasons their rescue from the ancient world was assured; and displayed prominently amid all this evil was magic. The roles of the demons here might change, however, as certain magical practices or practitioners aroused a greater or lesser abhorrence. Sometimes demons might seem to be most threatening when dealing in anxieties about the future, sometimes when tampering with human love and sexual potency, sometimes when inflicting diseases or affecting the weather and crops or even, on occasion, waking the dead. Changing views about those demonic magical activities thought to be most damaging will have a consequent effect on counters to them; and these will, in turn, vary in time. On some occasions angels might seem to be the only answer to demons, and so the need for the old bad daemones would lead to the rescue and the emphasis of the good ones too. On others science and reason might be invoked—astrology, for instance, against demonic powers of prediction, or scientific medicine against their ability to inflict disease. On other occasions still, men and women supernaturally reinforced might win unearthly battles against demons—and with the help of a Christian magic these same demons will do much to illuminate, and so, perversely and paradoxically, encourage. At an opposite extreme demons might bear the blame for apparent human faults. Nor must one forget that skepticism could be a lively force, and that evil magic demonically inspired could seem useful as a concept to counteract this too. Many and diverse factors conditioned the rise and the roles of demons within the period, and they could be remarkably variously employed; but that they had a place, and that this place was an important one, there is no doubt.

I propose at this point to look in a general way at some of our chief sources for the active rescue of demons in the cause of discrediting the non-Christian magic as a whole: sources in which magic and its demonic associations are a preoccupation, that is, and which found a wide audience in our period. We shall consider in later chapters those specific forms of magic which demons seem most to help to throw into relief, and then we shall look a little more closely at some of the reasons for which, and the places at which, demons were chosen to perform this service.

Foremost among the general treatises promoting the active rescue of demons is Augustine's *On the Divination of Demons*. Augustine wrote this treatise with the aim of isolating abhorrent magical practices in the face of their pressing persistence. It was, as I have already mentioned,[46] copied very nearly in its entirety into Rabanus's *On the Magic Arts*. Rabanus clearly revered it, and, taken from Rabanus, it went into Burchard's *Decretum*. Together, these three rescued demons with the greatest of vigor and associated them most firmly with the magical arts.

Demons live, all agreed with Apuleius and Plato, in a part of the cosmos superior to that inhabited by human beings (the air there may be murky in comparison with the pure spaces of the ether, but it is incomparably better as a habitation than the earth), and as physical beings they are superior too. Their bodies, for instance, are enviably lighter.

> The nature of demons is such that, through the sense perception belonging to the aerial body, they readily surpass the perception possessed by earthly bodies, and in speed, too, because of the superior mobility of the aerial body, they incomparably excel not only the movements of men and of beasts, but even the flight of birds. Endowed with these two faculties, in so far as they are the properties of the aerial body, namely, with keenness of perception and speed of movement, they foretell and declare many things that they have recognized far in advance.

These physical capacities and perceptions enable demons to outwit men and to hurt them.

[46] See above, chap. 3.

They often receive the power to induce diseases, to render the very air unwholesome by vitiating it, and to counsel evil deeds to men who are perverted and greedy for earthly gains. . . . They persuade them . . . in marvelous and unseen ways, entering by means of that subtlety of their own bodies into the bodies of men who are unaware, and through certain imaginary visions mingling themselves with men's thoughts, whether they are awake or asleep. . . . Sometimes they foretell, not the deeds which they themselves perform, but future events which they recognise in advance through natural signs which cannot reach the senses of man. [47]

In each of these passages, Augustine and his followers go a little further than did Apuleius in the *De Deo Socratis*, and than did the *Life of Saint Antony*, and further even than Cassian. Augustine stresses the superiority of demons to birds, but here it is a superiority in evil, and he associates demons with the misadventures of everyone, not just with those of monks. In this treatise Augustine is concerned to vilify all those religious practices Christianity had come to replace, but, as one who was himself preoccupied with the evils of augury and divination, he singles out augury and divination as activities peculiarly demonic. The copying and use of this little work may be a guide to the places and periods within which augury and those apparently expert in arts of this kind were most to be feared. [48] Augustine seems interested here also in the demonic causes of illnesses and dreams. Magicians might, as we shall see, be called upon especially in cases of illness and in the interpretation of dreams, and so demons might also appropriately be brought into service to discredit these practices especially, and perhaps even to draw both praise and fire away from the magician himself. [49]

Augustine, of course, has biblical precedents for the association of demons with illness and dreams, and many will make these associa-

---

[47] *The Divination of Demons* 3,5 (transl. R. W. Brown; in *edit.* R. J. Deferrari, *Saint Augustine, Treatises on Marriage and other Subjects* (Washington, 1955), pp. 426, 430.

[48] The earliest known manuscript, an eighth-century one, may be English: J. Zycha, *Sancti Aureli Augustini*, Corpus Scriptorum Ecclesiasticorum Latinorum 41 (Vienna, 1900), p. xxxviiii. Augustine associates demons with these peculiarly noxious forms of magic in many other widely popular works of course, for instance in the *De Doctrina Christiana* II,xx,xxiv and the *De Civitate Dei* VIII,xix.

[49] Demons, for Augustine, often explain away the apparent achievements of magicians, for instance those of the magicians of Pharaoh: *De Civitate Dei* XXII,X; *edit.* Green, *Saint Augustine*, vii,254–255. Augustine makes the same point in his *De Trinitate* III,vii, a passage often quoted. It is quoted, for example, by Hincmar of Rheims in his *De Divortio Lotharii et Tetbergae*; PL 125,676–677.

tions after him; but it is worth noting at this juncture that not every-one did. Medieval scientific treatises *De Natura Rerum* tended to stress natural (nondemonic) features, of airborne illnesses, for instance, and so to counter magical beliefs in a different way.[50] The energetic rescue of demons for these and allied purposes could, then, on occasion be tempered by an equally energetic rescue of natural knowledge, and a too great reliance on demons of the kind in which Augustine some-times indulged could induce an equally strong reaction. Demons, though a favorite answer to the problem of explaining away misfortune apparently magically induced, were certainly not the only one. Al-though our preoccupation here is with the rescue of demons, the pro-cesses which tempered the rescue or, on occasion, made it all the more forceful (sometimes through contrasting views of human psychology and the place of science) should constantly be borne in mind.

As well as Rabanus and Burchard, Caesarius of Arles stands out for his willingness to use, build upon, and bring into Europe Augustine's associations between demons and forbidden magic. In his most famous and most widely borrowed sermon against augury, he too connected demons most particularly with divination,[51] and this emphasis passed into the works of many of his admirers.[52] According to Caesarius, de-mons, led by the devil himself, also stand behind large numbers of other magical practices. "One who restrains men from observing omens, wearing phylacteries, or consulting magicians and seers is known to bear testimony to Christ when he speaks against these temp-tations of the Devil."[53] In this sermon he gives an especially full ac-count of those forbidden magical practices which most distress him and which the devil and his demons help him to illuminate. In one passage he shows just the same anxiety as Augustine about the involvement of demonically inspired magicians in cures. Mothers rush for the help of

[50] Isidore does not mention demons in his various efforts to explain airborne pesti-lence: *De Natura Rerum* XXXIX; *edit.* Fontaine, *Isidore de Séville, Traité*, pp. 302–305. Nor does Bede, *De Natura Rerum* XXXVII; *edit.* Jones, *Bedae Venerabilis*, p. 223. Cer-tain of the tenth-century glosses on Lucan contain a very down-to-earth explanation of dreams, too, in which heat and cold play a large part: *edit.* Usener, M. *Annaei Lucani*, pp. 220–221.

[51] ". . . diabolicas divinationes" (Sermon 54); *edit.* G. Morin, *Sancti Caesarii Are-latensis Sermones* i, CC (Turnholt, 1953), p. 236, *transl.* M. M. Mueller, *Saint Caesar-ius of Arles, Sermons* i (Washington, 1956), 266.

[52] Into the *Scarapsus* of Pirmin of Reichenau, for example, which uses many of the same words, *PL* 89,1041, and into Sermon xliii of Rabanus, *PL* 110,81.

[53] Sermon 52; *transl.* Mueller, *Saint Caesarius*, i,260.

such forbidden magicians for abortions, or when their sons are ill, instead of turning to the church.

> They do not ask for the church's medicine, or that of the author of salvation and the eucharist of Christ. Nor . . . do they ask the priests to anoint them with blessed oil, or place all their hopes in God. . . . They say to themselves: Let us consult that soothsayer, seer, oracle or witch ["illum ariolum vel divinum, illum sortilegum, illam erbariam"]. Let us sacrifice a garment of the sick person, a girdle that can be seen and measured. Let us offer some magic letters, let us hang some charms on his neck. In all this the Devil has one aim: either cruelly to kill the children by abortion, or to heal them still more cruelly with charms.[54]

At one point Caesarius bursts out, "If only they would seek that health from the simple skill of doctors!" We have a hint of an active counter to magic in the form of science here, as well as "church medicine," though, as we shall see later, doctors were not thought by everyone to be an appropriate answer. They were not by Gregory of Tours, for example. We have a similar appeal to reason as a counter in the same sermon, when Caesarius speaks of our now familiar old beliefs about the moon.

> How is it that foolish men think they should, as it were, help the moon in its eclipse? When its shining orb is covered at certain times by a natural condition of the air or is suffused with the nearby heat of the setting sun, they think that there is some conflict of incantations against heaven. This they imagine they can overcome by the sound of a trumpet or the ridiculous tinkling of bells that are violently shaken, through the vain persuasion of pagans believing they make the moon friendly to themselves by wicked shouting. Now, since at God's bidding it renders service to rational man, why does man render foolish obedience to it, to the insult of God? Let every wise and pious man, we beg you, avoid and detest these errors, or, rather, this madness, this shameful mockery. If the substance of this heavenly body is inferior to you, why do you fear to offend it by your silence? If it is superior to you why do you think it needs your help?[55]

Caesarius can reach for rational argument, as well as demons, as a corrective to forbidden magical beliefs, and he seems here, for a moment, to be a little closer to Sisebut than to Eligius. Demons come in

---

[54] Ibid., p. 262. I have emended the translation very slightly.
[55] Ibid., p. 261.

and out, as it were, as counters, depending partly upon the writer, partly upon the audience to be addressed, partly upon the political and psychological circumstances within which the pastor believes he operates. Belief in, and invocation of, demons is never universal and without its fluctuations, not even (especially not so) in the early Middle Ages. Astrology, not demons, will eventually take pride of place as a means of contesting those beliefs about the moon which were determined superstitious; and a greater skill in herb lore, at monastic hands perhaps especially, will come to replace Caesarius's "erbaria" and the other demonic seducers of anxious mothers. Sometimes science will work in tandem with a belief in demons in an effort to excite hostility to magic; sometimes science will be used directly to put demonic magic to flight, and demons then take second place to it; sometimes demons will be asked to do what reason cannot. For Caesarius particularly, much seems to have depended upon the audience to whom the sermon was addressed; the more intelligent and responsible the audience, perhaps the more possible it was for him to make an appeal to reason or science, confident that the appeal would not get out of hand. For certain audiences, however, and for his central pastoral purposes, Caesarius is as sure as anyone that demons must on occasion be invoked and so must be carefully preserved.[56] God is always liable to make use of the devil and his minions to try the virtue of Christian people (even the most rational of them). "Therefore avoid the Devil's tricks as much as you can."[57] Caesarius, like Augustine, drives the point home very hard.

A further firm believer in the association between demons and condemnable magic is Martin of Braga, in his sermon *Reforming the Rustics*. This is worth our pausing over, for Martin spelled the whole matter of demons out succinctly, and strictly within the context of a battle against magical beliefs. As a simplified rendering of Augustine's views it was an extremely forceful propellant of that demonization at which Augustine was adept, and it reached many readers and writers, such, for example, again, as Pirmin of Reichenau. Martin gives us a whole cosmology in reinforcement of his views. To Christians this is a familiar story, but it is pointed here in its reference to demonic magic in particular. Satan, for the sin of pride, "along with many other angels

[56] The sermon ascribed to Eligius in his *Vita* and referred to earlier is modeled upon one of Caesarius's, Sermon 13, designed for general parish use.

[57] Sermon 54; transl. Mueller, *Saint Caesarius*, i,268.

who had agreed with him was cast from that celestial abode into the air which is beneath the heavens; and he who had formerly been the archangel lost the light of his glory and became the devil, full of gloom and horror." Once men fell too, they became the prey of Satan and his demons, and the demons

> began to appear to them in various forms and speak with them and demand of them that they offer sacrifices to them on lofty mountains and in leafy forests and worship them as God. . . . [They] even persuaded them to build temples to them and to place therein images or statues of wicked men and to set up altars to them, upon which they should pour out for them blood both of animals and even of men. Furthermore, many of the demons who had been expelled from the heavens now preside over the sea or streams or fountains or forests, and in similar fashion ignorant men who do not know God worship them as gods and offer them sacrifices.[58]

We can see from this how quickly Martin leaves the Bible and plunges into post-Roman Spain, and also how, as he launches himself upon that condemnation of pagan practices which is his purpose, he launches the demons into the Christian world with him as he charges them specifically with the magical practices he abhors. Demons used to this end are, as it were, both rescued and recycled.

None of those I have cited as readily associating demons with the magic they condemned, and so as bringing demons through primarily for their services to this end, had any doubt that this magic was, at the same time, real. Happenings beyond human understanding and control did take place at the demons' hands. Augustine wrote his *On the Divination of Demons* in part to explain how it was that the destruction of the Temple of Serapis in 391 had been accurately predicted; and Caesarius spelled out clearly his own firm belief that magic can indeed have an effect. He did so, for instance, in a sermon on Num. 22–25, the story of Balaam the magician and Balak, king of Moab.

> This Balaam was exceedingly famous for his magical art, and very powerful with his harmful verses ["carminibus noxiis"]. He did not possess the power or skill of words in blessing but only in cursing, for the demons are invited to curse but not to bless. . . . Do not wonder if there is such a thing as

---

[58] *Reforming the Rustics*, transl. C. W. Barlow, *Iberian Fathers* i (Washington, 1969), 72, 74–75.

magical art. Even Scripture declares that this art exists but prohibits its use.[59]

Again:

> Perhaps someone says: What are we to do, for the magicians and seers often announce true omens to us? . . . Again you say: Sometimes many would run the risk even of death from the bite of a snake or some infirmity if there were no magicians. It is true, dearly beloved, that God permits this to the Devil . . . to try Christian people. Thus, when they sometimes are able to recover from sickness by these impious remedies, men see some truth in them and afterwards more readily believe the devil.[60]

Both Augustine and Caesarius were, of course, very quick to insist that demons do none of these things without divine permission. They denied them *truly* supernatural powers of any sort. Demons may only do that which is consistent with their natures, and they have no capacities which are of themselves divine. That being said, however, the demons they believe in and describe are so immeasurably greater in capacity than man, and so incalculably more adept at ambivalence and deception, that it is easy to believe their powers supernatural in comparison with his. Thus they remain a necessary part of the cosmos as long as irrational and forbidden magical divinations, marvels, and cures are sought after and are thought surely to work.

In this way, of course, demons both help man to allow that events beyond his understanding do take place, and they save him, weak as he is, from having to take upon himself full-scale responsibility for them. Thus a belief in demons can help to rescue man from excessive blame and its punishment. Demons work only under God. Man may, again under God, contend with them; but, without God's help, it goes almost without saying, man will never be their match. This dimension to the early medieval rescue of demons is an exceedingly important one. Demons do not here play that role for which they are later to become so famous in witchcraft trials; the role, that is, of active agents in a drama of fear and repression, and sometimes as assistants to so-called scientists in a process of proscription.[61] Rather, they play an

---

[59] Sermon 113; *transl.* Mueller, *Saint Caesarius*, ii, 156, 158.

[60] Sermon 54; ibid., i, 267.

[61] See, for example, the interesting remarks in W. Notestein, *A History of Witchcraft in England from 1558 to 1718* (New York, 1911), pp. 23, 76–77, on the tendency of professional physicians to lay the blame for difficult cases upon witchcraft diabolically

almost exactly opposite one. They are used to take the panic, much of the blame, and the extreme penalties from the accused *maleficus* upon themselves. This humane use of a belief in the magical powers of demons by the early medieval church is one deserving of some emphasis, for, in the light especially of later abuses, sight of it can easily be lost.

There are many examples of this motive for the rescue of demons, and of this way of employing them. A particularly vivid one may be found in the *Life of Bishop Ursmar* (abbot of Lobbes, d. 713). This is vivid because it conjures up so graphically the atmosphere of fear which might surround an instance of supposed diabolical possession, and the relief that the recognition and dismissal of the offending demon immediately occasioned. Here, a nun is so possessed as to be made to utter dreadful obscenities ("per os illius turpia loqui"). Her "consorores" blamed a demon but were unable of themselves to expel it. It needed Bishop Ursmar. He exorcised it accordingly, and immediately the terror it had inspired ("pavor tamen et horror") vanished with it. The sprinkling of blessed salt and water confirmed the expulsion and the cessation of fear. At no point was the nun seen as anything but a victim, and the exorcism ritual employed by the bishop was clearly associated with the restoration of serenity.[62] This, and stories like it, show us clearly how demons could be used, and why they were thought to be so necessary. They illustrate here the supernatural abilities of the bishop-saint and they promote, furthermore, the power of the particular ecclesiastical magic he purveys, in addition to saving the unhappy nun from obloquy. Vital to the elimination of non-Christian magic, demons were thus helpful, too, to the verification of its Christian counterpart.

The testimony of any one of the great preachers and storytellers I have cited would have been sufficient of itself to rescue magical demons for our period, and we have seen in the writings on magic of Rabanus and Burchard in particular how such a rescue was achieved.[63] Many further examples of these crucial associations—between demons, those different magical practices it was thought at various times necessary to outlaw with their help, and the Christian countermagic

---

inspired, even when such accusations were known possibly to lead to severe persecution.

[62] *Vita Ursmari Episcopi et Abbatis Lobbiensis* 4; *edit.* B. Krusch and W. Levison, *MGH SRM* vi (Hanover and Leipzig, 1913), 458–459.

[63] Isidore, too, faithfully follows Augustine. *Etymologiae* VIII, xi, 15–16; *edit.* Lindsay, *Isidori Hispalensis.*

whose usefulness they did so much to illustrate—can and will be found. I have chosen just one more to be looked at here, partly because it is to be found in one of the more famous of the texts concerning early medieval magic, but mainly because it too may be seen to draw the blame for magic from hapless humans by the invocation of a belief in demons, and to call upon demons largely for this service. The text is the famous *De Divortio Lotharii et Tetbergae* of Hincmar of Rheims (written ca. 860).

Hincmar's thoughts about (and obstruction of) the divorce of King Lothar II from his wife are among the more interesting of the surviving pieces of evidence for the belief that the magical arts could really work, and for the invocation of demons, both to account for this and to cope with some of the more frightening of its results. Hincmar is concerned, of course, to incriminate Waldburga, Lothar's mistress, but not, it seems, too severely. This fact is important. He expatiates, to this end, upon the apparent fact that some women (adulteresses especially, in Hincmar's view) could sow seemingly supernatural hatred or uncontrollable love between men and women. There are, of course, biblical precedents for such an ability. The devil incites such passions, says Hincmar, as he had in the case of Amnon's love for Tamar and his subsequent hatred of her (2 Sam. 13). Unhappily, however, these powers were manifest too in Hincmar's own day. In the archbishop's very diocese, indeed, the devil had provided a hostile mother-in-law with the means to render her son-in-law impotent. Only "ecclesiastical medicine" could mend the matter, Hincmar declared.[64] Adulteresses were still laying claim to such powers in the early eleventh century, according to Burchard.[65]

Though they are frequently (and rightly) given prominence in histories of witchcraft, it would be wrong to view either Hincmar's treatise or Burchard's observations here as directed only at the magical machinations of women. Hincmar happens immediately to be concerned with the problem of Waldburga, and so the possible malpractices of adulteresses occupy a great deal of his attention; but he is quite capable of ascribing magical malpractice in the matter of affairs of the heart to men (as when a little later in the treatise he tells the story of the young man accused of making a pact with demons to procure the

[64] *De Divortio* XV; PL 125,717.

[65] *Decretum* XIX (*Corrector*); PL 140,975. The supernatural capacities of adulteresses in matters of sexual love will be mentioned again in chaps. 8 and 9.

love of a girl).[66] The principal concern shewn here by both Hincmar and Burchard is with the *demonic* incitement to magical practice of both men and women. It is to this concern that I wish to draw particular attention, and, even more importantly, to the light it throws upon the helplessness of ordinary humans in the face of such incitement. To both Hincmar and Burchard humans are indeed helpless before such assaults, and in desperate need of the supernatural remedies for their plight provided by the church. In an earlier section of the same treatise Hincmar assembles for us a number of biblical, patristic, and early medieval references to demonic power, some of which are already familiar.[67] Everyone is vulnerable to it, he insists. Burchard is gentle in his penances. Hincmar's stories have happy endings, involving the humbling of the persons involved, and "ecclesiastical medicine" of a kind to which we shall come, but no great pain beyond that. The ability to cast the blame upon demons could help and here, it seems, once again did help most strongly to hold fiercer, perhaps secular, pressures for the persecution of magicians at bay, and to enable even those who felt themselves most harmed to recognize, in the one who worked for demons, a victim of demonic ill-doing rather than a wholly culpable perpetrator of it.

The service demons might render in such a cause as this helped also, then, to bring them through; and it is well to remember, and to emphasize, how important a service it was. We do have a little independent evidence, and from close to Hincmar's place and period, of the type of penalty to which persons accused, or even simply suspected, of magical practice might be subject if one could not, or would not, blame the wrong involved in the magic upon demons. I drew attention to it in an earlier section and shall have cause to mention it again when treating below of love magic. Gerberga, friend of Judith, the wife of the Emperor Louis the Pious, was actually drowned, "more maleficorum," on suspicion of tampering with the affections of her friend's husband; and Agobard of Lyons, of course, only just saved suspected cloud-borne harvest stealers from Magonia from being stoned to death.[68]

Aery demons then, flying about full of lightness and power in the

---

[66] PL 125,721–725.

[67] Interrogatio IX; PL 125,677–679.

[68] Nithard, *Historiarum Libri III* I,v; *edit.* G. H. Pertz, MGH SS ii (Hanover, 1829), 653; Agobard, *De Grandine et Tonitruis*; *edit.* L. Van Acker, *Agobardi Lugdunensis Opera Omnia*, CC (Turnholt, 1981), p. 4.

middle air, were a reality in our period, if a somewhat fluctuating and variably exploited one; and the particular ways in which they lent themselves as supports (both to Christian anxieties about and belief in magical practice, and to Christian reservations about penalties in times of threat) meant, paradoxically, that they were one of the features of the old pre-Christian magical world most enthusiastically transferred. Demons were thought to exist and were found to be necessary, sometimes (and this needs to be stressed again and again) for the most compassionate of reasons. Much of the magic in which they so greatly indulged, then, seemed real, and perhaps necessary, too. It might explain away (once more like astrology, but in different ways) any embarrassing successes soothsayers might have and at the same time isolate the objectionable features of their practice. It might preserve from excessive public punishment, or private vengeance, humans who could be supposed to be mere victims of demonic ill will. Belief in, and fear of, demons might profitably, even joyously (and this too needs emphasis), be manipulated for all of these ends. Demons were reduced, it is true, from the realm of the truly supernatural to that of the comparatively so. Their capacities, though extensive, were, when set against man's, limited both by Divine Providence and by their own natures. They were there as a sort of supernatural power nonetheless. And if the magical power of demons was truly there for all these reasons, then it had, for many of the same reasons, to be countered. Humankind evidently, however, could not counter it alone. Other heavenly agencies and other forms of Christian heavenly magic would become as important as the demons, and the rescue of the demons would lead to the rescue and elaboration of these agencies and practices in their turns. Thus, lastly and perhaps joyously too, the abetted persistence of the demons and the need to resist them would spawn many other rescues, rescues we might also with justice term risen Christian magic. We have had hints of these in the divisions between the supporters of different forms of astrology, in the story of the nun, and in Hincmar. We may follow them further very shortly.

ANGELS

In that early medieval Europe sustained a powerful belief in angels, it is true to say that the old good daemones were to some extent rescued in this form. In his *City of God* Augustine contributed some thoughtful chapters to an argument, clearly attracting attention among contemporaries, about whether Plato's "daemones" might be the same as the angels of Matt. 4:11 or Col. 1:16. These sections from the Scriptures underlay much subsequent discussion of the question. To a certain extent Augustine is happy with Plato's demons. Angels, like them, he agrees, do indeed live in the higher parts of the upper air, and they probably have superior fiery bodies as opposed to the merely aery ones of the wicked demons. They also, of course, have powers far superior to those of man. Unlike the older gods, however, and unlike the men called gods in Ps. 82:6, angels live with and in the knowledge of God himself. Unlike them too, angels will not encourage humans to worship them but will direct this worship to God alone. Provided this last distinction was clearly made, the cult of angels seemed to Augustine to be legitimate, and so angels were firmly fixed within the new supernatural heavenly hierarchy of the early Middle Ages.[69] Man, furthermore, might aspire to a place among the angels. He might, indeed, be called upon to fill the gap opened up in the heavenly city by the fall of those angels who became bad demons.[70]

Angels, like demons, then, and as a result of a parallel combination of philosophical, patristic, and scriptural (notably Hebrew) supports poured into our period rank upon rank.[71] It is hardly, in short, possible

[69] *City of God* IX,xxi–xxiii, X,i–iii; *edit.* D. S. Wiesen, *Saint Augustine*, iii,230–265. For Augustine's views on the fiery bodies of angels, see his *Eighty-Three Different Questions* 47; *transl.* D. L. Mosher, *Saint Augustine, Eighty-Three Different Questions* (Washington, 1982), p. 82. The problems of whether angels could be said to have bodies at all and, if they could, of the nature of these bodies, were much discussed in the Middle Ages. An introduction to some of the texts involved may be found in *edit.* and *transl.* A. de Gaudemaris and R. Gillet, *Grégoire le Grand Morales sur Job* i (Paris, 1975), 258–261. Fulgentius of Ruspe sums up a distinction widely accepted: angels have fiery and vaporous bodies, demons merely aery ones. *De Trinitate* IX; *PL* 65,505. It is not improbable that later tendencies to disallow fiery bodies to angels were prompted by associated anxieties about the reverence due to fire.

[70] One of the first exponents of this view was the *Life of Antony* 22–23; *transl.* R. T. Meyer, *St. Athanasius, the Life of St. Antony* (Westminster, Md. and London, 1950), pp. 38–39. Envy of human capacity to take up their lost places is held here to account for the extreme hostility of demons to human beings. Martin of Braga appeals to this view too in *Reforming the Rustics* 4 and 14; *transl.* Barlow, *Iberian Fathers*, pp. 72–73, 79. In this it forms a part of Martin's general onslaught upon outlawed magical practices. Gregory the Great gave the view a particularly wide appeal: e.g., *XL Homiliarum in Evangelia* II,xxxiv; *PL* 76,1249–1250. The further notion that each person had a guardian angel assigned to him or her was spread by Jerome's widely popular commentary on Matt. 3:18; *PL* 26,135.

[71] Col. 1:16 is a frequently cited source for the view that there were distinct ranks

to move far into the Middle Ages without falling over one.[72] All this is well known. Less generally remarked upon, however, and to us much more interesting, are the connections between these good angels, active as God's messengers and man's protectors in the world of the supernatural, and that good magic which was needed both as an illustration of, and as a counter to, the bad. Yet, as was the case with demons, early medieval angels are, within this context, often at their most energetic. Man, as a lesser creature than either angels or demons in the order of creation, was thought to be vulnerable to both of them in his relations with the supernatural.[73] He should choose, of course, to rely only upon the one, but this had its difficulties. Sometimes he would be unable to escape the magical tricks of demons without direct angelic intervention. In his attempts to evade the snares of demonic magical delusions, man must often both invite and receive angelic help, and God might, and very often did, use angels specifically to put a limit upon the games demons played with magic, and to suggest appropriate answers to these games.[74] Certainly I do not mean to claim, in drawing attention to this aspect of the activities of early medieval angels, that the need to combat the old magic, and encourage and illuminate the new, was the mainspring of medieval angelology. No more would I argue (as I hope I have made plain) that the survival of demons is wholly to be understood within this context. Both demons and angels sprang from a lineage, and sustained a being, larger than such anxieties; but this dimension of angelic activity is vital both to our understanding of many of the views early held about angels and to the survival of some of the old magical practices. And it has been, perhaps, a little understressed.

Angels contribute substantially to the rise of magic in early Europe,

---

of angels. Revelation was perhaps the most exploited biblical source of medieval angels.

[72] In addition to Jerome, Augustine, Gregory the Great, and the great commentary on the *Celestial Hierarchy* of the Pseudo-Dionysius by John Scotus Eriugena, Cassian is as important a conveyor of angels into the early Middle Ages as he was of demons. *Collations* VII,xiii; *edit. and transl.* E. Pichéry, *Jean Cassien Conférences* i (Paris, 1955), 257–258. A full collection of biblical references to angels and of references to angelic interventions in the Middle Ages may conveniently be found in the pages on the Feast of Michael and All Angels in *AS Septembris* viii (29 September), 4–39 and 89–109.

[73] This proposition, borrowed from Augustine, is to be found, once more, in Hincmar, *De Divortio; PL* 125,726.

[74] On the Divination of Demons 6 (*transl.* Brown); in *edit.* Deferrari, *Saint Augustine,* pp. 431–432.

and this on two levels, the first in general rather better explored than the second. Firstly, the old daemones are brought through, though in disguise, in angels as well as in demons. Secondly, angels in their new guises are used extremely forcefully as agents in the process of selecting that in the old magic which is to be welcomed in its Christian form, and in overcoming previous rejections. Demons distinguish both that in magic which is forcefully to be cast out, and that in human behavior which is to be saved from too harsh penalties, and they are in part preserved, as we have seen, for their services to these ends; angels, by "magical" victories over that which is harmful in supernatural exercises, and by use or approval of that which is helpful or inspiring, may fittingly point man to much that may be retained and reordered to his profit. They might help especially to distinguish those Christian supernatural powers that may be most effective against the demons. Some of the descriptions of angels and of their special capacities which early writers put before us, then, are more sharply imprinted with the negative image of contemporary demonic magic, and more urgently associated with hopes for joyful magical counters to this, than is, I think, generally realized. As with demons, so with angels, there is a psychological dimension to their employment. I have chosen to concentrate here upon those accounts of the actions of rescued angel-daemones which were most read in our period and which, to my mind, bear these imprints most clearly.

If we look again therefore at Augustine's treatment of angels and the "daemones" of Plato we may note that Augustine is especially concerned to emphasize the powers of wise and dependable farsightedness possessed by angels, and to contrast these with the much more limited (though still sought after) divinatory powers of demons. One passage in particular is worth quoting at some length.

The demons . . . do not fix their gaze on the eternal causes, the hinges as it were of temporal events, which are found in God's wisdom, though they do foresee many more future events than we do by their greater acquaintance with certain signs that are hidden from men. Sometimes too they announce in advance events that they themselves intend to bring about. Consequently the demons are often mistaken, the angels absolutely never. For it is one thing to guess at temporal matters from temporal, and changeable matters from changeable, and to introduce into them the temporal and changeable workings of one's own will and capacity, and this is a thing that the demons may do within fixed limits; but it is quite another to foresee in the light of the eternal and immutable laws of God, which derive their existence from his wisdom, the changes that time will bring, and to discern, by partaking of his spirit, the will of God, which is as absolutely certain as it is universally powerful. This gift has justly been reserved and bestowed upon the holy angels.[75]

Augustine expresses the same opposition and singles out this same particular aspect of angelic power in the On the Divination of Demons. "Demons foretell many events that will come to pass. Yet, far above them is the loftiness of that prophecy which God brings to pass through the holy angels and prophets. . . . Absolutely true are the pronouncements of the angels and the Prophets."[76] Angels here assist special humans, prophets, to outdo the demons in their divinatory skills. This same emphasis upon an angelic power to counter demonic foresight above all else is to be found elsewhere: in Bede, for instance, in his Commentary on Samuel (quoted with approval by Hincmar).[77] Bede clearly follows Augustine but lays an added stress on the belief that demons could only ever have learned such powers of prediction as they have from angels, and with the permission of these last. It may well be that both Augustine's influence and alarm at the activities of contemporary pagan diviners dictated this continued insistence by both Bede and Hincmar upon a foresight which angels alone have and in which man can and should trust. When demons use bad and fallible magic—here divination—angels will use good magic of a related type but one infinitely more rewarding. With a greater frequency than has been generally observed, God seems, as it were, to take his cue from the magical activities of demons as to when, and where, and in what manner he might license his angels to exercise their superior powers. Past and current demonic practices dictate the shape and purposes of the counterpractices angels might encourage humankind to share and to adopt. Particularly specialized forms of good magic may, as a result, be associated with and be seen to come from angels at particular times.

Augustine invests his angels here with a near monopoly of divinatory skills. Only prophets share them. By this device he contrives to

[75] City of God IX,xxii; transl. Wiesen, Saint Augustine, iii,234–237. Similar points about the limitations of demonic foresight and the contrasts between demonic and angelic behavior are made in the Life of Antony 31–37; transl. Meyer, St. Athanasius, pp. 46–51.

[76] Chapter 6 (transl. Brown); in edit. Deferrari, Saint Augustine, p. 431.

[77] Bede, In Primam Partem Samuhelis Libri IIII IV,xxviii; edit. D. Hurst, Bedae Venerabilis Opera, Opera Exegetica ii, CC (Turnholt, 1970), pp. 256–257.

leave no room for "scientific" or "natural" methods of prediction such as scientific astrology, which he had, of course, particular reason to hate. This too may be, on occasion, the role of angels in our period. They might be chosen to mediate the supernatural powers of God (the direct contemplation of whose face they never lose)[78] if need be as an alternative to, or at the expense of, natural human powers. They might even be used directly to criticize these natural powers. Paradoxically, the threats associated with the progress of certain sciences at hands deemed to be the wrong ones could contribute as much toward a belief in the angels, and in particular forms of their good magic, as could the need to counter the demons. Just as excessive emphasis upon demons sometimes compelled a turn to scientific answers, too great a reliance on these last could impel the invocation of angels. This particular use for angels in the service of Christian magic deserves a mention too.

Angels might always outdo pagan diviners and encourage Christians in their hopes about the future, and in a way more fulfilling than the diviners ever could. They might also outdo magicians engaged in other types of practice. By the time Isidore came to write his *Etymologies* angels had certain characteristics ascribed to them, such as wings with which to ride upon the winds (Ps. 103:3), an ordered hierarchy dividing them into nine ranks, and attested names and abilities.[79] Interestingly too, certain of the abilities Isidore singles out and ascribes to his named angels, though derivable independently from biblical, Rabbinic, and apocryphal traditions, do in fact have clear echoes in the world of the non-Christian magicians, including that of the magi Isidore himself describes. Like Augustine's angels, Isidore's prophesy first and foremost, and the first angel named is the prophetic angel Gabriel. Then comes Michael, "Qui sicut Deus," renowned for a strength close to that of God himself (Michael may here and frequently be placed with Gabriel because of the help he gave to the angel in Dan. 10:13). Raphael has the power to heal and indeed healed the blindness of Tobit (Tob. 6:5–9, 10:7–15). Uriel (taken perhaps from 4 Ezra:1 and notably abandoned in later lists of accredited angels) has power over fire and comes in fire. The rank of the Virtues governs all portents and wonders ("miracula"), and that of the Powers controls the malice of evil spirits. Some of the services people used to ask of Isidore's diabol-

[78] Gregory the Great, *Moralia in Job* II,iii; *edit.* de Gaudemaris and Gillet, *Grégoire le Grand*, i,258–259.

[79] VII,v,1–33; *edit.* Lindsay, *Isidori Hispalensis*.

ically assisted magi may thus, mutatis mutandis, be rendered by the angels instead, and in this way carefully selected angels might fill the gaps left by those magicians for whose downfall so many so fervently hoped.

Sometimes the invocation of angels in such causes could be a little overenthusiastic. At the end of the fifth century a Roman council had to rule against amulets which invoked, or were engraved with, the names of angels, and to insist that these names were merely a disguise for demons. Charlemagne, in the *Admonitio Generalis* of 789, and Ansegisus, in the collection of capitularies he made in the early ninth century, had to forbid the calling upon angels by names that were not scriptural.[80] But, interestingly, angels as healers are sometimes especially distinguished in early medieval literature for the medical orthodoxy of their treatments, as if to support points a little like those made by Caesarius about the unreliability of medical magic and the availability of respectable supernatural, as well as professional, alternatives to it. The healing angel in Sulpicius's *Life of Martin* is a case in point. In the cleaning of Martin's wounds and the expert application of salves, this angel could hardly have been more professionally respectable, or less tainted by contemporary magical practice.[81] Here, the angel dignifies acceptable science used in conjunction with appropriate supernatural power. Sulpicius seems to have been aware of the distinctions he was making here. Others use angels to emphasize the superiority of the purely supernatural healing power available within the Christian dispensation, and against the same enemies. Paul the Deacon tells a striking little story, for instance, about angelic measures against pestilence, one in which good angels are found to be entirely in command. A pestilence struck Rome in the year 680. It was inflicted, Paul tells us, by bad angels, but on the command of good ones. "A good and a bad angel proceeded by night through the city and as many times as, upon the command of the good angel, the bad angel, who appeared to carry a hunting spear in his hand, knocked at the door of each house with the spear so many men perished from that house on the following day."[82] This passage is a significant one, with many levels of interest. Eclipses of the moon and of the sun preceded

[80] *Council of Rome* 494; Mansi, VIII,152. The *Admonitio Generalis* and Ansegisus may be found in *edit.* G. Waitz, *MGH Leges* i (Hanover, 1835), 57, 276.
[81] *Vita S. Martini* 19,4; *edit.* and *transl.* J. Fontaine, *Sulpice Sévère, Vie de Saint Martin* i and ii (Paris, 1967–1968), 294–295, 888–892.
[82] *History of the Lombards* VI,5; *transl.* Foulke, *Paulus Diaconus*, p. 255.

the pestilence, says Paul, but angels were clearly operative, not the favored agents of non-Christian magical belief (eclipses themselves, that is) or the baneful influence of the moon charmed by the sorceress. Angels, in other words, had here replaced such possible sources of supernatural enchantment with a Christianized form of magical control. An angel it was, also, who listened to Saint Gall when he sought to release his people from the plague.[83]

Power over plague is sometimes attributed to an angel personally; to Saint Michael, for instance. When in 590 Pope Gregory the Great consecrated the Mausoleum of Hadrian to the Archangel Michael, a vision of the archangel was reported. A terrible plague had ravaged the city, and Michael was seen to be putting his sword back into its scabbard after it, as though he had presided over it.[84] The shadow of the avenging angel stands behind these stories, but so too does the view that, within the Christian dispensation also, powers far stronger than man intervene for and against him in supernatural affairs, and that there are mechanisms about which man both can and must learn in order to avail himself of their beneficence. The line between acceptable and unacceptable supernatural and natural agents, and between acceptable and unacceptable forms of magical intervention by them, was very hard indeed to draw;[85] but angels were vital to the task, and, above all, to the rescue of the acceptable.

The promise of the angel to Saint Gall to relieve his people from the plague was made good by a pilgrimage to the tomb of Saint Julian the Martyr at Brioude; and the angels who brought the pestilence to Rome in 680 were in fact so employed to point to the virtues of another martyr, this time Saint Sebastian. The passage from Paul the Deacon continues:

> Then it was said to a certain man by revelation that the pestilence would not cease before an altar of St. Sebastian the martyr was placed in the church of the blessed Peter which is called "Ad Vincula." And it was done, and after the remains of Saint Sebastian the martyr had been carried from the city of Rome, presently the altar was set up in the aforesaid church and the pestilence itself ceased.

[83] *Vitae Patrum* VI,6; transl. E. James, *Gregory of Tours: Life of the Fathers* (Liverpool, 1985), p. 57.

[84] AS Septembris viii (29 September), 72.

[85] Occasionally ecclesiastical councils had to rule against the excessive devotion given to certain angels, Michael in particular. For example, the Synod of Seligenstadt of 1012 did so in canon X; Mansi, XIX, 397–398.

We know from other sources about Saint Sebastian's supposed power over pestilence. His death by arrow shot was thought to give him special abilities in the matter of transforming the arrows of disease shot by elves or demons ("elfshot" in fact) into instruments for good. One legend about him would have it that he had, after all, recovered from his own arrow wounds,[86] and so who better to help others do the same? The idea that disease was shot through the air by malignant agencies did much to keep illness which was otherwise inexplicable within the sphere controlled by demons, and to that extent again demons did those liable to be accused of malevolent witchcraft a service; but then the cure of such illness might require, as a corollary, the intervention of angels—or extra-special humans. Martyrs and saints might have this power, or, for particular reasons, persons who followed the way of the cross. We shall consider why this was so in the chapter that follows this, and the impact made by this conviction upon medical magic especially in a later chapter again.[87] Here I would simply draw attention once more to the important, and complex, role rescued angel-daemones played in justifying Christian forms of magic, and to the ramifications this rescue may have had upon subsequent ones.

Among the many biblical references to angels, two Old Testament stories stand out as supports for those who would make connections between angels and outlawed demonic magic, and for those who would link angels and that magic which could bring supernatural blessings upon men. The first is the story of the battle between Moses and the magicians of Pharaoh (Exod. 7:8–13); the second is that of Balaam and the ass (Num. 22:21–35). Augustine insisted that it was angels who, through the power of God, in fact enabled Moses and Aaron to turn their rods into serpents, and this precisely to discomfit the demons who assisted Pharaoh's magicians.[88] Here Augustine introduced a dimension that is not to be found in the strict wording of the text and to which not everyone commenting on that text would resort.[89] Caesarius had similar points to make about the story of Balaam, and by similar

---

[86] AS Januarii ii (feast, 20 January), 278.

[87] Chap. 9.

[88] *City of God* X,viii; *edit.* Wiesen, *Saint Augustine*, iii, 282–283. The matter is the subject of more complex treatment in question 79 of Augustine's *Eighty-Three Questions*; *transl.* Mosher, *Augustine*, pp. 200–205. Here, angels are seen as exponents of that greater public generosity which magicians lack, and which earns angels and remarkable people special powers from God.

[89] Isidore, for example, does not when he mentions the battle in the *Etymologies* VIII,ix,4; *edit.* Lindsay, *Isidori Hispalensis*.

means. The king of Moab sends Balaam to curse Israel; an angel, seen first by the ass and not by Balaam, conveys God's command to Balaam to change his curses into blessings, which he does to appropriate effect. The angel is in the text—but Caesarius brings in demons and sees the story at this point as an account of a battle of magic between the two celestial supernatural powers. "[Balaam] climbed on his ass, and there met him an angel. . . . he sees the demons but not the angel who the ass beholds."[90] A human diviner or enchanter (which Balaam was) could never, says Caesarius, hope for angelic help. "None of the holy spirits obey a seer. He cannot invoke Michael or Raphael or Gabriel."[91] Such persons remain in the grip of demons unless angels or specially equipped persons close to the angels intervene on their behalf.

Both Augustine and Caesarius, we might remember, found their flocks to be peculiarly vulnerable to diviners and enchanters, and to pagan magicians and their practices in general. They delighted to translate the conflict to a higher sphere and so to represent it as one between angels and demons, which angels, predictably, win. Thus Caesarius could urge good Christians to range themselves confidently with the angels in their abjuration of condemned activities—"I exhort you, and before God and His angels I proclaim, that you should not come to those devilish banquets which are held at a shrine, or fountains or trees"[92]—and could imply that, by doing the will of the angels, they would be assured of the help of powers greater than their own, and greater too than those to which non-Christian magicians might pretend. Here was a proposition full of hope and capable of bringing great comfort to the hearer. Angels might both bear the burdens the old supernatural aids were to relinquish and outdo them in supernaturally beneficent power (just as Christianized demons might, as we saw, remove some of the blame from unhappy humans for failure). This dimension of the need for angels was never far from the minds of preachers such as Caesarius, and it was of immeasurable value for them to find how well the Bible provided for it. The story of Balaam and the ass was among the most popular of all Bible stories in the early Middle Ages.

The introduction of angels and demons into such biblical passages

---

[90] Sermon 113 (MT); transl. Mueller, Saint Caesarius, ii, 159–160.
[91] Ibid., 158.
[92] Sermon 54; ibid., i, 270.

was primarily a matter for those engaged in exhortation and inclined
to encourage a simple and hopeful response. One would not expect to
find it in serious works of exegesis and, for the most part, one does
not.[93] Just sometimes, however, it is possible to trace a clear connection
between biblical exegesis of this kind and the deeper anxieties aroused
by contemporary magical practice. Thus, in his *Commentary on Exodus*, Rabanus uses for his remarks upon the battle between Moses and
the magicians of Pharaoh exactly the same passage from Augustine on
Exodus he was to use again in his *De Magicis Artibus*.[94] This double use
of the passage has a double interest, for besides showing quite clearly
that this biblical story with its exegetical supports bore directly upon
Rabanus's own concern about magic, Augustine and Rabanus concentrate in it precisely upon angels. In explaining how it was that the rods
of Moses and Aaron were turned into serpents in a transformation exercise seemingly identical to that practiced by the condemned magicians of Pharaoh, both commentators emphasize a cosmic order in
which "occultae seminariae rationes" are hidden there by God, to be
activated at his command. Angels are all, good and evil alike, subject
to this command; but they are his chosen activators and thus have the
most prominent place of all created beings in God's dealings with that
in his cosmos which is supernatural in the sense that it is occult, or
hidden from man.[95] For Rabanus this section from Exodus, together
with Augustine's exegesis, is a vital support for his argument that God
has good magic, and, in the angels, unsurpassable operators of it to
advance against the evil kind with which he, Rabanus, felt himself
surrounded.

Finally, this early period produces one particularly vivid contemporary illustration, both of the need felt for the services of authentic

[93] Isidore, for instance, does not introduce angels into the discussion in his *In Exodum* viii, *PL* 83,290, nor does Bede into his, *PL* 91,300–301. Bede is reserved, too,
in his account of Tobit and the angel; *edit.* D. Hurst, *Bedae Venerabilis Opera, Opera
Exegetica* ii, CC (Turnholt, 1983), p. 10. He does, however, allow an angel to cure
Saint Cuthbert in the manner of Raphael. *Life* ii; *edit.* and *transl.* B. Colgrave, *Two
Lives of St. Cuthbert* (Cambridge, 1940), pp. 158–161.

[94] Rabanus, *Commentaria in Exodum* I,xii, *PL* 108,33, and *De Magicis Artibus*, *PL*
110,1099. The common passage reads, "Non . . . fuerunt creatores draconum . . .
seminarias rebus inseruit"; *edit.* I. Fraipont, *Sancti Aurelii Augustini Quaestionum in
Heptateuchum Libri VII*, CC (Turnholt, 1958), pp. 77–78.

[95] The whole discussion may owe a great deal to Origen (through Rufinus), especially *Contra Celsum* VIII,31–32; *transl.* H. Chadwick, *Contra Celsum* (Cambridge,
1953), pp. 474–476.

heavenly angels in conflicts over suspect practices and of the alarms this need could bring with it. It is to be found in the arraignment by Saint Boniface of one Aldebert, whom Boniface finally had brought to trial before Pope Zachary at Rome in 745,[96] and it deserves our special attention both because it is so striking in itself, and because it brings into the very sharpest focus so many of those aspects of angelic activity, in the cause of magic's rise within the new religion, which we have been trying here to follow. Aldebert was wandering about sowing dissension in the ranks of Boniface's hoped-for flock. He believed, we are told, that he was himself an angel, and that another angel had brought him relics of especial power. The Archangel Michael himself had somehow made available to him (via Mont-Saint-Michel) a letter from Christ which had fallen from heaven. Aldebert also conjured by the names of angels, some garbled and misremembered from Gnostic and Jewish sources: "I pray and conjure and beseech ye, Angel Uriel, Angel Raguel, Angel Tubuel, Angel Michael, Angel Adinus, Angel Tubuas, Angel Sabaoc, and Angel Simiel."[97] He claimed lastly, and most dangerously of all, that God himself had guaranteed to answer all such prayers. Aldebert had acquired a reputation for possessing remarkable supernatural powers, especially powers of healing, and a troop of devotees followed him about, to whom he distributed "relics" in the form of clippings from his nails and hair. Boniface tells us that he attracted multitudes of people to his public ceremonies which, he adds (significantly), took place in fields and at springs "or wherever he pleased."

Aldebert's infuriating capacity to empty nearby churches was in part the cause of Boniface's distress, it is true, but by far the larger measure of it seems to have stemmed from the means which Aldebert used. Aldebert appealed to many levels of the devotional instincts of the credulous, some pagan and some precariously Christian, but he appealed especially to a devotion to angels that was deep, and that was of importance to the authorities precisely because of the vital part the angels played on these delicately constructed, difficult to police, and ever-changing frontiers between Christian and non-Christian super-

---

[96] The letter from Boniface to Pope Zachary about Aldebert which was received at the 745 Synod of Rome, and also the process of condemnation there, is contained in transl. E. Emerton, *The Letters of St. Boniface* (New York, 1940), pp. 100, 106.

[97] The possible derivations of Aldebert's angels are interestingly discussed in J. B. Russell, "Saint Boniface and the Eccentrics," *Church History* 33 (1964), 237–238. An appendix (pp. 245–247) lists the further sources for the conflict between Aldebert and Boniface.

natural invocation and practice. Some of Aldebert's garbled names may have been drawn from a contemporary Soissons litany. Others are to be found in contemporary prayers.[98] In another part of the prayer in which he called upon the eight so-called angels, Aldebert made appeal, for instance, to God seated above the Seraphim and Cherubim, and so to a form of phrasing often found in exorcism formulae. As a way of dealing with malign spirits and maleficia, exorcism prayers and charms for health commanded an extraordinary importance in the early medieval church, and angels (especially the three, Michael, Gabriel, and Raphael, who came to be their named representatives, but unbiblical ones too, despite sporadic efforts to condemn them) were central to such exercises. We have, for example, a letter, written within twenty years at the most of the arraignment, and printed among the letters of Boniface and Lull, in which a sister invokes angels much as Aldebert does, but this time for her brother's health within the Christian fold.[99] A charm against fever, using these and further angel names, is to be found in the manuscript containing the Bobbio Missal, a manuscript possibly written in the early eighth century, and so close in time to Boniface's concerns.[100] The arraignment of Aldebert throws into dramatic relief how sensitive was the issue of angelic invocation, how closely linked it was with the world of forbidden magical practices, and how vital it was to the support of Christian magical ways of countering these.

Michael, Aldebert's supposed letter from Christ, and the shrine of Mont-Saint-Michel are matters which touch peculiarly delicate Christian sensibilities. The Archangel Michael seems to have occupied a prime position in the early medieval cult of angels and was, indeed, the only angel to be honored by a special feast until the ninth century. It is worth dwelling upon him for a moment, for of all the early medieval angels invoked he is perhaps the most instructive. The first reported appearance of Michael seems to have been that at Monte Gargano early in 493. It caused a great stir, and so we are quite well

[98] Ibid., and nn.

[99] Edit. E. Dümmler, MGH Epistolae Merowingici et Karolini Aevi i (Berlin, 1892), 429.

[100] Russell does not note these particular possible derivations, but, in the identifications of Adinus and Sabaoc, they support his conclusions. One such exorcism formula may be read in the collection made by Baluze: Mansi, XVIIIB,661–664. The charm is printed in edit. E. A. Lowe, The Bobbio Missal (London, 1920), p. 153.

informed about it.[101] Michael came to protect a bull from a herdsman, made angry because it had strayed into a remote cavern. We know about this cavern from an independent source. It had been the seat of an oracle, Calchas, and his cult, long preserved at Monte Gargano. Calchas required sacrifices, and those who wished to consult him had to spend the night on the mountain, lying upon the skin of the ram they had given to him.[102] Michael, however, did not want sacrifices. He intervened instead to protect the animal from the ferocious herdsman. Nor did he want persons prostrated upon a mountainside, but a church in which Mass could be said; nor, finally, anxious consultations with seers, but trust in the Christian way to salvation. Michael, in short, might look in some ways like Calchas,[103] but the form of behavior he encouraged could not be more opposed to that which was required by his pagan predecessor.

It is, sadly, very rare indeed for us to have clear record of such contrasts. We may, then, perhaps allow this one to stand out as an example of the sort of role angels might be asked to play in magical transference, and of the sorts of sensibilities that might be hurt by its abuse. It might illustrate, too, the kind of rational inquiry into prediction and forward planning it could inhibit. And, lastly, it can begin to show us how, deftly adapted, non-Christian magical interventions in human affairs can become Christian ones. Michael intervened at an important moment, early in the Middle Ages, and he was used to make clear Christian points about sacrifice, about the consultation of oracles, and about Christian dispositions toward the supernatural in general. We noted Michael's intervention in the matter of pestilence and on behalf of Saint Sebastian. Michael's methods and remedies could be a little extreme, but he is the prototype of the angel employed to advance the case for the rise of certain kinds of Christian magic.

In the eighth century Michael was held to have appeared to Autbert, bishop of Avranches, and to have ordered an oratory to be built at Mont-Saint-Michel for the special protection of sailors.[104] The Archangel Michael has long attracted the attention of historians of

---

[101] AS, Septembris viii (29 September), 60–62.

[102] Strabo tells of the cult of Calchas in his *Geography* 6.3.9; *edit.* and *transl.* H. L. Jones, *The Geography of Strabo* iii (Loeb Classical Library, 1924), 131.

[103] An engraved Etruscan image of Calchas shows him as winged, as Michael came to be. F. Lenormant, *A Travers l'Apulie et la Lucanie* i (Paris, 1883), 62.

[104] The Archangel required that his new shrine be at least up to the standard of that built for him at Monte Gargano; AS Junii iii (18 June), 602–603.

paganism and folk belief, and spirited attempts have been made to explain the popularity of his cult in general. This has been attributed variously to the forced encouragement of Constantine the Great, to the links that might be forged between Woden/Mercury and Michael protector of warriors,[105] and to the atmosphere of excitement generated by reported visions and appearances. Michael as protector of warriors from shrines high upon mountains is exceptionally well attested in the West. So too, and especially by the Carolingians, is Michael protector of pilgrims. Boniface himself favored the founding of shrines to the Archangel. It may not be wholly fanciful to connect Boniface's stress upon Michael's control over journeys with the concern shown by Pope Gregory III, for example, at the prevailing tendency to turn to pagan diviners for such help.[106] Michael's care, combined with that angelic skill in foresight so widely acknowledged in early medieval literature about angels, would, it seems to have been hoped, render such exercises obsolete. The form taken by the cult of Michael shows us with great clarity both the negative impress of forbidden demonic means of wielding supernatural power and the positive Christian one of how the wish for, and hope in, supernatural help might best be sustained in the face of this.

Boniface thought Aldebert was wicked and a heretic. Zachary thought he was mad. Both agreed that he should be silenced. He was accused, in the end, of "summoning demons to his aid under the guise of angels," and thus the affair was supposed to be ended (although Aldebert in fact remained at large, partly, it seems, through papal leniency). As I have tried to suggest elsewhere, it might to some have seemed more sensible to combat forbidden aery magic and deviant devotions with science, both natural and exegetical, rather than with charms and exorcisms dangerously like those condemned.[107] Bede himself, whom Boniface admired, may, indeed, have favored such a course in certain circumstances.[108] Boniface, however, clearly believed that

[105] Fundamental still to work upon Michael is O. Rojdestvensky, *Le Culte de Saint Michel et le Moyen Age Latin* (Paris, 1922).

[106] See above, chap. 5.

[107] V.I.J. Flint, "Thoughts about the Context," pp. 13–24.

[108] The commentary on Tobit by Bede was one of those most widely read by medieval exegetes. Tobit is the main biblical authority for Raphael's healing powers. Bede treats these wholly allegorically. It may be that he here deliberately avoided all entanglement with the idea that angels could assist in earthly healing, and that in part because he feared the type of confusion the contest between Boniface and Aldebert would bring to light.

the matter of Aldebert and, indeed, the matter of non-Christian supernatural practice in general, had gone beyond the arena of sober reason—an area of exercise never perhaps in any case of the first importance to the saint. In such a state of affairs good angels became the front line of attack, and their invocation by means of prayers, charms, litanies, and cult a matter of vital importance.

We touch here again upon the large issues of science and religion and upon those borderlines between the two which might have, on occasion, to be patrolled by angels. The confrontation between Boniface and Aldebert is a particularly stark and singular one, and many of the attitudes to which it draws attention were certainly forged by the peculiar conditions that confronted Boniface in early Carolingian Germany. We cannot generalize from it; but it does throw light upon many of the pressures which made angels necessary to the new good magic, and upon at least some of the disadvantages and complications attendant upon their employment in its aid. In addition to defeating the magic of the demons, angels were needed to distinguish those means of intervening in supernatural affairs which, in Christian hands, might compensate for the lost non-Christian ones (or those it was hoped would be lost); but simple helps such as angels could, among the unlearned, be as simply abused. The years ca. 740–745 seem to have been especially important in Boniface's struggle against the pagan magic of the Germans;[109] hence, perhaps, his stress upon the powers of rightful angels, but hence, too, the limit to his success. Angels needed better and more distinctive supports in their rescue of magic than Boniface could here give them, and pagan magic other counters too. Without these, angels might be dangerous aids to orthodoxy.

[109] These are the years which produced the *Indiculus Superstitionum*, for example, and during which anxieties about magic are to be found in the capitularies of Carlomann; *edit.* A. Boretius, MGH *Capitularia Regum Francorum* i (Hanover, 1883), 25.

CHAPTER

7

The Magic That Was
Needed: The Power of the
Cross in the Heavens

THE CROSS AGAINST THE DEMONS

THOUGH THE FIRST Council of Braga and its copyists
might inveigh against those who believed that the devil (and not God)
was in ultimate control of storm, drought, and pestilence bringers, and
of diviners and dream interpreters—and though man might expect,
(under certain circumstances), angelic help—the demons remained,
under God's licence, at least partially in command. Nor would the
waving of Old Testament figures at them and their accomplices necessarily have the impressive effect Agobard clearly hoped of such measures. In the matter of supernatural activities above the earth, demons
were manifestly adepts.

> It is with the spirits of darkness that we contend night and day, which bear
> rule over the damp and heavy clouded air. All this middle region, you must
> know, which stretches between the heavens above and the earth beneath
> and suspends the clouds in its great empty space, upholds the government
> of diverse powers and is the gruesome seat of wicked rulers under the com-
> mand of Belial.[1]

Gregory the Great put the position well: "One should not be surprised
that the devil, thrown from heaven, can excite storms in the atmosphere, when we see how it is that those condemned to work in the
mines still know how to use fire and water."[2] Though fallen, the demons had retained the capacities they had enjoyed in their unfallen
state. For man, then, to try to enter or to operate upon the murky and
turbulent air between the earth and the moon was both presumptuous
and highly dangerous. Only God, made man, had both entered into
and triumphed over these realms. Thus, according to the Christian

---

[1] Prudentius, *Hamartigenia* 11.514–520; *edit. and transl.* H. J. Thomson, *Prudentius*
i (Loeb Classical Library, 1949), 240–241.
[2] *Moralia* II,25; *edit. and transl.* A. de Gaudemaris, *Grégoire le Grand Morales sur Job*
i (Paris, 1975), 294–295 (MT).

dispensation, man had to be sure to be especially close to God and to his chosen ministers, the angels, were he to try to do so too.

This fact in part explains the extreme importance in all matters concerning the early medieval magic of the heavens of the symbolism of the cross raised high, and of the life of the cross which gave temporal expression to this symbolism. A passage from the *De Incarnatione* of Saint Athanasius gives eloquent expression to the feelings Christians had for the power of this cross. The *Life of Antony* had explained how the sign of the cross would frighten the turbulent demons away.[3] Here Athanasius explains a little more clearly why. The passage is vital to an understanding of the place occupied by the imagery of the cross in this period and so is worth quoting fully.

> The Lord came to overthrow the devil, purify the air, and open for us the way up to heaven, as the Apostle said, "through the veil, that is, his flesh." (*Hebrews* 10:20). This had to be effected by death, and by what other death would these things have been accomplished save by that which takes place in the air, I mean the cross? For only he who expires on the cross dies in the air. So it was right for the Lord to endure it. For being raised up in this way he purified the air from the wiles of the devil and all the demons, saying, "I saw Satan falling as lightning." (*Luke* 10:8). And he reopened the way up to heaven, saying again: "Lift up your gates, princes, and be raised, everlasting gates." (Psalm 23:7). For it was not the Word himself who needed the gates to be opened, since he is the Lord of all, nor was any part of creation closed to its Maker; but we were those who needed it, whom he bore up through his own body. For as he offered it to death on behalf of all, so through it again he opened the way up to heaven.[4]

The sacrifice of Christ, high on the cross and in the air, as Athanasius described it, was central to man's contest with the heavenly magic of the demons. This contest left its mark upon some of the high crosses that have survived, notably upon the Ruthwell cross with its runic script and seeming reference to Odin,[5] and it stands, furthermore, behind much of the material and emotional sacrifice endured especially

---

[3] *Transl.* R. T. Meyer, *St. Athanasius, the Life of St. Anthony* (Westminster, Md. and London, 1950), pp. 49, 65, 85–86.

[4] *De Incarnatione* 26; *edit.* and *transl.* R. W. Thomson, *Athanasius Contra Gentes and De Incarnatione* (Oxford, 1971), pp. 195–197

[5] For insights into such practices see A. G. Van Hamel, "Odinn Hanging on a Tree," *Acta Philologica Scandinavica* 7 (1932–1933), 260–288. For further discussion of the Ruthwell cross, see chap. 9.

by religious communities. It certainly explains much of the authority this suffering gave to those who did undertake to bear it. This point deserves great emphasis, for it is essential to our full appreciation of the means by which heavenly magic was both combated on the one hand and rescued on the other. If the cross put aery demons to flight as Athanasius said it did, then it behoved humankind to follow and use the cross with particular energy where demons were involved. Put briefly, if Christians were to aspire supernaturally to outdo the demons in their own element, and if, still more, they were to aspire to operate above them with the angels, then they must follow the full way of the cross, whatever this might mean. Only under the cross, furthermore, could supernatural measures to counter the magic of the demons be properly sanctioned.

This extreme concentration upon the sign and power of the cross is familiar enough, of course, to readers of medieval hagiography, sermons, and exegesis; so familiar, indeed, as to seem a little wearying and in no need of repetition here. But we do need to be reminded of it, precisely, and paradoxically, because of its very familiarity. These enthusiasms are often taken to be self-explanatory—the sort of thing one would expect of medieval Christians. Thus, they are rarely placed within a specific context, and certainly not (especially not, because of the distortingly adverse emotional charge so often attached to the term) within the context of anxieties about magic. When they are so placed, however, they take on new and vital meaning. The sign of the cross, when fears about magic are pressing, becomes primarily a way of exposing the demons, of making manifest their presence and the limitations of their power, and, most importantly, of selecting and invoking the best possible supernatural means of counteracting it. The use of the sign becomes, then, a means of demonstrating the Christian realization that such supernatural battles must and can be fought, and of adumbrating a Christian magical way of doing so.

Much was demanded of those who would wield the cross in the heavens against heavenly demons, and this precisely because of where these demons were. But the exalted region in which the struggle took place, and the superhuman capacities of the hosts engaged in it, gave the wielders great status and authority too. I dwell upon these points because they have a considerable impact upon our historical understanding of the rise of magic in the early Middle Ages and, in particular, of the institutional interests involved in this rise. As a result of the force of transmitted belief in both the existence and the habitat of

demons, the heavens were, quite simply, a more difficult sphere of supernatural operation for Christian invokers of supernatural forces than
was the earth. The man who, as it were, took on the demons in a
territory which was their own had a considerable standing in other
areas of supernatural exercise as a result of his presumed bravery. An
appreciation of this hierarchical subdivision, both of the cosmos itself
and of those at work within it, is of the utmost importance if we are to
understand the makeup and the power of the army, especially the monastic army, early medieval Christianity brought to the battle about
magic. This army fought both against the magic to be outlawed, and
on behalf of some of magic's acceptable Christian alternatives. The
combatants were selected with the greatest of care, and, once selected,
these powerful wielders of the cross came, in their turn, to be extremely influential. They early took the lead in the choosing of those
aspects of the supernatural manipulation of the heavens, and then also
of that of the earth, which might be retained by the church. They
could become also, it should be added, significant in the choice or
relegation of natural means of understanding and of operation. Little
less than the angels, they could decide to work, within this context,
in a way similar to them. This aspect of the rescued magic of the heavens is worth keeping in the forefront of the mind, for it is stamped
across the institutional responses of the church in the West, and across
much of its manuscript record. It helps us to understand how it was,
too, that when these so-called Christian superstitions came themselves
to be thought demonic, they could so easily be visited back upon the
Benedictines and advanced in support of the latter's demise.

The power the raised cross had against the demons active in the
skies is the very stuff of medieval melodrama, and it is rightly essential
to many of the pictures with which our minds are furnished of the
triumph of good magic against bad. Gregory of Tours enjoys them
greatly. Thus, demons vanish like smoke and into thin air when the
cross is held up in their paths.[6] Gregory revels in storms, and in the
power exerted against them by the image of the cross, made, as it
might be, by the crossing of the topmast and gaff-rig of a ship, stark
against the sky.[7] He is a rich source, too, of stories wherein the tremendous power of the cross vanquishes lesser forms of heavenly con-

---

[6] De Virtutibus Sancti Martini I,18; edit. B. Krusch, MGH SRM i(2) (Hanover,
1885), 165.

[7] Liber in Gloria Martyrum; De Virtutibus Sancti Martini I,9; ibid., 94, 143–144. His
evocations of seasickness in these passages are almost as compelling.

trol. A famous passage (and one which is informative too about pagan practices) dwells upon the discomfiture and defeat, by the mere sign of the cross made in the air, of the goddess Berecynth and her followers. In the time of the martyr Symphorian (possibly, that is, in the late second century) it was the custom at Autun, says Gregory, for people to wheel the statue of the goddess Berecynth on a cart about the fields, a ritual accompanied by much dancing and singing, and offered in the hope of good weather and so of a prosperous harvest. Symphorian objected. He made the sign of the cross against ("contra") the statue and it promptly fell off the cart. No amount of sacrificings of victims and beatings of the unfortunate traction animals could make the statue move again one inch. Many conversions to the powerful Christian God were made.[8] The raised cross might, according to Gregory, even be used by proxy.

> [Gregory, bishop of Langres] had the possessed come to him, and without touching them but simply making on them the sign of the cross, he ordered the demons to leave without a word. Immediately these demons, hearing his command, set free the bodies which their malice had enchained. Even in the holy man's absence men used the stick which he used to carry in his hand and expelled demons by raising it and making the sign of the cross.[9]

The imagery of the cross raised high against the demons was taken up with enthusiasm by hagiographers especially, but also by many other contenders against magic. Caesarius, for instance, sees an intimation of it in Jacob's ladder. "The ladder touching heaven prefigured the cross: the Lord leaning on the ladder is shewn to be Christ fastened to the cross." He plays too upon the association which can be made between the cross of Christ and that rod of Moses which miraculously turned into a serpent and devoured the serpents produced by the magicians of Pharaoh.

> We have mentioned that the staff prefigured the cross . . . after it was thrown on the ground, that is, prepared for the Lord's Passion, it was turned into a serpent or wisdom. This is that great wisdom which was to devour all the wisdom of the world. Finally, it devoured all the serpents which the magicians had made by their incantations. Now Egypt was

---

[8] In Gloria Confessorum 76; ibid., 343–344.

[9] Vitae Patrum VII,2; transl. E. James, Gregory of Tours: Life of the Fathers (Liverpool, 1985), pp. 61–62.

scourged by this staff, just as the world and the devil were completely conquered by the cross.[10]

These connections between Christ's cross and the respectable counter-magic of the rod of Moses recur in medieval commentaries upon the relevant parts of Exodus: in Bede's commentary, for example, and, once again, in that of Rabanus, which owes a lot to Bede,[11] and which has an echo, as we saw, in Rabanus's *On the Magic Arts*.[12] This part of Exodus obviously made Rabanus and others think quite hard about magic. Rabanus is exceptionally fond of the image of the rod of Moses held high and turned into the cross. He uses it again when commenting upon Exod. 17:9, "tomorrow I will stand on the top of the hill with the rod of God in my hand." Moses' rod here, says Rabanus, represents the devil, who wanted to block the way up into heaven, but who was overwhelmed by the sign of the cross.[13] Many more popular biblical passages and exegetes could readily be found to give these associations sustenance.[14] A remarkable treatise on the cross, generally known as the *De Laudibus Sanctae Crucis*, and by none other than Rabanus himself, expresses especially fully this sense of the completeness of the power of this instrument.

All things come together in this cross because on it suffered Christ, the creator of all things. For the Passion of Christ holds up the heavens, rules the world, and harrows hell. The angels are confirmed in their righteousness by it, the people are redeemed, the hostile are confounded. It secures the structure of the world, breathes life into the living, keeps feeling in the sentient, illumines the intelligent.[15]

This work enjoyed enormous popularity in monastic collections and found many there to share its sentiments. It is reflected, for instance,

[10] Sermons 87 and 95; *transl.* M. M. Mueller, *Saint Caesarius of Arles, Sermons* ii (Washington, 1964), 33, 68–69.

[11] Bede, *PL* 91,300; Rabanus, *PL* 108,33.

[12] *PL* 110,1099.

[13] *PL* 108,84–85.

[14] Such, for example, as Ps. 67:18, "Thou hast ascended on high, thou hast led captivity captive," in the commentary by Cassiodorus, *PL* 70,469.

[15] *PL* 107,158 (MT). Some impression of the vigor and immense popularity of Rabanus's view of the power of the cross may be gained from H.-G. Muller, *Hrabanus Maurus. De Laudibus Sanctae Crucis* (Dusseldorf, 1973), pp. 36–37, where the surviving manuscripts are listed. A full facsimile of the ninth-century Fulda manuscript, Vat. Reg. Lat. 124, is provided at the end of the book.

in the prayer to the cross of Odilo of Cluny; it is associated by him too with the physical ascension of the Savior, foretelling that of humankind, into the heavens.[16] The Feast of the Ascension was to play an extremely important part in decisions about magical practice.

Origen had early pressed the view that non-Christian sacrifices were a special help to the demons of the air. Indeed, demons had need of these.

> Some do not consider the truth concerning daemons, namely that if they are to remain in this gross air near the earth they need food from the sacrifices and so keep where there is always smoke and blood and incense. . . . Indeed, I think that because of the misdeeds committed by the daemons who work against mankind, those who feed them with sacrifices are no less responsible than the daemons who commit wicked deeds. For both the daemons and those who keep them on earth have injured men in like degree, since without the smoke and sacrifices and the food thought to be suited to their bodies the daemons would not be able to subsist.[17]

Thus sustained, these demons were able, according to Origen, to act as a kind of celestial customs barrier, stopping persons on their way up to heaven to demand that they paid their dues.[18] So physical a view of demonic relations with human beings was too extreme for many, and as the practice of animal sacrifice diminished, so condemnation of it as vivid as this grew less frequent. Caesarius, however, can still make telling points about it and with similar imagery. He states flatly that the eating of pagan sacrifice, combined with the making of the sign of the cross, will turn the sign against the culprit.[19] Such tampering and "devilish banquets" are to be renounced, and a life of greater sacrifice to be espoused instead. Sacrifice of a different kind was now required, one which affected the demons in a different way. Gregory of Tours told a story about Saint Patroclus that put the position well. The devil tried to block the way of the saint and prevent him from ascending to that place in the heavens from which he himself had fallen. Patroclus

---

[16] PL 142,1031,1037–1038. The cross was regarded at Cluny as carrying a greater weight of intercessory power than a saint. Udalricus, *Consuetudines Cluniacenses* I,xxxviii; PL 149,684–685.

[17] *Exhortation to Martyrdom*; transl. H. Chadwick, *Alexandrian Christianity* (London, 1954), p. 425.

[18] I have taken this felicitous phrasing from J. Daniélou, "Les démons de l'air dans la 'Vie d'Antoine,' " *Studia Anselmiana* 38 (1956), 142.

[19] Sermon 54; transl. Mueller, *Saint Caesarius*, i,270.

nearly succumbed; but fortunately he prayed, and an angel appeared to him in a dream. The angel showed him a column up which he might climb and see the world and the many temptations the celestial mountaineer must reject. Patroclus did so, and saw, and was repentant. Back in his cell, he found he had been left a heavenly gift: a tile with a cross upon it. He knew then how to circumvent the devil.[20]

It goes without saying, perhaps, that, when the question came to be asked as to what exactly constituted this way of the cross, there were many disagreements; and these disagreements necessarily affected, and are reflected in, decisions about Christian magic. A powerful line of argument would have it that the truest route lay through martyrdom, a form of sacrifice that not only would not feed the demons but would, in effect, starve them to death. Jerome made a famous claim, which had many echoes, about the supernatural power of the dust of martyrs' bones. This would always drive demons away—particularly those demons who dared to claim that martyrs were not special.[21] John Chrysostom gave currency to a story which described the effect of the smoke which rose from the voluntary submission of a martyr, in this case Drusus, to a death by burning. "And the smoke which rose up stifled the demons who were flying up there, put the devil to flight, and purified the air."[22] While the demons were given strength by the smoke of idolatrous sacrifices, smoke produced by this means had the reverse effect. The fate of Drusus (often in company with Zosimus and Theodore) was well known in the Middle Ages. He is in the so-called martyrology of Jerome, and in those of Florus, Rabanus, Ado, and Usuard.

The *passiones* of the martyrs are full of stories whereby the deaths of martyrs (in whatever manner) both overcome demons and, and most importantly, cause sudden "magical" reversals of the apparent laws of nature. Such deaths, indeed, were thought by the advocates of the way of martyrdom to release supernatural powers of extraordinary strength, capable of conversion to Christian uses of a particularly telling kind. Prudentius, for instance, tells of the fate and preternatural achievements of the body of Saint Vincent. This body wondrously resisted the efforts of Saint Vincent's slayers to destroy it. When weighted with stones it floated upon the water. When they exposed it to predators, a

---

[20] *Vitae Patrum* IX,2; transl. James, *Gregory of Tours*, pp. 80–81.

[21] *Contra Vigilantium* 9; PL 23,363–364.

[22] (MT.) The Latin version of the sermon in which he says this. (Sermon 71) is printed in full in T. Ruinart, *Acta Primorum Martyrum* (Amsterdam, 1713), pp. 536–538.

scavenging wolf was, to their annoyance, driven away by a mere raven. Prudentius on the sacrifice of the martyrs Emetrius and Chelidonius also sets the scene clearly.

> The offerings they sent up flew off through the air to shew, as they went shining on before, that the path to heaven was open. A ring, representing the faith of the one, was carried up in a cloud, while the other, as they tell, gave a handkerchief as the pledge of his lips, and they were caught up by the wind of heaven and passed into the depths of light. The glint of the gold was lost to sight in the vault of the clear sky, and the white fabric escaped from the eyes that sought long to follow it; both were carried up to the stars and seen no more.[23]

Heavy objects behave here in a wholly unnatural manner, and the murky realm of the demons presents no obstacle at all.

Death by martyrdom, then, was a sure way of cleaving a path past the demons in the manner of Christ, and, depending upon the manner of its accomplishment, perhaps of stifling a few demons on the way. Certainly it could change, when change was required, the operations of the observed laws of nature, both in the heavens and upon the earth, and it could replace both nature and the magic of the aery demons with a magic of its own. It was perfectly possible, in short, for it to have Christian magical effects. Much in the spirit of Jerome, Gregory of Tours and his relatives and friends accordingly use dust from the tombs of dead martyrs and saints, or oil from the lamps burning at their sides or wax from their candles, to overcome these laws of nature and produce wonders. Such powerful resources will even, magically and delightfully, cure toothache.[24]

There existed also, however, a form of sacrifice that did not require physical death for it to be effective against the demons. Bede speaks of it in his *Commentary on Luke*, when he discusses that same passage Athanasius had taken as his text (Luke 10:18): "And he said unto them, I beheld Satan as lightning fall from heaven." This passage and the comments upon it help us to understand how it was that many early medieval Christian exegetes could advance other (and equal)

[23] *Peristephanon* V, 396–503, I, 83–90; *transl.* Thomson, *Prudentius*, ii, 192–199, 104–105.

[24] *De Virtutibus S. Martini* III, 60; edit. Krusch, *MGH SRM*, i, 197. The description of toothache given in this passage seems to reflect vivid personal experience. Gregory's niece, Eustemia, applies oil from the light at Martin's tomb and wax from the candles burning there to a suffering friend, and she too recovers; ibid., IV, 36, 208.

forms of death as a means of confronting the power of Satan up above the earth.[25] Here Bede speaks of the effectiveness in supernatural matters of the death of pride, and he points out, furthermore, that it is this which distinguishes the "miracula" which God inspires from the mere "signa" which reprobates like Judas could manifestly perform.[26] A humble person, still on this earth but changed by a sort of death, can readily become the vehicle through which supernaturally charged spirits are made subject, because the names of such persons are "written in heaven" (Luke 10:20). Sulpicius speaks movingly of a vision he himself had of Saint Martin. He saw Martin in a dream, all dressed in white, his face and hair shining with light, his eyes sparkling like stars. Martin spoke of the cross, then rose into the air, vanishing from Sulpicius's sight. The latter is careful to explain how Martin would certainly have undergone a martyr's sufferings, had these been asked of him; but, as it was, his daily mortifications more than sufficed and enabled him to show Sulpicius a clear way upward through a kind of living death (the latter felt it was too difficult a climb, and that he would never get there; indeed, a slip downward by another route was much more likely).[27] This passage is a vivid evocation of that other type of sacrifice, short of death, which could allow those who made it also to follow the way of the cross, and so lay hold of the power it released.

Sacrifices, in or of life, of a special sort, then, distinguished those who were to do battle with the demons in the heavens by way of the cross and provided them with the sort of Christian magical powers they needed for success in this conflict. They and others might, as a result, wield the cross to good effect upon the earth as well. Gregory of Tours tells a revealing little story of a woman whose child was accidentally blinded in a dust storm. She was a countrywoman, and ill-educated, he says. Had she been better informed she would have known to make the sign of the cross for the protection of her child, and all would have been well.[28] Not every exercise of the cross in pursuit of supernatural

---

[25] The passage which succeeds this, Luke 10:19, contains the reference to the power Christ gave to his disciples to tread down serpents and scorpions, a passage again popular in the period and vividly represented upon, for example, the Ruthwell cross.

[26] In Lucae Evangelium Expositio III,x; edit. D. Hurst, Bedae Venerabilis Opera, Opera Exegetica ii (3) CC (Turnholt, 1960), 218–219.

[27] Ep. 2,X; edit. J. Fontaine, Sulpice Sévère, Vie de Saint Martin i (Paris, 1967), 324–325, 330–335.

[28] De Virtutibus Sancti Martini III,16; edit. Krusch, MGH SRM, i,186.

effects required, then, heroic sacrifice; but heroic sacrifice was the catalyst and symbol of their release. Agobard made some of the same points, in a rather backhanded manner, when speaking of the tempestarii. Sinners, he says, can neither raise winds nor command the evil angels in the heavens; they have not the necessary "virtus."[29] Agobard had, though, as we have seen, no contemporary Christian magic, no martyrs or saints or tomb dust or candle wax, to offer in their stead. His omissions are interesting in the context of contemporary hagiography and perhaps betoken a certain dislike of its exponents, and of the rights and supernatural powers they claimed. The problem was always apt to be divisive. Many hagiographers and some exegetes had, however, firm present-day answers (I have cited only very few among multifarious examples), and they made points about sacrifice and virtue, and about the forms of countermagic that might be validated and the kinds of person who might employ them, of the utmost importance to the rise of Christian magic as a whole.

These witnesses indicate that the problem of the magic of the heavens, when it called for an answer upon earth, was to be solved through the agency of particular ministers and persons. Martyrs, persons of especial sanctity, their remains, and the guardians, often monastic, of these (the latter are especially vital) could, under the all-embracing sign and way of the cross, neutralize malevolent magic. Humans who were saints already, like Martin, or well on the way toward the sacrifice of pride, or equipped with powerful relics of saints or martyrs (or dust or lamp oil or candle wax from their tombs, or the cross itself), might also, when they set out against storms, or wind-fanned fires, or hail or heaven-brought pestilences, expect supernatural success.

That belief in the powers of the demons of the air which, as we have seen, was so very vigorously retained in the Christian West, and that elaboration of counters to them we have begun to follow, brought, then, in its train a whole hierarchy of heavenly magical manipulators and tended to sustain this hierarchy in positions of authority and control. The fact that there was a hierarchy of influence of this sort, and one which reached deeply into the local level of society, into the village itself, indeed, is a fact that deserves great stress; for such a framework of power will generate in its turn certain attitudes. As, for instance, this particular hierarchy could neutralize malevolent magic, so

[29] *De Grandine et Tonitruis* XI; edit. L. Van Acker, *Agobardi Lugdunensis Opera Omnia*, CC (Turnholt, 1981), p. 11.

also could it deem certain types of magical intervention beneficial and consequently legitimize them. We shall turn shortly to these legitimations. And as they could legitimize, so also could they exclude. Three exclusions are especially important to our understanding of the historical place and status of legitimated Christianized magic, and we might review them here as a preface. Firstly, those who do not follow the life of the cross may not be allowed to exercise as much influence as those who do—not primarily because they are resented as insufficiently Christian, or as rustic, or lay, or cynical and hard to control (though such factors doubtless played their parts), but because they are too vulnerable to the devices of the demons. The demons are simply too strong and dangerous for their inadequate ministrations. Secondly, on this same argument, science, as we would define it, may have to take second place to sacrifice. We can see such an attitude expressed by both Gregory of Tours, once again, and by Sulpicius. Gregory is very distrustful, for instance, of ordinary medici, and delights to show how thoroughly his favorite relics and tomb dust (with water) can outshine all their best efforts.[30] Sulpicius, in a passage in the *Life of Martin* to which I have already drawn attention, tells of the exercise of great medical expertise; but by an angel.[31] Thirdly, it is such attitudes that make the greatest imprint upon our surviving written record, to the exclusion of much else; for major tomb churches, relic centers and monasteries will control this too. It is possible, indeed likely, that many of the choices these great centers of influence made in matters of magic did not go uncontested; but the other side is now very hard fully to recover. The rescue of astrology may have formed a part of it. So too, perhaps, did the writing of scientific treatises such as the treatises *De Natura Rerum*. The devotion of attention by persons such as Bede and Rabanus to matters exegetical rather than hagiographical may, like the views of Agobard, mark a similar turning away from the postures the hagiographers and homilists in particular recommended. Many of the selections of which we have most written record may reflect an internal struggle about the appropriate use of magic, and it is

[30] An epileptic whose condition had actually worsened at the hands of doctors was cured when he prayed at the tomb of Saint Nicetius. *Vitae Patrum* VIII,8; transl. James, *Gregory of Tours*, pp. 73–74. Afflicted with dysentery, Gregory appealed to a doctor, but in vain. Then he took a draught of the dust from the tomb of Saint Martin. Within three hours he was ready for a hearty meal. *De Virtutibus S. Martini* II,1; edit. Krusch, MGH SRM, i,159.

[31] *Vita S. Martini* 19,4; edit. Fontaine, *Sulpice Sévère*, i,294–295, ii,890–892.

worth reminding ourselves that, though a great deal of our "rescued magic" material comes from the great monastic centers, it is unlikely in the extreme that it represents fairly the true range of attitudes. We must explore it, for it is substantial, central to the process of the legitimation of magic, and, to modern eyes, good fun; but we may do so only with these limitations borne firmly in mind.

LEGITIMATE HUMAN MANIPULATORS OF THE HEAVENS

Through the interventions of legitimizers of this sort a singular transformation came about. While non-Christian tempestarii and augures and incantatores continued to be reviled, practices very similar to the outlawed ones came to be adopted by large sections of the Christian Church, and with enthusiasm. The secret lay in a manifestly acceptable performance in the matter of the way of the cross. These Christian methods of supernatural manipulation had to be modeled on, or the materials used derived from, someone who had gone this way if they were to be thus adopted; and the purposes for which the interventions were made must be deemed to be beneficial, and the deemers qualified (or thought to be qualified) to make such a decision by a sacrificial way of life. Of course, there was scope here both for retroactive canonization and for cynical self-regard. Because someone stilled a storm by "Christian magic," then he must have been a saint; because Brioude guards the tomb of Saint Julian, then Brioude must command respect and be a source of supernatural help. We cannot take all our accounts of legitimized magical operation at face value. But, this being said, we do seem to have convincing evidence of the energetic embracing by large parts of the Christian Church of practices unashamedly magical, provided only that they are practiced by the right people, fortified by the life and power of the cross. Once these criteria are met, the "right people" seem positively to have cornered the market in the matter of a Christianized magic of the heavens.

Rainmaking, and certain forms of wind and fire and storm control, are excellent examples. Take Saint Quintinianus, an early sixth-century bishop of Rodez, and a type of the kind of right person to whom I refer.

One day a great drought desolated the countryside of the Auvergne, and the grass dried up so that there was no pasture for the animals. Then the saint of God piously celebrated the Rogations, which are done before Ascension. The third day, as the procession was approaching the gate of the town, they urged the bishop himself to intone the antiphon that was going to be sung, saying, "Blessed pontiff, if you devoutly intone the antiphon, we trust so much in your sanctity, that we believe that the Lord will immediately deign to grant us abundant rain." The holy bishop prostrated himself on his cloak in the middle of the road, and prayed for a long time in tears. Then he got up and, as far as his strength allowed him, he intoned the antiphon which they had asked for. Its words were taken from Solomon as follows: "When the heaven is shut up and there is no rain because of the sins of the people, yet if they pray towards this place, then hear thou from heaven, and forgive the sins of thy servants, and send rain upon the land which thou has given unto thy people for an inheritance" (II *Chronicles* 6:26). And when they devoutly began to sing, the humble prayer of the confessor penetrated to the ear of Almighty God, and behold, the sky darkened and covered itself with clouds. And before they arrived at the gate of the town, a heavy rain fell upon the whole land, so that they were lost in admiration, and said that it was due to the prayers of this holy man.[32]

This passage has a great deal to tell us. Though prayers for rain and for appropriate weather for the harvest go back to our earliest surviving sacramentaries, this entry adds a little. The Rogations were three days of prayer and procession against damage to the harvest. Bishop Mamertus of Vienne (in ca. 470) ruled that they be held just before the Feast of Christ's Ascension.[33] The Major Rogation, of April 25th, seems to have been designed to echo exactly the timing of the old Roman *Robigalia*, supplications for the freeing of the standing corn from rust. The Rogations are specifically recommended by Carolingian synods,[34] and still, in the tenth century, the Feast of the Ascension was thought to be a suitable occasion upon which to contrast Christian weather-making procedures and beliefs with those ascribed to demons or to *malefici* and their incantations.[35] Quintinianus's intervention, then, is a vivid instance of the Christian remodeling of non-Christian methods of magical control.

Processions and singing bring back to mind not merely the *Robigalia*

---

[32] Gregory of Tours, *Vitae Patrum* IV,4; transl. James, *Gregory of Tours*, pp. 46–47.

[33] Gregory of Tours, *History of the Franks* II,34; transl. O. M. Dalton, *The History of the Franks by Gregory of Tours* ii (Oxford, 1927), 74.

[34] The 813 Synod of Mainz, for instance, and the Aachen Synod of 836 (canon X); edit. A. Werminghoff, MGH *Legum* III (2) *Concilia* (Hanover, 1898), 710.

[35] Thus Ratherius of Verona, in a sermon on the Ascension, inveighs against the "increduli" who believe in "tempestarii"; *PL* 136,739.

but peasant rainmaking processions. Burchard describes (for disapproval) one of these wherein women process with a virgin (and with special herbs and gestures) in a chant for rain.[36] Quintinianus's lying on his cloak is reminiscent of the posture required of the supplicant at the cave of the oracle Calchas, in which the skin of the sacrificial animal played an important part. In fact, when we look, we see that supplications for rain or against damaging storms throughout this period quite often involve the clothing of the saintly supplicants. Gregory the Great, for instance, tells us in his *Dialogues* of the rainmaking processions which were undertaken after the death of Abbot Eutichius. People carried the abbot's tunic round the fields after long droughts, and rain fell.[37] A later life of the seventh-century saint Deodatus of Nevers tells of how his tunic and that of his friend Hildulph were thought to be able to help in times of drought or flood or pestilence.[38] Adamnan's *Life of Saint Columba* is even more informative. Following a long and terrible drought the saint's community decided, after Columba's death, that

> some of our elders should go round the plain that had been lately ploughed and sown, taking with them the white tunic of St. Columba, and books in his own handwriting; and should three times raise and shake in the air that tunic, which he wore in the hour of his departure from the flesh; and should open his books and read from them, on the hill of angels, where at one time the citizens of the heavenly country were seen descending to confer with the holy man.[39]

Rain fell, of course, in torrents. The fact that the tunic was white brings back to mind the white-robed statues a previous system of invocation bore around the ploughed fields.[40] Christian accommodations to such practices may have been in Bede's mind, too, when he associated the conversion and baptism of the inhabitants of pagan Sussex with a sudden end to a long drought there. The newly baptized wore a white garment.[41] Invocations which parallel non-Christian weather

---

[36] *Decretum* XIX; *PL* 140,976.

[37] *Dialogues* III,xv,18; *edit. and transl.* A. de Vogüé, *Grégoire le Grand, Dialogues* ii (Paris, 1979), 326–327.

[38] AS Iunii iii,882.

[39] II,44; *edit. and transl.* A. O. and M. O. Anderson, *Adomnan's Life of Columba* (London, 1961), pp. 450–451.

[40] *Vita S. Martini* 12,2; *edit.* Krusch, MGH SRM, i, 278–279.

[41] *Ecclesiastical History* II,14, IV,13; *edit. and transl.* B. Colgrave and R.A.B. My-

magic in this way must be in changed hands, of course; but once they are it seems that many echoes and even imitations might be allowed.[42]

The same is true in the case of adverse winds and storms. Martin could turn back a raging fire against the wind that fanned it, by climbing up upon a rooftop and simply ordering it back. He could preserve fields from hailstorms throughout his entire life, by reason of his "virtus."[43] Saint Leoba could still a tempest that was blowing in windows and snatching the roofs from houses, by making the sign of the cross and holding up her hands against the skies.[44] Hugh of Cluny could make the sign of the cross against a storm and have it immediately subside.[45] Saint Florentius of Nursia could call down thunder and lightning to destroy the snakes that infested his cell.[46] Gregory of Tours kept hailstorms away from his fields by putting a candle from the tomb of Saint Martin upon the top of a tall tree.[47] Gregory's own mother, furnished with relics, was able to turn back a fire, caught by the wind, and save the family fields.[48] His mother was clearly a virtuous woman. He was not himself quite so effective. When, he goes on, he took the same relics with him on a journey and held them out against an oncoming storm, indeed, they worked. The storm divided and went round the company; but when he boasted that it was to his prayers that God in his heavens had responded, his horse threw him painfully to the ground.

A similar carefully orchestrated adaptation of practices otherwise associated with outlawed magic can be seen in the planting of weather crosses in the fields, in the dedications of bells, and in some of the blessings of holy water. Blessings for weather crosses, "against the aery

nors, *Bede's Ecclesiastical History of the English People* (Oxford, 1969), pp. 188–189, 374–375.

[42] The cloaks of saints and martyrs were allowed to affect the outcome of battles too; again perhaps a memory of the skins of sacrificed animals. Thus, for example, the tunic of the martyr Vincent, when carried round the walls of Saragossa, compelled the Franks to raise their seige. The action obviously had echoes, for it seemed to them to be a peculiarly powerful form of enchantment. Gregory of Tours, *History of the Franks* III,29; *transl.* Dalton, *The History*, ii,106–107.

[43] *Vita* 14,1–2; *transl.* Fontaine, *Sulpice Sévère*, i,282–283. *Dialogue* III,7; *transl.* A. Roberts, *The Works of Sulpitius Severus* (Grand Rapids, Mich., 1955), 49.

[44] AS, Septembris vii,766.

[45] *Vita* IV; *PL* 159,877.

[46] Gregory the Great, *Dialogues* III,xv,ll; *transl.* de Vogüé, *Gregoire le Grand*, ii, 320–323.

[47] *De Virtutibus S. Martini* I,34; *edit.* Krusch, MGH SRM, i,154–155.

[48] *In Gloria Martyrum* 83; *ibid.*, 94–95.

powers and evil spirits to whom power is given to harm the land," seem to have been popular, even encouraged.[49] A tenth-century formulary from Schaftlarn, for example, stresses the peculiarly strong protection of the cross, and the outstretched arms of Christ, in terms very like those of Rabanus, and it refers specifically to the power these have against ice and floods and the "murmurings of enchanters."[50] The practice of planting weather crosses goes back at least as far as the sixth century, for Bishop Caesarius of Arles, no less, condoned it. A mountainous region of the saint's diocese was constantly being laid waste by hailstorms. Caesarius allowed his own wooden staff to be made into a cross and put up on a high place; and the Lord, in turn, allowed the crops to be protected by it from the hail.[51] This gives us a little more insight into Caesarius's insistence upon the power of the cross, an insistence we have already noticed, for it is likely that in his diocese encounters between non-Christian weather magic and an alternative such as this one were especially direct.

Water, or salt and water, blessed and sprinkled to protect crops from thunder, lightning, birds, and other predators were acceptable too,[52] and so were bells, blessed to ring against tempests. The relics of Saint Salaberga (Sadalberga) of Laon (d. ca. 665), and bells blessed in her name, cured fevers and drove thunder away.[53] Sometimes, once again, angels were involved: the three respectable ones, Michael, Gabriel, and Raphael especially so, but stranger ones, such as Panchielus, Geruhel, Tubihel, and Rumihel, as well.[54] We are back again in that dangerous twilight which caused Boniface such clear distress but which, as clearly, attracted many inhabitants. The use of wood and water in such

[49] This invocation is to be found in an eleventh-century manuscript, possibly from Prül; A. Franz, *Die Kirchlichen Benediktionen im Mittelalter* ii (Graz, 1909), 14.

[50] Ibid, ii, 74–75. Such "murmurings" led to the invention of a special weather demon, called Mermeunt, against whom the might of the Creator was invoked; ibid., 56, 77.

[51] *Vita Caesarii* II, 27; edit. B. Krusch, MGH SRM iii (Hanover, 1896), 494.

[52] One of our earliest surviving sacramentaries, the so-called Gelasian sacramentary, preserves a blessing for water to be used against thunder and lightning: Franz, *Die Kirchlichen*, ii, 11–12, 47.

[53] AS, Septembris vi (feast, 22 September), 517. Bell ringing to chase away storms is still being chastised in Reformation Franconia in the mid-sixteenth century, together with other practices clearly traceable to the countermagic of the early Middle Ages: G. Hirschmann, "The Second Nürnberg Church Visitation," in edit. L. P. Buck and J. W. Zophy, *The Social History of the Reformation* (Columbus, Ohio, 1972), p. 371.

[54] Franz, *Die Kirchlichen*, ii, 11. Of course, there are Jewish and Gnostic echoes here, as well as those coming from the contemporary pagan world.

invocations bears also upon the magic of the earth, and that non-Christian reverence for the magic of sacred trees and fountains to which we shall shortly turn. Noise played an important part in both non-Christian and Christian practices. I say noise advisedly. Though the antiphons and psalmody sung by such as Quintinianus were doubtless more decorous than some of the other songs sung on such occasions, and though the bells (if well founded) may have produced a sound more modulated than that of the trumpets, horns, and conch shells that were characteristic of earlier and condemned methods of driving away tempests,[55] it was still a noise, and one which may well have amounted to "clamor" to some. Much is a matter of taste.

We are treading here on the margins of belief and practice, and the narrowness of the margins and the delicacy of the distinctions made between acceptable and unacceptable magic are very notable. Thus, and inevitably, there were difficulties. Charlemagne's capitulary of 789, for instance, had to forbid the actual baptizing of bells against the threat of hailstones.[56] That sympathetic attraction between the control of rainfall and the effects of baptism to which Bede had appealed, and "clamor," could easily be taken too far. An early eleventh-century council, similarly, had to rule against clergy who were misled into thinking that their clothing would produce miraculous effects such as the putting out of fires.[57] The events that must have preceded such a ruling stir the imagination. We have seen the trouble Boniface had in the matter of made-up angels. This finds a reflection in an eleventh-century manuscript containing blessings for the crops, in which the word "Panchielo" is replaced by the far safer "angelo et archangelo."[58]

Much more striking than the most vivid of these difficulties, however, is the willingness with which such risks of confusion were taken; and, above all, the trust reposed in those who were thought to have espoused the way of the cross in the making of decisions about them. Trusted as they were to defeat the demonic celestial customs officers, these saints, eminent monastic communities, and guardians of relics seem to have been commissioned to act as customs officers of a sort themselves, though this time on the frontier marking off non-Christian magic. So commissioned, they were afforded great scope for per-

[55] Ibid., ii, 39.

[56] Chapter 34; edit. A. Boretius, MGH *Capitularia Regum Francorum* i (Hanover, 1883), 64.

[57] Synod of Seligenstadt, 1012, canon vi; Mansi, XIX, 397.

[58] MS Bayerische Staatsbibliothek, Munich, clm. 100; cited in Franz, *Die Kirchlichen*, ii, 11.

sonal discretion, and, in the legitimate exercise of their duties, they allowed much magical material which could be viewed by many as frankly contraband to cross the borders.

One of the most remarkable of the magical admissions, an admission made possible primarily by the confidence monastic customs officers enjoyed, occurs in the matter of thunder prognostics. I mentioned in an earlier chapter the little ninth-century treatise *De Tonitruis*, once attributed to Bede. After a defense of his concern with prognostics which reads as a purely token one, the author proceeds with apparent assurance to inform his readers that thunder, heard coming from the four parts of the compass (here he echoes known Etruscan lore)[59] or in certain months, or on certain days of the week, is a guaranteed portent of definable events. Thus, thunder coming from the east portends an effusion of human blood, from the west, pestilence, from the south, slaughter, from the north, the deaths of sinners (here, the event arguably the most important to Christians is predicated upon a pre-Christian idea of significant direction). Thunder in April bodes ill for those at sea, but thunder in May means fertility and a copious harvest, and in June a great increase of fish. If it is heard upon a Sunday lots of clergy and women religious will die, if on a Wednesday lots of prostitutes and harlots will do so.[60]

We have only one surviving copy of this curious work,[61] but we have many more of related enterprises. English manuscripts, especially, are rich in them. One of the more striking examples is to be found in a tenth-century codex from Winchester, MS B.L. Titus D xxvi.

If it thunders[62] in the evening, this signifies the birth of a great man. If at the first hour of night, death. If at the third hour, the anger of the Lord, or his judgment made manifest in the world. If it does so at the fifth hour, in

[59] Such as that reported by Isidore in his *Etymologies* XV,4,7, for example, and expanded by Servius in his comments upon *Aeneid* II,693; edit. W. M. Lindsay, *Isidori Hispalensis Episcopi Etymologiarum sive Originum Libri XX* (Oxford, 1911). *Servianorum in Vergilii Carmina Commentariorum, Editionis Harvardianae* ii, Special Publications of the American Philological Association 1 (Lancaster, Pa., 1946), 488. Servius remarks that the augurer thought that thunder which came from the north was especially significant.

[60] *PL* 90,610–612.

[61] MS Stiftsbibliothek, Cologne, 102: a copy of the late tenth or early eleventh century and, interestingly, intruded into a text of Bede's *De Temporum Ratione* just before the chronicle section.

[62] fol. 9ᵛ. The text reads "notaverit" but this is clearly a scribal mistake for "tonitruit" or "tonitraverit." The second reading is to be found in the eleventh-century MS B. L. Cotton Tiberius A iii, fol. 35, from Saint Augustine's Canterbury (MT).

the middle of the night, then this means that someone is leaving this world or is being punished in this world. If at cockcrow, this means war and bloodshed. If at the morning hour, the birth of a king, if at sunrise, that a people is being converted to faith in Christ.

And so on. The Christian references hardly disguise the divinatory nature of the entry. In this codex, the thunder prognostics are immediately followed by a set of predictions about the future state of the weather, and so of the harvest, and about the possible deaths of kings and princes, reckoned from the days of the week upon which the first of January falls. Thus, if it falls upon a Sunday, this means a good warm winter and a dry summer with excellent crops and grapes, one in which cattle will fatten well and honey be abundant, and old men will die (here seen as an evident aid to prosperity) and there will be peace and plenty. If it falls on a Thursday, kings and princes will perish.

Often known in manuscripts as the *Supputationes Esdrae*, these purported to be signs given by God to the prophet Ezra, and so to be a part of that legitimate art of Christian prophecy of which even Augustine approved. We might remark that the author of the *De Tonitruis* also claimed to be inspired by the prophetic spirit.[63] The *Supputationes Esdrae* are widely to be found,[64] and they must have been used. In their emphasis upon the first of January they seem prepared to single out a time of the year significant in pre-Christian practice, and this despite the objections to such an emphasis Caesarius and Eligius had expressed. In the matter of the fates of kings and princes we might notice too that they pretended to pronounce upon precisely the subjects the *Laws* of the Visigoths forbade to the consulters of "ariolos, aruspices vel vaticinatores."[65] We seem to have here, in fact, a large measure of compromise in the matter of divinatory exercises concerning the heav-

---

[63] Preface; *PL* 90,609.

[64] In a second tenth-century Titus manuscript from Winchester, for example, MS B. L. Cotton Titus D xxvii, fol. 25. These two codices are described by W. de Gray Birch, "On Two Anglo-Saxon Manuscripts in the British Museum," *Transactions of the Royal Society of Literature*, n.s. ll (1878), 463–512. It is possible that they originally formed one book. The *Supputationes Esdrae* are also in MSS B. L. Harley 3017, fols. 63ʳ–64ᵛ, of the tenth century again, MS Vat. Pal. Lat. 235, fol. 39, of the turn of the tenth and eleventh centuries, MS Bayerische Staatsbibliothek clm. 6382, fol. 42, and MS B. L. Cotton Tiberius A iii, fol. 34ʳ, both of the eleventh centuries. The Tiberius manuscript repeats the prognostics in Anglo-Saxon.

[65] *Recc. Erv. Chind.* VI,2,1; edit. K. Zeumer, *MGH Legum 1, Leges Visigothorum* (Hanover and Leipzig, 1902), 257.

ens. Such compromise might not have met with the fullest approval at the highest level of ecclesiastical politics, but at a lower one it allowed to a local community divinatory prestige of a sort essential to its status and to its capacity to give the local population some solace for its un-resolved fears. This solace may not otherwise have been obtainable, save by recourse to non-Christian diviners; and this could, of course, by no means be permitted. Reasons such as these stood often, I am sure, behind such compromises.

The case is similar when we turn to heaven-borne illnesses. The codices that contain thunder prognostics and predictions associated with the first of January often include lunaria too. These lunaria are themselves, as we have already seen, a crude form of Christian magic, and intimately related to the history of the rise of astrology. We shall discuss the impact of illness upon the rise of magic much more fully when we come to consider the rescued magic of the earth; but these points might be made in preface. The incentive to turn to magic which unaccountable, and seemingly incurable, illness provides is one of the most powerful we have. Humanely speaking, too, it is one of the most difficult there is to resist; and, on a religious level, and if faith is to be sustained, needs of the order severe illness generates are among those most urgently demanding satisfaction. Some of the answers to the problem of heaven-borne disease given in our monastic manuscripts were, scientifically speaking, both inadequate and markedly close to condemned methods of divination. We might the better understand and make allowance for this inadequacy and this closeness, however, if we keep two things firmly in mind. Illness, demonically inflicted as perhaps it was, engendered a desperate fear. Monastic communities were in the front line of defense against both demons and competing non-Christian forms of cure; they must, therefore, carry both convic-tion and reassurance. Imitation was an effective means of conveying both. It may even have been the most effective there was available.

DREAMS AND THE FLIGHTS OF BIRDS

In these last two areas of outlawed heavenly magic, certain sections of the Christian Church allowed, once more, a great deal of the old faith and practice to filter through, and often for the very best of reasons. On one level again, of course, the ecclesiastical authorities could be fierce. They certainly were so in the matter of dreams, for pagans had set great store by them. Also, demons could excite them, as Augustine had pointed out—especially in his *De Divinatione Daemonum*. A famous passage in the *Dialogues* of Gregory the Great makes clear the latter's views on the matter. Dreams can come from a too full or too empty stomach, from demonic illusion (divinatory dreams in particular fall into this category), from reflection and anxiety, and from genuine revelation (perhaps involving reflection). It certainly is not easy to separate the genuine from the spurious, Gregory adds. Saints can do it, but others attempt it only at their peril. He contributes a chastening story about one of his friends who had saved up his money because he had dreamed that he would lead a long life, only to die quite suddenly.[66] A tenth-century gloss on Lucan, *Pharsalia* VII,8, is even more dampening. Dreams come from an imbalance of the elements in the body; when we are simply too hot we dream of soothing cold drinks, for example. Or we dream of something we have done or of something in the future about which we are anxious. Medieval scholars of Lucan had here cold scientific showers from Varro and Plato poured upon them.[67] Sources in addition to those passages in Regino and Burchard we have already discussed testify to an interest in dreams of a supernatural kind, and to a persistent tendency to dream in the wrong way and about the wrong things, and for, above all, the wrong ends, which needed correction.[68] And yet there was no doubt that the Bible gave credence to dreams, as Gregory himself pointed out, stressing those of Joseph, and that of Nebuchadnezzar and Daniel's excellence as an interpreter (Gen. 37:5–10, Dan. 2:29–47); and there is certainly no doubt that dream and vision literature occupies a place of very great importance in the literature of medieval instruction and authority.[69]

The correction, then, had to be most carefully administered, and it seems that some of it came, in fact, in the form of acceptable Christian "magical" dreams, dreams which involved a Christian heavenly magic. Christian corrective dreams such as these involve voyages up into the *Christian* heavens. Sometimes, and especially interestingly, their in-

[66] *Dialogues* IV,l–li; transl. de Vogüé, *Grégoire le Grand*, iii,172–177.

[67] H. Usener, *M. Annaei Lucani Commenta Bernensia* (Leipzig, 1869), pp. 220–221.

[68] The eighth-century *Libri Carolini* have an interesting discussion in them about right and wrong sorts of dreaming, and about the caution ecclesiastical authorities must exercise in their interpretation. *Edit.* H. Bastgen, MGH *Concilia* ii (suppl.) (Hanover and Leipzig, 1924), 158–161.

[69] An excellent summary article about this literature is that by M. Aubrun, "Caractères et portée religieuse et sociale des 'visiones' en occident du VIᵉ au XIᵉ siècle," *Cahiers de Civilisation Médiévale* 23 (1980), 109–130.

terpretation depends upon the phases of the moon. There are very many of them to be found in both hagiographies and histories; and I suspect that this proliferation and this popularity may be related, in part at least, to the need to counter that trust which was vested in such dreams as Diana's ride. Dream visions such as the famous *Vision of Fursey* reported by Bede, or the associated *Vision of Barontius*, for example (both of which have clear echoes of Saint Patroclus) set out for us the type of heavenly dream journey deemed to be appropriate.[70] Fursey and Barontius (both monks) dream of being taken to heights above the earth. Attempts are made by demons initially to block the paths of both, and angels come to clear the way (in Barontius's case Raphael plays an important part). Fursey and Barontius both see the choirs of angels, the joys of the blessed, the torments of the damned. Fursey is marked for life by a violent collision with the fiery body of a sinner with whom he had formerly colluded. The bearing of a scar from such an encounter for the rest of his life is not an uncommon experience for one who intervenes in the ways of the heavens,[71] and it may have some reference to the wounds inflicted and received of which Burchard so disapprovingly speaks. Barontius found reentry peculiarly difficult, and only with the help of a violent wind did he make his way back into his body: a warning, perhaps, that such journeys should not be undertaken lightly.

Such Christianized dreams do, I think, present a clear and edifying contrast to the type of heavenly ride both Regino and Burchard condemned. They seem, indeed, to have been designed to do so while, at the same time, sustaining belief in the possible validity of those dreams which were correctly begotten and employed. The celestial journeys (often specifically by night), physical horrors, and bodilessness of the forbidden magical dreams are all there in the new acceptable ones, but translated into a different form and with angels, not demons, as their governing spirits. It would be wrong to make too much of such juxtapositions, but at the same time they should not be ignored. Our surviving literature upon Christian dream journeys to the heavens suggests that those who wrote and received it might have valued both the

---

[70] For Fursey see Bede, *Ecclesiastical History* ii, 19; *transl.* Colgrave, *Bede's Ecclesiastical History*, pp. 270–275. For Barontius see edit. B. Krusch and W. Levison, *MGH SRM* v (Hanover and Leipzig, 1910), 377–394.

[71] Emperor Henry II, for example, was held to have been lamed because he had dared to attend the Mass, at night, of Saint Michael on Monte Gargano: *AS* Septembris, viii, 65.

accommodations with an older world it made possible and the points which could be made in it by speaking contrasts.

The same can also be said of the so-called lunaria de somnis we find frequently in monastic manuscripts (often together with the thunder prognostics and lunaria of the sick of which I have spoken). In these lunaria de somnis, dreams are interpreted in accordance with the days of the moon upon which they occur. A dream will come true if dreamed on the sixteenth or seventeenth day of the moon, for example, and so on.[72] Interpretations of this sort are not infrequently associated in early codices with more elaborate lists of subjects dreamed of (alphabetically arranged) and their meanings. Thus (beginning with A and "aves"), if one dreams of birds and has to fight them, this portends some sort of strife, if of doves, this means sadness, if of sun, or moon, or stars, joy.[73] This singularly jejune method of forecasting was given dignity by being ascribed to the prophet Daniel, and a guarantee of this quality was so readily produced, I suspect, once more because of the need to accommodate dream divination within the Christian dispensation. It was better to propitiate than to repress or ignore it, given, of course, the protection against demons afforded by the way of the cross.

The same may, finally, be true of divination from the flights and cries of birds. Saints, especially, show a particular interest in birds in our sources; and though the power of saints over animals of all kinds is a topos familiar to hagiographers in general, and though in the matter of birds such as doves or sparrows we would be right to suspect biblical influence,[74] sometimes the interest shown bears a recognizable relation to both earlier and, it seems, currently very widespread non-Christian magical beliefs. An incident in the *Life* of Saint Radegunde (d. 587) provides an instructive example. It involves the owl, thought in pre-Christian days to be an evil portent and seen, by Apuleius especially, as a bird that must be driven away from a dwelling house for fear it might bring death to its inhabitants.[75] When a horrified nun told Saint

[72] ms B. L. Cotton Titus D xxvi, fol. 9ᵛ. A similar dream lunary is to be found in the eleventh-century Worcester manuscript, Cambridge, Corpus Christi College 391, fol. 718ᵛ. Attached to the interpretations here are verses from the Psalms.

[73] A famous one, from ms B. L. Cotton Tiberius A iii, complete with interlinear glosses in Anglo-Saxon, is printed by M. Förster, "Beiträge zur mittelalterlichen Volkskunde iv," *Archiv für das Studium der neueren Sprachen* 125 (1910), 39–70.

[74] As in the case, for instance, of Remigius and the sparrows: *Vita Remigii* 5a; edit. Krusch, *MGH SRM*, iii,267.

[75] Apuleius, *Metamorphoses* (*Golden Ass*) III,23; edit. and transl. S. Gaselee, *Apuleius, the Golden Ass* (Loeb Classical Library, 1928), pp. 134–135. Also see Ovid,

Radegunde that there was an owl in the cloister, the saint made the sign of the cross over it and asked it to go away; and it did.[76] The belief was here respected. Only the manner of dealing with the evil portent had changed.

Other saints' lives also show a sensitivity to faith in such portents of an order we have not yet perhaps quite fully appreciated. When, furthermore, the non-Christian supernatural beliefs they register are thought to be destructive ones, the references to and changes they make in them are accordingly all the more forceful, or would have been so to a contemporary audience. Because of the slightness of the changes, the references can be a little hard to spot; but they are there. The treatment in our early medieval saints' lives of birds of prey contains many such references and changes. We have seen, for example, how birds of prey, and particularly the eagle, were sometimes viewed by non-Christians as portents of a very great stature indeed. They appear remarkably frequently in early saints' lives; but when they do so, they are represented not as awesome signs of an ineluctable destiny, and not as predators either, but as humble assistants, obedient to the saint in his pursuit of God's purposes alone, purposes of which they (and perhaps the saint) sometimes know nothing. The sea eagle who brought the fish to feed Saint Cuthbert is a famous example of a bird of prey who changed his way of life in deference to the needs of a saint; but there are very many others.[77] I certainly have not discovered them all, but I would cite here just a few of the more startling instances of birds of prey turned, by a saint, into obliging servants. I do so both to show how common is the theme, and to demonstrate how closely such stories may bear upon divination and its Christian alternatives.

Thus, an eagle brought food to Saint Desiderius of Vienne and his companions, as one did to Saint Cuthbert and his friend, but it did so here, and most interestingly, at the very moment when the company were discussing divine portents ("divinis oraculis"), as well as feeling rather hungry.[78] Heriger of Lobbes tells how an eagle protected Saint Servatius of Tongres (d. 384) when he was sleeping in the open air.[79]

Metamorphoses V,550; edit. and transl. F. J. Miller, Ovid, the Metamorphoses i (Loeb Classical Library, 1977), 276–277.

[76] Vita S. Radegundis II,19; edit. B. Krusch, MGH SRM ii (Hanover, 1888), 390–392.

[77] Anonymous Life of Cuthbert II,v, Bede's Life of Cuthbert xii; edit. and transl. B. Colgrave, Two Lives of St. Cuthbert (Cambridge, 1940), pp. 84–87, 194–197.

[78] Vita Desiderii Episcopi Viennensis 13; edit. Krusch, MGH SRM, iii,634.

[79] AS Maii, iii,216.

An eagle flew along with Saint Bertoul of Flanders (d. ca. 705) to shade his head from the sun and, when it rained, stretched its wings over him and acted as an umbrella.[80] To the monastic compiler of this life this service shows in fact the ministry of angels, made manifest by the servant eagle. An eagle as a sunshade can be found in the *Life* of Saint Lutwin, and, as an umbrella once again, in that of Saint Medard (d. 560).[81] Flodoard tells a story in his *History of the Church of Rheims* of an eagle choosing the site for a monastery. Saint Remigius had struggled up a wooded mountain to seek out a suitable position when an eagle flew down from the heights of heaven "to show the place where his disciple, Saint Thierry, ought to live on earth—he who one day was destined to mount to heaven." Then, four years later on Christmas Day, the same eagle reappeared, to show his approval (and confound the skeptics).[82]

Birds of prey, with eagles among them, also protect (rather than devour) the bodies of dead saints, and especially of martyrs. We saw how a raven guarded the body of Saint Vincent. Other such birds beat dogs and other beasts away from the body of Saint Bacchus.[83] An eagle cared for the body of Saint Vitus for three days (an eagle had earlier brought him food), and four eagles, coming from the four points of the compass in a manner reminiscent of the *De Tonitruis*, drove predators away from the body of Saint Stanislaus of Cracow (and for three days too).[84] The *Acts of Saint Florian* are especially informative. These, possibly put together in the eighth century, tell us, in the manner of many such *Acts*, how Saint Florian was accused, because of his extraordinary powers, of being a "magus." An eagle, however, guarded his body after he had been martyred, and this, to the compiler of the *Acts*, shows just the opposite, especially so in that the eagle spread out his wings in the sign of the cross.[85] This is a peculiarly vivid example of the uses to which such reversals could be put. Here a divinatory bird of prey both manifests a form of behavior in complete contrast with that which one

[80] AS Februarii, i,679.

[81] AS Martii, i,319; Iunii, ii,87.

[82] I,xxiv; *ed.* and *transl.* M. Lejeune, *Histoire de l'Église de Reims par Flodoard* i (Rheims, 1854), 194 (MT from the French).

[83] AS Octobris, iii,867.

[84] *Passio S. Viti* ii; AS Iunii, ii,1025–1026. Acta *S. Stanislai* xi; AS Maii, ii,231–232. The *Passio S. Viti* is a work of sixth- or seventh-century date. In the case of Saint Stanislaus the eagles were thought, once again, to be the servants of angels.

[85] AS Maii, i,465.

might normally expect of it and drives the difference home with the sign par excellence of the new magic. Yet, once again, the bird is allowed to occupy his familiar position as an object of reverent attention. His place in the hierarchy of the bird world is not seriously disturbed. The eagle *is* important; but his own special actions and the message he is allowed to convey through them are subtly, and crucially, altered.

Astrology, disguised as a form of science, was perhaps one of the most spectacular, and intellectually and institutionally complex, of the rescues of magic made in the period. Its scientific disguise, moreover, enabled its practitioners to claim that they were countering persistent and much more objectionable non-Christian magical pursuits, and were joining further scientific efforts, medical ones especially, to this end. Others took other ways. Those who felt themselves especially protected and sanctioned by the power and life of the cross seem to have been both inclined and encouraged to attempt the way of imitation of, and concession to, outlawed yet obdurate magical practices through similar Christian ones; and they publicized this way with considerable skill. They were helped toward this end, ironically, by the belief in demons they had so assiduously rescued too, for demonic magic required, after all, good magic of an adequately compensating kind to counter it.

The approach of medieval Christianity to the survival of belief in heavenly magic had, then, an enormous breadth about it, a breadth that ranged from the purely confrontational to the most intellectually testing, through, in enclaves which thought themselves especially protected by the cross, the most socially and emotionally indulgent. The problem of how best to harness and to Christianize the devotion the non-Christian magic of the heavens commanded did not lend itself to simple solutions. Yet such breadth of response could not but precipitate disagreements and disjunctions within the church; and, as a result, forms even of the rescued magic sometimes conflicted with, and ran up against, each other. The same will be seen to be true in the matter of the magic of the earth.

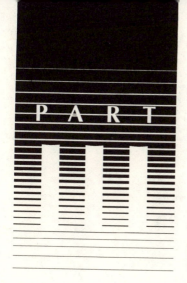

PART III

The Magic of the Earth

CHAPTER 8

Forbidden Magic:
The Focal Points of Christian
Disapproval

THE REVERBERATIONS of the conflicts we have just discussed echo across the world of earthly magic. Indeed, the ways in which the problems posed by heavenly magic were resolved were crucial to the solutions proposed for its earthly counterpart. The battle of the cross against the demons was central to all other battles about magic, and it led to the devolution of a great deal of authority upon certain Christian institutions in the matter of manipulating the supernatural—monastic institutions above all. I cannot sufficiently emphasize how important to the whole question of the rise of Christian magic was that cosmological borrowing from antiquity which placed the demons between the earth and upper air. The need to defeat the demons in their own element, the heavens, placed monks in the front line of the Christian warrior host. The strategic choices of the monks, therefore, and the disposition of their own particular troops, had a vital bearing upon supernatural action on the earth.

The Benedictine attitude, an attitude traceable, I would argue, at least as far back as the composition of the *Dialogues* of Gregory the Great in the last decade of the sixth century, was an especially vocal one. It is possible, I think, to say furthermore that most of the monastic evidence we have about earthly magic favored the "Christian substitute" approach to it—rather than the two alternatives of the outright repression and elimination of suspect supernatural practices, or their replacement by a form of science—and that, for the reasons I have given, this monastic material appealed to a very wide audience. This appeal came to be extremely costly. Many of those superstitious practices which gave armament to the enemies of monasticism during such periods as the English Reformation can be traced, in fact, back to this time; but they sprang, I shall argue, from efforts to cope with a difficult situation in the best available way, efforts which probed the problem deeply and, ironically, aimed above all at the avoiding of destructive confrontation. The positions were firm ones, but they did not incline to the simpler solutions; and they offered answers that were equally far removed from the merely superstitious in our sense. If by the sixteenth century the situation had so changed as to make of these practices fuel for conflict, this should not cloud our view of the very different context and intentions that had brought them into being.

Not that they wholly commanded the field. Again, in the magic of the earth, we find within the church different degrees of disapproval, and Christian substitutes in strife with more recondite or scientific methods of approach. The way of dealing with the supernatural opposition which the Benedictines, for the most part, adopted—the way of making common cause with them, where this was possible, and of attempting to win them over on their own ground without too much loss of face—was certainly not without its internal critics and opponents at the time (and opponents who, with hindsight, might have felt justified in their opposition); but these opponents had to work hard, and perhaps rightly so, to find an acceptable theoretical and institutional vehicle in which effectively to convey their objections. Those who espoused the scientific counter, especially, had to work harder in the matter of making reputable this approach to earthly magic than they had had to in the case of astrology, which appealed, after all, to forces physically above the demons, and which offered especially encouraging prospects of a reconciliation between Christian and non-Christian religious leaders on an intellectual level. Those who still obstinately believed in the wholesale elimination of the rival supernatural practices had to contend with the increasing numbers of those committed to a more diplomatic way.

CONDEMNED PLACES AND OBJECTS OF SUPERNATURAL COMMUNICATION

One of the most familiar of all the complaints about persistent non-Christian practice, a complaint found very widely in the sermons and in the legislation of the period, is that which deplores the reverence still displayed toward stones and trees and fountains, and poured out upon places where the ways on highroads forked or parted or crossed. All of these objects and places clearly occupied a position of immense importance in the competing ways of invoking supernatural assistance. Caesarius, as always, is explicit in his denunciation of such activities, giving evidence at the same time of the enthusiasm with which such invocation was made.

> We have heard that some of you make vows to trees, pray to fountains and practice diabolical augury. . . . What is worse, there are some unfortunate and miserable people who are not only unwilling to destroy the shrines of the pagans but even are not afraid or ashamed to build up those which have been destroyed.[1]

Martin of Braga, as so often, takes up the refrain. If, he inquired with some asperity, persons were asked to renounce, and did renounce, all cults and idols when they were baptized, how was it that they could still light candles and make little shrines at stones and trees and springs and crossroads?[2] To attend to such devotions was, he declared, simply to encourage those demons which inhabited such places to pursue their deceptions. In 597 Pope Gregory the Great wrote firmly to Brunhilda, ordering her to prevent her subjects from sacrificing to idols, worshiping trees, or exhibiting the sacrificed heads of animals.[3] Similar grumbles, as we might expect, are to be found in the *Life* of Eligius and in Pirmin's *Scarapsus* (Eligius's biographer adds a condemnation of "enclosures" to the standard one of lighted shrines at stones and trees and fountains, and at the places where roads meet, and Pirmin contributes "angulos"—turnings, perhaps, or hidden corners—to the list). They are found also in the *Homilia de Sacrilegiis*.[4] The strain recurs frequently among the canons of church councils, very often in the same words.[5] The *Indiculus Superstitionum* has prohibitions against "those things

---

[1] Sermon 53; transl. M. M. Mueller, *Saint Caesarius of Arles. Sermons* i (Washington, 1956), 263.

[2] *Reforming the Rustics* 16; transl. C. W. Barlow, *Iberian Fathers* i (Washington, 1969), p. 81.

[3] Edit. L. M. Hartmann, *Gregorii I Papae Registrum Epistolarum* ii (Vienna, 1899), 7–8.

[4] *Vita Eligii Episcopi Noviomagensis* II, 16a; edit. B. Krusch and W. Levison, MGH SRM iv (Hanover and Leipzig, 1902), 706. *Scarapsus*; PL 89, 1041. C. P. Caspari, *Homilia de Sacrilegiis. Aus einer Einsiedeler Handschrift des achten Jahrhunderts herausgegeben und mit kritischen und sachlichen Anmerkungun, sowie mit einer Abhandlung begleitet* (Christiania, 1886), p. 6.

[5] In canon xxii of the 567 Council of Lyons and canon iii of the 578 Council of Auxerre, xi and ii of the 681 and 693 Councils of Toledo, xii of the capitula of Gerbold of Liege (814), and in many mentioned by Regino and Burchard; Mansi, IX, 803, 912, XI, 1037, XII, 70, XIII, 1092. Regino, *De Ecclesiasticis Disciplinis* II, ccclix; PL 132, 351. Burchard, *Decretum* X and XIX; PL 140, 833–837, 964.

which they do upon stones" and "the fountains of sacrifices."[6] Penitentials recommend relatively heavy penalties for the making of, or releasing from, vows at such shrines,[7] and so do condemnations emanat-
ing from secular courts, especially those issued under the watchful eyes
of powerful churchmen.[8]

All such places were clearly focal points of reverent expectation.
They were places to which people came to stave off terrors and appease
their anxieties, to pour out the desires of their hearts (one dimension,
perhaps, to the phrase "reddere vota" so often found in the condemnations), and to seek comfort and help in sadness. The shrines at
stones and trees and fountains perhaps provided for anxieties of a general kind, those at the partings of the ways for those worries about
journeys to which papal rulings drew such repeated and hostile attention, and for which the Archangel Michael, among others, was supposed to provide an alternative solace. Crossroads evidently attracted
one form of the forbidden revered stones. Martin of Braga mentions
with dismay a habit travelers had of piling up stones into a cairn, for a
sacrifice in honor of Mercury, whenever they passed a crossroads,[9] and
Burchard, in the eleventh century, is still speaking with distaste in his
Corrector of the habit of carrying stones to cairns at such crossroads.[10]
The distinctions between types of shrine were not absolute ones. A
council held at Rouen, perhaps in the early seventh century, condemns ploughmen and hunters and herdsmen for their habit of hiding
enchanted ligatures in trees or at forked roads to protect the beasts on

---

[6] Chapters 7 and 11; transl. J. T. McNeill and H. M. Gamer, Medieval Handbooks
of Penance (New York, 1938), pp. 419–420.

[7] Latticed enclosures are occasionally mentioned in penitentials as places forbidden
to Christians, for instance in the so-called Roman penitential, chapter 38; ibid., p.
306.

[8] Chapter 21, of the Capitulary of Paderborn, 785, for example; transl. H. R. Loyn
and J. Percival, The Reign of Charlemagne (London, 1975), p. 53. Ansegisus, in his
ninth-century collection of capitularies I,62, records a similar prohibition, with a special reference to stones and to the lighting of lights at such places; edit. A. Boretius,
MGH Capitularia Regum Francorum i (Hanover, 1883), 402. See also the early eleventh-century so-called Canons of Edgar, chapter 16; edit. D. Whitelock, M. Brett,
C.N.L. Brooke, Councils and Synods i (Oxford, 1981), 320. Burchard takes up the
refrain, both in his Decretum proper and in his Corrector; PL 140,833–834, 964, transl.
McNeill and Gamer, Medieval Handbooks, p. 331.

[9] Reforming the Rustics 7; transl. Barlow, Iberian Fathers, p. 74.

[10] Transl. McNeill and Gamer, Medieval Handbooks, p. 334. He shows here that
crosses were put up at crossroads too but dislikes the idea of making "ligatura" for
them.

whom their livings depended from pestilence or death.[11] We are dealing here in large part again, of course, with practices that had been passed down through the generations, perhaps with very little change; with a form of pagan survival, that is. We have many witnesses to earlier forms of such devotions.[12] Yet, once more the fact that they were old, does not mean that the fervor invested in them had been at all attenuated by time. Pride in antiquity and ancestry seems, on the contrary, to have intensified it. One thing is abundantly clear, and this is that these shrines were places central to the lives of their adherents when these felt the need for supernatural assistance. Readily acceptable alternatives for such places and habits are never easily to be found.

Nor were these devotions in our period by any means confined to laypersons. Saint Valerius of Astorga (d. ca. 695), for instance, abbot of San Pedro de Montes, recounts with horror how the monks over whom he was placed as abbot welcomed magicians, along with a whole host of other malefactors, into the community, and how a local priest indulged in nocturnal forest rites accompanied, says the scandalized saint, by orgies of drunkenness and lascivious dancing.[13] The truth of this little tale, and of many others like it, may in fact be a little different. We may have here an indication both of a form of religious invocation far more ancient, and perhaps more innocent, than the saint's charged language would have us believe, and—instead of destruction (Valerius's answer)—of an effort on the part of the local religious at accommodation with it (for it was clearly held in high regard by the

[11] Canon 4; Mansi, x, 1200. Repeated in Burchard, *Decretum* X, 18; PL 140,836.

[12] Pliny, for example, speaks in his *Natural History* XII, ii of the dedication of particular trees to particular deities: oak to Jupiter, laurel to Apollo, olive to Minerva, myrtle to Venus, poplar to Hercules. These too often had carvings on them, and lights were burned in front of them. Varro, in his *De Lingua Latina* VI, 25, speaks of the sacrifices made to the Lares of the highways at crossroads. Transl. H. Rackham, *Pliny Natural History* iv (Loeb Classical Library, 1945), 4–5. Transl. R. G. Kent, *Varro on the Latin Language* (Loeb Classical Library, 1938), p. 199. Tacitus has some famous passages upon consecrated groves and coppices. *Germania* 9; transl. M. Hutton, *Tacitus. Agricola and Germania* (Loeb Classical Library, 1914), pp. 276–277. The consecrated chariot of the earth goddess, Nerthus, was kept in a holy grove: ibid., 40; pp. 320–321. Reverence for crossroads is clearly very ancient. It is to be found, for instance, in a love spell among the Greek magical papyri: H. D. Betz, *The Greek Magical Papyri in Translation, including the Demotic Spells* (Chicago and London, 1986), PGM IV, p. 94.

[13] PL 87,438,444.

local peasant population).[14] Such stories may give us an intimation of that monastic preparedness to compromise with earthly magic which was so to assist its rise.

It is difficult to describe in any detail the exact form taken by those shrines, but we have scraps of information from which we can piece together a picture. The famous (and beautifully excavated) Anglo-Saxon pagan temple at Yeavering in Northumbria, for instance, seems to have had a fenced enclosure abutting onto it. The shrine at Goodmanham, known to Bede, was apparently surrounded by such enclosures. Large standing posts stood near, or within, the enclosures at Yeavering, and bones and the skulls of oxen, which may be the remains of animal sacrifices, are to be found near the posts.[15] Latticed enclosures sometimes appear in early illustrations,[16] and the tenth-century Berne glosses on Lucan speak of the castration of pigs in "nemorosa loca," groves and enclosures full of trees.[17] Pliny, as we have seen, speaks of the dedication of particular trees to particular deities, and Saint Martin had a good deal of trouble with a revered tall pine, probably dedicated to the goddess Cybele and growing near a pagan temple. The pine tree very nearly fell upon the holy man, to the glee of his opponents. It was only persuaded to fall the other way (almost upon the gleeful opponents and giving them a scare) by the sign of the cross and a miraculously conjured up gale.[18] Great tree shrines were still giving trouble in the eighth century. Boniface felt called upon to chop down a particularly enormous and sacred oak at Geismar (in tell-

[14] The local population, Valerius reveals, did set great store by the ancient practices: ibid., 447. The account he gives here of rites practiced upon a mountaintop may be, thinks McKenna, a survival of the worship of Jupiter Candamius: S. McKenna, *Paganism and Pagan Survivals in Spain up to the Fall of the Visigothic Kingdom* (Washington, 1938), p. 131.

[15] B. Hope-Taylor, *Yeavering* (London, 1977), pp. 244–245, 258–260. The shrine at Goodmanham is described by Bede, in his *Ecclesiastical History* II, 13; edit. and transl. B. Colgrave and R.A.B. Mynors, *Bede's Ecclesiastical History of the English People* (Oxford, 1969), pp. 184–187. In the famous letter of Pope Gregory to Mellitus, which Bede reports, the pope speaks of the animal, especially oxen, sacrifices practiced by the English: ibid., I, 30; pp. 108–109.

[16] An especially fine one is to be found on the ninth-century Lothair crystal, at present in the British Museum, although here, of course, it represents the garden of Susanna.

[17] Commenting on Lucan VI, 41, "nemorosa," the glossator says, "Loca etiam aspera vel deserta ubi porci canstrantur. hic ideo 'nemorosa' dixit, quoniam hic locus sacratus est"; H. Usener, M. *Annaei Lucani Commenta Bernensia* (Leipzig, 1869), p. 191.

[18] *Vita S. Martini* 13; edit. and transl. J. Fontaine, *Sulpice Sévère, Vie de Saint Martin* i (Paris, 1967), 280–283.

ing the story, the saint's biographer seems to suggest in addition that the oak was an assembly point for diviners and enchanters of all kinds),[19] and the Irminsul destroyed by Charlemagne seems to have been a huge tree of a similar sort.[20] Sometimes the references to stones may have been to ancient sacrificial stones or great standing stones. The life of Saint Samson of Dol has a vivid description of pagans conducting ritual games and worshiping at a "simulacrum abominabile" standing on rising ground on Bodmin Moor.[21] Sometimes ancient and impressive stone ruins became important shrines[22] (pockets of reverence to these can be found spanning the period);[23] sometimes inscriptions, or marker stones, or stones with stories carved upon them may have done so.[24]

Carvings and images in wood or stone certainly seem to have been important to the atmosphere of reverence such places excited and to the expression of supplication. A great tree trunk, "carved with all kinds of images" confronted Saint Valery in the Bresle valley, and like ones seem to have been shown to Saint Amand.[25] Saint Martin's pine too may have been carved, and Boniface's oak, and the Irminsul, and we might perhaps legitimately picture, in these single massive holy posts and trees, memories of a divinized ancestral hall of fame. I have already drawn attention to the passage in Gregory of Tours's *Life of the Fathers* describing the sixth-century shrine Saint Gall of Clermont

[19] *The Life of Boniface by Willibald* VI; *transl.* C. H. Talbot, *The Anglo-Saxon Missionaries in Germany* (London, 1954), pp. 45–46.

[20] *Annals of the Kingdom of the Franks* 772; *transl.* P. D. King, *Charlemagne: Translated Sources* (Lancaster, 1987), p. 75.

[21] Chapter 48; *edit.* R. Fawtier, *La Vie de Saint Samson* (Paris, 1912), p. 144.

[22] For example, the *Vita Columbani Abbatis Discipulorumque Eius* I, 10 speaks of a crowd of stone statues ("imaginum lapidearum densitas") which formed a focal point for pagan worship; *edit.* Krusch and Levison, MGH SRM, iv, 76. The *Life* may refer here to the old Roman thermae at Luxeuil.

[23] Burchard, in his *Decretum*, still mentions disapprovingly the habit of showing reverence to stones in ruinous places: "Lapides quoque quos in ruinosis locis et silvestribus daemonum ludificationibus decepti venerantur"; *PL* 140, 834.

[24] Medieval glosses on Lucan point out that inscriptions marking the burial places of thunderbolts can still be seen: J. Endt, *Adnotationes Super Lucanum* (Leipzig, 1909), p. 35. Story stones depicting Welund or Sigurd are to be found, of course, in preChristian Scandinavia, notably Gotland.

[25] *Vita Walarici Abbatis Leuconaensis* 22: "Ad locum qui dicitur Augusta, juxta Auvae fluvium . . . juxta ripam fluminis stips erat magnus diversis imaginibus figuratus . . . qui nimio cultu more gentilium, a rusticis colebatur"; *Vita Amandi Episcopi* I, 13; *edit.* Krusch and Levison, MGH SRM, iv, 168–169, v (Hanover and Leipzig, 1910), 437.

found near Cologne. This had in it wooden models of those parts of the body for which supplicants sought a cure.[26] The Irish Saint Gall and Saint Columbanus, came upon three bronze statues, covered with gold, which they smashed up and threw into the lake,[27] and the *thermae* at Luxeuil, seemingly found by Saint Columbanus full of worshipers, were, of course filled with statues. Walfrid Strabo's *Life* of the Irish Saint Gall also mentions "simulacra" in the shrine the saint destroyed at Lake Tuggen. Sometimes we see great stone statues of the Roman Diana doing service as cult figures. The sufferings of the frozen Saint Walfroy took place near such a statue. The statue was clearly a stone one, for iron hammers were needed to smash it up.[28] The temple pulled down by Saint Bavo of Ghent (d. ca. 655) had statues in it, and the later life of Saint Hubert of Utrecht (d. 727) speaks too of the "simulacra" and "sculptilia" broken up by the saint.[29] The so-called Roman penitential of the mid-ninth century condemns the honoring of an image at a pagan sacred place.[30] A Slavic wooden temple described by the eleventh-century chronicler Thietmar of Merseburg was decorated with "wonderfully sculptured images of gods and goddesses," and more were to be found inside.[31]

[26] *Transl.* E. James, *Gregory of Tours: Life of the Fathers* (Liverpool, 1985), pp. 53–54.

[27] *Vita Galli Auctore Wettino* 6; *edit.* Krusch and Levison, MGH SRM, iv,260.

[28] "I found here [that is, near Trier] an image of Diana which the heathen people worshipped as a god. I also set up a column, on which I stood suffering great torture, with no covering for my feet. And so when winter came, in its due course, I was in such wise pinched with the icy cold that often the severe frost made the nails drop from my toes while frozen water hung from my beard like melted wax of candles." Walfroy, interestingly, had tried a sort of emulatory compromise first (in which bare and frozen feet played a prominent part), but it was of too demanding a kind to be permanent. It impressed some of the pagans sufficiently, however, for them to help him drag down the great statue with a rope and to smash it with the hammers. Walfroy also speaks of the many smaller idols he had broken up with rather less difficulty. *History of the Franks* VIII,15; *transl.* O. M. Dalton, *The History of the Franks by Gregory of Tours* ii (Oxford, 1927), 339–340.

[29] *Vita Galli Auctore Walahfrido* I,4; *edit.* Krusch and Levison, MGH SRM, iv,287. *Vita Bavonis Confessoris Gandavensis* 4; ibid., 537. *Vita Hugberti Episcopi Traiectensis* 3; *edit.* B. Krusch and W. Levison, MGH SRM vi (Hanover and Leipzig, 1913), 485.

[30] Chapter 42; McNeill and Gamer, *Medieval Handbooks*, p. 306.

[31] *Chronicle* VI,23(17): "In eadem est nil nisi fanum de ligno artificiose compositum, quod pro basibus diversarum sutentatur cornibus bestiarum. Huius parietes variae deorum dearumque imagines mirifice insculptae, ut cernentibus videtur, exterius ornant; interius autem dii stant manufacti, singulis nominibus insculptis, galeis atque loricis

Canon iii of that late sixth-century Council of Auxerre makes specific reference also to wooden carvings, either of a whole person or of a foot.[32] The *Vita Eligii* has Eligius object to the placing of images of feet at places where ways part,[33] Martin of Braga and Pirmin both object to "watching the foot,"[34] and the *Indiculus Superstitionum* (chapter 29) denounces "wooden feet or hands in a pagan rite."[35] Clearly, therefore, there were several types and forms of trees and of stones, and of wooden and stone carvings and statues to which that reverence the Christian Church claimed as its own could still be paid, around which non-Christian leaders, still held in great respect, assembled, at which great celebrations were held, and for the loss of which some compensation had to be provided.

Many different efforts were made to provide this compensation, and we shall follow some of them in the next chapter. Here, however, we may mention just one, for it illustrates rather clearly the dimensions of the problem and the many interests (and mistakes) involved in its resolution. It may help us, therefore, the better to understand the varied forms these resolutions took. This particular effort fell foul of the highest authority in that it was thought to be a little excessive. Pope Pelagius (d. 561) wrote to Sapaudus, bishop of Arles, complaining of a practice current within the latter's diocese, whereby wheat-flour cakes in the shape of ears, or eyes, or hands, or other parts of the body, were distributed as rewards to the faithful.[36] Pelagius obviously considered

---

terribiliter vestiti, quorum primus Zuarisici dicitur et pre caeteris a cunctis gentilibus honoratur et colitur." *Edit.* R. Holtzmann, *Die Chronik des Bischofs Thietmar von Merseburg und ihre korveier Überarbeitung* (Berlin, 1955), pp. 302–304. Thietmar says that there were many such temples. The Saxons across the Elbe were still cherishing "fana" with "simulachra" in 1069: *Annales Weissemburgenses; edit.* G. H. Pertz, *MGH SS* iii (Hanover, 1839), 71.

[32] Mansi, IX,912.

[33] *Vita Eligii* II,16a; *edit.* Krusch and Levison, *MGH SRM*, iv,708.

[34] *Reforming the Rustics*, 16; *transl.* Barlow, *Iberian Fathers*, p. 81. *Scarapsus; PL* 89,1041. This could conceivably be a reference to a practice mentioned by Burchard, whereby women watch a person's footprints, remove the trodden soil, and try to manipulate the fate of the person through it. *Decretum* XIX; *PL* 140,974. This, interestingly, and in common with many of the others, is a practice attested in African religion: A. J. Raboteau, *Slave Religion* (Oxford, 1978), p. 82. It is likely, however, that devotion to wooden images, perhaps placed to encourage the traveler, is meant here.

[35] McNeill and Gamer, *Medieval Handbooks*, p. 421.

[36] *Edit.* E. Dümmler, *MGH Epistolae Merowingici et Karolini Aevi* i (Berlin, 1892), 445. The letter is dated to the years ca. 558–560.

this too close to pagan practice to be tolerated,[37] but, equally obviously, the bishop was wrestling with a difficult local situation and one which required at least some kind of sympathetic attention. The problem lay in determining what, exactly, constituted attention of the right kind—a great problem indeed. It was perhaps exacerbated, furthermore, by interventions of this sort. Rulings from on high could not always be allowed to be absolute, nor accepted as appropriate to every local situation. They could result in reactions rendered all the more determined by the resentment aroused. This particular question had clearly not been solved by the mid-eighth century, for the *Indiculus Superstitionum* (chapter 26) is still to be found forbidding "idols made of moistened flour."

Springs and fountains are, of course, central to anxieties about fertility and prosperity. Martin of Braga speaks disapprovingly of the habit of throwing bread into fountains,[38] and a good sense of the reverence felt by agricultural communities for springs is conveyed by Alcuin in his *Vita Willibrordi*.[39] Willibrord came upon a pagan shrine on an island, close to the borders of Danish and Frisian territory. The cattle grazing there were sacred, and so was the spring. No one was allowed to draw water from this spring except in silence. Willibrord and his companions promptly performed baptisms in it (presumably noisily), then ate a few cattle with evident enjoyment—and survived unharmed. It was this last amazing circumstance that most astonished onlookers. They had expected him and all his company to be stricken either mad or dead. The little story is illuminating, not least in its emphasis upon the terror such places inspired. It is easier to understand the fury aroused by their violation if one remembers that the apparent respect in which they were held rested upon real fears. One appreciates a little better, too, how difficult it was for a religious organization, one of whose fundamental teachings was the duty to cast out fear, adequately to provide alternatives to such a form of devotion and to such a manner of enforcing respect. Non-Christian forms of reverence for

[37] Models made with bread dough are evident in ancient forms of pagan magic. Reference to them can be found, for example, once again among the surviving Greek magical papyri: "Put down a clean vessel and place the tablet under [it]; add barley meal, mix and form bread: twelve rolls in the shape of female figures. Say [the formula] three times, eat [the rolls] on an empty stomach, and you will know the power." Betz, *The Greek Magical Papyri*, PGM III, p. 29.

[38] *Reforming the Rustics* 16; transl. Barlow, *Iberian Fathers*, p. 81.

[39] *Vita Willibrordi Archiepiscopi Traiectesis Auctore Alcuino* I, 10; edit. B. Krusch and W. Levison, MGH SRM vii (Hanover and Leipzig, 1920), 124–125.

springs had, as we have seen, to be outlawed, and so too had many of the methods by which such a reverence was excited or compelled; but the springs themselves might sensibly and indeed justifiably be retained as the center of a differently directed devotion. This conversion, again, we shall follow.

One last prohibited place of resort was the pagan place of burial. We can glean from the *Corpus of Latin Inscriptions*, from the descriptions of tomb furnishings, excavated graves, and discovered grave goods, a most convincing picture of how vivid to both Roman and Germanic non-Christian peoples was belief in life after death. The quantities of Christian rulings we can find against them demonstrate in their turn, moreover, how alarmed the Christian authorities were by the tenacity of these beliefs and the ritual exercises that made them manifest. The prohibitions were uttered in part, of course, simply because the rituals observed at burial places were pagan ones, but also (and I think mainly) because the places containing (or, and more importantly, not always quite containing) the dead were held to exude such enormous amounts of supernatural power. Few moments, after all, so fill those left behind with so intense a sense of personal helplessness in the face of something beyond nature as does the moment of death. This sense left a peculiarly distinct impress upon the world the early European Christian Church confronted and upon its choice of places to revere.

Two strong strands of non-Christian belief in the supernatural needs and powers of the dead, part Greco-Roman, part "barbarian," seem to have persisted into the early Middle Ages. They are condemned by many of our familiar sources—and they are also allowed compensation, though to differing degrees. One was that dead members of a family still needed, and deserved, the services of the living, and that without these they might be impelled to revisit the living world. The second was that this impulsion to revisit might be manipulated by magicians. The first belief was made manifest in the Roman family *parentalia* (meals shared, perhaps at the tomb, on the anniversary of the death) and in the more general memorial celebrations of the dead that took place between 13 and 21 February. We also have magnificent information about both Anglo-Saxon and Viking graves, the latter replete with domestic animals and implements, weapons and food, and sometimes, of course, ships.[40] Martin of Braga, Ansegisus, Hincmar of Rheims, and Burchard all complain about practices which seem to

[40] See particularly H. R. Ellis, *The Road to Hel* (Cambridge, 1943), especially pp. 16–29, 39–50.

echo the parentalia, or similar Germanic or Viking customs,[41] and certain conciliar regulations appear to object to practices associated with the parentalia too.[42] Boniface may have in mind both Roman and Germanic customs, and, once more, overenthusiastic and spontaneous local efforts to come to terms with them, when he objects to the burying of the Eucharist, or clothing, with the dead,[43] and so may Burchard when he recounts, and condemns, a custom whereby water is poured beneath the body of a dead person as it is carried from the house, or corn burned where it lies.[44]

The second belief was certainly acted upon in the Greco-Roman world.[45] Dead persons (especially perhaps those who did not receive appropriate services at, or after, their deaths, or who had died "untimely")[46] were held not merely to be possessed of powerful supernatural abilities, but liable to be called upon to use them by supernaturally adept living persons. The *Recognitions* of Clement conveyed to the Middle Ages a clear picture of ancient necromancy in telling of Cle-

[41] Martin of Braga, *Capitula* 68 and 69; *edit.* C. W. Barlow, *Martini Episcopi Bracarensis Opera Omnia* (New Haven, 1950), p. 140. Ansegisus VI,cxcvii; Mansi, *Baluze*, i,957. Hincmar, *Capitula* xiv; Mansi, XV,478. Burchard, *Decretum* X and XIX; *PL* 140,838,964. In the second passage Burchard associates his prohibition of such tomb customs with his general condemnation of the reverence shown to stones and trees and fountains and crossroads, as though all could too easily still be approached in the same spirit.

[42] There are many rulings to be found against the mingling of milk or honey in the chalice with the wine in the sacrifice of the Eucharist: for example, canon viii of the 578 Council of Auxerre, canon ii of the 675 Council of Braga; Mansi, IX,913, XI,155. Milk and honey and wine were the most favored of the foods presented to the dead at Roman tombs. See on this F.V.M. Cumont, *Lux Perpetua* (Paris, 1949), pp 32–34. They were also favored magical ingredients: Betz, *The Greek Magical Papyri*, p. 3.

[43] Statutes of Boniface, xx; Mansi, XII,385. A related prohibition is to be found in canon xiii of the collection of Atto of Vercelli; Mansi, XIX,247.

[44] Burchard, *Decretum* XIX; *PL* 140,964–965. This prohibition is also found in the eighth-century so-called penitential of Theodore, XV,3, and in the penitential of Silos of the early ninth century, XI; McNeill and Gamer *Medieval Handbooks*, pp. 198, 289.

[45] The power of persons who had died "untimely" seems to have been thought, in Greek magic, particularly efficacious in the invocation of gods: Betz, *The Greek Magical Papyri*, p. 17.

[46] Virgil, of course, has Aeneas find the unburied on the near-side banks of the Acheron, after he has been refused passage across by Charon. Scarcely across the river are five other groups of persons who died untimely: infants ("biothanates"), persons falsely accused of crimes and killed, suicides, lovers who died of their love, and warriors killed in battle. *Aeneid* VI,318–546; *edit.* and *transl.* H. R. Fairclough, *Virgil* i (Loeb Classical Library, 1920), 532–543.

ment's instinctive manner of inquiry when he became curious about the immortality of the soul.

> 'I shall proceed to Egypt, and there I shall cultivate the friendship of hier-
> ophants or prophets, who preside at the shrines. Then I shall win over a
> magician by money, and entreat him, by what they call their necromantic
> art, to bring me a soul from the infernal regions, as if I were desirous of
> consulting it about some business.[47]

Clement's philosopher friend dissuaded him from this course of action but did not deny that it might yield results. Similar beliefs were acted upon in the Germanic world. Necromancers, those who conjure up the dead with blood and water to ask them questions, are the first named group of Isidore's condemned magicians, and this may bear wit-ness to a memory both of the family meals at tombs, at which the dead were fed in convivial company with the living,[48] and more sinister practices which had developed alongside the meals. An early Council of Elvira, in a ruling repeated by Burchard, warns against allowing women to watch in cemeteries for fear of the crimes they might com-mit there.[49] The calling up of demons for consultations by "pitonissae" (a term reminiscent of Saul and the witch of Endor, and attached alarms) is a matter for comment and disapproval in the *Homilia de Sacrilegiis*,[50] and necromancers are named among the persons to be sent to the ordeal in a conciliar canon which may be Carolingian.[51] Anglo-Saxon law codes contain specific condemnations of necromancy,[52] and necromancers may be subsumed, of course, below the general condem-nations of sortilegi. Hincmar speaks of conjuring with the bones of the

---

[47] I,v; *transl.* T. Smith, *The Writings of Tatian and Theophilus and the Clementine Recognitions* (Edinburgh, 1867), p. 145.

[48] Excavations at a Christian cemetery at Tarragona shows that these beliefs had persisted in Isidore's Spain at least into the fifth century: McKenna, *Paganism and Pagan Survivals*, pp. 35–37.

[49] *Decretum* X; PL 140,837.

[50] III,5; *edit.* Caspari, *Homilia*, pp. 6–7.

[51] *Edit.* A. Werminghoff, MGH *Concilia* ii (Hanover, 1906–1908), 215–219. In such objections as these, we may have an indication of those necromantic practices thought so abominable by Rabanus that he took the course of roundly declaring them incapable of truly waking the dead, no matter even that they seemed to have biblical support.

[52] For instance, the so-called *Canons of Edgar*, 16, and certain versions of the laws of Ethelred; *edit.* Whitelock, Brett, Brooke, *Councils and Synods*, i,320,371.

dead as one of the many practices of his witches.[53] Grave robberies and tomb violations are also penalized in law codes and papal rulings, and some of these robberies may have been carried out for magical as well as for material purposes.[54] Dead infants were, according to Burchard, still subject to objectionable procedures when he wrote, procedures devised to prevent them from doing harm to the living,[55] and so, it seems, were warriors.[56] One of the charges leveled against no less a personage than Pope Gregory VII at the Council of Brixen in 1080, and clearly thought capable of commanding credibility in some circles at least, was the charge of necromancy.[57]

Burchard also objects fiercely to the taking of death too lightly.[58] The deep emotions aroused by death were not to be diminished by Christians, nor were the reverence and hopes channeled through the condemned activities to be wholly lost. Tomb and burial places offered as great a range of supernatural opportunity and spiritual treasure as did shrines in general, and it was, once more, essential that, besides eliminating the worst, the medieval church preserve the best of it.

---

[53] *De Divortio Lotharii et Tetbergae* XV; *PL* 125,717. Hincmar's reaction was a little different from that of Rabanus, as we saw above. Hincmar, of course, had great faith in the ordeal. He explicitly opposes its (divinely assisted) veracity to the falsehoods sorcery could perpetrate; ibid., VI; 659. So fortified with a supernatural counter to it, he could, then, perhaps allow necromancy to be possible. The possibility that Hincmar and Rabanus, close as the two were in time and space, differed radically in their attitudes to condemned magic and its rightful counters, deserves further exploration.

[54] In the Visigothic *Forum Iudicum*, for example, a distinction is made between the person who robs to enrich himself (XI,2,1) and the one who does so for magical ends (XI,2,2); *edit.* K. Zeumer, *MGH Legum* 1, *Leges Visigothorum* (Hanover and Leipzig, 1902), 403. Bones, as well as jewels, were carried off by the robbers of the Oseberg ship burial: Ellis, *The Road to Hel*, pp. 17–18. See also the chapter (VI) on necromancy in the same work. Pope Gregory III rules against grave violation in a section of his legislation much preoccupied with magical practice; Mansi, XII,293.

[55] Penances of two years are prescribed for the driving of a stake through the hearts of a mother who dies in childbed and the dead child, and for doing the same to a child who dies without baptism: *Decretum* XIX; *PL* 140,974–975. A less severe one is prescribed for the furnishing of a dead child with a wax paten with a host on it, and a waxen cup of wine; ibid., 975.

[56] Burchard rules against providing a man who died of a wound with oil, as though the oil would heal the wound; ibid., 965.

[57] The decree spoke of "divinationem et somniorum cultorem manifestum, nicromanticum phitonico spiritu laborantem"; *edit.* L. Weiland, *MGH Constitutiones* i (Hanover, 1893), 119. Once more we have an echo of the story of Saul and the witch of Endor.

[58] *Decretum* X; *PL* 140,838.

CONDEMNED MAGICAL ACTIVITIES

Lot Casting and Conjuring

Next to the condemnations of the reverence shown to trees and stones and springs and fountains that we so often find in the legislation of the period and in the lives of its saints come similar prohibitions against lot casting for the purposes of divining. The two sets of objections may have been closely allied precisely because this lot casting tended to take place at revered places and shrines, so as to ensure for it an increased efficacy. A full complement of objectionable diviners and lot casters seems to have presented itself, as we saw, to Boniface when he came to destroy the pagan oak.[59] Lot casting and conjuration (sometimes involving sacrifices) clearly caused deep consternation. At the Council of Narbonne of 589, for example, in a decree that was often repeated, fierce fines are levied by ecclesiastical authorities for such activities,[60] and lot casting is again roundly denounced in penitential literature.[61] Lot casters, usually described as "sortilegi" or "caragii," appear frequently in the lists of magicians condemned in sermons, and secular legislators, as we have seen, take up the cry, especially when in the throes of cooperation with the Christian authorities.[62]

Lot casting can assume many forms, few of which are represented adequately by the terms used in the condemnations. Ancient sources provide information about certain of these forms, and, in default of clear descriptions in our medieval written sources (reluctant as these understandably were to elaborate upon anything so unpleasing—and familiar), we may look to these for some guidance to those practices which may have been remembered or transmitted from the past. Such sources indicate that sortilegium or caragium might involve the ran-

---

[59] *Life,* by Willibald, transl. Talbot, *Anglo-Saxon Missionaries,* p. 45. The full range is best conveyed in the original Latin: "Alii vero aruspicia et divinationes, prestigia atque incantationes occulte, alii quidem manifeste exercebant; alii quippe auguria et auspicia intendebant diversosque sacrificandi ritus incoluerunt"; *edit.* W. Levison, *Vitae Sancti Bonifatii Archiepiscopi Moguntini* (Hanover and Leipzig, 1905), p. 31.

[60] Canon xiv; Mansi, IX, 1017.

[61] In the mid-eighth century Burgundian penitential, for instance, chapter 28, in the penitential of Silos VII (104), and in the so-called Roman penitential of the ninth century, chapter 37; McNeill and Gamer, *Medieval Handbooks,* pp. 276, 288, 305–306.

[62] Charlemagne explicitly condemns lot casters of all kinds in his capitulary of 789, chapter 20; *edit.* Boretius, MGH *Capitularia,* i, 64.

dom casting of letters to form words, or the throwing of dice or knuckle-bones among, or to give numbers so as to choose from, directions already written (perhaps on stone or wooden tablets), or the throwing of bones or beans or pebbles, perhaps to give numbers, or the drawing of lots, or the plucking of dice or marked objects from containers. Lot casting containers of a kind perhaps currently in use appear in early illustrations to Ps. 21:19 (Vulgate) "and for my raiment they cast lots."

Third parties might choose the letters or words; birds (often cocks), for example, or small children, usually boys. Cicero speaks with great skepticism of the oak tablets kept in the temple of Fortuna at Praeneste. Words were engraved upon the tablets, and they were drawn at a sign from the statue of the goddess.[63] Macrobius tells of the carrying on litters of statues of those gods held to be possessed of divinatory powers, and of the responsiveness of the litter bearers to the directions of the statues.[64] These statues were thought sometimes to indicate their choices by leaning toward words made out for them. The opportunities for prejudgment and collusion here, on the part of the bearers or their employers, are very evident. Ammianus Marcellinus, under the years 371–372, tells of an unhappy lottery of a different kind, which, according to his account, had supported the aspirations of Theodorus to the empire, against Valens. A special tripod was made of laurel wood, and after suitable consecration by secret incantations, and the purification of its surroundings by perfumes, a round metal plate was placed upon it. Around the rim of the plate

the written forms of the twenty-four letters of the alphabet were skilfully engraved, separated from one another by carefully measured spaces. Then a man clad in linen garments, shod also in linen sandals and having a filet wound about his head, carrying twigs from a tree of good omen, after propitiating in a set formula the divine power from whom predictions come . . . stood over the tripod as priest and set swinging a hanging ring fitted to a very fine linen thread and consecrated with mystic arts. This ring, passing over the designated intervals in a series of jumps, and falling upon this or that letter which detained it, made hexameters corresponding with the questions and completely finished in feet and rhythm. . . . When we then and there inquired "what man will succeed the present emperor?" . . . the

[63] *De Divinatione* II,xli; *edit.* W. A. Falconer, *Cicero, De Divinatione* (Loeb Classical Library, 1923), pp. 466–469.

[64] *Saturnalia* I,23,12–13; *transl.* P. V. Davies, *Macrobius, The Saturnalia* (New York and London, 1969), p. 151.

ring leapt forward and lightly touched the two syllables [theo], adding the next letter [d]. Then one of those present cried out that by the decision of inevitable fate, Theodorus was meant.[65]

Ammianus says that the procedure was outlawed, and its proponents, including Theodorus, executed; but he is reserved about the credibility of the lottery itself. The letters and syllables pointed also, after all, to Theodosius, who did in fact succeed Valens.

Twigs from special trees played an important part in Germanic lot-casting practices, according to Tacitus.

To divination and the lot they pay as much attention as anyone: the method of drawing lots is uniform. A bough is cut from a nut-bearing tree and divided into slips: these are distinguished by certain runes and spread casually and at random over white cloth; afterwards, should the enquiry be official the priest of the state, if private the father of the family in person, after prayers to the gods and with eyes turned to heaven, takes up one slip at a time till he has done this on three separate occasions, and after taking the three interprets them according to the runes which have been already stamped on them: if the message be a prohibition, no enquiry on the same matter is made during the same day; if the message be permissive, further confirmation is required by means of divination; and even among the Germans divination by consultation of the cries and flights of birds is well known, but their special divination is to make trial of the omens and warnings furnished by horses.[66]

This is a famous passage, and one which shows yet again how interconnected were all methods of divination and the specially chosen diviners who engaged in them. The *Indiculus Superstitionum* (chapter 13) objects to auguries from birds and horses, some of which were perhaps sought through lots. Thietmar of Merseburg shows that similar customs had persisted among the Slavs of whom he writes, and that they too revered the horse as an intermediary.[67] Lot casting (perhaps of a similar

[65] *Rerum Gestarum* XXIX,1,29–32; *edit. and transl.* J. C. Rolfe, *Ammianus Marcellinus* iii (Loeb Classical Library, 1952), 202–207.

[66] *Germania* 10; *transl.* Hutton, *Tacitus*, pp. 276–279.

[67] Thietmar speaks of the procedures followed by the chosen lot casters at the temple described earlier. The passage is a difficult one, but I would render it thus: "Trembling, they make a trench in the earth, from which doubt-resolving lots are to be drawn. When the lots are placed, they cover them with green grass, and then they lead a horse (so important to these people that they consider him sacred) over the points of two crossed spears fixed upright in the earth, humbly asking of it answers. They then

sort again, but not described in any detail) clearly played a major part in the decision-making procedures of the northern peoples of the ninth century to whom Saint Anskar went as missionary.[68]

Among the Frisians human sacrifices could be chosen by lot. In a passage of great interest (for it deals with many levels and purposes of magic and countermagic), the *Life* of Saint Wulfram describes how the saint saved a young boy, upon whom the lot had fallen, from death "ad laqueum" (perhaps garroting). The saint prayed, and the bonds that bound the youth to the pillory fell off. The story perhaps had reference to the chains of Saint Peter, but it told also of the limitation (in Christian eyes) of the powers of non-Christian magical *defixio*. This was a kind of binding often attributed to non-Christian magic and magicians, one sometimes used to hold captives, and one to which Christianity needed to, and did, oppose a superior supernatural response. It will be discussed more fully below. Saint Wulfram's Christian supernatural powers, in the meantime, worked, to both personal and ecclesiastical advantage. His own recognizable, stronger, and, most important, differently aimed form of magic overcame both the powers of the pagan lottery and the captivity it ordered, and the boy became a Christian priest and valued scribe.[69] Duke Radbod himself proposed to use the procedure of the sacrificial lottery upon Willibrord after the latter had desecrated the sacred spring. Radbod only desisted because he was impressed by the sheer nerve of the saint.[70]

A unique manuscript record of the condemned practice of dicing for answers to questions about the future has survived into Christian Europe: the manuscript of the so-called *Sortes Sangallenses*. Written in uncials of the late sixth or early seventh century, and contained in some seventeen folios bound into the Saint Gall codex 908, this writ-

---

regard whichever of the planted lots he picks out first as the divine augury. If a like omen appears twice, the procedure is over [terram cum tremore infodiunt, quo sortibus emissis rerum certitudinem dubiarum perquirunt. Quibus finitis cespite viridi eas operientes, equum, qui maximus inter alios habetur et ut sacer ab his veneratur, super fixas in terram duarum cupides hastilium inter se transmissarum supplici obsequio ducunt et, praemissis sortibus, quibus id exploravere prius, per hunc quasi divinum denuo auguriantur. Et si in duabus hiis rebus par omen apparet, factis completur]." *Chronicle*, VI,23(17); *edit.* Holtzmann, *Die Chronik*, pp. 302–304.

[68] *Vita S. Anskarii* 18 and 19; *edit.* G. H. Pertz, MGH SS ii (Hanover, 1829), 701, 703.

[69] *Vita Vulframni Episcopi Senonici* 6; *edit.* B. Krusch and W. Levison, MGH SRM v (Hanover and Leipzig, 1910), 665–666.

[70] *Vita Willibrordi* I,10; *edit.* Krusch and Levison, MGH SRM, v,125–126.

ten lottery contains answers to questions about problems rangeable under 137 headings at least, and dealing with seemingly every aspect and
anxiety of life. The remaining manuscript folios are in disorder and
cannot be fully reconstructed,[71] and only about a quarter of the pos-
tulated original is now contained in the codex. The masterly efforts of
its editors, however, have shown that the lottery was designed to be
operated by dice, one or more, capable of delivering singly or in combination the numbers one to twelve.[72] The complete *Sortes* codex
probably had in it originally all the questions to be asked, together
with full directions for the throws each question required. We do not
have any of these, but it is clear from the replies that were one to defy,
for instance, the Council of Narbonne or Saint Eligius and ask for
omens, as it might be, for a journey, one throw or set of throws might
warn one not to go, another to expect a prosperous outcome to an early
start.[73] The inquirer might ask about harvests or lawsuits, love or en-
mity, health, surgery, inheritance, the gaining of public office,
whether to advertise his or her achievements or keep silent. The lottery was concerned, indeed, to provide for every conceivable source of
human anxiety requiring a difficult or worrying decision. We shall
never know why the great abbey retained such a record. Many of the
manuscript leaves seem to have been erased for reuse in the late eighth
or early ninth centuries, and the vellum recycled for the unassailably
respectable exercise of compiling vocabularies. Someone, perhaps,
had listened to Pope Gregory III. The sections that remain, however,
are invaluable, for they enable us not only to look more closely at a
certain type of non-Christian divinatory lot casting but to recognize,
also, how demanding and rewarding a process it was. This sortilegus
had valuable equipment, not easily come by. He was, in the sense that
his presence, his written records, his dice, and his expertise were all
essential, a local authority of some stature. This made him hard either

[71] A facsimile of a part of one leaf is to be found in *edit.* E. A. Lowe, *Codices Latini Antiquiores* vii (Oxford, 1956), 35. Lowe gives the late sixth century as its date.

[72] The text of the *Sortes Sangallenses* was first edited by H. Winnefeld, *Sortes Sangallenses Ineditae* (Bonn, 1887). Winnefeld printed the *Sortes* in the order in which they could best be reconstructed from the manuscript. His edition is reproduced and discussed by A. Dold and R. Meister, "Die Orakelsprüche im St. Galler Palimpsestcodex 908 (die sogennten 'Sortes Sangallenses')" *Österreichische Akademie der Wissenschaften. philosophisch-historische Klasse Sitzungberichte* 225, Abh. 4 (Vienna, 1948), 1–115. Dold reorders the responses under subject headings, in an effort to recover the original inquiries.

[73] So Dold, ibid., p. 21.

to silence or outdo. We can gain from a survival such as this a further insight into the quality of the opposition the Christian Church had to face. Lotteries were susceptible of a good deal of manipulation and chicanery, as Cicero, among many others, had been delighted to point out; but they could be taken very seriously too and were clearly a much cherished method of obviating stress. In the hands of an expert, lot casting could evidently be both impressive and convincing.[74]

The range of situations to which lot casting was seen to be appropriate, the awe and fervor so clearly invested in the practice, and the particular difficulties lot casters such as the Slavic or the *Sortes Sangallenses* diviners caused to the Christian authorities may account in part for the persistent popularity of a parallel Christian method of lot casting. Because this parallel process did not merely persist but operated extremely successfully, we shall follow its fortunes further in the next chapter. We may review here, however, the efforts made to stamp it out, for these latter efforts were, in some quarters, quite as unrelenting as the former efforts to perpetuate the practice, although they were a great deal less effective. We appear here to have once more a division within the ranks of the church of an illuminating kind: a division that should make us again wary of taking central rulings condemnatory of magic as the last word and should incline us to see them, in certain circumstances, as challenges rather than final solutions, and as challenges which were frequently, and rightly, taken up. Such divisions, and responses to the rulings, tell us yet more about the pressures upon Christian pastors in the mission field in matters of magical practice, pressures that encouraged negotiation and could bring about concession, compromise, and even the active encouragement of select and refurbished magical practices.

The parallel Christian method of lot casting that met the challenge here consisted in the casting of the *Sortes Biblicae* or *Sortes Sanctorum*. It involved the opening, usually upon the high altar of a church, of certain books of the Bible (most often the Gospels or the Psalter), or of sacred texts much revered (like Sacramentaries), or the placing there of scraps of vellum with possible directions on them, in the hope of drawing guidance from the passages chosen. Such Christian *Sortes*

---

[74] An excellent account of the training of a diviner in a present-day society is given in B. Tedlock, *Time and the Highland Maya* (Albuquerque, 1982), pp. 58–74. This training clearly calls upon great lot-casting skill and some austerity of life, and, most interestingly, produces diviners who have been able to survive in company with, and even draw upon, contemporary Roman Catholic practice.

also allowed the dicing for directions from holy books. One precursor of such practices seems to have been the so-called *Sortes Virgilianae*, the drawing of directions from the random opening of the poets, Homer and Virgil especially. As we have already noted, however, this was by no means the only precursor or pressure, and the *Sortes Virgilianae* may perhaps be seen now simply as one possible method to be groped for in a contemporary situation demanding of a quick response.

Christian lot casting is attested early, and condemnations of the *Sortes Biblicae* and the *Sortes Sanctorum* are found often in the rulings of ecclesiastical councils,[75] to be copied out once more by Regino and by Burchard,[76] and reflected by Isidore and his followers in the chapter *De Magis* of his *Etymologies*.[77] Charlemagne objects to them, and so, and rather fiercely, does the *Homilia de Sacrilegiis*,[78] and they are to be found, once more, in penitentials too.[79] There were, however, and again early, perceptible weaknesses in the wall of opposition. Saint Augustine, for instance, observed that, though distressing, the habit of resorting to the Gospels for "sortes" was slightly less so than that of resorting to other forms of prediction.

Now, regarding those who draw lots from the pages of the Gospel, although it could be wished that they would do this rather than run around consult-

[75] The Council of Venice in 465, for example, canon xvi; Mansi, VII,955. Also Agde, 506,xlii, Orleans, 511,xxx, Auxerre, 578,iv, the rulings of Gregory III,xxvi; Mansi, VIII,332,356, IX,912, XII,294.

[76] *De Ecclesiasticis Disciplinis* II,ccclviii, *Decretum* X,ix; *PL* 132,350–351, *PL* 140,834.

[77] VIII,28. The practice of casting the *Sortes Sanctorum* is the only practice Isidore associates specifically with his "sortilegi." He calls it "pretend reverence" ("ficta religio").

[78] "De tabulis vel codicibus requirendis, et ut nullus in psalterio vel in evangelio vel in aliis rebus sortire praesumat, nec divinationes aliquas observare." *Duplex Legationis Edictum* (789), chapter 20; *edit.* Boretius, *MGH Capitularia*, II(i),64. Caspari, *Homilia*, p. 7.

[79] The Burgundian penitential, the penitential of Silos, and the so-called Roman penitential condemn the *Sortes Sanctorum* and all other forms of lot casting in the same breath and insist on the same penance for all types: three years, with, in the Roman Penitential, one year on bread and water. The penitential formerly ascribed to Bede, and almost certainly of an eighth-century origin, expresses a particularly fierce objection to a person who observes the "Sortes Sanctorum or divinations, or utters things to come by looking at some sort of writings." Excommunication for both clerics and laymen is prescribed or, failing this, three years of penance for a cleric, two, or one and a half, years for a layman. McNeill and Gamer, *Medieval Handbooks*, pp. 228–229, 276, 288, 305–306.

ing demons, I do not like this custom of wishing to turn the divine oracles to worldly business and the vanity of this life, when their object is another life.[80]

This is a backhanded concession, but it is there. Such a suggestion may have done much to encourage those several unashamed early medieval Christian practitioners of the "lottery of holy things" of whom we have record and whose fortunes we shall follow further in the next chapter. There were worse forms of earthly magic abroad than the casting of the Christian *Sortes*, just as there had been worse forms of heavenly magic than astrology. The conjuring up of the dead by sortilegi may well have been one of these worse forms. If one could move the new faithful to the new Christian shrines, persuade them to abandon the more regrettable aspects of their so-called services to demons, and place this similar, yet subtly changed divinatory "technology" in converted or different hands, then the toleration of a pale imitation of some of those practices to which the adherents of the forbidden shrines had been attached, and at which their leaders were proficient, might be a harmless exchange to make and one that might bring with it palpable rewards. It might efface the threatened "dualism between converts and traditionalists" and bring about a shift "from an external opposition between institutions to an internal complementarity within a single institution."[81] It might thus contain much wisdom. Such a policy seems, on occasion, even to have been espoused by legislators. Burchard, for example, has two rulings in his *Corrector* against lot casting. The first is against those who practice lot casting in general for the purposes of prediction, and it carries a penance of two years (a penance that is, even so, less fierce, we may remark, than those in certain earlier penitentials).[82] The second, the one against the *Sortes Sanctorum* already mentioned, is extraordinarily slight, carrying a penance only of ten days on bread and water.[83] Lot casting of certain kinds was, among the various types of condemned earthly magic which still per-

---

[80] *Ep.* LV,xix, to Januarius; *transl.* W. Parsons, *Saint Augustine, Letters* i (Washington, 1951), 292.

[81] I take the quoted words from B. Tedlock, *Time*, p. 43. She gives (pp. 34–44) an account of a modern process of "negotiation" between a divided Roman Catholicism and native Guatemalan religious hierarchies and practices which has many parallels with, and light to cast upon, the one we are exploring here.

[82] *Decretum* XIX; *PL* 140,960.

[83] *Decretum* XIX; *PL* 140,961. This is all the more interesting in that in Book X,26–27 of the *Decretum*, Burchard records earlier, far fiercer, penalties; *PL* 140,836–837.

sisted, perhaps thought by Burchard, as it was by Saint Augustine, to be *relatively* harmless when set within the larger context of condemned magical practices. Properly used, it might well loosen the hold certain places, objects, and activities still exercised upon the religious sensibilities of hoped-for converts, and it might serve effectively to win persons away from the grosser forms of supernatural manipulation.

Among these grosser forms of supernatural manipulation by sortilegi we might number specifically divining by means of conjuring up images or ghosts, practices linked, of course, with necromancy. Images were called up by the condemned diviners in bowls of water or similar reflecting surfaces, such as mirrors, or even in the crystal balls popular in children's tales about magicians. Such practices were, once more, familiar to ancient magicians.[84] They seem frequently to have had as their object predictions about illness,[85] or the capturing and punishment of thieves.[86] Such efforts were again perhaps subsumed beneath the general distaste shown for sortilegi or caragii, but occasionally they are explicitly mentioned. Caesarius speaks of a means of conjuring up (under diabolical inspiration) "a person who can tell you who it is who stole your silver or your money."[87] The *Homilia de Sacrilegiis* objects to looking into a bowl (perhaps, indeed, the chalice) for answers.[88] Thieves were a perennial problem, and conjurations such as this were important strategies in default of a more orthodox form of policing. Thus, if such strategies were to be defeated, an acceptable substitute was required. As in the case of lot casting, so in the case of conjurations in the cause of thief divining, we shall see some members of the

[84] Betz, *The Greek Magical Papyri*, PGM IV, pp. 40 and 42.

[85] As in the case of Pausanias's account (vii,21) of Demeter's well, for example: "Here there is an infallible oracle, not indeed for everything, but only in the case of sick folk. They tie a mirror to a fine cord and let it down, judging the distance so that it does not sink deep into the spring, but just far enough to touch the water with its rim. Then they pray to the goddess and burn incense, after which they look into the mirror, which shews them the patient either alive or dead"; transl. W.H.S. Jones, *Pausanias Description of Greece* iii (Loeb Classical Library, 1977), 296–297. It is possible that the use of well- or springwater in this way stood behind some of those condemnations of pagan practices at springs reviewed above.

[86] "The names of the gods whom you seek when you are going to bring in a thief [by vase questioning]"; Betz, *The Greek Magical Papyri*, p. 246.

[87] Sermon 184; transl. Mueller, *Saint Caesarius*, ii,481.

[88] "Qui sortilegia observat, et qui manum hominis greve aut leve, [vel] quando accipit calicem, in ipso aspicet, iste sacrilicus est"; Caspari, *Homilia*, p. 7. Palmistry, as well as hydromancy, is condemned here, another sign that the copying of Isidore's section *De Magis* may have had reference to contemporary practices.

Christian Church taking to a form of slightly less offensive, but markedly similar, magic in response to these shared problems. Once again, pressing need, and the lack of any wholly convincing alternative in the face of it, would justify and encourage the adoption by this church of certain customary and familiar non-Christian magical procedures.

Weaving and Binding

Though surely useful and, one might think, every bit as innocuous as certain types of lot casting, weaving (or, more correctly, some of the activities seemingly connected with it) early drew down upon its head the outrage of concerned churchmen. Eligius objected to women who, when occupied at the loom, "or in dyeing, or in any kind of textile work," sought to exercise supernatural power, apparently through naming the unfortunate persons they sought to involve. The power may have been exercised by weaving a curse into a garment to be worn.[89] The penitential of Silos (attributed to a period close to the turn of the seventh and eighth centuries), associated weaving with a whole host of other outlawed magical activities.

> VII Of sacrilegious rites. If any Christian pays respect to diviners, enchanters, or fortune tellers to observe auguries, omens, or elements, or if they busy themselves with and seek after consultations of writings, dreams, woolen work, or magical practices, he shall do penance for five years. It is not permitted to observe [the customs connected with] wool at the kalends, or the collections of herbs, [or] to give heed to incantations except to perform everything with the creed and the Lord's Prayer.[90]

The Homilia de Sacrilegiis makes similar associations and expresses like alarms[91] and a rare piece of archaeological evidence, a weaving sley made of yew wood, datable perhaps to the late eighth century and with two names carved upon it in runes, may give us yet another indication of the association between magic and weaving.[92]

---

[89] "Nec in tela vel in tinctura sive quolibet opere Minervam vel ceteras infaustas personas nominare, sed in omni opere Christi gratiam adesse optare, et in virtute nominis eius toto corde confidere": Vita Eligii II, 16a; edit. Krusch and Levison, MGH SRM, iv,706–707.

[90] McNeill and Gamer, Medieval Handbooks, p. 288.

[91] Caspari, Homilia, p. 7.

[92] Westeremden A. R. W. V. Elliott, "Runes, Yews and Magic," Speculum 32 (1957), 256, is very cautious about this object and emphasizes its practical nature; but within the context of runic and yew-wood magic he describes there, and that of weaving magic here, a magical origin and use is far more likely.

Hincmar of Rheims, in his *De Divortio Lotharii et Tetbergae*, clearly thought of weaving skills and colored threads and garments as part and parcel of the equipment those witches who horrified him were wont to call upon to ply their trade.[93] He added, as we saw, to the section of this treatise he borrowed from Isidore, a passage similar to that in the *Life* of Eligius condemning the naming of unfortunates while weaving, and also one condemning measuring with threads.[94] In his *Decretum*, Burchard reiterated a prohibition issued at the Second Council of Braga, and contained in Archbishop Martin's own collection of canons, against women who "pursue vanities when they are weaving."[95] They should invoke God instead, he says, God who gave them, after all, their skill. In his *Corrector* Burchard elaborated upon the prohibition.

> Have you been present at, or consented to, the vanities which women practise in their woollen work, in their weaving, who, when they begin their weaving, hope to be able to bring it about that with incantations and with their actions that the threads of the warp and of the woof become so intertwined that unless (someone) makes use of these other diabolical counter-incantations he will perish totally? If you have been present or have consented, you must do penance for thirty days on bread and water.[96]

This seems similar, once more, to the activity to which Eligius drew attention; it might again refer to the casting of a spell, to be counteracted only by another, stronger, spell.[97] The appeal to prayers instead,

[93] *PL* 125,717–718.

[94] "Vel quibuscumque mensuris mensurandis," "et quas superventas feminae in suis lanificiis vel textilibus operibus nominant"; ibid., 719.

[95] *Decretum* X; *PL* 140,835. The prohibition is contained, too, in the *Capitula* (xxxviii) attributed to Archbishop Rudolph of Bruges, ca. 850; Mansi, XIV,960–961.

[96] "Interfuisti aut consensisti vanitatibus quas mulieres exercent in suis lanificiis, in suis telis; quae, cum ordiuntur telas suas, sperent se utrumque posse facere cum incantationibus illarum, ut et fila staminis et subtegminis in invicem, ita commisceantur [ut], nisi his iterum aliis diaboli incantationibus econtra subveniant, totum pereat?"; *PL* 140,961. I take the translation from A. L. Meaney, *Anglo-Saxon Amulets and Curing Stones* (Oxford, 1981), p. 185, who, with the help of Dr. John Ward, makes comparatively comprehensible the wholly incomprehensible translation in McNeill and Gamer, *Medieval Handbooks*, p. 330. It is impossible exactly to reconstruct the weaving techniques involved here, but a possible parallel, admirably described and explained, complete with the complex knots and textures involved, is to be found in K. P. Kent, *Navajo Weaving* (Santa Fe, 1985), pp. 23–47.

[97] Still, in the Val d'Aosta in the nineteenth century, a thread hidden above the

then, takes on an additional meaning and suggests that they were acceptable as a kind of countermagic to weaving here, as they would certainly come to be in the matter of healing charms and incantations (including those which used thread and spindles and to which we shall come). Prayers were even, on occasion, acceptable in love charms, despite a measure of reservation on all these fronts on the part of Saint Augustine.[98]

Weaving may have drawn upon itself especial condemnation because it could be associated with the *ligaturas*, plaits and bindings familiar to non-Christian magic (medical magic especially) and with those magical knots and binding-and-loosing charms and curses apparently common in ancient non-Christian magical practices.[99] Ancient magic sometimes speaks explicitly of the binding and unbinding of prisoners, a function which will find a further, and particularly striking, parallel in Christian magic.[100] Greek magic also speaks of binding the fate of a person by driving copper needles into a wax or clay figurine, and we have both archaeological and hagiographical evidence to prove that this was indeed done.[101] The word *defixio* most often represents a kind of binding curse. Defixiones were frequently found written upon a lead tablet and buried in a cold place, perhaps a well (to enhance the chill dread with which it was hoped the victim would be transfixed) or the grave of someone who had died untimely, and these tablets were believed to be possessed of a particular capacity for malevolent supernatural activity.[102]

---

doors was thought effective in preventing sorcerers from entering or leaving a church: P. Sébillot, *Le Folk-lore de France* iv (Paris, 1907), 138.

[98] See the closing section of this chapter, "Outlawed Medical Magic," for Augustine's hesitations.

[99] Again, many examples of binding-and-loosing charms are to be found in the Greek magical papyri: Betz, *The Greek Magical Papyri*, pp. 120, 128–129, 159, 180.

[100] For example, PGM i; Betz, *The Greek Magical Papyri*, p. 3. One has a Christian interpolation already intruded by the fourth century: PGM XIII; ibid., p. 180.

[101] PGM IV; ibid., p. 44. S. Kambitsis, "Une nouvelle tablette magique d'Egypte, Musée du Louvre, inv. e. 27145—iiie/ive siècle," *Bulletin de l'Institut français d'Archéologie Oriental* 76 (1976), 213–223. I owe this reference to Professor John Gager. For an attempt to hurt a saint by such a charm, see H. J. Margoulias, "The Lives of Byzantine Saints as Sources of Data for the History of Magic in the Sixth and Seventh Centuries A.D.: Sorcery, Relics and Icons," *Byzantion* 37 (1967), 237–238.

[102] See the illuminating remarks and translations of and comments upon "defixiones" in D. R. Jordan, "Defixiones from a Well near the Southwest Corner of the Athenian Agora," *Hesperia* 54 (1985), 205–252, and idem, "A Survey of Greek De-

We have not the same wealth of archaeological information for early Europe as we have for Greece and Rome, but we do have certain telling indications, especially in Germanic sources, of a reverence for non-Christian binding magic. Tacitus adds an interesting comment to his description of sacred groves.

> There is a further tribute which they pay to the grove: noone enters it until he has been bound with a chain: he puts off his freedom, and advertises in his person the might of the deity; if he chance to fall, he must not be lifted up or rise—he must writhe along the ground until he is out again.[103]

The capacity to weave binding fates for persons was one possessed by Valkyries and Norns.[104] The magus who confronted Bishop Wilfred, with results fatal to himself, sought to cast a binding curse upon the bishop, Eddius tells us. He stood, in addition, upon a high mound, perhaps a barrow grave.[105] Spells to bind and loose seem to have been familiar to the England Bede describes, for when his captors could not bind the captive thegn Imma effectively (his fetters kept falling off), their immediate reaction was to suppose him to have access to a powerful loosing charm.[106] The *Homilia de Sacrilegiis* seems actually to refer to surviving binding and cursing tablets (among other types of magical charm) when it condemns the use of plates of brass, or iron, or lead with writing on them, and the idea that written lead "laminae" were protection against hailstones.[107] The same *Homilia* shows too that

---

fixiones Not Included in the Special Corpora," *Greek, Roman and Byzantine Studies* 26 (2) (1985), 151–197.

[103] *Germania* 39; *transl.* Hutton, *Tacitus*, pp. 318–319.

[104] According to *Njal's Saga* the Walkyries weave the fates of people on the battlefield, and the Norns, too, weave destinies. The first of the famous Merseburg charms, a non-Christian binding-and-loosing charm in Old High German, and found in a tenth-century manuscript, may well call upon this tradition too: H. Bächtold-Staübli and E. Hoffman-Krayer, *Handwörterbuch des deutschen Aberglaubens* iv (Leipzig and Berlin, 1927–1942), 641.

[105] *Edit. and transl.* B. Colgrave, *The Life of Bishop Wilfred by Eddius Stephanus* (Cambridge, 1927), pp. 28–29.

[106] *Ecclesiastical History* IV,22; *edit. and transl.* B. Colgrave and R.A.B. Mynors, *Bede's Ecclesiastical History of the English People* (Oxford, 1969), pp. 402–403. The Anglo-Saxon translation here renders Bede's "literas solutorias" into "alysendlecan rune." "Ligaturas" (translated here as "amulets") and knots are condemned together in chapter 10 of the *Indiculus Superstitionum*; McNeill and Gamer, *Medieval Handbooks*, p. 420.

[107] The passage about hailstorms is an interesting addition to those already cited above concerning magical beliefs about the moon and about weather protection:

binding charms of this sort could be used for the binding of slaves, for it denounces in the very next breath a similar magical procedure, whereby written charms were used to conjure back fugitive slaves they had originally thought to entrap. These charms too were perhaps immersed in water. They seem even to have been placed in churches.[108] A persistent unease about that supernatural power which might lie in the hands of someone who had died untimely is reflected, as we saw, in certain sections of Burchard's *Corrector*.[109] Finally, defixio by means of a figurine was performed in Anglo-Saxon England in the reign of King Edgar.

> Then the bishop [Ethelwold of Winchester] gave the land at Yaxley to Thorney and that at Ailsworth to Peterborough. And a widow and her son had previously forfeited the land at Ailsworth because they drove iron pins into Wulfstan's father, Aelfsige. And it was detected and the murderous instrument dragged from her chamber; and the woman was seized, and drowned at London Bridge, and her son espcaped and became an outlaw. And the land came into the king's possession, and the king gave it to Aelfsige, and his son Wulfstan gave it to Bishop Aethelwold, as it says here above.[110]

This scrap of evidence is interesting in a number of ways. The supposed witch was drowned "more maleficorum," like Gerberga, an indication that this penalty was common to different societies and periods and so was perhaps to some extent standardized; and the king clearly profited

---

"Quicumque [in] deffeccionem lunae, quando scuriscere solet, per clamorem populi vasa lignea et erea amentea battent, ab strias depositam ipsa luna revocare in caelum credent[es], vel qui grandinem per laminas plumbeas scriptas et per cornus incantatos avertere potant, isti non christiani, sed pagani sunt," ". . . et qui caracteria in carta sive in bergamena, sive in laminas aereas, ferreas, plumbeas vel in quacumque christum vel scribi hominibus vel animalibus ad collum aligat, iste non christianus, sed paganus est." Caspari, *Homilia*, pp. 10–11.

[108] "Quicumque propter fugitivos petatia aliqua scribit vel per molina vel per basilicas ipsa petatia ponere presumit, non christianus, sed paganus est." Ibid., p. 11.

[109] "Hast thou done what some women do at the instigation of the devil? When any child has died without baptism, they take the corpse of the little one and place it in some secret place and transfix its little body with a stake, saying that if they did not do so the little child would arise and would injure many? If thou hast done, or consented to, or believed this, thou shouldst do penance for two years on the appointed days." McNeill and Gamer, *Medieval Handbooks*, p. 339.

[110] Transl. D. Whitelock, *English Historical Documents* i, 2d ed. (London, 1979), 563. The document is an old English deed of exchange and is dated 963–975.

from its application. It shows too that witches were alive and active in tenth-century England, a matter to which we shall return.

Such passages do much to make clear the fact that the close of antiquity had not brought the use of defixiones to an end. When medieval legislation and penitential literature condemns "incantatio," which it does very often, we might perhaps legitimately deduce that the cursing defixio was one of the enchantments it had in mind. Belief in magic such as this was clearly remembered vividly and perhaps was held widely in early medieval Europe. It can certainly be said that cursing and binding-and-loosing spells, whether physically woven into fabrics or not, constituted a lively part of the non-Christian magical practices current there, and that it behoved the Christian Church to take them into account. As in the case of Tacitus's grove and Willibrord's pagan spring, this belief seems often to have rested upon fear. Sometimes, as Eddius shows, a fear-inducing revenge was inflicted in return; but it perhaps behoved the answering Christian magic to depend in the main rather upon the loosing spell than upon the binding one or the primarily frightening response. And this, on the whole, with certain interesting exceptions, is, I think, the case.

CONDEMNED LOVE MAGIC

Love charms seem to have called especially often upon magical knots and upon binding-and-loosing spells, both in ancient[111] and in early medieval non-Christian magic. Though the blame is not exclusively reserved for them, women are often charged with involvement in love magic, and we may have here a further clue to one of the unacceptable powers women at their weaving were thought to exert. Both Hincmar and Burchard, as well as the many penitentials and some secular rulings to be cited below, are full of distaste for the nefarious activities of women in matters of love, and especially for the activities of those they call adulteresses. Hincmar tells a story in which a mother is able to render her daughter's husband impotent. Though the father of the bride had had his way in the matter of the original marriage ("which is rare"), the groom, through the malevolent power of his mother-in-

[111] "And take a lead tablet and write the same spell and recite it. And tie the lead leaf to the figures with thread from the loom after making 365 knots while saying as you have learned, 'Abrasax, hold her fast!' You place it, as the sun is setting, beside the grave of one who has died untimely or violently, placing beside it also the seasonal flowers." Betz, *The Greek Magical Papyri*, p. 44.

law, was unable to consummate it.[112] The superior "ecclesiastical medicine" of the local bishop was required for the undoing of such a diabolically assisted love charm: prayers and blessings and exorcisms, or
even, in the face of the husband's threat of divorce or murder, invocation of the binding spell of Christian marriage (we shall come to
this). The Ramsey Chronicle tells a story, set in the early eleventh century, wherein a jealous stepmother (the second wife, indeed, of Cnut's
sometime friend and ally, Thorkell the Tall) employs a witch (at some
expense) to divert her husband's love. He is to lose his love for his son
by his first marriage and devote it wholly to herself. The witch administers a potion, which works.[113] Burchard notes too that women are
thought to have special powers in matters of love.

> Hast thou believed or participated in this infidelity, that there is any
> woman who through certain spells and incantations can turn about the
> minds of men, either from hatred to love or from love to hatred, or by her
> bewitchments can snatch away men's goods? If thou hast believed or par-
> ticipated in such acts, thou shalt do penance for one year in the appointed
> fast days.[114]

He, like Hincmar, is especially critical of adulteresses.

> Hast thou done what some adulteresses are wont to do? When first they
> learn that their lovers wish to take legitimate wives, they thereupon by
> some trick of magic extinguish the male desire, so that they are impotent
> and cannot consummate their union with their legitimate wives. If thou
> hast done or taught others to do this, thou shouldst do penance for forty
> days.[115]

[112] De Divortio Lotharii et Tetbergae XV; PL 140,717.
[113] "Confectum ergo nefariae medicamen scientiae in cibo vel potu viro porrigitur
ignoranti"; edit. W. D. Macray, Chronicon Abbatiae Rameseiensis, RS (London, 1886),
pp. 129–134. Though put together in the main in the late twelfth century, the Chronicle certainly draws upon earlier material. The stepmother pressed matters too far when
she murdered the stepson and persuaded the witch to help her bury him. The witch
then, and interestingly, betrayed her to the local bishop (Ethelric of Dorchester).
Clearly there was a point at which certain magical practitioners could be persuaded to
cooperate with the church, should too much be asked of them and should they trust
the local dignitary. Ethelric, when the whole plot was revealed, including the murder,
administered only penance—again, a leniency which may well have done much to
encourage cooperation on both sides.
[114] Decretum XIX (Corrector); McNeill and Gamer, Medieval Handbooks, p. 331. A
similar passage is to be found in Regino, De Ecclesiasticis Disciplinis II,45 and in the
Decretum X,29; PL 132,284, PL 140,837.
[115] McNeill and Gamer, Medieval Handbooks, p. 340.

Women, then, are seen as particularly prone, through magic, to disrupt the proper course of human love and Christian marriage.

Condemnations of love magic treat in general of two kinds of exercise (although the two are in fact often thought of and condemned together). Firstly, there are potions and spells to excite or quell love: magical aphrodisiacs and procedures which so act upon the emotions of the persons involved that their wills are made subject, and their capacities to consummate their marriages either precociously forced or altogether inhibited. Such spells are to be found once more both in the surviving Greek magical papyri and among defixiones.[116] It was upon a spell of this kind, seemingly, and perhaps one handed down, that Hincmar's hostile mother-of-the-bride depended. Such spells are remembered, too, in the sagas. Queen Gunnhild, for instance, laid one upon Hrut to make him impotent when he left her to marry Unn. It worked.[117] Impotence spells are peculiarly inimical to that strong bond of marriage Christians sought to promote, as I shall try to make more clear below, and the fiercest condemnations of women's powers here seem to be expressed within this context. Secondly, there is birth magic: contraceptive magic, that is, or magic which prevents a woman from carrying her child to full term, or magic which procures abortion. It is difficult to draw an adequate distinction between contraceptive and abortion magic, and indeed the same potion or suppository seems on occasion to have been capable of procuring either effect.[118]

In addition to the sources mentioned above, there are many surviving early medieval poems, sermons, penitentials, and secular law codes that mention love magic, and love magic of both these kinds. The earlier and Greco-Roman ones, interestingly, are not quite so insistent upon the power of women as are the Germanic. The Christian poet Prudentius of the fourth/fifth centuries, for instance, tells of how adept

[116] One demotic spell for separating lovers involves the writing of the spell upon papyrus and burying it under the doorsill of a house: PDM xii; Betz, *The Greek Magical Papyri*, pp. 169–170. Surviving Greek love defixiones seem contrived primarily to disrupt relations between lovers, although outside Greece there are to be found some which provoke, rather than disrupt, love: Jordan, "Defixiones," p. 222.

[117] Njal's Saga VI; transl. M. Magnusson and H. Palsson, *Njal's Saga* (Harmondsworth, Middlesex, 1960), pp. 49–51.

[118] So Burchard, in his *Corrector*, seems to imply; PL 140,972. In a paper he was kind enough to make available to me in draft, "Oral Contraceptives and Early Term abortifacients during Classical Antiquity and the Middle Ages" (to be published in *Past and Present*), Professor John Riddle advances impressive evidence to show that this was indeed the case. Pomegranate peel and rind, "giant fennel," rue, myrrh, and black pepper, for example, can be used to produce such potions or suppositories.

Cyprian of Antioch was at breaking up marriages by spells (necromantic ones, it seems). "He was pre-eminent among young men for skill in the perverse arts ["artibus sinistris"], would violate modesty by a trick, count nothing holy and often practise a magic spell amid the tombs to raise passion in a wife and break the law of wedlock."[119] Assaults upon the virtue of married women seem, indeed, early to be seen as a special skill of those magicians most to be discredited. The Clementine *Homilies* contain passages both interesting and amusing about the magical adventures of would-be adulterers. Appion, a friend of Clement's father, discusses his own adulterous adventures with Clement. "Having fallen in with a certain Egyptian who was exceedingly well versed in magic, and having become his friend, I disclosed to him my love, and not only did he assist me in all that I wished, but honouring me more bountifully, he hesitated not to teach me an incantation by means of which I obtained her." Clement is appalled, though less, and significantly, at the adultery than at the violation of the woman's free choice the spell involved.

> I do not admit that it is a righteous thing to compel to adultery a woman who is unwilling; but if anyone will engage to persuade her, I am ready for that. . . For he who constrains an unwilling woman by the force of magic subjects himself to the most terrible punishment, as having plotted against a chaste woman; but he who persuades her with words, and puts the choice in her own power and will, does not force her.

In the event, the two put Appion's arts of persuasion (unassisted this time by magic) to the test, and, in an episode that approves feminine assertiveness in a manner hard to equal, Appion is sent about his business.[120] The author of the *Homilies*, however, clearly believed in the efficacy of such spells, and, as we have seen, the Clementine literature was widely available in the early Middle Ages. Love magicians were readily to be found, plying their popular trade. Caesarius condemns the seeking out of magicians "harmful to chastity and virtue," and Aelfric that of women who "devise drinks for their wooers, or some mischief that they may have them in marriage."[121]

[119] *Peristephanon* xiii; *edit.* and *transl.* H. J. Thomson, *Prudentius* ii (Loeb Classical Library, 1953), 329–331.

[120] V,iii–vi; *transl.* T. Smith, *The Clementine Homilies* (Edinburgh, 1870), pp. 102–104.

[121] Caesarius, Sermon I; *transl.* Mueller, *Saint Caesarius*, i,12. *Edit.* W. W. Skeat, *Aelfric's Lives of the Saints* (London, 1881), p. 375.

Clerics might be accused in early penitentials of indulging in love-arousing and love-quelling activities (though not all of these indulgences were equally discouraged).

> If any cleric or woman who practises magic have led astray anyone by their magic, it is a monstrous sin, but it can be expiated by penance (six years—three on bread and water). . . . If, however, such a person has not led astray anyone but has given [a potion] for the sake of wanton love to someone, he shall do penance for an entire year on an allowance of bread and water.[122]

It may be that we have here a distinction between a procedure or philter that led to adultery and one that did not. As well as the philters, there are well-attested enchantments "ad fascinum"[123] and love foods,[124] and there are ways of preparing these of a decidedly curious kind.[125] Many are held to produce singularly remarkable effects. The

---

[122] From the sixth-century penitential of Finnean; L. Bieler, The Irish Penitentials (Dublin, 1963), pp. 80–81.

[123] "If anyone sings enchantments for infatuation or any sort of chantings except the holy symbol or the Lord's prayer, he who sings and he to whom he sings shall do penance for the three forty-day periods on bread and water"; Saint Hubert penitential of ca. 850, chapter 54; McNeill and Gamer, Medieval Handbooks, p. 294. A similar ruling is to be found in Burchard's Decretum X, 49, where it is ascribed to the Council of Chalons.

[124] The philter mentioned in the Confessional of Egbert 29 may be a love philter. The penitential attributed to Theodore rules (canon 15) against a practice whereby a wife mixes her husband's semen in food so as to induce him to love her more fervently. Three years' penance seems to be adjudged. McNeill and Gamer, Medieval Handbooks, pp. 196, 246. This way of exciting love, and another which involves the mixing of menstrual blood with food and drink, is referred to again by Rabanus in his Poenitentiale ad Heribaldum xxv, xxx; PL 110,490,491. It finds its way into both Regino and Burchard. Rabanus mentions too the practice of administering a dead man's testicles, ground to powder, as an aphrodisiac, and this also concerns Burchard; see C. Vogel, "Pratiques superstitieuses au début du XIᵉ siècle d'après le Corrector sive Medicus de Burchard évêque de Worms (965–1025)," in Études de civilisation médiévale (IXᵉ–XIIᵉ siècles), Mèlanges offerts à Edmond-René Labande (Poitiers, 1974), 751–761.

[125] "Hast thou done what some women are wont to do? They take off their clothes and anoint their whole naked body with honey, and laying down their honey smeared body upon wheat on some linen on the earth, roll to and fro often, then carefully gather all the grains of wheat which stick to the moist body, place it in a mill, and make the mill go round backwards against the sun and so grind it to flour; and they make bread from that flour and then give it to their husbands to eat, that on eating the bread they may become feeble and pine away. If thou hast [done this], thou shalt do penance for forty days on bread and water." Burchard, Corrector; McNeill and

Visigothic laws speak of adulteresses who manage by witchcraft to persuade their husbands by magic to turn a blind eye to their activities.[126]

Contraceptive and abortion magic are both very roundly penalized in ecclesiastical legislation, often in the words of the Fathers or Caesarius[127] and with a singular consistency.[128] The bewitching of a pregnant woman so that her child is born dead or lives only for a short time is condemned in the Alamannic laws,[129] and the laws of the Salian and Ripuarian Franks rule against a woman who has committed "maleficium," with the result that she cannot bear children,[130] and against women who give magic potions to other women so that the latter cannot.[131] Later preachers also deal with the problem. Birth and abortion witchcraft is attacked, for example, in the *Homilia de Sacrilegiis*,[132] perhaps again following Caesarius's strictures.

A part of this disapproval stemmed, of course, from simple objections to interferences of this kind with the production of children, but it sprang too from the fact that some of the procedures and potions,

---

Gamer, *Medieval Handbooks*, pp. 340–341. In an earlier passage Burchard refers to women who have bread kneaded upon their bare backs and then cooked to increase their husbands' ardor; PL 140,974. These procedures, interestingly, seem to have an echo of certain ones found in the Greek magical papyri which also use honey: PGM VII, PDM XIV; Betz, *The Greek Magical Papyri*, pp. 120, 245.

[126] "Quia quorundam interdum uxores, viros suos abominantes seseque adulterio polluentes, ita potionibus quibusdam vel maleficiorum factionibus eorundem virorum mentes alienant adque precipitant, ut nec agnitum uxoris adulterium accusare publice vel defendere valeant, nec ab eiusdem adultere coniugis consortio vel dilectione discedant." *Recc. Erv. Chind.* III,4,13; *edit.* K. Zeumer, *MGH Legum 1, Leges Visigothorum* (Hanover and Leipzig, 1902), 152.

[127] As in the late seventh- or early eighth-century Irish collection of canons, XLV,4,5; *edit.* F.H.W. Wasserschleben, *Die Irische Kanonensammlung* (Leipzig, 1885), p. 181.

[128] Numerous rulings may be found in McNeill and Gamer, *Medieval Handbooks*. Regino's strictures against it (PL 132,282) reappear in Burchard, PL 140,933. In his *Corrector* Burchard speaks of the use of "maleficia" and herbs to prevent conception or bring about an abortion; PL 140,972.

[129] *Transl.* T. J. Rivers, *Laws of the Alamans and the Bavarians* (Philadelphia, 1977), p. 93.

[130] *Pactum Lex Salicae* 19,4; *edit.* K. A. Eckhardt, *Pactus Legis Salicae* (Göttingen, 1954–1956; repr., Hanover, 1962), p. 82.

[131] 19,4; *transl.* T. J. Rivers, *Laws of the Salian and Ripuarian Franks* (New York, 1986), p. 63.

[132] "If any poisoner or wizard ["maleficus"] or anyone who does things to women through witchcraft so brings it about that women fail to conceive or miscarry their offspring, they are not Christians but pagans." Caspari, *Homilia*, p. 11 (MT).

aphrodisiac ones included, were thought to be dangerous; and doubtless many were, and in many different ways. Magic potions from which
death resulted could, after all, in some early law codes, mean death for
the person who administered the potion,[133] as well as death for the
victim, should the abortion itself be fatal or the potion be too strong
or wrongly prepared. Should they go wrong, then, such magical activities could have repercussions of a very serious kind, as they can in
more modern societies.[134] Before dismissing all of this disapproval,
then, as obdurately antagonistic to the rights of women, we must consider this aspect of it. The Penitential of Columban of ca. 600 (seemingly following that of Finnean) includes a regulation which is often
repeated, and in markedly similar words, whereby comparatively heavy
penances are prescribed for a person who acts as a magician "for the
sake of love but destroys nobody,"[135] as though the danger of destroying
somebody were really rather high. Rulings of this kind, which deal
with "magic which does not cause anyone's death," may often have
both love philters and contraceptive or abortion procedures in mind,
for they frequently have an additional puzzling clause which speaks of
the deceiving of a woman "with respect to the birth of a child." Contraceptive magic and love-arousal or fertility magic could clearly be
connected, and their very connection could call down upon them both
severe objections, but for reasons of physical peril as well as moral and
material disapproval. Gerbold of Liege (d. 810) condemns in the same
breath both women who administer potions for the destruction of em-
bryos and those who make magic of a kind which will cause their husbands to love them more.[136]

The reasons behind these perceptions, and the highly varied penances we can find prescribed for such delicts, are complex and inter-
woven, and—given the tumbled and scattered state of the surviving
sermons, and secular and ecclesiastical legislation on the subject, and
the difficulty of deciding exactly upon the sources of each type—it is

[133] *Laws of the Salian and Ripuarian Franks* 19,1; transl. Rivers, *Laws*, p. 62.
[134] See R. Bowden, "Sorcery, Illness and Social Control in Kwoma Society," in *edit.*
M. Stephens, *Sorcerer and Witch in Melanesia* (Melbourne, 1987), p. 190.
[135] Five years for a priest, then steadily down the scale to six months for a layman.
McNeill and Gamer, *Medieval Handbooks*, pp. 252–253. This ruling is also found in
the Burgundian Penitential of ca. 700–725 and in the ninth-century so-called Roman
Penitential; *ibid.*, pp. 274, 305.
[136] Diocesan Statutes; *edit.* C. De Clercq, *La Législation Religieuse Franque* (Louvain,
1936), p. 360.

at present impossible, even with the most relentless diligence, adequately to describe and place all early medieval attitudes to love magic. There are, however, certain observations we can make about these with relative security, and they are all observations which bear upon the rise of Christian magic in general. Firstly, it does seem true to say that some of the concern the early European Christian authorities expressed about the activities of women at their weaving may have been connected with a larger concern they certainly did feel about the magical expertise displayed by women in matters of human love; and that woman were, in the period, generally thought to be preeminent in this last sphere as well. Secondly, it also seems that the interventions of women in matters of love earned them a form of censure which was widely supported and especially severe. Indeed, were we to set ourselves to search for a type of magic with which no Christian accommodation seemed possible, our search could well appear to have come to an end with love magic. Such an appearance is, however, deceptive, and probing beneath it is, in this case, exceptionally instructive. A form of Christian love magic made respectable did come to be encouraged, and the apparent repression and vilification of women needs here most particularly to be placed within a much larger social context—a context in which, I hope to argue, this vilification was neither in every way repressive of every type of love magic, nor, on all counts, of the well-being and social positions of women. On the contrary, it in fact supported a Christianized love magic of a kind and was designed to do so, and that precisely because of this larger social context within which women operated, and, even more importantly, because of the oppressions, indeed injustices perhaps, to which they were vulnerable. The "ecclesiastical medicine" administered by the bishop in the early mother-in-law story told by Hincmar, for example, seems to have included a form of Christian magic of a more powerful type, yet one at the same time far less dangerous to the accused, than the condemned magic purveyed by the supposed witch. A particular kind of Christian countermagic may, in short, have had as its object rather the saving of women from the results of prohibited love magic's successes (death by poison or punishment, that is), than the condemnation of love magic in its every form.[137] We shall return to this.

[137] It is possible, too, to look at the ecclesiastical condemnations of women's making magic in their weaving in this light. Involvement in love magic while at their weaving may have rendered them vulnerable to fierce secular retribution.

Once more, it is worth taking general note that not all ancient love-magic beliefs were frowned upon with equal harshness, and this again for complex and well-considered reasons, reasons often associated with the preservation of persons accused of magic from too severe a form of revenge. A memory of the magical incubi and succubi of a pagan past, demons thought capable of assuming a human shape and seducing their victims (called among the Franks "Dusii"), for instance, persisted; it was even indulged by no less a figure than Saint Augustine.[138] It is spoken of, again, by both Hincmar and Rabanus,[139] and Burchard mentions a belief in "sylvan ones" who make love, then vanish—a belief for which he prescribes a very light penalty indeed.[140] The belief persisted well into the twelfth century.[141] Dusii or *sylvaticae* could be blamed for a state of affairs, an adulterous pregnancy, perhaps, which might bring down a savage penalty at purely secular hands. There were, then, sound Christian reasons for perpetuating belief in magic of this sort, as there had been for bringing the demons through as a whole. Certain love spells were also brought through, and under a like impulsion. Finally, and paradoxically, the need to obliterate the wholly destructive aspects of non-Christian belief in love magic may have provided for the Christianization and rise, in certain circles, of a quite startling number of other less alarming forms of supernatural exercise. These included Christianized sortes, weaving, and certain types of binding-and-loosing spells, and they served both as an attempted corrective to these misdirected love spells in compensation for their loss, and in protection of some of the losers. Love magic, though an important part, was still only a part of a great complex of interrelationships between unacceptable and acceptable practice. We shall deal with all these questions more fully in the next chapter.

[138] *City of God* XV,23; *edit.* and *transl.* P. Levine, *Saint Augustine the City of God Against the Pagans* iv (Loeb Classical Library, 1966), 548–551.

[139] Hincmar, *De Divortio* XV; *PL* 125,725. Rabanus, *Commentaria in Genesim* II,v; *PL* 107,512.

[140] *Corrector*; McNeill and Gamer, *Medieval Handbooks*, p. 338.

[141] Guibert of Nogent, for instance, tells us that "stories about demons who covet the love of women and even [have] intercourse with them are widely circulated, and if it were not shameful, we could tell a great many of them. There are some who are barbarous in inflicting their wickedness, and others who are content with sport alone." He was sure, moreover, that his own mother had been attacked by one. *De Vita Sua*, I,13, III,19; *transl.* J. F. Benton, *Self and Society in Medieval France* (repr., Toronto, 1984), pp. 69–70, 223.

OUTLAWED MEDICAL MAGIC

Pliny, in a passage at the very beginning of that book of his *Natural History* which he devotes to magic, insists that magic as a whole took its origins from medicine. It yoked itself, he suggests, and for its own nefarious purposes, to those especially deep human fears and desires the onset of illness arouses.

> Nobody will doubt that [magic] first arose from medicine, and that professing to promote health it insidiously advanced under the disguise of a higher and holier system; that to the most seductive and welcome promises it added the powers of religion, about which even today the human race is quite in the dark; that again meeting with success it made a further addition of astrology, because there is nobody who is not eager to learn his destiny, or who does not believe that the truest account of it is that gained by watching the skies. Accordingly, holding men's emotions in a three-fold bond, magic rose to such a height that even today it has sway over a great part of mankind.[142]

The religious element of medical magic, so clearly recognized here by Pliny, meant that the problem of medicine was absolutely central to the struggles of the medieval church with magical practice in general. As we have seen, predictive and curative medical magic, both that which was rejected and that which was brought through, made up an exceedingly important part of the magic of the heavens, and it will inform some of the capacities allowed to the rescued magus too (and constitute, indeed, one reason for his rescue). Furthermore, as Pliny also pointed out, astrology could easily be annexed to medicine, for illness might be both caused and affected by the heavenly bodies, the moon especially. The recognition of this fact did much, of course, to bring about the rescue of astrology itself. Much illness, "pestilence" particularly, was, in addition, associated with the demons of the air, with the noxious vapors which they stirred up as they flew, or with the arrows which they shot.

There is much, then, to suggest that Pliny is right, and that it is to medicine and healing as a whole that we should look for our truest guides to all those processes whereby magic came to be incorporated into the Christian religion, with the greatest part of our attention de-

---

[142] XXX,l; *edit. and transl.* W.H.S. Jones, *Pliny Natural History* viii (Loeb Classical Library, 1975), 278–279.

voted to the medical magic of the heavens and its manipulators. To treat of medical magic, then, as a subsection of the magic of the earth is not to do it justice. I do nonetheless propose to treat it here in this subsection, and for one very particular reason. To be sure, medical matters constitute an important part of that earthly magic we have already discussed. Anxieties about pain and sickness were prominent among those whose relief was sought at shrines, and the shrine destroyed by Saint Gall of Clermont seems, indeed, to have been chiefly given over to such anxieties. So does that destroyed by Saint Amand near Beauvais. Lots were frequently cast to give answers to questions about the course and outcome of an illness,[143] the sick could have magical enchantments woven for them and amazing potions brewed, and the illnesses brought about by love unrequited or unwanted were, and are, too evident to be in need of further rehearsal here. My main reason for treating of medical magic now and in this place, however, is a different one. I hope, by focusing upon those medical practices in which earthly ingredients and contact with the earth predominate, to draw sharp attention to certain special features of it—features that offer, in their turn, support for those general propositions about the rise of Christian magic I have been trying throughout to advance. The first proposition has been perhaps sufficiently stressed already, but I stress it again for good measure. It is that saints and religious communities were able to exercise a tremendous influence over the rise of magic, because, once more, of their ways with the demons. The idea that earthly illness of the most serious sort came from the aery regions in which demons were so overwhelmingly strong, and humankind so unbearably weak, helped to give those who followed the way of the cross an exceptional authority here, and this authority is imprinted especially clearly upon this aspect of the surviving medical evidence. A second, much more important, proposition follows from the first. It is that these saints and religious communities, embedded as they were within the life of the localities, exercised their influence with a surpassing sensitivity to local needs. This sensitivity is also in fact most clearly made evident in the magical medical practices they condoned.

We are not, perhaps, quite as well-conditioned to accept this prop-

---

[143] At least three sections of the *Sortes Sangallenses*, according to Dold, were devoted to questions about illness: Dold and Meister, "Die Orakelsprüche," pp. 50–51. Gregory of Tours speaks of a "hariolus" called in to attend a boy stricken with plague, a part of whose pretended cures consisted in the casting of lots: *Liber de Passione et Virtutibus Sancti Iuliani Martyris* 46a; *edit.* Krusch, MGH SRM, i(2), 132.

osition as we might be, schooled as we often are to think rather in terms of monastic ignorance than of monastic pastoral and medical adroitness, and of the survival rather than the conscious deployment of "superstitious" practices; and my reiterated view that such communities were, instead, exceptionally skillful, and that their skills are best shown in their preservation of earthly magico-medical practices, is, I think, a new one. Also new is a third proposition connected with this second one: that the pastoral sensitivities of these saints and communities for whose pressing importance I would argue are especially vividly to be seen in that medical evidence which survives from Anglo-Saxon England, and among English Benedictine communities. Evidence of such capacities is not, of course, confined to the English material and communities; but it is registered upon this record particularly sharply. I have chosen, therefore, to single it out. In order fully to appreciate it, however, we must look at the Anglo-Saxon magico-medical texts (in which we are exceptionally rich) from a perspective rather different from that we have been accustomed to use. This fresh perspective may, I hope, lead us at least to consider two further propositions. These are, that the monastic choices made in matters of medical magic, and the medicinal disguises provided, may have had a fundamental effect upon the rise of Christian magic in general. These disguises best guaranteed the crossing of the frontier between condemned and acceptable supernatural practice; and their success helped other magical practices to cross it too. Pliny *is* right; medicine *is* our best clue. But, fundamental though it is, it forms only a part of a great and intricate complex; and though we might best start to make out its impact with the help of the English material, this is the first, and not the last, corpus to which we should look.

I use this subsection of a truly mighty question, then, contentiously. I shall discuss here, with these propositions in mind, therefore, only selected kinds of condemned yet partly rescued earthly medical magic—kinds that illustrate peculiarly vividly the strength of monastic influence, the thoughtfulness with which it was deployed, the possible impact of rescued medical magic upon other aspects of rescued magic (and upon science), and the contortions and divisions of opinion which the problem of selecting from magic could, in general, bring about. Monks might have been in the majority as far as Christian written record goes, but they were certainly not alone; this fact needs also to be kept constantly in mind. The specific kinds are medical ligatures and amulets, curing stones, charms,[144] prescriptions to be swallowed, and curious medico-magical methods and views upon time.

Two elements among the practices of non-Christian magicians unfailingly drove pastors into a fury. These were, firstly, the habit of tying, or binding, or putting onto sick or injured people supposedly curative ligatures; and, secondly, the administering to them of "execrable remedies" in potions or powders (perhaps involving these same ligatures).[145] One need only turn to Pliny, once more, for an idea of why these remedies were thought to be so execrable.

> I shall include several of the magicians' remedies, and in the first place the amulets they recommend [remedia . . quae adalligari iubent]: the dust in which a hawk has rolled himself tied in a linen cloth by a red thread, or the longest tooth of a black dog. The wasp they call pseudosphex, that flies about by itself, they catch with the left hand and hang under the chin, and others use the first wasp seen in that year; a severed viper's head attached in a linen cloth, or the heart taken from the creature while still alive; the snout and ear tips of a mouse, the mouse itself being allowed to go free; the right eye gouged out of a living lizard; a fly in a bit of goat skin, with its head cut off; or the beetle that rolls little pellets . . . four joints of a scorpion's tail, with the sting, wrapped in black cloth, care being taken that the sick man does not see, for three days, either the scorpion when set free or him who attaches the amulet.[146]

The last recommendation is perhaps the most readily understandable of all. Pliny has many more such illustrations, and endless prescriptions for magical potions, of which the following (for epilepsy) might give the general flavor. "Some are of opinion that a vulture's breast should be taken in drink in a cup made of Turkey-oak wood, or the

[144] Here again the Latin terms are not always used uniformly, and they have not always a clear modern English equivalent. *Ligatura*, for instance, need not mean something actually tied, and it could mean the same as amulet, as it does, it seems, occasionally when Saint Augustine uses it. *De Doctrina Christiana* II,20; transl. J. J. Gavigan, *Saint Augustine, Christian Instruction* (Washington, 1947), p. 88. I use these terms here simply to designate objects, applied and used very variously, but all meant to protect or cure from illness.

[145] "Ad haec omnia pertinent [to the activities of magicians, that is] et ligaturae execrabilium remediorum, quae ars medicorum condemnat, sive in praecantationibus, sive in characteribus, vel in quibuscumque rebus suspendendis atque ligandis." Isidore, *Etymologiae* VIII,ix,30; edit. W. M. Lindsay, *Isidori Hispalensis Episcopi Etymologiarum sive Originum Libri XX* (Oxford, 1911).

[146] *Natural History* XXX,xxx,98–101; transl. Jones, *Pliny*, viii,340–343.

testicles of a cock in water and milk, after abstinence from wine for five days; for this purpose the testicles are preserved. There have also been some who give in drink twenty one red flies, and that too from a corpse, but fewer to weak patients."[147]

Augustine has a fierce and illuminating passage upon such magical medicinal remedies in his *De Doctrina Christiana*, bringing in demons, as usual, to drive his message home.

> Whatever has been conceived by men for fashioning and worshipping idols is superstitious, since it concerns the worship of a created thing, or some part of it, as God, or else concerns communications and certain arrangements and pacts with demons about portents. . . . To this category belong . . . all amulets and charms, of which the science of medicine also disapproves, whether these involve enchantments, or certain signs called "characters," or the hanging, attaching, or even in a way the dancing of certain objects, not in relation to the bodily condition, but according to certain portents, either obscure or evident. These are more leniently termed "physics," that they may seem as if they were not involved in superstition, but only profiting by nature. Instances of these are earrings hung at the tip of each ear, or small rings of ostrich bone worn on the fingers, or telling a person with hiccups to hold the left thumb in the right hand.[148]

He condemns them also in his *Enarratio in Psalmos*[149] and has an even more ferocious section upon them in his *Treatise on Saint John's Gospel*, in which he warns Christians against the seductive power of such remedies, and especially against the tendency to substitute a Christian prayer for an attached incantation—a wholly futile attempt to render the process respectable, according to the saint.[150] Isidore possibly relies

[147] *Natural History* XXX,xxvii,92 ; ibid., viii,336–337.

[148] II,20; transl. Gavigan, *Saint Augustine*, p. 88.

[149] Commenting upon Ps. 33:13, "keep your tongue from evil"—"Tales sunt homines, qui et facere volunt mala, et iurare mendacium, et blasphemare contra Deum, et murmurare, et fraudem facere, et inebriari, et litigare, et adulterari, *et ligaturas adhibere, et ire ad sortilegos*"; edit. E. Dekkers and J. Fraipont, *Sancti Aurelii Augustini Enarrationes in Psalmos I–L*, CC (Turnholt, 1956), p. 294.

[150] "Fingunt enim spiritus mali umbras quasdam honoris sibimetipsis, ut sic decipiant eos qui sequuntur Christum. Usque adeo, fratres mei, ut illi ipsi qui seducunt per ligaturas, per praecantationes, per machinamenta inimici, misceant praecantationes suis nomen Christi, quia iam non possunt seducere christianos, ut dent venenum, addunt mellis aliquid, ut per id quod dulce est, lateat quod amarum est, et bibatur ad perniciem"; edit. A. Mayer, *Sancti Aurelii Augustini In Iohannis Evangelium Tractatus CXXIV*, CC (Turnholt, 1954), p. 70.

upon Augustine for the section of his *De Magis* mentioned above in which he castigates such ligatures.

As well as Augustine, Isidore, and their immediate emulators, most of our other now familiar sources of prohibition condemn curative practices such as these explicitly, along with other forms of objectionable magical activity. Caesarius, predictably, is as appalled by them as is Isidore.

> If you still see men . . . hanging devilish phylacteries, magic signs, herbs, or [amber] charms on themselves or their family, rebuke them harshly.

> Do not hang on yourself and your family diabolical phylacteries, magic letters, amber charms and herbs.

> Let noone in any sickness dare to summon or question sorcerers or seers or magicians in wicked pleasure. Noone should hang phylacteries or charms on themselves or their possessions.[151]

He speaks of persons being tempted into the wrong type of behavior, and in two passages he is helpfully explicit about the form this wrongfulness took.

> Let us consult that soothsayer, seer, oracle or witch. Let us sacrifice a garment of the sick person, a girdle that can be measured. Let us offer some magic letters, let us hang some charms upon his neck.

> It usually happens, brethren, that a persecutor on the side of the devil comes to a sick man and says: If you had summoned that magician, you would already be cured. If you had been willing to hang those superstitious signs on you, you would already have recovered your health. . . . Perhaps another man comes and says; Send to that soothsayer, transmit your cincture or fillet to him so he can measure it and look at it. Then he himself will tell you what to do, or whether you can escape. Still another says: That man knows very well how to fumigate; and everyone for whom he has done this immediately felt better, and every attack left his house. . . . The devil is wont, in this way, to deceive careless and lukewarm Christians.[152]

And if Caesarius, of course, then Eligius. Curative "ligamina," bits of amber, as it might be, hung round the necks of people or animals, are inadmissible, says Eligius, even if they are put together by clerics who

---

[151] Sermons 13, 14, 19; *transl.* Mueller, *Saint Caesarius*, i,78,82,101. The Latin "sucinos" in the original, translated by "charms" here, in fact means amber charms.

[152] Sermons 52 and 184; ibid., i,262, ii,481.

say that such things are holy, and even if the writings they contain are "lectio divina" (presumably passages from Scripture).[153] Eligius's biographer here, of course, reveals that there were in fact "clerici" who were prepared to make compromises in such matters. Martin of Braga, too, tackles the problem of clergy who seem to wish to be thought of as magicians and to make amulets, and with a similar firmness.[154]

We seem to be seeing in such condemnations, once again, reactions to an obstinate effort at adaptation not unlike that which Pope Pelagius condemned in the case of Sapaudus and the wheat-flour images, and traceable, in fact, in much of the evidence to be explored in the next chapter. Anxieties about healing were clearly appallingly difficult to quell, and traditional remedies such as these equally difficult to outlaw. The condemnations continue unabated nonetheless. The Visigothic laws object to the use of ligatures, perhaps with letters on them thought to be magical, and so does the Carolingian recension of the *Lex Salica*.[155] Boniface berates them in sermons,[156] and they appear as chapter 10 of the *Indiculus Superstitionum*. Boniface is clearly supported by a comprehensive ruling made at the 747 English Council of Clovesho against "divinos, sortilegos, auguria, auspicia, fylacteria, incantationes."[157] The anonymous *Homilia de Sacrilegiis* becomes quite ex-

---

[153] "Nullus ad colla vel hominis vel cuiuslibet animalis ligamine dependere praesumat, etiamsi a clericis fiant, etsi dicatur quod res sancta sit et lectiones divinas contineat, quia non est in eis remedium Christi, sed venenum diaboli. . . . Nulla mulier praesumat sucinos ad collum dependere." *Vita Eligii Episcopi Noviomagensis* II, 16a; *edit.* Krusch and Levison, MGH SRM, iv, 706. We know from archaeological sources that amber was exceptionally popular as a curative and protective substance, and Pliny, of course, reports as much: Meaney, *Anglo-Saxon Amulets*, pp. 67–71 and nn.

[154] He does so in canon 59 of his capitula, compiled from the Greek and attached to the rulings of the Second Council of Braga; *edit.* Barlow, *Martin Episcopi Bracarensis*, p. 138.

[155] *Recc. Erv. Chind.* VI, 2, 5: "Iubemus, seu ingenuus sit, sive servus utriusque sexus, qui in hominibus vel brutis animalibus omnique genere, quod mobile esse potest, seu in agris vel vineis diversisque arboribus maleficium aut diversa ligamenta aut etiam scriptis in contrarietatem alterius excogitaverint facere aut expleverint, per quod alium ledere vel mortificare aut obmutescere vellint, ut damnum tam in corporibus quam etiam in universis rebus fecisse repperiuntur"; *edit.* Zeumer, MGH *Legum*, i, 260. "Si quis alteri aliquod maleficium superiactaverit sive sum ligaturis in quolibet loco miserit, IIMD den(arii) qui f(aciunt)"; *edit.* K. A. Eckhardt, *Lex Salica*, MGH *Legum* iv (Hanover, 1969), 66.

[156] Sermons VI and XV; *PL* 89, 855, 870.

[157] A. W. Haddan and W. Stubbs, *Councils and Ecclesiastical Documents Relating to Great Britain and Ireland* iii (Oxford, 1869–1878), 363–364.

pansive on the matter of pagan incantations and ligatures for healing, and it condemns explicitly one form of neck amulet (containing a snake's tongue) which is reminiscent of the severed viper's head in Pliny. It also objects to "salomoniacas scripturas" and amulets with writing on them, hung round the necks of men or beasts, and the use of gold rings for eye afflictions, and all forms of remedy of this sort describable as pagan.[158] Hincmar specifies the tying on of ligatures among the many bewitchments to which he draws attention, and he also denounces cures that involve the measurement of the patient, perhaps with thread, as a form of talismanic protection.[159] Capitularies and councils, admirably summed up by Burchard, reissue regulations against "phylacteria" and "incantationes" along with the magicians who presumably tie them on, apply them, and chant them,[160] and penitentials, once more, are full of quite fierce penances for their use. The eighth-century so-called Bedan penitential prescribes a five-year penalty for clerics who attach "diabolical amulets whether of grass or amber to their people or to themselves" and a five- or three-year one for a layman.[161] Aelfric also objects to amulets and ligatures.[162]

The condemnable ligatures were, however, still certainly very widely applied. We might deduce as much from the repetitive rulings, but there is much extra evidence too. Caesarius in his sermons is clearly inveighing against very common practices, and the "If only you had . . ." style of argument he denounces has power over the vulnerable. When Gregory of Tours tells us that "harioli" came to attend to the sick wife of Serenatus, or to the boy ill with the fever, or to the young man who became faint while hunting, and when the biographer of Iunianus the Confessor describes how his "fideles" called "malefici" to the rich Ruricius,[163] all show that ligatures formed an essential part

[158] Caspari, Homilia, pp. 9–12.

[159] De Divortio; PL 125,719.

[160] For instance the ca. 769 code of Charlemagne, chapters 6 and 7, repeating earlier rulings, especially those of Carloman; edit. Boretius, MGH Capitularia, ii(1)25,45. Burchard summarizes the rulings of selected earlier councils in Decretum X,18,23,33; PL 140,835–838.

[161] Chapters 4 and 5; McNeill and Gamer, Medieval Handbooks, p. 229. Burchard, in the Corrector, however, asks only forty days on bread and water; PL 140,964.

[162] In his sermons on the passion of Saint Bartholomew and on the Nativity of Saint Stephen; edit. and transl. B. Thorpe, The Homilies of the Anglo-Saxon Church i (London, 1844), 476–477, ii (London, 1846), 29–30.

[163] De Virtutibus S. Martini I,26, IV,36, Liber de Passione et Virtutibus Sancti Iuliani

of the treatments proposed by such healers, accompanied in some cases with lot casting, brews, and incantations. In his *History of the Franks* Gregory describes the large following two such "malefici" attracted to them, and the collection an outraged bishop confiscated from the second. "There was found on him a large bag full of the roots of various herbs; there were also in it moles' teeth, bones of mice, and the claws and grease of bears. Seeing that all these things were instruments of witchcraft, the bishop ordered them to be thrown into the river."[164] Baggage of a seemingly similar type, this time belonging to an enchantress called in to heal the son of a local prince, so incensed Saint Corbinianus (d. 725) that he forgot himself and physically ejected her and all her equipment from the precincts of the palace.[165] The saint was very nearly murdered by the prince's following for his pains. Hincmar of Rheims speaks of the use by witches of bones, ashes, coals, hair, bits of colored thread, herbs, snail shells, and snakes, all sometimes employed as "medicamenta."[166]

We might perhaps see something similar to the remedies proscribed by Gregory and Hincmar (even to those thrown out by Saint Corbinianus) in the little bags or boxes of Anglo-Saxon and Germanic curative equipment so revealingly described by Professor Meaney, and often to be found in women's graves of a somewhat exceptional kind. Such assemblages would also include animals' teeth (in one case that of a bear) and headbones, and such possible instruments of witchcraft as rings (perhaps iron)[167] and pierced coins.[168] Sometimes the forbidden amber beads are found in the same graves as the amulet bags. Certainly very many amber beads are to be found in early European graves,

---

Martyris 46a; *edit.* Krusch, MGH SRM, i(2),132,151,208–209. *Vita Iuniani Confessoris Commodoliacensis* 6–7; *edit.* B. Krusch, MGH SRM iii (Hanover, 1896), 378–379.

[164] IX,6; *transl.* O. M. Dalton, *The History*, ii,374. The charge that they were merely animal bones was, ironically, one frequently levied against Catholic relics at the time of the Reformation. It was levied, for example, against the relics stolen by the Protestant mob from the Carmelite monastery of Albiac in 1561: N. Z. Davis, *Society and Culture in Early Modern France* (London, 1975), p. 157. By then, of course, the circumstances which had dictated the original collection of such bones by the orthodox (and to which we shall attend in the next chapter) had vanished.

[165] *Vita Corbiniani Episcopi Baiuvariorum Retractata* B; *edit.* B. Krusch and W. Levison, MGH SRM vi (Hanover and Leipzig, 1913), 624–625.

[166] *De Divortio*, XV; PL 125,717.

[167] Iron rings are mentioned in the *Homilia de Sacrilegiis* VI,22 as instruments in pagan rites against demons; *edit.* Caspari, *Homilia*, pp. 11–12.

[168] Meaney, *Anglo-saxon Amulets*, pp. 249–262.

and so too are amethyst and crystal beads, almost certainly as magical, and so forbidden, as amber. Rock crystal beads are to be found in tenth-century Viking women's graves.[169] A famous chapter in Bede's *Life of Saint Cuthbert* tells how persons afraid of the plague took immediately to "incantationes vel alligaturas," to that saint's distress.[170] Aelfric too, though clearly he knew of the condemnations uttered both by Augustine and by Caesarius and depended upon both writers for many of his descriptions, seems, in his Sermon on the Nativity of Saint Stephen, to express disapproval of a contemporary ring-amulet that was chosen and worn with care.[171] As well as berating ligatures and phylacteries, Burchard, in his *Corrector*, refers to some strikingly "execrable remedies" that apparently still had currency.[172]

It is not difficult to find reasons, both scientific and aesthetic, for the sustained loathing with which ligatures and amulets such as those described by Pliny and excoriated by Christian hagiographers and pastors were viewed. Also, many of their supposedly supernatural curative powers sprang from religious dispositions Christianity was anxious to displace. I mentioned the problem of fear in the matter of Willibrord and the sacred spring. Fear seems to have prompted the adoption of many of these protective and healing remedies. Fear of the illness the

[169] Pliny, *Natural History* XXXVII,xl, traces the magical qualities attributed to amethyst and its inferior form, rock crystal, back to the magi; *transl.* D. E. Eichholz, *Pliny*, x,264–267. The beads may possibly have been used in a form of lot casting similar to that described by Tedlock, *Time*, pp. 62–64.

[170] IX; *edit.* and *transl.* B. Colgrave, *Two Lives of St. Cuthbert* (Cambridge, 1940), pp. 158–159. Bede clearly felt strongly about this, for he mentions the matter again in his *Ecclesiastical History*, IV, 27, referring to the "fylacteria" and "incantationes" as "erratica idolatriae medicamina"; *edit.* and *transl.* B. Colgrave and R.A.B. Mynors, *Bede's Ecclesiastical History of the English People* (Oxford, 1969), pp. 432–433.

[171] *Edit.* and *transl.* Thorpe, *The Homilies*, ii,29. Meaney, *Anglo-Saxon Amulets*, pp. 77, 108–109. This whole book bears witness to the enormous numbers of amulets currently in use in Anglo-Saxon England, and it shows both how very well based Bede's alarms were and how urgent and difficult the problem of persistent non-Christian curative magic certainly was, both there and in many other parts of early Europe.

[172] "Comedisti scabiem corporalem pro aliqua sanitate, aut bibisti propter solutionem vermiculos qui pediculi vocantur, vel bibisti urinam humanam, sive stercora aliqua comedisti pro sanitate aliqua?"; "Fecisti quod quaedam mulieres facere solent? Tollunt testam hominis, et igni comburunt, et cinerem dant viris suis ad bibendum pro sanitate?"; *PL* 140,968,974. "Leavings" and bodily remains may have been the common stock-in-trade of the early medieval sorcerer as they can be of more modern ones: A. Forge, "Prestige, Influence and Sorcery. A New Guinea Example," in *edit.* M. Douglas, *Witchcraft Confessions and Accusations* (London, 1970), pp. 261–262.

evil eye and *fascinatio* might inflict[173] perhaps stood behind the possession of whorled rings and shining deflecting stones and substances, fear
of the ferocious attack of disease behind the treasuring of boars' teeth
and bear claws, fear simply of great, and potentially hostile, strength
and power behind much of the reverence shown for iron. Fear and
disgust, too, seem deliberately to have been aroused by many of the
creatures and materials the magi chose to use. Christianity at its best,
of course, had no wish to rule through the raw emotion of fear, or to
trade upon the repellent. Yet the real reason for the horror expressed
at these cures lies, I suspect, in a third area. Non-Christian magicians
(and quite often it seems, in Germanic areas, female ones) were in very
great demand in matters of medicine, and obviously legerdemain of a
serious kind was involved, at least on the face of it, in such exercises
as catching a wasp with the left hand—a dexterity impressive, perhaps,
to many, and understandably so. Also, some of the purveyors of the
medical ligatures at least pretended to a particular austerity of life.[174]
Magical ligatures and remedies were execrable because of the horrors
they normally contained, and the wrongful play upon the emotions
these horrors involved, but much more so because they formed an important part of the stock-in-trade of the numerous supernatural opposition; and, in default of remedies more convincing still, it was difficult
and perhaps cruel to detach people wholly from them.

Other magico-medical practices also clearly caused objections.
Some of these can be found in penitentials. Placing a child "upon a
roof or into an oven for the cure of a fever" could earn the miscreant a
penance of seven years.[175] The *Indiculus Superstitionum*, chapter 17,

[173] Fascinatio of this sort seems to have affected no less a personage than King Alfred; *edit*. W. H. Stevenson, *Life of King Alfred* (Oxford, 1904), p. 55.

[174] Gregory of Tours claims that such pretences were fake. "He wore a tunic and
hood of goat's hair, and in public practised abstinence in the matter of food and drink.
But in private, at the inn, he gorged himself to such a point that the servant waiting
on him could not keep pace with his greed." *History of the Franks* IX,6; *transl*. Dalton,
The History, i,373. We may, perhaps, suspect special pleading, for, fake or not, they
clearly carried an alarming measure of conviction.

[175] The so-called penitential of Theodore, I,xv,2 (a compilation possibly of the late
seventh century); McNeill and Gamer, *Medieval Handbooks*, p. 198. The same prohibition occurs in the eighth-century Egbert penitential, VIII,2, and in the so-called
confessional of Egbert, found in the eleventh-century MS Corpus Christi College,
Cambridge, 190, one of Leofric's gifts to Exeter; ibid., pp. 246–247. Burchard, in
Book X,14 of his *Decretum*, reduces the penance to one year, and in the *Corrector*, to
twenty days; *PL* 140,835,964.

speaks "De observatione pagana in foco." A curious little passage in Burchard's *Corrector* suggests that the practice may still have been current in the early eleventh century.[176] Also forbidden was an apparently popular method of curing children of illness by drawing them through some sort of aperture (perhaps a sort of simulated rebirth)—most often one made in the earth. This too is banned in penitentials and is specifically prohibited in the so-called Canons of Edgar of the early eleventh century,[177] and by Aelfric.[178] MS Corpus Christi College, Cambridge, 190, of the eleventh century, condemns the practice too.[179] Burchard, in the *Corrector*, objects to women doing it to stop their babies' crying.[180]

One of the answers was, once more, an answer of the order proposed by Sapaudus: the provision, that is, of a parallel kind of seemingly harmless Christian magic, one with sufficient echoes to attract, but one imprinted most of all with Christian messages. Answers such as this were given; spectacularly so, I will shortly argue. Another answer, however, lay in medical science, and we may briefly look at this answer here, for it, as usual, complicated the situation, and it does a great deal

[176] "Posuisti infantem tuum juxta ignem, et alius caldariam supra ignem cum aqua misit, et ebullita aqua superfusus est infans, et mortuus est. Tu autem qui infantem septem annos in tua custodia debuisti habere, tres annos per legitimas ferias poenitere debes. Ille autem qui aquam in caldarium misit, innocens erit"; *PL* 140,974. The person addressed is a woman. Interestingly, the person who places the kettle on the stove appears to be a man ("alius"). The woman is the guilty party, but the lenient penances prescribed by Burchard above, when death was not involved, suggest that the bishop was inclined to be indulgent toward practices he regarded as *comparitively* innocent.

[177] "That devil's craft which is performed when children are drawn through the earth"; *edit. and transl.* Whitelock, Brett, Brooke, *Councils and Synods*, i, 320 and nn.

[178] "Likewise some witless women go to cross-roads, and draw their children through the earth, and thus commit themselves and their children to the devil." *De Auguriis*; *edit. and transl.* Skeat, *Aelfic's Lives*, pp. 374–375. Eligius's biographer drew attention to a seemingly parallel practice whereby herdsmen passed their flocks through a hole in the earth or in a hollow tree, presumably for their health and protection. *Vita Eligii* II, 16a; *edit.* Krusch and Levison, *MGH SRM*, iv, 706.

[179] "If anyone passes his child for the sake of its health through a hole in the earth, and then fills the hole behind him with thorns, he shall do penance for forty days on bread and water"; quoted and translated in W. Bonser, *The Medical Background of Anglo-Saxon England* (London, 1963), p. 240, together with a similar prohibition in the same manuscript. Some of the penitential material contained in Corpus 190 goes back to the seventh century at least.

[180] "Fecisti quod quaedam mulieres facere solent? Illas dico quod habent vagientes infantes, effodiunt terram, et ex parte pertusant eam, et per illud foramen pertrahunt infantem, et sic dicunt vagientis infantis cessare vagitum"; *PL* 140,974.

to explain both the enthusiasm and the care that would come to be devoted to the choice and adoption of the magical type of Christian remedy. As was the case with astrology, so here, medical science—the learning and practice, that is, of the early medieval *medicus*—could be at root critical both of non-Christian and of Christian supernatural answers to anxieties about health. It could be used, therefore, to inhibit the development of Christian medical magic; but it could also provoke, in its turn, a renewed reaction toward this medical magic, and toward other forms of Christian magic too.

The problem of the exact effect this scientific medical practitioner had upon the rise of magic within Christianity is a many-faceted one, and perhaps incapable of resolution; but we may make certain observations about it. The medicus was thought to be important; but, to Christian leaders, only within certain limits. These limits might be themselves, moreover, matters for dispute. Caesarius saw this medicus as one of the counters to the diabolical cures against which he inveighed;[181] but there were others who saw in him a threatening figure, and one potentially hostile to the reverence accorded to (or hoped for by the guardians of) Christian shrines, and so to the proper appreciation of, and faith in, Christian miracles and grace. The denigration of the physician's healing abilities against those of a given saint is a familiar topos of early medieval hagiography, and Gregory of Tours, among others, is particularly good at deploying it.[182] The reasons that underlay this attempted diminishing of the physician's role are not in all respects, however, quite so familiar as is the topos. They are extremely important to our understanding of the rise of Christian medical magic. I have recently argued that they were born, in the main, of insecurity. The early medieval doctor could upset the social status of (and the rewards due to) Christian saints and healing shrines, in two main ways. He could, through superior remedies, cast doubt upon the efficacy of the cures they offered, and rob them of revenue; or, and still more alarmingly, he could ally with that non-Christian healing oppo-

---

[181] Sermon 52; *transl.* Mueller, *Saint Caesarius*, i,262.

[182] See, for example, the story of the cure of the epileptic, whose condition had worsened at the hands of doctors, at the tomb of Saint Nicetius of Lyons, or his own cure from "dysentery," again after the unsuccessful ministrations of his doctors, by dust from the tomb of Saint Martin. *Life of the Fathers* VIII,8; *transl.* James, *Gregory of Tours*, pp. 73–74. *Liber II de Virtutibus S. Martini* I; *edit.* Krusch, *MGH SRM*, i(2),159. Also, *History of the Franks* V,6; *transl.* Dalton, *The History*, ii,175–176.

sition the church sought so avidly to defeat. Occasionally he might do both.[183]

It behoved Christian purveyors and defenders of nonscientific curing powers, then, to elaborate especially convincing supernatural means of attracting support. By taking to imitative magical healing practices, suitably adapted, they might hold scientific competition at bay, and they might tap a following already in place.[184] They might also, it should be added, provide comfort of a sort when the scientific kind was too expensive or was simply unavailable. For all these reasons we see science, this time in the form of the early physician and sometimes clearly despite himself, helping Christian magic once more upon its way. Religious communities and, indeed, some physicians would come later to regret their opposition to science, and these communities would in the end be rendered doubly vulnerable as a result of it; but in the meantime it had benefits to offer. We may now turn to the positive aspects of monastic enthusiasm for Christian earthly magic.

[183] V.I.J. Flint, "The Early Medieval 'Medicus,' the Saint—and the Enchanter," *Social History of Medicine* 2 (1989), 127–145. As in the case of astrology, the "scientific" opposition to magic could come from within religious communities themselves. Such divisions and reactions were often rendered all the more energetic because they occurred within the heart of the Christian community.

[184] Thus, when Hugh of Cluny cures someone of fever by means of a drink of wine with relics immersed in it, he is described by his biographer as "*beatus* medicus": *Vita* IV; *PL* 159,873–874. The contrast between Hugh's methods and those of the ordinary "medicus" would not have been lost upon a contemporary audience, no more than would the (qualified) resemblance between them and those of the contemporary witch-doctor.

CHAPTER 9

Encouraged Magic:
The Process of Rehabilitation

CHRISTIAN PLACES AND OBJECTS

O N THIS SUBJECT, at last, we have an abundance, almost an embarrassment, of evidence. Archaeological, chronicle, and hagiographical sources, separately and together, tell a single story. When non-Christian shrines were destroyed, they were wherever possible replaced by Christian ones: oratories, churches, and monasteries, erected upon the selfsame spot and made up sometimes of the very same materials (those, at least, which had managed to survive the first fine fury of destruction). Saint Martin, for example, made a point of placing churches and monasteries where pagan sanctuaries had stood before,[1] and those distinguished holy vandals of whom I spoke in the preceding chapter, Saint Amand, Saint Bavo, and Saint Hubert of Utrecht, made sure that they set up Christian communities complete with religious edifices, or oratories in honor of the holy martyrs, upon the demolition sites they created.[2] Boniface used the wood of the sacred oak of Geismar for the construction of an oratory (apparently the tree was so big that it sufficed for the whole building).[3] Gregory of Tours recounts in his In Gloria Confessorum a tale of name, as well as place, substitution of a most ingenious sort. There was a mountain in the Gevaudan called Mons Helarius, and it held a lake, he recalls, that was thought to be sacred. This lake was the focal point of a three-day

[1] Vita S. Martini 13,9; edit. and transl. J. Fontaine, Sulpice Sévère, Vie de Saint Martin i (Paris, 1967), 282–283. See also C. Stancliffe, St. Martin and His Hagiographer (Oxford, 1983), pp. 332–334.

[2] Vita Bavonis Confessoris Gandavensis 4; edit. B. Krusch and W. Levison, MGH SRM iv (Hanover and Leipzig, 1902), 537 (with reference to the Life of Saint Amand). Vita Hugberti Episcopi Traiectensis; edit. B. Krusch and W. Levison, MGH SRM vi (Hanover and Leipzig, 1913), 484–485.

[3] Edit. W. Levison, Vitae Sancti Bonifatii Archiepiscopi Moguntini (Hanover and Leipzig, 1905), pp. 31,135. Transl. C. H. Talbot, The Anglo-Saxon Missionaries in Germany (London, 1954), p. 46.

festival, complete with animal sacrifices and offerings of many kinds.[4] The bishop of Mende was at a loss as to how to curtail the practice (since no one took the slightest notice of his sermons against it), until at last divine inspiration came to his aid. Suddenly, he conceived the idea of building a chapel to Saint *Hilarius* by the lakeside, placing relics in it, and explaining to the populace that Saint Hilary of Poitiers would intercede far better for them with God than any old pool of water. "Conpuncti corde," the people brought their offerings to the chapel of Saint Hilary instead.[5] Examples such as these could readily be multiplied. The physical adoption by the new religion of the place and materials occupied by the old is not, then, hard to demonstrate.

Of course, stones, trees, and fountains are, in various proportions, absolutely necessary to the completion of buildings and in the establishment of communities. At the simplest level, therefore, the taking over of a place and the transference of building materials can be understood in purely practical terms. Also, the scouring of "devils" from a shrine and their replacement by the people and emblems of the new religion was an activity medieval Christians might hear of from the heroic days of Rome and therefore be proud to emulate.[6] Once again, however, though satisfying, such explanations for the transferences we

[4] Offerings, that is, of woven stuffs, men's clothes, tufts of unspun wool, and many shapes and kinds of cheese and wax and bread. We seem to have here again reference to votive images, perhaps wax cursing figures even, and the bread-dough models we have already seen condemned, and also supernaturally charged weaving. The relevant passage reads: "Ad quem certo tempore multitudo rusticorum, quasi libamina lacui illi exhibens, lenteamina proieciebat ac pannos, qui ad usum vestimenti virili praebentur; nonnulli lanae vellera, plurimi etiam formas casei ac cerae vel panis diversasque species, unusquisque iuxta vires suas, quae dinumerare perlongum puto. Veniebant autem cum plaustris potum cibumque deferentes, mactantes animalia et per triduum aepulantes."

[5] And were miraculously freed from the attentions of a troublesome storm which customarily brought the older celebration to an end. *Liber in Gloria Confessorum* 2; *edit.* B. Krusch, MGH SRM i(2) (Hanover, 1885), 299–300.

[6] Paul the Deacon, for instance, recalls the conversion of the Pantheon and tells how the Emperor Phocas "commanded at the request of . . . Pope Boniface, that the church of the Ever-blessed Virgin Mary and of all the Martyrs should be established in the old temple which was called the Pantheon, after all the uncleanness of idolatry had been removed, so that where formerly the worship, not of all the gods, but of all the devils was performed, there at last there should be a memorial of all the saints." *History of the Lombards* IV,xxxvi; *transl.* W. Foulke, *Paulus Diaconus, History of the Lombards* (Philadelphia, 1907), p. 178. The passage is reminiscent of Bede, *Ecclesiastical History* II,4; *edit.* and *transl.* B. Colgrave and R.A.B. Mynors, *Bede's Ecclesiastical History of the English People* (Oxford, 1969), pp. 148–149.

seek to retrace here are not quite complete. The motives and processes that went into the reconstruction of such places and objects are a little more intricate, and illuminating therefore, than this; and, once more, cross-references to pressures coming from the world of contemporary non-Christian supernatural belief and practice, and cross-references of a rather more detailed kind than we usually make, are necessary to their proper understanding.

In reality, it seems that in the adaptation of many of the old revered places and objects, extra-special efforts were made toward preservation of a most careful sort, and toward the careful preservation of more than mere materials. This, furthermore, often in the sympathetic ways and for the lasting ends Pope Gregory had proposed. The old shrines and objects were, after all, as I suggested in Part I of this inquiry, and as we have just seen, already impregnated with sources of supernatural power much sought after, and they were called upon by persons whose habits were already formed. The new religion was therefore confronted with a set of cultural customs bearing upon the supernatural and a following that it would do well to try to make its own if it could. The force of formed habit was perhaps especially compelling and should never be underestimated, though it can be hard to reconstruct it, given our necessarily telescoped view of the past. Under such conditions it is not hard to see that it made excellent sense deliberately to build the old shrines into the new as closely as conceivable, and consciously to provide a particular place in them (and in the stories attached to the saints associated with them) for revered stones and trees (carved stones and trees perhaps especially) and fountains. Such efforts would beguile the eye, and perhaps the heart, and so would make that fundamental alteration of allegiance which was essential to the new religion a good deal easier to achieve.

And this is what we find. Because the old shrines already incorporated within themselves a well-tried means of drawing persons toward the supernatural world, the signs and emblems of supernatural communication they contained were not simply incorporated into the Christian system; they *dictated*, for many of the wise, the placing, the contents, and sometimes even the shape and environs of the new places of recourse. We are not dealing here, then, simply with material replacement, nor even with the studied imitation of the heroic days of Christian Rome. Still less are we watching the "trickling down" of pagan memories and practices. Our new shrines provide us instead with evidence of carefully, even cunningly, considered borrowings, and adaptations of a very high artistry indeed.

Impressive oratories and shrines, carvings in stone and wood (sometimes quite daring ones),[7] and wells and springs of especial holiness were thus brought actively into the system of communication with the supernatural espoused by Christianity, precisely because they had played, and still did play, so important and so lively a part in the competing system; but they came through with their import prudently, and often subtly, adjusted. With this competing system in mind, we might recognize all the more clearly how desirable it was to incorporate Christianized figural sculpture, especially representations of parts of the body or of whole persons, into the new shrines, and to defend its presence there; and how diplomatic to include tall stones or towers, or forms of enclosure. There were, once more, dangers attendant upon certain sorts of incorporation. A famous early fourth-century ruling against the placing of representational paintings in churches for fear of idolatry was often repeated;[8] but we have mountainous evidence that such rulings were much more often ignored.

It is not possible, within the compass of so broad a study, to try to open more than a small window into the surviving physical evidence for such borrowings and adaptations. The window I have chosen to open here is an Anglo-Saxon one—this partly because the Anglo-Saxon evidence is being so splendidly cataloged and described, partly because it is in itself so revealing and indicative.[9] Some of the most spectacular surviving manifestations of a desire to tap the reverence given to condemned great trees and enclosures, and wooden and stone pillars, and to *sculptilia* and *simulacra* in stone and wood, are to be found in the yew enclosures of Christian churchyards, and in the recorded and surviving wooden crosses and carved stone high crosses of Anglo-Saxon England. King Oswald, for instance, set up a great

[7] We may better understand the appearance, often in church buildings, on quoins, and over church doorways, of the Sheela-na-Gig, for example, within this context. The Sheela-na-gig, a displayed nude female figure, early seen as a fertility symbol, has lately, and convincingly, had apotropaic or healing functions attributed to her. A catalog of known surviving examples is contained in J. Andersen, *The Witch on the Wall* (Copenhagen, 1977), pp. 138–158 (with, at no. 12, a possibly Anglo-Saxon one). Traceable perhaps to the ninth century in medieval Europe (ibid., p. 25), such figures could well have been adopted from nearby non-Christian models.

[8] Council of Elvira, 305, canon 36; Mansi, II, 11.

[9] See, for instance, R. Cramp and R. N. Bailey, *Corpus of Anglo-Saxon Stone Sculpture* (Oxford, for the British Academy, 1984–1988, ongoing).

wooden cross as an omen of victory before his last battle at Heaven-field, against the heathen Penda—a procedure not too greatly removed from the seeking of omens before battle at a sacred oak. Bede allows that the cross was indeed a "praesagium," although the victory was, of course, a heavenly one, for the king himself was killed.[10] High crosses seem to have marked monastic centers in Northumbria in the pre-Viking period[11] and may often have been placed within the enclosure of the church itself, or that of its cemetery, just as great trees and sculptured stones marked contemporary non-Christian shrines and enclosures. They were also set up at the sides of roads, and perhaps at crossroads. Sometimes, in addition, they seem to have been designed to be used much as non-Christian sacred objects had been. Take, for instance, the early ninth-century stone shaft topped by a cross from Rothbury. This had provision made for lights to be attached to it, apparently in the manner of the lighted trees condemned in conciliar legislation, and, in the same way, to have been dressed in foliage.[12] Supernatural ways of providing food and healing, but ones within the Christian scheme of things, seem also to be consciously evoked on such crosses; a striking echo of the powers attributed to, and requests made of, the old shrines of which we have spoken.[13]

The Ruthwell cross of the late seventh/early eighth century, with its runic inscription consisting of lines from an early version of the Anglo-Saxon poem *The Dream of the Rood*, is well known.[14] The messages of

[10] *Ecclesiastical History* III,2; *transl.* Colgrave, *Bede's Ecclesiastical History*, pp. 214–217. When Brother Bothelm of Hexham slipped on the ice and broke his arm, Bede tells us, moss which had grown on the cross healed the break. A large wooden cross, possibly also of the seventh century, was buried beneath the tenth-century church of Saint Bertelin, Stafford; *edit.* A. Oswald, *The Church of St. Bertelin, Stafford, and the Cross* (Birmingham, 1955), pp. 15–16, 26–27.

[11] Cramp, *Corpus*, i,2–3, and fig. 2.

[12] Ibid., p. 221.

[13] The Rothbury cross has on it the miracle of the healing by Christ of the blind man, and the healing of the woman with the issue of blood, and the Ruthwell cross the healing of the blind man and also the breaking of bread in the desert by Paul and Anthony; ibid., pp. 220–221. Archers are not infrequently to be found upon sculptured monuments from this period, and one is to be found on the Ruthwell cross. The Ruthwell archer might be Ishmael, many might well be derived from classical models (for example the putto from Hexham, ibid., pp. 185–186, and ii, pls. 179, 961), and their meaning might, in any case, be purely decorative and secular—but it is just possible that they might also have reference to elfshot, that demon-borne pestilence whose ravages the cross and Christian healers sought to undo.

[14] On this see M. Swanton, *The Dream of the Rood*, rev. ed. (Exeter, 1987). I am heavily dependent here upon this masterly discussion of the subject.

both cross and *Dream* (and especially the complex and sophisticated artistry detectable in each) deserve a little extra emphasis, however, within the particular context of the non-Christian beliefs and practices they hoped to replace. The fact that, in *The Dream of the Rood*, the healing message to Christians comes in a dream, the nature of the adornments of the wooden cross so movingly described in the dream, and the standing, surviving Ruthwell cross itself, bearer of a reminder of the dream and of so much other imagery besides, recall very many features of the ancient and contemporary magical world and its shrines. Incubation at temples frequently produced prophetic or healing dreams, for instance, and the proximity of the dreamer to a special sort of wood was thought markedly beneficial.[15] *The Dream of the Rood* mentions the decking of crosses with foliage. The cross in the *Dream* is jeweled, hung with garments and "drenched with gold," as were some of the simulacra and trees in the non-Christian shrines, and as too were certain other of the crosses known in the period.[16] The cross in the *Dream* is described also as soaked with blood, again a characteristic it has in common with other examples.[17] The association of blood with magic, and with necromancy especially, was a familiar one to readers and borrowers of Isidore, and to inveighers against witchcraft, as we have seen. Though the poet's evocation here of the power of Christ's blood hardly needs reference to the contemporary magical scene to explain it, the references were, nonetheless, there to be made.[18] That they were made with such clarity and directness suggests a high degree of conscious appeal to it, across the borders of the Christian world.

Further reference of this kind is to be found on the Ruthwell cross itself. Birds and beasts are transformed from portents into adoring subjects (as they were in some of the saints' lives we have already re-

---

[15] A. Bouché-Leclercq, *Histoire de la Divination dans l'Antiquité* iv (Paris, 1882), 287. Sanctuaries to Asclepius, perhaps the most frequent places of resort for healing dreams, came to be replaced by sanctuaries to Saint Martin of Tours, complete with incubation. Alcuin makes the connection; *ep.* 245; *edit.* E. Dümmler, MGH *Epistolae Karolini Aevi* ii (Berlin, 1895), 397.

[16] They might be jeweled, and contain crystals too, like the one referred to in the tenth-century so-called Egbert pontifical; Swanton, *The Dream*, p. 52.

[17] Ibid., p. 49.

[18] This emphasis does seem to be a vernacular one; ibid., p. 46 n. 3. The cross in the poem is also described as shedding its own blood, "stricken with shafts." This puts the reader in mind of the spear-throwing horse-games described, for instance, in the *Life of Saint Barbatus*, below.

viewed), sometimes with crossed paws. The scene depicting Paul and
Antony breaking bread in the desert would have recalled, to those who
knew their Jerome, the raven who, against nature, originally brought
them the bread; it would also have recalled the *confractio* of the Christian Sacrifice of the Mass.[19] *Unguentum*, a potentially magical application sometimes explicitly associated with the magical arts[20] is, in the
panel on the cross representing Mary Magdalen (one framed in a Latin
inscription allowing of no mistake), shown in the service of Christ. As
in Luke 7:37–38, Mary dries Christ's feet with her hair, an action scru-
pulously in accord, of course, with the biblical passage, but still an
arrestingly different form of "watching the foot" and of that conjuring
with hair attributed by Hincmar to witches. When healing the blind
man, Christ heals not with his fingers, as in the biblical text, but with
a wand.[21]

The ring chains and plaits and braids and knots characteristic of the
carvings upon freestanding crosses of this type and period are relatively
familiar to us; yet our appreciation of these too might gain a little from
the setting of contemporary non-Christian magic. The ninth-, tenth-,
and early eleventh-century crosses of Aycliffe, Chester-le-Street,
Gainford, and Sockburn are spectacular examples of knotted and ring-
braided crosses, and these come from a period in which, and places
where, anxieties about the incorporation of pagan Scandinavian set-
tlers were perhaps especially intensely felt.[22] As impressive memories
of non-Christian hanging sacrifices, special stones and woods, omens,
and supernatural means of healing are carried vividly and carefully into
the monuments proclaiming Christianized supernatural power at the
new shrines, then, so too, on a rather smaller scale, are echoes of other
forms of supernatural practice, such as amuletic rings and knots, weaving, and binding. All of these, obviously, are to be rendered subordinate to the new ways of invoking the supernatural; yet also they are

[19] Ibid. p. 15.
[20] By, for example, Gregory of Tours. In a story dealing principally with miracles
associated with the ordeal, he tells how one participant-to-be anoints his arm with oil
as a precaution, before plunging it into the cauldron of hot water. He is immediately
accused by his opponent of taking to magic: "Magicis artibus te elitandum putasti, ut
haec unguenta diffunderis, nec valebunt ista quae agis." *Liber in Gloria Martyrum* 80; *edit.*
B. Krusch, *MGH SRM* i(2) (Hanover, 1885), 92.
[21] Swanton, *The Dream*, p. 17.
[22] See Cramp, *Corpus*, i, 42–46, 53–59, 80–86 (especially Gainford 4 and 5), 135–
140.

still to form a part of it, where this is possible. This second function is less obvious; but it is extraordinarily important.

To be sure, the problem of the iconographic lineage that stood behind the carvings found upon such crosses (ivories, metalwork, illuminated manuscripts) is a most complex and taxing one in its own right, filled with a variety of pressures and possible choices. This variety of possible previous models and influences, rich as it is, should not be allowed to divert our view totally, however, from the immediate situation within which such works were undertaken. Crosses of this kind certainly owed much to earlier artists and to "the stone triumphal pillars or columns of the Roman world,"[23] but in making his selection each given sculptor might, as a person of stature within the community, be expected to have had an eye to more than his iconographic models. His gaze seems frequently, in fact, to have rested upon a lively contemporary magical scene, and perhaps for even more reasons than we have already reviewed. Artistry of a very high order indeed was involved in the carrying of the eye of the non-Christian devotee through to the Christian sanctuary, and in the incorporation there of symbols of the supernatural which were familiar; symbols which did not demand too great an aesthetic disjunction, and yet were acceptable to Christians. This was a challenge worthy of the mettle of a great wood or stone carver. We should not overlook the part played by sheer challenge in the calling forth of artistry of the quality we find in so many of the standing crosses.

Surviving dedications to early medieval saints too might tentatively be allowed to indicate a process of substitution that took place equally consciously and early, and again in the face of pressing need. Great standing stones are still to be found dedicated to such saints as Vaast, Radegunde, and Hubert. Hollows and cavities in stones are still popularly thought predominantly to bear the impress of exceptionally early saints. Some of these impresses are held to be those of footprints, footprints often of such saints as Martin or Hilary or Julian of Brioude, or their mounts.[24] Christianized footprints remind us once more of that non-Christian cult of the foot which we saw in our condemnations,

[23] Ibid., p. 5.

[24] J. G. Bulliot and F. Thiollier, *Le Mission et le Culte de Saint Martin d'après les Légendes et les Monuments Populaires dans le Pays Eduen* (Autun and Paris, 1892), pp. 8–10. The inclusion of the horses of these saints is interesting, given the place of horses in lot taking and the evidence for horse races in the ritual celebrations held at the competing shrines.

and the names of the saints to which such footprints are attributed take us back once again to that testing period in which the deliberate Christian substitutions are most likely to have been made.[25]

Thus, although on the one hand, of course, they condemn such shrines and sources and objects of devotion, on the other, Christian pastors recognize that they have power and are persistent, and so the churchmen try to incorporate their strength. Some such incorporations are even to be found, and quite quickly, within the bounds of that body of ecclesiastical regulation which so often contains the condemnations. We are early informed, for example, of a deep reluctance on the part of adherents of the old shrines, and even on the part of Christians too, to destroy the old sacred trees entirely. Caesarius complained about Christians who hesitated to destroy the wood of ancient shrines,[26] and similar hesitations (complete with penances for them) are registered by Burchard.[27] Yet, in an interesting entry to be found in the eighth-century so-called penitential of Theodore, such reverence has been turned to Christian purposes. This rules that wood used in the construction of churches may only be reused for other churches, or for the needs of a religious community. Otherwise, it must be burned. It may not fall into lay hands.[28] Yew trees, so familiar a feature of early churchyards, may similarly have been quite intentionally allowed to live on from the pre-Christian grove.[29]

Holy springs and wells are too familiar a feature of the early Christian landscape to be in general cause for comment. Once again, however, we can, if we will, draw a direct link between early medieval Christian associations and ways with water, and that outlawed non-Christian reverence for the element which so preoccupied pastors. In the Limousin, the name of Saint Eligius, that scourge of non-Christian

[25] On such dedications see also S. Reinach, "Les monuments de pierre brute," *Revue Archéologique* 21 (1893), 195–226.

[26] Sermon 53; transl. M. M. Mueller, *Saint Caesarius of Arles, Sermons* i (Washington, 1956), 263.

[27] Burchard, *Decretum* X; *PL* 140,834.

[28] II,3; J. T. McNeill and H. M. Gamer, *Medieval Handbooks of Penance* (New York, 1938), p. 199.

[29] E. A. Philippson, *Germanisches Heidentum bei den Angelsachsen* (Leipzig, 1929), p. 184. In an illuminating few pages upon Anglo-Saxon reverence for the True Cross, Swanton draws attention to that Anglo-Saxon riddle (LV) according to which this cross was made of "maple, oak, the hard yew and pale holly" (an adaptation of the customary inference from the Pseudo-Chrysostom): *The Dream*, p. 46. The last three of these, of course, are woods attestedly revered by non-Christians.

magical practice, stands now behind a great many Christian healing wells and fountains, and we may have in this fact too, then, record of an adaptation process that reaches back to the seventh century at least.[30] Many well dedications seem, indeed, to take us back precisely to this early period, and so do some of the wishing and divinatory offerings still made.[31] Well-dressing ceremonies seem often even now to be associated with Ascension Thursday.[32]

Condemned magic in general and that special grace conferred by the waters of baptism were seen as direct counters one to the other by Caesarius, Eligius, and Martin of Braga. Resort to such magic meant the loss of baptismal grace. Baptism, again, hardly needs the world of early European outlawed magical beliefs to account for its importance, but, in its concentration upon the element of water, it was an attractive method of invoking the supernatural within this context, and this lively non-Christian reverence for water does perhaps at least help to explain the enthusiasm with which Christian missionaries and Christian kings insisted upon baptism as a paramount sign both of conversion and of victory. As we shall shortly see, baptismal water could serve as ordeal water and so could play its part in that process of calming reconciliation by consensus so vital both to small rural enclosed communities and to their leaders, a mode of social organization which, once again, it behoved the Christian order rather to involve itself in, and reinforce, than to upset. Miracles involving water, and baptism, were also early built into the liturgy for the Feast of the Epiphany in the medieval West, the feast that first focused discussion upon the role in Christian revelation and the release of supernatural power of the Christian Magi.[33]

Physically and liturgically, then, that non-Christian reverence for stones and trees and fountains so vigorously condemned in councils,

[30] L. de Nussac, "Les fontaines en Limousin," *Bulletin du comité des travaux historiques et scientifiques* (1897), 153–159.

[31] See, for example, the names contained in the index to R. C. Hope, *The Legendary Lore of the Holy Wells of England* (London, 1893), pp. 214–215. The great majority of the dedications listed there take us back to early Europe. Hope also attests to practices such as the throwing of pins into wells, in order to make predictions from the ways in which they turn, to the hanging of scraps of linen upon trees, perhaps reminiscent of votive offerings of magical weaving, to the hanging on them of garments representing affected parts of the body brought for healing, and to the timing of well-dressing rituals; ibid., pp. xiii,83–84,180.

[32] ibid., p. 47.

[33] See below, chap. 11.

penitentials, and sermons was in fact called upon and incorporated within the European Christian dispensation, seemingly very early and with great care and determination. I have argued above that, in certain instances of condemned heavenly magic, saints' lives and miracle stories were used with a surpassing subtlety to refer to, and to retranslate, many of the magical associations which had been condemned yet required treatment of a sympathetic kind. Only an exhaustive analysis of sources such as these will even begin to establish whether all earthly magic was subject to the same system of retranslation; but there are indications that it was, and we shall explore a number of them below. The condemned influences exerted by shrines and objects, in the meanwhile, do seem to have been recognized and countered with energy by supernatural interventions recounted as miracles, and very carefully devised in detail to incorporate, yet change, the old beliefs and practices.

The dedications of completed churches provided an occasion for complex stories of this kind, an occasion that was seized upon;[34] and stones and trees and special wood and water are speakingly manipulated by certain hagiographers. Celtic saints, for instance, are noted for their ways with stones, and especially for the ease with which they sail about on them in default of more customary modes of water trans-

---

[34] See, for example, a story in the *Frankish Royal Annals* under the year 773 (the year after Charlemagne destroyed the Irminsul): "When the Saxons in their savagery began to burn the houses outside [the castle of Buraburg], they came upon a church at Fritzlar which Boniface of saintly memory, the most recent martyr, had consecrated and which he said prophetically would never be burnt by fire. The Saxons began to attack this church with great determination, trying one way or another to burn it. While this was going on, there appeared to some Christians in the castle and also to some heathens in the army two young men on white horses who protected the church from fire. Because of them the pagans could not set the church on fire or damage it, either inside or outside. Terror-stricken by the intervention of divine might they turned to flight, although nobody pursued them. Afterward one of these Saxons was found dead beside the church. He was squatting on the ground and holding tinder and wood in his hands as if he had meant to blow on his fuel and set the church on fire"; *transl.* B. W. Scholz and B. Rogers, *Carolingian Chronicles* (Ann Arbor, Mich., 1970), p. 50. There is a great deal in this short passage. As well as the obviously magical wood, charged this time with Christian supernatural power, the saint's divinatory capacity is stressed, and the protectors of the church are on special horses. In his *Ecclesiastical History* V,4, Bede tells how water, consecrated for the dedication of a church built by a *gesith*, heals the *gesith*'s sick wife, a healing miracle using an old element of healing but associated with a brand new shrine; *transl.* Colgrave, *Bede's Ecclesiastical History*, pp. 462–463.

port. The many stories wherein such saints use great stones effortlessly as boats[35] may have reference to the consultations of, and offerings made to, sortilegi and magi at such standing stones for safe sea journeys. On occasion the saintly sailors were themselves mistaken for magi.[36] Before contemporaries they claimed a magician's powers: they tapped the supernatural energies of the stones yet used them for clearly Christian ends (Enda got some land for a monastery). These saints could render such stones immovable too, or, on the contrary, move them in superhuman ways, but again, of course, for Christian purposes.[37] One such saint's life actually tells outright of the substitution for a pagan sculpture of a carved cross. When Saint Samson confronted the "simulacrum abominabile" on Bodmin Moor, his first response was to take up an iron tool, carve a cross on a nearby standing stone, and order that it be revered instead. When that measure failed he brought back to life a young boy killed in the horse-games. The combination worked, the competing simulacrum was destroyed, a form of conjuring with the untimely dead was successfully performed at the new substitute stone monument, and many converts were made.[38]

When we turn to sacred trees, sometimes the recognitions and changes advanced in such works are simple, even crude, ones. Saint Amand, for example, attributed a certain woman's blindness to her reverence for a particular tree, and he cured it miraculously when she had the tree cut down; but then Saint Amand (or his biographer) did, it seems, favor the simpler oppositions.[39] At other times they are much more elaborate and careful, and evince a high degree of calculated and convincing substitution. We might look once more with profit, in this context, at the *Lives* of Saint Boniface, with their description of the careful use the saint made of the sacred oak, and see there an example of a complex and considered response to a prevailing belief in the magic inherent in wood. A whole "multitudo" of pagans was involved, as we saw, in the conversion for which he contended and which, the

[35] Saints Ciaran and Lasrian, for instance, climbed upon a "lapis magnus" and "saxum grande" standing by the seashore and sailed away; C. Plummer, *Vitae Sanctae Hiberniae* i (Oxford, 1910), 227, ii,137.

[36] *Vita Sancti Endei* xv; ibid., ii,67.

[37] Ibid., i,clv–clvii.

[38] *Vita S. Samsonis* 48–49; edit. R. Fawtier, *La Vie de Saint Samson* (Paris, 1912), pp. 144–145.

[39] *Vita Amandi Episcopi* I,24; edit. B. Krusch and W. Levison, MGH SRM v (Hanover and Leipzig, 1910), 447.

Lives claim, he brought about.[40] To preserve the wood, but in Christian buildings, then, made excellent supernatural sense, both from the point of view of retaining for the new religion that reverent attention such a material commanded, and from that of securing the new buildings against hostile attack, arson attack especially. Such motives may have stood behind the entry in the so-called penitential of Theodore already cited. Again, Saint Odile of Hohenburg, when given three linden rods to plant and warned by one of her nuns of their evil supernatural associations, planted them nonetheless, but, in the incantation with which she accompanied the replanting, she invoked the name of the Trinity.[41] A Christian leader here recognized a belief in the magical power of the wood, once more, and allowed that it needed a spell to neutralize it, but of a clearly Christian kind and one which reinforced a belief central to the Christian faith. The *Life* (most probably a ninth-century compilation) of Saint Barbatus of Benevento (d. 682) tells how this saint, in his struggle against pagan practice, destroyed both a great sacred tree (hung with the skin of a sacrificed wild beast and shot at by riders in the horse-games) and a golden image of a viper. The latter he melted down and had remade into a chalice and paten for the greatest sacrifice of all, the Sacrifice of the Mass.[42]

Trees planted by holy men, on the other hand, partake of their especial goodness, deserve reverent treatment, and should not be cut down.[43] Trees also, spectacularly so, of course, in *The Dream of the*

---

[40] *Edit.* Levison, *Vitae*, pp. 31, 135.

[41] *Vita Odiliae Abbatissae Hohenburgensis* 15; *edit.* B. Krusch and W. Levison, MGH SRM vi (Hanover and Leipzig, 1913), 45.

[42] *Vita Barbati Episcopi Beneventani* 1,7,8; *edit.* G. Waitz et al., *MGH SS Rerum Langobardicarum et Italicarum Saec. VI–IX* (Hanover, 1878), 557, 560, 562. This short *Life* is interesting for a number of reasons. It tells how Barbatus took care first of all to calm the fears of the Lombard Duke Romuald's wife, before she would dare have the image melted down, and it shows the importance of the Eucharist as a substitute propitiation. This is a large subject in its own right and has received full treatment in P. Browe, *Die Eucharistischen Wünder des Mittelalters* (Breslau, 1938), and idem, "Die Eucharistie als Zaubermittel im Mittelalter," *Archiv für Kulturgeschichte* 20 (1930), 134–154. The *Vita Barbati* shows also, once more, how important horses were in such rituals and so may give us an extra reason for the appearance of sculptured horsemen in early churches.

[43] Such a tree was cut down at a holy man's death and made into a saw-bench, but then the perpetrator of this act realized his error, chopped off the legs of the saw-bench, and replanted the tree, which flourished. Gregory of Tours, *In Gloria Confessorum* 23; *edit.* B. Krusch, MGH SRM i(2) (Hanover, 1885), 312–313. A famous story in Bede tells how the beam of wood against which Saint Aidan leaned when dying was

Rood, can be singled out by God to convey a supernatural message. A pear tree figures prominently in the *Life* of Saint Heribert of Cologne (d. 1022). None of the saint's carpenters was able to find wood suitable for the great crucifix the saint had commissioned for the abbey of Deutz. While enjoying a picnic in a local orchard, however, the saint came upon the pear tree, all shaped and ready for the crucifix. The saint's biographer here seized the opportunity to explain that this marvel could be attributed neither to man nor (still less) to the power inherent in the wood. Only the power of the Christian God could bring about in trees such singular and salvific effects.[44] To regard such stories as directed at least in part toward contemporary non-Christian magical practice is not to deny the influence upon them of ancient or Eastern exempla, or to exclude other points of reference. It merely gives them an additional context and purpose.

The story of the lake on Mons Helarius is a good example of the sort of new uses to which a reverence for water might be put.[45] In many *Acta* and saints' lives healing springs gush forth in profusion at the places where martyrs and saints fall.[46] We sometimes glimpse in these a possibly deliberate reversal of expectation. The devotees of Willibrord's spring feared that violators of holy springs might be killed; but in the Christian stories the deaths of saints actually draw forth these sacred (and healing) springs from the ground. Sometimes we can find also a rearrangement, as it were, of supernatural rank. In the case of Charlemagne's destruction of the Irminsul, Christian supernatural control over water replaces, and outdoes, Saxon reverence for wood. A miraculously produced spring of water ends the prevailing drought

---

proof against fire: *Ecclesiastical History* III, 17; *transl*. Colgrave, *Bede's Ecclesiastical History*, pp. 263–265. Splinters from the beam healed the sick.

[44] "Recte ergo huius veritatis, hujus divinae electionis meminisse nos facit res ipsa, quae pene similiter accidit, dum non qualecumque lignum, non quodcumque volebant homines artifices, sed quod nutu divino monstratum est, ad eiusmodi operis effectum perduci potuit." *Vita S. Heriberti Archiepiscopi Coloniensis* iv; AS Martii ii,482.

[45] The lives of Celtic saints also are especially full of water miracles: Plummer, *Vitae* i,cxlvii–clii.

[46] For example, Gregory of Tours, *Liber de Virtutibus S. Iuliani* 3; *edit*. B. Krusch, MGH SRM i(2) (Hanover, 1885), 115. And see R. von Antropoff, *Die Entwicklung der Kenelm-Legende* (Bonn, 1965), pp. 109 and XII. My attention was drawn to this by Mr. Paul Hayward. Such stories are again, of course, hagiographical commonplaces, as Hope clearly showed: *The Legendary Lore*, pp. 65–67, 94. In many of these instances it is possible that we have an attempt to Christianize an established pre-Christian sacrificial and healing place.

at the sanctuary (a drought against which, it is implied, the Irminsul had been unable to provide a remedy).[47]

The sacrament of baptism too is often used, in such sources, to Christianize non-Christian magical springs, and it is possible, as I have already suggested, that the nature of this sacrament allowed Christians to be especially at ease when allowing magical power to water. Willibrord, of course, converted the Frisian sacred well, a well previously associated with fertility magic, to Christian uses by means of baptism.[48] According to a remarkable story in Gregory of Tours's *In Gloria Martyrum* an ancient sacred fountain is made to behave, in association with the sacrament of baptism, in a manner wholly unnatural and clearly magical.[49] It is allowed to retain, moreover, its power over fertility. Gregory tells how those who assembled at the spring on Easter Sunday, all ready for baptism, found the water all piled up into a heap, "like wheat piled into a measure." Many people took it away in amphoras and poured it over their fields and vineyards to ensure their prosperity. Even when huge numbers of such vessels had been filled, the heap stayed high and undiminished, and the waters only went back to their proper limits and behaved like water when the baptisms began.[50] Here Christian magic greatly outdoes the non-Christian variety, but without losing the non-Christian spring's power to command attention and devotion. Examples of transforming miracles such as these can readily be multiplied, and they are surely suggestive.[51] Hagiographical correspondences and counters of this kind are revealingly to be found in many other cases of earthly magic, and especially so in matters of magical medicine.

[47] *Frankish Royal Annals*; transl. King, *Charlemagne*, p. 75.

[48] *Vita Willibrordi Archiepiscopi Traiectensis Auctore Alcuino*; edit. B. Krusch and W. Levison, *MGH SRM* vii (Hanover and Leipzig, 1920), 124–125.

[49] A Christian baptistery had apparently been constructed over the spring: "Piscina namque est apud Osen campum antiquitus sculpta et ex marmore vario in modum crucis miro composita opere. Sed et aedes magnae claritatis ac celsitudinis desuper a Christianis constructa est." *In Gloria Martyrum* 23; edit. B. Krusch, *MGH SRM* i(2) (Hanover, 1885), 51–52.

[50] In a similar story Gregory tells how a declivity, usually dry, filled with water for Easter baptisms in response to the prayers of Saint Marcellinus: *In Gloria Confessorum* 68; ibid., p. 338.

[51] Thus I have found myself wondering in addition whether topoi familiar to Celtic lives of saints, whereby the discovery of a sow and a litter of pigs, or the actions of oxen or horses, decides the site for a monastery (Plummer, *Vitae* i,cxliv) might not refer back to the sacrifices and games of the displaced rituals, as site-finding eagles echo divinatory birds of prey.

When we turn to that last place redolent of forbidden supernatural energy and power, the domain of the dead, we find a markedly similar pattern of qualified adoption and change. Of course, the great gospel story of the Resurrection from the tomb, and its celebration at the feast of Easter, were absolutely central to the Christian message, and, whatever the state of affairs outside it, Christianity necessarily focused its devotion upon these events. This being said, however, we can make out once more careful echoes of the contemporary magical world. We have seen how the Acta of martyrs, for example, provided opportunities for the remodeling of the supernatural expectations visited upon beasts and birds. The tombs of martyrs, together with these same Acta, also helped to shift the direction of behavioral habit toward the dead. The anniversaries of martyrs' deaths (called birthdays) were kept by a feast and liturgical celebration at the tomb, observances which echoed those of the pagan parentalia, and the general celebrations of the Roman parentalia were refocused upon Saint Peter, no less, in a feast remembering the inauguration of his apostolate on 22 February. It was on this day that Saint Eligius delivered his famous sermon against magical practice, according to his Vita. The changes did not always have the happy effects expected of them.

> There are some people who come to the birthday festivals of the martyrs for this sole purpose, that they may destroy themselves and ruin others by intoxication, dancing, singing shameful songs, leading the choral dance, and pantomiming in a devilish fashion. . . . What is worse, there are many people who not only get drunk themselves but also beg others to drink more than is proper: moreover (so much the worse!), even some of the clergy do this.[52]

Here the compromise had perhaps proceeded a little far and the wrong habits been retained; but the aims were clear for all that. The celebrations focused upon the "family" tomb were preserved, but directed toward the most distinguished of the dead of the Christian family. Martyrs' feasts served another purpose too. They brought back to mind, and vividly, the deaths of those who had died untimely, even of those who had committed crimes against a given government, but made it abundantly clear at the same time that these particular victims would act in ways the reverse of harmful. Bede is one of the more famous

[52] Caesarius, Sermon 55; transl. Mueller, Saint Caesarius, i,271–273.

examples of hagiographers who allowed extra-special supernatural powers to the Christian untimely dead, and to their relics.[53]

The relics of a dead saint were commonly employed to make complete the transference of a pagan place of worship to a Christian use (they are mentioned in the cases I have cited), and tombs placed in tomb churches were a central source, of course, of miracles, particularly of miracles of healing. The *Anglo-Saxon Herbal* attributes a special power to plants grown upon burial places.[54] Herb tea made from the grass covering the body of Saint Gall (to keep it cool in the heat), and herbs and flowers strewn upon his tomb, and absentmindedly chewed, produced the most beneficent effects.[55] Accounts of healing miracles that take place after a period of incubation at the tomb of a saint are, in Gregory of Tours, very frequent. The deep trust Gregory had in wax from tomb lamps and his partiality for a drink of tomb dust in water are well known, but he supplies us also with other anecdotes whose true appreciation needs the context of pre-Christian attitudes toward the dead. Those without proper burial are allowed still to exercise an influence, for example—but an influence helpful to Christians. Gregory tells of two holy virgins who were annoyed that their tombs lacked adequate shelter from the rain. They promptly reappeared to the living and not only procured new roofs from the terrified peasants who saw them but had an oratory built nearby. The virgins dealt also in short order with the weather, allowing the elderly Bishop Euphronius to come and dedicate the oratory—and apologize for his initial reluctance to go out in a downpour. The earlier *Life* of Saint Germanus of Auxerre includes a chilling story of a dilapidated haunted house. Two ghosts

[53] Saint Oswald's victory cross performed miracles, as we saw. After his death at the hands of the heathen Penda, the soil on which his body lay cured sick people and horses and protected wood from fires. Soil washed with the water which had cleansed the saint's bones drove away devils and healed. The oak on which the saint's head was fixed by Penda effected cures and so did the saint's tomb. *Ecclesiastical History* III,9–13, transl. Colgrave, *Bede's Ecclesiastical History*, pp. 241–255. Here an enormous amount of non-Christian magical reference is involved in, and retranslated by, the power Bede attributes to the King-Martyr.

[54] XIX,1, XXIX,1, XLIV,1; edit. O. Cockayne, *Leechdoms, Wortcunning and Starcraft of Early England* i, RS (London, 1864), 112–113, 124–125, 146–147.

[55] Gregory of Tours, *Vitae Patrum* VI,7; transl. E. James, *Gregory of Tours, Life of the Fathers* (Liverpool, 1985), p. 59. The holy Meratina collected some of the grass and prudently planted it in her garden, whence it provided herb tea for many of the sick. After the holy virgin's death the practice unaccountably lapsed. For further examples of relic and tomb healing, see the section on Christian medical magic, below.

prowl about in it, to the dread of nearby inhabitants. One appears to the saint in a dream and tells him that they were convicted of crimes and so cast into an unconsecrated grave. Germanus is led to it and finds the jumbled bones. He gives them Christian burial and prays over them, with the happy (and practical) result that the house is repaired and lived in. The convict-ghosts and the two ill-buried virgins terrorized the living, it is true, as did the non-Christian untimely and ill-buried dead, but to the best and most Christian of ends.[56]

Paul the Deacon tells also of how the Christian dead can help warriors in battle. The martyr Sabinus fought alongside Duke Ariulf of Spoleto, defending him fiercely in the thick of the melee, and saving his life. The duke realized that it was Sabinus who had defended and saved him when he saw the martyr's picture in his church.[57] The Christian dead can also come back and frighten greedy persons into good behavior, rather as the non-Christian dead can identify thieves.[58] Gregory again, for example, has an unnamed holy man uncover the truth about a malefactor by throwing him off his tomb (with a great shaking and rattling) when the unfortunate miscreant sits down upon it.[59]

The Christian dead were not actually called up and persuaded to be helpful, according to such anecdotes as these. They offered their assistance voluntarily—a very pointed difference—but they were supernaturally effective all the same. In that effective operations were so clearly permitted to the dead in such stories, however, and to the saintly dead especially, we may also consider their bearing upon non-Christian nec-

[56] *Vita S. Germani* I,v; AS Iulii vii,210–211. The story is based upon Letter VII of Pliny the Younger. Gregory of Tours, *In Gloria Confessorum* 18; *edit.* Krusch, MGH SRM, i,307–308.

[57] *History of the Lombards* IV,xvi; *transl.* W. J. Foulke, *Paulus Diaconus, History of the Lombards* (Philadelphia, 1907), pp. 161–162. A similar story is told of the war, early this century, between Guatemala and El Salvador, and again within the context of an ordered compromise between Christianity and the native religion. This time Saint James fought with the Momostecans, flying above them on his horse and urging them on with his sword: B. Tedlock, *Time and the Highland Maya* (Albuquerque, 1982), p. 21.

[58] Saint Nicetius appeared in a dream to Dado who had not delivered on his promise to donate two silver chalices to the saint's church: Gregory of Tours, *Vitae Patrum* VIII,11; *transl.* Krusch, MGH SRM, i,75–76. See also, below, Gregory's story about the dead husband who reveals to his wife in a dream that his mass wine has been stolen.

[59] *In Gloria Confessorum*, 35; ibid., p. 320.

romancy and the problem of its correction. The stress placed in some of our sources upon the willingness of dead saints to return of their own volition may in part reflect efforts to discredit the necromancer and make him or her redundant. The ability wholly to call back the dead to life, an ability attributed to certain saints in these same sources, may represent an effort to outplay that non-Christian manipulator of the supernatural. The tangled problem of necromancy called forth many and complex responses, as we saw it did in our major sources about magic, and as well it might. Could such an ability ever be possessed by humans, the God-Man, Christ, apart? Augustine, as we saw, and Rabanus thought that it could not; but as the non-Christian necromancer seems to have been considered by others, (I have instanced Isidore and Hincmar) the worst type of condemned magician, both persistent and effective, so the capacity to bring the dead back to life seems, in some quarters, to have been attributed readily to selected saints.[60] The differing distribution in saints' lives of the ability of saints to call back the dead may, in its turn, represent divided answers to (and a varying incidence of) necromancy in action.

Necromancy and the resuscitation of the dead are, of course, opposites. One submits the dead person to magical manipulation; the other actively restores life to him, complete with free will. For that very reason, the condemned practice and such stories of resuscitation are extremely likely to be related. Aldhelm knew about the opposition between the two. Informed by the Clementine *Recognitions*, he was able to distinguish between the accusation of necromancy leveled by Simon Magus against Peter and that saint's real and positive ability to bring the dead back to life.[61] Samson of Dol's raising up of the boy untimely dead, related above, may have been aimed, as a story, against Druidic sacrificial and necromantic practices, as well as sculptured stone shrines. Saint Amand resuscitated a thief who had been condemned to the pillory by a mob of pagans and killed there. Here the miracle both turns the early death of a criminal to Christian uses (people rush to become Christians, pagan shrines are destroyed and religious communities are installed in their place) and accords the enormous power of bringing back the dead to Christian leaders, but, once again for

---

[60] And to be refused to others. On this see especially J.-C. Poulin, *L'Idéal de Sainteté dans l'Aquitaine Carolingienne* (Québec, 1975), pp. 111–114. He argues, for instance, that it was not a characteristic of Merovingian saints.

[61] Letter to King Gerontius and the priests of Britain, ca. 675–705; *edit.* E. Dümmler, et al., *MGH Epistolae Merowingici et Karolini Aevi* i (Berlin, 1892), 232.

clearly Christian purposes.[62] Certain saints, notably Saint Martin, were especially distinguished for bringing the dead back to life.

One story in Sulpicius takes us directly into an even deeper dimension of the Christian magical replacement for necromancy, and especially informatively. Sulpicius reports how Martin engaged in an inquiry that closely paralleled the practice of the ancient necromancer. The story is not about the complete resuscitation of a dead person, nor, still less, does it tell of the return of a dead saint, or worthy Christian person, of his own volition. It does, however, convey with a striking vividness the ferocity with which the rights of the Christian dead to their particular kind of rescued magic are defended. Martin here calls up a shade, the shade of a suspect martyr, who confesses that he was in fact a brigand, executed for his crimes. Martin accordingly, and very publicly, destroys the counterfeit cult.[63] This is a startling example of a dramatized Christian magical role reversal of a particularly thoroughgoing kind. The man's untimely death was just, yet he claimed the services due to the unjustly martyred, the Christian untimely dead, and their supernatural powers too. A Christian necromancer, therefore, intervenes (using a similar, though appropriately adjusted, ritual)[64] and restores the rightful state of affairs by ensuring that devotion and expectation are directed toward the authentic untimely dead. Layer upon layer of transformed practice are involved here, but all to the end of bringing to Christianity the best of the supernatural expectations visited upon the dead and their places of burial. Once more, non-Christian magical practices both inform the activities of the Christian magician and dictate to him the differences he must act out.

SANCTIFIED MAGICAL ACTIVITIES

Lotteries and Conjurations

Though lot casting in general was entirely forbidden, as both pagan and destructive of the proper and responsible operation of the will, and though the *Sortes Biblicae* and *Sortes Sanctorum* were so often condemned in church councils in company with all other forms of divi-

---

[62] *Vita Amandi Episcopi* I, 14–15; *edit.* B. Krusch and W. Levison, MGH SRM v (Hanover and Leipzig, 1910), 438–439.

[63] *Vita S. Martini*, 11, 1–5; *edit. and transl.* J. Fontaine, *Sulpice Sévère, Vie de Saint Martin* i (Paris, 1967), 276–277, ii (Paris, 1968), 692–712.

[64] Ibid., ii, 700–701. The resuscitation described in the *Vita* 7 is only very slightly less spectacularly geared to a contending world; ibid., i, 267–269, ii, 607–633.

nation, these *Sortes* enjoyed nonetheless a seemingly wholly secure existence. Their security appears, furthermore, not merely to have been unhindered, but in some quarters (and notably clerical ones) positively encouraged. There are excellent reasons for this. Firstly, Augustine had given his permission, albeit tentatively. Secondly, *Sortes* such as these were indeed relatively harmless when set beside the far worse forms of magic that threatened in our period, as Augustine had foreseen. Augustine had himself received directions crucial to his life and happiness through the seemingly random opening of the New Testament, or at least through the chance lighting of his eye upon particular passages in it, and this story had been made widely available in his *Confessions*.[65] And then again, it is hard to perpetuate a joyous belief in Divine Providence and yet totally to deny to that Providence all possibility of interventions of this kind. Lotteries could (and can) keep hope alive, and a faith in the conceivably beneficial effects of chance can do much to lift the spirits. It can be unwise, then, to discourage resort to such sources of hopeful human expectation when they are comparatively innocent—and perhaps even foolish when this resort might help in deeper ways to keep religious aspiration both alive and open to negotiation. This many early medieval churchmen saw.

Casting the Christianized *Sortes* took, in the main, three forms. Possible solutions to the particular problem for which divine direction was sought might be written upon slips of parchment or vellum, and the slips placed upon a holy place, probably the altar and usually under the cloth, to be drawn at a specified time. Books of the Bible, or service books, might be used, opened on the altar, or perhaps on a tomb, at random; or dice might still be cast (two or three, perhaps, of six sides each) and the answers read from an accompanying codex, rather in the style of the *Sortes Sangallenses*. Such *Sortes* did have certain built-in advantages. Attention was drawn through them to Christian shrines, and in particular to the especially holy parts of these. It was drawn also, of course, to the Christian holy book; and it was perhaps unlikely,

---

[65] *Confessions* VIII, 12, 9. On this episode, and for some insight into the complexity and care with which Augustine's experience here was built into Christian expectations of divine guidance little removed from the pagan, see P. Courcelle, "Source Chrétienne et allusions paiennes de l'episode du 'Tolle, lege' (Saint Augustin, Confessions VIII, 12, 19)," *Revue d'Histoire et de Philosophie Religieuses* 32 (1952), 171–200, and idem, "L'enfant et les 'sorts bibliques,' " *Vigiliae Christianae* 7 (1953), 194–220. The crucial passages came from Rom. 13:13–14 and 14:1, and encouraged Augustine to follow a life of continence.

in addition, that the slips of vellum, or the chosen books of the Bible (the Psalter, as it might be, or the Canticles or Gospels), or the pre-written Christian answers to the throwing of dice, would order too dreadful a course of action upon those who asked them for guidance. Further, though I have said that these books were opened at random, the process certainly provided an opportunity for a little theatrical manipulation, and one cannot escape the suspicion that this opportunity was on occasion seized—for, of course, the very best of reasons.[66] More important than these three reasons, however, is a fourth. These Christianized *Sortes* provided a relatively innocuous, yet strikingly imitative mechanism. Here was a device encouragingly similar to those operated by non-Christian practitioners, in the details both of the simple and of the complex forms of its operation; yet this device was operated by differently sanctioned leaders, and, as I have said, at a different shrine. The encouragement of such familiarities, with these crucial distinctions made, was a most adroit and sympathetic pastoral method of going about the transference of religious affection, one that was, I shall shortly argue, especially evident in the realm of supernatural curative practices. It was a means of changing in its essence the manner in which communication with the supernatural was customarily conducted, while maintaining many of the old and familiar appearances and habits. Hostility is kept at bay, and conversion is often more lasting, when custom and affection are thus respected and preserved.

There are many examples of the ways in which such *Sortes* actually operated. I shall recount a few of them here so that we can begin to understand more fully why they enjoyed such encouragement, and appreciate more clearly the services they provided. The simpler forms are attested early. Saint Patroclus, for instance, (d. 576), when wondering whether or not to go out into the desert, "for an auspice wrote out little notes, and placed them on the altar. Then he watched and prayed for three nights, so that the Lord might deign to reveal clearly to him what He ordered him to do. But the great mercy of divine goodness had decreed that he would be a hermit, and made him take the note which hastened his departure for the desert."[67] Patroclus's own notes replace the Bible here. Books were not always necessary to the Christian *Sortes*, but the altar or a special holy place is still important

<hr>

[66] Especially when it came to arousing support for a candidate for ecclesiastical office. See the remarks upon the election of Saint Anianus to the See of Orleans in Courcelle, "L'enfant," p. 202, and below.

[67] *Vitae Patrum* IX,2; transl. James, *Gregory of Tours*, p. 80.

(and seems usually to be so in Christianized lotteries), as are, of course, the verbal directions and the intervention of God. When, again, Bishop Leudgar of Autun died, there was some anxiety as to who should have the body of the saint, and there were three contestants for it. Once more, the possibilities were written down on slips of vellum and placed upon the altar for God to do the choosing. They were left all night, and the next day, after fasting and prayers and Mass, a priest was ordered to go and draw one from beneath the altar cloth; and Leudgar's body was, in accordance with its directions, returned to the first contestant. A night's incubation and, seemingly, fasting were required here for the lottery to work, and also a cloth, all preparations clearly similar to those needed in the pre-Christian invocation of an oracle. Only the different place and the special drawer of the lots mark a clear change from the non-Christian style of lot taking.[68] Just sometimes it was necessary only to hear the Psalms sung for the message to be received as a divine one. Early in the sixth century, Bishop Sollemnis of Chartres was quick to take advantage of the belief in auspices manifested by King Clovis and his army. On their way to do battle with the Goths, they heard Ps. 35:2 being chanted in church: "Take hold of shield and buckler, and rise for my help." Sensibly, they consulted the bishop, who both signed them with the sign of the cross (explaining that this was the true armament through which victory was assured) and advised them on strategy, successfully, of course.[69]

In his *History of the Franks* Gregory of Tours tells two particularly clear stories, both with morals attached, about the use of the full biblical form of the Christianized *Sortes*. They were consulted, for instance, by the clergy of Dijon (under the tutelage of the visiting bishop of Langres) in the making of a crucial political decision. The wicked Chramm, rebellious son of Lothar I, king of the Merovingian Franks (d. 561/62), was at the city gates.

The clergy placed on the altar three books, namely, those of the Prophets, the Epistles, and the Gospels, and prayed the Lord to reveal what should befall Chramm; they asked the divine power to declare whether he should prosper, and whether he should ever reign. At the same time it was agreed between them that each should read at Mass the passage which he found

[68] *Passio Leudgarii Episcopi Augustodunensis* II,24; *edit.* B. Krusch and W. Levison, MGH SRM v (Hanover and Leipzig, 1910), 347–348.

[69] *Vita Sollemnis Episcopi Carnoteni* 7–9; *edit.* B. Krusch and W. Levison, MGH SRM vii (Hanover and Leipzig, 1920), 316–318.

on opening the book. The book of the Prophets was opened first, and there they found this verse; "I will take away the wall thereof, and it shall be broken up; because it should have brought forth grapes, and it hath brought forth wild grapes." Then they opened the Epistles, and found this: "For ye yourselves know perfectly, brethren, that the day of the Lord shall come as a thief in the night. When they shall say Peace and safety, then sudden destruction shall come upon them as the pains of a woman in childbirth, and they shall not escape." And through the Gospels the Lord said; "He who heareth not my words shall be likened unto a foolish man who built his house upon the sand. And the rain descended, and the river-floods came, and the winds blew and beat upon that house, and it fell, and of it there was made great ruin."[70]

The choice of three books here is reminiscent of Tacitus's description of the choice of three directions by the Germanic priestly diviner. The consensus of the three books was that Chramm was not to be trusted, and he was not admitted to Dijon. This decision proved wise, for Chramm came to an exceedingly sticky end. He was strangled to death, and his body was then burned, together with those of his wife and daughters.

The *Sortes Biblicae* were cast also by Merovech, son of King Chilperic, in order to discover whether he would inherit the kingdom. He placed the Psalter, the Books of Kings, and the Gospels upon Saint Martin's tomb, spent a night there in prayer, and then endured a further three days of fasting and watching and praying before he returned to open them. He was immediately deeply depressed, Gregory tells us, by the direful pronouncements of all three, and by the gloomy morals they all drew from his discreditable past activities.[71] Merovech did not, of course, inherit the kingdom. This second story holds all the more interest for us by reason of some extra little pieces of information Gregory gives. Merovech, he says, had consulted the *Sortes Biblicae* explicitly to verify the predictions of a soothsayer. The latter had foretold that he would indeed succeed his father Chilperic. The Merovech presented to us by Gregory of Tours was clearly not wholly confident of the powers of such a seer. Gregory himself knew that Merovech would not succeed to the kingdom, for he had been told so by an angel in a

---

[70] IV,10; *transl.* Dalton, *Gregory of Tours* ii,130. The passages were, in order, Isa. 5:4–5 (not the Vulgate version), 1 Thess. 5:2–3, Matt. 7:26–27.

[71] *History of the Franks* V,8; ibid., pp. 181–183. The passages in this case were 1 Kings 9:9, Ps. 17:18, Matt. 26:2.

dream. Here we have a fine example of the service the Christianized *Sortes* (and here prophetic angels as well) might, by alert churchmen, be made to render to the Christian Church. In this story the Christian *Sortes* both take advantage of a moment of doubt about the older ways and insert themselves successfully by means of strikingly similar ones, together with a Christian "daemon" and dream. The whole perhaps gathers even more force from the fact that it is performed upon a tomb, haunt of outlawed sorcerers and necromancers.

The part-biblical, part-liturgical *Sortes* are described in the ninth-century *Life* of Bishop Hubert of Liège (d. 727) by Jonas of Orleans, and with every sign, once more, that these *Sortes* were approved. In this case they deal directly with death and burial (as did the simpler type called upon in the case of Leudgar's body), matters of pressing concern to certain categories of non-Christian magician, as we have seen, and susceptible of varied responses on the parts of Christian leaders. The *Sortes* response here, then, is a further example of the Christianization of one kind of condemned magic to defeat another, wholly unacceptable, kind. According to this account, the clergy of Liège felt, some sixteen years after the death of their saint, in need of guidance about a suitable setting for his remains. Operating on the basis of Matt. 10:26, "For there is nothing covered that shall not be revealed; and hid that shall not be known," they fasted for three days and, on the last of the three, placed the Gospels and a Sacramentary upon the altar. The Gospels fell open at Luke 1:10: "Fear not, Mary, for thou hast found favor with God." The Sacramentary gave the message "Guide the path of thy servant." Encouraged by both, the clergy set off in full procession to the Basilica of Saint Peter in Liège and there found the body of the saint to be incorrupt. The remains were reburied and Saint Peter's richly endowed accordingly.[72] The last event, of course, affords us a motive for the giving of this full account, and one might once more suspect a certain measure of manipulation. Equally, it shows in what high regard such proceedings were still held. The reason for an endowment rested upon a message given in the *Sortes*; what greater tribute to the *Sortes* could be given than this?

The Christian *Sortes* could also usefully (and dramatically, when employed in the midst of a great ceremony) confirm electors in their choice of prelate and give comforting prognostications about the char-

---

[72] *Vita Secundi Sancti Huberti* III,xv; AS Novembris 1,815–816.

acter of his rule.[73] In this way they could gladden the heart, not by fulfilling its dreams so much as by delivering those charged with making an important decision from too crushing a burden of responsibility. Of course, this was not a method of decision making calculated everywhere to command support, and we have seen that there were quarters in which it distinctly did not; but it is easy to see its attractions and, in difficult circumstances, its sense. Occasionally, chroniclers tell us of the Christian God's actively patronizing, for the time being, lot-casting procedures that are purely pagan, in order to turn them to his own use. One such story is to be found in Rimbert's *Life of Saint Anskar*. Here God allows the pagan procedure to turn a hostile army from Birka, to the great profit of Anskar's convert Christians.[74] This is a large and risky step to take into pagan supernatural territory, and one that illuminates all the more vividly the horror such contrivances evoked in official ecclesiastical circles. It was so very easy, after all, to overstep the mark. The smaller steps seem, however, to have enjoyed a distinguished following.

In order the better to appreciate the reasons for this following, it is worth dwelling for a moment, lastly, upon the complexities that could be involved in the casting of the full biblical *Sortes*; for these demonstrate both how well fitted these *Sortes* were to succeed the kinds of practices we find in the *Sortes Sangallenses* and with what good cause, in their seeming command of a special expertise, they might have been expected to gain for their practitioners an esteem at least equal to that of their non-Christian opponents. A British Library manuscript, MS B.L. Royal 7 D xxv, has an especially clear account of one set of the rules for casting the *Sortes* of the Psalter.[75] Interestingly, too, it in-

[73] As they did in the case of Heribert of Cologne (d. 1020). At his consecration the Gospels and Isaiah fell open at the most pleasing of places; AS Martii ii,479. The later *Life* of Lietbert of Cambrai (d. 1076) has his election confirmed by the opening of Matthew at 17:5; PL 146,1459. Tension over the election of no less a person than Saint Martin of Tours to his bishopric was resolved by a chance reading (in full congregation) of a passage from the Psalter. *Vita S. Martini* IX,5–7; *edit.* Fontaine, *Sulpice Sévère*, ii,654–656.

[74] Another story, in the *Annales Xantenses* (under the year 845), is interesting too. According to this, a Christian captive persuades his pagan captors to turn to a Christian method of lot casting, with the most felicitous results; *edit.* G. H. Pertz, MGH SS ii (Hanover, 1829), 228, 703. Both stories have about them an air of special pleading.

[75] Fol. 75ᵛ. This is a codex of great interest, containing material perhaps originally put together for the renowned scholar and astrologer Adelard of Bath. It is a small handbook, peculiarly apt for practical use.

cludes these directions together with a set of medicinal recipes, a carefully drawn sphere of life and death (together with all the numerical equivalents for the letters in that person's name whose fate was to be determined through its help), and a lunarium of the sick: one more indication of the fact that imitative mechanisms of this sort might be combined with imitative medical procedures and might be manipulated by a practitioner seeking leadership in both spheres of pastoral action. Here are the directions for these particular *Sortes* of the Psalter:

> If you need to find something out, you may do so in this way. Sing first of all a psalm on the first of the altar steps, that God will reveal to you that which you seek. Then open the Psalter, and look to it for the first letter, and you will find the answer to your question in this way.[76] A means life and power, B means power over the people, C some man's death, D trouble and death, E joy and happiness, F noble blood, G the slaying of a man,[77] H the slaying or death of a woman, I a good life, K a foolish conflict, L joy or honor, M some sorrow, N a return visit, O power, P health, Q life, R estates secure or plundered (?),[78] S the soul's salvation, T anger and change, V death, X a meeting with a relative, Y whatever you want will be told to you, Z money or some increase.

The procedure was hardly a difficult one to manage, but, contained in a book and manipulated, once again, by an ordained and literate Christian leader, it could easily seem as impressive as at least some of the mechanisms of the competition.

Another important manuscript containing directions for the casting of the *Sortes Sanctorum* survives from the library of the distinguished south German Benedictine abbey of Saint Emmeramm's, Regensburg. This is the tenth-century MS Bayerische Staatsbibliothek, clm. 14846.[79] Bound together with a copy of the *Ars Minor* of Donatus and a poem apparently in praise of Charlemagne, these directions seem both to have an ancestry stretching back possibly to the late eighth century (and to an exemplar complete with Old Irish and Old Breton glosses) and to be designed to be taken seriously. Again, the rules are for consulting the Psalter, and again the directions are taken from the

---

[76] "Si de aliqua re scire volueris, hoc modo scire poteris. Canta in primis aliquem psalmum ad primum altaris gradum, ut deus manifestet quod queris. Postea aperto psalterio in eo tibi per primam litteram aperte cognosce hoc modo quod queris" (MT).

[77] Reading "viris" for "unius" in the manuscript.

[78] "rurum restitutum vel vulneratum."

[79] Fols. 106–121.

first letter of the first word upon which the eye falls. For instance, in the case of questions about illness (fol. 108v), "E in the first part [of the page] means blood, in the head or in the feet, or an outpouring of it, or a mass of it in the stomach."[80]

A much more sophisticated manuscript exemplar of the casting of the *Sortes Biblicae* survives from the ninth century in MS Paris, B.N. lat. 11553. This is, furthermore, clearly a conflated copy of earlier exemplars. It contains a text of the Gospel of John divided up into 316 sections, and no fewer than 185 of these have written against them little indicatory notes (in Latin) that bear no relation at all to the Gospel text. They say such things as "If you are going to lie, they will catch you" or "It will work out."[81] The notes clearly respond this time to a very complex method of casting the *Sortes Biblicae*, probably by means of dice.[82] The Gospel of John also had an important role to play in Christian healing magic, as we shall see.

The early medieval church could offer, then, and did offer a whole range of derivative and imitative lotteries and conjurations. Much ancient and contemporary non-Christian lot casting and divination was aimed at the detection of criminals, and, in a rare revelatory moment, the *Lex Frisionum* tells of a murder case resolved by a process which is in fact a magnificent mixture of earlier forms of non-Christian lot casting, of reverence for wood, and of a form of the *Sortes Sanctorum*. The case is to proceed in this way. When seven suspects have been accused and have sworn oaths as to their innocence, two slips of wood, one marked with a cross, are to be wrapped separately in cloths and laid upon a church altar, or, failing that, upon some relics. A Christian priest (or a young boy, if there is no priest) is then to choose one. If the one with the cross on it is drawn, then the oath swearers are to be

---

[80] (MT.) These directions are set out in *edit.* J. Delumeau, *Documents de l'Histoire de Bretagne* (Toulouse, 1971), p. 98, together with interesting instructions on thief divining by means of the *Sortes*.

[81] This codex (together with its relationship to earlier exemplars) is discussed, and some of the notes printed, in J. R. Harris, "The Sortes Sanctorum in the St. Germain Codex ('g')," *American Journal of Philology* 9 (1888), 58–63.

[82] "The most probable method of using the *Sortes* would be by the selection of a number, for there are objections to the method of opening the book at random where the margins are thickly studded with sentences. Probably, therefore, a number was selected, and the pages of the Gospel of St. John were turned until the sentence was found to which that number was attached"; ibid., p. 60. A segmented wheel on fol. 89ᵛ, each segment containing numbers, 316 in all, suggests that several stages of computation were needed for the casting of the numbers required by these particular *Sortes*.

believed, and other suspects are to be asked to swear. If the unmarked one is drawn, however, then each person must write his own sign upon another slip of wood. These seven will all be wrapped, placed, then drawn again in turn; and the owner of the last lot to be drawn must make reparation for the murder.[83] This seems to have been a fine combination of pagan and Christian magical sanctions, worked out with care and acceptable to both sides. MS. CLM. 14846 included also, we might remember, a means of thief divining.

Gregory of Tours has an account of successful thief divining which actually involves a chalice, though in a way very different from that condemned in the *Homilia de Sacrilegiis*. A much-loved husband dies, and his wife makes a present of a special wine for masses for his soul. A certain subdeacon keeps the wine for himself and substitutes vinegar for it, knowing that the wife does not always take communion. The husband, however, appears to her in a dream and upbraids her for the quality of the wine. The next day she takes the chalice. The thief is revealed and is forced to make amends.[84] This is dream divination with a special dimension to it. Gregory carefully points out that such a discovery would not have been possible had the wife not been a person of great good works. We seem to have here, in short, a Christianized and very studied type of thief divining: it calls upon instruments familiar to a kind of non-Christian thief divining we know was practiced and condemned but uses them in a different way, through a morally irreproachable intermediary, and for a far more acceptable purpose. The similarities render the differences all the more striking within this particular context and are surely meant to do so. On another occasion, Gregory tells how a thief is brought to confess through the miraculous action of holy water in a water jar. In the press of a crowd of people, all coming to have their jars filled with the holy water, a man steals a knife from another's scabbard and hides it in his own. When he holds out his hands to receive his full jar, however, the water in it immediately disappears, in full sight of everybody. He confesses to the theft, and the water returns.[85]

[83] *Lex Frisionum* XIV,i; *edit*. G. H. Pertz, MGH *Leges* iii (Hanover, 1863), 667–668. And see P.C.J.A. Boeles, "Zu den friesischen Runendekmälern," *Runenberichte* 2/3 (1941), 122.

[84] "Quae tam ferventem acetum hausit ex calice, ut putaret sibi dentes excuti, si haustum segnius deglutisset." Gregory of Tours, *In Gloria Confessorum* 64; *edit*. Krusch, MGH SRM i(2), 335–336.

[85] *In Gloria Martyrum* 25; ibid., p. 53.

Gregory adds that a recalcitrant people needs such signs; and the signs are indeed, when set against non-Christian procedures, clear, for the parallels, once we look to these last, serve to throw them into especially sharp relief. In yet another story, a letter wielded by a bishop throws a thief into a fit and so induces him to confess to his crimes.[86] As in the case of the Christianized *Sortes*, so in divinations of this latter kind, some of the practices legitimated in stories about holy persons and saints reflect remarkably closely both the kinds of conjuring condemned and the purposes behind them; and they seem also to have been deliberately contrived to do so. Such stories regale us once more with evidence of victorious Christian attitudes and supernatural powers; but the deceptively simple impression they make at first sight is promptly dispelled when they are set within this deeper context.

One further spectacular example of Christianized magical manipulation in the matter of divining for criminals is the ordeal. The early medieval ordeal took several forms. It might involve the casting of the suspect, or the suspect's champion, or even the suspect's accuser, into a deep pool of water to see whether the element would reject him or not. It might involve the gripping of a heated iron bar, or walking across heated ploughshares (usually nine of them), to see whether the subsequent healing process would be sufficiently quick and thorough to prove the subject worthy. The ordeal might even follow a form of *Sortes Biblicae* whereby the Scriptures are called into play to declare upon guilt or innocence. If, for example, the Psalter were to rotate of its own volition at the approach of the supposed culprit, then guilt was proven.[87] Again, the Eucharist might be taken as a test of innocence or guilt.[88] All of these procedures clearly call upon the supernatural, indeed upon God himself, to divine who is the malefactor.

---

[86] Gregory of Tours, *Vitae Patrum* VIII; transl. James, *Gregory of Tours*, pp. 74–75. This power in written form recalls those written "petatia" condemned, once again, in the *Homilia de Sacrilegiis* and associated with the capture of fugitive slaves and thieves; edit. C. P. Caspari, *Homilia de Sacrilegiis. Aus einer Einsiedeler Handschrift des achten Jahrhunderts herausgegeben und mit kritischen und sachlichen Anmerkungen, sowie mit einer Abhandlung begleitet* (Christiania, 1886), pp. 11 and 40.

[87] W. Duerig, "Das Ordal der Psalterprobe in Codex Latinus Monacensis 100. Ihr liturgietheologischer Hintergrund," *Münchener theologische Zeitschrift* 24 (1973), 266–278.

[88] Bishop Abraham of Freising used it in this way to exculpate the Empress Judith in the face of rumors of her sexual misconduct with him. He swallowed it at her Requiem Mass, clearly calling upon the Host to damn him were either of them guilty. His innocence was vindicated. Thietmar of Merseburg, *Chronicle* II,41; R. Holzmann, *Die*

Indulgence in non-Christian divinatory practices would lose, it was declared, the participant the grace of baptism.[89] Given this stricture, it is at first sight both puzzling and ironic that a great pool meant for baptism should also be used, and frequently, for the administering of the ordeal by water;[90] and that that great inveigher against witchcraft and divination, Archbishop Hincmar, could use baptism as a model for (and justification of) that calling upon God to protect the righteous the ordeal required.[91] In fact, when placed within the setting of magical competition, the Christian ordeal is just one other instance, although a very deft and striking one, of the care which went into the replacement of outlawed magical procedures, and their practitioners, with similar, Christian, kinds, and of the assistance given to this replacement by belief in baptismal rituals and graces. The services this Christian ordeal procedure might render to a small village community, in the way of "objectifying" its tensions, allowing time for destructive emotions to cool, and saving those involved from loss of face or from too great a burden of responsibility, have been recently, and most expertly, made clear.[92] They were services of the greatest possible importance to that society of close-knit small rural settlements we know prevailed in early medieval Europe, and it would have been difficult in the extreme to find an adequate substitute for them. All we need here to add is the fact that they were themselves a substitute. The Christian ordeal procedures provided a substitute of a wholly like kind for those services the village diviners had previously rendered to the cause of

---

Chronik des Bischofs Thietmar von Merseburg und ihre korveier Überarbeitung (Berlin, 1955), p. 90.

[89] Caesarius, Sermon 53; transl. Mueller, Saint Caesarius, i,263–265.

[90] The pool in the baptistery of Canterbury, for instance, was so used in the eleventh century: R. W. Southern, St. Anselm and His Biographer (Cambridge, 1963), p. 265.

[91] De Divortio VI; PL 125,668–669.

[92] Peter Brown, "Society and the Supernatural: A Medieval Change," in idem, Society and the Holy in Late Antiquity (Berkeley, 1982), 302–332 (reprinted from Daedalus 104 [1975]). "An ordeal is a tacit 'defusing' of the issue. It is not a judgement by God; it is a remitting of the case ad iudicium Dei, 'to the judgement of God.' This is an action tantamount to removing the keystone of the arch on which, hitherto, all pressures had converged. Once removed, a decision can be reached quickly and without loss of face by either side. For by being brought to the judgement of God, the case already stepped outside the pressures of human interest, and so its resolution can be devoid of much of the odium of human responsibility"; p. 313. For a singularly sympathetic defense of the ordeal as a valid judicial process, see also R. V. Colman, "Reason and Unreason in Early Medieval Law," Journal of Interdisciplinary History 4 (1974), 571–591.

"objectification," a substitute requiring, once again, the smallest possible change and dislocation. Apparently a spectacular manifestation of medieval "superstitious" beliefs (and a manifestation about two forms of which we now know quite a lot),[93] the adoption of the ordeal by the early medieval church is no sign of superstition *tout simple*; nor is it to be dismissed as a weak compromise with barbarism. Though striking and inclined to catch the eye, it is in fact just one more indication of the sober care the organization came to take in the preserving, in as intact a state as possible, of those prevailing non-Christian magical procedures which sustained both the fabric of village society and the credibility of many of its much needed leaders.

Once again, sympathetic adaptations of this sort were apt to cause confusion. We often find rulings against the carrying of sacred objects, holy oil for instance, or the Eucharist itself, as amulets against the ordeal: of one form of Christian magic, that is, being used to neutralize another. Burchard, a notable defender of the ordeal, decrees a seven-year penance for such a delict.[94] Such confusions are understandable. Magical neutralization procedures of this sort had, after all, been a feature at least of sections of the old rejected magical world, if we are to believe the sagas.[95] Sometimes a Christian king, such as Olaf Tryggvason, was depicted as defeating hostile magic by a stronger magic of his own,[96] and the *Sortes* could themselves be used as a kind

[93] See R. Bartlett, *Trial by Fire and Water: The Medieval Judicial Ordeal* (Oxford, 1986), especially pp. 1–90.

[94] "Hast thou drunk the holy oil in order to annul a judgement of God or made or taken counsel with others in making anything in grass or in words or in wood or in stone or in anything foolishly believed in, or held them in thy mouth, or had them sewn in thy clothing or tied about thee, or performed any kind of trick that thou didst believe could annul the divine judgement? If thou hast, thou shouldst do penance for seven years on the appointed days." Burchard, *Corrector*; *transl.* McNeill and Gamer, *Medieval Handbooks*, p. 339. Other references are given in Browe, "Die Eucharistie," 134–135. His argument that the Eucharist came only to be employed as a protection of this kind late in the eleventh century is not, I think, fully convincing. Regino seems to rule against it, and there is, of course, the precedent of Saint Ambrose; see below.

[95] Magic to enable a criminal to escape justice is not infrequently found in the sagas. In the *Eyrbyggja Saga* XX, for example, Katla conceals her son Odd from his pursuers by creating illusions so that they cannot see him. This works until a better magician defeats her; *transl.* P. Schach, *Eyrbyggja Saga* (Lincoln, Nebr. 1959), pp. 37–39. Katla spins as she performs her magic. In *Njal's Saga* XII the wizard Svan magically conceals a murderer; *transl.* M. Magnusson and H. Palsson, *Njal's Saga* (Harmondsworth, Middlesex, 1960), pp. 60–63.

[96] As when, the *Heimskringla* tells us, he turns their conjured-up mists and dark-

of neutralization procedure, as we have seen and shall see. This is, however, very dangerous ground, strewn with hazards of many different types. Above all, the lines that delimit the areas of the rescued and condemned forms of magic respectively can be so very easily lost to sight. It is this that seems to cause pastors unease, an unease which would not, perhaps, have been quite so deeply felt had the efforts at accommodation not been espoused with such hope and enthusiasm, and had they not, also, met with redoubtable opposition within the church itself.[97] The severity of the penalties (for seven years is an exceptionally heavy penance for Burchard to inflict) may perhaps be a measure both of the investment made in such efforts and of the strength of the internal opposition. It is one thing to encourage a parallel, and to some questionable, Christian means of invoking the supernatural in the pursuit of justice; it is quite another to have it pervert justice's course and gratuitously give fuel to one's adversaries. Abuses of this order could bring the whole idea of accommodation and assimilation into jeopardy. They had therefore to be treated seriously.

The ordeal was neither universally, nor long, supported as the best demonstration of the justice of the Christian God. In the early Middle Ages, however, it may well have been, in some areas, the most suitable available: the least offensive to local sensibilities, that is, and the most protective of local mores that the church could find. With a struggle, then, it acquired a place in the world of magic-made-respectable; and efforts to have other forms of magic-made-respectable neutralize its power were, as a result of this struggle, especially savagely condemned.

Weaving and Binding

I have mentioned the fact that an altar cloth or a tomb cloth occasionally played a part in the consutation of the Christian *Sortes*. Altar and tomb cloths, *Godwebbe*, were important in many other forms of Christianized magic too. They feature especially often in stories about su-

---

nesses back upon the original magicians and the criminals they had protected by it; *transl.* L. M. Hollander, *Heimskringla* (Austin, Tex., 1964), pp. 213–214.

[97] Especially, once more, from Archbishop Agobard of Lyons (d. 840). His *De Divinis Sententiis Contra Iudicium Dei*, though directed largely against trial by battle, objects in principle to that quasi-divinatory manipulation of God which was demanded by other forms of ordeal too: *De Divinis Sententiis* I,II; *edit.* L. Van Acker, *Agobardi Lugdunensis Opera Omnia*, CC (Turnholt, 1981), pp. 31–32. The difference between the position he adopts and that adopted by his near contemporary in space and time, Archbishop Hincmar, shows vividly again how divisory was the problem of the accommodation of magical practice.

pernatural curative practices, and some of their interventions (together with the sources that speak of them) will be discussed more fully below in the section on Christian supernatural healing. It is worth noting here, however, how very narrowly allied the use of Godwebbe often is, not merely to the casting of the *Sortes Sanctorum* and *Sortes Biblicae*, but to the use of other quasi-magical Christian specifics, and how closely matched they all can be seen to be to those ways of invoking the supernatural which were condemned. It is thus, once again, hard to avoid the conclusion that, like the Christian *Sortes*, many of these uses of Godwebbe were meant to be a sensitive substitute for magical activities which had, in the end, to be outlawed.

On certain occasions Godwebbe seems to have been used directly as a counter to the condemned magic associated with weaving and ligatures. Take, for instance, this charm for cattle:

> For lung trouble in cattle: The plant found in homesteads; it is like the plant "hound's stale"; there grow black berries of the same size as other peas. Pound; put into holy water; put into the mouth of the cattle. Take that same plant; put upon burning coals; and fennel and hassock and fine linen ["Godwebbe"] and incense. Burn all together on the windward side; make it smoke upon the cattle.[98]

Here are the coals with which Hincmar saw witches conjuring, and smoke, and herbs—and weaving. Wool often also seems to be allowed to play in itself an important part in healing "loosing" spells. "For a woman suddenly going dumb: Take pulegium, and grind to dust and wrap up in wool. Lay it under the woman. Soon will she be better."[99] This hardly seems far removed from the applications used by those harioli who were called in to minister to the wife of Serenatus, stricken in just the same way. Again: "For cheek disease, take the whorl, with which a woman spinneth, bind on the man's neck with a woollen thread, and swill him on the inside with hot goats milk; it will be well

---

[98] *Lacnunga* CXLIb. Also, CXLIIb: "Make five Christ-crosses of hassock-grass; set on four sides of the cattle and one in the midst. Sing around the cattle: 'I will bless the Lord at all times' (Psalm 34) to the end, and 'Benedicite' and litanies and Pater Noster; sprinkle holy water on them; burn around them incense and fine linen [Godwebbe]; and let the cattle be valued. Give the tenth penny for God; and after that leave them to mend; do thus thrice"; *transl.* J.H.G. Grattan and C. Singer, *Anglo-Saxon Magic and Medicine* (Oxford, 1952), pp. 176–179.

[99] CLIIa; ibid., pp. 180–181.

with him."[100] Once more, a source of enchantment fiercely condemned is, while retaining many of the same materials, translated into another dimension. Its beneficent aims and different wielders make it now a respectable form of magic.[101] There are great numbers of such examples, especially among the abundant surviving evidence of Christian curative charms and practices, and more will be mentioned in the final section of this chapter. It is tempting, too, to connect an emphasis on ecclesiastical textiles with a desire to associate these with, yet distinguish them from, contemporary weaving of a magical sort. When King Athelstan of the Anglo-Saxons, for instance, went north in 934 to give gifts to the shrine of Saint Cuthbert, among these gifts was a stole: a beautifully textured and colored and woven ecclesiastical vestment, that is, and bestowed upon a population at least partly composed of non-Christians with a belief in magical weaving.[102] A similar effort at transformation without too much loss may stand behind the emergence of women especially (or, in the case of the Anglo-Saxon *Elene*, angels) as peace-weavers.

When speaking of the way in which Saint Wulfram defeated the pagan lottery, and of the release of the captive thegn Imma, I touched upon the subject of Christianized binding-and-loosing spells. An ability to break the bonds of a captive seems to have been a characteristic of early medieval sanctity and a highly respectable end for Christian magic to pursue.[103] Christian binding and loosing, of course, has ex-

---

[100] *Leech Book* III,vi; transl. O. Cockayne, *Leechdoms, Wortcunning and Starcraft of Early England* ii (London, 1864), 310–312. The Anglo-Saxon supplement to the *Herbarius* recommends, also, this way of using milotis: "This wort thou shalt take up in the waning of the moon, in the month which hight August; take then the root of this wort, and *bind it to a yarn thread*, and hang it to thy neck; that year thou shalt not feel dimness of thine eyes, or if it befall thee, it suddenly shall depart, and thou shalt be hale. This Leechcraft is a proved one." Ibid., i,320–321.

[101] It is true that "classical borrowings" may account for some of the uses of fine linen we find in these sources—in the *Medicina de Quadripedibus* of Sextus Placitus, for example. Cockayne, *Leechdoms*, i,326–329. They do not, however, account for all of them, and it seems proper in any case to ask on such occasions quite why specific "classical borrowings" were chosen. That such classics were quarried merely because they *were* classics is, I think, both unproven and unlikely.

[102] This stole survives. In the list of gifts given, the vestments and altar cloths (three) are accorded a high priority, preceded only by the Gospels. *Historia de Sancto Cuthberto* 2b; *edit.* T. Arnold, *Symeonis Monachi Opera Omnia* i, RS (London, 1882), 211.

[103] The saintly Queen Mathilda of Germany (d. 968) was also able to release captives from their bonds through her attendance at Mass, according to Thietmar, *Chron-*

plicit gospel support. It has it in Matt. 18:18, for instance, where Christ grants to his disciples the powers of binding and loosing on earth and in heaven, and in John 20:23, in which these powers are associated with the loosing and binding of sin. The powers involved in the gospel grants, and devolved in the early Middle Ages upon priests, are similar in many ways to those of a pagan defixio. It should not, then, perhaps be a matter for too much surprise that we can find them deployed specifically against pagan binding spells. We do, indeed, find them so deployed; but, and interestingly, not so much in association with the original biblical permissions as with the contemporary magical scene. Bede's story of Imma is particularly vivid and instructive. Imma's captors are unable to bind him, for the fetters will keep falling off. The captors suspect, as we saw, that Imma must have access to powerful runic spells; but Imma has, in fact, a stronger source of supernatural power. His brother is having masses said for him. [104] Bede does not here appeal to the gospel grant at all but instead ranges this loosing power directly against Imma's captors' clear belief in a non-Christian form of magic. Though gospel authority is at hand, it is the pressure of non-Christian magical belief and practice that actually induces Bede to bring this countering Christian form of magic to the fore, and to emphasize it.

The original opposition between the pagan and the Christian defixio is carried forward here into circumstances in which magic posed similar threats, and Christian binding and loosing is accorded a magical role again appropriate to these immediate circumstances. The same may be said, perhaps, of that most famous of all Christian means of cursing: excommunication. Though of a long and unimpeachable ancestry, such ceremonies take on an extra meaning when set against parallel contemporary ones, and the pressure of these last gives us an additional explanation for the shape and form of such ceremonies, and for the enthusiasm with which they continued to be used.

---

icle I, 21; edit. Holtzmann, *Die Chronik*, p. 26. The church of Saint Nicetius of Lyons contained a whole heap of iron chains and fetters broken by the saint: Gregory of Tours, *Vitae Patrum* VIII, 10; transl. James, *Gregory of Tours*, p. 75. See the section to follow on Christian medical magic for the releasing capacities of the tomb cloth of Saint Martin and of the relics carried by Bishop Wilfred. There are many such examples. One effect of the Christian *Sortes* recommended by the captive in the *Annales Xantenses* (edit. Pertz, MGH SS, ii, 228) was the release of all the Christian captives.

[104] *Ecclesiastical History* IV, 22; edit. Colgrave, *Bede's Ecclesiastical History*, pp. 402–403.

CHRISTIAN LOVE MAGIC

Of all the areas of magical activity that provoked the rise of a Christian form of countering magic, this is perhaps the most contentious and hard to deal with. The discouraging attitude of sections of the medieval Christian Church to human sexual love is well attested, both in those writings of Saints Jerome and Augustine for which the church expressed so great an enthusiasm[105] and in the institutions and offices for which it required a celibate life. Again, there are flawless biblical and patristic authorities for the attitude the medieval church so publicly adopted. And yet, we can detect once more in this attitude pressures which sprang from non-Christian beliefs in love magic: pressures that were immediate and found echoes accordingly in Christian ways of dealing with this problem too. There is a sense, for instance, in which certain of the gospel supports for Christian marriage can be said to impose a binding of a magical kind, one not at all unlike that to be found in the Greek magical papyri. The passages declaring that what God had joined together no man might part (Matt. 19:6, Mark 10:9) seem to denote a power of this sort and could certainly be used to enforce it. It is worth looking, therefore, first of all at some of the ways in which early medieval Christian marriage was viewed, and its rules formulated, if we are to try to answer questions about how the early medieval church contended with non-Christian love magic. Some of these answers might have surprises in them.

One of the most important sources of information about early medieval Christian attitudes to marriage is Archbishop Hincmar of Rheims. Archbishop Hincmar set out his position most clearly in two treatises, in the *De Divortio Lotharii and Tetbergae*, that is, and in his *De Nuptiis Stephani et filiae Regimundi Comitis*.[106] The *De Divortio* has already been heavily quarried, of course, but I propose to depend upon Hincmar exceptionally heavily here once again for three particular reasons. Firstly, he felt so strongly about non-Christian love magic, and wrote with such passion, that his views upon it and his ways of countering it deserve to be taken with the utmost seriousness. Sec-

---

[105] See especially on this subject P. Delhaye, "Le dossier anti-matrimonial de l' 'Adversus Jovinianum' et son influence sur quelques écrits latins du XIIᵉ siècle," *Medieval Studies* 13 (1951), 65–86.

[106] The *De Nuptiis* is to be found in *PL* 126, 132–153. Other references to Hincmar's views on marriage are collected together in J. Devisse, *Hincmar Archévêque de Reims 845–882* i (Paris, 1973), 379–416.

ondly, the case he puts forward for the indissolubility of Christian marriage once validly contracted, advanced as it is within the particular context of his belief in (and extreme distaste for) non-Christian love magic, takes on a new meaning and might lead us to think new thoughts about the place and origins of clerical attitudes to Christian marriage at other times. Hincmar places great trust in the ritual binding power of Christian marriage, for instance, and seeks to reinforce it with "ecclesiastical medicine" of a kind very akin to pure magic.

Thirdly, and perhaps most interestingly of all (especially when placed against this particular background), there are further, and possibly rather novel, suggestions to be made about Hincmar himself. Hincmar clearly believed in the maleficent power of witches in general, and in that of women in matters of love magic in particular. But it may be that his enthusiasm for the binding power of Christian marriage, and for the types of Christian countermagic he advances here in its service, spring in part from a desire to protect these very women, much as he disliked them—to protect them, that is, from the effects of malevolent magical power in other hands, and also against secular accusations of their use of it, along with the penalties liable to follow the successful pursuit of such accusations. This third possibility adds a large and complex dimension to the problem of the means by which non-Christian love magic could be, and was, countered by Christians. Such aspects of early medieval Christian marriage rules and Christian responses are not those generally foremost to the modern mind. But they might well, I propose to argue, have been foremost in the mind of Hincmar, and this precisely because of the magical context within which he had to operate. They might have been present, then, in the minds of others too. We shall look first here at Hincmar's rulings upon marriage within their immediate context, and then at the possible application to the wider scene of his particular emphases.

Although it is hard to be sure which rules and practices applied to which specific area, it seems that the marital rules current among the Franks in general could allow of divorce, and indeed of both divorce and remarriage on the part of either man or woman. There were four main grounds for divorce. A man might divorce his wife on grounds of adultery, witchcraft (maleficium), or the violation of graves. A woman might divorce her husband on the latter two grounds and on that of homicide.[107] Certain of the other secular codes make it clear that false

---

[107] *Leges Burgundionum* XXXIV (2): "Si quis vero uxorem suam forte dimittere vol-

and deeply damaging accusations on these grounds, and especially on the grounds of adulterous maleficium, were not uncommon.[108] The seriousness with which the violation of graves was viewed is interesting in the context of the alarms about haunting and necromancy reviewed above; divorce on grounds of adultery or witchcraft, however, interests us here. It would be wrong, I think (despite an observation made by Hincmar and to be noted below) to deduce that divorce for adultery was a device available *solely* to men against women. *Maleficium* is an imprecise term, after all, and it could include magically induced adultery. It seems nonetheless true to say that women, given their predominance in those condemnations of love magic I have already recounted, were in general more vulnerable than were men to divorce on these grounds.

Christian marriage, as Hincmar described it in his treatise and his letter, differed from the prevailing contemporary secular practices and contracts in two particular respects. The original Christian marriage contract depended for its validity upon the free will of both contracting parties;[109] and it allowed, once the marriage had been validly contracted, only for separation (on biblically based grounds of unchastity). It did not allow for divorce or for remarriage. Hincmar spells out resoundingly the case against divorce once the marriage has been solemnized (calling upon Matt. 19:6 and a whole array of patristic and papal views, among them the famous letter of Pope Nicholas I to the Bulgars), and he objects specifically to the notion that barrennness or adultery on the woman's part might constitute such grounds. Men might have no license not allowed to women, he points out.[110] Each party had to be treated equally in this respect. Nor could a union be

---

uerit et ei potuerit vel unum de his tribus criminibus adprobare, id est: adulterium, maleficium vel sepulchrorum violatricem, dimittendi eam habeat liberam potestatem." *Leges Burgundionum—Lex Romana* XXI (3): "Quod si mulier nolente marito repudium ei dare voluerit, non aliter fieri hoc licebit, quam si maritum homicidam probaverit, aut sepulchrum violatorem, aut veneficum." *Edit.* L. R. De Salis, *MGH Leges Nationum Germanicarum* ii (1) *Leges Burgundionum* (Hanover, 1892), 68, 144. Here I take "veneficus" to be equivalent to "maleficus," an equivalence which seems justified by the other readings in the apparatus.

[108] *Recc. Erv. Chind.* VI,1,6 prescribes fierce penalties for those who accuse others falsely of "veneficium, maleficium, adulterium," resulting in death or loss of property; *edit.* Zeumer, *MGH Legum*, i,255.

[109] "voluntas propria suffragaverit, et vota succurrerint legitima": *De Divortio* IV; PL 125,649.

[110] Ibid., V; 652.

dissolved because it had not yet been consummated. Provided that certain conventions were observed (approaches to and acceptance by the guardians of the bride, betrothal, *dotatio*, and *traditio*), and that there was no barrier of relationship within the prohibited degrees (often termed incest) or irremediable impotence, once the betrothal blessing, the dotatio, and the sealing nuptial mass had been completed, no breaking of the marriage bond could be permitted.[111]

The two matters of the prohibited degrees and irremediable impotence claim our attention within this particular context. The presence of either of these conditions, on Hincmar's ruling, would render the marriage in effect no marriage at all, and the apparent union "dissoluble" (such a dissolution was not, of course, divorce, but merely an authoritative assertion that no marriage had ever taken place); and the second condition, "irremediable impotence" gave a special power over this dissolution to women. Hincmar did, indeed, in theory seem to have found it readily acceptable for a woman to be allowed to break an apparent marital union should her partner prove wholly incapable of consummating the union sexually;[112] but he was careful about it in practice. And to the service of this care he harnessed a form of Christianized magic interesting both in itself and for the information it has to offer about the many different ways in which Christianized magic might be used.

As we have already seen, Hincmar truly believed that witches were very widely to be found, that they could exercise a real and preternatural power, and that they were usually female. He was certain too that among their many capacities lay the power to inflict impotence upon a hapless male; and, furthermore, that abandoned and malevolent mistresses and adulteresses (like Lothar's Waldburga) were especially inclined to resort to such a measure as a means of redress. Thus, when expanding upon his allowable reasons for the dissolution of an apparent marital union ("incest," that is, and impotence), Hincmar draws a markedly careful distinction between that incapacity on the part of the man to consummate a marriage which springs from natural causes and which is to be presumed incurable (from his being born a eunuch,

[111] One widely read ruling, found in the *Hispana,* would have it that the marriage became indissoluble once the betrothal blessing had been given by the priest; PL 84,632.

[112] *De Nuptiis;* PL 126,137. Also K. Ritzer, *Le Marriage dans les Églises Chrétiennes du 1e au 11e Siècles* (Paris, 1970) (translated from the 1962 German edition), pp. 355–356.

for example) and that impotence which is inflicted by witches (with diabolical assistance). This second type of impotence *might* be cured. It might not readily, then, render a marriage null or allow of a "divorce." And as a means toward its cure he advocates resort to a particular brand of "ecclesiastical medicine." He specifies within this context the loosing powers of confession, exorcism, and other kinds of priestly help (perhaps the blessed oil and salt that worked such wonders on other occasions). Only if the "ecclesiastical medicine" fails, and does so unmistakably, can the afflicted couple break the marriage bond; and, once they have done so, they may not marry subsequently, no matter that the power to consummate the marriage may have returned to them.[113] This last point is crucial. It provides a sharp and most valuable insight into the intricacy of social motive which impelled the espousal of certain Christian forms of magic. The Christian magical prescriptions are here to be followed absolutely, and their verdict is to be the final one.

Now at first sight, as impotence, according to Hincmar, allowed for a marriage to be made null, one might expect that Hincmar's manifest belief in the powers of maleficent women (especially adulteresses) magically to inflict impotence upon their unfortunate foes would have increased the possible incidence of marital dissolution.[114] Again, in that

---

[113] "nuptias quas concubitus pro quibusdam causis non sequitur, solvi posse, et propter incontinentiam feminas ad alias convalere valet. Sed subtilis investigatio et rationabilis discretio in his prius est adhibenda, utrum quasi naturalis in viris sit hujusmodi commixtionis impossibilitas (quia et sunt eunuchi, sicut scriptum est, qui de matris utero sic nati sunt) an hoc impedimentum operatione diaboli, sicut fieri adsolet, illis accidit. Quod si per sortiarias, atque maleficas, occulto, sed nunquam vel nusquam iniusto, Dominici judicio permittente, et diabolo operante, accidit, hortandi sunt quibus ista eveniunt ut corde contrito, et spiritu humiliato, Deo et sacerdoti de omnibus peccatis suis puram confessionem faciant, et profusis lacrymis, ac largioribus eleemosynis, et orationibus, atque jejuniis, Domino satisfaciant . . . et per exorcismos, atque caetera medicinae ecclesiasticae munia ministri ecclesiae tales, quantum annuerit Dominus . . . sanare procurent. Qui si forte sanare non potuerunt, separari valebunt. Sed postquam alias nuptias expetierint, illis in carne viventibus, quibus iunctae fuerint, prioribus, quos reliquerunt, etiamsi possibilitas concumbendi eis reddita fuerit, reconciliari nequibunt." *PL* 126,151. He specifies holy oil and salt in the *De Divortio*; see below.

[114] Gratian seems to have thought so, for he has difficulty with this last section of Hincmar's ruling and points out that it is inconsistent with papal policy. *Decretum* 2.33.1.4; *edit.* E. A. Friedberg, *Corpus Iuris Canonici* i (repr., Graz, 1955), 1150. Hincmar's works are sorely in need of a good modern edition, and it is by no means certain which of them were available to Gratian, and in what form he had them. From

maleficium constituted grounds for secular divorce, then it might seem that, by expressing his belief in maleficium Hincmar made such maleficae more vulnerable, both to secular divorce and to secular punishment for their malfeasance. I would suggest that, in fact, the opposite is the case; and "ecclesiastical medicine," stronger Christian magic, holds the balance. This is a straight battle of magic—a battle of a most revealing kind, and one in which a certain type of Christianized magic plays a part that both explains and justifies its adoption.

Through the general emphasis Hincmar places upon the permanence of the ritual binding power of Christian marriage, through his specific stress upon the power the ecclesiastical countermagic he prescribes can wield against the magical "knot" of impotence, Hincmar declares it to be virtually impossible for such witches to inflict this impotence irremediably. Christian magical *medicamenta* so neutralize the abilities witches have to procure impotence, in short, that they render them wholly unable to threaten the Christian marriage knot. The argument is an extremely ingenious one; it is one, also, that could only have been elaborated, and can only be perceived as powerful, within the context of the presence of witchcraft, and of Hincmar's belief in it. And there is yet more to this argument. In that maleficium of this type is so eminently well able to be neutralized by means of ecclesiastical countermagic, then this fact renders it all the harder for those who practice maleficium to be divorced for it at secular law. Thus, in broadening the church's authority and power in such matters, Hincmar manages to some extent to correct the disability that women suffered under the contemporary secular dispensation. We may find in this particular context, moreover, one more reason for Hincmar's support of the ordeal. The ordeal was not infrequently used as a device for the detection of adultery.[115] Here was another form of Christian magic that might serve to keep so sensitive a matter as love magic within the church's control, and by a means as little offensive as possible to contemporary belief in the power of adulteresses. The ordeal was a valuable weapon in Hincmar's armory.

Layer upon layer of meaning attach to Hincmar's rulings upon marriage and to his patronage of Christianized love magic, and we can

---

the copies we have, however, it seems unlikely in the extreme, as I shall shortly argue, that Hincmar could easily have pronounced "ecclesiastical medicine" a failure and so permitted such a dissolution. Gratian, at a distance of three hundred years, may perhaps have misunderstood the context within which Hincmar operated.

[115] Bartlett, *Trial*, pp. 16–20.

penetrate only a few of them. These few do, however, cast additional light upon those circumstances which can both provoke and justify the rise of Christian magic at certain times. Christian marital binding, and "ecclesiastical medicine" of a quite clearly magical kind, are called in here to defeat a form of non-Christian magic that was forceful and believed in, and for many ends. These ends included, and this should be doubly stressed, the active protection of the rights of women—even of those of women witches. Hincmar devised his measures to defeat, on the one hand, the much feared powers of these witches over human love, and, on the other, the penalties they themselves might suffer for their efforts, or supposed efforts. Once more, assertive, and in this case deeply dangerous, contemporary non-Christian magic stands behind a magical response on the part of the church.

Hincmar, then, set himself to nullify non-Christian love magic by stronger Christian kinds. And, further, he rendered love maleficium incapable of providing an excuse for divorce, or persecution, by his firm assurances (set out especially clearly in the *De Divortio*) that such non-Christian magic, strong as it was, sprang not from human capacities, but wholly from the devil. Hincmar devoted a long section of this treatise to proving this point.[116] Here, once more, we have the rescued demons of the old magic invoked rather to save than to condemn (as were, as I suggested, the tolerated *Dusii*); and here, and interestingly, they were invoked especially to save women accused of love magic from subjection to savage penalties, rejection from the marriage bed and the marriage property included. Blessed salt and holy oil were to be applied to the haplessly afflicted by magic, freeing them from the demons that attacked them. An illuminating extra passage in this same treatise shows an appreciation of the need, in the battle against these magically adept demons, for the unbinding of confession and absolution as well.[117] A little more reparation was required from obdurate cooperators with the demons than from the simply unfortunate (confession and heavy disciplinary penances for free persons, and beatings for slaves), but never the heavy penalties of secular law, still less drowning "more maleficorum"; and the ordeal, especially the ordeal by water, was a particularly speaking counter to punishments such as this last.

Supernatural Christian binding-and-loosing powers and Christian-

[116] PL 125,720–725.
[117] PL 125,725.

ized magical means of judgment are, then, here given prominence in a context charged with opposing love magic. They are called upon expressly to contend both with it per se and, and especially interestingly, with its possibly fatal consequences at the hands of secular judges. Early medieval attitudes to the strix or striga become all the more illuminating against this background. Certain well-respected Roman authors—Ovid, Petronius, Festus, Apuleius—preserved a memory of a ravenous bird-sorceress, especially inclined to devour children or to render men impotent or eat them. The belief still clearly had life in it in the early Middle Ages. One passage in the laws of the Salian and Ripuarian Franks suggests that a "strix" can in fact be proved to have eaten someone (in which case she is liable for a huge fine),[118] and Charlemagne's Saxon Capitulary of 785 suggests that the Saxons still believed in the "striga" (man or woman), for he prescribes execution for anyone who has committed murder on that account.[119] Rothair's Edict is especially anxious about any woman accused of being a "strix."[120] Clearly women were greatly vulnerable to accusations such as these, and it seems reasonable to suppose that secular divorce customs played, once more, a large part in rendering them thus vulnerable. "Strigae" too are named among the witches Hincmar mentions. In this specific context again, Christian supernatural belief and practice had an important place in the protection of women accused of love maleficium. Even though women are clearly thought by pastors such as Hincmar especially effective in this branch of magical exercise, it is better for them to be thought subject to the power of demons, and for both to be overcome by a more powerful form of ecclesiastical countermagic, than for such women to be submitted to the penalties available to the secular authorities.[121] We have an interesting contrast here again with certain of the courses of action toward such "witches" favored in later periods.

[118] 64,3; transl. T. J. Rivers, The Laws of the Salian and Ripuarian Franks (New York, 1986), p. 109.

[119] Chapter 6: "Si quis a diabulo deceptus crediderit secundum morem paganorum, virum aliquem aut feminam strigam esse et homines commedere, et propter hoc ipsam incenderit vel carnem eius ad commedendum dederit vel ipsam commederit, capitali sentientiae punietur"; edit. A. Boretius, MGH Capitularia i (Hanover, 1883), 68–69. Loyn and Percival translate the term "striga" simply as "witch"; transl. H. R. Loyn and J. Percival, The Reign of Charlemagne (London, 1975), p. 52.

[120] 197; transl. K. Fischer Drew, The Lombard Laws (Philadelphia, 1976), p. 90.

[121] Hincmar was, in general, notably sympathetic to women; Devisse, Hincmar, i,401.

It would be ridiculous, of course, to relate the sort of ecclesiastical medicine Hincmar recommends, still more the liturgical ceremonies and regulations of early medieval Christian marriage and continence in general, solely to the insistent presence of that love magic which pressed upon such pastors. Nonetheless, it did press; and it did have a place in decisions about the permissibility of retaliatory supernatural activity. And some of the permissible Christian magical counters were less cruelly destructive of the place of magicians in society, and still less so of that of women magicians, than might at first appear. Again, they could be misunderstood. The church's emphasis in affairs of the heart both upon the binding power of the nuptial mass and upon its power against maleficium seems to be reflected in one of the more revolting of the miracle stories recorded by Peter Damian. According to this, a woman who fears she has an adulterous husband consults a neighboring woman about a cure. The latter advises her to reserve a portion of the Host from her communion and to administer it to the erring husband "non sine quibusdam maleficiis." She does so—and the reserved section of the Host reveals its strength in such matters by turning into flesh.[122] Here we have, once again, love magic, marriage, the Mass, and even a form of the Eucharistic ordeal. The Christian functions of marriage, the Mass, and the ordeal as measures against adultery are very evidently misconstrued in this eleventh-century tall tale; but, and equally evidently, the story carries an echo of supernatural operations in matters of love magic which were remembered as helpful to women. The point must be made once again that later misunderstandings and abuses should not be allowed to detract from our appreciation of the care with which such measures were originally devised.

Finally, certain love spells, some to excite love or to overcome impotence inflicted by witchcraft, some concerned to prevent miscarriage and to enable a child to be brought to full term, also managed to cross the frontier between forbidden and accepted, even encouraged, magic. There are particularly engaging ones to be found among the material that has survived from Anglo-Saxon England.[123] A few are preserved

---

[122] Peter Damian, *Opuscula* XXXIV; *PL* 145,572–573. I have this reference from Browe, "Die Eucharistie," 134–154, but he does not mention this aspect of the story.

[123] "If to anyone anything of evil has been done [by a knot], so that he may not enjoy his lusts, then seethe a coillon of brock [deer] in running spring water and in honey and let him partake of it, fasting for three days; soon he will be better." Cockayne, *Leechdoms*, i,330–331.

in *Lacnunga* (some involving textiles).[124] Such spells were copied and administered under auspices to be discussed more fully in the section that immediately follows, and those which involved prayers were provided for in certain penitentials.[125] It may even be possible to see, in the liturgically carefully regulated periods prescribed for continence,[126] the reflection of an anxiety about the ill effects, legal and physical, of magical contraceptive and abortion practices.

It was well, in fact, for the medieval church to have some positive supernatural help to offer in matters of love magic, and for reasons additional to the ones already mentioned; for as this church could accuse persons of unacceptable witchcraft in sexual concerns, so its own leaders could be the object of such accusations, especially when, in recommending the religious life, they sought to remove persons, and especially women, from the accepted forms of matrimonial commerce. Few kinds of interference with prevailing custom were so calculated to inflame feelings as was this, and these were feelings within which fears of magical intervention were especially intricately woven. Two striking little episodes from early saints' lives provide a further illustration of these tensions and these fears, along with a little more insight into the ways in which the Christian Church called upon its own magic to contend with them. The *Life* of Saint Lonoghyl tells how Saint Agnofleda had been persuaded by Saint Lonoghyl not to accept an offer of marriage, but to espouse the religious life instead. Her disappointed suitor promptly accused him, before the king, of acting upon his betrothed "per artem maicam." Both Saint Lonoghyl and Saint Agnofleda were called to the palace to answer to the charge. It was cold waiting for the king to come back from his hunting, and Saint Lonoghyl asked Saint Agnofleda to carry in some coals to warm his feet. She did so—in her apron. Both linen cloth and carrier were unharmed. The charge of malevolent love magic was rescinded, when the king came back, in response to this clear demonstration of a superior form of supernatural power, and the king offered a sum large enough in expiation to enable Saint Longhyl to found a small monastery.[127] This is a story that has many dimensions to it, some of which

[124] CLXIX,XX,XXI,XXIIb; *transl.* Grattan and Singer, *Anglo-Saxon Magic*, pp. 188–191.

[125] See the Saint Hubert penitential, for example, chapter 54; McNeill and Gamer, *Medieval Handbooks*, p. 294.

[126] Set out in J. L. Flandrin, *Un Temps pour Embrasser* (Paris, 1983), pp. 8–40.

[127] *Vita Lonoghyli Abbatis Buxiacensis* 6; *edit.* B. Krusch and W. Levison, *MGH SRM* vii (Hanover and Leipzig, 1920), 436–437.

can, once more, be appreciated fully only when set against this specific background. We might note, for instance, that conjuring with coals in the wrong way was one of the charges Hincmar leveled against his witches; conjuring in the right way, however, freed a suspected witch from this same charge. Again, we might suggest that such spells, and such stories of justified magical activity, were fabricated deliberately to help in the Christian responses to love magic, and as a result of complex calculations about the pastoral benefits that might accrue from such indulgence.

The second story is even more illuminating. This comes from the *Life* of the late sixth-century saint Consortia of Cluny. Consortia was pursued by one Aurelius, a most determined suitor, and one supported, moreover, by diverse unnamed (but formidable) "matronae." Consortia was unconvinced and sought escape—and she sought it by means of the *Sortes Biblicae*. She had a copy of the Gospels placed upon the altar during Mass, and when the Common of the Mass was over she had the Gospels opened. They opened at that passage in Matt. (19:21) wherein direction was given to follow only Christ.[128] Happily, Consortia then dismissed her suitor. Christianized emulatory magical procedures, here the *Sortes*, justify once more a Christian breach of customary social practice, free the individual from too crushing a burden of personal responsibility (especially in the face of the pressing matronae), and perhaps here offer a special supernatural defense against other forms of magical operation, forms hostile to Consortia's decision. What Aurelius or the matronae, unchecked by the Christian *Sortes*, would next have done, we cannot, of course, know; but neither physical threats nor love spells can wholly be ruled out. The bringing to bear of the Christian *Sortes* upon such a situation is, of course, of particular interest.

I am sure that there are many similar examples of Christianized magical interventions of this kind to be found, and especially in vivid little local scenes such as this, set within the village community and involving choices between marriage and the religious life. Both of these stories illustrate especially well the supernaturally charged atmosphere within which such decisions were taken, and how vital it could be to be able to produce a Christian magical procedure such as the *Sortes Biblicae* to help to resolve the tensions, no matter how loudly conciliar

---

[128] This was the passage which had prompted the conversion of Saint Antony. This connection may not have been lost upon the audience of this later *Life*.

thunderings rang in the ears. We see in the case of Consortia how, in addition, a lightening of the heart may well have been the aim (and the result) of certain kinds of imitative Christian magic.

CHRISTIAN MEDICAL MAGIC

Should the spirit of creative compromise come to prevail in the matter of "pagan" magical curative procedures too, then, once again, Augustine provides a welcome loophole. He provides it in a section of his *De Doctrina Christiana* later than the one condemning amulets outright, and he makes it possible there for certain simple practices, practices very similar to the magical ones that had been outlawed, to become acceptable.

> It is one thing to say: "If you drink the juice crushed from this herb, your stomach will not pain you"; and quite another to say: "If you hang this herb round your neck your stomach will not pain you." In the first instance, a suitable and salutary mixture is recommended; in the second a superstitious token deserves censure. And yet, where there are no enchantments, invocations, or characters, we can ask these questions. Is the object which is tied or fastened in any way to the body for the restoration of its health efficacious by virtue of its own nature? (If so, we may use this remedy unrestrictedly.) Or, does it succeed because of some signifying bond? The more effectually this seems to do good, all the more cautiously should the Christian beware of it. But, when we do not know the reason for the efficacy of a thing, the intention for which it is used is important in so far as concerns the cure or alleviation of bodies, whether in medicine or in agriculture.[129]

This is a passage full of riches, and capable of a very wide interpretation, for so much depends upon the accepted goodness of a specific intention, as well as upon current notions of, and authorities for, the "scientific" nature of a given ligature or charm. It is, in short, an enormous loophole, and one with which many more liberties could be taken than the saint intended. The *De Doctrina Christiana* was, in addition, a very well known work. Whether as a direct result of access to this passage or not, we can certainly see in early medieval Europe a tremendous diversity of Christian attitudes toward protective and cu-

[129] II,29; transl. J. J. Gavigan, *Saint Augustine, Christian Instruction* (Washington, 1947), pp. 100–101.

rative ligatures, amulets, and charms. It seems, indeed, from much of our surviving written evidence, that there was a very strong tendency to Christianize a form of ligature very close to the condemned non-Christian species—this, furthermore, not always under a guise of science recognizable as such to Augustine.[130]

Once again, we see most active in this process in the early Middle Ages those who were most confident of their right to wield the power of the cross, and those who at a local level seem to have been most troubled by active enchanters. There are numbers of instances to be found, especially in Merovingian saints' lives. A revealing tale about intention occurs in the *Vita Menelei*. Meneleus is a healer, and the wicked Brunhilda (seemingly one of many "perversitatis cultores") accuses him of using diabolical enchantments. No, says her sister, Dotiva; he does so much good, his methods must be good ones.[131] Meneleus's intentions (and the obvious benefits that resulted from his treatments—a somewhat dangerous means of judgment, and deeply dependent upon the current observer) gave him, in short, legitimacy. Here a fictitious sister stood to his defense, but large and important monastic *familiae* could do the same and so sanction the efforts of favored individuals and communities whose efforts appeared to them capable of being judged beneficial.

One of the most striking examples of well-adapted and sanctioned *ligaturae* comes from the *Life* of Saint Monegunde (d. 570). The saint is called upon to cure a youth who has been made ill by drinking a potion prepared by "maleficium."[132] She takes a vine leaf, moistens it with saliva, and lays it upon his stomach, making over it the sign of

---

[130] As well as the loophole opened by Augustine in the *De Doctrina Christiana*, Saint Ambrose provides an excuse for the use of protective talismans in his funeral oration for his brother Satyrus, and perhaps an even larger one. He tells how Satyrus once escaped drowning in a shipwreck: "He asked members of the faithful . . . for the Blessed Sacrament . . . he had it wrapped in a napkin, and tied the napkin around his neck, and so cast himself into the sea. He did not look for a plank loosened from the ship's structure, floating upon which he might save himself, for he had sought the arms of faith alone. And so believing that he was adequately protected and defended by these arms, he desired no other aid"; *transl.* J. J. Sullivan and M.R.P. McGuire, *Funeral Orations by Saint Gregory Nazianzen and Saint Ambrose* (Washington, 1953), p. 180. This oration was not, however, quite so widely known as Augustine's treatise.

[131] *Vita Menelei Abbatis Menatensis* II,9–10; *edit.* B. Krusch and W. Levison, *MGH SRM* v (Hanover and Leipzig, 1910), 153.

[132] "Puer vero loci incola maleficium in potione libavit, de quo medificatus": Gregory of Tours, *Vitae Patrum* XIX,3; *edit.* Krusch, *MGH SRM*, i(2), 288–289. The translation offered by James, *Gregory of Tours*, pp. 127–128, does not, I think, quite convey the air of active magic against which the saint contended here.

the cross. He is cured. But for the accepted status of the saint and (perhaps) the sign of the cross, such a process would have been hard to distinguish from the binding on of an herbal cure by a wise woman, or the defeat of a bad witch by a good one.[133] Again, a passage I have already cited as evidence of that sustained belief in the moon's power which helped toward the rehabilitation of astrology, and allied to those I have mentioned in the context of justified weaving, gives further evidence of a willingness to compromise in the matter of ligatures. "Against a lunatic. Take this herb [clovewort], and wreathe it with a red thread about the man's neck when the moon is waning, in the month of April or early in October. Soon he will be healed."[134] There are many more such passages to be found, both in the *Herbarius* and in other sources, especially Anglo-Saxon ones.[135] The link between applications such as these and Augustine's legitimate medicinal herbs is a very slender one. There are further opportunities here for blurred lines of demarcation, both between magic and science, and between the specifics prescribed by condemned *malefici* and those of Christian leaders. We seem in this particular instance to have, once again, a measure of parallel magical practice (in the case of the *Herbarius* and such texts, one seemingly made acceptable under the guise of science), but very differently legitimated practitioners.[136] Once more, the practices might resemble the condemned ones very closely indeed, provided that the practitioners were beyond doubt respectable in Christian eyes; and this resemblance might well help, in its turn, to preserve and extend the credibility of such Christianized magical practices to persons less than totally convinced of it.

Those Christian supernatural curing practices in which the most speaking parallels with condemned magical practices are to be found, and in which a legitimated, yet imitative, Christian magic seems most conspicuously to have been encouraged, are the ones which involve relics (sometimes used in potions), Christian *characteres* (or writings), and Christian incantations. The reverence given to such Christian ob-

---

[133] Saint Radegunde was given to vine-leaf cures too: *Vita S. Radegundis* I,20; *edit.* B. Krusch, *MGH SRM* ii (Hanover, 1888), 371.

[134] *Anglo-Saxon Herbarium Apulei* X,2; *edit.* Cockayne, *Leechdoms*, i,100–101, also *transl.* G. Storms, *Anglo-Saxon Magic* (The Hague, 1948), p. 10.

[135] "In case a man ache in the head; take the netherward part of crosswort, put it on a red fillet, let him bind the head therewith"; Cockayne, *Leechdoms*, ii,305.

[136] The *Herbarius* allows the use of a gold ring in a cure for eye afflictions, for instance; XIX,5; Cockayne, *Leechdoms*, i,113. In doing so it legitimizes a practice explicitly condemned in the *Homilia de Sacrilegiis*; Caspari, *Homilia*, p. 11.

jects and activities meant that they offered a magnificent opportunity for such adaptations—an opportunity which was seized upon, and early, with a manifest enthusiasm.

Objects deemed by Christians to have a special power (the Eucharist in the case of Ambrose's brother Satyrus, for instance) were certainly considered by many extremely efficacious as protective talismans in our period. Relics might be hung in little caskets or bags around the neck, just like those amulets we find the likes of Caesarius and Gregory of Tours condemning so forcefully. Gregory's own parents wore relics round their necks, in a little gold reliquary shaped like a wolf, and with the happiest of results in the matter of wind-blown fires, as we have seen. They did not even know the names of the saints whose relics they were, having accepted them purely upon the authority of a local priest. Gregory wore them himself, albeit, on occasion, a little less successfully.[137] Saint Avidius (Avitus, d. ca. 530) wore relics of Saint Julian in a little golden casket around his neck,[138] and Germanus of Auxerre wore mixed ones in a bag.[139] One of the most spectacular reliquary necklaces was that purportedly worn by Charlemagne, the so-called amulet of Charlemagne. This consisted of two crystal hemispheres enclosing (supposedly) portions of the True Cross and of the hair of the Virgin Mary. It was bound with gold and worn round the neck on a chain.[140] The combination here of non-Christian and Christian magical ingredients, such as special wood and hair, is again very remarkable and enjoyed, we must presume, the approval of Charlemagne's clergy.[141]

[137] In Gloria Martyrum 83; edit. Krusch, MGH SRM, i(2),94–95. Gregory's parents considered them proof against lots of dangers, including thieves, floods, treachery of every kind, and sword blows, as well as fires; ibid., p. 94. The text speaks of a "lupino aureo." This is extremely reminiscent of the magical protection supposed to spring from fierce beasts. Pliny speaks of the protective and curative powers of wolf amulets: Natural History XXVIII,lxxviii,257; transl. W.H.S. Jones, Pliny Natural History viii (Loeb Classical Library, 1963), 172–173.

[138] Vita Avidii Abbatis Lemovicini 13,45; edit. B. Krusch, MGH SRM iii (Hanover, 1896), 586, 598. The biography is most probably of a ninth-century date.

[139] Bede, Ecclesiastical History I,xviii; edit. Colgrave, Bede's Ecclesiastical History, pp. 58–59.

[140] P. E. Schramm, "Der 'Talisman' Karls der Grossen," in Herrschaftzeichen und Staatsymbolik i (Stuttgart, 1954), 309–311. Another spectacular survival is the mid-ninth-century Lothair crystal, engraved with the Legend of Susannah, and at present in the British Museum.

[141] If so, then we might compare Charlemagne in this respect with Clovis. One argument (and a not wholly unconvincing one, despite its rejection in modern translations) would have it that the words spoken to the first Christian king of the Franks,

Bishop Wilfred of Ripon, his biographer Eddius tells us, also wore relics round his neck.[142] This passage is a particularly interesting one. The queen of Northumbria stole the relics from Wilfred, says Eddius, when King Oswiu imprisoned the obstreperous bishop. She clearly meant the stolen relics to keep her safe, for she carried them round with her "like the ark of God." Instead she became desperately ill. Only when the relics were returned to their owner and the owner released from prison did she recover. Much play is made by Eddius here of the supernatural binding-and-loosing power possessed by both bishop and relics, a binding-and-loosing power, of course, superior to that of mere physical imprisonment, and potent both against the latter (in ways similar to those we have already discussed) and in the infliction of and the release from illness. Many examples of the influence the binding-and-loosing power had over illness can be found.[143] Here, once more, this power is very much akin to the non-Christian power of the magical knot yet is its counter.[144] The queen was clearly partially convinced of this countering Christian magic at the beginning of the episode, and presumably fully so at its end. The opportunities provided

---

Clovis, by Saint Remigius at his baptism (and recorded by Gregory of Tours), "Mitis depone colla, Sicamber, adora quod incendisti, incende quod adorasti" (*Historia* II,31), meant "Humble yourself, take off your necklaces, Clovis; revere that which you have burned and burn that which you have revered." Thus it referred to the magic talismanic necklaces Clovis (Sicamber) and his nobility were accustomed to wear, necklaces of which we have good archaeological evidence, and which sometimes incorporated crystal pendants. J. Hoyoux, "Le collier de Clovis," *Revue Belge de Philologie et d'Histoire* 21 (1942), 169–174. In this context, the substitutions allowed to Charlemagne and to Lothair become all the more striking—the outward forms and even the purposes of the necklaces remained, but the emblems, and so the deeper messages they contained, became Christian ones.

[142] *Life* 39; edit. and transl. B. Colgrave, *The Life of Bishop Wilfred by Eddius Stephanus* (Cambridge, 1927), pp. 78–79.

[143] The association of Christian binding-and-loosing powers with release both from illness and from physical imprisonment, through the intermediacy of relics, is made by Gregory of Tours. When (ca. 550) the son of the Visigothic King Chararich fell ill, for instance, and a silken cloth from Martin's tomb was brought to heal him, Gregory tells how prisoners burst out of prison as it passed. *De Virtutibus S. Martini* I,11; edit. Krusch, MGH SRM, i(2),145. A recent, and most interesting, reappraisal of an Anglo-Saxon obstetrical charm (probably against miscarriage and misinterpreted by the editors of *Lacnunga*) shows that this too called upon Christian loosing powers, this time those of Saint Peter's Chains, and that it employed, indeed, some of the words contained in the liturgy for the Feast: G. H. Brown, "Solving the 'Solve' Riddle in B. L. MS. Harley 585," *Viator* 18 (1987), 45–51.

[144] Pliny, *Natural History* XXVIII,xvii,64; transl. Jones, *Pliny*, viii,46–47.

by half-beliefs of this sort to Christian missionaries prepared to cooperate with them in their form, but outplay them in their effect, were
very great.

It is hardly surprising, then, to find that such relics were widely used
in adaptive magical curative practices. There are, indeed, so many examples of such parallel practices and adaptations to be discovered,
once we look for them from this angle and with the condemned practices of the non-Christian opposition in mind, that it is only possible
to include the most indicative here. On this subject Gregory of Tours
is perhaps at his very best and most revealing. His story of the sudden
and unaccountable illness of the wife of Serenatus, for instance, which
I have already cited as evidence of the speed with which recourse was
had to non-Christian "witch doctors," of the availability of these last,
and of the ligatures they so often produced, is an especially striking
and informative one. Gregory's niece, Eustemia, does not merely detach the offending ligatures; she applies new ones of another kind, oil
and wax from the lamps and candles burning at the tomb of Saint
Martin—clearly here meant to outdo the efforts of the harioli by a
stronger magic.[145] The replacement was, however, both procured and
harnessed with a similar care, and it closely resembled in content that
of the opposition, for we know from Gregory that grease could be included in the equipment of the enchanter, and wax was a common
element in magical ointments. The actions and ingredients seem
sometimes in such substitutions strikingly the same; only the actors
and the sources of their applications differ from those prominent in the
opposing scene.

This story, bringing, as it does, the harioli so forcefully into the
picture, spells out both similarities and contrasts with a particular
trenchancy; but there are many comparable tales in the sources, tales
in which Christian relics, used as cures, are tied or laid upon the ill

---

[145] *De Virtutibus S. Martini* IV,36; *edit.* Krusch, MGH SRM, i(2),208–209. This
story, it might be noted, contains remarkable parallels with later situations, in which
illness which was sudden and unaccountable was liable to provoke accusations of
witchcraft, and so sometimes to impel persons to turn in the first instance to counter-
witchcraft: R. C. Sawyer, " 'Strangely handled in all her lyms': Witchcraft and Healing in Jacobean England," *Journal of Social History* 22 (1989), 466–467. Similar fears
of bewitchment may have provoked the calling in of the witch doctors to the wife of
Serenatus. We may see in the provision here of a form of Christian countermagic
evidence, once again, of a gentler and less socially divisive answer than witchcraft
accusations pursued to their full conclusion were later to be, and as they might have
been here had the cure not been effective.

person, just as non-Christian ones are (and often round the neck) and have words written on them, like pagan magical charms, or are made of special woods, or are used in potions to be swallowed, like curing stones. Germanus used the relics he carried, pressing them upon her eyelids, to heal a blind girl whose parents had been urged to take her to Germanus's opponents. Sulpicius praises the efficacy of the fringes of Saint Martin's cloak, when attached to the fingers or placed upon the necks of sufferers, and he also tells of a letter from Saint Martin (presumably a piece of parchment or vellum with characteres upon it) that, when laid upon a girl stricken with quartan fever, cured her.[146] The Anglo-Saxon Lacnunga recommends the hanging round the neck of an angelic letter from Rome as a specific against loose bowels.[147] Gregory of Tours's father, Florentius, was cured of an attack of gout, says his son, by a mysterious figure who gave directions for this cure. Gregory himself (then a child) was directed to write the name of Joshua upon a piece of wood and place the piece under his father's pillow. He recovered (though evidently not permanently).[148] Splinters from the thatch that covered the roof of Saint Medard's tomb (before his tomb church was built) cured toothache when placed upon the offending tooth. When Saint Medard's church was built, the same power attached to the wood of its doors.[149] The sudarium from the head

---

[146] Vita S. Martini 18,3, 19,1; edit. Fontaine, Sulpice Sévère, i,292–293. I confess that I find the careful distinction between condemned magic and this form of curing made by Fontaine in his commentary a little strained (ibid., ii,870–877), and, in fact, unnecessary. Similarity, rather than distinction, was surely Saint Martin's aim. The idea of the curative letter goes back at least to Eusebius and was condemned both by Pope Gelasius I (d. 496) and in the late eighth-century Libri Carolini: L. Gougaud, "La prière dite de Charlemagne et les pièces apocryphes apparentés," Revue d'Histoire Ecclésiastique 20 (1924), 212–213.

[147] CLXVIII: "This epistle did the angel bring to Rome, when they were grievously afflicted with loose bowels. Write this on a vellum sheet as long as may surround the head, and hang it on the neck of whatsoever man needeth it. He will soon be better. 'Ranmigan adonai eltheos mur O ineffabile Omiginan midanmian misane dimas mode mida memagartem. Orta min sigmone beronice irritas venas quasi dulath fervor fruxantis sanguinis siccatur fla fracta frigula mirgui etsihdon segulta frautanur in arno midoninis abar vetho sydone multo saccula pp. pppp sother sother miserere mei deus deus mini deus mi Amen Alleliuiah' "; transl. Grattan and Singer, Anglo-Saxon Magic, pp. 188–189, and n.

[148] Liber in Gloria Confessorum 39; edit. Krusch, MGH SRM, i(2),322. On a successive occasion, recounted in the same paragraph, the remedies came more directly from Tobit, 6:8–9.

[149] You cut off a splinter with your knife and applied it to the offending tooth. Gregory of Tours, In Gloria Confessorum 93; edit. Krusch, MGH SRM, i(2)357–358.

of Saint Ouen healed the fever.[150] Saint Cuthbert's linen girdle restored Abbess Aelfleda of Whitby to health (she tied it round herself), and his shoes cured a paralyzed boy.[151] Saint Guthlac wrapped his belt round the hapless warrior Ecga, brought to him suffering from speechlessness (perhaps a stroke). Ecga recovered and wore the belt as an effective protection for the rest of his life.[152] Fringes from her clothes and drinks of water signed with the sign of the cross healed the sick who thronged to Saint Genevieve.[153] Water in which the burned hair of Saint Rusticula had been immersed effected a cure from the attacks of the midday demon.[154] The *Life of Saint Columba* by Adamnan, informative as we saw in the matter of Christianized rainmaking, is instructive in this matter too. Columba had a white curing stone, whose powers in general defied the laws of nature (for it could float on water), and whose curative effects persisted after the saint's death. The stone, moreover, is in this story used specifically to confound a competing "magus."[155]

Tomb dust in water was, as we have seen, one of Gregory's favorites (certainly not far removed from curing stones), and so again, as applications, were altar cloths, and woven cloths covering tombs.[156] Tomb

[150] *Vita Audoini Episcopi Rotomagensis* 19; *edit.* B. W. Krusch and Levison, MGH SRM v (Hanover and Leipzig, 1910), 567.

[151] Bede, *Life of St. Cuthbert* xxiii, xlv; *edit. and transl.* B. Colgrave, *Two Lives of St. Cuthbert* (Cambridge, 1940), pp. 230–234 and 298–300. This is reminiscent of a practice Caesarius condemns (Sermons 52 and 184) whereby girdles are taken to enchanters in the hope that their owners might be healed. Girdles and shoes are still thought capable in England of effecting supernatural cures in the fifteenth and sixteenth centuries, although by then their manipulators are without strong social or institutional defenses: K. Thomas, *Religion and the Decline of Magic* (Harmondsworth, Middlesex: Penguin, 1978), p. 217.

[152] *Felix's Life of Saint Guthlac* xlii; *edit. and transl.* B. Colgrave, *Felix's Life of St. Guthlac* (Cambridge, 1956), pp. 130–133.

[153] *Vita Genovevae Virginis Parisiensis* 38; *edit.* B. Krusch, MGH SRM iii (Hanover, 1896), 231.

[154] *Vita*, IV,27; AS Augusti ii,662. The process seems similar to the fumigations Caesarius condemned.

[155] I,i, II,33; *edit. and transl.* A. O. and M. O. Anderson, *Adomnan's Life of Columba* (London, 1961), pp. 196–197, 400–405. The defeat of the magus, Broichan, involved the release of a captive, showing, once more, that the saint's power to loose from illness could loose from other wrongful bonds as well.

[156] The cloth covering Saint Senoch's tomb cured a paralytic who kissed it: *Vitae Patrum* XVI,4; *transl.* James, *Gregory of Tours*, p. 108. There are many such stories in Gregory. One of the most remarkable concerns the sick son of King Chararich, mentioned above. Chararich's messengers insisted, when asking Martin for a cure, that the

dust in a container and the fringes of tomb cloths might also be hung round the neck.[157] The tomb of that same Saint Gall who destroyed the pagan curing shrine at Cologne seems to have acquired a curing power of its own, one communicated through herbs. A certain Valentinianus, who came to the saint's tomb seeking a cure for fever, picked up some of the herbs strewn there by Saint Gall's followers; he chewed them and was instantly restored to health.[158] More Augustinian than simulacra perhaps, such a remedy was still remarkably close to some of the ones that were still being so fiercely outlawed in councils and in penitentials. Aelfric, perhaps acting under the pressure of a long tradition, and now, and importantly, with experience of the inefficacy of purely repressive methods, offered a specific alternative to those who wished to turn to "unallowed practices" (such as the amuletic ones he had condemned), or enchantment, or witchcraft for their health. He suggested recourse instead to "holy relics." He declared too that "noone shall enchant a herb with magic, but, with God's word shall bless it and so eat it."[159] He refers to Augustine's loophole in the *De Doctrina Christiana* here, though not, and interestingly, to the saint's warning in his commentary on John against wrongfully attaching the name of Christ to such activities.

To be sure, there are obvious scriptural precedents, both for healing miracles, and for some of the materials used. Cloths that have touched a holy person, for instance, have, as instruments of healing, clear ech-

---

virtue of the tomb of Saint Martin be communicated to a silken cloth. Martin obliged, the son recovered, and so did many others. *De Virtutibus S. Martini* I,xi; *edit.* Krusch, *MGH SRM*, i(2),145–146.

[157] Gregory of Tours, *De Virtutibus S. Iuliani*, 24, *De Virtutibus S. Martini* IV,43; *edit.* Krusch, *MGH SRM*, i(2),124–125,210.

[158] Gregory of Tours, *Vitae Patrum* VI,7; *transl.* James, *Gregory of Tours*, p. 59. The herbs had perhaps lain there for some time, and, if so, the power they then communicated seems similar to the power expected of pagan incubation practices (although Gregory carefully associates it with the raising of Lazarus): A. Delatte, *Herbarius. Recherches sur le Cérémonial usité chez les Anciens pour la Cueillette des Simples et des Plantes Magiques*, 3d ed. (Paris, 1961), p. 40. The power communicated to the cloth laid overnight on Martin's tomb, and which cured Chararich's son and released prisoners, is similar. Altar cloths strewn with herbs are proof against fire, according to Gregory's *History of the Franks* VII,12; *transl.* Dalton, *Gregory of Tours*, ii,293–294.

[159] *The Passion of St. Bartholomew the Apostle*; *edit.* and *transl.* B. Thorpe, *The Homilies of the Anglo-Saxon Church* i (London, 1844), 475, 477. For this reason I find it hard to believe, with Meaney, that when Aelfric condemned non-Christian amulets he condemned Christianized charms and amulets as well. *Anglo-Saxon Amulets*, pp. 20–21. Rather, he seems to have opened a way for these.

oes in Acts (19:11–12). Such examples as these, those found in Matthew, and the directions of the Archangel Raphael in Tob. 6:8–9 as to the healing efficacy of a fish's heart and liver clearly gave much scope.[160] Belief in the possible power of stones, especially white ones like rock crystal and with characteres written on them, and other precious stones and metals, finds a justification in Rev. 2:17 and 27:19–21. To stress this ancestry at the expense of contemporary pressures is, however, I would suggest once more, to distort our historical understanding of the situation we confront here. It can, indeed, do as much violence to the proper interpretation of these early medieval texts as the taking of biblical passages out of their own historical contexts does to them. Though biblical precedents and Augustinian loopholes were doubtless a relief, these Christian amuletic practices may only be appreciated fully when set against their immediate background: the background, that is, of that forbidden curative magic I have tried to describe, of firm residual belief in it, of relatively ineffective condemnation, and of those practitioners of it who refused to relinquish their influence. Supernaturally (electromagnetically, we might say, in the case of crystal) charged necklaces, power-drenched herbs and textiles, threads and bindings, necks and fingers, precious metals, special woods and writings, even, perhaps (as in the case of Florentius's wolf-shaped reliquary), protective animals—all of these resources, so evident in the Christian species of curative magic, bear in fact the imprint of the outlawed, yet threatening and fiercely defended, contemporary non-Christian form.

Nor, let me emphasize again, are we dealing here simply with memories of paganism, filtering through into a weak, unformed, and unresistant Christianity. To none of the hagiographers and historians I have instanced could such terms even remotely be applied; and it is inconceivable that pastors of the stamp of Germanus, or Gregory, or Wilfred, or Cuthbert, or Guthlac, or Bede, or Aelfric (to name but a few) could have confused, all unwittingly, pagan echoes with Christian truths. This fact needs to be appreciated fully. What we see, in the writings of these advocates, and in the healing practices they so clearly described and recommended, is a form of Christian resistance

---

[160] Matt. 4:23–25 was a favorite passage for healing in early missals. Acts 19:12 told of how cloths which had touched Saint Paul's body healed the sick. Tobit figured in Gregory of Tours's mother's remedy for gout. *Liber in Gloria Confessorum* 39; *edit.* Krusch, *MGH SRM*, i(2),322.

to pagan competition as skillful as it was vigorous, one not averse to calling upon scriptural example when it could, but one, in truth, activated by far more immediate and pressing pastoral anxieties. Non-Christian habits were strong; they needed a stronger alternative, but not, in a matter so desperate and so delicate as that of healing, one that relied primarily upon disapproval, nor one which alienated more than it attracted, with all the attendant loss. Better treatment in every sense than this was possible; and often it was achieved.

Sometimes, the strength of the non-Christian opposition at the village level, the urgency of the need for a discernibly Christian and creative answer to it, and the skill and immediacy with which this answer was produced are made particularly explicit. Take another of Gregory of Tours's stories. A traveling "clericus," bearer of the relics of Saint Julian, is suddenly overcome by the heat and calls at a roadside cottage for a drink. A youth coming to serve him faints and seems, to his relatives, close to death. They immediately (and again revealingly) suspect the traveler of practicing magic on him, and they start to carry the boy away.[161] The boy declares, however, that it is the "virtus" of Saint Julian, not witchcraft, which has made him faint. At this, the clericus promptly places the casket containing the saint's relics upon the victim's head and prays, and the victim is cured, vomiting up blood and demons.[162] The little anecdote is enormously instructive. Healing comes, once again, through a Christian form of amulet, laid upon the head and with a prayer, this time clearly in the face of an accusation of evil supernatural practice. The counterpractice was, in appearance, similar to the one expected of a hariolus, the result very markedly different. The vomited demons reveal the true source of the evil: not any person but a spirit. The supposed witch is then freed, not merely from blame, but also from its punishment at the hands of the victim's relatives, and shows himself instead to be a beneficent wielder of supernaturally much more powerful healing and demon-defeating ligatures.

Christian curative incantation, in the form of prayers (of the kind seemingly sanctioned by Aefric in the face of Augustine's doubts) and charms containing quite as much mumbo jumbo as any non-Christian enchanter could ever have commanded, was also a response widely and enthusiastically adopted, and once again, it does seem, in the face of

[161] "Concurrentes autem parentes eius, calumniabant hominibus, adserentes parentum suum eorum magicis artibus fuisse peremptum."

[162] *Liber de Virtutibus S. Iuliani* 45; *edit.* Krusch, MGH SRM, i(2),131.

persistent, and condemned, non-Christian incantatory practices.[163] Charms and incantations of this sort are especially marked in the wealth of curing material that has come down to us from English sources, both Anglo-Saxon and Latin, compiled at periods (I think of the tenth and early eleventh centuries especially) when non-Christian opposition was especially fierce, and when Christian effectiveness against supernatural threats to health was still far from being proven— a major reason again for us to believe that Aelfric's views sprang from, and extended, a tolerance meant to conciliate and attract, rather than a spirit of outright condemnation meant only to repress. Aelfric objected to unhallowed amulets, as we have seen, but not their hallowed substitutes. *Lacnunga*, already briefly mentioned,[164] is a veritable quarry of such adaptations, and one that Aelfric's permissions may, indeed, have done much to make possible. It is impossible to refrain from quoting here more fully some of the choicer examples, well publicized as these now are. Thus:

> XXVc. Sing this prayer upon the black blains nine times; Firstly Paternoster. "Tigath tigath tigath calicet aclu cluel adclocles acre earcre arnem nonabiuth aer aernem nidren arcum cunath arcum arctua fligara uflen binchi cutern nicuperam raf afth egal uflen arta arta trauncula trauncula. Seek and ye shall find. I adjure thee by Father, Son and Holy Ghost that thou grow no greater, but that thou dry up. Upon the asp and the basilisk shalt thou tread and upon the lion and the dragon shalt thou trample. Cross Matthew, cross Mark, cross Luke, cross John."

Again:

> XXIXc. This is the holy drink against elfin enchantment and for all temptations of the Fiend: Write upon the housel-dish: "In the beginning was the Word" as far as "comprehended it not," and again "And Jesus went round all Galilee teaching" as far as "and there followed him great crowds" (and again) "God in Thy name" until the end (and again) "God have mercy upon us" until the end (and again) "Lord God to our aid" until the end. Take cristalan and disman and zedoary and hassock and fennel. And take a sester full of consecrated wine, and bid one without blemish fetch in silence against stream half a sester of running water. Take then and lay all

---

[163] See on this a valuable article: J. Klapper, "Das Gebet im Zauberglauben des Mittelalters," *Mitteilungen der schlesischen Gesellschaft für Volkskunden* 18 (1907), 5–41.

[164] MS Harley 585, fols. 130–151ᵛ, 157–193, put together perhaps around the year 1000, or in the early eleventh century; see, for a description of this codex, N. R. Ker, *A Catalogue of Manuscripts Containing Anglo-Saxon* (Oxford, 1957), no. 231, pp. 305–306.

the plants in that water and wash off very clean therein the writing from the housel-dish. Pour then the consecrated wine from above upon the other liquid. Bear then to church. Have masses sung thereover: firstly Omnibus Sanctis, secondly Contra tribulationem, thirdly Sancta Maria. Sing these psalms of supplication: Misere mei deus, Deus in nomine tuo, Deus misereatur nobis, Domine deus, Inclina domine, and the Credo and Gloria in excelsis deo, and litanies and Paternoster. And bless earnestly in the name of the Lord Almighty, and say "In the name of the Father, and of the Son, and of the Holy Ghost be it blessed." Then use it.[165]

Caesarius, of course, specifically recommends the saying of prayers over a sick person (after James 5:14–15) as an alternative to "diabolical phylacteries" and sorcerers, and Aefric singles out the Creed and Paternoster as protective prayers.[166] Lacnunga is magnificent, but similar counter-charms and adaptations are richly to be found elsewhere, and especially in compilations springing directly from late tenth- and early eleventh-century English monastic houses. Other striking examples are the so-called Leechbook of Bald, or MSS Cotton Titus D xxvi and xxvii (perhaps originally the same manuscript), from Hyde Abbey, Winchester, and already mentioned in the matter of the movement for the Christianization of astrology and of prognostics from the heavens.[167] There are charms to be found in the Leechbook that show an especially judicious combination of ancient magic and tender care. Take this one, for instance:

> Against dysentery, a bramble of which both ends are in the earth, take the newer root, dig it up, and cut nine chips on your left hand, and sing three times: Miserere mei deus. And nine times the Our Father. Take then mug-

[165] Grattan and Singer, Anglo-Saxon Magic, pp. 107–111. The reference to the lion and the dragon comes from Ps. 90:13 (Vulgate). Other scriptural references are to John 1:1–5, Matt. 4:23–25, and Psalm 53 (Vulgate), used in exorcism rituals. The use both of the housel-dish and of the consecrated wine imply the permission of a priest.

[166] Caesarius, Sermons 13, 184; transl. Mueller, Saint Caesarius, i, 77, ii, 482. Aelfric, De Auguriis; edit. and transl. W. W. Skeat, Aelfric's Lives of the Saints, EETS (London, 1881), pp. 370–371.

[167] The Leechbook is to be found in MS B. L. Royal 12.D.xvii, perhaps datable to the second half of the tenth century, and again from Winchester (from the Benedictine Cathedral). Ker, A Catalogue, pp. 332–333. The standard translation is still that by O. Cockayne, Leechdoms, Wortcunning and Starcraft of Early England ii, RS (London, 1865). The compilation as it stands was not all put together at the same time, and at least one section of Book II seems to go back to King Alfred. The copy we have, however, seems to have been compiled for late tenth- or early eleventh-century pastoral use.

wort and everlasting and boil these three in several kinds of milk until they become red. Let him then sup a good bowl full of it fasting at night, some time before he takes other food. Make him rest in a soft bed and wrap him up warm. If more is necessary, do so again; if you still need it then, do so a third time, it will not be necessary to do so more often.[168]

Psalm 56 (Vulgate), the Paternoster, a strangely grown bramble, the numbers nine and three, the color red,[169] brewing and incantation— all go together here to make a concoction that seems actually to work (and may have been a little more palatable than some of Pliny's remedies, or burned hair or tomb dust in water).

Both of the Titus codices, with their *Supputationes Esdrae*, *Lunaria de Somnis*, predictive spheres of life and death, and lunaries of the sick, are excellent examples of the kind of little pocket book a Christian pastor and healer might have about him. Such directions would be of great service to him if he wished to carry conviction against that witchcraft of which Aelfric and Wulfstan complained, yet was ill-equipped to take too recondite an approach, or ill-convinced, indeed, of its efficacy and acceptability. Such codices too might help to place *Lacnunga* within a larger context, and one rather different from that sometimes assigned to it.[170] The first little Winchester book has in it (fol. 3), besides the lunaria and spheres of the sick, a protective and health charm very reminiscent of condemned measuring witchcraft, one meant probably to be worn upon the person, and based upon the measurement of Christ's body (projected from that of a drawn cross).[171] It

[168] Leechbook II,lxv; Cockayne, *Leechdoms*, ii,290–293. In Storms, *Anglo-Saxon Magic*, no.26.

[169] Associated with blood in magical procedures, of course, and, therefore, powerful; see W. L. Hildburgh, "Psychology Underlying the Employment of Amulets in Europe," *Folklore* 62 (1951), 238.

[170] See, for the Cotton Titus manuscripts, W. de Gray Birch, "On Two Anglo-Saxon Manuscripts in the British Museum," *Transactions of the Royal Society of Literature*, n.s., 11 (1878), 463–512, and Ker, *A Catalogue*, pp. 264–266. The context proposed for *Lacnunga* by Grattan and Singer, *Anglo-Saxon Magic*, pp. 16–17, of either monastic "blank misunderstanding" of the non-Christian element in the charms they included, or lay leechcraft comparatively free of a narrow Christian affiliation, is not, I am convinced, the right one for such a text.

[171] Birch, "On Two Anglo-Saxon," pp. 470–472. Measuring witchcraft of this sort is mentioned by Hincmar, and described and denounced in Sermon 184 of Caesarius; transl. Mueller, *Saint Caesarius*, ii,481. See also L. Gougaud, "La prière," pp. 216–223.

has also a remedy for boils that, if it lacks the elaborations of the *Lacnunga* one, still conjures with numbers.[172] The two potions prescribed, both that in *Lacnunga* and that in Titus (but especially, perhaps, the Titus one, which seems to resemble nothing so much as an early form of sweetened mayonnaise), must again have been a good deal more palatable than some of the treatments Pliny recommended, and certainly more so than some of those he ascribed to the magi.[173] The *Leechbook*, too, was happy to combine holy water with ale.[174] This aspect of the contemporary competition and of Christian answers to it should not, perhaps, be underestimated and may reward a little (guarded) practical research. The first few verses of the Gospel of Saint John, as required in *Lacnunga* against "elfin enchantment," are written out, also, at the end of this Titus manuscript.

The second Titus codex shares prognostics and lunaries with the first, and it adds a list of the names of the Seven Sleepers (fol. 14).[175] The Seven Sleepers of Ephesus, who miraculously escaped the Decian persecution by retiring to a cave until aroused by the Christian Theodosius, were figures familiar to Eastern magical formulae.[176] They seem

[172] "Against blains, take nine eggs and boil them hard, and take the yolks and throw the white away, and (beat up) the yolks in a pan, and wring out the liquor through a cloth; and take as many drops of wine as there are of the eggs, and as many drops of unhallowed oil, and as many drops of honey; and from a root of fennel as many drops; then take and put it all together, and wring it out through a cloth and give to the man to eat, it will soon be well with him." Birch, "On Two Anglo-Saxon," p. 484. The same charm is also printed in Cockayne, *Leechdoms*, i, 380–381.

[173] Although for "superficial abscesses" Pliny, like *Lacnunga* on "dwarf," below, recommends the intervention of a virgin, he advises the swallowing, too, of "mandrake root in water, a decoction of scammony root in honey, sideritis crushed with stale grease, marruviun with stale axle grease." *Natural History* XXVI,lx; *transl.* Jones, *Pliny*, vii,334–335. The magi treat boils, he tells us, in this way: "by a spider, applied before its name has been mentioned and taken off on the third day, by a shrew mouse, killed and hung up so that it does not touch earth after death and passed three times round the boil, both the attendant and the patient spitting the same number of times, by the red part of poultry dung, best applied fresh in vinegar, by a stork's crop boiled down in wine, by an odd number of flies rubbed on with the medical finger, by dirt from the ears of sheep, by stale mutton suet with the ash of woman's hair, and by ram's suet with ash of burnt pumice and an equal quantity of salt." Ibid., XXX,xxxiv; viii,346–349.

[174] In charms against chicken pox, against the devil and insanity, against typhoid, for example: Storms, *Anglo-Saxon Magic*, nos. 5, 28, 33

[175] "Haec sunt nomina septem dormientium qui ccclxxiii annos dormierunt, Maximianus.Malchus.Martinianus.Dionisius.Iohannes.Serapion.Constantinus."

[176] See R. Pietschmann, "Les inscriptions coptes de Faras," *Receuil de Travaux Re-*

to have been especially effective against fever. *Lacnunga* advises that their names be written on seven Mass wafers, that a charm be sung into the right and left ears and above the head of a given sufferer, and that the wafers be hung round the neck by a virgin as a specific against goblin-induced nightmares or fevers. We have, then, in this at least one reason for their listing in Cotton Titus D.xxvii.[177] It is perhaps no accident that both Gregory of Tours and Aelfric pay the legend of the Seven Sleepers serious and respectful attention.[178] Their names are found in one other late tenth- or early eleventh-century English man- uscript known to me, MS B.L. Cotton Vitellius C iii from Christ Church, Canterbury,[179] this time clearly as a part of a charm against fever, and one that could, again, evidently be applied to the patient in written form.[180] The Seven Sleepers (and, perhaps, their story) clearly seemed better as cures in Christian eyes than placing the sufferer upon the roof or near the fire. This last codex contains, too, a charm to staunch blood which involves the reciting—nine times—of precisely that section of the beginning of John's Gospel prescribed in *Lacnunga* against enchantment, and available, as we saw, in Cotton Titus D xxvi.[181] Bede's *Life of Saint Cuthbert*, in the chapter immediately pre- ceding the one in which Cuthbert condemns amulets, shows that this saint was especially instructed in the Gospel of John, and John of Sal- isbury, in the twelfth century, reports that he healed with it, laying

---

latifs à la Philologie et à l'Archéologie Egyptiennes et Assyriennes 21 (1899), 175–176.

[177] XCIIIb; Grattan and Singer, *Anglo-Saxon Magic*, pp. 160–163. There are diffi- culties about the exact meanings of "dweorh" and "spiden" or "inwriden" in this charm. "Dweorh" may mean fever; see the alternative translation and notes in Storms, *Anglo-Saxon Magic*, pp. 167–173, and also his references to other charms, chiefly against fever, calling upon the Seven Sleepers. Storms (p. 171) also argues that the amulet was made up of two spiders in a bag, hung round the neck, but for many reasons Grattan's interpretation seems preferable.

[178] Gregory of Tours, *Passio Septem Dormientium*; edit. Krusch, MGH SRM, i(2), 398–403. Aelfric gives his account of them in the *Lives of the Saints*; edit. Skeat, *Ael- fric's Lives*, pp. 488–541.

[179] Neither this nor the Titus manuscripts are cited by Storms.

[180] Fol. 79ᵛ. "Qui ista verba poterit tenere *aut super se habuerit scripta* [my emphasis] non debet febres habere." The same charm calls upon the "angelus domini."

[181] Fol. 79ᵛ. "Carmen contra sanguinis fluxum sive de naribus sive de plaga vel de omnibus locis. In principio erat verbum .ix. vicibus. Deus propitius esto huic peccatori famulo tuo N. vel peccatori famule tue N. et de suis vel de quacunque corporis membra sive de plaga gutta sanguinis amplius non exeat sic placeat filio dei sancteque genetrici eius marie." The careful reference here to male *or* female sufferers gives the lie to the notion that such material was meant solely for monastic use.

the Gospel Book upon the patient.[182] Such memories and prescriptions, and especially the conciliatory purposes that stood behind them, lend a peculiar poignancy to one of the cases of sixteenth-century English witchcraft persecutions recounted by Notestein. A woman was accused (by a contemporary physician) of bewitching a sick boy by reading out verses of the first chapter of Saint John. She died in prison.[183]

It is possible that the special emphasis upon these particular verses from John had an effect upon their inclusion in the Ordinary of the Mass, for Mass, or the presence at least of the mass-priest, was often thought in this material essential to the completion of such a charm and cure.[184] The feast of Saint John (27 December) was, however, also close to the winter solstice, and midwinter, like midsummer, had an ancient importance in the matter of magical intervention.[185] Bald's *Leechbook*, for example, requires that certain curative herbs for jaundice (and for other infirmities, including "evil air") have three masses said over them on three days in midwinter, one of which is John's feast.[186]

These codices are outstanding ones, but there are many many more instances (especially in English sources contemporary with them, or nearly so) of closely Christianized parallels to cherished non-Christian magical ways of healing. MS B.L. Cotton Caligula A xv[187] has in it, as

[182] *Life of St. Cuthbert* viii; *edit. and transl.* B. Colgrave, *Two Lives of Saint Cuthbert* (Cambridge, 1940), pp. 182–183. *Policraticus* II,i; *edit.* C.C.J. Webb, *Joannis Sarisberiensis Episcopi Carnotensis Policratici sive De Nugis Curialium Libri VIII* i (Oxford, 1909), 66. It is now thought unlikely that Cuthbert was actually taught from the surviving copy in the Stoneyhurst Gospels (Colgrave, *Two Lives*, p. 346), but this may have been the copy he used in healing.

[183] W. Notestein, *A History of Witchcraft in England from 1558 to 1718* (New York, 1911), p. 77.

[184] Sections of the Mass were vital, for example, to the correct preparation of the butter needed in a "holy salve" in *Lacnunga*, and a mass-priest had to bless the whole concoction and say prayers over it: Grattan and Singer, *Anglo-Saxon Magic*, pp. 124–127.

[185] The eve of the Feast of the Nativity of Saint John the Baptist (24 June) conveniently replaced the summer solstice and could be an important substitute occasion for gathering medicinal herbs, notably Saint-John's-wort. The prescription in *Lacnunga* XIVa may refer to this time, *pace* Grattan and Singer, ibid., pp. 100–103.

[186] II,lxv; *transl.* Cockayne, *Leechdoms*, ii,294–297. The prayer of Saint John was thought effective against snakebite: ibid., I,xlv; pp. 112–113.

[187] An eleventh-century codex, from Christ Church, Canterbury; Ker, *A Catalogue*, pp. 173–176. This codex also has in it lunaries of the sick, the sphere of Apuleius,

well as unexceptionable prayers for health, one charm the meaning-
lessness of which must have outdone anything a non-Christian enchanter bent on mystification could devise,[188] and another (brought
once more by an angel in a letter, and laid upon Saint Peter's altar in
Rome) that, sung over water (which was then drunk), or over butter
subsequently smeared on the affected part, cured anything.[189] The list
of English manuscripts coming from the tenth and eleventh centuries
and setting out parallel Christian charms and incantations of this sort
could become exceptionally long. ms Cotton Vitellius C iii, in the
main a distinguished late tenth- or early eleventh-century English
medical codex, also from Christ Church, contains, as we saw, a charm
against fever in which it calls upon the Seven Sleepers, and which can
also clearly be bound upon the patient as a ligature with characteres;
the manuscript has also a Latin charm against an "issue of blood" (in
men or women) in which the "In principio" verse has to be repeated,
once more, nine times.[190] A further eleventh-century Christ Church
codex, ms B.L. Cotton Tiberius A iii has a fine mixture of prayers,
charms, and prognostics (thunder and moon and dream and pregnancy
prognostics, for example), together with a copy of the *Regularis Con-
cordia*.[191] ms Cotton Vitellius E xviii, an eleventh-century codex possibly from the cathedral priory at Winchester (and containing notable
parallels with Cotton Caligula A xv)[192] has, again with the Sphere of
Apuleius, medical charms for cattle and sheep.[193] Eleventh-century

---

and lists of lucky and unlucky days for bloodletting and health and journeys. It will be
discussed more fully below.

[188] Fol. 125 (129): "In nomine domini nostri Ihesu Christi.tera.tera.testis.
contera.taberna.gise.ges.mande.leis.bois.eis.audies.mandies.moab.lib.lebes." This is
against fever and is printed in Storms, *Anglo-Saxon Magic*, no. 68.

[189] Ibid., no. 34. Storms prints one more from this manuscript, no. 69 (to obtain
favors). Some of the charms printed by Storms are in direct contravention of prohibitions issued in the *Homilia de Sacrilegiis*, for instance no. 3, against a "furuncle"; *edit.*
Caspari, *Homilia*, p. 9.

[190] Fol. 79ᵛ.

[191] Ker, *A Catalogue*, pp. 240–248. Cockayne, *Leechdoms*, iii,144–158,169–215.

[192] On these parallels, and parallels with other English manuscripts of the same period, see especially M. Förster, "Die altenglischen Verzeichnisse von Glücks- und Unglückstagen," in *edit.* K. Malone, et al., *Studies in English Philology. A Miscellany in
Honor of Frederick Klaeber* (Minneapolis, 1929), pp. 258–277.

[193] Storms, *Anglo-Saxon Magic*, no. 50. Cockayne, *Leechdoms*, i,388–389. On the
explanation of the secret writing see M. Förster, "Ae.fregen 'Die Frage,'" *Englischer
Studien* 36 (1906), 325. This codex, the main part of which is occupied by a copy of
the Psalter and Canticles, seems admirably constructed, too, for the taking of the
Sortes Sanctorum.

Worcester possessed manuscripts with charms in them.[194] A number of charms (two for sore eyes and earache that call upon Raphael as in Tobit), together with less exceptionable prayers, are to be found in MS Corpus Christi College, Cambridge, 41, one of the books Bishop Leofric (d. 1072) gave to Exeter.[195] This is of great interest, both because of its reputable pastoral source and because, given its inclusion of the "Missa contra paganos," its owners clearly had the threats of non-Christians in mind.[196] Another of Leofric's gifts contained charms,[197] and there are many more such eleventh-century examples.[198] The practice, moreover, of setting out in order and describing in detail the parts of the body for which a given supplicant requested protection from sickness—a practice particularly evident in English so-called Lorica material, and reflected, once more, in *Lacnunga*[199]—bears an uncanny resemblance to that non-Christian one of which we learned from the *Life* of Saint Gall of the Auvergne, whereby carefully carved models of those parts of the body most in need of help are placed in pagan healing shrines.[200]

I have laid some emphasis upon late tenth- and early eleventh-cen-

[194] MS Corpus Christi College, Cambridge, 190, for example, MS Worcester Cathedral Q 5, and two Cotton manuscripts now lost, Cotton Otho A xii and xiii; Ker, *A Catalogue*, pp. 70–73, 221–222, 467.

[195] Cockayne, *Leechdoms*, i, 384–393. Storms, *Anglo-Saxon Magic*, nos. 1, 12, 13, 15, 16, 43, 48, App. 4. This codex is carefully described by R. J. S. Grant, *Cambridge Corpus Christi College 41: The Loricas and the Missal* (Amsterdam, 1979). The charms, some of which concern theft as well as healing, are printed and discussed on pp. 1–26.

[196] Ker, *A Catalogue*, pp. 43–45.

[197] Oxford, Bodleian Library, MS Auct. F.3.6; Storms, *Anglo-Saxon Magic*, nos. 77, 78.

[198] E.g., Oxford, Bodleian Library, MSS Barlow 35 and Junius 85 and 86; Ker, *A Catalogue*, pp. 355–56, 409–411, Storms, *Anglo-Saxon Magic*, nos. 41, 45, 49. No. 45 is a pregnancy charm, and this again suggests that such codices were meant to serve a world greater than that bounded by the monastery. MS B. L. Sloane 475, a small medical handbook, would richly repay detailed study. It has, for example, among many medical prescriptions, a charm against fever invoking the Seven Sleepers (fol. 22ᵛ—unknown to Storms) and seems, like the Cotton Titus books, admirably adapted to being carried around on consultations.

[199] In the *Lorica of Gildas*, for example, inserted into *Lacnunga*; Grattan and Singer, *Anglo-Saxon Magic*, pp. 137–147.

[200] In that the origins of such *Loricae* are generally believed to have been Celtic, they may well have been in operation in the Celtic missions to the Continent. A variation whereby Christ himself, together with distinguished Old Testament figures, protects named parts of the body is to be found in the famous eighth-century *Book of Nunnaminster*, MS B. L. Harley 2965, fol. 40ᵛ.

tury English sources, partly because the magical elements in them are so evident and have been so much a matter for remark, but mainly, of course, because they throw into such clear relief so many of the points I have been laboring to make. Gregory the Great's advice to Augustine concerning conciliation had not been forgotten in England. It had, instead, been given new life by the reappearance of conditions similar to those which had faced the first Christian pastors, and in a country proud in any case of being so addressed by the great pope. All of the texts I have cited here as evidence of deliberately Christianized magical compromises come from a place where, and a period when, the opposition of non-Christian practices and practitioners was provably causing alarm.[201] A revealing little note in Latin, added in the surviving manuscript copy of Bald's *Leechbook* II,lxiv (a drink "against a devil and dementedness"), speaks specifically of "maleficiatorum" when it affirms the need for holy water (with ale) in such potions.[202] The *Leechbook* itself shows that witches and enchantment were much in its compiler's mind when it offers a prescription against them. "Against every evil rune-lay and one full of elvish tricks, write for the bewitched man this writing in Greek letters 'alpha, omega, Iesum, Beronikh.' "[203]

---

[201] See, for example, the intensification of alarms against witchcraft illustrated in Whitelock, Brett, and Brooke, *Councils and Synods*, i,320,344–345,366,371, as well, of course, as the pronouncements of Aelfric and Wulfstan in their sermons. The story of Thorkell's second wife and the witch, cited earlier, is set in this period.

[202] "quia omni potu et omni medicinae maleficiatorum et demoniacorum a(d)miscenda est aqua benedicta, et psalmis et orationibus vacandum est, sicut in hoc capitulo plene docetur"; Cockayne, *Leechdoms*, ii,preface,xxx.

[203] The last word is most probably a reference to Saint Veronica. More is required to undo the witchcraft than the mere writing of a charm. A complex potion must be made up, laid under the altar, have nine masses sung over it, and be taken at specified hours; Cockayne, *Leechdoms*, ii,138–141. Anxiety about being "restrained by worts," by a hostile witch, runs through the *Leechbook* (e.g., xlv; ibid., ii,115). It even elaborates upon a passage it borrows from Marcellus Empiricus, rendering a cure for eyeache and fever one also for "night visitors," "bewitchment," and "evil incantational arts"; Grattan and Singer, *Anglo-Saxon Magic*, pp. 37–38. It is worth recalling, in this context, one possible interpretation of an incident told in the first *Life* of the great tenth-century English saint, Saint Dunstan. The saint's irritated (and less piously inclined) kinsmen, seeking a way to bring him down, accuse him of learning pagan incantations. The accusation may be one of excessive indulgence in pagan learning; but it may also refer to witchcraft. The editor certainly thinks so. If so, then in singling out witchcraft as the first, and most obvious, accusation for which to reach, the passage is most instructive. *Edit.* W. Stubbs, *Memorials of St. Dunstan Archbishop of Canterbury*, RS (London, 1874), p. 11.

When speaking of the rescue of astrology, I suggested that contemporary witchcraft was the context for the compilation of lunaria. The English evidence again is extraordinarily rich in lunaria, perhaps the most spectacular examples being MS Cotton Tiberius A iii and its congener MS Cotton Caligula A xv.[204] This should not surprise us. It is rich too, lastly, in certain other forms of curative earthly magic crucial to our understanding of magic's rise: forms I will call here "neutral practices" in that they seem to inhabit the borderland between non-Christian and Christian practice, neither wholly separate from nor wholly associated with either. I would place in this neutral category those ancient, yet hardly execrable, remedies we find in our manuscripts, and the many lists we also find in them of lucky and unlucky days.

The *Leechbook* and *Lacnunga*, once again, are splendid sources for such material, and Grattan and Singer, on the level of description at least, most helpful guides. Beyond the positively Christianized counter-incantations we have already seen, they single out a whole series of other instances of incorporated magical practices, practices that have both northern and Mediterranean echoes. One of these is the use of the number nine, so prominent in Germanic magical tradition. This was particularly widely adopted in Christian charms, and we have seen examples of its adoption already. Another is the reverence shown for iron. Iron is an ancient source of magical power,[205] and it is frequently specified in these records as either forbidden or necessary to the cutting of a particular plant. Sea holly, for instance, was, in the Anglo-Saxon supplement to the *Herbarium Apulei*, to be cut "with a crooked and very hard iron."[206] Further examples of the incorporation of such practices within the Christian dispensation are the respect shown for silence and for certain times of the day and the week for picking and applying simples,[207] the inclusion of taboos against looking back-

[204] The prognostics and lunaries from Cotton Tiberius A iii, with much comparative material, have been exhaustively printed by M. Förster in a magisterial series of articles, the references to which may be found in Ker, *A Catalogue*, bibliography. Small sections in (charming) English translation are to be found in R. T. Hampson, *Medii Aevi Kalendarium* i (London, 1841), 133ff., and longer ones in Cockayne, *Leechdoms*, iii, 144–158, 169–215.

[205] There is a taboo against it in Deut. 27:5 and Josh. 8:31.

[206] Cockayne, *Leechdoms*, i, 318–319. Iron taboos may be found in *Lacnunga* XIV and LXXVIII; Grattan and Singer, *Anglo-Saxon Magic*, pp. 100–101, 150–151

[207] "Against elf-disease. . . . Go on Thursday evening, when the sun is set, where thou knowest that helenius stands, then sing the 'Benedicite' and 'Paternoster' and a

ward,[208] the care for "sympathetic" colors and shapes,[209] and an anxiety about, and curious ways with, blood.[210]

Foremost among the unlucky days, especially for bloodletting, were the so-called Egyptian Days. Tables listing these days, and verses reminding one of their existence and malevolence, are very widespread indeed in the manuscripts of this period.[211] There were thought to be two of them in each month, and though the lists vary in detail somewhat, a fair guide to them is to be found in Cotton Caligula A xv (fol. 130).[212] The Egyptian Days were considered unsuited to all great enterprises, including medical ones. On the verso of the same leaf the Cotton manuscript then proceeds to list twenty-four different days, found specially inauspicious for drugging or for bloodletting. These lists vary too (and, confusingly, these days can also be known as Egyptian Days),[213] but they often constitute a separate and additional set, as they do here, and so add an extra two hazardous days to each month.[214] The picture of calendrical alarm is completed by the so-

---

litany, and stick thy knife into the wort, make it stick fast, and go away: go again, when night and day just divide; at the same period go first to church and cross thyself and commend thyself to God; then go in silence, and though anything soever of an awful sort or man a meet thee, say not thou to him any word." *Leechbook* III,lxii; Cockayne, *Leechdoms*, ii,346–347.

[208] "The woman who cannot nourish her child; let her take in her hand milk of a cow of one colour, and then sip it up with her mouth, and then go to running water and spew therein the milk. . . . When she goeth to the brook, then let her not look round, nor again when she goeth hence." *Lacnunga* clxxi; Grattan and Singer, *Anglo-Saxon Magic*, p. 191.

[209] Yellow for jaundice, for instance, or brown, the color of clotted blood, to staunch blood flow.

[210] For example, *Leechbook* I,xl: "For fellons [seizures], take, to begin, a hazel or an elder stick or spoon, write thy name thereon, cut three scores on the place, fill the name with the blood, throw it over thy shoulder or between thy thighs into running water and stand over the man. Strike the scores and do all that in silence"; Cockayne, *Leechdoms*, ii,104–105. We have here too, of course, silence, and magical twigs and marks.

[211] Thorndike provides a helpful preparatory list: L. Thorndike, *A History of Magic and Experimental Science* i (New York, 1923), 695–696. He conflates in the list, however, the Egyptian Days with unlucky days of other kinds.

[212] They are: 3, 4 January; 5, 7 February; 6, 7 March; 5, 8 April; 8, 9 May; 5, 27 June; 3, 13 July; 8, 13 August; 5, 9 September; 5, 15 October; 7, 9 November; 3, 13 December.

[213] See H. Henel, "Altenglischer Mönchsaberglaube," *Englischer Studien* 69 (1934–1935), 339–340.

[214] Cockayne, *Leechdoms*, iii,153.

called dog days, the days of the moon forbidden for medicinal treatment, and the three critical Mondays.[215] There were lucky days too, though not, it seems, so many.[216]

All of these reckonings of lucky and unlucky days may have seemed to come close to science and may have been, indeed, the more acceptable to some for this reason. In their references to the Egyptians, however,[217] in their jugglings with the lunar and solar calendars and with numbers, in the need for books and the written words hidden in them that they imposed, and even, perhaps, in the atmosphere of awe they sought to create, such lists encouraged a form of medico-magical practice (and dependence) which must have been very like that purveyed by the ligature-tying, spell-binding, and lot-casting harioli they attempted to replace. One passage in the Cotton Caligula manuscript shows that its writer was both aware of the presence of witchcraft and conscious of how close the two forms of activity had drawn. "This is no sorcery, but wise men have made experiment of it, through the holy wisdom, as God Almighty dictated to them."[218]

These magical curative practices for a time occupied a no-man's-

[215] Henel, "Altenglischer," pp. 331–333, 340–341. The dog days were reckoned from the heliacal rising of Sirius and stretched from ca. 14 July to ca. 5 September. There were generally thought to be seven days of the moon unsuitable for medical treatment (the fourth, fifth, tenth, fifteenth, twentieth, twenty-fifth, and thirtieth days of the moon). The three critical Mondays were usually the first Monday in April, the second Monday in August and the last Monday in December. The acceptance of these Mondays as bad days in the English manuscripts seems to be in defiance of Aelfric: "Many are also possessed with such great error, that they regulate their journeying by the moon, and their acts according to days, and will not undertake anything on Monday, because of the beginning of the week." Homily on the Circumcision; Thorpe, The Homilies, i, 101. Presumably respected Christian monastic authority made all the difference. The dog days and unlucky days of the moon appear in Bald's Leechbook I, lxxii; Cockayne, Leechdoms, ii, 146–149.

[216] "There are three days in the twelvemonth with three nights, on which no woman is born; and whatever man is born on those days never putrifies in body in the earth, nor turns foul till dooms day. Now one of those days is in the latter part of December, and the remaining two are in the early part of January, and few there are who know or understand these mysteries"; Cockayne, Leechdoms, iii, 154–155 (from the Cotton Caligula manuscript). Other references are to be found in M. Förster, "Die altenglischen Verzeichnisse," pp. 259–261.

[217] Egyptians were known widely in the early Middle Ages for their magic, not merely from the story of Moses and the magicians of Pharaoh, but also from Lucan (Pharsalia iii, 224) where he speaks of Egyptian hieroglyphs as "magicas linguas," and from the Clementine literature.

[218] Cockayne, Leechdoms, iii, 155.

land between magic clearly outlawed and science, a no-man's-land similar to that inhabited for a while by the lunaria. By inhabiting this land and allowing precious time for thought and negotiation, they rendered crucial assistance to those who wished to preserve supernatural manipulations of a magical sort more largely; and we might reasonably suppose, although we cannot prove it, that persons of good will who wished for this lived on the non-Christian, as well as the Christian, side of the borders. These practices may legitimately be described as magical ones, in that they certainly have in them echoes of earlier pagan magic, and they tend to be described (and sometimes dismissed) as mere pagan survivals (presumably of a weak sort in that they escape explicit outlawry). They deserve, however, far better than this. When such practices are set alongside the forms of earthly magic that were explicitly forbidden, when they are placed within the context of contemporary witchcraft, and when, furthermore, their patrons (those who recorded them and allowed their use, that is) are allowed to advance more clearly into the light, their function becomes almost the exact reverse of that which is usually assigned to them. These were not survivals, tolerated on account of their relative unimportance; they were opportunities, seized upon and savored. These magical healing practices are transformed, in this light, from unwelcome remnants of a religion wholly to be dispossessed into welcome and amenable holders of a ground that Christianity wanted badly to annex, and to annex securely. They were preserved then, even cherished, in the English material, as residents of areas within which compromise was still possible, and as a means by which (like the *Sortes Sanctorum*) waverers, especially wavering leaders, might still be won over, bringing their followers with them.

With the help of such practices, furthermore, such leaders might be persuaded to make common cause with Christians without either that loss of pride, that loss of status, or that loss of respected expertise that so often defeats less skillful efforts at conversion. Take iron, for instance, and carefully gathered herbal applications. We might perhaps with reason suppose that an iron knife and special herbs frequently formed a part of the witch doctor's equipment (as it did of that of the professional medicus). Christianizing and paying attention to their use was an easy and tactful method of giving status to the user under the Christian dispensation. Looked at in this way such practices become active helpers, recognized as such and seized upon with enthusiasm by those in the forefront of effective pastoral care.

That special interest in medico-magical practice that we find so copiously illustrated in the English evidence is best understood, therefore, when we place it within the immediate context of opposing, yet similar, methods of solacing those deep anxieties aroused by sickness. In order truly to appreciate its message, we need to take account of the role of its compilers, and of the sensibilities both of respected non-Christian healers and (most important) of those of people as yet uncommitted to either side. When we do so place this evidence, and when we do take such account, it tells us much indeed about the origins and purposes of such so-called superstitious healing practices, and about the sensitivities shown in them toward contemporary social pressures above all. Monastic followers of the way of the cross had, we know, in the wake of the tenth-century monastic reform in England, taken upon themselves especially great burdens of local pastoral authority and responsibility. They were determined to confront the problem of resistant non-Christian supernatural curing practices both directly and effectively; and the confidence their way of life could give the monks against the demons allowed them to confront it in a particular way. They encouraged and adopted magical healing practices in a Christianized form very widely indeed; and the more closely they could emulate the methods of the opposition, of course, the better. Thus, imitations and adaptations of this kind are imprinted with an outstanding vividness upon this particular record.[219] Political and social strength of a special kind fostered in England at this period an extraordinary flowering of sympathetic magical practice.

Evidence of this kind is by no means unique to England. Admirable diligence in the examination of surviving manuscript material from the periods of Regino and Burchard would, I am sure, show up much more, in Latin as well as that of which we know already in Old High German.[220] The importance of the tenth/eleventh-century English mate-

[219] Some of the manuscripts I have cited combine this material in a spectacular way with prayers and invocations to the cross, and with illustrations of it. Cotton Titus D xxvii, for instance, fols. 65ᵛ–73ᵛ, has a fine Christ on the cross, accompanied by prayers and pronouncements of the power of the cross over the demons: "Si primum opus tuum tibi sit ad crucem omnes demones si fuissent circa te non potuissent nocere te" (fol. 70). B. L. Sloane 475 has (fol. 23) a pregnancy charm which recommends the binding of a cross onto the pregnant woman.

[220] The tenth-century manuscript of the famous Merseburg Charms (the second of which is curative) is, of course, an extraordinarily important record of preserved non-Christian practice and comes again from a sensitive frontier area. See on these charms G. Eis, *Altdeutsche Zaubersprüche* (Berlin, 1964) and H. P. Schlosser, *Althochdeutsche*

rial lies rather in the fact that, springing as it does from a situation recognized as one of particular delicacy in the matter of non-Christian and Christian competition for forms of supernatural control, it can alert us to the type of material we might in general legitimately take as an effort at magical compromise.[221]

Efforts so forceful as these at parallel, attractive, and yet Christian processes of magical curing did not, either in early Europe as a whole, or in England, go unremarked or unopposed. Anxieties are quickly expressed about them, much in the manner of Augustine, in his commentary on the Gospel of John. We saw in the case of Gregory of Tours's Desiderius, who claimed to carry efficacious relics (and must have looked as though he did, for he had a cross in addition to his teeth and bones and bear claws), and in that of Gregory's second "imposter," who carried flasks of oil claiming that they were holy, and in that of Saint Boniface's Aldebert, that the possibilities for confusion were very great.[222] Adamnan shows that he too was sensitive to these possibilities, for, in another passage showing how closely Saint Columba competed in his measures with opposing sorcerers, he makes a special point of the fact that the saint's specifics were *not* sorcery.[223]

Literatur (Frankfurt-am-Main, 1970). Further references to non-English curative material with magical echoes are collected together in the valuable compilation by A. Delatte, *Herbarius. Recherches sur le Cérémonial usité chez les Anciens pour la Cueillette des Simples et des Plantes Magiques*, 3d ed. (Paris, 1961), but, tantalizingly, he does not date or place his manuscript sources, nor examine their interrelationship.

[221] In the case of the second Merseburg charm, that in which Woden healed Balder's lamed horse, we know that a Christian holy man came to be substituted promptly for Balder, and Christ for Woden, but that the curing charm itself once more remained markedly similar: J.L.K. Grimm, *Kleinerer Schriften* ii (Berlin, 1865), 1–29, and H. Bächtold-Staübli and H. Hoffman-Krayer, *Handwörterbuch des deutschen Aberglaubens* viii (Leipzig, 1936–1937), 1147–1149.

[222] *History of the Franks* IX,6; transl. Dalton, *Gregory of Tours*, ii,373–374. Transl. E. Emerton, *The Letters of St. Boniface* (New York, 1940), pp. 98–106. Aldebert, as well as conjuring with pretended relics and angelic names, also laid claim to a letter from the tomb of Saint Peter in Rome, all very close to the legitimated charms we have discussed.

[223] The passage is a very interesting one, and worth dwelling on a little, for it has in it so many magical ingredients. Columba is asked to judge a dispute between two "rustics," one of whom is a sorcerer. He does so by making the sorcerer prove his skill by drawing milk from a bull, then making the magic milk revert to its original demonic substance—blood. He did this, says Adamnan, "not in order to confirm the sorceries (let it not be thought), but in order to confound them before the crowd," ("non ut illa confirmaret maleficia fieri jussit, quod absit, sed ut ea coram multitudine distrueret"). *Life of Columba* II,17; ed. and transl. Anderson, *Adomnan's Life*, pp. 362–363.

The decision, on the part of the local bishop, to pronounce Desiderius's "relics" witchcraft demonstrates how closely together Christian magic and its opposition had drawn in fact, and how great an authority was vested in whoever defined the line between them. To some, these possible confusions between Christian and non-Christian medical magic (and perhaps, too, the authority they gave to powerful local clerical figures in the matter of pronouncing upon them), and the dangers that always attend the choice of the lesser of two evils (in this case the outplaying of, or the cooperation rather than outright conflict with, the opposition), clearly outweighed the advantages sympathetically managed reconciliations could bring with them. Thus, Alcuin objects specifically to the wearing of little bags of relics (he mentions the bones of saints) or texts from the Gospels round the neck like "ligaturas." Such "philacteria" are pure superstition, which the truth defies, he says. The condemnation is a firm one, and he repeats it in a second letter. Even Gregory of Tours, or Aelfric, might have quailed at this.[224]

Many may have felt as Alcuin did. Gregory of Tours at his most robust was widely read, of course, but we cannot be sure that all of his copyists and readers copied and read him with sympathy or felt that his heroes should always be emulated. The great abbots of tenth- and eleventh-century Cluny were worried about an excessive emphasis on "miracula"[225] and wary of anything that could be seen as "superstitio."[226] Many of the charms found in the English codices I have men-

---

[224] "Multas videbam consuetudines, que fieri non debebant. Quas tua sollicitudo prohibeat. Nam ligaturas portant, quasi sanctum quid estimantes. Sed melius est in corde sanctorum imitare exempla, quam in sacculis portare ossa; evangelicas habere scriptas ammonitiones in mente magis, quam pittaciolis exaratas in collo circumferre. Haec est pharisaica superstitio; quibus ipsa veritas improperavit philacteria sua." This, the first, letter was written to Archbishop Adelard of Canterbury, between the years 793 and 804, and the second may have been similarly directed. *Edit.* E. Dümmler, MGH *Epistolae Karolini Aevi* ii (Berlin, 1895), 448–449.

[225] "Our virtues demonstrate our degree of perfection, not our power to work signs and miracles"; *PL* 142,913 (MT). Jotsald, in this his prologue to Book II of his *Life of Odilo*, also quotes Luke 10:20: "Nevertheless do not rejoice in this, that the spirits are subject to you; but rejoice that your names are written in heaven"; ibid., 914. The same warning had been given by Gregory the Great, of course, to Augustine of England, in company with the famous letter in which he advocates a form of compromise. Bede, *Ecclesiastical History* I,xxxi; *transl.* Colgrave, *Bede's Ecclesiastical History*, pp. 110–111.

[226] "Nullam pestem plus perhorrebat quam superstitionem vanamque laudem."

tioned are entered in a hand different from that of the body of the text[227]—a good use for spare space, perhaps, but possibly also a sign that such matters were not yet thought quite orthodox enough, even within certain sympathetic institutions, to be given the dignity of careful codification and collection. A preferred answer might be, as I have shown, recourse to natural healers and scientific remedies, even, if one were very pressed, to astrology, even though these also had their disadvantages. Alcuin certainly approved of orthodox medical practitioners,[228] and much of the medical material copied in late Anglo-Saxon England, including that put out in the vernacular, echoes Cassiodorus's ideal of a scientifically informed monastic curing shrine, magical in its echoes as some of it was.[229]

Scientia understood as wisdom had many dimensions, some of which countered Christian magical substitutes. It would be foolish to suppose that a single, or simple, approach to the problem of magical medical adaptations held undoubted sway, even in a single community. In matters of health, above all things, substitute magic was a dangerous commodity, exceptionally powerful in its implications and to be chosen, distributed, handled, and controlled with the greatest of care. On occasion, however, it was clearly a desirable one too. It is not surprising to find that opinions as to the proper use of adaptive medical magic varied greatly; but neither is it hard to explain, nor indeed to justify, the evidence of enthusiastic compromise we do meet.

Epistola Gilonis De Vita Hugonis Cluniacensis Abbatis; edit. A. L'Huillier, *Vie de Saint Hugues* (Solesmes, 1888), p. 595.

[227] This is so in the case of the Seven Sleepers charm in the Vitellius manuscript and the charm for catching a thief in Titus D. xxvi.

[228] *Ep* 213 (dated 801); *edit.* Dümmler, *MGH Epistolae*, ii, 356–357.

[229] *Institutes* I, xxxi, 2; *transl.* L. W. Jones, *An Introduction to Divine and Human Readings by Cassiodorus Senator* (New York, 1946), pp. 135–136. Essential here is the article by L. E. Voigts, "Anglo-Saxon Plant Remedies and the Anglo-Saxons," *Isis* 70 (1979), 250–268.

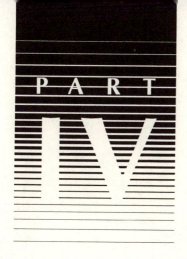

PART

IV

The Magus

CHAPTER 10

The Discredited Practitioner: Charlatans

IT WILL have escaped no one that I have been inclined to write so far as though magician and magic could be treated together and amounted to much the same thing. To some extent, this is not unreasonable, for their fates can of course be very closely connected. If, for instance, the office of the magus is itself a matter for offense, then no matter how beneficial his activities may be, or how unexceptionable his materials, they will cause offense too. Many a non-Christian magus was, together with his materials, discounted by Christians through sheer prejudice. At the opposite extreme, the practitioner of the supernatural can be exalted well beyond his or her human worth by practices deemed to be effective or socially helpful. This practitioner and his or her materials can, however, also work in opposition to one another. The development of a scientific understanding will rob certain materials of their association with magic and accordingly diminish the status and authority of the magus, and this magus, non-Christian or Christian, may then be tempted in turn to inhibit the growth of a scientific understanding. In short, in that magicians and their materials can react upon each other in so many different ways, and the more so over several hundred years, it is misleading to treat them always as a unity.

That being said, I propose now promptly to fall into the opposite error, and, as a postscript, to touch here upon certain individual and named magi as figures in their own rights. I do so for three reasons. Firstly, the need for a single transcendent human being as a focus for expectation and devotion seems to have been keenly felt throughout the societies we have attempted to survey, and this need bore heavily upon the problem of magic. I say "single transcendent" in order to contrast this magus both with those many nameless and faceless practitioners who opposed the Christian organization and with the multitude of competing lesser Christian manipulators of the supernatural, many of whose activities we have already followed. This brings me to my second reason. The greater magi need to be singled out, for the two levels of magus on each side should be looked at in tandem. Each influenced the other's position in important respects. The memory of the major non-Christian figures could, and did, help to keep the minor non-Christian ones within a correct perspective, and to alert medieval Christians to that which, practiced by the less publicly eminent, might allow room for compromise, as well as to the first symptoms of serious deviation. The conjuring up of the specters of the major discredited practitioners encouraged, then, the distinguishing of that which was *relatively* harmless in the lesser ones and the Christianization of some of the magical practices of lesser village healers or diviners, many of which, as we have seen, were welcomed in. Much the same might, mutatis mutandis, be said of the Christian magi of eminence, though this time the great would guide the less.

Thirdly, given the picture of Christian vigilance on all these fronts I have tried here to convey, it is possible that the memory of many non-Christian magi persisted so very firmly into the Christian dispensation, and was so carefully recorded by it, *precisely* because it could help in these processes of selection. The figure of the discredited magus is for the most part portrayed in the Christian sources extremely vividly, and by persons who were appalled, and yet who rejoiced in explaining the reasons for their horror in the most exact detail. We do well to be a little guarded against this heady combination, and to be alerted once more to the danger of depending literally upon sources which are both so firmly Christian and often so very polemical. We cannot assume that everyone felt as the apologists did, and there may, by reason of the very hyperbole some of these apologists used, be grounds for supposing that many did not. Some of the ferocity with which the discredited magi are denigrated at certain times is often, then, a guide rather to the deficiencies of the contemporary Christian answer than to the ways in which these magi were truly viewed. Through all the vilification and humiliation of the discredited figure we can sometimes make out, though dimly, an old magus who did not merely refuse to die, but with whom, as with many of his condemned magical practices, it distinctly behoved the new to come to terms. The familiar Christian magi often, in their turn, reflect this extra need and borrow some of their features from it. This is, then, an instructive way in which to view these figures too. All of these magi may have been made great in our Christian sources (and, once again, the Christian records are the ones upon which we must rely) to keep the lesser ones in their appropriate places, to help to heal the divisions within the Christian ranks that the encouragement of certain types of magic might excite and, once more, to assist in the projection of that magic deemed by the early medieval church to be most helpful to Christianity as it progressed in strength. Thus, the named magi had, on each side, exacting and ever evolving functions to fulfill.

In addition to the distinctions to be observed in the hierarchical roles played by the greater magi, and the points to be made about the selective and purposeful memory the Christian sources practiced, there can be found differences between the separate members of each category of eminent magus, non-Christian and Christian. These differences too, when marked, can greatly increase our understanding of the processes of Christian magical choice. Simon Magus, for instance, did not occupy the same role nor present the same danger to Christian society as did the magus by blood. On the Christian side, Saint Benedict and the sacral king are wholly distinct. A heightened appreciation of these internal differences might help to keep us aware of the dangers of taking too monolithic an approach to the problem of early magic, and of how recognizedly complex a problem it was, capable of manifold different solutions through many and diverse leaders and lesser figures on each side.

From among all the many possible nameable supernatural figures, non-Christian and Christian, I have chosen to single out here persons who do seem, indeed, to have acted one upon another. And, among the Christian figures, I have chosen to pay most attention to those who seem to echo, and counter, the discredited memory of their opponents.

HAM

The figure of Ham, one of the three sons of Noah, came to the Middle Ages firstly through the Book of Genesis. Interest in this, the first book of the Old Testament, never waned in our period, and fascinated discussion of the fundamental problems, especially the moral problems, it posed never ceased. Indeed, it is fair to say that were we in the unhappy position of having to choose a single deposit of materials through which to understand this period, then Genesis and its commentaries should be our choice. Ham appears in Gen. 5:32, with the beginning of the story of the Flood, and within one of the most difficult sections of all. Indisputably, Ham, with his father Noah and his brothers Shem and Japheth, was one of the four male heirs of the race of

Adam. Exactly what he came to inherit, however, and exactly what he might be allowed to do with it, was not so clear. The arguments about the natures both of Ham and of his inheritance which occupied the attention of preachers and commentators upon Genesis have much to tell us about the early medieval magus. They are of great importance to our understanding of the position, and the behavior demanded, of the respectable magical adept, and especially of the learned one.

The episode of the Flood is introduced in Gen. 6:1–4 in this way:

> And it came to pass, when men began to multiply on the face of the earth, and daughters were born unto them, that the sons of God saw the daughters of men that they were fair; and they took them wives of all which they chose. . . . There were giants in the earth in those days; and also after that, when the sons of God came in unto the daughters of men, and they bare children to them, the same became mighty men which were of old, men of renown.

We may perhaps allow the orthodox early medieval Christian interpretation of this passage to be summed up for us by John Cassian, writing in the late fourth century. The "sons of God," says Cassian, were in fact the sons of Seth, third son of Adam and Eve, and were conceived in order that the human race might be renewed after the slaughter of Abel by Cain. These sons of Seth were so virtuous that they deserved their special name on account of their special goodness. The "daughters of men," on the other hand, were the daughters of Cain, degenerate as was their father. For a long time the sons of Seth resisted the blandishments of Cain's daughters, but at last they fell, and the union of the two lines begat children so wicked that the earth had to be cleansed of them by the Flood—cleansed, that is, of all save Noah and his family and the chosen animals.

Here we arrive at Ham, and Cassian goes on. At first, Seth's children had been endowed with all knowledge, including the knowledge of the properties of trees and plants and stones. They had also the gift of prophecy. When, however, they allied themselves with the daughters of Cain, they turned all this learning to profane uses. With the help of demons they dabbled in the malefic arts, in wonders, and the illusions of magic, and they turned from God to the worship of fire and devils. All this Ham saw. Alone of the family of Noah, Ham became expert in magic. Knowing that his father would allow no record of this knowledge into the ark, however, he had it engraved upon plates of metal and tablets of stone, both proof against the action of water. He hid the plates and tablets and found them again after the floodwaters had subsided. From then on Ham was launched upon his nefarious career, parts of which we learn about in Genesis itself.[1]

It is a marvelous story, and Cassian was not alone in his early report. Ham was similarly associated with the preservation of magic after the Flood by the author of the Pseudo-Clementine *Recognitions* (on whom Cassian perhaps drew). This takes us a little further into Ham's family's supposed later career. The *Recognitions* also tell how the Flood destroyed all save Noah, his three sons, their wives, and the chosen animals. Then:

One of them, by name Ham, unhappily discovered the magical art, and handed down the instruction of it to one of his sons, who was called Mesraim, from whom the race of the Egyptians and Babylonians and Persians are descended. Him the nations who then existed called Zoroaster, admiring him as the first author of the magic art; under whose name also many books on this subject exist. He therefore, being much and frequently intent upon the stars, and, wishing to be esteemed a god among them, began to draw forth, as it were, certain sparks from the stars, and to shew them to men, in order that the rude and ignorant might be astonished, as with a miracle.

Zoroaster met a fiery death at the hands of a demon, but this made little difference to his followers, who chose to regard him as having been carried up to heaven in a chariot of lightning. Next in succession came the biblical Nimrod, whose support of the magical arts was much assisted by the provision of drunken banquets. According to the *Recognitions*, Ham's magic involved sexual depravity and blood sacrifices, in addition to wonders, tricks, and illusions.[2]

---

[1] *Collations* VIII,xxi; *edit.* and *transl.* E. Pichéry, *Jean Cassien Conférences* ii (Paris, 1958), 28–31. The idea that the condemnation of magic goes back to the ark became attractive to homilists. Chromatius of Aquileia, for example, says that the raven which Noah threw out of the ark to its death was a type of Simon Magus; J. Lemarié, *Chromace d'Aquilée, Sermons* i (Paris, 1969), 141. I owe this reference to Mr. Stephen Benson.

[2] IV,xxvii–xxx; *transl.* T. Smith, *The Writings of Tatian and Theophilus and the Clementine Recognitions* (Edinburgh, 1867), pp. 297–299. The notion that Nimrod was similarly depraved gained much support from an old Latin mistranslation of Gen. 10:9, according to which Nimrod was described as a mighty hunter *against* the Lord. This mistranslation was given currency by Augustine, *City of God* XVI,iii and iv; *transl.*

Of course, the associations of Ham and Mizraim and Nimrod with magic are not biblical; they are expansions, rather, of hints given later in Genesis about the character of Ham. It was Ham who came upon his father drunk and naked after Noah had planted his vineyard, and who failed to cover him (Ham's brothers, according to Gen. 9:22, when told, did cover their father). For this, Noah cursed Ham's line through Ham's son Canaan. Ham himself and Ham's line are now ready targets for the worst of accusations, and among these worst lay, equally ready, magic.[3] We do not know quite when these particular expansions of the biblical story, and their application to magic, were first made, but their effect upon the practitioner of magic in the early Middle Ages, especially through the intermediacy of the *Recognitions* and Cassian, was devastating. A literally antediluvian wickedness survived the Flood, was given the name of magic, and lay there to be picked up and used by the likes of Ham. The likes of Ham, in the persons of his son and grandsons, did, indeed, use it. We begin to know a little more, moreover, about the type of person we should suspect of being a spiritual heir of Ham. Sexual aggression and irresponsibility are singled out from the more general aggressions and irresponsibilities of the discredited magus for special stress; and this magus is credited with a very powerful (and recondite) form of learning. Many legends about Ham pursue these themes, and stories of Ham's vicious behavior to his father, his athletic sexual prowess in the ark, his catholic tastes in the matter of sexual partners, and his general depravity and self-indulgence abound.[4]

Both the magus's sexual irresponsibility and the power of his learning receive reinforcement, furthermore, from the apocryphal scrip-

E. M. Sanford and W. M. Green, *Saint Augustine City of God* v (Loeb Classical Library, 1965), 16–17, 28–31.

[3] Other societies would have other targets for the curse of Noah. In New Guinea, for instance, it deprived Ham's followers of much wanted cargo: P. Lawrence, *Road Belong Cargo* (Manchester, 1964), p. 76. I owe this reference to my colleague Dr. Hugh Laracy. The story was, and is, capable of infinite manipulation. The notion, traceable to the Christian Fathers, that Ham received Africa to rule, led early, when coupled with the curse of Noah, to the view that Ham and his descendants were black and were slaves—a notion which has done much, of course, to support the concept of apartheid. On this see J. B. Friedman, *The Monstrous Races in Medieval Art and Thought* (Cambridge, Mass., 1981), pp. 100–101 and nn.

[4] See, for example, Francis Lee Utley, "Noah's Ham and Jansen Enikel," *Germanic Review* 16 (1941), 241–249, and S. Gero, "The Legend of the Fourth Son of Noah," *Harvard Theological Review* 73 (1980), 321–322.

tures. Cassian seems to have had some of these in mind when he wrote of the original learning of the "sons of Seth." I have already mentioned the passage in the apocryphal Book of Enoch according to which these sons of Seth were angels who fell through their lust for the daughters of Eve and brought the teaching of enchantments with them in their fall.[5] There were many such stories. They occupied the attentions of Jewish as well as Christian exegetes and reached the Middle Ages often as a result of contemporary conflict between the two. Like the Book of Enoch, these stories spread a view of magic even more alarming than the one Cassian and the *Recognitions* tell. Such angelic knowledge is again associated with sexual malpractice, and it is knowledge that transcends the merely human capacity of Seth. Its menace is commensurately greater. In this context, the actions of such a character as Ham become all the more dreadful, and their consequences in the matter of magic all the more greatly to be feared. We know, furthermore, that the *Collations* of Cassian, in which the tale is recounted so vividly, occupied a position of extraordinary privilege in this period, for in chapters 42 and 73 of his *Rule* Saint Benedict prescribes them for his monks,[6] and we may charitably suppose that this order was frequently followed. We might therefore expect many monks, and many of those whom they taught and to whom they talked, to have been especially familiar with Ham's treachery, and with the principal features of its probable heirs. Thus we may presume them to have formed particular views about a possible Christian antidote, views some of whose expression we have already attempted to trace.

Ham, then, occupied a central place in the early Middle Ages as a type of the discredited magus, and because his story had a basis in Genesis and was retold in expanded form in widely read and respected writings, he was a type to be taken very seriously indeed. The figure of the discredited magus projected through him is enormously powerful. Its learning is, at the very least, that of giants among men, and it goes back to the very beginnings of time. Thus, it helps to distinguish many later figures for discredit, and for discredit particularly in the eyes of Benedictine monks. This magus is supremely self-serving. His selfishness is, furthermore, contrasted sharply with the innocence of Noah[7]

---

[5] Above, chap. 2.

[6] *Transl.* J. McCann and P. Delatte, *The Rule of St. Benedict* (London, 1921), pp. 283, 492–493.

[7] Angelom of Luxeuil, writing in the mid-ninth century, observed charitably (as

and with the humble willingness of the latter to listen to God, by being primarily sexual, and deeply, and arrogantly, intellectual. We begin to have a foreshadowing of, and at least one explanation and reinforcement for, the special anxieties expressed by certain medieval churchmen, monks prominent among them, about the learning and sexual behavior of Christian priests. We may find here further reasons too for the priority accorded to the order of Saint Benedict in the legitimation of humbler Christian supernatural practitioners.

SIMON MAGUS

Ham became a figure of fear and distaste largely through expansions of Genesis. Parallel expansions of the New Testament brought to the Middle Ages a markedly similar model of the discreditable magus in the person of Simon Magus. Simon Magus looms over this whole period and, behind Faust, well beyond it; but, in the early medieval literature about him, he becomes at some points less a figure of fear than a figure of fun, despite the fact that a major medieval sin went by his name. The tone of the Simon Magus literature is a good example of that spirit of precocious self-confidence the New Testament church could breed in its early adherents. Precocity can make for good entertainment, however, and in this case it served a serious purpose too. The entertainment value of this literature greatly helped to ensure that Simon was well known—and, when it became important to stress this too, so dangerous a figure as urgently to demand a powerful answer.

The life span, indeed the very existence, of Simon and the interrelationship of the quite numerous texts which deal with him are still matters which provoke discussion. It is generally agreed, however, that the bulk of the evidence we have was put together during the operational disputes of the early Christian Church, and in support of the supernatural authority of Peter. The picture it paints of both Simon and Peter was prepared for a public which was, this literature hoped, avid to hear about all that was dreadful in the old magi and all that was admirable in the new; and the Simon who passed into the early Middle Ages did so because of a continued interest in these same problems of authority, and, especially, in the credit to be attached to supernatural abilities.

---

indeed had Jerome) that Noah's drunkenness, and subsequent unconscious nakedness, were caused by his being wholly unused to wine: *Commentarius in Genesin*; PL 115,162.

Simon's notoriety and his predilections, taken together, are of immense importance to the process by which magic became validated in the early Middle Ages. All of the accounts of him to which I shall give weight here are well represented in early medieval manuscripts. The most respectable source for Simon Magus is a passage in Acts 8:9–24. In the Vulgate, Simon is described as a "magus" engaged in seducing the people of Samaria. He is rebuked by the apostle Peter for his attempt to buy from Peter the power of the Holy Spirit. This and a rather less respectable source have already been briefly mentioned.[8] Several more sources which fall into the category of less respectable were widely popular in the Latin West. An especially gripping account of Simon and Peter's contest is to be found in the Passion of Peter and Paul (also known as *Marcellus*).[9] The action takes place in Rome in the reign of Nero, where Simon is already established as a wonder-worker but is becoming envious of the reputation of Peter. The stage is gradually set for a battle royal between the two. *Magus* is used as a term of abuse by both contestants, Peter's followers hurling it at Simon and Simon's at Peter; but the case is quite other with the actual magic involved. Some supernatural exercises are neither admissible nor praiseworthy; but some are both. This is the crux of the message delivered by this literature. Magical ability is expected of a great religious leader; objections arise only when he uses it in unacceptable ways and for unacceptable ends.

We learn from the subsequent narrative what it is about Simon's supernatural activities which provokes objections on the Christian side, and what it is about Peter's this side approves. Further illuminating information upon these points is to be gleaned from the Clementine literature, both *Recognitions* and *Homilies*.[10] The Clementine literature is preoccupied with Simon's heretical teaching and has

[8] See above, chap. 2. The version of the apocryphal Acts of Peter mentioned there, also known as the Vercelli Acts, is extant in a Latin manuscript of the late sixth or early seventh century.

[9] There are several early manuscripts of this, a list of which may be found in R. Lipsius and M. Bonnet, *Acta Apostolorum Apocrypha* i (Leipzig, 1891), LXXV–LXXXIII, with the Latin text at pp. 119–177. This particular text has not been translated into English, but it is very like the Greek Acts of Peter and Paul which has: A. Walker, *Apocryphal Gospels, Acts and Revelations* (Edinburgh, 1873), pp. 262–276. My references here will be to the Latin text.

[10] Again, the surviving manuscript evidence of medieval knowledge of these texts is early, and widely disseminated. See B. Rehm, *Die Pseudoklementinen* (Berlin, 1965), pp. XVII–XCIC.

passages of a philosophical kind that are singularly lacking in the Passion of Peter and Paul, but it portrays a person markedly similar in outline to the Simon of this last. None of these nonbiblical sources has the slightest doubt about the reality of Simon's magical power, which they all describe, nor about the efficacy of the countering magical power of Peter. Thus, Simon could make brazen serpents move, and bronze or stone statues laugh and walk about, and he could take a short run and himself fly up into the air. He could turn himself into a boy, and an old man, and back into a young one. He could change sex as well as age, and so convincingly that Nero was convinced that Simon must be a god.[11] Simon could make himself invisible and could pass through rocks and prison doors. He could throw himself down from mountains and escape unhurt, jump into fires without being burned, turn himself into fire, make new shoots and trees spring up, turn stones into bread, order farm implements to do jobs by themselves, put beards on boys, heap up gold, make or unmake kings. The Vercelli Acts attribute to him the alarming capacity to produce, at short notice, ghostly guests for dinner.[12] On one occasion, Simon professed to have made and unmade a boy out of thin air, explaining that this was a far greater achievement than that of God, who had had, after all, the solid earth to start with; and he used the soul of this boy, who had met a violent death in a previous incarnation, to help him in his magic.[13] There seems to have been no limit to his magic. Some of it is clearly reminiscent of the idolatry condemned in the Old Testament, some, of the challenges of the devil condemned in the New, and some, of the effects sought through ancient magical defixiones, necromancy, and spells.

The apocryphal Passion takes us in detail into the responses of Peter and Paul. In this there are two dramatic trials of strength, staged in the presence of Nero; and in each of them Peter, predictably enough, is the winner. The first involves the vanquishing of Simon's savage dogs by the production of blessed bread from Peter's sleeves (he had hidden it there before, just like a conjuror and with the connivance of Nero—here somewhat disingenuously depicted as a childlike figure, anxious only for the truth). The second entails the familiar demon-

[11] Lipsius and Bonnet, *Acta Apostolorum*, pp. 131–132.

[12] Transl. M. R. James, *The Apocryphal New Testament* (Oxford, 1924), p. 331.

[13] *Recognitions* II,ix,xiii,xv; transl. T. Smith, *The Writings of Tatian and Theophilus and the Clementine Recognitions* (Edinburgh, 1867), pp. 197–198, 200, 202.

stration of Simon's powers of flight. Simon has Nero build him a great wooden tower on the field of Mars. He puts on a laurel crown, climbs up, extends his arms, and (no one is in doubt about it) flies. Peter's answer is to command that the angels who hold him up let him fall. They do so and he dies. Here the Passion differs a little from the Vercelli Acts, according to which only Simon's leg is broken in his fall. His death comes later, as a result of the attentions of the medical profession.

All of the magic is portrayed as real. The powers involved are matters of fact; and they are not, of themselves, occasions for alarm. With the possible (though disputable) exception of the conjuring up of the dead child's soul, it is arguable, on the basis of these accounts, that everything Simon did Peter could perfectly well have done too, had he seen the need. As it was, Peter did perform some remarkable feats of magic. In the Passion he did not merely defeat Simon's dogs with the blessed bread; he made them vanish. In the Vercelli Acts Peter performed another wonder with a dog. He made Simon's guard dog talk, and to such effect that the animal delivered himself of a few home truths about his master which went well beyond the saint's original commission.[14] In the *Recognitions*, Peter is represented as using Simon's own magical powers against the magus himself. Simon, fleeing from Caesar's inquisition, visits his own face upon Faustinianus, father of Clement; this so that Faustinianus might be mistaken for Simon himself, and so take Simon's place should anything untoward occur. Faustinianus's wife faints at the sight; his family despairs. Peter steps in. He promises to restore the hapless victim to his former appearance if only Faustinianus will forswear Simon and take Peter's part in Antioch. Faustinianus agrees, and Peter performs the countering shape shift accordingly.

The objections raised against magic and its practitioners in this literature, then, are directed solely at the object of the practices and at the aims of the practitioners. In that he seeks to be revered as a god, Simon's aims are blasphemous.[15] His practices, on the other hand, are objectless and therefore vain. The *Recognitions* have Peter make these points quite clearly.

---

[14] *Transl.* James, *The Apocryphal*, p. 314.

[15] His imitation of Christ so convinced Nero, according to the apocryphal Passion, that the emperor waited hopefully after Simon's death for him to rise again in three days' time.

For tell me I pray, what is the use of shewing statues walking, dogs of brass or stone barking, mountains dancing or flying through the air and such like things that you say that Simon did? But those signs which are of the good one are directed to the advantage of men, as are those which were done by our Lord, who gave sight to the blind and hearing to the deaf, raised up the feeble and the lame, drove away sickness and demons, raised the dead and did other like things as you see also that I do. Those signs, therefore, which make for the benefit of men and confer some good upon them the wicked one cannot do, excepting only at the end of the world.[16]

So do the *Homilies*. Simon, they have Peter say,

works wonders to astonish and deceive, not signs of healing to convert and save. Wherefore it behoves you also from the miracles that are done to judge the doers, what is the character of the performer, and what of the deed. If he do unprofitable miracles, he is the agent of wickedness; but if he do profitable things, he is a leader of goodness. . . . I say that making statues walk, and rolling himself on burning coals, and becoming a dragon, and being changed into a goat, and flying into the air, and all such things, not being for the healing of man, are of a nature to deceive many. But the miracles of compassionate truth are philanthropic, such as you have heard that the Lord did, and I after him accomplish by my prayers; at which most of you have been present, some being freed from all kinds of diseases, and some from demons, some having their hands restored, and some their feet, some recovering their eyesight, and some their hearing, and whatever else a man can do, being of a philanthropic spirit.[17]

Herein lies the central point. The harnessing of magical abilities to selfish ends renders the practice of magic wholly objectionable. Some feats of magic seem peculiarly susceptible of such harnessing (perhaps flying was one of these, for it certainly seems to be singled out as deserving of special punishment); but magical powers of a wide variety emerge from the Simon literature as legitimate, provided only that they are employed for the clear benefit of human beings. They may even be necessary to humanity. Here we have an enormous change from Ham, whose activities had seemed to render magic totally illicit, and we secure carte blanche for the new dispensation. The fact that this literature, and the Clementine literature in particular, found so

[16] III,lx; *transl.* Smith, *The Writings*, p. 271.
[17] II,xxxiii–xxxiv; *transl.* T. Smith, *The Clementine Homilies* (Edinburgh, 1870), pp. 48–49.

wide a readership is extremely important to our understanding of the rise of magic in the early Middle Ages; for the way in which the downfall of the condemned magus, Simon, was presented in it acted as a most potent stimulus to the rise of magi of a different kind. Simon was a wicked magus, it is true[18] but this treatment of him helped powerfully to demonstrate that there could, and must, be better ones on the excellent precedent of Peter. We might recognize, indeed, in those aspects of Peter's miraculous activity which were singled out for special praise, a blueprint, almost, for much of that earthly magic the early Middle Ages made so much their own.

Blasphemous impersonation of the Redeemer, magic used against Christ's apostles, selfish arrogance, wasteful means, and, once more, a dissolute sexual life,[19] then, disqualified Simon from a role in Christian society—not his magic as such. And the Simon literature made it clear that there was plenty of room for magic in the Christian Church *with* Peter's authority. More important even than this, however, and extremely so for our purposes, is the fact that the question as to which type of person might in the future become the Christian magus (perhaps with the help of authority of other kinds) here remains an open one. The circumstances under which this literature was produced and its very forcefulness allowed, and allow, for doubts about the precedence of Peter as an absolute model for the Christian magus. While the Passion of Peter and Paul, for instance, has Simon reject Peter as lowly born and poorly tutored, an impossibly superior stance according to its author, we might see underlying this vehemence a view that was not universally shared. Not everything about the magus Peter projected here was seen by everyone as good. Nor is everything about

[18] The manner of Simon's death is sometimes drawn out with a view to demonstrating the particular vileness of his life. Arnobius, for instance, has him live on a little after his fall and broken leg, in the manner of the Vercelli Acts, but then, in shame, commit suicide by throwing himself from the roof of a high house. *Against the Heathen* II,xii; transl. H. Bryce and H. Campbell, *Arnobius, Against the Heathen* (Edinburgh, 1871), p. 77. Arnobius's treatise is extant in a ninth-century manuscript.

[19] Later accounts of Simon expand upon hints given in the Clementine literature about sexual malpractice. The *Ecclesiastical History* of Eusebius, for instance (made popular through the translation by Jerome) has Simon partnered in his activities by a certain Helena, a prostitute from Tyre, and encouraging in his followers "unspeakable conduct that cannot be mentioned by the lips of decent men": II,13; transl. R. J. Deferrari, *Eusebius Pamphili Ecclesiastical History* (Washington, 1953), pp. 106–107. The epicene atmosphere often evoked by literature of this kind is well captured by Anita Mason in her novel about Simon, *The Illusionist* (London, 1983).

Simon bad. There is an interesting silence, for example, about Simon's monetary greed, and the Clementine literature in particular allows him considerable, and admirable, intellectual ability. In short, a shadow of a different Christian magus can be seen to form behind the figures both of Simon and of Peter, a shadow that carries with it something of the old-world magus not yet entirely discredited, not even by Simon's excesses. This shadow Christian magus is educated, thoughtful, experienced, and perhaps open-minded on a number of issues, the positive aspects of the non-Christian world, it may be, included.

The discrediting of the figure of Simon, then, though exceedingly forceful, was not total, and its very tone and energy, if it ensured it a readership, also gave food for further thought. Such thought may, paradoxically, have done much to provoke many of those reactions we have followed in earlier chapters, especially the reactions against Petrine regulation, and on behalf of local, even local episcopal, decision making. It is always possible to protest too much, and it can often be argued that the more shrill the detraction, the less likely is it that it will be listened to in the spirit for which it hopes. This particular discrediting process involved exceptionally clear value judgments, and literature of the kind we have for the most part been examining here can bring down vengeance upon its own head. Then, discredit can be turned to credit with an equal energy. The discrediting of Simon Magus had wide repercussions upon the diverse choices of Christian leader made by the early medieval church and may help, indeed, to account for many of these diversities.

THEOPHILUS

The story of Theophilus became widely known in the West far later than the story of Simon Magus. It tells of a magus whose activities and encounters differed from those of Simon in important details, details that were perhaps seen, by its translator into Latin, as apposite to the later circumstances affecting magic in the West. The central message this story conveys, however, when viewed from the point of view of Christian magic's rise in general, is as much a reinforcement of the tendency to encourage the adoption of certain aspects of opposing supernatural practices, suitably changed, as is that of Simon; and this fact makes the attested popularity of the Theophilus story doubly informative and important for our particular purposes.

The oldest Latin version of the story we have is to be found in a ninth-century translation, by Paul the Deacon, of an earlier version from the Greek.[20] Many similar accounts circulated subsequently, and the story became a favorite with preachers. It is set in the period before the Persian invasion of the Byzantine Empire—probably sometime in the sixth century, therefore—and its major characters are appropriate to the time and circumstances of its composition. They are: Theophilus of Adana, a steward in the service of a Christian bishop; a Jew (unnamed); the devil himself—and the Virgin Mary. Theophilus was, according to the legend, the very model of a Christian steward, practical and kindly.

> Quietly and with all moderation he managed most excellently the sheepfold of Christ and the business pertaining to the church, so that the bishop, because of his happy discretion, depended upon him in all business of the church and of the people in general. Wherefore all, great and small, were grateful to him and esteemed him highly. For to orphans and widows and the needy he administered alms very prudently.

At the death of the bishop, and in an interesting account of the processes of the subsequent election, we are told that the clergy and people of Adana wished for Theophilus to succeed to the see, and that they managed to persuade the metropolitan that his candidacy would be acceptable. At the last minute, however, and just before his consecration, Theophilus indulged in a show of self-abasement which infuriated his supporters, and withdrew. A second candidate was consecrated forthwith, and not only was Theophilus given no time for second thoughts, but his very stewardship was taken from him by his outraged former friends.

Theophilus's second thoughts, when he did have them, were prompted by the devil; and they arose not out of true compunction but from the pangs of frustrated ambition. "He sought not for divine but human glory and strove for vain and transitory honour more than divine." He yearned to be restored to his former high position. His desperation led him to consult a Jewish sorcerer, who took him, in turn, to the devil, appropriately installed in the circus building, and surrounded by white-robed minions clutching lighted candles and "uttering loud cries." In return for supernatural help, the devil required of Theophilus that he renounce Christ and Mary and seal the renuncia-

[20] A translation into English of the relevant portions of Paul's Latin version is contained in P. M. Palmer and R. P. More, *The Sources of the Faust Tradition from Simon Magus to Lessing* (New York, 1936), pp. 60–75. My quotations will be taken from this.

tion in a written bond. The pact was made, and the very next day Theophilus was reinstated by a repentant bishop in his former position and given double preferment. Theophilus was not, however, happy, and he prayed, in his remorse, to the Virgin Mary. She heard him, appeared to him in a vision, and, after delivering him a good long lecture upon his sins, agreed to intercede for him if he would again declare his Christian faith. He did so, and, after three days, she delivered him back the bond. Amid great demonstrations of public enthusiasm the bond was burned before the bishop, and Theophilus's countenance was seen to shine like the sun. He returned to the church in which the Virgin had appeared to him, and there he died.

When Paul the Deacon chose this particular story to translate, he was prompted, it seems, by considerations interestingly larger than those which sprang simply from sorcery. Theophilus, through Paul's agency, was to become a major figure both in the bringing to the forefront of the Virgin's miraculous powers and in the denigration of Jews; but these are different (and enormous) issues. In the immediate matter of the rise of magic, and for our present purposes, the points the Theophilus story makes are these. Sorcery can be effective, for it can call upon the devil; and when it does so, it demands a supernatural counter. Once again, there is no doubt here at all about the power inherent in magic, only about the motives of its practitioners. Nor is there any doubt about the acceptability of a supernatural response, provided that the motives which guide it are changed. Jealousy, pride, and greed predominate among the motives condemned, and so also here does damaging irresponsibility and the refusal to face up to the results of free choice. Theophilus had, after all, given up his position of his own free will, and there is every reason to believe that his successor was elected in a right and proper manner. Thus, Theophilus's restoration was short-lived. Generosity and kindliness, by contrast, inform the Christian response, and Christian supernatural power, complete with the restored and destroyed bond, is revealed, in addition, as responsibility personified. This is an important extra dimension to the matter. A proper responsibility toward the operations of human free will, and toward the free will of women especially, played, as we saw, an important place in the Christianization of counters to condemned love magic. Such considerations may also have done much to precipitate the Virgin Mary into prominence.

The stories of Simon and Theophilus, in contrast to that of Ham, allow to the New Testament church—indeed demand of it—wide-ranging magical powers. However, the question as to which human Christian intermediaries might best be trusted with the wielding of these powers is still left interestingly open; indeed, there remains great and enriching scope for disagreement. The figures of the discredited magi here, by the very fact that they are so clearly delineated and so widely publicized, rather stimulate than repel the provision of many Christian answers to them.

ASCLEPIUS

We have discussed in the main, so far, some of the more rabble-rousing pictures of the discredited magus, pictures passed on by polemical, apocryphal, and popular literature. There survives evidence too, however, of a more learned brand: one less given to spectacular exhibitions, adulteries, and pacts with the devil, and more to what we might describe as the intellectual branch of the art of magic. Ham and Simon Magus fall to some extent, of course, into both categories, but the intellectual branch of non-Christian magic is well represented without them, and by persons more impressive in their lineages and more respectable in their pursuits than they. Not surprisingly, the evidence dealing with this branch is more recondite than that we have just left, but it seems to have been widely accessible nonetheless.

Typical of this branch is the figure of Asclepius. Asclepius was, in many ways, the most difficult of all of the outlawed magicians for early Christian Europe to deal with; indeed, he is remembered rather as the object of attempts to discredit him than as discredited in fact. A picture of him appears in one of the earliest and most important of the Anglo-Saxon medico-magical codices,[21] and, though he was not perhaps quite so well known as Simon Magus, Theophilus, or Ham, there was certainly a wide awareness of his extraordinary abilities. This awareness could be, to some, alarming, for Asclepius was a god-hero of Homeric ancestry, renowned through the ancient world for his supernatural healing power—a type of supernatural power, of course, exceptionally deeply treasured and sought after. There was a statue to Asclepius in Rome at the time of Suetonius,[22] and the memory of his

---

[21] The eleventh-century MS B. L. Cotton Vitellius C iii, from Christ Church, Canterbury.

[22] E. J. and L. Edelstein, *Asclepius: A Collection and Interpretation of the Testimonies* i (Baltimore, 1945), 349. This is a careful anthology of evidence about Asclepius, and I shall draw here upon it greatly.

name and semidivine origins and abilities was kept alive in the reading and teaching of the early medieval schools: in Hyginus, for example, and Virgil, and the *Fasti* and *Metamorphoses* of Ovid,[23] all sources capable of exciting the imaginations of more readers and listeners than we always realize. Pliny, too, was impressed by the medical expertise of Asclepius, and Isidore gave Asclepius a simple but telling place in his *Etymologies*. "The founder and purveyor of the art of medicine among the Greeks appears to have been Apollo, an art his son Asclepius worked upon and added to in a most eminent manner."[24] Isidore reduces both Asclepius and Apollo to the status of mere human medical experts, an excellent way of dealing with would-be gods in general, and one followed with enthusiasm by hagiographers when they had to deal with the medical profession. This method was not, however, universally effective in Asclepius's case. Alcuin, in the early ninth century, is still to be found implying that the heights to which the cult of Asclepius attained tower even over that of Saint Martin.[25]

One obstacle stood firmly in the way of the effective reduction of Asclepius to the status of medicus rather than magus. The Fathers remembered him as a magician. Origen spoke of his habit of appearing "like a firebrand down on the floor,"[26] and, more importantly, Jerome described Asclepius and his priests as effective in the magical arts. Jerome tried to discredit Asclepius's expertise by having him exercise it in forbidden ways and with the help of demons.

A nun from . . . Gaza was desperately loved by a youth from the vicinity. When he had accomplished nothing by frequent touching, joking, nodding, whistling and other things of a similar kind which are wont to be the first steps in the loss of virginity, he went to Memphis so that after confessing his unhappy plight he might return to the nun, armed with magic devices. When, therefore, he had been instructed for a year by the priests of Asclepius, the god who does not cure souls but destroys them, he came back, flaunting the dishonour he had taken upon himself.[27]

---

[23] Ibid., pp. 42–43, 45.

[24] *Etymologiae* IV,iii; *edit*. W. M. Lindsay, *Isidori Hispalensis Episcopi Etymologiarum sive Originum Libri XX* i (Oxford, 1911) (MT). This is one of the few occasions on which I part from Edelstein, for the translation of Isidore they advance (p. 186) does not adequately represent this passage.

[25] *Ep.* 245; *edit*. E. Dümmler, *MGH Epistolae Karolini Aevi* ii (Berlin, 1895), 397.

[26] *Contra Haereses* IV,32–33; Edelstein, *Asclepius*, i,167–168.

[27] Jerome, *Life of Hilarion*; Edelstein, *Asclepius*, i,169. Hilarion, of course, put a stop

The expertise itself remained potent nonetheless, and such stories have indeed something of an air of desperation about them. It seems, in truth, to have been hard to find firm evidence upon which to convict Asclepius of pure trickery. And he could, as a healer, and as son of a divine father (Apollo) and human mother (usually Coronis), in addition sustain comparison with Christ.[28] The story of the death of Asclepius (he was struck down by a thunderbolt from Zeus, on account of his healing too many people for that god's peace of mind),[29] in its aura of injustice and unmerited violence, only reinforced the sense of similarity. The Christian Fathers were exasperated. "To Asclepius let them grant that he revived the dead, provided only that they admit that he himself did not escape the lightning."[30] This is a tremendous concession to Asclepius's supernatural powers, and not a wholly damning one, for Christ himself, of course, did not escape his crucifixion. Origen attempts a distinction, but not, it must be said, a completely successful one. "His [i.e., Christ's] death was indeed the result of a conspiracy of men, and bore no resemblance to the death of Asclepius by lightning."[31] The memory of the reputation of the magus Asclepius was, ironically, kept very much alive through these efforts to decry it, and it was a memory that had carried with it, in addition, evidence of the exercise of those healing powers Peter himself had approved.

If the discrediting of Simon Magus bequeathed to the early Middle Ages a shadow figure impossible wholly to outlaw, much more so did that of Asclepius. Asclepius could not be simply discounted, for the Fathers, though grudgingly, admitted that he was effective, and he had virtues and powers very like the Christian ones. He had, therefore, to be outshone. There were in place already plentiful pressures upon the Christian Church either to produce a healing magic of its own or to heal by natural means, as we have seen. The memory of Asclepius added to these, and the emphasis laid upon Asclepius's supernatural healing abilities by the Fathers may have tilted the balance toward a response, in matters of healing, which rested very heavily indeed upon supernatural means. It was not a response wholly to the taste of such

---

to it all, but not without a severe struggle against the demons of debased love. The rest of the story may be read in *PL* 23, 39–40.

[28] Ibid., ii, 132–138.

[29] A story popularized, for instance, by Servius, in his commentary on Virgil's *Aeneid* VI, 398; Edelstein, *Asclepius*, i, 55.

[30] Ambrose, *De Virginibus* III, 176; Edelstein, *Asclepius*, i, 56.

[31] *Contra Celsum* III, 23; Edelstein, *Asclepius*, i, 56.

as Isidore. He favored, as we have also seen, the scientific healing offered by the professionals, and he included Asclepius among these last.
We may remind ourselves once more, however, that not everyone
thought as Isidore did. The need to counter the magus Asclepius, a
magus so convincingly depicted, may have offered to the opponents of
Isidore and his fellow supporters of science a powerful extra incentive
to the encouragement, in its stead, of an appropriate, and similar,
Christian medical magic.

THE MAGUS BY BLOOD

Each of the magi we have discussed so far, disparate are they are, have
one feature in common. Many of the supernatural activities and capacities these magi manifested could be, and were, absorbed by Christianity; and, given the right conditions, each could have done as
Theophilus did: turn from his evil ways. The case of this last non-
Christian magus figure I propose to discuss is rather different, for he
had his magic built in.

The importance of blood in magic is very old and very understandable. Well into and beyond our period, Germanic gods were still demanding blood sacrifices in return for the release of their supernatural
powers, and war leaders seemed more than prepared to produce the
sacrifices, especially from their captives. Procopius (d. ca. 562), for
instance, tells of the practices of the inhabitants of Thule.

> And they incessantly offer up all kinds of sacrifices, and make oblations to
> the dead, but the noblest of sacrifices, in their eyes, is the first human being
> that they have taken captive in war; for they sacrifice him to Ares, whom
> they regard as the greatest god. And the manner in which they offer up the
> captive is not by sacrificing him on an altar only, but also by hanging him
> on a tree, or throwing him among thorns; or killing him by some of the
> most cruel forms of death.[32]

Such passages, myth-making though they can sometimes be, help one
to understand all the better why Christians advanced and emphasized
a Christian magical loosing power and associated it with the Mass, and
why saints liked to release human sacrifices decided upon by Germanic
kings. Odin/Woden was a master magician: a shape shifter, flier,
calmer of fires, seas, winds, and storms, raiser of the dead, diviner,

---

[32] The Gothic Wars VI, 15; edit. and transl. H. B. Dewing, Procopius, History of the
Wars iii (Loeb Classical Library, 1928), 421.

giver of speech, controller of the runes, as well as governor of victory. He could blunt swords, bind with spells, and make earth and mountains and burial mounds open and reveal their treasures. Thus, the *Aesir*, the gods of whom he was the most prominent, were all skilled in the magical arts, for he taught them, and so were his sacrificial priests, for he taught them too.[33] His lust for blood in return was prodigious. He would require it simply for a fair wind, or in recompense for a good harvest, but most especially for victory in battle.

Early barbarian kings were often chosen in time of war, and this association between the war leader and the powerful blood required for victory may, on occasion, have exerted an especially strong influence upon the emergence of a royal family, set apart by blood with a supernatural character. Tacitus seems to have such special blood in mind when he says of the Germans that they "take their kings on ground of birth, their generals on the basis of courage," and when he adds that the help of these kings was called upon in the interpretation of the auguries proclaimed by the neighing of the sacred white horses.[34] Certainly, when we do have such a person distinguished by his blood in this way, he becomes a conductor, rather in the manner of a lightning conductor, of all manner of those magical powers necessary to the procuring of good fortune for his people. And should the power of his blood fail in a single hapless individual, then it might be thought wise to replace this source of it with a stronger one. Ammianus Marcellinus tell us that the Burgundians did just this. "In their country a king is called by a general name, Hendinos, and, according to an ancient custom, lays down his power and is deposed, if under him the fortune of war has wavered, or the earth has denied sufficient crops."[35] Justinian came up against a pretence, at least, to such a belief in the case of the Heruli, when they rejected his candidate for the kingship in favor of a distant member of their own royal house.[36] Sometimes (and perhaps here) one is tempted to suspect, in addition to myth making, the manufacture of tribal convictions for the discomfiture of a gullible imperial commander. The temptation must often have been irresistible; but the idea could not, for the same reason, have been wholly incredible. The

[33] Transl. L. M. Hollander, *Heimskringla* (Austin, Tex., 1964), pp. 10–11.

[34] *Germania* 7,10; *edit.* and *transl.* M. Hutton, *Tacitus. Germania* (Loeb Classical Library, 1914), pp. 274–275, 278.

[35] XXVIII,5; *edit.* J. C. Rolfe, *Ammianus Marcellinus* iii (Loeb Classical Library, 1939), 168.

[36] Though they had murdered the existing incumbent in a momentary lapse. Procopius, *The Gothic War* VI,15; *transl.* Dewing, *Procopius*, ii,423.

idea of the magical blood of royalty may never have been far from the minds of certain of the early European peoples, and for some it was in the forefront.

The magus by blood in early medieval Europe, then, is most readily to be found in that pool of leading families from which the king might be drawn. He is an extraordinarily important figure, and it is possible that the obduracy with which his supernatural powers were defended compelled the Christian Church to be a good deal more flexible in its own approach to magic in general than it might otherwise have been. On occasion, and in the postmigration period especially, this powerful blood was thought to be derived directly from a supernatural source: from Woden himself, in the case of the early Anglo-Saxon kings, from a state of semideification in the case of the kings of the Ostrogoths, from an extraordinary sexual alliance between their mother and a sea monster in the case of the Merovingians.[37] It is possible that the special blood of the blood magus was, on occasion, seen as magically manifest in his hair. Gregory of Tours, for instance, has much to say about the importance to the Merovingian royal house of their long hair as a sign by which their royalty was known, and by the loss of which they could be deeply humiliated. We shall never know for certain whether this long hair was simply a badge of status, or whether it represented a deeper belief in the potency and supernatural quality of the person upon whose head it grew. The latter is at least a possibility, however, and Clovis seems to have inclined to this last view, for when he cut off the hair of the Merovingian Chararic and his son, he was still afraid lest "they threatened to let their hair grow again, and compass his death."[38] He therefore had them killed. The idea of long hair as a sign of royal stock and strength of a particular kind goes back at least as far as Tacitus's Civilis, who, "in accordance with a vow such as these barbarians make, had dyed his hair red, and let it grow long from the time he first took up arms against the Romans."[39] Why red? Striking, cer-

[37] Bede, *Ecclesiastical History* I,15; *transl.* B. Colgrave and R.A.B. Mynors, *Bede's Ecclesiastical History of the English People* (Oxford, 1969), p. 51. Jordanes, *History*, XIII; *transl.* C. C. Mierow, *The Gothic History of Jordanes* (Princeton, 1915), p. 73. Fredegar, *Chronicle* III,9; *edit.* B. Krusch, MGH SRM ii (Hanover, 1888), 95. The idea of the monstrous husband has its parallels in Shamanism: M. Éliàde, *Le Chamanisme et les Techniques Archaïques de l'Extase* (Paris, 1951), pp. 407–408.

[38] Gregory of Tours, *History* II,30; *transl.* O. M. Dalton, *The History of the Franks by Gregory of Tours* ii (Oxford, 1927), 80.

[39] *Histories* IV,lxi; *edit.* C. H. Moore, *Tacitus* ii (Loeb Classical Library, 1931), 116–117. Civilis was of royal blood; ibid., IV,xiii,23. The nineteenth-century excavators

tainly; but also, perhaps, the color of the blood that set him apart. Whether colored or not, however, there are indications that the length of his hair could be of importance to the blood magus, and perhaps of magical importance.[40]

Their especially remarkable beginnings seem to have sown in the Merovingians especially the conviction that, so extraordinary was their stock, the utmost license should be allowed them in the interest of preserving and extending it. Indeed, such efforts were a positive duty. Thus when Saint Columbanus, for example, refused to bless two young princes because they were born out of Christian wedlock, there was outrage. They had the blood. The blessing should, then, follow automatically or, if not, could be dispensed with.[41] In such circumstances women could claim a prominent place in the passing on of this blood. For practical purposes, of course, well they might; but Friga, Woden's consort, goddess of childbirth (and associated sometimes with the Roman Venus), was possessor of Woden's skill in magic and foreknowledge too. This state of affairs both intensified those alarms about feminine magical interventions we saw expressed in the preceding chapter and required that counters involving a Christianized magic must also, at least to some extent, involve women. Against this background we may again the better understand the reasons for the bringing forward of the Virgin Mary's miraculous powers.

The problem of the magus by blood was an enormously difficult one for the early medieval church to contend with, and we may begin to make out some of the deeply different ways by which it did so. The reasons for the bringing to prominence of this magus by blood, the supports upon which he relied, and the times at which his prominence was thought most desirable are complex and interrelated. The presence of hereditary witches within the community may have helped in the emergence of an internal hierarchical counter to them of this sort, a counter that, in its turn, acted upon the Christian world.[42] There are

---

of the early seventh-century ship burial at Snape, in England, found in it hair of a "dirty red" color, though it seems likely that this came from a fur cloak: R. Bruce-Mitford, *Aspects of Anglo-Saxon Archaeology* (London, 1974), p. 117.

[40] Such considerations may throw at least a little more light upon Christian anxieties about the hair of its priests, and about the shape and cut of the clerical tonsure—perhaps as a denial of magical power of this kind.

[41] *Vita Columbani* I, 18–19; *edit.* B. Krusch and W. Levison, MGH SRM iv (Hanover and Leipzig, 1902), 86–87.

[42] A belief in hereditary witchcraft, common among other societies, may not have

many possibilities, few of which the surviving sources enable us fully to test. Claims to magical power were certainly common to them all, however, and in the early Middle Ages the princely magus by blood was firmly in position and posed, if not always a direct threat, certainly a challenge to Christian supernatural authority and a need for careful negotiation. In a letter to King Ethelred of Northumbria, written in 793, Alcuin sums up the position succinctly. "All his people's prosperity, his army's victories, the temperateness of the seasons, the fruitfulness of the earth, the benison of sons, the health of his workers rests upon the goodness of the king."[43] Unless things went very wrong, and Woden, as it might be, became especially demanding, or bloodletting on the part of skeptics or rivals was provoked too easily, few kings can have found it objectionable to have their blood and its associated powers seen as magical, and there could be excellent political reasons for insisting upon it. Such a state of affairs will exercise the Christian Church greatly and will, indeed, encourage it to protect magical blood kings of its own, as well as to produce means of containing them, as we shall see.

***

Learning in a type of magical lore too powerful for humans to handle, magic practiced for frivolous or selfish reasons, magic whose exercise involves a lack of respect for the free judgment of others (especially their free judgment in matters of love), magical powers built into the blood and bones of a given individual—all of these activities and attributes made for a magic abhorrent to the Christian order, though abhorrent to different degrees and in different ways. As in the case of magic in general, the problem posed to the early medieval Christian Church by the memory and the presence of the greater of the individual non-Christian magi was one of horrifying intricacy. No wonder, then, that markedly different individual solutions were advanced. One of the ways of grappling with the problem lay in the inventing of, or falling with relief upon, a person who would neutralize the evil, or who would substitute, for an inadmissible figure replete with supernatural power, an acceptable one instead. This last option was perhaps the most optimistic and was, in fact, the one most enthusiastically, and encouragingly, pursued.

been unknown in early medieval Europe. We know too little about it to be sure that this category was absent from the scene.

[43] Ep. 18; edit. E. Dümmler, MGH Episolae Karolini Aevi ii (Berlin, 1895), 51.

CHAPTER 11

The Figure of Esteem: Christian Counterparts

FOR CHRISTIANS, of course, the greatest of all wielders and mediators of supernatural power was Christ, whose coming transcended the powers of the old magi and heralded a new age of wonders. Although anxieties about the scope and nature of these wonders were felt from the very beginning and left, indeed, an indelible mark upon the New Testament itself, the new religion had no doubt about its need to manifest its supernatural strength by means of distinguished personal action, and efforts to meet this need opened the way for a new form of magus (though rarely, of course, one distinguished by that name). The early Middle Ages in Europe are studded with this new form, and we have already come upon many named exponents of it. Here I shall try to distinguish a little more clearly the principal ones. We shall be concerned with outstanding persons, those whose names and actions seem to have found the widest audience, who acted as models for some of the others, and who (perhaps most important of all) bear most insistently the mark of the magi they oppose.

THE CHRISTIAN PRIEST

To persons brought up within a northern protestant tradition, however diluted, the medieval priest can be understood almost instinctively as the archetypal repository of the Christian "superstitious" tradition. It can come as something of a shock, therefore, to find that, in the early European Middle Ages, the reverse was meant to be the case. I say "meant to be." Councils and penitentials contain many condemnations of priests who did engage in condemned magical pursuits,[1] and we have touched upon certain cases of this, not all of them unedifying.

---

[1] A useful collection of references to such rulings may be found in D. Harmening, *Superstitio. Überlieferungs—und theoriegeschichtliche Untersuchungen zur kirchlich-theologischen Aberglaubensliteratur des Mittelalters* (Berlin, 1979), pp. 222–225.

On the face of it, however, the office of the medieval Christian priest was extremely carefully defended against all suspicion of resemblance to that of the discredited magus. This fact needs to be borne carefully in mind because, paradoxically, the exclusion of the priest from this role can throw much welcome light upon those who did come forward to accept it. If the Christian priest proved unacceptable as the main vehicle for that magic the church chose to make its own, then other figures would have to be prompted forward to take up the burden with an urgency all the greater.

The Bible provided many models and precedents for the possible supernatural activities of the medieval priesthood; but, and interestingly, these were very variously balanced and acted upon. The Old Testament spoke of the priesthood in four main places: in Exodus (28–30) and Leviticus (28), in Genesis (14:18–20) and Psalm 109 (Vulgate). The first two passages described the vesting and anointing by Moses of his brother Aaron and his sons, and the requirements and rituals of the particular priestly office to which they were anointed (complete with blood sacrifice). The passage in Genesis tells of a different precursor of the priesthood of Christ: Melchizedek, king of Salem. Melchizedek (described in this passage as both king and priest of God) provides food and drink for Abraham and his men as they bring back the rescued people of Sodom. He blesses Abraham, and Abraham, in his turn, gives Melchizedek tithes of his booty. In Psalm 109 the unknown successor of King David, of whom the psalm speaks, is addressed as a "priest forever after the order of Melchizedek," a phrase which entered the canon of the medieval Mass.

The passages in Exodus and Leviticus did provide a loophole whereby the priest might be seen as a Christian magician. They provided it in the priority they gave to Moses and Aaron (a priority that came to be much emphasized by the Fathers of the Church), in their mention of blood sacrifices, and, above all, in the memory evoked of the battle of Moses and Aaron against the magicians of Pharaoh. The loophole was, however, a small one, and it was not one that early medieval writers upon the priesthood were to exploit. Quite the contrary. When they turned at all to Old Testament sources they showed themselves far fonder of the Melchizedek tradition; and they may, indeed, have turned to this for reasons of great interest both to the present study and to the history of the medieval priesthood itself. That view which saw Melchizedek as the direct precursor of the priesthood of Christ could be used to cast the Christian priest as a direct counter to Ham. When, in Gen. 9:26–27, Noah blessed Shem, he placed Shem in direct opposition to Ham by cursing at the same time Ham and his descendants. According to a strong tradition of Jewish teaching, the descendants of Shem were given a special place in the passing on of Jewish law and learning; and many of these traditions, in addition, gave Shem the office of high priest and identified him with Melchizedek.[2] This identification was accepted by certain of the Fathers, and it was, with certain modifications to which we shall come, passed on to influential medieval exegetes.

That stream of Old Testament tradition which became the most popular one, then, gave Ham and his particular magical predilections a specific counter which was priestly. It is possible that this need to counter Ham conditioned the selection, at least in part,[3] and that this selection and this need are responsible for some of the more puzzling of the manifestations of, and limitations placed upon, the office and functions of the early medieval priesthood. Once more, alarms about contemporary magic might help us to understand a little better the multiple functions the priest fulfilled, and we may even have again an example of the subordination of biblical and patristic sources to immediate requirements. Melchizedek had two roles to play: one in which he replaced the legacy of Aaron, Jewish and magical, and a second in which he focused the attention of the Christian priesthood upon its main enemy in the realm of supernatural practice, Ham, his adherents, and those who imitated him.

Supports for the office of Christian priest in the New Testament are to be found first and foremost in the Epistle to the Hebrews (believed in the early Middle Ages to be an authentic letter from Saint Paul), then in 1 and 2 Timothy (4:14 and 1:6–8, respectively), and in Acts (1:26). The main theme of Hebrews is the priesthood of Christ himself, a priesthood which encompasses, yet surpasses, all that had gone before in the shape of Aaron and the Levites; and (5:6, 10 and 7:17) it associates this priesthood explicitly with the order of Melchizedek. Hebrews (7:3) sees in the lack of a genealogy for Melchizedek in Gen-

---

[2] L. Ginsberg, *The Legends of the Jews* i (Philadelphia, 1909), 173–174, 233, v (Philadelphia, 1925), 187, 192, 197.

[3] In part only, of course. The wish to dissociate the Christian priesthood from the Jewish is the chief reason for the interest of the early Fathers in Melchizedek, and this wish too acounts for their influence on medieval exegetes. See on this M. Simon, "Melchisedech dans la polémique entre juifs et chrétiens et dans la légende," *Revue d'Histoire et de Philosophie Religieuses* 17 (1937), 58–93.

esis, and in the failure to mention his death, references to the eternity of the priesthood of Christ. We begin to have here a foreshadowing of the many unresolved problems that troubled medieval commentators upon the priestly office. Melchizedek, and Christ, and their successors are both priest and king. In what exactly did their respective powers reside? How were they shared? And, and most important for us, in what spheres of action might king and priest justly expect to receive supernatural reinforcement? Hebrews gave no firm answers. All depended upon the nature of the powers delegated to Christ's successors, and upon how widely distributed these delegated powers might be taken to be.

The references to Melchizedek in Hebrews give us an extra reason, of course, for the turning of medieval exegetes to the Melchizedek tradition of the Old Testament priesthood; but it is hard to see it as determining. The choice of Hebrews, after all, as the New Testament source upon which chiefly to rely was itself a conditioned one and involved the relegation, in their turn, of the passages in the Epistles to Timothy, and of the episode in Acts. All of these last sources in fact open up a much larger conspectus upon the supernatural capacities that might be given to the priest. The Epistles to Timothy speak of "the gift you have, which was given you by prophetic utterance" and of a "spirit of power and love and self-control," both imparted by the laying on of hands. That sacrificial element of the priesthood which can be found in Hebrews is lacking here, and we have different charismata, both clearly linked with power of a supernatural kind and passed on by a ritual ordination. In one homily on this section of Timothy (known to the Middle Ages in an old Latin translation) John Chrysostom more than kept the matter of the powers of the priesthood open. "This is the grace of the Spirit which you have received, so that you may preside in the church, show forth signs, and offer divine worship of every kind."[4] Such a passage held out large possibilities for the operation of priestly powers; but these possibilities were, officially at least, left undeveloped in the West. The passage in Acts, in its turn, speaks of the choosing of the apostle Matthias—but by lot. The anxieties engendered by this far larger conspectus and range of supernatural power, given the particular political conditions within which the early medieval priest had to work, may have contributed to the comparative relegation of these passages.

[4] PG 62,603 (MT).

Few early medieval Christian exegetes thought it necessary to write a commentary upon Hebrews or Timothy, but Alcuin (d. 804) was the most influential of these few. By placing him within his larger pastoral context, we can begin to understand both why he chose Hebrews in the first place as the text upon which chiefly to rely, and why he set out certain clear views upon the priesthood, views which came to be influential. Alcuin's views are distinguished for the severity with which he confines his priests purely to their sacramental functions. He expands upon the Melchizedek tradition to this end. In harmony with the Fathers, but a step along the way from the author of Hebrews, he sees the giving of food and drink by Abraham to Melchizedek as a type of the Eucharist,[5] the central concern of his priest, and he deals in short order with the problem of Melchizedek as king. Alcuin follows (without comment) Jewish tradition in his insistence that Shem and Melchizedek were one and the same; but Melchizedek, he insists, was not king of Jerusalem, but Sichem,[6] and his kingship was, as an office, unimportant. The implications of this insistence will become clearer when we turn to the sacral king, but Alcuin presents us here with a fine summary of the orthodox early medieval position on the functions, and especially the limitations, of the Christian priestly office. As Alcuin associates the bread and wine of the Eucharist with the food and drink given by Abraham to Melchizedek, so he contrasts this service specifically with the sacrifices and activities asked of Aaron and his sons. The principal way in which the Christian priest stands between God and his people lies, according to Alcuin, in the offering of this wholly new kind of sacrifice. The supernatural powers of Alcuin's priests are here very rigidly circumscribed indeed. There are no battles of magic in the past he allows for them, and they may expect no special abilities beyond the strictly sacramental in the future.

Thus, Alcuin keeps the charismata of the Epistles to Timothy firmly within bounds, and in a way that differs significantly from that of John Chrysostom, whose homilies and commentaries (in their Latin translations) he knew and on occasion used. This same rigid circumscription, with perhaps the same reasoning behind it (alarm, that is, about confusions between the office of the Christian priest and that of the

[5] After John 6:53–54.

[6] He clinches the argument by declaring that the ruins of Melchizedek's palace are still to be seen in Sichem. *Expositio in Epistolam Pauli Apostoli ad Hebraeos* VII,i; *PL* 100,1062. He draws heavily here upon parts of the Latin translation of John Chrysostom's commentary on Hebrews, a commentary he clearly knew.

non-Christian magus) characterizes the most influential of the early medieval commentaries upon the relevant passage of Acts—that by Bede. Bede felt called upon to state quite categorically that interventions of a magical kind in the advancement of persons to the priesthood, choices by lot, were confined to the pre-Pentecostal church. As we saw above when discussing some of the operations of the *Sortes Sanctorum*, such interventions were by no means so confined by everyone, and they were sometimes actively invoked when it came to the validation of bishops. Bede's insistence,[7] then, like Alcuin's, is perhaps best understood when placed against the background of a different, pressing, and controversial state of affairs.[8]

Pope Gregory the Great, in his classic treatise upon the sacerdotal office, the *Pastoral Rule,* is perhaps the most stalwart of all the advocates of restrictions; and this book (completed by 591) was foremost among the early medieval treatises devoted to the office of priest or bishop. It was carried to England by Augustine of Canterbury, translated into Anglo-Saxon by King Alfred, and at least supposed to be issued to every bishop appointed in ninth-century Francia. Indeed, almost as soon as it was written, and for the whole of the rest of the period with which we are here concerned, it would have been very difficult indeed for any priestly aspirant to have avoided the *Pastoral Rule*; and there is a singular irony in the fact that, although this treatise was composed to show that almost no one could fulfill the requirements of this office, so impossibly demanding were they, it nonetheless became the standard manual for those who strove to do so. The *Pastoral Rule* is a masterpiece of practical priestmanship; but for our purposes it is more informative in that which it does not say than in that which it does. One looks to it in vain for the priest-king Melchizedek, for the crucial sections of Hebrews, and for any discussion of the full extent of the supernatural powers which might come to the priest from

---

[7] *Expositio Actum Apostolorum* I,26; *edit.* M.L.W. Laistner, *Bedae Venerabilis Opera, Opera Exegetica* ii(4), CC (Turnholt, 1983), 14–15. The passage is a most interesting one and seems in fact to be written with an eye at least in part to the discrediting of those lot-casting practices in connection with episcopal elections we discussed in chap. 10. It appears from Bede's phrasing that the defenders of these lot-casting practices sometimes justified them on the grounds of apostolic precedent. Bede will not allow it. After Pentecost, says Bede firmly, such choices were to be made by means of prayer and proper electoral practices. Even in apostolic times, he adds, such methods always took precedence.

[8] Regino, for instance, seems to see no difficulty in describing a bishop as "sortitus" to his church: *De Ecclesiasticis Disciplinis* I,ccxlix; PL 132,238.

ordination. The emphasis of the work is wholly other and, predictably, especially pleased Alcuin. He wrote of it to Archbishop Eanbald of York, "The book is a mirror of the life of a bishop, and a medicine for all the wounds inflicted by the devil's deception."[9] Gregory envisages his priest and bishop as first and foremost a preacher and giver of guidance (even going so far as to advance a distinctly curious etymology in his support).[10] We search without success for deeper, or wider, supernatural abilities. All the powers Gregory attaches to the priest as follower of Aaron are moral ones, concerned with the subduing of vice. His comments upon the significance of the sacred vestments of Exod. 28:15 are especially striking in this respect.[11]

Gregory, of course, intended the *Pastoral Rule* to be a practical handbook for the office, not an analysis of it, and a handbook in which the powers accorded to priests through ordination could be taken somewhat for granted; but, even with this in mind, the strictness with which the role is curtailed is still very remarkable. Gregory tells us a great deal about the "love and self control" of the Epistle to Timothy, but almost nothing of the concomitant "spirit of power." As we have seen, and as we shall see further when we come to his *Life of Saint Benedict*, Gregory held complex and somewhat anxious views upon the place of signs and wonders and Christian magic. A superfluity of contemporary wonder-workers, and a profound desire to ensure that the Christian response to these was an appropriately nuanced one, may have led him therefore to have been even more than normally restrictive of the charismata of his priests. We do well to bear this possibility in mind when tempted to treat the *Pastoral Rule* as a timeless work.

The Christian priest of the *Pastoral Rule* had, then, perhaps the least chance of anyone to compete in a common arena with the non-Christian *magus*, and fear lest the two roles might seem to run together appears, in all formal descriptions of the early medieval priestly office, to have taken clear precedence over the idea of a possibly successful competition for supernatural power in the tradition of Moses and Aaron's contests with the magicians of Pharaoh. We need to keep the reality of the pressing presence of the non-Christian magician in the forefront of our minds, if we are to understand the very particular po-

---

[9] *Transl.* H. Davis, *St. Gregory the Great Pastoral Care* (London, 1950), p. 11.

[10] "Sacerdotes," he says, take their name from "sacrum ducatum": ibid., II,7; p. 74.

[11] Ibid., II,2–3; pp. 46–49. John Chrysostom, *De Sacerdotio*, especially III,4, on the sheer power of both the old and new priesthood is, once more, far more vivid. Again, though known, this work was little copied in our period.

sition on the priesthood adopted by those who took the trouble directly to write about it. At some point a sharp line had to be drawn between the non-Christian and the Christian wielder of supernatural authority, and the figure of the priest seems to have been chosen by certain outstanding spokesmen as that best fitted for the drawing of this line. The extra-special nature of the Eucharistic Sacrifice may account at root for the choice of the priest for this dividing role. At all events, the priest could, in the early Middle Ages, be expected to play it, and his withdrawal, at least in theory, from the center of the competition left the way open for others to fill the gap.

The fear of a possible total confusion of roles within a situation intensely delicate—and one made all the more so by the fact that in certain circles the need to preserve a place for *some* kind of Christian magus was very deeply felt—may in part account for the extraordinary preoccupation, in conciliar rulings, with the problem of simony. Simony, of course, was the name for the sin of purchasing ecclesiastical office and was derived from Simon Magus's great sin of seeking to buy from the Apostle Peter the secret of the supernatural charismata of his followers. The ferocity with which simony was condemned in early medieval councils is familiar; but, again, the full context of this condemnation is not always wholly appreciated. Simon Magus, of course, as Peter's competitor for authority in supernatural affairs, plays an important part in it; but so too (and as a backdrop to the medieval importance of Simon himself) do the generality of those early non-Christian medieval magi who were held to follow him, and who competed with Christian priests. We have some evidence, moreover, that, as Acts kept alive the memory of the wicked expense of the older outlawed magic (in both 8:18–24 and 19:13–19), so these contemporary magi both could and did charge highly for their attentions.[12] It was of redoubled importance, then, within this context, that the medieval priest be freed from this particular stigma.[13] Pressing non-Christian

---

[12] When Ruricius fell sick, and his anxious household consulted "medici" and also "malefici" and "praecantatores," they cost a lot of money. *Vita Iuniani Confessoris Commodoliacensis* 6–7; *edit.* B. Krusch and W. Levison, MGH SRM iii (Hanover and Leipzig, 1896), 378–379. Saint Iunianus healed him without charge. The Ramsey Chronicle witch (mentioned above in chap. 8) had been expensive and had apparently also indulged in blackmail; *edit.* W. D. Macray, *Chronicon Abbatiae Rameseiensis*, RS (London, 1886), pp. 129–134.

[13] Richard M. Meyer, in his *Altgermanische Religionsgeschichte* (Leipzig, 1910), p. 150, touched upon this point, but I have not seen it discussed since.

magic and magicians, great and small, once more encouraged the distancing of the role of this priest from that of his competitors, and the fierce and consistent condemnations of simony become the more comprehensible against this background. So, perhaps, do the rulings enforcing celibacy. The celibate priest made again for a clear contrast with both Ham and Simon Magus; and he was removed too, and firmly, from many of the condemned operations of love magic and its practitioners, operations which, as we saw, gave rise to especial alarms. It would be hard for the priest to operate against love magic, even at the sacramental level Hincmar advocated, if he made himself vulnerable to its snares. Though such pressures were not, perhaps, the most compelling of the reasons for the insistence upon priestly celibacy, it is at least arguable that they had a part to play.

It is equally clear, however, that not every priest accepted this official distance. The canons of early councils, full as they are of rulings against simony, are full also, as we have seen, of condemnations of priests who associate with, or try themselves to be, magicians—condemnations that are readily echoed in later compilations.[14] Some legislators find it necessary to specify both clergy and laity in their general prohibitions against magic, and to make the penalties for clerical involvement far higher ones. Martin of Braga includes in his collection of the canons of Greek councils one from the council of Laodicea. This declares roundly that "sacerdotes" and "clerici" who try to be "incantatores" abuse the binding-and-loosing power itself, an abuse which results in the "colligatio animarum."[15] Such clerics are to be ejected from the church. Isidore finds it necessary to specify all ranks of the clergy (lest there be any mistake) when he outlaws magical practice, and to insist upon a lifetime of penance for any cleric who so much as consults a magician.[16] Similar condemnations, taken both from councils and from penitentials, recur in Burchard, who is inclined to the

---

[14] For example, the 506 Council of Agde, canons xlii and lxviii; Mansi, viii,332,336. Caesarius of Arles himself presided over this council. And see Harmening, *Superstitio*, pp. 222–225.

[15] Canon LIX; *edit.* C. W. Barlow, *Martini Episcopi Bracarensis Opera Omnia* (New Haven, 1950), p. 138.

[16] Canon xxix of the 633 Council of Toledo: "Si episcopus, aut presbyter, sive diaconus, aut quilibet ex ordine clericorum, magos, aut aruspices, aut ariolos, aut certe augures, vel sortilegos, vel eos qui profitentur artem aliquam, aut aliquos eorum similia exercentes consulere fuerit deprehensus, ab honore dignitatis suae depositus monasterii poenam excipiat, ibique perpetuae poenitentiae deditus scelus admissum sacrilegii luat." Mansi, x,627.

degradation and excommunication of clerics who indulge.[17] Repetitions and ferocities of this nature indicate that the problem was widespread and thought to be a very serious one. Yet, once more, we may find sometimes in such rulings evidence of an extended sympathy that outran the limits of prudence, and an interpretation of the priestly office that rested upon a more liberal tradition than that currently espoused, rather than an outright rejection by clerics of the Christian priestly ideal or a backsliding and craven submission to paganism.[18] Local clergy found themselves in a difficult position, one made perhaps all the more difficult by the attempted severe confinement of their functions.

Despite these resistances, however, the casting of the priest as countermagus was not to find orthodox sanction in early medieval Europe. Thus, those who saw the need for such a Christian role had either to defy the official circumscriptions of the priesthood, with all the risks this entailed, or to look to figures other than the priest for its fulfillment. When circumstance rendered the second of these options the more desirable one (and here once more, it is worth noting, weight could fall upon the monastic orders, not all of whose members were candidates for ordination), these alternative figures bore a burden all the greater as a result.

THE MAGI OF MATTHEW

In many ways, the best model for the Christian countermagus was to be found in Matt. 2:1–12.

> Now when Jesus was born in Bethlehem of Judea in the days of Herod the king, behold, there came wise men from the East to Jerusalem, saying, where is he that is born king of the Jews? For we have seen his star in the East, and are come to worship him . . . and, lo, the star which they saw in

---

[17] *Decretum* X,27; *PL* 140,837. Excommunication seems to be the standard penalty and is presumably the canonical one to which chapter xxxiii of the so-called statutes of Boniface (745) consigns a priest or "clericus" for such a delict; Mansi, xii,386.

[18] Not always, of course. The 683 Council of Toledo contains a canon (vii) condemning the stripping of altars and the closing of churches by priests when they have a grievance (a form of conjuring with God described as magic by Gratian); Mansi, xi,1069. That of 694 (canon v) records the censure of priests who celebrate mass for a living person in order to procure his death; Mansi, xii,99. Perversions such as these, however, tend to be clearly described in the canons and so seem to stand apart from those associations with magicians which may in intention be sympathetic.

the East went before them, till it came and stood over where the young child was. When they saw the star, they rejoiced with exceeding great joy . . . and when they had opened their treasures, they presented unto him gifts; gold and frankincense, and myrrh.

As with the Simon Magus literature, so with this passage we tread upon difficult textual and theological ground, but the message that came through to the early Middle Ages was relatively clear, and, for the positions of the magical wonder-worker of the early Middle Ages and of those who observed the stars in the hope of supernatural direction from them, it was of the greatest importance.

The Vulgate allowed that these men might be called "magi." They were obviously, however, neither blinded by their learning, nor destructive or selfish in their employment of their powers. Thus, they hardly deserved to be called "malefici," even though, equally clearly, they exhibited skills that were pre-Christian and beyond the natural. This passage, then, in contrast with both the multifarious examples of wicked Old Testament magi and the Simon Magus of Acts, stands out as giving uncompromising scriptural support to a type of magus able from the first to be incorporated within the Christian dispensation. Matthew's story of the Magi gave a golden opportunity to take stock, to measure the gulf between the old magus and the possible new one, and to become alive to the means whereby this gulf might be crossed.

We might note that the Magi in the gospel are not royal, nor, in the West, did they immediately become royal. Although the liturgy will come to associate them with Ps. 71:10–11 (Vulgate), "The kings of Tarshish and the Isles shall bring presents; the kings of Sheba and Seba shall offer gifts," early representations show them merely in the Phrygian bonnet, and their subsequent regal office seems to have been fastened upon them largely as a result of political circumstance.[19] Nor were they invariably thought to be three in early sources.[20] That they became three seems to have been in part due to an efficient and economical distribution of Matthew's three gifts, in part to the ease with which the number three could be interpreted allegorically.[21] In their

[19] Tertullian claimed that they were kings; *edit.* E. Evans, *Tertullian, Adversus Marcionem* i (Oxford, 1972), 208. He had some few followers in this, notably Pope Leo the Great and Caesarius of Arles, but the kingship of the magi was only widely emphasized after the translation of their presumed bodies from Milan to Cologne in 1164.

[20] Some early medieval writers were convinced that there must have been very many of them, for example, Paschasius Radbert, *Expositio in Mattheum* II,ii; *PL* 120,127.

[21] For example, by Haimo of Auxerre in his *Homilia xv In Epiphania Domini; PL*

earliest medieval form, Matthew's Magi seem simply to have been just and learned and generous persons, and persons with access also to supernatural direction of a Christian kind: the ideal, that is, of the helpful and dignified counterpart to such as Simon Magus, and an ideal, it seems, also open to many followers.

We can measure to some extent the impact the story of the Magi had upon the early Middle Ages, and upon early medieval ideas about possible Christian countermagi, by following them through two different kinds of record, liturgical and literary (the latter mainly in the form of sermons and comments upon this passage in Matthew). There was, of course, very little firm liturgical unity in early Europe, but from as early as the late fourth century, Matthew's Magi had the foremost place in a great feast on 6 January.[22] They were not, however, alone. Two other events in which magic in the form of miraculous prediction and practice played a great part (and which were thought to have taken place on the same day of the year) were also celebrated on this feast, especially so in northern Italy and Gaul. One was the baptism of Christ by John the Baptist, the other the gospel miracle of the changing of the water into wine at the marriage feast of Cana, a miracle of social grace and kindliness strong in contrast to Simon Magus's ghostly dinner guests.[23] The inclusion of the marriage feast helped, also, to introduce the idea of the marriage between Christ and his church, commemorated in the Roman antiphon of the *Benedictus*. Thus, the new Magi take part in the general joyful evocation of a marital union of a most sacred kind; they provide a speaking, and we may suppose conscious, contrast with the dubious sexual activities often associated with the old magi, not least with Ham. A third event sometimes grouped with these was the miracle of the loaves and fishes, a type of the Eucharistic sacrifice. All added up to a considerable celebration of supernatural power, and of those wielders and objectives of this power which were thought appropriate to Christianity.

The Feast of the Epiphany demonstrated too the determination with which the church set itself to rival older joys.[24] It did so very success-

---

118,111. Their three names, Caspar, Melchior, and Balthasar, are to be found in the West at least as early as the eighth century, and sporadically before: D. M. Dumville, "Biblical Apocrypha and the Early Irish: A Preliminary Investigation," *Proceedings of the Royal Irish Academy* 73 (1973), 316.

[22] B. Botte, *Les Origines de la Noël et de l'Épiphanie* (Louvain, 1932), pp. 40–44.

[23] Paulinus of Nola, *Poema* xxvii; *PL* 61,649 (ll. 47–53).

[24] Close to this Christian feast there were pagan ones, to Dionysius and to the sun

fully in this case. Few pieces of medieval chant are more moving than the settings of the response, verse, and psalm passages of the liturgy for the day, insofar as we are able to reconstruct them, even though the verse especially (Isa. 60:1: "Arise, shine, for thy light has come") has some particularly stiff later competition. Music of this quality and, in the pre-eleventh-century Offertory, the congregation's presentation of gifts of bread and wine, made the whole enactment of the journey of the Magi to the Christ Child and that of the people to the altar emotionally deeply compelling and kept Matthew's Magi firmly in the forefront of devotional attention. And it kept in the forefront too, with them, the image of the good magus. In the later Middle Ages this feast became the ideal occasion for the coronation of a king, and the moment of the Offertory a fine media moment, as it were, for the king to stand in the tradition of these Magi and bring gifts of many kinds, including, perhaps, supernatural ones. We might also assume that a good deal of literal feasting, on the excellent precedent of the feeding of the five thousand, took place when the liturgical ceremonies were over, coronation or no coronation.

The liturgy stressed, then, miracles of supernatural and virtuous prevision and provision, miracles introduced by those Magi who were present at Christ's nativity. This stress is reinforced in medieval sermons on the Epiphany and commentaries upon Matthew. With these materials we enter into a complex dimension of the question, but in that these complexities spring directly from those anxieties about the magician's position in the Christian dispensation which we seek here to examine, they are in themselves illuminating. Three questions tended to be asked about Matthew's Magi in these sermons and commentaries. They constitute in fact a microcosm of that larger inquiry we have been in general undertaking and were, I am sure, formed against its background. They are these. How far must the new order seek entirely to eliminate the old? Is it possible that their magical learning had actually helped the Magi to welcome the new order, and that it might, therefore, still be of assistance? Were the Magi magicians of a kind wholly impossible for the Christian dispensation to absorb? Were they malefici, evil magicians, that is, whose conversion had to be total and must include the rejection of all their former supernatural

god, Aion (on its eve). Epiphanius of Salamis (d. 402) gives a vivid description of the latter, involving as it did a night watch at a sanctuary, with chants and flutes and, at cockcrow, a torchlight procession to an underground cavern, carrying a gilded wooden image of the god on a bier: Botte, *Les Origines*, pp. 74–75.

powers; or could they, with profit to all, be encouraged to bring some of their pre-Christian ways with them? Opinions varied greatly; yet, and most interestingly, the further we venture into the early Middle Ages in Europe, the more ready are some to admit that the Magi of Matthew might have, through their supernatural abilities, a great deal to offer to Christianity.

One apparently overwhelming obstacle stood initially in the way of such an accommodation. This lay in the possibility that the Magi were astrologers, and that, in their recognition of the star, they were living proof that the stars were indeed a guiding principle in the lives of men. This view, given their objections to astrology in all its aspects, the Fathers could not abide. Nothing short of the complete conversion of the Magi from their old ways could satisfy them. John Chrysostom (d. 407) expressed himself particularly forcibly on this subject in his sixth homily on Matthew (which, with many others of his homilies, was translated into Latin in the early fifth century and enjoyed a wide following). Whatever their skills, astrology did not help the Magi this time, he pointed out.[25] Astrology as an exercise is simply absurd. John was not above sarcasm; few of the Fathers were when pressed, least of all Augustine. Augustine's own position on the Magi of Matthew is a similar one, as we might expect, and it is in some places even sharper.[26] To Augustine, as to John, the star was not a governing principle but a sign, and astrology not only had nothing to do with the discovery the Magi made, it has nothing to do with anything. To make their discovery and, above all, to profit by it, these Magi had to abandon their suspect astrological skills. Jerome puts the matter with trenchant simplicity: "Christ, by his coming, destroyed the tricks of the magi in their entirety."[27] Pope Gregory the Great reinforced this view,[28] and one might, with good reason, have expected the matter to end there.

In fact, the Fathers did not end the matter. True, their attitudes to astrology were, for the time being, allowed to pass; but not their views

[25] Astrologers, says John, try to predict not who will be born but what will happen to them; the magi knew only of the birth. They could not even foretell what might happen to them at the hands of Herod! Nor was the star a real star, but simply a sign sent to astonish them into action. Transl. G. Prevost, The Homilies of St. John Chrysostom on the Gospel of St. Matthew (Oxford, 1843), 36–43.

[26] For instance, in his Sermon 199 on the Epiphany, translated as Sermon 18 in T. C. Lawler, St. Augustine. Sermons for Christmas and Epiphany (London, 1952), pp. 157–158.

[27] Ep. xcvi; PL 22,786 (MT).

[28] Homilia x; PL 76,1112.

on Matthew's Magi. Two refinements of these views become evident as we press on through later comments on Matthew's story. One refinement dignifies the science of the stars in those ways and for those ends we have already tried to examine.[29] A second dignifies the Magi and makes them, indeed, possible precursors of a new style of Christian magus, given to the attraction to themselves of wondrous signs from heaven and possessed of the ability to make use of these supernatural aids—and thus, able actively to outplay the non-Christian opposition.

A beginning was made by Prudentius. He agreed with Augustine that the new star threw into confusion the calculations of astrologers, and he did so vividly and beautifully. It is easy to see why Prudentius was so popular as a school text, and why his views deserve notice and, it seems, gained it.

> The astrologer watching all night on a height in Chaldea felt his blood curdle with alarm when he saw that the Serpent had given place, the Lion taken to flight, the Crab drawn in his feet in a crippled row along his side, that the Bull was roaring in defeat, his horns broken, the constellation of the Goat, with his hair torn, fading away. Here slides off in retreat the boy with the Water Pot, there the Arrows, the Twins wander apart in flight, the false maiden deserts her silent wooers in the vault of heaven, and the other blazing orbs hanging in awful clouds have feared the new Morning Star.[30]

The Magi however, says Prudentius, stood apart from this confusion. They identified the star as the Christ Child from the first. "We have seen . . . this child passing over the sky, and outshining the trains of the ancient stars." Yet they did believe in star lore. Prudentius calls them "skilled interpreters" and has them take the star sign as confirmation of God's promise to Abraham that his children "must one day be equal to the stars."[31] There is much more respect here for the Magi, and for their knowledge of the stars, than Augustine will allow them, and the reverse of a suggestion that this knowledge was in any way alarming or should be abandoned.

The problem was a difficult one, and we can see it occupying the minds especially of those who wrote formal commentaries on the Gospel of Matthew, the most important of which (and indeed for many

---

[29] See above, chap. 6.

[30] *Apotheosis*; *edit.* and *transl.* H. J. Thomson, *Prudentius* i (Loeb Classical Library, 1949), pp. 166–167.

[31] *Apotheosis* ll. 615–616, *Cathemerinon* ll. 26, 46; ibid., pp. 166–167, 104–105.

the model) was the commentary by Jerome. Jerome's exegesis of Matthew's Magi was short and ripe for expansion. It received it—partly, it is true, from remarks Jerome had made in his other works, but partly, and for us most illuminatingly, because of the changed needs and experiences of Jerome's European successors. The first of these to claim any wide impact was Rabanus Maurus, whose own commentary was completed by the 850s (just, perhaps, as he completed his *De Magicis Artibus*). Rabanus makes one particularly firm preliminary statement about the Magi. They are not magicians in the sense of "malefici."[32] This puts Rabanus in immediate, and surely conscious, opposition to Augustine, whose famous propositions on the Magi he knew well. Augustine had been in no doubt that the Magi were magicians, and of the very worst kind. He speaks of their "irreligion" and "unholy practices," of their conversion from the "curse of their superstition" and of their having been previously "burdened with sins."[33] Rabanus accepts none of this. Matthew's Magi can easily be confused by the commonalty with "malefici," he admits, but they were in fact philosophers, men whose learning was held in great respect in their own land, Chaldea. Their three gifts presented to Christ represent, among other things, "physica, ethica, logica."[34]

These Magi, then, with all their learning and even with their astrological lore, begin to be rehabilitated in the mid-ninth century, and it is hard to resist the view that this movement for the rehabilitation of the Magi was intimately associated with that undertaken for the rehabilitation of astrology which, as I have suggested, may have begun to develop precisely at this time. It is more than possible, moreover, that the two movements were meant to achieve the same ends. It was peculiarly vital, in the barely Christianized Carolingian Empire, and in the face of the determined official withdrawal of the priesthood from this role, for the Christian Church to find a convincing countermagus, one equipped with appropriate skills and free of too close a resemblance to his unskilled local magician opponent. In this context, it is unsurprising that Rabanus, alarmed as we know he was by the grosser

[32] *Commentaria in Mattheum* I,ii; PL 107,756.

[33] Transl. Lawler, *St. Augustine. Sermons*, nos. 19, 21, 22, pp. 163, 171, 175.

[34] Here Rabanus draws out other observations from Jerome. The latter had been prepared to allow that the Magi (from Persia) were learned and respectable, moderate in their eating habits (a great thing with Jerome), and far from the common run of "malefici." *Adversus Jovinianum* II; PL 23,317. *Commentaria in Danielem Prophetam Liber*, cap. II, 2; PL 25, 498–499.

magical practices he saw around him, should turn with relief to such figures and to their astrological expertise. Matthew's Magi were not everyone's answer to the problem; but they could be to some a convincing one, as could astrology itself. It is also worth noticing that, as the three Magi came to be seen as New Testament successors to the three sons of Noah (ruling the three parts of the world and leading the human race to its redemption), one of the Magi, Caspar, lay ready as another answer to Ham.[35] Caspar's name and Ham's appeared second in their respective groupings, and both men were, in legend, supposed to be black.[36] Caspar was in a position, then, to save the human race through his particular form of magic, rather than condemn it to the kind of subjection and slavery to which Ham had confined it.[37]

From Rabanus onward, Matthew's Magi take on a role very different from that assigned to them by the Fathers. Rabanus's views color the rendering of Matthew contained in the popular Old Saxon poem *Heliand*, and Rabanus's influence can be clearly seen in the widely read commentary on Matthew of the Pseudo-Bede.[38] Nor does that discredit earlier heaped upon the Magi before their conversion return in the later commentaries produced within our period. Some may take the opportunity to condemn astrology in passing[39]—there remained many

[35] As early as the late seventh or early eighth century *Expositio Quattuor Evangeliorum* of the Pseudo-Jerome, the three Magi are seen as the New Testament successors of the three sons of Noah; *PL* 30,537.

[36] The idea that Caspar was black, as was Ham according to certain commentators, goes back at least to Sedatus (fl. ca. 500) and was possibly familiar to Caesarius: A. Wilmart, "Une homélie de Sedatus évêque de Nîmes pour la nativité de notre Seigneur," *Revue Bénédictine* 35 (1923), 5–6. *Edit.* A. Englebrecht, *Fausti Reiensis et Ruricii Opera* (Vienna, 1891), p. 253.

[37] Ambrosiaster, in his commentary on Phil. 2: 7, dilates upon the slavery to which Ham had consigned the human race; *edit.* H. J. Vogels, *Ambrosiastri qui dicitur Commentarius in Epistulas Paulinas* iii (Vienna, 1969), p. 140. Rabanus, we might remember, showed in his concerns about magic a particular predilection for the works of Ambrosiaster.

[38] *In Matthaei Evangelium Expositio* I,ii; *PL* 92,12–13. Again, we are told, the Magi were never magicians or diviners of a reprobate kind, but philosophers who responded appropriately to respectable prophecy, in this case to the prophecy of Balaam (Num. 24:17): "A star shall arise from Jacob and a man shall come forth from Israel, and he shall rule all nations." Once more, their gifts are "physica, ethica, logica," and they rule the three parts of the world (Asia, Africa, Europe), as successors respectively to Shem, Ham, and Japheth.

[39] Thus Smaragdus (after Augustine) in his *Collectiones in Epistolas et Evangelia quae per circuitum anni leguntur*; *PL* 102,72, and Christian of Stavelot (d. post 880) in his *Expositio in Matthaeum* II; *PL* 106,1281. This commentary is here wrongly attributed

different views about the exact position of astrology even, perhaps especially, after its return to respectability had begun—but the learning and star lore of the Magi becomes now a matter rather for optimism than alarm, and so does their capacity to exercise a respectable form of divination when it comes to interpreting prophecy.[40] Matthew's Magi thus become fine New Testament supports for later types of Christian magus similarly equipped. Once again, we wrestle best for an understanding of this transition and of the need for it against the background of certain named condemned magi, against that of the lively activity of their contemporary non-Christian successors, and against that also of the staged withdrawal of the Christian priest from the fray.

One of the most vivid, fascinating, and contentious evocations of the place given to the Magi of Matthew in our period is to be found on the front panel of the Franks Casket. This priceless little box of carved whalebone is an object to which no justice can be done within small compass. It is so important a relic, however, and it sums up so succinctly the crucial position of these Magi as intermediaries and possible vehicles of compromise between condemned and respectable magic, that it deserves the utmost emphasis. Datable to the turn of the seventh and eighth centuries, long thought to be Northumbrian, and certainly European in origin, the Franks Casket has on its front panel a representation of Matthew's Magi (here three) seemingly deliberately ranged both against and within that magic they have come to replace. On the right-hand side of the panel these Magi bring their gifts to the Virgin and the Christ Child. On the left, the non-Christian magician of Germanic legend, Welund the Smith, practices his supernatural arts in pursuit of a dreadful revenge upon King Nithud who had harmed him.[41] It is, indeed, arguable that the supersession of that magic which pursued revenge and power over human destiny by a gentler order of intervention (though still a supernatural one) is the theme of the whole casket.[42] Christ's coming made for this different order of super-

to Druthmar of Corvey; see M.L.W. Laistner, "A Ninth Century Commentator on the Gospel according to Matthew," *Harvard Theological Review* 20 (1927), 129–145.

[40] Smaragdus, *Collectiones*, p. 72.

[41] Plates of all the panels of the Franks Casket may conveniently be found in G. Baldwin Brown, *The Arts in Early England* vi(1) (London, 1930), but his commentary is now somewhat out of date. An excellent, if controversial, more recent one may be found in K. Schneider, "Zu den Inschriften und Bildern des Franks Casket und einer ae. Version des Mythos von Balders Tod," in *edit.* H. Oppel, *Festschrift für Walther Fischer* (Heidelberg, 1959), pp. 4–20.

[42] Thus, for example, on the much discussed right-hand panel we seem to have

natural power, and that advent is associated here with Matthew's Magi, its chief participants.[43]

As a postscript, I would draw attention to certain other apocryphal and legendary views about these Magi. These are principally to be found in a sermon popularly (though falsely) attributed to Saint John Chrysostom,[44] and in the apocryphal Cave of Treasures (sometimes known as the Book of Adam and Eve).[45] There is no certainty that these views were widely disseminated in the West in the early Middle Ages,[46] but the dates at which some of them became current in the East, their attractiveness, and their correspondence at certain points with observations made in the Pseudo-Bedan commentary on Matthew make them worth some little notice. In both of them, rehabilitated Magi play a central role. The first makes a special point of the fact that Matthew's Magi are not magicians or astrologers in the bad sense, but

---

reference to the legend of Balder and its supersession, and also to the three Norns of northern literature (women supposed to be able to influence the destiny of any child) or the Parcae of classical mythology, similarly influential, and especially so upon the destiny of a newborn boy. All were clearly without influence in the matter of the Christ Child, but the new Magi might partake instead of a Christian kind of supernatural power. The Parcae, and the frightening part non-Christians still believed they played in human destiny, are mentioned by Burchard in his *Corrector*; *PL* 140,971. They are mentioned too by Aldhelm, and in the same breath as he mentions those forbidden "mathematici" of ancient astrology whom the Magi and their astrological successors would come, if I am right, to be allowed to replace; *edit.* R. Ehwald, *De Metris et Enigmatibus ac Pedum Regulis, MGH Auctorum Antiquissimorum* xv (Berlin, 1919), 72–73.

[43] This different order of magical power is perhaps accepted also on the casket by a repentant Germanic magical bird, which leads the Magi in their obeisance. This bird seems certainly to be an intrusion into an otherwise familiar iconography: P. W. Souers, "The Magi on the Franks Casket," *Harvard Studies and Notes in Philology and Literature* 19 (1937), 249–254.

[44] This is printed as the *Opus Imperfectum in Matthaeum, Homilia ii*, of Chrysostom; *PG* 56,637–638. Known only in Latin, it is possibly the work of a fifth-century Arian.

[45] *Transl.* S. C. Malan, *The Book of Adam and Eve* (London, 1882). This is a Christian work, possibly of the fifth or sixth centuries, and currently known only in an Arabic or Ethiopic version. In this, it is distinct from the Jewish apocryphal lives of Adam and Eve, some of which were certainly early known in Latin.

[46] Thorndike is certain that the Pseudo-Chrysostom sermon was widely known, and he gives a summary of it in his *A History of Magic and Experimental Science* i (New York, 1923), 474–475. It is perfectly possible that it was, of course, but I have been able to find no sure evidence for early medieval Europe, although I have looked for it. Some of the stories in the Cave of Treasures, however, can be found in the Talmud, and it is certainly legend of a genre much to the taste of our period.

wise men ready to learn from the prophecy of Balaam (as the Pseudo-Bede also tells us). They had assistance from a writing attributed to Seth (the son of Adam born to replace the degenerate line of Cain) in which were described the star and the gifts to be offered. As in the Pseudo-Bedan commentary, we are taken back before the Flood and to a writing which, attributed as it is to Seth, deserves credence, unlike the forbidden written magical lore Ham is supposed to have preserved. Seth's generation had not, as yet, fallen prey to the wrong sort of enchantment. As a result of Seth's writing, these Magi (there were twelve of them) were able to recognize the star and see in it the Christ Child and the cross. They followed it for two years, miraculously provided with food and drink along the way. They found the Child, presented the gifts, and eventually became helpers to the apostle Thomas. If this work was indeed well known, then both the ancient dignity and recent respectability of the services rendered by such Magi were strongly reinforced by it, and it adds to the picture we have so far.

According to the second set of stories, the gifts of the Magi and all they represent go back even further than Seth. They derive from Adam himself, and they come from paradise. The gold, frankincense, and myrrh were brought by angels as presents to Adam for his marriage to Eve.[47] At Adam's death, they were taken, with Adam's body, into the ark by Noah and his three sons,[48] to be brought out after the Flood by Melchizedek and Shem (here distinct personages). Led by an angel, the two took the whole to Golgotha, where the rock opened of its own accord to take the body and the gifts.[49] The close of the story has the Magi taking these gifts to the Christ Child and recalls associations which run through the Western medieval tradition.[50] The Cave of Treasures, once more, sees Matthew's Magi both as playing a central part in the redemption of the human race and as heirs to a supernatural tradition of the very highest authority.

Seen in this way, the Magi are not merely links between the old magic and the new; they are bringers of gifts from the one dispensation

[47] I,lxxiii; transl. Malan, The Book, p. 90.

[48] Shem had the gold, Ham the myrrh, Japheth the frankincense.

[49] III,xix; transl. Malan, The Book, p. 169. We might note, once more, how in this transference the role of the Christian priest is somehow left to one side. Melchizedek and Shem are separate, and Shem has the royal gold.

[50] "Gold, namely, as unto a king; frankincense as unto God; myrrh for his death": ibid., IV,xiv; p. 205. Cf. Gregory the Great, Homilia X, PL 76,1112, and Rabanus, Commentaria in Mattheum I,ii, PL 107,759.

to the other and, as such, are allowed both to do honor to certain aspects of the divinatory learning of the pre-Christian world and to make this learning relevant to the redemption. Such Magi make it appropriate for predictions later to be made and interpreted by authorized figures, and they thus pave the way for the emergence of many disparate new Christian magicians, equipped with many different supernatural skills.[51] The materials for such a rehabilitation lay ready in the Scriptures, but to be brought forward in all its strength, it required both the active pressure of the non-Christian magus and careful thought about how this pressure might best be combated.

SAINT BENEDICT

In bringing their three gifts, the Magi of Matthew brought with them also dramatic possibilities magnificently open to exploitation. Thus, for instance, the three vows of the religious life—poverty, chastity, and obedience—came to be associated with the Magi's three gifts,[52] and it is arguable that Saint Benedict himself, so influential in the fostering of this life, was the Christian magus par excellence.

Benedict of Monte Cassino (d. ca. 547), founder of the Benedictine Order, deserves to be given a central place here as a Christian magus for many reasons. Firstly, his name was a byword throughout the period of our concern. Secondly, he was certainly associated with supernatural achievement to a degree remarkable even for this period. Thirdly, he may have grown in importance as a Christian magus because of the limits placed upon the magical operations of priests—a factor that may have been of far more importance than we have in general recognized. Fourthly, he was projected forward, once again, by the vital part played by the religious in general in the supernatural battle against demons. Most important of all of the reasons, however, is, perhaps, this fifth one. Benedict's particular means of operating within the supernatural dimension was publicized by no less a person than Pope

[51] Matthew's Magi were early associated with supernatural healing, and their names are to be found on amulets. Descriptions of some of these are given in H. Kehrer, *Die heiligen drei Könige in Literatur und Kunst* i (Leipzig, 1908), p. 76. By the eleventh century they were in wide demand as healers.

[52] The Epiphany was one of the days deemed most suitable by the tenth-century Romano-German Pontifical, for example, for the consecration of virgins: C. Vogel and R. Elze, *Le Pontifical Romano-Germanique du Dixième Siècle* i (Vatican City, 1963), 38.

Gregory the Great. Thus, it was elaborated upon, and so became best known, at a time, in a place, and by a spokesman peculiarly vital to the working out of good relations between non-Christian and Christian magic.

Between 593 and 594 Pope Gregory wrote his *Dialogues*. These are preserved in an exceptionally large number of copies (many of them early ones), and they were written precisely to tell early Western Europe, and Italy in particular, about the standard of supernatural achievement the good Christian might expect, and from among his very own people.[53] Through the eighth-century translation into Greek by Pope Zachary (friend to Boniface, scourge of Aldebert and all non-Christian magical practice, and evident admirer of Gregory's efforts) they told the East too. A speaking example of this standard of achievement was, for Gregory, Saint Benedict. Book II of the *Dialogues* is devoted to Benedict's life and works, and it both dictated to a very large extent the way in which the memory of the saint reached the early Middle Ages and, I suspect, played a crucial part in the encouragement of the Benedictine Order in those liberal and responsible attitudes to non-Christian magic we have been following.[54] Also, it would be extremely hard to find a more complete contrast between Gregory's Benedict and the rational, sober, and industrious ideal pastor of the *Pastoral Rule*. It is tempting to suggest that the difference between the two was conscious and was deliberately contrived, and that the wonder-worker Benedict was launched into the Christian magical world as the Christian priest was withdrawn from it.

The most striking characteristic of the *Dialogues*, and of the *Vita Sancti Benedicti* in particular, is their absolute obsession with wonders. Benedict can hardly move without performing a miracle. Obsessions can, of themselves, be very tiresome, and one that results in a surfeit of miracles particularly so. Thus, the *Dialogues* have posed problems for admirers of the great pope. They have seemed so singularly lacking in the balance and finesse of his other works, and at times so oppres-

[53] A recent discussion of the *Dialogues*, which is now a sine qua non for students of this work, draws special attention to Gregory's wish to locate the saint's contribution firmly within his own time and place. J. M. Petersen, *The Dialogues of Gregory the Great in Their Late Antique Cultural Background* (Toronto, 1984), p. 117.

[54] There are many translations into English of the *Dialogues* to be found, but the best translation of all (accompanied by an edition of the Latin, introduction, and notes) is the one cited in the chapter on sources, namely, that into French by A. de Vogüé and P. Antin, *Grégoire le Grand, Dialogues* (Paris, 1978–1980).

sively naive, as to be incapable of having been written by him. We now know, however, how deceptive such appearances can be. Far from being merely simple tales, directed at a rustic audience by a spasmodically credulous pontiff, the *Dialogues* are a tapestry of references that must be read at many levels of understanding. Their structure is complex, their Latin is polished, and Gregory's interlocutor, Peter the Deacon, was a person of considerable learning and experience of the world, high in Roman counsels.[55] The *Dialogues* were presented, also, to Queen Theudelinda of the Lombards (perhaps as a kind of phylacterium for her), and thus they were aimed at least in part at her court, not all of whose members could with exactitude be described as Christian. The *Dialogues*, then, were in all probability directed to a wide and varied audience, one ranging from those committed to non-Christian magical practice, both at its least sophisticated and its most refined, through Christians who were themselves in need of reassurance, to the worldly wise, indeed world-weary. Put at its simplest, their message is this. The Christian religion is rich in much-needed supernatural power, and true *virtus* and the receipt of the fruits of this power go together. Put in another way, it is extremely difficult to attain to virtue and to lack a capacity for reverent wonder and miraculous achievement. Where there is such a lack the Christian dispensation will readily supply it. This is a very deep message indeed, and especially so for those heavily involved in matters of state. Taken to its logical conclusion, it means that government without these capacities can never be good government. This is reminiscent of Augustine at his best and may, indeed, be one of the most politically and socially relevant messages Gregory had to offer. The prevalence of magic, and the cherishing, especially, of magic of a Christian kind, are crucial to it.

It is impossible, of course, to prove whether the miracles of which Gregory writes actually happened, or whether Gregory himself truly believed in them. Nor does it greatly matter. He asks his audience to trust only that, given the right intermediary, supernatural interventions of this kind are possible; and that Benedict is the type of the right

[55] Ibid., i, 51–77. A recent attempt to prove, on these grounds and others, that the *Dialogues* are not in fact an authentic work of Gregory has been unsuccessful. On this see P. Verbraken, "Les Dialogues de Saint Grégoire le Grand, sont-ils apocryphes?," *Revue Bénédictine* 98 (1988), 272–277; A. de Vogüé, "Grégoire le Grand et ses 'Dialogues' d'après deux ouvrages récents," *Revue d'Histoire Ecclésiastique* 83 (1988), 281–348; P. Maeyvaert, "The Enigma of Gregory the Great's Dialogues: A Response to Francis Clark," *Journal of Ecclesiastical History* 39 (1988), 335–381.

intermediary. Gregory is struggling to keep the Christian practitioner of the supernatural alive in a kingdom beset by non-Christian magicians and obsessed with statecraft. His Christian magician here is pitted both against the forces of the non-Christian opposition—to Gregory, the forces of darkness—and against too human and too limited a form of light. The miracle workers of the *Dialogues* distance themselves from the achievements of the great non-Christian magicians of the past, and perhaps from those of the present; and they afford no solace to the grand pretensions of the secular rulers of Gregory's own day.

Benedict's miracles begin the moment he abandons his formal studies in Rome and sets off, accompanied by his old nurse, upon his spiritual quest. These miracles have two outstanding characteristics. The first is their preoccupation with the relief of ordinary, practical anxieties. Wonder in the sense of rapt and ineffectual ecstasy is emphatically not encouraged. Thus, Benedict's first miracle concerns a sieve, borrowed and accidentally broken by the nurse, and a cause to her of great consternation. It is mended by Benedict's prayers. Seemingly immovable stones are lifted to help humble builders, springs are discovered to save monks a tiresome scramble to the lake for water, wants of lighting oil are marvelously supplied.[56] There is a bustling everyday quality about the whole which gives the lie to the idea that Gregory's magus could ever be the lofty wonder-worker beloved of the followers of Zoroaster, or Simon Magus, or even Asclepius. The story of the helpful Goth is an excellent case in point, and one charming from many points of view. This Goth wanted to enter Benedict's community and so strove to make himself useful. In transports of enthusiasm, he set about clearing some land by the lake for a garden. The strength of his sickle was not, however, equal to his own, and at the end of one particularly vigorous sweep of the arm, the blade flew from the wooden handle and sailed into the seemingly bottomless depths of the lake. The hapless Goth was horrified; but no matter. Benedict took the handle from him and lowered it into the water's edge. Instantly the blade returned to the handle. "There now, work on and don't worry," said the saint, handing it back.[57]

---

[56] II,i,1–2,viiii,v,1–3,xxviiii,1–2; de Vogüé, *Grégoire le Grand*, ii,128–131,170–173,152–155,218–221.

[57] "Ecce, labora, et noli tristari." II,vi; ibid., ii,154–157. This story is a useful reminder of the many levels at which the *Dialogues* can be read. Though making a simple point about the ready supply of supernatural help a holy man could mediate, it was also clearly directed to those who knew the passage in 2 Kings 6:4–7 (the story of

This story is a good example of the second characteristic of Benedict's miracles (and, indeed, of those of the other books of the *Dialogues*); for the Goth is described as having the soul of a poor man (a quality seemingly rare among Goths). These miracles always spring from, and serve, humility. They reinforce this virtue above all, and they single out, too, the materially poor and the financially and emotionally underprivileged for their practical help. In one strikingly feminist moment, Benedict's own pride is humbled by the prayer and virtue of his sister. Benedict had left his monastery for his yearly visit to his sister, Scholastica, in a nearby dependency of the monastery. His sister exclaimed at how long it had been since last she saw him, and she begged him to stay the night. He pronounced such a stay impossible. She prayed. Instantly, the heavens opened, and the resulting storm was so violent that the saint had no alternative but to remain. Thus, comments Gregory, was Benedict miraculously prevented from rejecting the call of his sister's affection.[58]

Each of these stories is deeply instructive. Doubtless both the practical interests and the concern for humility echo Gregory's own predilections and are in part products of the situation with which he was immediately faced; but there is a larger message too, and one directed far further. It is that the Christian wonder-worker will stoop to the smallest problems and still not exalt himself. There is no limit to the supernatural capacities of this wonder-worker, least of all a limit that would confine them to grand enterprises or great persons; yet he or she will ask in return no more than the poorest human being has to offer. There are signs of this message in the battle between Peter and Simon Magus, but here it is inescapable, and so are the oppositions to which it points. Non-Christian magi too might, of course, be storm bringers, but not, it seems generally, in the services of sisterly affection. Nor did they, as far as we know, often stoop to the mending of sieves or garden implements. In contrast to the number of miracles of practical assistance marked by the *Life of Saint Benedict*, there are, we should note, only two miracles of healing, and one of these concerns the healing of a slave.[59] It is hard to account adequately for this lack. It may spring

Elisha and the sons of the prophets, in which an ax head fell into the Jordan and Elisha drew it to the surface with a stick), and who would thus cast Benedict, with Elisha, as a type of Christ. See J. H. Wansborough, "St. Gregory's Intention in the Stories of St. Scholastica and St. Benedict," *Revue Bénédictine* 75 (1965), 145–151.

[58] II,xxxiii–xxxiiii; de Vogüé, *Grégoire le Grand*, ii,230–235.

[59] II,xxvi; ibid., ii,214–215.

from a desire to protect the priority, in this special art, of Christ and his apostles. Benedict himself may not in truth have been a healer. It seems at least possible, however, that Gregory feared the special onslaught upon the virtue of humility the power of healing might make within a single person, and that he was reluctant, for this reason, to emphasize this power.

For our own purposes, the most important message about the Christian magus the *Dialogues*, and the *Life of Saint Benedict* in particular, have to convey is this. The quality of the person involved in the exercise of supernatural power is all-important. Wonder-working is never to be admired simply for itself. "Do not spend your time admiring the external actions Sanctulus performed with the help of the Saviour; pay attention rather to what he was within himself."[60] Thus, it is the quality of the person, and never the office he holds, that provides the graces necessary for the performance of Christian supernatural acts. If peasants, for example, could employ the tunic of Abbot Euthicius in successful rainmaking ceremonies (and there is every sign that this was acceptable to Gregory), this was because of the abbot's inner merit.[61] As the pope seems to have been especially wary, in his *Pastoral Rule*, of the idea that the ritual of ordination could have a crucial part to play in the passing on of special supernatural charismata, so, in contrast, he seems here to be concerned to emphasize how very widely distributed, and how deeply imitative, such charismata might be, provided only that they are merited by a special style of life. The touchstone is charity. The poorest human being might, then, become a Christian magus. The wonders he or she might perpetrate could never, of course, be called magic, but the way of Saint Benedict is open to everyone and is to be encouraged.

This "democratization" of the Christian magus in the Christian dispensation, and in the name of Saint Benedict, is of surpassing importance. It bears upon both the nameable and the unnameable non-Christian opposition, and upon the positions of other Christian mediators of supernatural power. It was no accident that Gregory conjured up the image of Benedict for the edification of the Lombard royal house. Among the many magical figures with whom the saint had to compete was the Christian sacral king.

[60] III,xxxvii, 9; ibid., ii,416–417.
[61] III,xv,18–19; ibid., ii,326–327.

THE SACRAL KING

Pope Gregory delivered to his readers a double message about Christian magic. On the one hand, "signa" and miraculous powers were
quite worthless in themselves.[62] On the other, such graces were
clearly, in his *Dialogues*, freely available to all those worthy enough to
wield them. This was not a message all of Gregory's listeners would
have wished to hear. The criteria for worthiness involved humility and
a distinctive, and often uncomfortable, style of life. Thus, they ruled
out certain sorts of non-Christian magus as receptors of these graces. I
suspect that Gregory devised these excluding criteria at least in part
because so many people were willing and anxious to play the excluded
roles, and to play them, indeed, in a manner that did not involve them
in the meeting of minor domestic emergencies or in energetic garden-
ing. One of the foremost of those so willing was, of course, the magus
by blood.

The magus by blood, possessed as he was through this blood of a
special and superior kind of supernatural potency, enjoyed, as did the
harioli, a position of high respect in early medieval society; and he,
like them, resolutely refused to relinquish this position. Pope Gregory
himself was among the many prominent witnesses to the power and
tenacity of the barbarian magical blood kingship,[63] and it was a power
felt by many far to exceed that offered, for instance, by ecclesiastics.
The *Life of Saint Columbanus* bears witness to such feelings. Columbanus had suggested to King Theudebert that the latter might with
profit become a monk, but this suggestion "seemed to the king and to
all those standing around to be the height of absurdity. It was out of
the question, they said, for a Merovingian once raised to the kingship
to choose to become a member of the clerical order."[64] One understands a little better from such passages why certain clerics exhibited a
high degree of impatience, accompanied by a desire to demonstrate a
measure of magical power themselves. And we are provided with yet

[62] This message is best summed up in his *XL Homiliarum in Evangelia* xxix,4; *PL*
76,1216.

[63] "In the Frankish realms kings are taken from royal stock" (MT)—a statement
attributed to Gregory by Charles the Bald; *edit.* A. Boretius and V. Krause, *MGH
Legum* ii(2), *Capitularia Regum Francorum* ii (Hanover, 1893), 450.

[64] *Vita Columbani Abbatis Discipulorumque Eius* I,28; *edit.* B. Krusch and W. Levison,
MGH SRM iv (Hanover and Leipzig, 1902), 105 (MT).

one more reason for the church to evolve a forceful magic of its own, a magic that, in the end, would have no place for kings.

In the meantime, however, this king had to be accommodated, for he was one of the most persistent in his claims to supernatural ability of all the major discredited magi. If he could not be removed entirely, then he must be realigned; and realigned he was. The early medieval church grappled with the determined persistence of this supernatural figure in two main ways. It attempted to change the powers attached to the blood kingship into something resembling special graces or the rewards of Christian virtue (and, in doing so, promoted all the more strongly some of its own carefully elaborated magical specifics); and it promoted checks and balances to these powers. Gregory of Tours's "Good King Guntram" (d. 594)[65] and King Sigismund of Burgundy (d. 552) are excellent examples of blood kings whose supernatural capacities were susceptible of the type of transformation the church so badly needed to be able to demonstrate. Both were powerful healers (the latter specializing in fevers). The merest fragment from the fringe of Guntram's robe could, when soaked in water and administered to the sick, produce a life-restoring draught.[66] Thus, it equaled the supernatural effects of altar cloths and tomb cloths, and it was, like them, a conductor of the virtus of the object it covered. The invocation of the royal name could cause demons to confess to their crimes. Guntram had little luck with his wives, one of whom, Marcytrude, was described by Fredegar as a witch ("herbaria" and "meretrix"),[67] and the second of whom, Austrechilde, seems to have involved her husband in her vengeances.[68] This "good" king foreswore allegiances (marital and military); he was vain, and cruel, and bad tempered, and ill-behaved in church. He was not, in short, an obvious candidate for an award for Christian virtue; but his *comparative* suitability for the role of Christian magician-king seems, in the face of something of a dearth of suitable figures, to have allowed Gregory of Tours to overlook these small deficiencies. He mentions them, as a historian with a claim to honesty (and one who wrote in the hope of being in general believed) had to;

[65] Guntram was so evidently virtuous as to prompt Michelet to describe him as "ce bon roi a qui on ne reprochait que deux ou trois meurtres." Quoted by O. M. Dalton, *The History of the Franks by Gregory of Tours* i (Oxford, 1927), 52.

[66] *History of the Franks* IX,21; ibid., ii,395.

[67] *Chronicle* iii,56; edit. B. Krusch, MGH SRM ii (Hanover, 1888), 108.

[68] Her dying wish was that her unsuccessful doctors be slaughtered, a wish Guntram fulfilled. *History of the Franks* V,27; transl. Dalton, *The History*, ii,206–207.

but they must be rendered of little account. Gregory may personally have approved (on the whole) of both Guntram and Sigismund, but there is certainly a measure both of distortion and of relief to be found in the enthusiasm with which he assigns acceptable supernatural powers to them and singles out justifying acts of kindness when he can. Such a state of affairs is only truly understandable within the context of the church's desperate need, in circumstances that were pressing, to acquire a respectable royal blood-magus for itself; and it may be taken as rather striking extra evidence of this. Here we have Christian compromise with non-Christian magical belief arrayed before us in a less than edifying form. Bede had an easier time with King Oswald of Northumbria, who seems to have been, in himself, a far more impressive man. It is, then, all the more interesting to mark to what extensive purposes Bede puts this king's evidently greater virtue. Oswald's blood gives special healing powers to soil and to water (the resources used in fertility magic, we may note), healing powers employed upon a goodly range of ills and sufferers. Soil taken from the place where Oswald fell proofs buildings against fire. Splinters from the wooden stake upon which Penda fixed Oswald's head cures people of the plague.[69] The beneficiaries of Oswald's powers are Christian, but the vehicles whereby these powers are conveyed are not; or rather, they are not so in origin. They belong to the competing magical world, but they have, once more, been annexed with care to an accredited leader and reordered. Bede seemingly feels so sure of Oswald that he can tell both of his dismembered body and of its burial in different places, much in the manner of a fertility-bearing pagan good luck king.[70]

Kings such as Oswald, however, were not too readily to be found, and, for the most part, shift had to be made with what there was. A well-told later story of Christian compromises over kingship takes on a new dimension when it is set against this backdrop of persistent alarms about the tenacity of non-Christian magical kingship, and of the need the church had to seize every chance it could find to refashion it. This is the story of the transference of royal power from the Merovingian royal house to the ancestors of Charlemagne. At the abbey of

[69] *Ecclesiastical History* III,ix–xiii; *edit.* and *transl.* B. Colgrave and R.A.B. Mynors, *Bede's Ecclesiastical History of the English People* (Oxford, 1969), pp. 240–255.

[70] III,xii; ibid., pp. 250–253. The body of the pagan Halfdan the Black, for example, was dismembered and buried in different places in order to ensure the fertility of each separate region; *transl.* L. M. Hollander, *Heimskringla* (Austin, Tex., 1964), p. 58.

Saint Denis, in 754, Pope Stephen II anointed the Carolingian Pippin, together with his wife and sons, to the Frankish kingship, and
with holy oil analogous to the type Hincmar placed among his "anti-
dota catholica." The history of royal inauguration rituals is murky, and
this was certainly not the first anointing of a king, not even of Pippin.[71] Nor, in all probability, did it cause a great stir among contemporaries; but it is much wrestled over by historians of Carolingian politics. Its significance will be the better appreciated, however, if we
remove it from an arena primarily political and set it instead within
the Christian Church's struggle for the annexation of assimilable
magic to itself. The events of 754 meant most, it seems, to the Benedictine abbey of Saint Denis. This anointing marks, then, just one
more stage in this particular struggle for monastic magical annexation.
Such events show, above all, just how little the church could do; and
how, on occasion, non-Christian magic, allowed through under Christian auspices because of its sheer tenacity, could outstay its welcome
and generate a need for a still stronger Christian magic in order to
outplay it. The pope, it seems, had to declare when he anointed Pippin
that future kings were to spring from Pippin's stock alone.[72] Pope Stephen explained that it was "divina pietas" which set Pippin's family
apart in this way, but this explanation has, like Gregory on Guntram,
an air of special pleading about it; and the power of the royal blood
remains. The ceremony containing the unction is akin to that used in
Francia for the ordination of priests, Old Testament models of kingship
are freely invoked in papal correspondence with the king, and Pippin,
like his more famous son Charlemagne, is set firmly in the line of King
David. To that extent any pre-Christian supernatural power still
claimed by Pippin was Christianized, and so neutralized and robbed of
its competitive edge. But the superior royal blood of the pre-Christian
dispensation remained paramount, and for all we know Pippin may
have gone away and promptly grown his hair and dyed it red.

This great moment at which the papacy stepped in to promote a

[71] On Pippin, and on Carolingian royal anointings in general, see the valuable remarks in J. L. Nelson, *Politics and Ritual in Early Medieval Europe* (London, 1986),
especially pp. 289–293.

[72] "No one may ever presume to elect a king sprung from any loins but those of this
family, for the tenderness of God himself has raised them to this height, and, in response to the prayers of the holy apostles, has seen fit to confirm and consecrate them
by the hands of their vicar, the pope" (MT). *Clausula de Unctione Pippini; edit.*
B. Krusch, *MGH SRM* i(2) (Hanover, 1885), 15–16.

change of dynasty had political implications and repercussions of the gravest kind; but for our purposes its significance is of a different order. The anointing of Pippin is a forceful reminder of the persistent power of blood defined as royal. Pope Stephen may have altered, for the moment, the source of this blood and the means of its definition; but the essence of the older magic stayed in place, and the supernaturally charged holy oil of the Christian rite seems rather to be annexed to it than the reverse. For all the Old Testament trumpetings (and partly, perhaps, because of them), the magical blood kingship of the Franks was, in essence, very little changed. It is difficult to know quite who used whom here, pope or king; but there was much that redounded to the advantage of the old-style blood magus. One could argue, as Gregory of Tours had and others would, that true royal magic displayed itself only in Christian ways. One could provide telling examples of those ways which were acceptable, as Pope Gregory did for Theudelinda in the *Dialogues*; but behind all that, the magical blood king triumphed. It was even hard to limit the proliferation of the magical blood by an insistence on Christian marriage. Anxieties on this front again may help to explain the special stresses placed both upon Christian marriage and upon priestly celibacy, at certain points in the period; and in this respect, of course, some of the Old Testament precursors of the Christian kingship were less than no help at all.

The old magus by blood played, then, a central role in the rise of magic in early medieval Europe. His rehabilitation as a sacral king has about it certain external resemblances to the rehabilitation of astrology. This living magus was rescued because the threatened alternative was unimaginably worse; but he was extremely hard satisfactorily to assimilate and still harder wholly to realign, and some of the efforts to do this threatened to recoil upon the church itself. I hinted at checks and balances, instead of complete assimilation and refashioning, as a second possible way of dealing with the blood king. This way was attempted. Some of the needed checks could be found, of course, in any form of explaining away seemingly supernatural phenomena by "scientific" means. In this context the rehabilitation of astrology may be seen in a different light. Its analogous role may be less important than its active, and indeed opposing, one, for the transformation of the scientific Magi of Matthew into kings may have been in part impelled by the need to counteract this tenacious blood magus, to whom so many and such great concessions had been made. Other (and perhaps more easily available) checks could be found in other people, holding other offices and differently deployed. The shadow of the blood magus stands in fact behind the emergence of all of the other accredited magi I have mentioned—but especially, perhaps, behind the one to whom we shall now turn.

THE BISHOP

The office of the early medieval bishop could, if one looked hard, be provided with a scriptural basis; and the emergence to power of this bishop was described by both Isidore and Rabanus in works that were widely read, and in a way that gave great satisfaction. "When the apostles died, bishops succeeded them and were set up in place of them all over the world. These bishops were not chosen for the blood in their veins, as was the case with Aaron's dispositions, but on that merit which divine grace produced in them."[73] This description is, however, as we know and as they knew too, incomplete. The process by which the early medieval episcopal office was forged is a complicated one, and the result was an alloy compounded of many and diverse elements. We may number among these the early need felt by Christian communities for some sort of sanctioned superintendence, the administrative requirements of the *civitates*, and the ambitions felt by families of prestige for suitable positions in the new order. But in addition to these elements, we must number also the challenge presented by the persistence of non-Christian magic in general, and especially by the peculiar brand of magic retained by the barbarian king. This last brand of magic seems to have been Christianized only with the greatest of reluctance, and we left it in grave need of a stronger Christian counter: a need rendered all the more urgent by the relative ineffectiveness, as counteracting agents to this king, of those other Christian magi we have discussed. They might attract the attention and even the admiration of this king. Such persons as Saint Vaast and Saint Llonoghyl evidently did so; but it was very hard effectively to displace or to outdo him.

Once he had been declared and accepted as the true successor of the apostles, the bishop could be accepted as the successor to their thaumaturgical powers too;[74] but the wonder-working abilities attributed to its leaders had been a problem for the Christian Church from its very

---

[73] *De Ecclesiasticis Officiis* II,6; PL 83,782 (MT). The passage is repeated by Rabanus in his *De Clericorum Institutione* I,iv; PL 107,300.

[74] In Mark 16:17–18, for example, or Acts 13:6–12.

beginnings, and there are those who would argue that certain New Testament accounts of it are, like the Peter/Simon Magus literature, polemical ones, furnished in support of a position already beleaguered. The passage toward the institutional acceptance of thaumaturgy in the medieval church was never in danger of being a smooth one, even without the complications we have begun to unfold in these pages,[75] and we may find in the critical views of thaumaturgy one further explanation for the firm refusal of supernatural powers to Christian priests. Yet they were extended at times with great enthusiasm to early medieval bishops. Indeed, at certain points in the early Middle Ages spectacular moves were made to put bishops, implicitly ex officio, into a position denied to others on the loudly bruited theory that supernatural ability could never be attributed to anyone on the grounds of office alone.

Inconsistencies of this order are not uncommon in human institutions subject to political pressure, and it is to political pressures, and especially to those pressures exerted by the office of the early barbarian king, that we should chiefly look for an understanding of this one. Politically, the bishop was an essential counter to the power of the king—and magically, then, as well. This aspect of the evolution of the bishop's office must be taken fully into account if we are truly to understand its historical development. Against such a background the office of bishop may be allowed to take on yet one more new dimension. He was sometimes precipitated by circumstance into the very front ranks of those thought capable of practicing Christian magic, and he thus, like the monastic followers of the cross, became a strong influence upon the making of choices about it. It becomes possible, in fact, that the early medieval bishop was potentially one of the most important single Christian magi of them all. Moreover, in that his selection of persons and practices for acceptability within the church were often made primarily with an eye to the competition of the blood magus and sacral king, he was bound to have clear priorities, and perhaps to cause offense. His importance for the rise of magic undoubtedly rests in part, therefore, upon the reactions he inspired in other leaders. It is fitting that we end this study with this bishop, for he is the very embodiment

---

[75] Not least because Augustine himself changed his mind about it. *In Iohannis Evangelium* xiii; *edit.* R. Willems, *Sancti Aurelii Augustini In Iohannis Evangelium Tractatus CXXIV*, CC (Turnholt, 1954), pp. 39–40. *De Civitate Dei* XXII,8; *edit. and transl.* W. M. Green, *Saint Augustine, the City of God Against the Pagans* vii (Loeb Classical Library, 1972), 208–251.

of those tensions and difficulties we have been attempting throughout to unravel.

Merovingian hagiographers in general, and Gregory of Tours in particular, are rich in stories about the supernatural abilities of bishops, and about the impression these made upon kings. Unsurprisingly, Gregory the Great also expressed views independent of the *Pastoral Rule* upon the position of the bishop in supernatural affairs. His views did much to confirm such stories, and they were extremely influential. Bishops were heirs to the apostles, this was certain. Certain too was the fact that they possessed apostolic binding-and-loosing powers.[76] Much else could then follow. Although, as we have seen, Gregory was ready to acknowledge that thaumaturgical powers might be widely distributed on the basis of Christian merit, his bishops are very well represented among those who deserve to exercise them, and particularly so, it seems, when powers of healing are at issue.[77] Pope Gregory's exact views upon the place of bishops as wonder-workers in the church, vis-à-vis that of Benedict and his monks, are not easy to ascertain. It may be that through the attribution of healing powers rather to bishops than to Benedict he meant to point to a division of rank. It is certain that he gave much thought to the establishment of appropriate relations between bishops and barbarian kings, and that he saw that appropriate supernatural ability played an essential part in such relations. He was sometimes measured in his approval of the attitudes of his bishops to their miracles,[78] but he saw that these bishops must be allowed special supernatural abilities, and on political as well as on scriptural grounds. "God's servants can do more through miracles than the powers of this earth can do through anger."[79] So great and so revered a spokesman had admirers and followers in this matter, as in so many others. Thus we might note that the only persons whom Bede, in his *Ecclesiastical History*, allows to have performed miracles of heal-

---

[76] *XL Homiliarum in Evangelia* xxvi,5; PL 76,1200.

[77] Ibid., iv; 1090–1091. Bishops are accorded a distinguished place as healers in the *Dialogues* too. Acts 19:20 provides excellent grounds for this, but the similarity between this passage and the powers ascribed to King Guntram should not be overlooked. Competition over healing power was perhaps the bitterest of all.

[78] He reproaches Augustine of Canterbury, for instance, for his excessive elation at his own miracles. Bede, *Ecclesiastical History* I,xxxii; *edit.* and *transl.* Colgrave, *Bede's Ecclesiastical History*, pp. 108–111.

[79] *Moralia in Job* Book IX,x,11; PL 75,865. The context shows that Gregory is speaking of the apostles and their successors. See also ibid., Book XXX,i,5; PL 76,525.

ing during their lifetimes are bishops, for instance John of Beverley, bishop of Hexham and archbishop of York.[80]

Bishops, then, were allowed under certain conditions to become Christian magi in the early Middle Ages, and they were encouraged to seize the opportunities allowed to them most particularly when it came to dealing with barbarian sacral kings. The Carolingian kingdom, set up so shakily by Pope Stephen II and Pippin, was a rich area for experiments in this respect. The 754 settlement, which intruded a ceremony akin to episcopal ordination, was not, as we saw, wholly successful in neutralizing the magical power of royal blood. Other means had to be tried, and the apostolic capacities available to bishops lay ready to hand for the battle. The distinction made, for example, by Isidore, between the blood priesthood of Aaron and that apostolic tradition which so palpably renounced the blood-line was an additional, and crucial, source of strength. A fine example of the deployment of this particular Christian magus's power against the competition of the sacral king is to be found in the De Institutione Regia of Bishop Jonas of Orleans (written most probably in 831). Jonas lays especial stress upon two aspects of the bishop's office. He recalls Isidore in the first one. Bishops are chosen by merit alone, and not by blood. And, secondly, they are possessed of powers to bind and loose. Through these especial emphases he contrives to advance a theory that is both critical of the traditional power of the Frankish king by blood and suggestive of a superior supernatural ability, transmitted by bishops alone. Writing to a later (but still difficult) Carolingian, King Pippin of Aquitaine (d. 838), Jonas makes some thunderous points about the sole right of bishops to dispense the binding-and-loosing power, and the superiority of the episcopal order to the royal, and, indeed, to every other order. He mounts a spirited attack, too, upon the idea that Carolingian power may be founded at all upon blood. On the contrary, says Jonas (hereby contradicting, of course, the concession made by Stephen to that other Pippin), royal authority is God-given, is subject to God's ministers, and can be forfeited by the royal family for misbehavior, as it was in the case of Solomon.[81]

These views were expressed in circumstances of great provocation, and they are distinguished rather for the energy with which they were

[80] V,ii–vi; transl. Colgrave, Bede's Ecclesiastical History, pp. 456–469.

[81] De Institutione Regia ii, iii, vii; edit. J. Reviron, Jonas d'Orléans et son "De Institutione Regia" (Paris, 1930), pp. 135–137,141.

injected into the struggle than for the impact they made upon the kings concerned. For our purposes, however, they show with great clarity to what purposes the bishop's office might be turned, and what the place of supernatural capacities might be in these. Like Peter when confronted with Simon Magus, or indeed, with a credulous Nero, the early medieval bishop could be expected to exercise a supernatural power of an evidently superior kind.[82] He must, indeed, employ magic of a sort, and magical ability will remain an essential part of his equipment as long as non-Christian magic, and especially that of the blood king, remained a threat.

It is possible that some even of the most apparently ordinary and everyday exercises of the bishop's power have, in the early Middle Ages, this dimension to them. Take, for instance, the insistence on preaching, so evident in Gregory's *Pastoral Rule*. The status of orator carried great prestige, and especially so in a preliterate society, and the church wished its most distinguished officers both to be able to communicate with their congregations and to share in that prestige; but there is more. To kings who claimed ancestry from supernatural figures such as Woden, excellence in speech and writing were not merely natural powers, but supernatural ones. Tacitus, in his *Germania*, equated Woden with Mercury, the god of eloquence. Anglo-Saxons credited Mercury with the first setting down of letters, and Woden was the controller of the runes.[83] Thus, Anglo-Saxon kings spoke first in the declaring of the laws. Gregory's insistence upon the preaching authority of his bishops should be seen to rest upon conditions such as these, as well as upon the more familiar directives of the Gospels. Take too the blessings reserved to the bishop in early sacramentaries and pontificals. These are vitally concerned with fertility—an obvious enough concern

---

[82] In the case, once more, of the Ramsey witch, he did so. When Thorkell swore upon his beard that his wife was innocent of the murderous magic, and did so before Bishop Ethelric of Dorchester, his beard came away in his hand; *edit*. W. D. Macray, *Chronicon Abbatiae Rameseiensis*, RS (London, 1886), p. 134. The extent of the bishop's magical power will be the better appreciated when it is remembered that an oath upon a beard was a very serious oath indeed; see G. Constable in *edit*. R.B.C. Huygens, *Apologiae Duae* (Turnholt, 1985), pp. 64–65.

[83] *Edit*. J. M. Kemble, *The Dialogue of Solomon and Saturn* (London, 1848), p. 192. The association between Woden and Mercury is not mentioned in the commentary upon this dialogue by J. E. Cross and T. D. Hill, *The Prose Solomon and Saturn and Adrian and Ritheus* (Toronto, 1982), pp. 122–123, and instead Mercury is here associated with the equally formidable Hermes Trismegistus. I confess that I find the latter association, at this period, unconvincing.

in itself, but striking in the context of this particular competition. Take lastly the insistence upon celibacy. No one could begin to argue that the threat of royal blood-magic pressed upon attitudes to episcopal celibacy at every point; but at the same time it must be admitted that the latter was a powerful check to the former, and the more so if the celibate magus could produce a more powerful magic. It is worth remarking that the extreme vehemence expressed by Archbishop Boniface on the matter of clerical celibacy was contemporary with some of the forced concessions by the papacy to the bloodline of Pippin.[84]

The early medieval bishop, then, was an important member of the confraternity of Christian magi, and his public eminence as an heir to the apostles, combined with his theoretical remoteness from a power derived from blood, made him an especially important figure in the competition with the sacral king. Miracles of some grandeur, healing miracles especially, came thus to be associated with living episcopal power. Again, we catch a glimpse of a competition for magic within the church itself. Perhaps it was the weight of this responsibility, and not mere curiosity, that led Archbishop Gerard to his ill-fated interest in the *Mathesis* of Julius Firmicus Maternus. Perhaps it was this competition too that provoked some Anglo-Saxon monks to take to curative medical magic of a different and contentious kind. It was always possible for a bishop to define the line between respectable and outlawed magic in a way unacceptable to some of his diocesan subjects, monks among them, and so to provoke the offering of alternative solutions to the problem, perhaps under the cloak of the different magus, Benedict. Such speculations may perhaps be pressed further at another time. For now we may record that the early medieval bishop was deeply, and crucially, involved in the rise of magic, and his involvement is reflected in some even of the most familiar of his activities.

I have been able to do no more here than produce a sketch of the more eminent of the early medieval magi we can find in the sources, and of

[84] The famous *Indiculus Superstitionum* is, in the only surviving manuscript, attached to a copy of the first four canons of the Council of Leptinnes. Three of these condemn clerical marriage with ferocity, and the fourth provides Pippin with a tax for subscribing to the condemnation. The combination may be an accidental one; but if it was not, then we have here a startling example of an association between sexual malpractice on the part of the clergy and magical malpractice on the part of all, with perhaps the pious hope that the reform of the first might lead to the reform of the second.

the effect they had upon the magic of early medieval Europe. There are in this sketch, however, features upon which I think we may rely. Some magi in each of the dispensations are treated more seriously than are others, as though their respective threats and contributions in truth meant more. Again, as one individual is drawn forward upon the stage, at a certain time and in a certain place, so another is drawn back. All of these prominent figures, in other words, are as deeply interrelated and interdependent as are the various branches of magic itself. This conclusion, if it is in certain respects a somewhat punishing one, opens up to the inquiry limitless horizons.

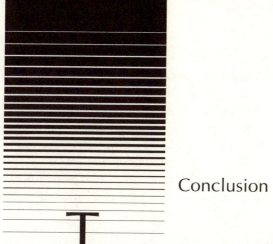

Conclusion

TWO PASSAGES from two separate (and deeply different) books first prompted this inquiry. The first of these passages is to be found in an edition and translation of the Anglo-Saxon *Lacnunga*, published by two undoubted experts upon early medieval magic and science. This passage was intended to serve as a working generalization about "barbarian" literary remains, and as an introduction to an examination of Anglo-Saxon magico-medical texts. It reads as follows:

> For the period with which we are concerned—that is the seventh to the twelfth century—the main agent in the spread of Mediterranean culture was the Church, and its instrument, for our purpose, the written word. Consider the literary sequences when a non-literate people is converted, by force, by imitation, or by persuasion, to the religion of a higher culture. Prayers, liturgies, and sacred works, translated from the language of the higher invading civilisation, are the first documents in the native tongue in the new medium of writing. These, as they circulate, will often be misunderstood; they will certainly become corrupted; they will inevitably be put to magical uses. Native magic, by gathering liturgical catch-phrases, will assume a Christian color, while Christian symbols will gain a wonder-working repute. This is the result in the modern missionary field; so it was in A.S. England. [1]

The second passage is to be found in an enormously impressive, and justifiably admired work upon the fate of magic in a later period. Again, it is introductory, and again it is a generalization, this time about the attitude to magic of the medieval church as a whole.

> There were several circumstances which helped to consolidate the notion that the Church was a magical agency, no less than a devotional one. The

[1] J.H.G. Grattan and C. Singer, *Anglo-Saxon Magic and Medicine* (Oxford, 1952), pp. 6–7.

first was the legacy of the original conversion. It was not just that the leaders of the Anglo-Saxon Church had laid so much stress upon the miracle-working power of their saints, and had disseminated anecdotes illustrating their superiority to any magic the pagans had to offer; though this in itself made difficult the later efforts to purge religious teaching of any "grossness." The real difficulty stemmed from the notorious readiness of the early Christian leaders to assimilate elements of the old paganism into their own religious practice, rather than pose too direct a conflict of loyalties in the minds of the new converts.[2]

Each of these passages provides yet one more vehicle for a perspective upon the Middle Ages that is widely shared. It is the product of a diminishing exercise, not unlike that achieved by looking the wrong way down a telescope. Sometimes, as in the first of the passages, this diminishing exercise is directed at the reduction of rather frightening textual and codicological difficulties to manageable proportions. Sometimes, as in the second, it aims at the encouragement of modern "rational" persons in their hope that they have progressed at least a little with time. A combination of puzzlement at, yet indulgence toward, a period and a people remote from our own and less technologically successful than we, inclines the onlooker to see the inhabitants of this early period as less subtle, even less humane, than ourselves. In that they are so very much less sophisticated, their responses must be crude and outdated—in a word, "medieval." This inclination is surely largely unconscious; but it is pervasive for all that. It is apt to cause medievalists (and not only medievalists) deep unease.

In the case of medieval magic, this exercise has indeed, as we have seen, allowed difficulties within single texts to be reduced to the dimension of unfortunate mistakes (and rendered a great deal less discomfiting into the bargain), and the greater part of the inhabitants of early medieval Europe to be seen as smaller in capacity (especially in rational capacity), and assuredly less refined, than their Renaissance and still more modern successors. Medieval Europeans were, the argument proceeds, necessarily unable adequately to distinguish, and deal appropriately with, "superstition" when it reared its ugly head. Pagan magical beliefs and practices sneaked through into the early Christian West because too few of Christianity's adherents were alert or astute enough to stop them at the borders, and too many were too

---

[2] Keith Thomas, *Religion and the Decline of Magic* (Harmondsworth, Middlesex: Penguin, 1973), pp. 53–54.

benighted to see magic and "grossness" for the affronts to human dignity they were. As for those compromises with, and admissions of, non-Christian magic which were engineered apparently deliberately—they could have been so only through weakness. It was easier for the medieval church, nascent as it was, supinely to give in to pressure, than to take to the stonier path of truth and righteousness. A third approach to the period seeks to attribute all compromises, all coming to terms by the medieval church with non-Christian religious culture and behavior, to pressure from "the people," a description that implies "the mob."[3] The notion that a delicate social sensitivity or extended reasoning at the highest levels could have played a part in the compromises and admissions made, let alone that these capacities could have predominated in the choices taken about magic, is, within this perspective, scarcely to be conceived.

This book has been an attempt to think again about the hardly thinkable, and, as far as possible, to demonstrate both its thinkability and its likelihood. I have tried to turn the telescope round once more, and, in addition (and yet more hazardously), to reassess the importance of some of the actors and the objects in the scene at which it looks. The exercise has involved, therefore, rather more than an alteration of focus. It was that "notorious readiness" in the second passage which first gave me pause. Was the early medieval Christian Church all that ready to let the old magical practices slip across its borders? Consulters of the canons of early medieval ecclesiastical councils and of Regino and Burchard, not to speak of readers of Caesarius, Martin of Braga, Isidore, Eligius's biographer, Rabanus, and Hincmar (to recall only a very few), could be forgiven for not thinking so. Certain very vocal forces within the church were not ready at all; but then again, and equally clearly, their words of condemnation were not always the final ones. Indeed, they seem to have been honored more often in the breach than in the observance. For those who were ready (and sometimes a single person could hold different positions, depending upon the type of magic to be accommodated), was their readiness always in truth "notorious," infamous in the sense of its being wickedly collusive, or the result of a craven inability to resist? And

---

[3] "Le peuple, cherchait-il à gazer sa conversion et peut-être a préserver les témoins et les instruments des superstitions en les cachant sous le manteau du saint-apôtre [St. Martin]?"; J. G. Bulliot and F. Thiollier, *La Mission et le Culte de Saint Martin d'après les Légendes et les Monuments Populaires dans le Pays Eduen* (Autun and Paris, 1892), p. 18.

those practices which did indeed cross the frontier and establish themselves firmly within the Christian community: did they do so largely as a result of treachery within that community, or because the frontier guards were asleep? There were, I am certain, sleeping guards and traitors in the ranks. They would perhaps reward a separate study. But the assumption that they predominated, or (still less) that they determined events, was not an assumption easy to accept.

The inquiry began, then, because of niggling doubts: doubts about the general suitability of the adjective *notorious* and the noun *readiness* to the decisions made about the assimilation of magic within the early European Christian Church. It has ended by my trying to remove the adjective entirely but retaining the noun as absolutely central to our understanding of the period. Many members of this early medieval church were markedly ready both to compromise (another loaded term, we might remark) with magic, and, and far more importantly, to encourage it—but for the best, not the worst, of reasons.

One account of the rise of the medieval Christian Church upon the remains of its non-Christian predecessors has long been accepted and is reasonably familiar. It tells of how Christian saints and shrines and relics stood in for non-Christian ones, and how Christian feasts replaced the earlier and non-Christian celebrations. It has much about it that is true, and I have retraced a little of it. My main aim here has been, however, to overlay it with another. According to this second story, the main lines of force are horizontal, coming from the present; not vertical, coming from the past. The most compelling of the pressures upon the Christian Church, those which obliged it to consider the problem of magic with the greatest urgency, stemmed from the immediate contemporary context of its operations. The responses demanded of it were, then, far more complex than the linear story has been able to suggest. This second situation required less the replacement of past practices than the levering into mesh of parallel, and potentially or actively competing, systems of communication with the supernatural; and, through this levering, the annexing of the strengths of the parallel systems to the Christian cause. It presented a task of social and religious engineering daunting in its dimensions, requiring an enlarged understanding which was reciprocal. I have argued that the most discerning of the early Christian leaders in the mission field realized that this daunting task must be undertaken, and this reciprocation fostered, for there were enormous energies to be tapped. They set about it, therefore; and it is to their courageous insight, to their recognition of the strengths and weaknesses both of the competing system and of their own, and to their dexterous manipulation of the levers that we owe, for the greatest part, the rise of magic.

The most insistent of these horizontal lines of force sprang from the sheer liveliness and energy of the non-Christian spiritual world of Western Europe, full as it was of practitioners in the realm of the supernatural, practitioners much sought after and respected, and sometimes with good cause. Here lay opportunities for the removal of earlier inhibitions, and for the making of common ground; removals were accomplished, and common ground was made. Christian leaders actively invited non-Christian magic of certain sorts into the medieval Christian community, and they did this, in the main, for three reasons, all of them positive ones. They did so in the first place because they came to realize that deep social and cultural dislocation, and the discomfiture of respected opposing leaders, religious or political, rarely helps a new religion to put down firm roots; in the second, because non-Christian magic already gave consolation and attracted loyalty where consolation and loyalty were badly needed; and in the third, because they valued established devotional habit and spiritual aspiration above some of the manifestations of "reason" they saw about them, and they had need of such devotion. Christian leaders struck active bargains, therefore, in the localities in return for the acceptance of their own leadership and for the transfer of loyalties, and much of the Christian magic that in the end emerged did so as a result of prolonged and skillful negotiations in place and time. Magic was allowed to rise in importance in the early medieval West as a result of profound and careful thought, and for the good it could do.

The levering into mesh, and the tapping of energies for the Christian cause, called into play impressive diplomatic and artistic talents. These manifested themselves most often in the making of extremely small, but also extremely crucial, adjustments to old or contemporary non-Christian magical beliefs and practices. The levering might be managed, for example, by the bringing through of demons, who looked familiar to the older magical world, but who could now both frighten and deflect blame from humans;[4] or by the acceptance of cer-

---

[4] Here, some of the early medieval uses for demons, especially as ultimate bearers of blame, resemble some of those made of them by Protestant reformers in a later age of witchcraft persecution: S. Clark, "Protestant Demonology: Sin, Superstition, and Society (c. 1520–1630)," in *edit.* B. Ankarloo and G. Henningsen, *Early Modern European Witchcraft: Centres and Peripheries* (Oxford, 1989), pp. 59–60. Nor, on the other

tain sorts of lot casting; or by the elaboration of judicial processes, like the ordeal, magically based but conducted under Christian auspices; or by the offering of remedies for ill health reassuringly like the old ones, and possibly more accessible (and less expensive) than professional medicine. This last purpose may help to explain the inclusion, at first sight a puzzling one, of magico-medical remedies in many of the surviving codices of the period, *Lacnunga* included. These should now be seen as the work not of ignorant, but of remarkably aware, compilers and scribes. Skilled hagiographers preserved the type of religious leader who had been prominent in the non-Christian magical scene and made him prominent in the Christian one too, but with his activities and obediences deftly changed. That which was objectionable in the opposing practices was left behind, and that which was acceptable retained. Thus, certain birds and beasts, and woods, and writings, and medical specifics were, because they were favored in the competing systems, actively chosen to mediate a supernatural message in the Christian one too; but in Christian ways, and for Christian ends.

By such means the older players, man and animal, the materials, and sometimes the gestures retained their places on the stage; but the roles of these players, and the objectives of their gestures and materials, were altered and even reversed. I have suggested that these slight adjustments were deliberate, and that they were slight precisely because this made them all the more acceptable and therefore effective. They could retain the attention of the audience while giving small or no cause for offense. To ally a secured attention with a dramatic performance fundamentally altered can bring great rewards in its train. Many writers of saints' lives and many compilers of miracle collections knew this. The artistry exhibited by hagiographers in pursuit of such role reversals and transferences, and which can be seen to stand even (especially?) behind some of the simplest of their anecdotes, was often, then, of a very high order indeed—much higher than we are accustomed to allow. Hagiography, as a genre of literature displaying social sensitivity at its most refined, and one which manifests artistic dexter-

---

hand, was the Protestant (and Counter-Reformation) expedient of transferring the blame ultimately to the individual conscience without parallel in this early period, as many of the sermons and penitentials I have cited make clear. The medieval conscience was, however, differently informed and reinforced, and practices later condemned as idolatrous, as lacking in biblical authority, and as demonically inspired were, in these early and differing circumstances, seen as helpful to this conscience. I am grateful to Dr. Clark for an illuminating conversation on this point.

ity of a remarkable kind, emerges from this study as a historical source of the first importance: a source deserving of a far closer, and more painstaking, reading between the lines than we are accustomed to give to it.

Such endeavors could not but produce divisions within the Christian ranks, divisions which seem to have sprung partly from the inapplicability of central regulations to the needs of a distant mission field, partly from the tenacity of the earlier inhibitions and partly from the threats of real enemies. I have tried to sketch in the lines of these divisions and the variety of the responses to magic they generated, but they would richly repay more detailed studies. Very occasionally a practice that had been described (and condemned) as a magical one was brought through into early medieval Europe fully and aggressively, and not by hagiographers this time, but by "scientists." It might, indeed, be brought through to hold at bay "superstitious" and hagiographical excesses within the Christian Church itself. Astrology falls into the category of magico-scientific counters to a too enthusiastic espousal of magically inspired devotions. Here we touch upon disagreements within this church about priorities, about the kinds of magic to be considered admissible, the sorts of "Christian substitute" to be allowed, and the space, physical and educational, to be given to these allowances. Some of the divisions within the ranks of the Christian Church were caused, then, by subdivisions of opinion of another type, once the fundamental decision to bring in magic had been made. None of this activity bears the stamp of notoriety or of weak irrationality.

I have striven also to make clear that some of the forms of non-Christian supernatural practice which were encouraged into the West were so encouraged in compensation for the more effective outlawry of other forms, forms thought to be peculiarly hostile to Christian principles, and yet peculiarly insistent also in their presence. This is another aspect of the bargaining process about priorities, and one to which those who would rightly understand the place of "superstitious" practices—within both the early medieval church and its Reformation successor—should be especially alert. *Superstition* and *grossness* are, after all, relative terms.[5] Practices which, when set against the refine-

[5] And were at the beginning of the period we have considered here, as well as at its end. A fascinating discussion of those social and political circumstances which could give the word *superstitio* pejorative connotations, yet of differing degrees and for differing ends, is to be found in M. Salzman, "Superstitio in the Codex Theodosianus, and the Persecution of Pagans," *Vigiliae Christianae* 41 (1987), 172–188.

ments of a later age, may deserve to be described as gross, might, in an earlier one, have been devised in exchange for grossnesses beside which they themselves paled, and for which there was, at the time, no other effective answer. This state of affairs was, I have argued, to be found often in early Europe. Sometimes a choice between multiple seeming evils had actively to be made. Thus certain Christianized forms of magical activity (storm direction, rainmaking, lot casting, incantation, binding and loosing, as it might be) came in part to be adopted in return for the abandonment of supernatural practices considered especially hurtful: practices that involved, for instance, the calling up of the dead, or the use of repugnant materials; or practices which aimed at control of human emotions, wills, and livelihoods of a kind that was thought to be damaging. Some of the non-Christian magic which came into the Christian Church is best understood, then, as borrowed and encouraged not merely in the spirit of creative compromise, nor only for its amenability to skillful adjustment to the Christian cause, but in return for the elimination of other types. This process led eventually to the making of distinctions between maleficent and beneficent magic, distinctions which would, of course, be lost in a later age when the need for such bargains had passed.[6] Certain forms of Christian magic (and I have placed the Christian *Sortes* especially firmly within this category) have, then, an extra dimension to them. They were remarkably imitative, yet could be rendered harmless, even helpful, when firmly Christianized. They could readily be adopted as bargaining counters, therefore, in return for the repudiation of practices which were wholly unamenable to Christian use. The *Sortes* had the particular advantage, furthermore, of bringing the Bible firmly before the eyes of those involved.[7] The elaboration and encouragement of some medieval Christian magical practices can only be fully understood if one bears such local negotiations and debts in mind. They should not be valued, or devalued, outside this immediate context. There were, in short, excellent reasons for supporting, in sev-

---

[6] Thus could both Protestant and certain Counter-Reformation pastors condemn them all together: Clark, "Protestant Demonology," pp. 78–81. The threat posed by the magi, sortilegi, harioli of the early medieval period, however, was different in degree and proportion from that posed by the later village "cunning man" or woman. This difference has to be borne constantly in mind.

[7] I owe this observation to Mr. Jonathan Elukin, who allowed me to read his paper on the *Sortes*.

enth-century Europe, systems of invocation that had, by the seventeenth century, become matters for reproach.

In the making of such bargains about magic, deep and detailed decisions about rightful and wrongful fear and hope, about the relative importance of coercion and example, and about the operations of Divine Providence were involved. This is an extraordinarily important aspect of the question, and I have attempted to identify moments at which Christian magic seemed actively to replace terror with a less numbing emotion, and so bolster a hopeful trust in Providence. The borrowing of the less repugnant non-Christian specifics and aids to health (astrology among them), and the benevolent use of them, especially by religious communities not in need of immediate financial reward, might greatly have helped to give the Christian God of early medieval Europe an appearance kindlier than that of some of his competitors when death threatened. This motive may have stood behind much borrowing of this kind. The Christian command of magic could be used by the wiser of Christian leaders, furthermore, to diminish the severities which suspicions of magical malpractice might call forth (often randomly) from mobs, or from societies differently regulated from the Christian ones. Leniency of this sort might bring about a greater and more hopeful enthusiasm for Christian rulings, especially for those issued by God's bishops. As I have suggested, Archbishops Agobard of Lyons and Hincmar of Rheims were, in their different ways adept at leadership of this kind. The loosing of the young boy by Saint Wulfram, and the saint's transmutation of him from human sacrifice into Christian priest and scribe,[8] though spectacular, is only one example of Christian magic used to redefine the role of fear in intercession. Sometimes, we catch a distant echo of fear-inducing pagan "magical" sounds. The anonymous *Homilia de Sacrilegiis* speaks of hissings in connection with the taking of auguries,[9] and Thietmar, in his description of the lot-casting procedures followed among the Slavs, speaks of the low murmuring or hissing that accompanied the burying of the lots and made people tremble.[10] Whatever the impression upon some persons

---

[8] *Vita Vulframni Episcopi Senonici* 6; *edit.* B. Krusch and W. Levison, MGH SRM v (Hanover and Leipzig, 1910), 665–666.

[9] III,9 ; *edit.* C. Caspari, *Homilia de Sacrilegiis. Aus einer Einsiedeler Handschrift des achten Jahrhunderts herausgegeben und mit kritischen und sachlichen Anmerkungen, sowie mit einer Abhandlung begleitet* (Christiania, 1886), p. 7.

[10] "et invicem clanculum mussantes terram cum tremore infodiunt." *Chronicle*

of the supernatural sounds at which early medieval chants and church music aimed, they were scarcely designed for discomfort. Again, though appearances may have been retained, the effect of entering a Christian yew enclosure, or the sanctuary of a Christian church, must have been rather different from that produced by entering a sacrificial grove.

Augustine was, as we saw at the beginning, an enthusiast for wondering hope. Caesarius too worried openly about the balances between fear, hope, and despair to be struck in Christians by their pastors,[11] and for him, as for Augustine, Christian magic, in the form of baptismal grace, shrines, relics, and miracles, clearly played an important part in the delicate adjusting of this balance, in the diminishing of wrongfully aroused alarms, and in the reinforcing of appropriate ones. Pope Gregory the Great expressed like anxieties, especially about the dangers of despair, and it is possible, indeed, that such anxieties were seminal to the production of the sympathetic responses that we can trace to him. Thus, hopefulness, and even humor, found a place in the pictures certain hagiographers liked to paint of certain saints at certain times: in the *Lives*, for instance, of Saint Vaast and Saint Remigius, and in many more early hagiographical materials than I have been able here to explore. Urges for change such as this, then, change that would actively lighten the heart, also encouraged the rise of Christian magic.

At an opposite extreme, of course, certain Christian writers on the Christian use of the supernatural within the period seemingly allowed the saints to operate, and be operated upon, by means of condemned *defixiones*, cursings and terrors and threats to life, in a manner similar to that of many of the condemned and fear-inducing magicians.[12] Coercive magical practices of this kind, which reduced the saints as magical operators to the level of some of the worst of the opposition, and

---

VI,24; *edit*. R. Holzmann, *Die Chronik des Bischofs Thietmar von Merseburg und ihre korveier Überarbeitung* (Berlin, 1955), pp. 302–304.

[11] Sermons 1, 12, 160, 184; *transl*. M. M. Mueller, *Saint Caesarius of Arles, Sermons* i (Washington, 1956), 7, 72, ii (Washington, 1964), 371–372, 483–484.

[12] Plummer long ago drew attention to the vindictiveness apparent in the activities of early Irish saints, and the willingness with which they resorted to curses: C. Plummer, *Venerabilis Bedae Opera Historica* ii (Oxford, 1896), 260. See on this subject the seminal articles of P. Geary, "La coercition des saints dans la pratique religieuse médiévale," in *edit*. P. Boglioni, *La Culture Populaire au Moyen Age* (Montreal, 1979), pp. 147–160, and "Humiliation of Saints," in *edit*. S. Wilson, *Saints and their Cults* (Cambridge, 1983), pp. 123–140.

hardly helped in the refining of the emotions of fear and hope, were certainly adopted by some Christians. There was tension here, then, too, and we have evidence once more of disagreements within the ranks of those who stood for Christian magic within the medieval church, disagreements that added to the kaleidoscopic complexity of the choices to be made and understood. Anxieties about the correct ordering of fear and hope played a vital and constantly active part in the making of all of these choices and divisions. In the Europe of which Delumeau writes, the Europe of the fourteenth to the eighteenth centuries, that is, fear appears to have won the day, and through the agency of some of those very beliefs and practices the earlier church accommodated.[13] It is not possible to make an accurate and quantifiable comparison between this later period and the one we have surveyed; but it is arguable that in earlier medieval Europe the barriers against terror of an overwhelming kind held out, and that Christian magic in the form of these beliefs and practices made an important contribution toward helping them to do so.

I have suggested every so often that some of the decisions in favor of non-Christian magic's reception were made possible because there were acceptable biblical and literary (especially patristic) loopholes for them. I have set out the more striking of these; but I have found myself putting them last in line. As a corollary of this attempt to readjust the stature, and stress the wisdom and circumspection, of the early medieval Christian leader, this point needs to be pressed a little further. As this Christian leader should not be dwarfed in his achievement alongside his more modern successor, neither, I would argue, should this achievement be seen as governed primarily by the directions of his predecessors—not even when these directions are enshrined in the Bible and the Fathers. It was certainly helpful that, when he needed them, biblical precedents and patristic authorities for much of what he wanted to do lay ready to hand; but they were not the decisive factors. The hopeful section of the legacy of attitudes set out at the beginning of this exercise was filled with possibilities rather than determinants, possibilities exploited in the light of needs that were overwhelmingly contemporary. Similar observations might be made about the uses, by hagiographers, of typology and exempla.[14] Early medieval authors,

[13] J. Delumeau, Le Peur en Occident, XIVᵉ–XVIIIᵉ Siècles (Paris, 1978), especially pp. 54–74.

[14] By typology I mean the presentation of an event as echoing, or fulfilling, a similar type of event in Scripture, and the taking, therefore, of the biblical past, and not the

hagiographers especially, certainly employed typology and drew greatly upon exempla, and a great deal of testing and valuable work has been devoted to discovering which sources provided the greater medieval authors with their supplies, especially which Eastern and biblical sources.[15] Without diminishing the importance of such investigations, I would suggest that they tend, once again, to portray the medieval writer rather as overshadowed than as self-acting, and that, in so doing, they may distort. For the historian, the most important part of the information may lie less in the origins of the stories told (Eastern or Western, biblical or classical or "popular"), and in the forerunners of the types chosen, than in the immediate conditions and purposes for which these particular selections of stories and types were made.

In the last event, it has to be said that the hypotheses I have here advanced cannot be conclusively proved. The evidence I have brought forward, drawn as it is from such a number of different areas, is primarily analogous, cumulative, and suggestive—not definitive. I would, however, draw particular attention, finally, to certain of the more striking aspects of it. Take, first of all, the argument from analogy. Much of this attempt to drive back the frontiers of a faintly condescending colonialism in history has been both inspired and assisted by parallel postcolonial efforts in another discipline: the discipline of social anthropology. I am sure that it is toward the social anthropologists that medievalists must now, and increasingly, turn for help, perhaps even offering a little of their own in return. However, there are very many examples of sympathetic adjustments to preexisting and competing magical beliefs, adjustments made designedly and as a result of hard experience and intelligent choice, to be found in other early historical periods. In the period of which Betz treats, for example (Greco-Roman Egypt from the second century B.C. to the fifth century A.D.), the Greek magical papyri are thought themselves to be evidence of a carefully thought out working syncretism. They are described as products of a deliberate scheme of action, one elaborated by Hellenizing magicians confronted by the obduracy of their Egyptian forbears.[16]

present, as the primary point of reference. By *exempla*, I mean well-used model stories, or *topoi*.

[15] For example A. M. Cameron, "The Byzantine Sources of Gregory of Tours," *Journal of Theological Studies* 26 (1975), 421–426, and J. M. Petersen, *The Dialogues of Gregory the Great in their Late Antique Cultural Background* (Toronto, 1984), passim, but especially pp. 27–55, 116–121.

[16] "In this syncretism, the indigenous ancient Egyptian religion has in part survived,

The parallels between this state of affairs and that for which I have argued in the early Middle Ages are inescapable, and the early Middle Ages contained echoes, as we have seen, of much of the magic of the papyri. Given the evidence coming from other times and places of an intelligently manifested sensitivity to the social advantages of competing magic deliberately transferred, it seems at least permissible to ask why the early Middle Ages should be thought bereft of it.

In support of the more positive argument, the argument from sheer accumulation, it might be pointed out once again that the many names of those cited as leading the way in compromises with magic, and in the encouragement of the rise of certain sorts of it, are not the names of persons confused or supine in other aspects of their known work. Saints Martin and Benedict, Caesarius of Arles, Gregory of Tours, Martin of Braga, Gregory the Great, Isidore, Bede, Boniface, Alcuin, Agobard, Rabanus, Hincmar, Regino, Burchard, Aelfric, Wulfstan (it becomes a litany) were pastors and directors of great experience. The balance of probabilities alone, then, renders it unlikely that the choices they made were predominantly simple, or uninformed, or insensitive. Those who have made the most enduring impact on popular memory and who may therefore have been the most vigorous of the actors upon the barbarian magical stage (arguably Saints Martin and Benedict, and Pope Gregory the Great) seem, furthermore, to have been *precisely* those for whose sympathetic approaches to the problem of magic we have the most convincing record. Again, many of the communities from which I have drawn material suggestive of an ingeniously constructed syncretism, the Benedictine communities of late tenth- and early eleventh-century Anglo-Saxon England in particular, were communities deeply involved in the life of the localities. Thus, they were communities to which, simply on the face of it, compromise with and adjustment toward local customs might be presumed to have

---

in part been profoundly Hellenised. In its Hellenistic transformation, the Egyptian religion of the pre-Hellenistic era appears to have been reduced and simplified, no doubt to facilitate its assimilation into Hellenistic religion as the predominant cultural reference. . . . There are texts reflecting perhaps a different type of magician, a type we know from the Greek religious milieu. This type of wandering craftsman seems keen to adopt and adapt every religious tradition that appeared useful to him. . . . He could tap, regulate and manipulate the invisible energies. He was a problem solver who had remedies for a thousand petty troubles plaguing mankind; everything from migraine to runny nose to bedbugs to horse races, and, of course, all the troubles of love and money." H. D. Betz, *The Greek Magical Papyri in Translation, including the Demotic Spells* (Chicago and London, 1986), pp. xlvi–xlvii.

been a more attractive and a more probable course of action than either confrontation or capitulation.

It is undoubtedly true that magic adopted in these ways and for these ends can become redundant when the conditions which prompted the original rescues no longer apply. Then it can indeed degenerate into superstition and grossness in our sense: irrationality, that is, damagingly upheld. Such a degeneration (though we might quarrel still about when, and in what circumstances, it takes place) will rightly discredit early European Christian magic; but this should not imperil our appreciation of the conditions in which this Christian magic first took shape. Nor should it blind us to the fact that these same conditions might reemerge and equally rightly demand (and receive) the same responses, no matter even that the opposition to them may have redoubled within the Christian fold. In this context, it is of surpassing interest to observe that some, perhaps much, of the magic preserved and Christianized in the early period we have discussed fulfilled once more a function remarkably similar to that I have here ascribed to it, and in a period far closer to our own. African "slave religion" has, at its roots, magic which has much in common with that early European non-Christian variety I have described in this book. And, among the many factors that contributed to the survival of this slave religion, (especially in such areas as Brazil, or Cuba, or Haiti), there are to be found a large number of those early medieval Christian practices which, I have argued, were originally elaborated precisely as sympathetic responses to magic of this very kind.[17] Largely expelled from post-Reformation northern Europe and its North American heirs, these saints and relics, rituals and feast days, conjurations and charms and talismans served once more (at a remove from their origins, and operated this time perhaps a little more automatically and with less direct intent)[18] to preserve the devotions of a culture markedly like that for which they were, at the outset, devised.

[17] A. J. Raboteau, *Slave Religion* (Oxford, 1978), pp. 16–25, 34–35, 87–89. For an account of non-Christian magical practices markedly similar to those we can trace to early medieval Europe, see especially pp. 80–87, 275–288. They include the use of clothes and hair and nail clippings in conjurations (like Aldebert), and reverence for trees and stones and springs and crossroads, as well as more striking similarities such as the practice already mentioned as condemned by Burchard—the scraping up of the soil from a person's footprint for use in spells.

[18] Though it is hard to be sure about this, and missionary enterprise and adaptations would surely reward investigation here.

My main purpose here has been to attempt to recover those pristine skills and enthusiasms which were originally involved in the devising of these complex responses, and so to rehabilitate the so-called medieval approach to magic in modern eyes. Many later "grossnesses," were, at their origins, products of high devotional excitement and sophisticated religious sensitivity. In terms now familiar to the modern anthropologist and social historian, these practices served, in the early Middle Ages, to hold the forces of too rapid an "acculturation," or cultural dominance, at bay, to prevent the complete "deculturation" of the subject culture, and, through extended exercises in "negotiation," to bring about an enduring fusion of religious sensibilities and behavior instead.[19] The culture engaged in becoming dominant, in this case the culture of the early European Christian Church, had both to make concessions and invent attractions if its aims were to be fulfilled. Many of its leaders and spokesmen saw this. I have suggested that the concessions and inventions were wisely, and often willingly, made (perhaps all the more wisely and willingly in the face of the resounding conciliar condemnations of them, for irritation with ossified regulation can, after all, be a great stimulus to creativity); and that the attractions were effective, not least because of the existence of a cooperative spirit on the non-Christian side as well, if only this spirit could be appropriately unlocked. Magic was important to many in the medieval church because it was already believed in by the peoples to whom its missionaries came, and because some of this belief gave hope and supported happiness. The church had need of these peoples. It too supported this hope and happiness; and it could find echoes of this magic, furthermore, when it looked for them, within its own dispensation. Much magic was, then, rescued in the service of human aspiration, and, certainly, in defiance of certain aspects of reason and regulation. However, I trust it will be difficult to continue to insist that magic's rise in the early medieval church defied right reason in all of its forms.

[19] I draw here upon the definitions given in P. Burke, "A Question of Acculturation," in edit. P. Zambelli, Scienze, Credenze Occulte, Livelli di Cultura (Florence, 1982), pp. 197–204. My attention was drawn to this article by my colleague Dr. Barry Reay.

Bibliography

PRIMARY WORKS

Individual authors

The works of each author are ordered in the first place alphabetically and then, when more than one edition of the same work is cited, in order of date of publication.

ADAMNAN
Edit. and transl. Anderson, A. O., and M. O. *Adomnan's Life of Columba.* London, 1961.

ADAM OF BREMEN
Edit. Schmeidler, B. *Adam von Bremen. Hamburgische Kirchengeschichte.* Hanover and Leipzig, 1917.
Transl. Tschan, F. S. *History of the Archbishops of Hamburg-Bremen.* New York, 1959.

ADHÉMAR OF CHABANNES
Edit. Waitz, D. G. *Adhemari Historiarum Libri III. MGH SS* iv, 106–148. Hanover, 1841.

AELFRIC
Edit. and transl. Skeat, W. W. *Aelfric's Lives of the Saints.* 2 vols. EETS. London, 1881.
Transl. Thorpe, B. *The Homilies of the Anglo-Saxon Church.* 2 vols. London, 1844–1846.
Edit. Pope, J. C. *Homilies of Aelfric. A Supplementary Collection.* 2 vols. EETS. Oxford, 1967–1968.

AGOBARD OF LYONS
Edit. Van Acker, L. *Agobardi Lugdunensis Opera Omnia.* CC. Turnholt, 1981.

ALCUIN
Edit. Dümmler, E. *Alcuini sive Albini Epistolae. MGH Epistolae Karolini Aevi* ii, 1–481. Berlin, 1895.
Expositio in Epistolam Pauli Apostoli ad Hebreos; PL 100, 1031–1086.

ALDHELM
Edit. Ehwald, R. *De Metris et Enigmatibus ac Pedum Regulis. Epistulae. MGH Auctorum Antiquissimorum* xv, 35–58, 475–503. Berlin, 1919.

AMBROSE

Transl. Sullivan, J. J., and M.R.P. McGuire. *Funeral Orations by Saint Gregory Nazianzen and Saint Ambrose.* Washington, 1953.

AMBROSIASTER

Edit. Vogels, H. J. *Ambrosiastri qui dicitur Commentarius in Epistulas Paulinas.* 3 vols. Vienna, 1966–1969.

Edit. Souter, A. *Pseudo-Augustini Quaestiones Veteris et Novi Testamenti CXXVII.* Vienna and Leipzig, 1908.

AMMIANUS MARCELLINUS

Edit. and transl. Rolfe, J. C. *Ammianus Marcellinus.* 3 vols. Loeb Classical Library. 1935–1939.

APULEIUS OF MADAURA

Transl. Butler, H. E. *The Apologia and Florida of Apuleius of Madaura.* Oxford, 1909.

Edit. Thomas, P. *Apulei Platonici Madaurensis Opera Quae Supersunt.* Stuttgart, 1970.

Edit. and transl. Gaselee, S. *Apuleius, the Golden Ass.* Loeb Classical Library, 1928.

ASSER

Edit. Stevenson, W. H. *Life of King Alfred.* Oxford, 1904.

ATHANASIUS

Edit. and transl. Thomson, R. W. *Athanasius Contra Gentes and De Incarnatione.* Oxford, 1971.

AUGUSTINE

Transl. Gavigan, J. J. *Saint Augustine, Christian Instruction.* Washington, 1947.

Edit. and transl. McCracken, G., W. M. Green, et al. *Saint Augustine City of God.* 7 vols. Loeb Classical Library.

Transl. Pine-Coffin, R. C. *Saint Augustine Confessions.* London, 1961.

Edit. Mutzenbecher, A. *Sancti Aurelii Augustini De Diversis Quaestionibus ad Simplicianum.* CC. Turnholt, 1970.

Edit. Mutzenbecher, A. *Sancti Aurelii Augustini De Diversis Quaestionibus Octoginta Tribus.* CC. Turnholt, 1975.

Edit. Zycha, J. *Sancti Aurelii Augustini De Fide et Symbolo. . . .* Vienna, 1900.

Transl. Mosher, D. L. *Saint Augustine. Eighty-Three Different Questions.* Washington, 1982.

Edit. Dekkers E., and J. Fraipont. *Sancti Aurelii Augustini Enarrationes in Psalmos.* 3 vols. CC. Turnholt, 1956.

Edit. Willems, R. *Sancti Aurelii Augustini In Johannis Evangelium Tractatus CXXIV.* CC. Turnholt, 1954.

Transl. Parsons, W. *Saint Augustine, Letters.* 5 vols. Washington, 1951–1956.

Edit. Fraipont, I. *Sancti Aurelii Augustini Quaestionum in Heptateuchum Libri VII.* CC. Turnholt, 1958.

Transl. Lawler, T. C. *St. Augustine. Sermons for Christmas and Epiphany.* London, 1952.

Edit. Deferrari, R. J. (*transl.* R. W. Brown). *Saint Augustine. Treatises on Marriage and Other Subjects.* Washington, 1955.

Avienus

Soubiran, J. *Les Phénomènes d'Aratos/Avienus.* Paris, 1981.

Bede

Edit. and transl. Colgrave, B., and R. A. B. Mynors. *Bede's Ecclesiastical History of the English People.* Oxford, 1969.

Edit. Jones, C. W. *Bedae Opera De Temporibus.* Cambridge, Mass., 1943.

Edit. Jones, C. W. *Bedae Venerabilis Opera, Opera Didascalica* i. CC. Turnholt, 1975.

Edit. Jones, C. W. *Bedae Venerabilis Opera, Opera Didascalica* ii. CC. Turnholt, 1977.

Edit. Hurst, D. *Bedae Venerabilis Opera, Opera Exegetica* ii. (2). CC. Turnholt, 1970.

Edit. Hurst, D. *Bedae Venerabilis Opera, Opera Exegetica* ii. (2B). CC. Turnholt, 1983.

Edit. Laistner, M. L. W. *Bedae Venerabilis Opera, Opera Exegetica* ii. (4). CC. Turnholt, 1983.

Boethius

Edit. and transl. Stewart, H. F., et al., *Boethius.* Loeb Classical Library. 1973.

Boniface

Edit. Dümmler, E. S. *Bonifatii et Lulli Epistolae. MGH Epistolae Merovingici et Karolini Aevi* i, 215–433. Berlin, 1892.

Transl. Emerton, E. *The Letters of St. Boniface.* New York, 1940.

Burchard of Worms

Decretum; PL 140, 537–1058.

Caesarius of Arles

Edit. Morin, G. *Sancti Caesarii Arelatensis Sermones.* 2 vols. (CC. Turnholt, 1953).

Transl. Mueller, M. M. *Saint Caesarius of Arles, Sermons.* 3 vols. Washington, 1956–1973.

Cassian

Edit. and transl. Pichéry, E. *Jean Cassien Conférences.* 3 vols. Paris, 1955–1959.

Edit. and *transl.* Guy, J. C. *Jean Cassien Institutions Cénobitiques.* Paris, 1965.

CASSIODORUS

Edit. Mynors, R. A. B. *Cassiodori Senatoris Institutiones.* Oxford, 1937.
Transl. Jones, L. W. *An Introduction to Divine and Human Readings by Cassiodorus Senator.* New York, 1946.

CATO

Edit. and *transl.* Hooper, W. D. and H. B. Ash. *Marcus Porcius Cato On Agriculture, Marcus Terentius Varro On Agriculture.* Loeb Classical Library. 1934.

CATULLUS

Edit. and *transl.* Cornish, F. W. *The Poems of Gaius Valerius Catullus.* Loeb Classical Library. 1914.

CHRISTIAN OF STAVELOT

Expositio in Evangelium Matthaei; PL 106, 1261–1594.

CICERO

Soubiran, J. *Aratea; Fragments Poétiques.* Paris, 1972.
Edit. and *transl.* Falconer, W. A. *Cicero.* Loeb Classical Library. 1923.

COLUMELLA

Edit. and *transl.* Forster, E. S., and E. H. Heffner. *Lucius Junius Moderatus Columella on Agriculture and Trees.* Loeb Classical Library. 1955.

EDDIUS

Edit. and *transl.* Colgrave, B. *The Life of Bishop Wilfred by Eddius Stephanus* Cambridge, 1927.

EUSEBIUS

Transl. Deferrari, R. J. *Eusebius Pamphili Ecclesiastical History.* Washington, 1953.

FELIX

Edit. and *transl.* Colgrave, B. *Felix's Life of St. Guthlac.* Cambridge, 1956.

FLODOARD

Edit. and *transl.* Lejeune, M. *Histoire de l'Église de Reims par Flodoard.* Rheims, 1854.

GERBERT

Transl. Lattin, H. *The Letters of Gerbert.* New York, 1961.

GERMANICUS

Edit. Breysig, A. *Germanici Caesaris Aratea cum Scholiis.* Berlin, 1867. Reprint. Hildesheim, 1967.
Edit. Gain, D. B. *The Aratus Ascribed to Germanicus Caesar.* London, 1976.

GREGORY OF TOURS
Edit. Krusch, B. *Gregorii Episcopi Turonensis Opera*. MGH SRM i(1). Hanover, 1885.
Edit. Krusch, B. *Gregorii Episcopi Turonensis Miracula et Opera Minora* MGH SRM i(2). Hanover, 1885.
Transl. Van Dam, R. *Gregory of Tours Glory of the Confessors*. Liverpool, 1988.
Transl. Van Dam, R. *Gregory of Tours Glory of the Martyrs*. Liverpool, 1988.
Transl. James, E. *Gregory of Tours: Life of the Fathers*. Liverpool, 1985.
Transl. Dalton, O. M. *The History of the Franks by Gregory of Tours*. 2 vols. Oxford, 1927.

GREGORY THE GREAT
Edit. and transl. de Vogüé, A., and P. Antin. *Grégoire le Grand, Dialogues*. 3 vols. Paris, 1978–1980.
Edit. and transl. de Gaudemaris, A. and R. Gillet. *Grégoire le Grand Morales sur Job*. 3 vols. Paris, 1975.
Transl. Davis, H. *St. Gregory the Great Pastoral Care*. London, 1950.
Edit. Ewald, P., and L. M. Hartmann. MGH *Gregorii I Papae Registrum Epistolarum*. 2 vols. Vienna, 1887–1899.
XL Homiliarum in Evangelia; PL 76,781–1312.

GUIBERT OF NOGENT
Edit. Bourgin, G. *Guibert de Nogent: Histoire de sa Vie*. Paris, 1907.
Transl. Benton, J. F. *Self and Society in Medieval France*. Reprint. Toronto, 1984.

HERODOTUS
Edit. and transl. Godley, A. D. *Herodotus*. 4 vols. Loeb Classical Library. 1920–1924.

HINCMAR OF RHEIMS
De Divortio Lotharii et Tetbergae; PL 125,619–772.
De Nuptiis Stephani et filiae Regimundi Comitis; PL 126,132–153.

ISIDORE OF SEVILLE
Edit. Lindsay, W. M. *Isidori Hispalensis Episcopi Etymologiarum sive Originum Libri XX*. Oxford, 1911.
Edit. Fontaine, J. *Isidore de Séville, Traité de la Nature*. Bordeaux, 1960.
Quaestiones in Vetus Testamentum; PL 83,207–424.

JEROME
Adversus Jovinianum; PL 23,221–352.
Commentaria in Danielem; PL 25,491–581.
Commentaria in Evangelium Matthaei; PL 26, 15–218.

JOHN CHRYSOSTOM
    Transl. Prevost, G. *The Homilies of St. John Chrysostom on the Gospel of St. Matthew.* Oxford, 1843.

JOHN OF SALISBURY
    Edit. Webb, C.C.J. *Joannis Sarisberiensis Episcopi Carnotensis Policratici sive De Nugis Curialium Libri VIII.* 2 vols. Oxford, 1909.

JONAS OF ORLÉANS
    De Cultu Imaginum; PL 106,305–388.
    Edit. Reviron, J. *Jonas d'Orléans et son "De Institutione Regia."* Paris, 1930.

JORDANES
    Transl. Mierow, C. C. *The Gothic History of Jordanes.* Princeton, 1915.

JUVENAL
    Edit. Mayor, J.E.B. *Thirteen Satires of Juvenal with a Commentary.* London, 1900.

LUCAN
    Edit. Endt, J. *Adnotationes super Lucanum.* Leipzig, 1909.
    Edit. and transl. Duff, J. D. *Lucan.* Loeb Classical Library. 1928.
    Edit. Usener, H. M. *Annaei Lucani Commenta Bernensia.* Leipzig, 1869.

MACROBIUS
    Transl. Stahl, W. *Macrobius, Commentary on the Dream of Scipio.* New York, 1952.
    Transl. Davies, P. V. *Macrobius, The Saturnalia.* New York and London, 1969.

MARTIN OF BRAGA
    Transl. Barlow, C. W. *Iberian Fathers* i. Washington, 1969.
    Edit. Barlow, C. W. *Martini Episcopi Bracarensis Opera Omnia.* New Haven, 1950.

MAXIMUS OF TURIN
    Edit. Mutzenbecher, A. *Maximi Episcopi Taurinensis Collectionem Sermonum Antiquam.* CC. Turnholt, 1962.

NITHARD
    Edit. Pertz, G. *Historiarum Libri IIII. Vita Hludovici Imperatoris* MGH SS ii,604–672. Hanover, 1829.

ORIGEN
    Transl. Chadwick, H. *Contra Celsum.* Cambridge, 1953.

OVID
    Edit. and transl. Frazer, J. G. *Ovid's Fasti.* Loeb Classical Library. 1951.
    Edit. and transl. Showerman, G. *Ovid, Heroides and Amores.* Loeb Classical Library. 1977.

Edit. and *transl.* Miller, F. J. *Ovid, The Metamorphoses.* 2 vols. Loeb Classical Library, 1977.

PASCHASIUS RADBERT
Expositio in Matthaeum; PL 120,31–994.

PAUL THE DEACON
De Gestis Longobardorum; PL 95,433–673.
Transl. Foulke, W. J. *Paulus Diaconus, History of the Lombards.* Philadelphia, 1907.

PIRMIN OF REICHENAU
De Singulis Libris Canonicis Scarapsus; PL 89, 1029-1050.

PLINY
Edit. and *transl.* Rackham, H., et al. *Pliny Natural History.* 10 vols. Loeb Classical Library. 1938–1963.

PROCOPIUS
Edit. and *transl.* Dewing, H. B. *Procopius, History of the Wars.* 7 vols. Loeb Classical Library. 1914–1954.

PRUDENTIUS
Edit. and *transl.* Thomson, H. J. *Prudentius.* 2 vols. Loeb Classical Library. 1949–1953.

PSEUDO-BEDE
De Auguriis et Divinationibus; PL 94,573.
De Minutione Sanguinis sive de Phlebotomia; PL 90,959–962.
De Tonitruis Libellus ad Herefridum; PL 90,609–614.
Edit. and *transl.* Burnett, C. *Pseudo-Bede: De Mundi Celestis Terrestrisque Constitutione. A Treatise on the Universe and the Soul.* Warburg Institute Surveys and Texts x. London, 1985.
In Matthaei Evangelium Expositio; PL 92,9–132.

RABANUS MAURUS
Commentaria in Matthaeum; PL 107,727–1156.
De Magicis Artibus; PL 110,1095–1110.
De Universo; PL 111,9–614.
Homiliae 16, 42-43; PL 110,33–34,78–81.
Poenitentiale; PL 110,467–494.

RATHERIUS OF VERONA
Praeloquia; PL 136,145–344.

REGINO OF PRÜM
De Ecclesiasticis Disciplinis; PL 132,185–400.

RIMBERT
Edit. Pertz, G. H. *Vita Sancti Anskarii.* MGH SS ii,683–725. Hanover, 1829.

SENECA

Edit. and transl. Corcoran, T. H. Seneca, Natural Questions. Loeb Classical Library. 1972.

SERVIUS

Edit. Thilo, G., and H. Hagen. Servii Grammatici qui feruntur in Vergilii Carmina Commentarii. 3 vols. Hildesheim, 1878–1902.

Edit. Rand, E. K., et al. Servianorum in Vergilii Carmina Commentariorum, Editionis Harvardianae ii. Lancaster, Pa., 1946. iii. Oxford, 1965.

SUETONIUS

Edit. and transl. Rolfe, J. C. Suetonius. Loeb Classical Library. 1941.

SULPICIUS SEVERUS

Edit. and transl. Fontaine, J. Sulpice Sévère, Vie de Saint Martin. 3 vols. Paris, 1967–1969.

TACITUS

Edit. and transl. Hutton, M. Tactitus. Agricola and Germania. Loeb Classical Library. 1914.

Edit. and transl. Jackson, J., and C. H. Moore. Tacitus. The Histories. The Annals. 4 vols. Loeb Classical Library. 1925–1937.

TERTULLIAN

Edit. and transl. Evans, E. Tertullian, Adversus Marcionem. 2 vols. Oxford, 1972.

THIETMAR OF MERSEBURG

Edit. Holzmann, R. Die Chronik des Bischofs Thietmar von Merseburg und ihre korveier Überarbeitung. Berlin, 1955.

VARRO

Edit. and transl. Kent, R. G. Varro on the Latin Language. Loeb Classical Library. 1938.

On Agriculture. See under Cato.

VIRGIL

Edit. and transl. Fairclough, H. R. Virgil. 2 vols. Loeb Classical Library. 1920.

Edit. and transl. Rieu, E. V. Virgil, the Pastoral Poems. Harmondsworth, Middlesex, 1967.

WILLIAM OF MALMESBURY

Edit. Hamilton, N.E.S.A. Willelmi Malmesbiriensis Monachi De Gestis Pontificum Anglorum. RS. London, 1870.

Edit. Stubbs, W. Willelmi Malmesbiriensis Monachi de Gestis Regum Anglorum. 2 vols. RS. London, 1887.

WULFSTAN

Edit. Bethurum, D. The Homilies of Wulfstan. Oxford 1957.

Collected and Unattributable Works

Edit. Arnold, T. *Symeonis Monachi Opera Omnia.* 2 vols. RS. London 1882.

Transl. Attenborough, F. L. *The Laws of the Earliest English Kings.* Cambridge, 1922.

Transl. Betz, H. D. *The Greek Magical Papyri in Translation, including the Demotic Spells.* Chicago and London, 1986.

Edit. Beyerle, F. *MGH Leges* iii (2). *Lex Ribuaria.* Hanover, 1954.

Edit. Bieler, L. *The Irish Penitentials.* Dublin, 1963.

Edit. Boretius, A., et al. *MGH Legum* ii *Capitularia Regum Francorum.* 2 vols. Hanover, 1890–97.

Edit. Caspari, C. P. *Homilia de Sacrilegiis. Aus einer Einsiedeler Handschrift des achten Jahrhunderts herausgegeben und mit kritischen und sachlichen Anmerkungen, sowie mit einer Abhandlung begleitet.* Christiania, 1886.

Transl. Charles, R. H. *The Apocrypha and Pseudepigrapha of the Old Testament.* 2 vols. Oxford, 1913.

Edit. and transl. Cockayne, O. *Leechdoms, Wortcunning and Starcraft of Early England.* 3 vols. RS. London, 1864–1866.

Edit. and transl. Colgrave, B. *Two Lives of St. Cuthbert.* Cambridge, 1940.

Edit. Conrat (Cohn), M. *Breviarium Alaricianum.* Aalen, 1963.

Edit. Cook, A. S., and C. B. Tinker. *Select Translations from Old English Prose.* Cambridge, Mass., 1908.

Edit. Cross, J. E., and T. D. Hill. *The Prose Solomon and Saturn and Adrian and Ritheus.* Toronto, 1982.

Edit. De Clercq, C. *La Législation Religieuse Franque.* Louvain, 1936.

Edit. De Salis, L. R. *MGH Leges Nationum Germanicarum* ii(1). *Leges Burgundionum.* Hanover, 1892.

Transl. Drew, K. F. *The Burgundian Code.* Philadelphia, 1949.

Transl. Drew, K. F. *The Lombard Laws.* Philadelphia, 1976.

Edit. Dümmler, E. *MGH Epistolae Merowingici et Karolini Aevi* i–vi. Berlin, 1892–1939.

Edit. Eckhardt, K. A. *Lex Salica.* Weimar, 1953.

Edit. Eckhardt, K. A. *MGH Leges Nationum Germanicarum* iv(1). *Pactus Legis Salicae.* Göttingen, 1954–1956. Reprint. Hanover, 1962.

Edit. and transl. Edelstein, E. J. and L. *Asclepius: A Collection and Interpretation of the Testimonies.* 2 vols. Baltimore, 1945.

Ekhart, J. G. *Commentarii in Rebus Franciae Orientalis.* Würzburg, 1729.

Edit. Fawtier, R. *La Vie de Saint Samson.* Paris, 1912.

Edit. Friedberg, E. A. *Corpus Iuris Canonici* i. Reprint. Graz, 1955.

Grattan, J.H.G., and C. Singer. *Anglo-Saxon Magic and Medicine. Illustrated Specially from the Semi-Pagan Text Lacnunga.* Oxford, 1952.

Edit. Haddan, A. W., and W. Stubbs. *Councils and Ecclesiastical Documents Relating to Great Britain and Ireland.* 3 vols. Oxford, 1869–1878.

Edit. Hartmann, W. *Concilia Aevi Karolini 843–859.* Hanover, 1984.

Transl. Hollander, L. M. *Heimskringla.* Austin, Tex., 1964.

Edit. Howald E., and H. Sigerist. *Antonii Musae De Herba Vettonica, Liber Pseudoapulei Herbarius, Anonymi De Taxone Liber, Sexti Placiti Liber Medicinae Ex Animalibus. Corpus Medicorum Latinorum 4.* Teubner-Leipzig, 1927.

Edit. Huillier, A. *L' Vie de Saint Hugues.* Solesmes, 1888.

Transl. James, M. R. *The Apocryphal New Testament.* Oxford, 1924.

Transl. James, M. R. *Latin Infancy Gospels.* Cambridge, 1927.

Edit. Kemble, J. M. *The Dialogue of Solomon and Saturn.* London, 1848.

King, P. D. *Charlemagne: Translated Sources.* Lancaster, 1987.

Edit. Krapp , G. P., and E.V.K. Dobbie. *The Anglo-Saxon Poetic Records. A Collective Edition.* 5 vols. London and New York, 1931–1953.

Edit. Krusch, B. *MGH SRM* i–iii. Hanover, 1888–1896.

Edit. Krusch, B., and W. Levison, *MGH SRM* iv–vii. Hanover and Leipzig, 1902–1920.

Edit. Lehmann, K. *MHG Leges Nationum Germanicarum v. Leges Alamannorum.* Hanover, 1888.

Edit. Levison, W. *Vitae Sancti Bonifatii Archiepiscopi Moguntini.* Hanover and Leipzig, 1905.

Edit. Lipsius, R., and M. Bonnet. *Acta Apostolorum Apocrypha.* Leipzig, 1891.

Edit. Lowe, E. A. *The Bobbio Missal.* London, 1920.

Transl. Loyn, H. R., and J. Percival. *The Reign of Charlemagne.* London, 1975.

Edit. Maass, E. *Commentariorum in Aratum Reliquiae.* Berlin, 1898.

Edit. and *transl.* McCann, J., and P. Delatte. *The Rule of St. Benedict.* London, 1921.

Transl. McNeill, J. T., and H. M. Gamer. *Medieval Handbooks of Penance.* New York, 1938.

Edit. Maccray, W. D. *Chronicon Abbatiae Rameseiensis.* RS. London, 1886.

Transl. Magnusson, M., and H. Palsson. *Njal's Saga.* Harmondsworth, Middlesex, 1960.

Transl. Malan, S. C. *The Book of Adam and Eve.* London, 1882.

Edit. Massen, F. *MGH Concilia Aevi Merovingici i.* Hanover, 1893.

Transl. Meyer, R. T. *St. Athanasius, the Life of St. Antony.* Westminster, Md. and London, 1950.

Edit. Mohlberg, L. C. *Missale Gallicanum Vetus.* Rome, 1958.

Edit. Mohlberg, L. C. *Liber Sacramentorum Romanae Ecclesiae Ordinis Anni Circuli.* Rome, 1960.

Edit. Mohlberg, L. C. *Missale Gothicum.* Rome, 1961.

Edit. Pertz, G. H. *MGH SS* i–vii. Hanover, 1826–1846.

Transl. Pharr, C. *The Theodosian Code.* Princeton, 1952.

Edit. Plummer, C. *Vitae Sanctae Hiberniae* 2 vols. Oxford, 1910.

Edit. Rehm, B. *Die Pseudoklementinen.* Berlin, 1965.

Transl. Rivers, T. J. *Laws of the Alamans and the Bavarians.* Philadelphia, 1977.

Transl. Rivers, T. J. *Laws of the Salian and Ripuarian Franks.* New York, 1986.

Transl. Roberts, A. *The Works of Sulpitius Severus.* Grand Rapids, Mich., 1955.

Transl. Robertson, A. J. *The Laws of the Kings of England from Edmund to Henry I.* Cambridge, 1925.

Edit. Ruinart, T. *Acta Primorum Martyrum.* Amsterdam, 1713.

Edit. Sackur, E. *Sibyllinische Texte und Forschungen.* Halle, 1898.

Transl. Schach, P. *Eyrbyggja Saga.* Lincoln, 1959.

Edit. Schneemelcher, W. (*transl.* R. McL. Wilson). *New Testament Apocrypha.* Philadelphia, 1963.

Transl. Scholz, B. W., and B. Rogers. *Carolingian Chronicles.* Ann Arbor, Mich., 1950.

Edit. Schwerin, C. MGH *Fontes* iv. *Leges Saxonum und Lex Thuringorum.* Hanover, 1918.

Transl. Scott, S. P. *The Visigothic Code.* Boston, 1910.

Edit. Silk, E. T. *Saeculi Noni Auctoris in Boetii Consolationem Philosophiae Commentarius.* Papers and Monographs of the American Academy in Rome, 9. 1935.

Transl. Smith, T. *The Writings of Tatian and Theophilus and the Clementine Recognitions.* Edinburgh, 1867.

Transl. Smith, T. *The Clementine Homilies.* Edinburgh, 1870.

Edit. Stubbs, W. *Memorials of St. Dunstan Archbishop of Canterbury.* RS. London, 1874.

Transl. Talbot, C. H. *The Anglo-Saxon Missionaries in Germany.* London, 1954.

Edit. Waitz, G. MGH SS *Rerum Langobardicarum et Italicarum Saec. VI–IX.* Hanover, 1878.

Edit. Wasserschleben, F.W.H. *Die Bussordnungen der abendländischen Kirche.* Halle, 1851.

Edit. Wasserschleben, F.W.H. *Die Irische Kanonensammlung.* Leipzig, 1885.

Edit. Werminghoff, A. MGH *Concilia Aevi Karolini* ii. (1 and 2). Hanover, and Leipzig, 1869–1898.

Transl. Whitelock, D. *English Historical Documents* i. 2d ed. London, 1979.

Edit. and *transl.* Whitelock, D., M. Brett, C.N.L. Brooke. *Councils and Synods* i. Oxford, 1981.

Edit. Winnefeld, H. *Sortes Sangallenses Ineditae.* Bonn, 1887.

Edit. Wright, T. *Popular Treatises on Science Written During the Middle Ages in Anglo-Saxon, Anglo-Norman and English.* London, 1841.

Edit. Zeumer, K. MGH *Formulae Merowingici et Karolini Aevi.* Hanover, 1886.

Edit. Zeumer, K. MGH *Legum 1, Leges Visigothorum.* Hanover and Leipzig, 1902.

SECONDARY WORKS

Allen, D. C. *The Legend of Noah.* Urbana, Ill., 1949.

Anawati, G. "Introduction bibliographique à l'étude de la magie dans l'Islam." In *Études de Philosophie Musulmane,* 411–432. Paris, 1974.

Anderson, J. *The Witch on the Wall.* Copenhagen, 1977.

Edit. Anderson, G. H. *Studies in Philippine Church History.* Ithaca, N.Y., 1969.

Antropoff, R. von. *Die Entwicklung der Kenelm-Legende.* Bonn, 1965.

Assmann, B. "Eine Regel über den Donner." *Anglia* 10 (1888), 185–193.

Aubrun, M. "Caractères et portée religieuse et sociale des 'visiones' en occident du VIe ou XIe siècle." *Cahiers de Civilisation Médiévale* 23 (1980), 109–130.

Bächtold-Staübli, H., and E. Hoffman-Krayer. *Handwörterbuch des deutschen Aberglaubens.* 10 vols. Leipzig and Berlin, 1927–1942.

Balfour, H. "Concerning Thunderbolts." *Folklore* 40 (1929), 37–49.

Baltrusaitis, J. *Le Moyen Age Fantastique.* Paris, 1955.

———. *Reveils et Prodiges. Le Gothique Fantastique.* Paris, 1960.

Barb, A. A. "Birds and Medical Magic." *Journal of the Warburg and Courtauld Institute* 13 (1950), 316–322.

Bardy, G. "Melchisédech dans la tradition patristique." *Revue Biblique* 35 (1926), 496–509 and 36 (1927), 25–45.

Baring-Gould, S. *Curious Myths of the Middle Ages.* London, 1884.

Barley, N. F. "Anglo-Saxon Magico Medicine." *Anthropological Society of Oxford Journal* 3(2) (1972), 67–76.

Baroja, J. C. *Les Sorcières et leur Monde.* Paris, 1972.

Bartlett, R. *Trial by Fire and Water: The Medieval Judicial Ordeal.* Oxford, 1986.

Baur, C. S. *Jean Chrysostome et ses Oeuvres.* Louvain, 1907.

Bayerschmidt, C. F. "The Element of the Supernatural in the Sagas of Icelanders." In *edit.* C. F. Bayerschmidt and E. J. Friis. *Scandinavian Studies. Festschrift for Henry Goddard Leach,* 39–53. Seattle, 1965.

Beccaria, M. A. *I Codici di Medicina del Periodo Presalernitano.* Rome, 1956.

Bezold, F. von. "Astrologische Geschichtsconstruction im Mittelalter." *Deutsche Zeitschrift für Geschichtswissenschaft* 8 (2) (1892), 29–72.

Birch, W. de Gray. "On Two Anglo-Saxon Manuscripts in the British Museum." *Transactions of the Royal Society of Literature,* n.s., 11 (1878), 463–512.

Bischoff, B. "Die lateinischen Übersetzungen und Bearbeitungen aus den Oracula Sibyllina." *Mittelalterliche Studien* 1 (1966), 150–171.

Blau, L. *Das altjüdische Zauberwesen.* Berlin, 1914.

Bloch, R. *Les Prodiges dans l'Antiquité Classique.* Paris, 1963.

Blumenkranz, B. *Les Auteurs Chrétiens Latins du Moyen Age.* Paris, 1963.

Boas, G. *Essays on Primitivism and Related Ideas in the Middle Ages.* New York, 1948.

Bober, H. "The Zodiacal Miniature of the Très Riches Heures of the Duke of Berry—Its Sources and Meaning." *Journal of the Warburg and Courtauld Institute* 11 (1948), 1–34.

Boer, E. "Aus der Arbeit am Katalog der astrologischen Handschriften des lateinischen Mittelalters." *Helikon* 4 (1964), 392–396.

Boese, R. *Superstitiones Arelatenses e Caesario Collectae.* Marburg, 1909.

Boglioni, P. "Miracle et nature chez Grégoire le Grand." In *Cahiers d'Etudes Medievales* 1. *Épopées, légendes et miracles*, 11–102. Montreal, 1974.

Edit. Boglioni, P. *La Culture Populaire au Moyen Age.* Montreal, 1979.

Boll, F., C. Bezold, and W. Gundel. *Sternglaube und Sterndeutung.* Leipzig and Berlin, 1931.

Bolte, J. "Zur Geschichte der Losbücher." In *Georg Wickrams Werke IV. Bibliothek der lit. Vereins in Stuttgart*, 276–348. Tübingen, 1903.

Bonnard, R. "Notes sur l'astrologie latine du VIe siècle." *Revue Belge de Philologie et d'Histoire* 10 (1931), 557–577.

Bonner, C. *Studies in Magical Amulets, Chiefly Greco-Egyptian.* Ann Arbor, Mich., 1950.

Bonser, W. "The Significance of Colour in Ancient and Medieval Magic, with Some Modern Comparisons." *Man* 25 (1925), 194–198.

———. "The Dissimilarity of Ancient Irish Magic from That of the Anglo-Saxons." *Folklore* 37 (1926), 271–288.

———. "Magical Practices against Elves." *Folklore* 37 (1926), 356–363.

———. "Survivals of Paganism in Anglo-Saxon England." *Transactions of the Birmingham Archeological Society* 56 (1932), 37–70.

———. "Anglo-Saxon Laws and Charms Relating to Theft." *Folklore* 57 (1946), 7–11.

———. *The Medical Background of Anglo-Saxon England.* London, 1963.

Botte, B. *Les Origines de la Noël et de l'Epiphanie.* Louvain 1932.

Bouché-Leclercq, A. *Histoire de la Divination dans l'Antiquité.* 4 vols. Paris, 1879–1882.

Boudriot, W. *Die altgermanische Religion in der amtlichen kirchlichen Literatur des Abendlandes vom 5. bis 11. Jahrhundert.* Bonn, 1928.

Boyancé, P. "La religion astrale de Platon à Ciceron." *Revue des Études Grecques* 65 (1952), 312–349.

Braekman, W. L. "Fortune-telling by the Casting of Dice." *Studia Neophilologica* 52 (1980), 3–29.

Brooke, C. and R. *Popular Religion 1000–1300*. London, 1984.

Browe, P. "Die Eucharistie als Zaubermittel im Mittelalter." *Archiv für Kulturgeschichte* 20 (1930), 134–154.

———. *Beiträge zur Sexualethik des Mittelalters*. Breslau, 1932.

———. *Die Verehrung der Eucharistie im Mittelalter*. Munich, 1933.

———. *Die Eucharistischen Wünder des Mittelalters*. Breslau, 1938.

Brown, G. B. *The Arts in Early England*. 6 vols. London, 1903–1937.

Brown, G. H. "Solving the 'Solve' Riddle in B.L. MS. Harley 585." *Viator* 18 (1987), 45–51.

Brown, P. *Augustine of Hippo*. London, 1967.

———. *Religion and Society in the Age of St. Augustine*. London, 1972.

———. *Society and the Holy in Late Antiquity*. Berkeley, 1982.

Bruce-Mitford, R. *Aspects of Anglo-Saxon Archaeology*. London, 1974.

Edit. Buck, L. P., and J. W. Zophy. *The Social History of the Reformation*. Columbus, Ohio, 1972.

Buhler, C. F. "Prayers and Charms in Middle English Scrolls." *Speculum* 39 (1964), 270–278.

Bulliot, J. G., and F. Thiollier. *La Mission et le Culte de Saint Martin d'après les Légendes et les Monuments Populaires dans le Pays Eduen*. Autun and Paris, 1892.

Burke, P. "A Question of Acculturation." In *edit.* P. Zambelli. *Scienze, Credenze Occulte, Livelli di Cultura*, pp. 197–204. Florence, 1982.

Butler, E. M. *The Myth of the Magus*. Cambridge, 1948.

———. *Ritual Magic*. Cambridge, 1949.

Cameron, A. M. "The Byzantine Sources of Gregory of Tours." *Journal of Theological Studies* 26 (1975), 421–426.

Cameron, M. L. "Bald's Leechbook: Its Sources and Their Use in its Compilation." *Anglo-Saxon England* 12 (1983), 153–182.

Edit. Caquot A., and M. Leibovici, *La Divination*. Paris, 1968.

Carcopino, J. *Études d'Histoire Chrétienne. Le Christianisme Secret du Carré Magique. Les Fouilles de Saint Pierre et la Tradition*. Paris, 1953.

Carmody, F. J. *Arabic Astronomical and Astrological Sciences in Latin Translation. A Critical Bibliography*. Berkeley and Los Angeles, 1956.

Cawte, E. C. *Ritual Animal Disguise*. Cambridge, 1978.

Chadwick, H. *Alexandrian Christianity*. London, 1954.

———. *Priscillian of Avila*. Oxford, 1976.

Chaney, W. A. "Paganism to Christianity in Anglo-Saxon England." *Harvard Theological Review* 53 (1960), 197–217.

Charmasson, Th. *Recherches sur une Technique Divinatoire: la Géomancie dans l'Occident Médiéval*. Paris, 1980.

Clark, S. "Protestant Demonology: Sin, Superstition, and Society (c. 1520–1630)." In *edit.* B. Ankarloo and G. Henningsen, *Early Modern European Witchcraft: Centres and Peripheries*, 45–81. Oxford, 1989.

Cohn, N. *Europe's Inner Demons*. New York, 1975.

Colman, R. V. "Reason and Unreason in Early Medieval Law." *Journal of Interdisciplinary History* 4 (1974), 571–591.

Combarieu, J. *Études de Philologie Musicale*. 3. *La Musique et la Magie*. Paris, 1909.

Cooper, H. "Magic That Does Not Work." *Medievalia et Humanistica* 5 (1976), 131–146.

Courcelle, P. "Source Chrétienne et allusions paiennes de l'episode du 'Tolle, lege' (Saint Augustin, Confessions VIII, 12, 19)." *Revue d'Histoire et de Philosophie Religieuses* 32 (1952), 171–200.

———. "L'enfant et les 'sorts bibliques.' " *Vigiliae Christianae* 7 (1953), 194–220.

Cramp, R., and R. N. Bailey. *Corpus of Anglo-Saxon Stone Sculpture*. Oxford, for the British Academy, 1984–1988, ongoing.

Crawford, J. "Evidences for Witchcraft in Anglo-Saxon England." *Medium Aevum* 32 (1963), 99–116.

Cumont, F.V.M. "Astrologica." *Revue Archéologique* 5 (1916), 1–22.

———. *Lux Perpetua*. Paris, 1949.

d'Alverny, M.-Th. "Recréations monastiques. Les couteaux à manche d'ivoire." in *Recueil de Travaux Offert à M. Clovis Brunel* i, 10–32. Paris, 1955.

———. "Les anges et les jours." *Cahiers Archéologiques* 9 (1957), 271–300.

———. "La Survivance de la magie antique." In edit. P. Wipert, *Antike und Orient im Mittelalter*, 154–178. Berlin, 1962.

———. "Astrologues et théologiens au XIIe siècle." In *Mélanges offerts à M.D. Chenu*, 31–50. Bibliothèque Thomiste 37. Paris, 1967.

Daniélou, J. "Les démons de l'air dans la 'Vie d'Antoine.' " *Studia Anselmiana* 38 (1956), 136–147.

———. (transl. D. Heimann). *The Angels and Their Mission*. Westminster, Md., 1957.

Davis, N. Z. *Society and Culture in Early Modern France*. London, 1975.

Delatte, A. *Herbarius. Recherches sur le Cérémonial usité chez les Anciens pour la Cueillette des Simples et des Plantes Magiques*. 3d ed. Paris, 1961.

Delaunay, P. *La Médicine et l'Église*. Paris, 1948.

Delehaye, H. *Les Légendes Hagiographiques*. Brussels, 1906.

Delhaye, P. "Le dossier anti-matrimonial de l' 'Adversus Jovinianum' et son influence sur quelques écrits latins du XIIe siècle." *Medieval Studies* 13 (1951), 65–86.

Delumeau, J. *Documents de l'Histoire de Bretagne*. Toulouse, 1971.

———. *La Peur en Occident XIVe-XVIIIe Siècles*. Paris, 1978.

———. *Le Péché et la Peur. La Culpabilisation en Occident XIIIe-XVIIIe Siècles*. Paris, 1983.

de Mély, F. *Du Rôle des Pierres Gravées au Moyen Age*. Lille, 1893.

de Mély, F., M. H. Courel, and C. E. Ruelle. *Les Lapidaires de l'Antiquité et du Moyen Age*. 3 vols. Paris, 1898–1902.

de Nie, G. *Views from a Many-Windowed Tower: Studies of Imagination in the Works of Gregory of Tours*. Amsterdam, 1987.

de Nussac, L. "Les fontaines en Limousin." *Bulletin du comité des travaux historiques et scientifiques* (1897), 153–159.

Deonna, W. "Abra, Abraca, la croix talisman de Lausanne." *Genava* 22 (1944), 116–137.

Destombes, M. "Un astrolabe carolingien et l'origine de nos chiffres arabes." *Archives Internationales d'Histoire des Sciences* 58–59 (1962), 3–45.

Devisse, J. *Hincmar Archévêque de Reims 845–882*. 3 vols. Paris, 1973–1976.

de Vogüé, A. "Grégoire le Grand et ses 'Dialogues' d'après deux ouvrages récents." *Revue d'Histoire Ecclésiastique* 83 (1988), 281–348.

de Vries, J. *Altgermanische Religionsgeschichte*. 2 vols. 2d ed. Berlin, 1956–1957.

Diepgen, P. "De improbatione maleficiorum." *Archiv für Kulturgeschichte* 9 (1912), 385–403.

———. *Traum und Traumdeutung als medizinisch-naturwissenschaftliches Problem im Mittelalter*. Berlin, 1912.

Doble, G. H. "Hagiography and Folklore." *Folklore* 54 (1943), 321–333.

Dold, A., and R. Meister. "Die Orakelsprüche im St. Galler Palimpsestcodex 908 (die sogennten 'Sortes Sangallenses')." *Österreichische Akademie der Wissenschaften. philosophisch-historische Klasse Sitzungsberichte* 225, Abh. 4. Vienna, 1948.

Dornseiff, F. *Das Alphabet in Mystik und Magie*. Berlin, 1922.

Edit. Douglas, M. *Witchcraft Confessions and Accusations*. London, 1970.

Douglas, M. "The Problem of Evil among the Lele. Sorcery, Manicheeism and Christian Teaching in Africa." Unpublished paper.

Duerig, W. "Das Ordal der Psalterprobe in Codex Latinus Monacensis 100. Ihr liturgietheologischer Hintergrund." *Münchener theologische Zeitschrift* 24 (1973), 266–278.

Eis, G. *Altdeutsche Zaubersprüche*. Berlin, 1964.

Eisler, R. *Weltenmantel und Himmelzeit*. 2 vols. Munich, 1910.

Éliàde, M. *Le Chamanisme et les Techniques Archaïques de l'Extase*. Paris, 1951.

———. "Some Observations on European Witchcraft." *History of Religions* 14 (1975), 149–172.

———. "History of Religions and 'Popular' Cultures." *History of Religions* 20 (1980), 1–26.

G. Ellard. "Devotion to the Holy Cross and a Dislocated Mass Text." *Theological Studies* 11 (1950), 333–355.

Elliott, R.W.V. "Runes, Yews and Magic." *Speculum* 32 (1957), 250–261.

Ellis, H. R. *The Road to Hel*. Cambridge, 1943.

Evans J., and M. S. Serjeantson, *English Medieval Lapidaries*. London, 1933.

Evans-Pritchard, E. E. *Witchcraft, Oracles and Magic among the Azande*. Oxford, 1937.

Fehr, B. "Altenglische Ritualtexte für Krankenbesuch, heilige Ölung und Begräbnis." In *edit*. M. Förster et al. *Texte und Forschungen zur englischen Kulturgeschichte. Festgabe für Felix Liebermann*, 20–67. Halle, 1921.

Fernandez, P. *The History of the Church in the Philippines (1521–1898)*. Manila, 1979.

Finch, C. E. "Excerpts from Pliny's *Natural History* in Codices Reg. Lat. 309 and Vat. Lat. 645." *Transactions and Proceedings of the American Philological Association* 96 (1965), 107–117.

Fischer, A. *Aberglaube unter den Angelsachsen*. Meiningen, 1891.

Flade, G. "Germanisches Heidentum und christliches Erziehungsbemühen in karolingischer Zeit nach Regino von Prüm." *Theologische Studien und Kritiken* 106 (1934–1935), 213–240.

Flandrin, J. T. *Un Temps pour Embrasser*. Paris, 1983.

Flint, V.I.J. *Ideas in the Medieval West* III. London, 1988.

———. "The Early Medieval 'Medicus,' the Saint—and the Enchanter." *Social History of Medicine* 2(2) (1989), 127–145.

———. "The Transmission of Astrology in the Early Middle Ages." *Viator* 21 (1990), 1ff.

Flom, G. T. "On the Old English Herbal of Apuleius, Vitellius C.III." *Journal of English and Germanic Philology* 40 (1941), 29–37.

Fontaine, J. "Isidore de Séville et l'astrologie." *Revue des Études Latines* 31 (1953), 271–300.

———. *Isidore de Seville et la culture classique dans l'Espagne Wizigothique*. 2 vols. Paris, 1959.

Förster, M. "Ae. fregen 'Die Frage'." *Englischer Studien* 36 (1906), 325–328.

———. "Beiträge zur mittelalterlichen Volkskunde." *Archiv für das Studium der neueren Sprachen* 120 (1908), 43–51; 121 (1908), 30–46; 125 (1910), 39–70; 128 (1912), 31–84; 285–308; 129 (1912), 16–49; 134 (1916), 264–293.

———. "Die Weltzeitalter bei den Angelsachsen." *Neusprachliche Studien. Festgabe K. Luick dargebracht*, 183–203. Marburg, 1925.

———. "Die altenglische Traumlunare." *Englischer Studien* 60 (1925–1926), 58–93.

———. "Die altenglischen Verzeichnisse von Glücks- und Unglückstagen." In *edit*. K. Malone, et al. *Studies in English Philology. A Miscellany in Honor of Frederick Klaeber*, 258–277. Minneapolis, 1929.

———. "Zwei kymrische Orakelalphabete für Psalterwahrsagung." *Zeitschrift für Celtische Philologie* 20 (1935), 228–233.

———. "Zur Geschichte des Reliquienkultus in Altengland." *Sitzungsberichte der Bayerische Akademie der Wissenschaften, phil.-hist. Klasse* (1943), 1–148.

Förster, M. "Vom Fortleben antiker Samellunare im Englischen und in anderen Volkssprachen." *Anglia* 67 (1944), 1–171.

Edit. Forster R., and O. Ranum, *Ritual, Religion and the Sacred.* Baltimore, 1982.

Fournier, P. "Études critiques sur le Décret de Burchard de Worms." *Nouvelle Revue Historique de Droit Francais et Etranger* 24 (1910), 40–112, 213–221, 289–331, 564–584.

———. "Le Decret de Burchard de Worms. Ses caractères, son influence." *Revue d'Histoire Ecclésiastique* 12 (1911), 451–473, 671–701.

Fowler, R. "A Late Old English Handbook for the Use of a Confessor." *Anglia* 83 (1965), 1–34.

Frank, R., and A. Cameron. *A Plan for the Dictionary of Old English.* Toronto, 1973.

Franz, A. *Die Messe im Deutschen Mittelalter.* Freiburg-im-Breisgau, 1902.

———. *Die Kirchlichen Benediktionen im Mittelalter.* 2 vols. Graz, 1909.

Fridrichsen, A. *Le Problème du Miracle dans le Christianisme Primitif.* Strasbourg, 1925.

Friedman, J. B. *The Monstrous Races in Medieval Art and Literature.* Cambridge, Mass., 1981.

Fryer, A. C. "Theophilus the Penitent as Represented in Art." *Archeological Journal* 92 (1935), 287–333.

Gaiffier, B. de. "L'hagiographe et son public au XIᵉ siècle." In *Miscellanea L. Van der Essen* i, 135–166. Brussels, 1947.

———. "De l'usage et de la lecture du Martyrologie." *Analecta Bollandiana* 79 (1961), 40–59.

———. *Études Critiques d'Hagiographie et d'Iconologie.* Brussels, 1967.

Geary, P. *Furta Sacra.* Princeton, 1978.

———. "La coercition des saints dans la pratique religieuse médiévale." In *edit.* P. Boglioni, *La Culture,* 147–160.

Geertz, H., and K. Thomas. "An Anthropology of Religion and Magic. Two views." *The Journal of Interdisciplinary History* 6 (1975–1976), 71–109.

Gero, S. "The Legend of the Fourth Son of Noah." *Harvard Theological Review* 73 (1980), 321–330.

Gerould, G. H. *Saints' Legends.* Boston, 1916.

Ginzberg, L. *The Legends of the Jews.* 7 vols. Philadelphia, 1909–1938.

Ginzburg, C. *The Night Battles.* London, 1972.

Goldschmidt, A. *Die Elfenbeinskulpturen aus der Zeit der karolingischen und sächsischen Kaiser.* 3 vols. Berlin, 1914–1923.

Gougaud, L. "La Danse dans les Églises." *Revue d'Histoire Écclésiastique* 15 (1914), 229–245.

———. "La prière de Charlemagne et les pièces apocryphes apparentés." *Revue d'Histoire Ecclésiastique* 20 (1924), 211–238.

Grant, R.J.S. *Cambridge, Corpus Christi College 41: The Loricas and the Missal.* Amsterdam, 1979.

Grendon, F. "The Anglo Saxon Charms." *Journal of American Folklore* 22 (1909), 105–237.

Grimm, J.L.K. (transl. J. S. Stalybrass). *Teutonic Mythology,* 4 vols. London, 1880–1888.

———. *Kleinerer Schriften.* 8 vols. Berlin, 1865–1890.

Gundel, W. *Neue astrologische Texte des Hermes Trismegistos, Abhandlungen der Bayr. Akad. d. Wiss.* Munich, 1936.

Hair, P. *Before the Bawdy Court.* London, 1972.

Hamilton, G. L. "Storm-making Springs." *Romanic Review* 2 (4) (1911) 355–375; 5 (3) (1914) 213–237.

Hampson, R. T. *Medii Aevi Kalendarium.* 2 vols. London, 1841.

Hansen, J. *Zauberwahn, Inquisition und Hexenprozess.* Munich, 1900.

Harmening, D. *Superstitio. Überlieferungs—und theoriegeschichtliche Untersuchungen zur kirchlich-theologischen Aberglaubensliteratur des Mittelalters.* Berlin, 1979.

Harris, J. R. "The Sortes Sanctorum in the St. Germain Codex ('g')." *American Journal of Philology* 9 (1888), 58–63.

Hart, C. "The Ramsey Computus." *English Historical Review* 85 (1970), 29–44.

Harvey, E. R. *The Inward Wits: Psychological Theory in the Middle Ages and Renaissance.* London, 1975.

Haskins, C. H. "The Reception of Arabic Science in England." *English Historical Review* 30 (1915), 56–69.

Henel, H. "Altenglischer Mönchsaberglaube." *Englischer Studien* 69 (1934–1935), 329–349.

———. *Studien zum altenglischen Computus.* Leipzig, 1934.

Hildburgh, W. L. "Psychology Underlying the Employment of Amulets in Europe." *Folklore* 62 (1951), 231–251.

Hill, T. D. "The Aecerbot Charm and Its Christian User." *Anglo Saxon England* 6 (1977), 213–221.

Hine, H. W. "Seneca and Anaxagoras in Pseudo-Bede's De Mundi Celestis Terrestrisque Constitutione." *Viator* 19 (1988), 111–127.

Holthausen, F. "Rezepte, Segen und Zaubersprüche aus zwei Handschriften." *Anglia* 19 (1897), 75–88.

Hope, R. C. *The Legendary Lore of the Holy Wells of England.* London, 1893.

Hope-Taylor, B. *Yeavering.* London, 1977.

Edit. Horstmann, C. *The Three Kings of Cologne.* EETS. London, 1886.

Hoyoux, J. "Le collier de Clovis." *Revue Belge de Philologie et d'Histoire* 21 (1942), 169–174.

Hübner, W. "Das Horoskop der Christen." *Vigiliae Christianae* 29 (1975), 120–137.

Hübner, W. *Zodiacus Christianus*. Beiträge zur klassischen Philologie 144. Konigstein, 1983.

Hurt, J. *Aelfric*. New York, 1972.

James, E. O. "The Influence of Christianity on Folklore." *Folk-lore* 58 (1947), 361–376.

——. *Seasonal Feasts and Festivals*. New York, 1962.

James, M. R. "Apocrypha Anecdota." *Texts and Studies* 2:3, v. 5 (1891).

Jolly, K. L. "Anglo-Saxon Charms in the Context of a Christian World View." *Journal of Medieval History* 11 (1985), 279–293.

Jones, C. W. *Bedae Pseudepigrapha*. New York, 1938.

Jordan, D. R. "A Survey of Greek Defixiones Not Included in the Special Corpora." *Greek, Roman and Byzantine Studies* 26 (2) (1985), 151–197.

——. "Defixiones from a Well near the Southwest Corner of the Athenian Agora." *Hesperia* 54 (1985), 205–252.

Joret, C. *Les Plantes dans l'Antiquité et au Moyen Age, Histoire, Usages et Symbolisme*. 2 vols. Paris, 1897 and 1904.

Jungmann, J. A. (*transl.* F. A. Brunner). *The Mass of the Roman Rite*. 2 vols. New York, 1951–1955.

Kambitsis, S. "Une nouvelle tablette magique d'Egypte, Musée du Louvre, inv. e. 27145–iiie/ive siècle." *Bulletin de l'Institut français d'Archéologie Oriental* 76 (1976), 213–223.

Edit. Kaplan, S. L. *Understanding Popular Culture*. Berlin, 1984.

Karras, R. M. "Pagan Survivals and Syncretism in the Conversion of Saxony." *Catholic Historical Review* 72 (1986), 553–572.

Katzenstein, R. *The Leiden Aratea: Ancient Constellations in a Medieval Manuscript*. J. Paul Getty Museum. Malibu, 1988.

Kee, H. C. *Miracle in the Early Christian World*. New Haven, 1983.

——. *Medicine, Miracle and Magic in New Testament Times*. Cambridge, 1986.

Kehrer, H. *Die heiligen drei Könige in Literatur und Kunst*. 2 vols. Leipzig, 1908.

Keller, H. "Zum sogennanten Reliquienschrein Ottos des Grossen in Quedlinburg." *Dumbarton Oaks Papers* 41 (1987), 261–264.

Kent, K. P. *Navajo Weaving*. Santa Fe, 1985.

Ker, N. R. "An Eleventh Century Old English Legend of the Cross before Christ." *Medium Aevum* 9 (1940), 84–85.

——. *A Catalogue of Manuscripts Containing Anglo-Saxon*. Oxford, 1957.

Kiessling, E. *Zauberei in den germanischen Volksrechten*. Jena, 1941.

Kiessling, N. *The Incubus in English Literature: Provenance and Progeny*. Washington, 1977.

King, C. W. *The Natural History, Ancient and Modern of Precious Stones and Gems*. London, 1865.

King, V. H. *An Investigation of Some Astronomical Excerpts from Pliny's Natural*

History Found in Manuscripts of the Earlier Middle Ages. Unpublished Oxford B.Litt., 1970.

Kitson, P. "Lapidary Traditions in Anglo-Saxon England." *Anglo-Saxon England* 12 (1983), 73–123.

Kittredge, G. L. *Witchcraft in Old and New England.* Cambridge, Mass., 1927.

Klapper, J. "Das Gebet im Zauberglauben des Mittelalters." *Mitteilungen der schlesischen Gesellschaft für Volkskunden* 18 (1907), 5–41.

Klibansky, R., E. Panofsky, and F. Saxl. *Saturn and Melancholy.* London, 1964.

Kottje, R. *Die Bussbücher Halitgars von Cambrai und des Hrabanus Maurus.* Berlin, 1980.

Kunz, G. F. *The Curious Lore of Precious Stones.* Philadelphia, 1913.

———. *The Magic of Jewels and Charms.* Philadelphia, 1915.

Labriolle, P. de "Le 'Demon de Midi.' " *Bulletin du Cange* 9 (1934), 46–54.

Lascault, G. *Le Monstre dans l'Art Occidental.* Paris, 1973.

Laistner, M.L.W. "A Ninth Century Commentator on the Gospel according to Matthew." *Harvard Theological Review* 20 (1927), 129–145.

Laistner, M.L.W. "The Western Church and Astrology during the Early Middle Ages." *Harvard Theological Review* 34 (1941), 251–275. Reprinted in idem. *The Intellectual Heritage of the Early Middle Ages,* 57–82. New York, 1959.

Lawrence, P. *Road Belong Cargo.* Manchester, 1964.

Lea, H. C. *Materials towards a History of Witchcraft.* 3 vols. Philadelphia, 1939.

Leclercq, J. "Aux origines du Cycle de Noël." *Ephemerides Liturgicae* 60 (1946), 7–26.

Lecouteux, C. "Hagazussa-Striga-Hexe." *Études Germaniques* 38 (1985), 161–178.

Le Diable au Moyen Age: Doctrine, Problèmes Moraux, Representations. 3ᵉ Colloque organisé par le Cuerma, Aix-en-Provence les 3–4–5 Mars 1978. Aix-en-Provence, Paris, 1979.

Lemarié, J. *La Manifestation du Seigneur.* Paris, 1957.

Lenormant, F. *A Travers l'Apulie et la Lucanie.* 2 vols. Paris, 1883.

Levison, W. *England and the Continent in the Eighth Century.* Oxford, 1946.

Lewis, J. P. *A Study of the Interpretation of Noah and the Flood in Jewish and Christian Literature.* Leiden, 1968.

Liebermann, H. *Die heiligen Englands.* Hanover, 1889.

Liebeschütz, H. "Windkräfte und Sternenkräfte." In idem, *Das allegorische Weltbild der heiligen Hildegard von Bingen,* 72–86. Leipzig and Berlin, 1930.

Lieftinck, G. I. *Manuscrits Datés Conservés dans les Pays Bas* i. Amsterdam, 1964.

Lloyd, G.E.R. *Magic, Reason and Experience.* Cambridge, 1979.

Loewenthal, L.J.A. "Amulets in Medieval Sculpture." *Folklore* 89 (1978), 3–12.

Loomis, C. Grant. *White Magic. An Introduction to the Folklore of Christian Legend.* Cambridge, Mass., 1948.

Lucius, E. *Die Anfänge des Heiligencultus in der christlichen Kirche.* Tübingen, 1904.

Luck, G. *Hexen und Zauberei in der römischen Dichtung.* Zurich, 1962.

McCall, A. *The Medieval Underworld.* London, 1979.

McGurk, P. "Germanici Caesaris Aratea cum Scholiis: A New Illustrated Witness from Wales." *National Library of Wales Journal* 18 (1973–1974), 197–216.

McKenna, S. *Paganism and Pagan Survivals in Spain up to the Fall of the Visigothic Kingdom.* Washington, 1938.

MacKinney, L. C. *Early Medieval Medicine, with Special Reference to France and Chartres.* Baltimore, 1937.

———. "An Unpublished Treatise on Medicine and Magic from the Age of Charlemagne." *Speculum* 18 (1943), 494–96.

———. "Medical Ethics and Etiquette in the Early Middle Ages: The Persistence of Hippocratic Ideals." *Bulletin of the History of Medicine* 26 (1952), 1–31.

McNeill, J. T. "Folk Paganism in the Penitentials." *Journal of Religion* 13 (1933), 450–66.

Maeyvaert, P. "The Enigma of Gregory the Great's Dialogues: A Response to Francis Clark." *Journal of Ecclesiastical History* 39 (1988), 335–381.

Magie, Sorcellerie, Parapsychologie. Editions de l'Université de Bruxelles. Brussels, 1984.

Majno, G. *The Healing Hand: Man and Wound in the Ancient World.* Cambridge, Mass., 1975.

Manitius, K. "Magic und Rhetorik bei Anselm von Besate." *Deutsches Archiv* 12 (1956), 52–72.

Manselli, R. "Simbolisme e magia nell' alto medioevo." In *Simboli e Simbologia nell' Alto Medioevo,* 293–348. Spoleto, 1976.

Margoulias, H. J. "The Lives of Byzantine Saints as Sources of Data for the History of Magic in the Sixth and Seventh Centuries A.D.: Sorcery, Relics and Icons." *Byzantion* 37 (1967), 228–269.

Marsh-Edwards, J. C. "The Magi in Tradition and Art." *Irish Ecclesiastical Record* 85 (1956), 1–9.

Maurice, J. "La terreur de la magie au IVᵉ siècle." *Revue Historique de droit Francais et Etranger* 4 (1927), 108–120.

Maury, L.F.A. *La Magie et L'Astrologie dans l'Antiquité et au Moyen Age.* Paris, 1860.

———. *Croyances et Légendes du Moyen Age.* Paris, 1896.

Mead, G.R.S. *Simon Magus.* London, 1892.

Meaney, A. L. "Aethelweard, Aelfric, the Norse Gods and Northumbria." *Journal of Religious History* 6 (1970), 105–132.

———. *Anglo-Saxon Amulets and Curing Stones.* Oxford, 1981.

———. "Variant Versions of Old English Medical Remedies and the Compilation of Bald's Leechbook." *Anglo Saxon England* 13 (1984), 235–268.

———. "Aelfric and idolatry." *Journal of Religious History* 13 (1984), 119–135.

———. "Aelfric's Use of his Sources in His Homily on Auguries." *English Studies* 66 (1985), 285–295.

Meier, C. *Gemma Spiritalis: Methode und Gebrauch der Edelsteinallegorese vom frühen Christentum bis ins 18. Jahrhundert i.* Munich, 1977.

Mercier, C. A. *Astrology in Medicine.* London, 1914.

Meyer, R. M. *Altgermanische Religionsgeschichte.* Leipzig, 1910.

Mirmont, H. de la Ville de. *L'Astrologie chez les Gallo-Romains.* Bordeaux, 1904.

Morin, G. "The Homilies of Caesarius of Arles." *Orate Fratres* 14 (1938–1940), 481–486.

Morris, R. *Legends of the Holy Rood.* EETS. London, 1871.

Muller, H.-G. *Hrabanus Maurus. De Laudibus Sanctae Crucis.* Dusseldorf, 1973.

Münter, D. F. *Der Stern der Weisen. Untersuchungen über das Geburtsjahr Christi.* Copenhagen, 1827.

Napier, A. S. *History of the Holy Rood Tree.* EETS. London, 1894.

Nauert, C. G. "C. Plinius Secundus (Naturalis Historia)." In *edit.* P. O. Kristeller, *Catalogus Translationum et Commentariorum: Medieval and Renaissance Translations and Commentaries* 4,296–422. Washington, D.C., 1979.

Naumann, H. *Notker's Boethius.* Strassburg, 1913.

Nelson, J. L. *Politics and Ritual in Early Medieval Europe.* London, 1986.

Edit. Newall, V. *The Witch Figure.* London, 1973.

Nielsen, K. M. "Runen und Magie: ein forschungsgeschichtlicher Uberblick." *Frühmittelalterliche Studien* 19 (1985), 74–97.

Nikolskii, N. M. (transl. G. Petzold). *Spüren magischer Formeln in den Psalmen.* Giessen, 1927.

Edit. Niles, J. D. *Old English Literature in Context.* Cambridge, 1980.

Nilsson, M. P. "Problems of the History of Greek Religion in the Hellenistic and Roman Age." *Harvard Theological Review* 36 (1943), 251–275.

Noonan, J. T. "Power to Choose." *Viator* 4 (1973), 419–434.

Nordenfalk, C. "A Tenth Century Gospel Book in the Walters Art Gallery." In *edit.* U. E. McCracken et al., *Gatherings in Honor of Dorothy E. Miner*, 139–170. Baltimore, 1974.

North, J. D. "Astrology and the Fortunes of Churches." *Proceedings of the Second International Colloquium on Ecclesiastical History*, 181–211. Oxford, September, 1974.

Notestein, W. *A History of Witchcraft in England from 1558 to 1718.* New York, 1911.

Edit. Oswald, A. *The Church of St. Bertelin, Stafford, and the Cross.* Birmingham, 1955.

Owen, G. W. *Rites and Religions of the Anglo-Saxons.* London and Totowa, N.J., 1981.

Page, R. I. "Anglo Saxon Runes and Magic." *Journal of the Archaeological Association* 27 (1964), 14–31.

Palmer, P. M., and R. P. More, *The Sources of the Faust Tradition from Simon Magus to Lessing.* New York, 1936.

Pannier, L. *Les Lapidaires Français du Moyen Age.* Paris, 1882.

Paul, L. and B. D. "The Maya Midwife as Sacred Professional: A Guatemalan Case." *American Ethnologist* 2 (1975), 707–726.

Pépin, J. *Théologie Cosmique et Théologie Chrétienne.* Paris, 1964.

Peters, E. *The Magician, the Witch and the Law.* Philadelphia, 1978.

Petersen, J. M. *The Dialogues of Gregory the Great in Their Late Antique Cultural Background.* Toronto, 1984.

Petraglio, R., et al. *L'Apocalypse de Jean. Traditions Exégetiques et Iconographiques IIIᵉ–XIIIᵉ Siècles.* Actes du Colloque de la Fondation Hart 29 Fevrier–3 Mars 1976. Geneva, 1979.

Phelan, J. L. *The Hispanization of the Philippines. Spanish Aims and Philippine Responses 1565–1700.* Madison, 1959.

Philippson, E. A. *Germanisches Heidentum bei den Angelsachsen.* Leipzig, 1929.

Pingree, D. "The Diffusion of Arabic Magical Texts in Western Europe." In *La Diffusione delle Scienze Islamiche nel Medio Evo Europeo,* Accademia Nazionale dei Lincei, 57–101. Rome, 1987.

Pinto, L. B. "Medical Science and Superstition: A Report on a Unique Medical Scroll of the Eleventh–Twelfth Century." *Manuscripta* 17 (1973), 12–21.

Piper, F. *Mythologie und Symbolik der christlichen Kunst von der altesten Zeit bis ins sechzehnte Jahrhundert.* Weimar, 1847–1851. Reprint. Ann Arbor, Mich., 1978.

Plessner, M. *Picatrix.* Warburg and London, 1962.

Poulin, J.-C. *L'Idéal de la Sainteté dans l'Aquitaine Carolingienne.* Québec, 1975.

———. "Entre magie et religion. Recherches sur les utilisations marginales de l'écrit dans la culture populaire du haut moyen age." In *edit.* P. Boglioni, *La Culture,* 123–143.

Poulle, E. "Les instruments astronomiques de l'occident latin au XIᵉ et XIIᵉ siècles." *Cahiers de Civilisation Médiévale* 15 (1972), 27–40.

Puhlmann, W. "Die lateinische medizinische Literatur des frühen Mittelalters." *Kyklos* 3 (1930), 395–416.

Raboteau, A. J. *Slave Religion*. Oxford, 1978.

Raith, J. *Die altenglische Version des Halitgarischen Büssbuches*. Hamburg, 1933.

Regnault, J. *La Sorcellerie: ses Rapports avec les Sciences Biologiques*. Paris, 1897.

Reinach, S. "Les monuments de pierre brute." *Revue Archéologique* 21 (1893), 195–226.

Reinsma, L. M. *Aelfric. An Annotated Bibliography*. New York and London, 1987.

Reviron, J. *Jonas d'Orléans et son 'De Institutione Regia.'* Paris, 1930.

Richards, H. J. "The Three Kings." *Scripture* 8 (1956), 23–28.

Riché, P. "La Magie a l'époque Carolingienne." *Académie dans Inscriptions et Belles-Lettres, Comptes Rendue des Séances de l'année 1973, Janvier-Mars*, 127–38.

Riddle, J. "The Introduction and Use of Eastern Drugs in the Early Middle Ages." *Sudhoffs Archiv für Geschichte der Medizin* 49 (1965), 185–198.

———. "Theory and Practice in Medieval Medicine." *Viator* 5 (1974), 157–184.

———. "Oral Contraceptives and Early Term Abortifacients during Classical Antiquity and the Middle Ages." Unpublished paper.

Riesman, D. *The Story of Medicine in the Middle Ages*. New York, 1935.

Ritzer, K. *Le Marriage dans les Églises Chrétiennes du 1ᵉ au 11ᵉ Siècles*. Paris, 1970.

Rocquain, F. "Les sorts des saints ou des apôtres." *Bibliothèque de l'École des Chartes* 41 (1880), 457–474.

Rojdestvensky, O. *Le Culte de Saint Michel et le Moyen Age Latin*. Paris, 1922.

Roques, R. *L'Univers Dionysien*. Paris, 1954.

———. *Denys L'Aréopagite La Hierarchie Céleste*. Paris, 1958.

Roscher, W. H. "Ephialtes." *Abhandlungen der philologisch-historischen Klasse der königlich sachsischen Gesellschaft der Wissenschaften* 20 (Leipzig, 1900–1903), 3–17.

Ross, A. *Pagan Celtic Britain*. London, 1974.

Rousset, P. "Le sens du merveilleux à l'époque féodale." *Le Moyen Age* 62 (1956), 25–37.

Rubin, S. *Medieval English Medicine*. New York, 1974.

Rück, K. "Auszüge aus der Naturgeschichte des C. Plinius Secundus in einem astronomisch-komputistischen Sammelwerke des achten Jahrhunderts." *Programm des königlichen Ludwigs-Gymnasiums für das Studienjahr 1887–'88*. Munich, 1888.

———. "Die Naturalis Historia des Plinius im Mittelalter: Exzerpte aus der Naturalis Historia auf den Bibliotheken zu Lucca, Paris, und Leiden." *Sitzungsberichte der philosophisch-philologischen und der historischen Klasse der k. Bay. Akademie der Wissenschaften zu München*. Munich, 1898.

Russell, J. B. "Saint Boniface and the Eccentrics." *Church History* 33 (1964), 235–247.

———. *Witchcraft in the Middle Ages*. Ithaca, 1972.

Rutledge, D. *Cosmic Theology: The Ecclesiastical Hierarchy of Pseudo-Denys: An Introduction*. London, 1964.

Rydberg V. (*transl*. A. H. Edgren). *The Magic of the Middle Ages*. New York, 1879.

Saint-Denis, E. "Les énumerations de prodiges dans l'oeuvre de Tite-Live." *Revue de Philologie* 16 (1942), 126–142.

Saintyves, P. *Essais de Folklore Biblique*. Paris, 1922.

———. *L'Astrologie Populaire. Études Specialement dans les Doctrines et les Traditions Relatives à l'Influence de la Lune*. Paris, 1937.

Salzman, M. "Superstitio in the Codex Theodosianus, and the Persecution of Pagans." *Vigiliae Christianae* 41 (1987), 172–188.

Sawyer, R. C. " 'Strangely handled in all her lyms': Witchcraft and Healing in Jacobean England." *Journal of Social History* 22 (1989), 461–485.

Saxl, F., and H. Meier. *Verzeichnis astrologischer und mythologischer illustrierter Handschriften des lateinischen Mittelalters*. 3: Handschriften in englischen Bibliotheken, herausgegeben von Harry Bober. Warburg Institute London, 1953.

Schlette, H. R. *Epiphanie als Geschichte. Ein Versuch*. Munich, 1966.

Schlosser, H. D. *Althochdeutsche Literatur*. Frankfurt-am-Main, 1970.

Schneider, K. "Zu den Inschriften und Bildern des Franks Casket und einer ae. Version des Mythos von Balders Tod." In *edit*. H. Oppel, *Festschrift für Walther Fischer*, 4–20. Heidelberg, 1959.

Schramm, P. E. *Herrschaftszeichen und Staatssymbolik*. 3 vols. Stuttgart, 1954–1956.

Schramm, P. E., and F. Mütherich. *Denkmale der deutsche Könige und Kaiser*. Munich, 1962.

Schrire, T. *Hebrew Amulets: Their Decipherment and Interpretation*. London, 1966.

Sébillot, P. *Le Folk-lore de France*. 4 vols. Paris, 1904–1907.

Simon, M. "Melchisédech dans la polémique entre juifs et chrétiens et dans la légende." *Revue d'Histoire et de Philosophie Religieuses* 17 (1937), 58–93.

Singer, C. J. "A Review of the Medical Literature of the Dark Ages with a New Text of About 1110." *Proceedings of the Royal Society of Medicine* 10 (1917), 107–160.

———. *Studies in the History and Method of Science*. 2 vols. Oxford, 1917–1921.

———. *Early English Magic and Medicine*. London, 1920.

———. "The Herbal in Antiquity and Its Transmission to Later Ages." *Journal of Hellenic Studies* 47 (1927), 1–52.

———. *From Magic to Science*. London, 1928.

Singer, C. J., and D. W. Singer. "Byrhtferth's Diagram." *Bodleian Quarterly Record* 2 (1920), 47–51.

Singer, D. W. *Catalogue of Latin and Alchemical MSS. from Before the Sixteenth Century.* 3 vols. Brussels, 1928–1931.

Souers, P. W. "The Magi on the Franks Casket." *Harvard Studies and Notes in Philology and Literature* 19 (1937), 249–254.

Spence, L. *The Magic Arts in Celtic Britain.* London, 1945.

Stahl, W. H. "Dominant Traditions in Early Medieval Latin Science." *Isis* 50 (1959), 95–124.

Stancliffe, C. *St. Martin and His Hagiographer.* Oxford, 1983.

Stanley, E. G. *The Search for Anglo Saxon Paganism.* Cambridge, 1975.

Stannard, J. "Greco-Roman Materia Medica in Medieval Germany." *Bulletin of the History of Medicine* 46 (1972), 455–468.

——. "Marcellus of Bordeaux and the Beginning of Medieval Materia Medica." *Pharmacy in History* 15 (1973), 47–53.

——. "Magiferous Plants and Magic in Medieval Medical Botany." *Maryland Historian* 8 (2) (1977), 33–46.

Stegemann, V. *Aus einem mittelalterlichen deutschen astronomisch-astrologischen Lehrbüchlein.* Hrsg. E. Schwarz and E. Trunz. Hildesheim, 1973.

Edit. Stephen, M. *Sorcerer and Witch in Melanesia.* Melbourne, 1987.

Stevens, W. M. "Isidore's Figure of the Earth." *Isis* 71 (1980), 268–277.

Storms, G. *Anglo-Saxon Magic.* The Hague, 1948.

Stuart, H. "The Anglo Saxon Elf." *Studia Neophilologica* 48 (1976), 313–320.

Svenberg, E. *Die Latinska Lunaria.* Gothenburg, 1936.

——. "Quelques remarques sur les 'Sortes Sangallenses.' " *Eranos* 38 (1941), 68–78.

——. *Lunaria et Zodiologica Latina.* Gothenberg, 1963.

Swanton, M. *The Dream of the Rood.* Rev. ed. Exeter, 1987.

Talbot, C. "Some Notes on Anglo-Saxon Medicine." *Medical History* 9 (1965), 156–169.

——. *Medicine in Medieval England.* London, 1967.

Tavenner, E. *Studies in Magic from Latin Literature.* New York, 1916.

Taylor, A. R. "Hauksbok and Aelfric's *De Falsis Diis.*" *Leeds Studies in English* 3 (1969), 101–109.

Tedlock, B. *Time and the Highland Maya.* Albuquerque, 1982.

Temkin, O. *The Falling Sickness.* Baltimore, 1915.

Tester, S. J. *A History of Western Astrology.* Boydell, Suffolk, 1987.

Thee, F.C.R. *Julius Africanus and the Early Christian View of Magic.* Tübingen, 1984.

Thomas, K. *Religion and the Decline of Magic.* Harmondsworth, Middlesex: Penguin, 1973.

Thorndike, L. *The Place of Magic in the Intellectual History of Europe.* New York, 1905.

Thorndike, L. "The Attitude of Origin and Augustine toward Magic." *The monist* 19 (1908) 46–66.

———. "Some Medieval Conceptions of Magic." *The Monist* 25 (1915), 107–139.

———. *A History of Magic and Experimental Science* i. New York, 1923.

———. "Imagination and Magic: Force of Imagination on the Human Body and of Magic on the Human Mind." In *Mélanges Eugène Tisserant* vii(2), 353–358. Vatican City, 1964.

Thun, N. "The Malignant Elves." *Studia Neophilologica* 41 (1969), 378–396.

Trachtenberg, J. *Jewish Magic and Superstition.* New York, 1939.

Turville-Petre, E.O.G., and A.S.C. Ross. "Agrell's 'Magico Numerical' Theory of the Runes." *Folklore* 47 (1936), 203–213.

Utley, F. L. "Noah's Ham and Jansen Enikel." *Germanic Review* 16 (1941), 241–249.

Vacandard, E. "L'Idolatrie en Gaule au VIe et VIIe siècles." *Revue des Questions Historiques* 1 (1899), 424–454.

Van de Vyver, A. "Les oeuvres inédites d'Abbon de Fleury." *Revue Bénédictine* 47 (1935), 125–169.

———. "Les plus anciennes traductions latines médiévales (x–xi siècles) de traités d'astronomie et d'astrologie." *Osiris* 1 (1936), 655–691.

Van Hamel, A. G. "Odinn Hanging on a Tree." *Acta Philologica Scandinavica* 7 (1932–1933), 260–280.

Verbraken, P. "Les Dialogues de Saint Grégoire le Grand, sont-ils apocryphes?" *Revue Bénédictine* 98 (1988), 272–277.

Vézin, G. *L'Adoration et le Cycle des Images dans l'Art Chrétien Primitif.* Paris, 1950.

Vogel, C. *Le Pécheur et la Pénitence au Moyen Age.* Paris, 1969.

———. "Pratiques superstitieuses au début du XIe siècle d'après le Corrector sive Medicus de Burchard évêque de Worms (965–1025)." In *Études de civilisation médiévale (IXe–XIIe siècles). Mélanges offerts à Edmond-René Labande*, 751–761. Poitiers, 1974.

Vogel, C., and R. Elze. *Le Pontifical Romano-Germanique du Dixième Siècle.* Vatican City, 1963.

Vogels, J. "Scholia in Ciceronis Aratea aliaque ad astronomiam pertinentia e codice Musei Britannici, Harleiano 647." In *Wissenschaftliche Beilage zum Programm des Real-Gymnasiums zu Crefeld Ostern I and II.* Crefeld, 1884 and 1887.

Voigts, L. E. "The Significance of the Name 'Apuleius' to the Herbarium Apulei." *Bulletin of the History of Medicine* 52 (1978), 214–227.

———. "Anglo Saxon Plant Remedies and the Anglo-Saxons." *Isis* 70 (1979), 250–268.

———. "The Latin verse and Middle English Prose Text on the Sphere of Life and Death in Harley 3719." *Chaucer Review* 21 (1986), 291–305.

Vreese, L. de *Augustine en de Astrologie*. Maastricht, 1933.

Wagner, R. L. *Sorciers et Magiciens, Contribution à l'Étude du Vocabulaire de la Magie*. Paris, 1939.

Wallis-Budge, E. A. *Amulets and Superstitions*. Oxford, 1930.

Walsh, J. J. *Medieval Medicine*. London, 1920.

Wansborough, J. H. "St. Gregory's Intention in the Stories of St. Scholastica and St. Benedict." *Revue Bénédictine* 75 (1965), 145–151.

Ward, B. *Miracles and the Medieval Mind*. Philadelphia, 1982.

Ward, J. O. "Witchcraft and Sorcery in the Later Roman Empire and the Early Middle Ages." *Prudentia* 12 (1980), 93–108.

————. "Women, Witchcraft and Social Patterning in the Later Roman Lawcodes." *Prudentia* 13 (1981), 99–118.

Wedel, T. O. *The Medieval Attitude toward Astrology*. New Haven, 1920.

Weinstock, S. "The Geographical Catalogue in Acts II, 9–11." *Journal of Roman Studies* 38 (1948), 43–46.

Welborn, M. C. "Lotharingia as a Center of Arabic and Scientific Influence in the Eleventh Century." *Isis* 16 (1931), 188–199.

Weston, L.M.C. "The Language of Magic in Two Old English Metrical Charms." *Neuphilologische Mitteilungen* 86 (1985), 176–186.

White, L. "Eilmer of Malmesbury, an Eleventh Century Aviator." *Technology and Culture* 2 (1961), 97–111.

————. "Medical Astrologers and Late Medieval Technology." *Viator* (1975), 296–308.

Wickersheimer, E. "Figures medico-astrologiques des IXe, Xe et XIe siècles." *Janus* 19 (1914), 157–177.

————. *Les Manuscrits Latins de Médécine du Haut Moyen Age dans les Bibliothèques de France*. Paris, 1966.

Wilmart, A. "Une homélie de Sedatus evêque de Nîmes pour la nativité de notre Seigneur." *Revue Bénédictine* 35 (1923), 5–16.

Edit. Wilson, S. *Saints and their Cults*. Cambridge, 1983.

Wulff, A. *Die frauenfeindlichen Dichtungen in den romanischen Literaturen des Mittelalters bis zum Ende des XIII Jahrhunderts*. Halle, 1914.

Wünsch, R. *Sethianische Verfluchtungstafeln aus Rom*. Leipzig, 1898.

Edit. Xella, P. *Magia: Studi di Storia delle Religioni in Memoria di Raffaela Garosi*. Rome, 1976.

Index